The Gun and the Olive Branch

Born in 1936, David Hirst first acquired his interest in the Middle East during two years of national service in Egypt and Cyprus. After Oxford, he returned there as a student at the American University of Beirut and has remained ever since. Having drifted, almost accidentally, into journalism, he became the Middle East correspondent of the *Guardian*, and, from the 1967 Arab-Israeli War onward, covered all the main events in the recent history of this turbulent region. David Hirst now works as a freelancer and is the author of two other books, *Sadat* (1981) and *Oil and Public Opinion in the Middle East* (1966).

The GUN and the OLIVE BRANCH

The Roots of Violence in the Middle East

David Hirst

Thunder's Mouth Press · Nation Books
New York

THE GUN AND THE OLIVE BRANCH: *The Roots of Violence in the Middle East*

First published in England in 1977 by Faber and Faber
Second Edition published in 1984 by Faber and Faber
First published in the United States in 1977 by Harcourt Brace Jovanovich

Published by
Thunder's Mouth Press/Nation Books
An Imprint of Avalon Publishing Group, Inc.
161 William St., 16th Floor
New York, NY 10038

Nation Books is a co-publishing venture of the Nation Institute and Avalon Publishing Group Incorporated.

Library of Congress Cataloging-in-Publication Data

ISBN 1-56025-483-1

9 8 7 6 5 4 3 2

Book design by Simon M. Sullivan
Printed in the United States of America
Distributed by Publishers Group West

CONTENTS

AUTHOR'S NOTE

There have been three editions of *The Gun and the Olive Branch*. The first, published in 1977, comprised chapters one to nine. The second, published in 1984, saw the addition of chapters ten to twelve. All, as well as the epilogue to the second edition, have been kept unchanged in this third edition, whose Foreword brings the book up to date. The author invites the reader to look on the Foreword as a short, separate book that is complete in itself but also, he hopes, whets the appetite for the larger history that follows.

In the few months between writing and publication, there was one major development in the Arab-Israeli conflict: the diplomatic initiatives known as the 'road map.' Both sides have accepted it, and in the wake of Anglo–American conquest and occupation of Iraq, President Bush, formerly so shy of close involvement in the 'peace process,' has thrown his personal power and prestige behind it. But, despite all the professed hopes and expetations which this ostensible breakthrough has aroused, there is in fact precious little ground for believing that it will go on to prevail against those perennial, intractable realities—rooted in Israeli excess, Palestinian grievance, and American partisanship—which have defeated the most earnest and illustrious peace-makers of the past.

* * *

For her help and encouragement, I owe a special debt to my very old friend Leila S. Kadi. My thanks are also due to Linda Butler, Michele Esposito and Jeannette Seraphim, of the Institute for Palestine Studies, for their assistance in research; to Carl Bromley, of Nation Books, for proposing a project that I would not otherwise have undertaken; and to Danny Trad, for rescuing it from the near-fatal vicissitudes of a suddenly moribund computer.

DAVID HIRST
June 2003
Beirut

FOREWORD TO THE THIRD EDITION

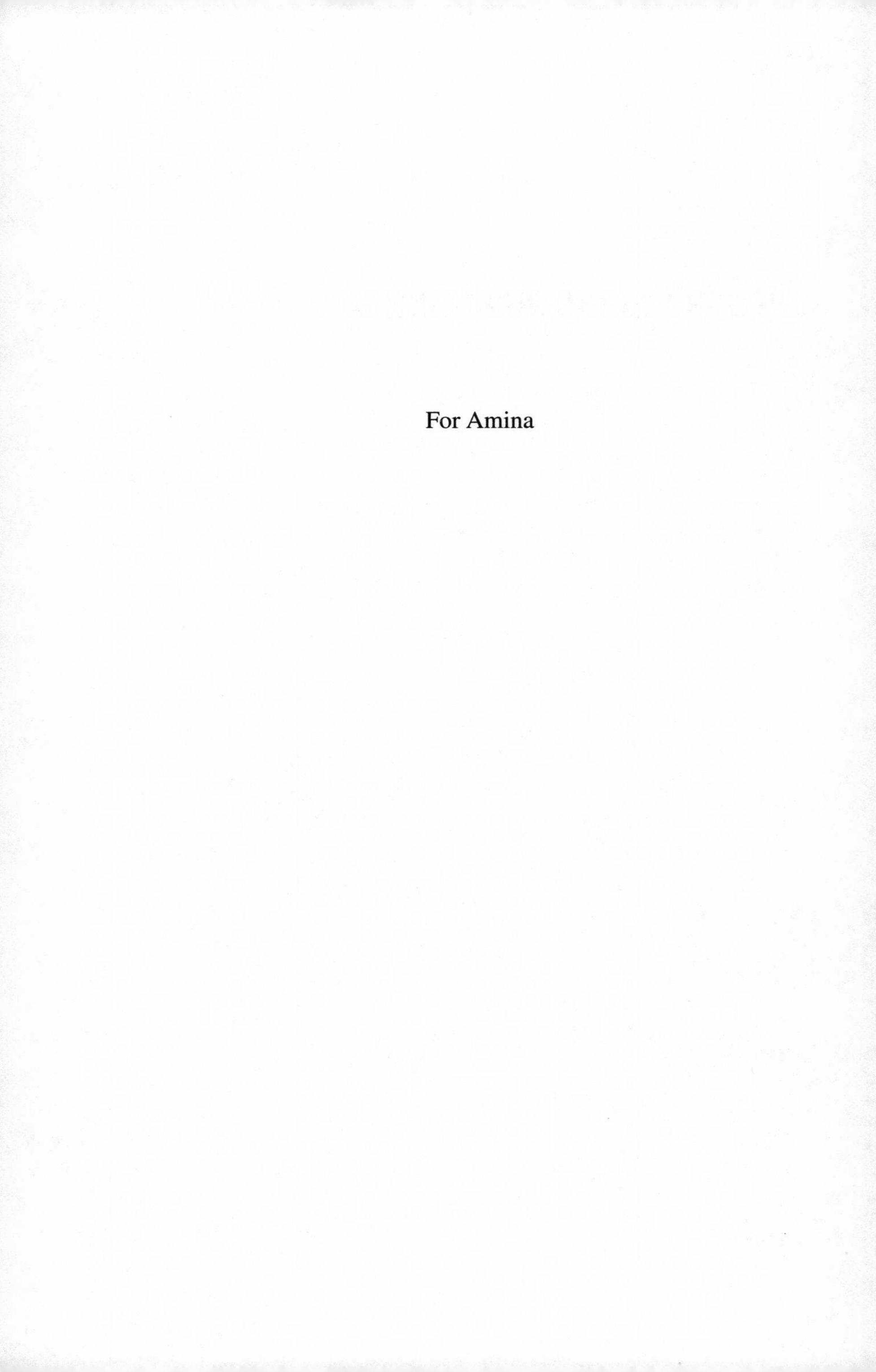

For Amina

i · THE RAVAGES OF A PURBLIND ORTHODOXY

'A Resounding and Puzzling Silence'

This is the third edition of a book that was first published, in the United States and Britain, in 1977, on the eve of that historic breakthrough in Middle East peace-making, the pilgrimage which President Anwar Sadat of Egypt made to Jerusalem and the first-ever peace treaty between Israel and an Arab state to which it led. To some, especially in the United States, it looked as though a solution to the world's longest-running, most implacable and dangerous of conflicts was finally coming into view. But that could only have been at best a part, and a small part, of the reason why—in the United States in contrast with Britain—the book was greeted with what its publisher, Harcourt Brace Jovanovich, called a 'resounding and puzzling silence'.[1]

The only major newspaper to touch it at the time—the *Washington Post*—was derisive. Conceding that histories of the Arab-Israeli conflict were apt to be *a priori* partisan, with the Arabs usually cast as the 'designated villain', novelist Roderick MacLeish called *The Gun and the Olive Branch: The Roots of Violence in the Middle East* 'yet another attempt at that which is both absurd to try and impossible to achieve—to identify a starting point for the violence of recent Middle Eastern history'; to identify it as a period in the late nineteenth century, even before the publicist Theodor Herzl 'fully conceived the Zionist dream of a return to Palestine and the establishment of a Jewish homeland', and then to 'cast a preponderance of blame' on one side, the Zionists and the Israelis, for all that happened subsequently. In any case, he said, it 'could not have appeared at a more inappropriate time'; Sadat's descent on Jerusalem had reduced it to 'an accusative sniffle amid the opening chords of an anthem of hope'.[2]

Among other hostile mentions, the *New Republic* lent its pages to perhaps the most personally scurrilous. British writer David Pryce-Jones, himself the author of a book which attributed Palestinian tales of Israeli torture to an Arab 'cultural' propensity for make-believe and self-delusion, called it 'the most malignantly anti-Israeli book ever to be published in English by someone with claims to be a serious commentator'. However, he explained, this was 'temperamentally' consistent in one on whom, before Sadat was assassinated, he had managed to 'eavesdrop'—metaphorically speaking, of course—'discussing how [his] murder [would] introduce democracy' in Egypt.[3] Although, among the immediately discernible evidence that it was the fruit of considerable labour, *The Gun and the Olive Branch* contained some 800 references to works in five languages, the supposedly judicious and authoritative *Library Journal* warned its subscribers against this 'partisan quickie' and its 'misuse of relatively limited sources'.[4]

Curiously, none of America's Jewish journals, normally so preoccupied with Middle Eastern affairs, deigned to notice it—if only, like their British counterparts, to savage it. Somehow or other, it was even missing from *Books in Print*, the catalogue of all published works. That this did amount, in one illustrious quarter at least, to a conspiracy of silence is not in doubt. At the *New York Times*, most famous and august of American newspapers, the books editor had commissioned what, unexpectedly, turned out to be 'a favorable, indeed enthusiastic' review. But on the point of publication it was withdrawn by order from on high.[5] This was not surprising, perhaps; as the columns he was to write in later years showed, the editor, Abe Rosenthal, was more extreme, in Israel's cause, than a great many Israelis themselves; but it was surely at variance with his paper's masthead motto, 'All the News That's Fit to Print'.

The silence may have been resounding, but it should not have been particularly surprising. For the book went against a dominant orthodoxy, and did so—or so critics like Pryce-Jones averred—in outrageous fashion. I had not sought furore for its own sake. However, I certainly had set out to 'tell the other side of the story', for the simple reason that, as it seemed to me, it had not been properly told, or won anything like the attention it deserved; I wanted to help redress a balance that was strongly, if not outrageously, tipped in the opposite direction.

America and Israel: An Affair of the Heart

Normally, in a democratic society, the novel or the unexpected, even the willfully provocative and polemical, is, or should be, welcomed as the essence of debate and controversy, out of which grows greater understanding, and ultimately, if it is misguided, a shift in the dominant orthodoxy. But that is probably less true of the debate about the Arab-Israeli conflict than it is of almost any other, or at least it is of those, Israel and the 'friends of Israel' in the United States, who dominate the debate, and make it their business to shape and preserve the orthodoxy. In the circumstances, it was perhaps lucky that *The Gun and the Olive Branch* was even published, however unsuccessful it might have been when it was. About the time it appeared, the celebrated Jewish commentator, I. F. Stone, was lamenting how very difficult it had become for an alternative point of view on the Middle East to win a hearing at all. Thirty years earlier, Stone had earned heroic status among American Jewry for his first-hand reporting on the post-war flight of European Jews to Palestine, and won a medal for it from the pre-state Zionist militia, the *Haganah*. But now he was moved to write: 'Freedom of debate on the Middle East is not encouraged; it is only rarely that we dissidents can enjoy a fleeting voice in the American press. . . . Finding an American publishing house willing to publish a book which departs from the standard Israeli line is about as easy as selling a thoughtful exposition of atheism to the *Osservatore Romano* in Vatican City.'[6] What is not in doubt is that, historically, the Zionists have everywhere been quite extraordinarily successful in winning and maintaining international support for their point of view, but in no country more so than in the United States, where Israel has always enjoyed a unique predisposition in its favour.

This benevolence issued from much the same reservoir of emotional and cultural sources as it did elsewhere in the West, ranging from Christian belief—and the sentimental idea that the 'return' of the Jews to the 'Land of their Ancestors' would be a fulfillment of biblical prophesy—to Gentile guilt over their persecution down the ages. But it was more intense than anywhere else, and America's Jewish community was peculiarly effective in converting it into governmental support. In her book *Perceptions of Palestine*, Kathleen

Christison, a former CIA analyst, argues that 'most of America literally fell in love with Israel'. Others said that 'Americans and Israelis [were] bonded together like no two other sovereign peoples', or that the identification was so close that Israel took part 'in the "being" of American society'.[7] Israel was 'one of us', an outpost of Western civilization, a bastion of democracy, and a key ally in an alien, often hostile and turbulent region. America, unquestioningly embracing the Zionist historical narrative, more or less viewed Israel as Israel viewed itself. Its birth was restitution for the great, cosmic disaster of the Holocaust, a triumph of the human spirit over terrible adversity; and its 'War of Independence', an epic struggle against enormous odds, was so inspiring that, fifty years on, Vice President Al Gore could say, in a not untypical flight of rhetoric: 'The Americans feel our ties with Israel are eternal. Our founders, like yours, also made an errand into the wilderness in search of a new Zion. Our struggle, like yours, has been with the divine, as well as the human. Our prophets, and yours, have told us they had a dream and have summoned us with their dream to this struggle for justice and peace'.[8]

Yet what, to American admirers, might have appeared noble and uplifting was, for the Palestinians, a catastrophe. And indeed *al-Nakba*, the Catastrophe, is what, quite simply, they called it ever after. For the fact is that the 'Jewish state', however estimable an aspiration it might have been in itself, was also, in its origins, birth and subsequent growth, a colonial enterprise; it was different, perhaps, in its initial impulse, from that broad movement of nineteenth-century European colonization from which it sprang, but, in method and results, it was inescapably a part of it, and no less unjust or harsh in its impact on the inhabitants of the land it colonized.

This is the historical reality on which *The Gun and the Olive Branch* rested its central argument. The continuing violence in the Middle East takes on a very different complexion from the one the dominant orthodoxy adorns it with, if to lay bare its roots is also to demonstrate that the greatest act of violence in the history of the Arab-Israeli struggle—Israel's 'War of Independence'—was in reality a massive act of ethnic cleansing on which the Zionists had been resolved, and girding for, ever since they set foot in Palestine that the official Zionist narrative surrounding this event is a myth of gigantic proportions: the myth, that is to say, which broadly speaking contends that—as a celebrated maxim had it—Palestine was 'a land without a people, waiting for a people without a land'; that, in the war which broke out in the war of 1948 the Palestinians fled the country on the orders of their leaders; that the Jewish soldiers, faithful to their 'purity of arms', perpetrated no wilful atrocities against them, vanquishing a hugely superior coalition of Arab armies bent on Israel's destruction; and that, after its establishment, the newborn state earnestly sought peace with its neighbors, only resorting to military force in self-defence against on-going, unprovoked Palestinian terror and Arab aggression.

Like any colonial enterprise, Israel was dependent for its very existence on the support of an imperial, or metropolitan, sponsor. Thanks in particular to the Jewish Diaspora, and its geographic diversity, it was able, uniquely, to rely on more than one. In pre-state days, the sponsor was Britain, the leading imperial power of the age; with the Balfour Declaration of 1917, it opened the gates of Palestine to Jewish immigration and then protected the growing settler community in their inevitable conflict with the indigenous people until they were strong enough to deal with them on their own. But, after 1948, sponsorship shifted essentially to the newly emergent superpower, the United States.

To foster and preserve this support, Israel-the-Jewish-state, and Zionists everywhere, have had at all costs to keep international public opinion sufficiently on their side to offset the negative consequences for themselves of whatever moral and material wrongs Israel-the-colonial-enterprise might have been inflicting on the Palestinians.

From the very beginning, they were so very good at doing it—and Palestinians and Arabs, lacking any remotely comparable representation within the domestic politics of the metropolitan sponsor, so ineffectual in opposing it—that the doyen of Palestinian scholars, Walid Khalidi, elevates this factor to a position of pre-eminent importance in the whole history of the conflict. 'Western purblindness', he wrote in the brief but masterly account of the rise of Israel that accompanies his anthology *From Haven to Conquest*, 'is itself a hallmark of the Palestine problem.' For there was never 'any mystery' as to how it came about:

> The Palestine tragedy, for that is what it is, did not unfold in some obscure era of history, in an inaccessible frontier area of the world. It has been enacted in the twentieth century, within the life-span and under the observation of thousands of Western politicians, diplomats, administrators and soldiers, in a country, Palestine, well within reach of modern means of communication. Nor was it the spontaneous outcome of fortuitous circumstances and uncontrollable forces. It was initiated by deliberate acts of will. The major decisions which brought it about were taken in two Western capitals—London and Washington—by constitutional leaders. . . . These decisions were taken in the teeth of the existing realities in Palestine, and against both the agonized appeals of the Palestine Arabs and the warnings and counsels of Western expert observers. . . . The Palestinians are not the first and will probably not be the last people to be dispossessed and banished; but so far they are, perhaps, in the unique position where not only is their catastrophe ruled out of the Western court as being irrelevant to their reactions against its perpetrators but where these very reactions are held to incriminate them. It is this self-same Western purblindness that has been the indispensable environment for the actualization of the Zionist venture.[9]

Reinforcing the Zionist Myth: The Joan Peters Affair

The purblindess persists to this day, as does the need for it—or rather for the partisanship which is its foster-child. Israel has grown immeasurably stronger, but it is no less dependent on its metropolitan sponsor than it ever was, on the enormous influence which, either directly or in concert with the 'friends of Israel' in America, it has acquired over it.

That in turn makes it dependent on the esteem of the American public at large, which ultimately shapes American foreign policy, or at least deters it from courses it will not accept. Israel's standing can always, of course, affect some immediate political issue, but, on a deeper, long-term basis, it is about preserving, in American eyes, the integrity, the moral foundations, of the whole Zionist enterprise.

Although *The Gun and the Olive Branch* obviously had very little to do with it, since it appeared there has been some erosion of the dominant orthodoxy. Yet just how strong this remained, or rather, perhaps, just how efficiently, and automatically, the intelligentsia, academe, the media and opinion-moulders in general could be mobilized in its defense, was made very clear with the appearance seven years later of another book, which got an illuminatingly different reception from mine. In 1984 Joan Peters published her *From Time Immemorial: The Origins of the Arab-Jewish Conflict over Palestine.*[10] This work set out not merely to defend the orthodoxy, to sustain the myth, but, with an immense display of research and erudition, to render it impregnable. Ever since 1948, it had been generally accepted that the Palestinian refugees who came into being as result of the creation of Israel were indeed refugees, whatever one's interpretation of the events that brought this about. But here came a scholar to proclaim, in a study of demographics and migration in the late nineteenth and early twentieth century, that, in essence, they were really no such thing. They had not inhabited Palestine 'since time immemorial'; they were, in effect, hardly more native than the Zionist 'immigrants' who had flocked to Palestine since the Balfour Declaration. They were 'immigrants' themselves. Most of these so-called refugees had actually come to Palestine in the immediately preceding years. They had been drawn there by the prosperity and work opportunities created by those other, industrious, efficient, enterprising immigrants, the Zionists, who, be they from Russia, Europe or the United States, had consequently acquired as much, if not more, right to the territory of Palestine than these Palestinian 'newcomers' themselves.

Here was a revolutionary new thesis indeed, astonishing, original, missed by every single scholar, journalist or traveller, Zionist or anti-Zionist, who had dealt with the subject in the past hundred years, one which, if true, virtually demolished the Arabs and Palestinians' case at a stroke. 'No longer', said the distinguished Palestinian critic and commentator Edward Said, 'could a scholar or propagandist argue that "the Palestinians" were in fact a real people with a real history in "Palestine." Her book asserted that their national, as well as actual existence, and consequently their claims on Israel, were at best suspect and at worst utter fabrication . . . the Palestinians are and have always been propaganda.'[11]

This was immensely important, for its own sake, for the conflict and for the attitude that the United States should adopt towards it. And the keepers of the Zionist flame immediately saw it as such, along with just about the entire politico-cultural establishment. Peters became an instant celebrity, in perpetual demand from radio and TV talk shows, with some 250 speaking engagements in 1985 alone. Her *magnum opus* was an instant publishing triumph. It swiftly won the prestigious National Jewish Book Award. It went into seven editions within eight months of its first appearance, each emblazoned with endorsements from the great and the good, from renowned historian Barbara Tuchman, who called it an 'historical event in itself', to novelist Saul Bellow, who said that 'millions of people the world over, smothered by false history and propaganda, will be grateful for this clear account of the origins of the Palestinians'.[12]

It was reviewed by virtually every important journal of opinion. The critics were united in awe at the epic scale, thoroughness and—they frequently asserted—the accuracy of her research and scholarship. For Ronald Sanders, author of a monumental study of the Balfour Declaration, these demographics 'could change the entire polemic over Palestine'. Martin Peretz, editor of the *New Republic*, declared that it 'will change the mind of our generation. If understood, it could also affect the history of the future.'[13]

How was it possible, asked Said, that in the United States, the very citadel of free expression and healthy debate, 'normally competent editors, historians, journalists and intellectuals could go along with the fiction that *From Time Immemorial* is a wonderful work of historical discovery?' Had it 'come to this, then: an unconsciously held ideology that permits the most scandalous and disgusting lies—execrably written, totally disorganized, hysterically asserted—to pass as genuine scholarship, factual truth, political insight, without any significant challenge, demurral or even polite reservation?'[14]

It had. For when it comes to Palestine, the United States is quite different from anywhere else, including its closest, Anglo-Saxon ally, Britain, and even the ostensible beneficiary of this purblind partisanship, Israel itself. The influence which the Zionists of Britain had once brought to bear when it, as the Mandatory power in Palestine, was playing the decisive, metropolitan sponsor's role in their fortunes had always been impressive, but it paled in comparison with the subsequent achievements of their counterparts in the United States. Not surprisingly, when it appeared in Britain in 1985 *From Time Immemorial* was swiftly and ignominiously demolished. 'Ludicrous and worthless', concluded the eminent Middle East historian Albert Hourani; 'the only mildly interesting question', he said, was how it could possibly have earned such encomiums on the other side of the Atlantic. 'Preposterous', enjoined Sir Ian and David Gilmour in an 8,000-word hatchet job in the *London Review of Books*. In Israel, the Labour party daily *Davar* likened it to the more lamentable of the country's past propaganda exercises; and Avishai Margalit, head of the Philosophy Department at the Hebrew University, called it a 'web of deceit'.[15]

Meanwhile, back in the United States, partly in response to this foreign ridicule, the welcome which had been so fulsomely heaped on the great work was becoming a major embarrassment and a potential literary scandal, only surpassed in recent times by Clifford Irving's fake biography of the eccentric billionaire recluse Howard Hughes.

Initially, only radical or little known publications had ventured any criticism at all. In the Chicago-based newsweekly, *In These Times*, the scholar Norman Finkelstein, beginning to make his name as a ferocious scourge of the Zionist establishment, wrote a devastating critique not merely of Peters's 'theses', but of the Herculean feat of research that others had discerned in it. Her investigations, he concluded, had been neither first-hand, original or rigorous, but merely a delving into 'half a century's Zionist propaganda tracts'. The result was 'among the most spectacular frauds ever published on the Arab-Israeli conflict'; 'no mean distinction', he added, 'in a field littered with crass propaganda, forgeries and fakes'.[16]

But finally a weighty journal, the *New York Review of Books*, stepped in. True, it took it nine months to publish the indictment it had commissioned, but eventually, amid rumours that the scandal was being suppressed, it did so. Even then, however, the author of it, the noted Israeli scholar Yehoshua Porath, discredited Peters's 'theses' only; he did not impugn her mendacious scholarship. And, emulating her publisher, Harper and Row, which had defended her right not to 'reply to published attacks on her work, regardless of their nature or provenance', the *Review* refused to accept any correspondence that raised this crucial question. Eventually, after more than a year of foot-dragging, the *New York Times* itself saw fit to run a story on the 'controversy'—in the Thanksgiving Day (non-) issue, on the theatre page, without even a listing in the index—in which Porath's view that it was a 'sheer forgery', 'almost universally dismissed' in Israel as 'sheer rubbish', was set against Barbara Tuchman's stubborn contention that the Palestinian people were a 'fairy tale', and that of Martin Peretz that the arraignment of Peters was part of a calculated left-wing plot.[17]

Burying the Myth Once and for All: Israel's 'New Historians'

It was from Israel itself that, a few years later, there came the most definitive rejoinder to Peters, and the kind of historical falsification that was her stock-in-trade. This was characteristic; the harshest and most cogent critics of Israel are very often Israelis themselves. The opening, in 1978, of Israeli archives had presented whole new opportunities for research into the creation of the Jewish state. A group of 'new historians', as they came to be known, profited from them to produce a thorough-going, revisionist account of 1948 and its antecedents. They explored the typically colonialist origins of Israel which the traditional, mainstream historians had for so long obscured. In doing so, they corroborated, in authoritative detail, what *The Gun and the Olive Branch* had earlier said, as well, of course, as the original studies, by scholars such as Khalidi, on which it had largely drawn. Works like Benny Morris's *Birth of the Palestinian Refugee Problem, 1947–1949*, Avi Shlaim's *Collusion Across the Jordan* and Ilan Pappé's *The Making of the Arab-Israeli Conflict, 1947–1951*[18] challenged 'the most sacred truths' of Zionism, the 'ideological and mythical certainties' that arose from the apparently sure knowledge that Israel's cause was and always had been entirely just and its behavior above reproach.[19] In the words of Benny Morris, the 'new history' showed that Israel was 'born in original sin,' not 'pure and innocent'.[20] It made clear that the Jewish community had never been in danger of annihilation on the eve of the 1948 war, and that the Arab armies, poorly trained and equipped, operationally incompetent, and even inferior in numbers, stood virtually no chance of defeating the new-born state.

The Palestinians did not flee on orders from their leaders, but because of the often deliberate terror, the violence and atrocities perpetrated against them by Jewish militias. Moreover, in its early years, Israel was never interested in making peace with its neighbours, and its so-called 'retaliatory' policies were really brutal and aggressive forms of expansionism that led, deliberately, to another war. There were conflicting interpretations among the 'new historians', with the doyen of them, Morris, arguing—often, it seemed, in the teeth of all the evidence he himself had adduced—that there had been no premeditated scheme to drive the Palestinians out: the refugee problem had been 'born of war, not by design'.[21] But others, such as Pappé, disputed this; essentially, they accepted that the Palestinian version of events—that of deliberate, long-planned ethnic cleansing—first put forward by Khalidi in 1961 had all along been the correct one.

But this radical re-assessment of the origins of the conflict—by Israelis in favour of the Palestinians—had few, if any, significant, practical consequences for its subsequent course. It led to no discernible change in Israel's policies, or diminution of the support which these won from its metropolitan sponsor.

True, it could not but contribute to the better understanding, among the American public at large, of the conflict's real nature. This did not add up to much. But for what it was worth, it had come about, in part at least, because of the sheer prominence, and impact on the public consciousness, of the 'peace process' over which, since the seventies, the United States had presided. To no world problem did American governments, Republican or Democrat, devote such disproportionate political resources as they did to this one, so important did they regard it. At its core, the conflict encompassed a very small portion of mankind; yet, in pursuit of peace, one Administration after another spent extraordinary amounts of time and energy launching 'initiative' after previously failed initiative, hosting conferences, dispatching emissaries, or, in the person of the legendarily 'hands-on' President Clinton, familiarizing itself with the minutiae of West Bank geography or the medieval alleyways of Jerusalem's Old City. The leaders of small, or otherwise rather inconsequential Middle East states and societies, the Palestinians' Yasser Arafat, the late Hafiz Asad of Syria or the late King Hussein of Jordan, became household names. The process acquired an almost sacrosanct quality, with men of good will everywhere stepping in to help where America faltered. It had looked decidedly hopeless in earlier years. But in 1977—without any help or encouragement from America, but revered by it ever since—Sadat had changed all that. To be sure, the process suffered severe setbacks; violence, insurrection, even full-scale war, often impeded its path; but conventional piety had it that it was irreversible, that a 'just, lasting and comprehensive' peace between Arab and Jew would assuredly one day come to pass.

In principle, at least, better understanding could not but work in favour of the Palestinians. For hitherto, in the eyes of the vast majority of Americans, including reasonably well informed ones, the Palestinians had simply never had a history; 'they were never there,' as Kathleen Christison put it, 'until, apparently out of the blue, they began to prey on Israel.'[22] Their dispossession and dispersal in 1948 had become 'an unrecognizable episode', not only in the sense that it had been forgotten, but that it had been erased from any moral accountancy of the conflict. It followed that Palestinian claims had been 'artificially and mischievously inspired' and Palestinian 'resistance' was the fruit of unreasoning hatred and the unreasonable Arab refusal to accept Israel's existence.[23] Policy-makers had pandered to a pitifully ill-informed, or wilfully distorted, domestic reading of the situation far more readily than they addressed the real one on the ground. They barely paid any attention to the strictly Palestinian dimension of the conflict; all they chose to see was an Arab-Israeli, inter-state conflict in which the refugees were simply a nuisance or the pawns of larger players.

Better understanding could not but entail, for the fair-minded at least, sympathy for the Palestinians as victims with a genuine grievance, as a people with national cause and a right to 'self-determination' which, in the end, might even take the form of independent statehood. Yet the shift in perceptions, such as it was, could have little or no practical consequences so long as the policy-makers continued to be so much better disposed towards the Israeli than the Palestinian point of view, so much more responsive to domestic pressures on Israel's behalf than to feeble or all but non-existent counter-pressures on behalf of the other side. And continue they did; fair-mindedness was far from being their dominant trait. In general, in fact, there was an ever-growing cleavage between what the policy-makers should have done—in the light of the growing understanding—and what they actually did, between what a doubtless small, but growing, number of the now better informed public were beginning to expect of them and what they got.

Indeed, the cleavage was all the greater in that Israel itself was steadily growing more extreme. In the first thirty years of its existence, the (relatively speaking) moderate wing of the Zionist movement, embodied by Labour, had dominated public life. Although it had been responsible for the 'original sin' of Palestinian ethnic cleansing, and all the abuses that flowed from it, it did at least officially espouse contemporary Western ideals of democracy, social justice, equality and human and civil rights, and sought to present a civilized face to the world. But after the victory of Menachim Begin in the 1977 general elections, governments alternated between Labour and *Likud*—which embodied Zionism in its extreme, ultra-nationalist form and cared much less about ethical appearances or international opinion—or coalitions of the two. This secular right was greatly reinforced by the religious right, or Israeli/Jewish fundamentalists, who, matching the rise of other fundamentalisms in the region, became a powerful new actor on the Israeli political and electoral stage.

The United States did not react with any seriously reproving vigour against the growing militancy, and excesses, of its protégé. And it did not do so, in good measure, because of a parallel process that was at work in Washington too: in its centres of power, in both executive and legislature, the metropolitan sponsor was itself being

'Zionized' to a greater and greater degree. The resulting partisanship was all the more striking in that, by contrast with the Israelis, the Arabs and Palestinians were growing increasingly moderate and accommodating, and behaving in a way that was quite exceptional in the history of indigenous peoples' responses to European colonialism.

ii · ARAFAT'S HISTORIC PEACE OFFER

The Palestinians Renounce 78 per cent of Palestine

Generally speaking, in the great process of European withdrawal from empire the conflicts, sometimes violent and sometimes peaceable, that set native against foreign master, led to a complete victory and emancipation of the colonized. By that criterion, Israel, the settler-state, was unique in that it continued not merely to grow and thrive, but to exist at all. All other such polities disappeared in the anti-colonial struggle. Those who peopled them were either, like the million French *colons* of Algeria, driven out in a bloody liberation war, or, like South Africa's whites, they yielded their political supremacy to majority rule.

In the quarter century since *The Gun and the Olive Branch* was written, the indigenous victims of Israel—the colonial enterprise—have recognized Israel—the Jewish nation-state—and its right to exist in perpetuity. They have formally renounced what, from both the standpoint of international jurisprudence and established anti-colonial norms, they were entitled to claim as their right: the recovery of their usurped homeland, the return of the refugees and the dismantling of the whole Zionist-colonial apparatus of immigration, settlement and political control. This Israeli achievement was all the more remarkable in that, in this case, the victims were not just those, the Palestinians, who had been expelled from their native land, but a much larger, less directly affected, community, the Arabs, who, impelled by ties of common nationhood, identified with them in their anti-colonial struggle. It was an acceptance that certainly did not come about voluntarily, out of any affection or good will towards the intruder, any sense that this was what it merited, or had the moral right to demand. At every stage of a long and bloody conflict, Arabs and Palestinians would, if they could, have denied pre-state Zionism, then the Israeli state itself, the legitimacy they craved; they would have undone them both. It came out of defeat, weakness, and a sense of the futility of continuing the struggle. Nor was the acceptance universal; though the accepters became the dominant players in the region, many were the 'rejectionists', Arabs and Palestinians, who could not stomach the idea of such an alien aggressor forever in their midst. Furthermore, the actual process of acceptance was itself incomplete. Most Arab states subscribed to a broad consensus as to what constituted a 'just, lasting and comprehensive' settlement. But the settlement became accomplished fact only in the case of those, Egypt in 1979 and Jordan in 1994, which signed full and final peace treaties. It remained only an intent with those, 'Palestine', Syria, Lebanon, which had yet to do so.

At the heart of the peace-seeking Arab consensus was the notion of a Palestinian state to be established in those territories, the West Bank and Gaza, which Israel had conquered in the 1967 Arab-Israeli War and occupied ever since. Arab East Jerusalem would be its capital. This was enshrined in the Oslo agreement of 1993. Oslo did not formally spell it out, but, for Palestinians and Arabs, that was its ultimate meaning.

The agreement was the climax of Yasser Arafat's moderation. When, in the early sixties, Mr Palestine, as he came to be known, first emerged on the public stage, it was as the leader of the guerrilla organization *Fatah*, and, as with all such resistance movements, his goal was absolute and uncompromising: the liberation, through 'armed struggle', of the whole land of Palestine. Israel would cease to exist and the only Jews permitted to remain would be those who had settled in the country prior to the Zionist 'invasion.' But ever since the 1973 Arab-Israeli War and the peace process that then began in earnest, he had—in accordance with a 'doctrine of stages'—been staking out ever more moderate positions, implying that Israel, in some form or other, was there to stay, and resorting to diplomacy as well as violence to achieve his aims.

Indeed, in view of all the strategic and military defeats which, as a guerrilla chieftain, he had suffered, and more particularly his expulsion from Lebanon in 1982, Mr Palestine had precious little ability to pursue an armed struggle of any kind. But in 1987, after years of seemingly growing irrelevance in his remote, Tunisian exile, his own people came to the rescue—or at least an important segment of them did.

These were the inhabitants of the West Bank and Gaza, be it those who were still living in their own homes, or those who, though refugees from 1948, had fetched up outside the borders of original Israel, but inside this newly occupied remainder of historic Palestine. In the earlier years of Palestinian resistance, it had been the 'outsiders', armed with Kalashnikovs, who bore the main burden of the struggle. Arafat's guerrillas hailed mainly from the squalid refugee camps that lay outside this *Greater*-Israel of 1967. The 'insiders' had been largely quiescent, waiting upon deliverance by their Diaspora brethren. But with Arafat's setbacks, and the scattering of his troops, deliverance never came, nor ever looked like doing so. Finally, exasperated by twenty years of occupation, they took matters into their own hand; without any prompting from the exile leadership, they spontaneously erupted in what became known as the *Intifada*. This one—unlike its now more famous sequel that broke out in 2000—was essentially non-violent, or at least unarmed. As such, the 'uprising of stones' proved more effective, in terms of its political impact on Israeli society and the international community, than the 'outsiders' Kalashnikovs had done. It could not be portrayed as that 'terrorism' which, in American eyes, de-legitimized any cause, however otherwise just it might be. Furthermore, the brutality of Israel's response did serious damage to its international reputation. It had been quite early on that the defence minister of the time, Yitzhak Rabin, decreed his policy of 'force, might, beatings', a policy that led, and was intended to lead, to breaking the bones, deliberately and systematically, of bound and shackled men.[24] The commander of the elite *Givati* Brigade would order his soldiers 'to break their [rioters'] legs so they won't be able to walk and break their hands so they won't throw stones'.[25] The practice became so institutionalized in another regiment, the *Golani*, that medical orderlies were instructed to be present at bone-breakings, considered to be 'educational' in purpose, so as to ensure that no 'irreversible medical damage was caused'.[26]

Armed with this miraculous new asset, Arafat felt able to offer the historic compromise towards which all his growing moderation had been tending. In 1988, the Palestine National Council, the Palestinian parliament-in-exile, formally proposed a 'two-state solution'. Henceforth, it decided, the Palestinians would confine their struggle to the establishment, by peaceful means, of a state on that 22 per cent of historic Palestine constituted by the occupied territories, while ceding the remaining 78 per cent, once theirs too, constituted by the original Israel of 1948. A few weeks later, at Geneva, the Palestinian Liberation Organization formally 'renounced' terrorism, and recognized Israel's right to exist. It thereby earned that 'dialogue' with the United States which it had so long sought. A spokesman called it the Palestinians' 'passport to the world'.

But the offer was a gamble that didn't pay off, such was the continuing weakness of both Palestinians and Arabs. For Israel, Arafat was the unregenerate terrorist still; and Washington, in its ever-deepening partiality, would not gainsay its imperious protégé.

In 1991, following the Iraqi invasion of Kuwait, its liberation, in Desert Storm, by an American-led military coalition and the great enhancement of American influence in the region which that ushered in, the United States stage-managed an international peace conference in Madrid. There, for the first time, Israel and its Arab neighbours talked to each other across the same table. The Palestinians were there too—but at the price of great concessions. For it was the Israelis who, with American backing, decided *which* Palestinians they should be, and they did not include Arafat, or even members of the PLO. The Israelis also largely set the agenda; they refused to discuss anything suggesting that the Palestinians might be entitled to the same fundamental, twentieth-century right to 'self-determination' as other peoples were.

Madrid, and the subsequent Palestinian-Israeli negotiations that flowed from it, got nowhere. Arafat slipped further into the wilderness—until, going behind the back of his official negotiators, and unbeknown even to the Americans, he embarked on those highly secret talks that were to astonish the world in the form of the Oslo agreement.

The Oslo Agreement

On 13 September 1993, Arafat won his accolade as world statesman and peace-maker cast in an almost Sadat-like mould. In a signing ceremony on the White House lawn, the 64-year-old former 'terrorist' chieftain shook hands with Yitzhak Rabin, prime minister of the Jewish state which he had once made it his sacred mission to remove from the face of the earth.

In what one of the 'new historians', Avi Shlaim, called 'the mother of all breakthroughs in the century-old conflict between Arabs and Jews in Palestine', the two leaders redrew the geopolitical map of the entire region.[27] It was, or so it seemed at the time, an historic reconciliation between two peoples whose attitude towards each other ever since Zionist settlement began had been one of complete reciprocal denial. For the first time they effectively recognized one other's existence, and their right to self-determination, as peoples, on the land of Palestine.[28] They abandoned the ideological dispute over who was Palestine's rightful owner and turned to finding a practical solution, based on the old idea of partition, to the problem of sharing the cramped living space between the Jordan River and the Mediterranean.

It was the first, formal step in that process of de-colonization to which all such European colonial enterprises had submitted. And yet, at the same time, the Jewish state being that great exception which proved the rule, it was also to be a last and very limited one. For it was of course the Palestinians who, on any true historical reckoning, had made the real concession; for them, historically, it was pure loss against pure Israeli gain. By his own standards, Arafat's retreat had been breathtaking, incomparably greater, in fact, than Sadat's, which, sixteen years before, he had denounced as an 'apostasy.' His formal renunciation of 78 per cent of historic Palestine had been foreseen. But, in addition, he had virtually given up the idea of the 'Return' for all those, half the Palestinian people, who had been driven out in 1948 and 1967 and ever after regarded it as the supreme goal of the struggle. He himself was to return, along with the high officials and bureaucracy of PLO, to head the 'interim self-government', or Palestine Authority, that was to be established in the territories. But for the Palestinian Diaspora, *his* return, and that of his cronies, amounted to the final abandonment of theirs. Furthermore, he had thrown away two of the most potent weapons in his hands, a physical and a diplomatic one. On the one hand, he abjured violence of all kinds. Indeed, he turned himself into collaborator as much as liberator. For the Israelis, security—theirs, not the Palestinians'—was the be-all-and-end-all of Oslo; his job was to supply it on their behalf. Israel's 'right to exist in peace and security' took clear precedence over the Palestinians' right to continue the struggle for any rights Israel persisted in denying them. The whole *raison d'être* of the 'strong police force' Arafat was entitled to set up was to 'discipline violators' who might disturb that Israeli 'security'. On the other hand, he effectively abandoned the whole, accumulated corpus of United Nations jurisprudence which constituted the one sure, incontrovertible, internationally recognized testimony to the justice of the Palestinian cause. In addition, the agreement was in it itself incomplete. He had made these retreats for nothing in return—or at least nothing guaranteed.

He, of course, claimed otherwise. He assured his people that Oslo's five-year 'transitional period' would lead, via a series of negotiations on successive 'interim arrangements' and then on so-called 'permanent status' questions such as the refugees, to the end of the whole conflict. As the negotiations proceeded and the Israelis withdrew, the Palestine Authority, starting off in part of Gaza and the small West Bank town of Jericho, would gradually expand to incorporate the whole of the territories. It was supposedly an inexorable momentum that he had set in motion. Nothing could now impede the inevitable march towards statehood; he himself already saw in his mind's eye the beckoning spires and minarets of his future capital, East Jerusalem.

But it was not to be. The very nature of the American-sponsored peace process negated it. With his separate peace, Sadat had acquiesced in the one great indispensable stratagem that sustained it ever afterwards: the deferral of the most intractable, 'permanent status' issues to the end. But the deferment was invariably at the Palestinians', not the Israelis', expense. That had always been true, but, with Oslo, it was more than ever so. For, given all that Arafat had renounced there, the balance of power was now weighted even more overwhelmingly in Israel's favour. His precious 'momentum' worked against, not for him. The 'interim arrangements' which were supposed to advance his conception of 'permanent status' only advanced the Israelis' conception of it instead. Obeying the logic of 'take what you can now and seek the rest to later', which weakness thrust upon him, he acquiesced in accumulating concessions that only widened the gulf between what he was actually achieving and what he assured his people he would achieve, by this method, in the end. It became more and more obvious that even the modest goal which he had set himself, statehood in a very small portion of original Palestine, was unattainable, and that Israel, far from genuinely accepting the historic compromise, was merely exploiting the interminable, tortuous and acrimonious negotiations to consolidate its hold on its *Greater*, post-1967 self.

With almost total impunity, it persisted in all those traditional colonizing and expansionist policies, the creation of yet more Zionist 'facts on the ground', that made an ever greater mockery of the Palestinian state-in-the-making. The establishment of settlements had always been at the heart of these policies, and its inevitable corollary, Palestinian dispossession and dispersal. Those which had already taken root in the occupied territories were illegal under international law and repeatedly condemned as such by the United Nations. For the Palestinians, and indeed much of the world, it was all but axiomatic that, by virtue of Oslo, they were either to be dismantled or fall under eventual Palestinian sovereignty. Thus, upon the agreement's signing, an end to all new settlement activity would have constituted the most reassuring single indication of Israel's readiness for a partition leaving the Palestinians in possession of that part of their ancestral homeland to which they were ready to confine themselves, the continuation of it the most disturbing indication of the contrary.

It continued with a vengeance. In spirit, if not in letter, Oslo had ruled against any changes, at the Palestinians' expense, in the 'integrity and status' of the West Bank and Gaza. But Rabin himself, in effect, expressly repudiated the idea that this should apply to the settlements: 'we told them that we would not negotiate over the territories but that we are ready to discuss land and we are willing to make a division: land intended for Jewish settlement and land under Palestinian ownership.'[29] Between 1993 and the present day, Labour governments which officially supported Oslo pursued settlements with even greater vigor than *Likud* governments which, though formally committed to it, undisguisedly abhorred it. This was a yardstick of the growing ambition and intransigence of both. Between 1967 and 1982, a mere 21,000 settlers had moved into the West Bank and Gaza. In 1990, the figure stood at 76,000. By 2000, it had risen to 213,000, and that did not include the 170,000 who had settled in an Arab East Jerusalem long since annexed to Israel proper. For the two million Palestinian inhabitants of the West Bank, the areas denied to them by reason of the settlements themselves, purpose-built settler roads, confiscation or military use now amounted to 59 per cent of the whole. Seven thouand settlers controlled 20 per cent of Gaza, which, with 1.1 million Palestinian inhabitants packed into 140 square kilometers, ranked as the most densely populated territory in the world.[30] General Ariel Sharon summed matters up with characteristic candour, and—given that he was foreign minister at the time—contemptuous disregard for the lawful authority of his own government: 'Everybody has to move, run and grab as many hilltops as they can to enlarge the settlements because everything we take now will stay ours. . . . Everything we don't grab will go to them.'[31]

The despair to which this led, as the Palestinians witnessed the last vestiges of their homeland disappear and continued to endure all the vicissitudes and humiliations of a barely lightened occupation, made an explosion all but inevitable. It came hard on the heels of the Camp David summit conference of July 2000, an attempt to replicate the one which, twenty two years before, had produced that first great breakthrough in Middle East peace-making. President Clinton presided over it. But it was actually the brainchild of Israeli prime minister Ehud Barak. The interim phases of the Oslo agreement had ground to a halt, as they had been all but bound to do, and so, in a fantastically ambitious gambit, he had proposed to telescope both those and the permanent-status negotiations into one last, grand, climactic conclave. With Clinton's blessing he laid before Arafat and his negotiating team a take-it-or-leave-it compromise. In return for 'the most generous offer' Israel had ever made, or was ever likely to, the Palestinians were to have renounced all further claims. It was to have marked 'the end of the [100-year] conflict', and the priceless, existential gain of Israel's full and formal integration into the region.

It might well have been Israel's most generous offer, but it was not nearly generous enough, in no way comparable, in historical terms, to the generosity which, at Oslo, the Palestinians themselves had displayed. Barak still demanded much more than the 78 per cent of original Palestine which Arafat had offered him, plus a whole gamut of other ideological or security-related gains, which would have reduced his state to a pathetic, powerless simulacrum of the real thing. What he was ready to 'give' the Palestinians was actually much less than the percentages in the lower-to-middle nineties which Israel claimed they were, because, even before its calculation of the dimensions of the West Bank began, it always left out certain areas, such as the unilaterally expanded municipality of East Jerusalem, which amounted to 5.4 per cent of the whole.[32] In order to retain the vast bulk of the settlements under its sovereignty, Israel would have annexed valuable or strategically important territories cutting deep into the Palestinian state, and dividing it into three disconnected cantons in such a way that every time its citizens wanted to cross, or transport goods, from one to another they would have had to pass through Israeli territory on roads that Israel could close at will. These, and other exactions and indignities, would have locked in place many of the very worst aspects of the occupation the Palestinians were seeking to end. Camp David collapsed without any agreement at all.

The *Intifada*

Within two months, on 29 September 2000, the second *Intifada* broke out. Whether, or to what extent, by putting 2,000 soldiers, with Apache helicopters overhead, at the disposal of his right-wing political rival, General Sharon, and a phalanx of *Likud* deputies for a deliberately provocative, 'right-of-ownership' walk-about at the

Temple Mount—which is also the site of the mosques of al-Aqsa and the Dome of the Rock, Islam's third most holy place—Barak actually triggered it for his own purposes, or whether Arafat encouraged it as a means of strengthening his otherwise desperately weak diplomatic hand, is a matter of historical controversy. It was coming anyway, and, in essence, it was a spontaneous, popular revolt directed first against Israel's continued occupation, and the realization that Oslo could never end it, and, implicitly, against Arafat and his Palestine Authority, which had so obstinately connived in the fiction that it could.

It was, in effect, the Palestinians' 'war of independence', albeit an independence confined to 22 per cent of their original homeland. Some of its participants, especially the fundamentalist 'rejectionists' of *Hamas* and *Islamic Jihad*, were still in principle wedded to the old Arafatian concept of 'complete liberation', and to the hope that, exploiting the logic of violence, they could turn it, Algerian-style, into an existential, all-or-nothing struggle. But its mainstream, 'young guard' leaders—notably the subsequently imprisoned Marwan Barghouti—and the organizations they headed—the *Tanzim* or the *al-Aqsa* Brigades, both of them offshoots of Arafat's original *Fatah* movement—repeatedly and emphatically proclaimed no ambition beyond that 22 per cent. They wanted their independent state to co-exist with Israel, not to destroy it.

If the aim was still Oslo, the renewal of violence to achieve it was, of course, a clear violation of it. It was also, or was soon to become, atrocious, as atrocious as any which it has been the task of this history of violence to record. The terrorism which had often marred the Palestinians' struggle reached new and barbarous heights with what they called their 'martyrdom operations'. There had been suicide, or quasi-suicide attacks before.[33] But it was only with the second *Intifada* that, mainly but by no means exclusively the handiwork of the Islamic militants, they became a principal, systematic and strategic weapon in the Palestinians' arsenal. The readiness of young men—and women—to sacrifice their lives in this dreadful fashion was certainly a measure not merely of their own, individual despair, and the fanaticism it had bred, but of that of the whole society which threw them up in such fearfully large numbers. It was also perceived, by those who justified them, as the only way in which the Palestinians, so very inferior, technically, organizationally and diplomatically, could redress the strategic and military balance at least some way in their favour.

There was undoubtedly some logic in that. The bombings shook Israel to its foundations; the damage, mainly psychological, which they inflicted was great. But, in the end, they did not work. They were not only morally repugnant, they were operationally counterproductive. If violence there had to be, some Palestinians believed, its targets should have been strictly confined to the self-same territorial bounds this 'war of independence' had officially set itself, to the soldiers and settlers who were both the symbols and instruments of the occupation it aimed to throw off. In cold logic, perhaps, it should not have, but, in practice, it did impair the anti-colonial legitimacy of the whole struggle. And the more abhorrence it generated, both in Israel itself and in the rest of the world, the easier it became for Israel to make full, unfettered use of the vastly superior, high-tech, American-supplied arsenal of violence which it could bring to bear in the suppression of the rebellion.

The error was all the more egregious—if also more understandable—in that it had actually been the Israelis themselves who first resorted to violence, and massively disproportionate violence at that. Immediately after the Sharon walk-about, the army opened fire on crowds of non-violent demonstrators; Palestinian civilians, a high proportion of them children, died in far higher numbers than Israelis did. This was deliberate, and it was more the army's than the government's doing. For 'when the *Intifada* erupted', wrote *Maariv* commentator Ben Kaspit, 'it was finally clear to all: Israel is not a state with an army, but an army with a state. . . . For many years the Israeli Defence Forces had been waiting for this *Intifada*, and when it erupted, it unleashed all its frustrations on the Palestinians, who did not know what had hit them. . . . "Tell me", General Amos Malka [head of Military Intelligence] said to Yosi Kopperwasser [a District Intelligence Officer], "how many bullets has the IDF fired since the beginning of the *Intifada*?" Kopperwasser was dumbfounded. He did not have a clue. Malka asked him to find out. When the answer arrived by noon, most of the officers who were present . . . turned white. In the first few days the IDF had fired about 700,000 bullets and other projectiles in Judea and Samaria [the West Bank] and about 300,000 in Gaza. Someone in the Central Command later quipped that the operation should be named "a bullet for every child".'[34]

'What's the matter with you?' high Palestinian officials protested to their Israeli counterparts. 'You are breaking all the rules of the game!' But the army continued shooting, relying mainly on snipers.[35] The shock to the Palestinians was profound, and the desire for revenge intense. It led to more effective and murderous forms of Palestinian violence which eventually came to their grisly climax in the suicide bombers. But as it did so, the Israeli public, in its turn, only closed ranks amid a growing clamour for punishment and revenge. That public was in any case deeply imbued with the disdainful attitudes towards a subject people typical of colonial societies anywhere, and very receptive to the archetypal colonial slogan: 'the only language they understand is force'. For those, on the left, who self-righteously considered that they had done so much to promote the peace process, the *Intifada*, even without the suicide bombers, was a kind of betrayal; the Arafat in whom they had placed their trust had, they lamented, grievously disappointed them. They bought Barak's contention that, with the rejection of his 'generous offer', he had 'exposed Arafat's true face'. The genuine, hard-core 'peace camp' dwindled almost into non-existence. For the right, it was the fulfilment of all their prophecies: the Palestinians never wanted peace anyway, and Arafat remained the 'killer and murderer' bent on Israel's 'destruction' they always said he was. Before long both left and right were ready for the 'saviour' who promised them a simple military solution. In the general elections of February 2001, and by an overwhelming margin, they chose Sharon to replace Barak at the head of the most extreme, bellicose government in Israel's history.

Sharon occupies a unique place in *The Gun and the Olive Branch*. This is not merely because, in such a history of violence, he inevitably figures as one of Israel's most prominent, dedicated and archetypal practitioners of it. It is because, alone among them, he figures in almost all its representative phases, from the so-called 'retaliatory' raids of the state's earliest years—of which he was the audacious and murderous leader—through the massacre of civilians in the Lebanese refugee camps of Sabra and Chatila—for which he still risks trial as a 'war criminal' before an international court—to this, his last great battle, in the capacity of the prime minister which few, even in Israel, had expected so reckless, fanatical and sanguinary a man ever to become. His mere appointment was a portent of ferocious deeds to come. And, in fact, it was only after Sharon took office that *Hamas* turned to what one Israeli military analyst called 'the Palestinian H-bomb: exploding human beings'.[36]

For Sharon, the *Intifada*, and the terror that accompanied it, was the opportunity he had been waiting for. Here was an Israeli leader who had opposed every single stage of the peace process, from the first Camp David of 1978 to Oslo. He had done so because he knew that these compromises involved, or at least portended, the 're-division' of *Eretz Israel*, or the 'Land of Israel'—an area generally deemed, in the current thinking of the mainstream Israeli right, to be coterminous with historic Palestine—which, since 1967, had become one and whole. For him, as for many others, *Likud* party members, settlers, secular-nationalist and religious extremists in general, Oslo was the 'greatest misfortune ever to have befallen Israel',[37] a negation of Zionism as they understood it.

The ground was already prepared. As early as 1996, the Israeli military had drawn up a contingency plan, called Field of Thorns, whose execution would, in effect if not perhaps in explicit intent, bring the destruction of Oslo and all it stood for: the very idea of Palestinian self-determination, leading to eventual statehood, on any portion of historic Palestine, and any legitimate, representative, internationally recognized institution—such as Arafat and his Palestine Authority—empowered to bring it about. All that was needed was the pretext. The *Intifada* furnished it. So eager were the proponents of this plan to exploit the pretext that they went into action even before *Hamas* or *Islamic Jihad* had perpetrated their first serious act of terror, a bomb blast which killed two persons in Jerusalem; by the time this took place, on 2 November, the Palestinian casualty toll had reached 145 dead compared with 14 Israelis. On 15 October, at the request of Prime Minister Barak, the security services had already published a report which stated that 'Arafat the person is a severe threat to the security of the state and the damage which will result from his disappearance is less than the damage caused by his existence'. This was followed by the release of a 60-page 'White Book' entitled *PA Non-Compliance: A Record of Bad Faith and Misconduct*. Accusing Arafat of 'orchestrating the *Intifada*', it said that this was just the last in a long series of proofs that he had never abandoned the 'option of violence and "struggle" ', and his oft-repeated 'green light' to Islamist terror. It produced no serious evidence for this claim; moreover, the claim was wholly at variance with what, in the years before the *Intifada*, the Israeli security services, amply cited in the Israeli media, had themselves long been saying about Arafat and his efforts to protect Israel from Palestinian violence. He 'is doing his job—he is fighting terror—and puts all his weight against *Hamas*,' Ami Ayalon, head of the *Shabak* secret service, told the government in 1998. He was even ordering assassinations of *Hamas* terrorists which were disguised as 'accidents'; doing a better job, it was conceded, than the Israelis ever did themselves.[38]

From the outset, then, not just Sharon was complicit in, or supportive of, this long-matured, Machiavellian scheme; this latest of Israel's so-called 'chosen wars', of which Sharon's 1982 invasion of Lebanon, with very similar aims, had been the last one;[39] this was *Evil Unleashed*, as one of Israel's most forthright commentators, Tanya Reinhart, entitled her investigation into its hidden origins, motives and methodology.[40] So, too, was a whole coterie of the generals and generals-turned-politicians who were actually, and increasingly, making the real decisions in Israel; and not the least among them, his 'most generous' peace offer notwithstanding, was his political rival, but admiring disciple, outgoing premier Barak. But it was Sharon, the last, legendary leader from the 'generation of 1948', to whom it now fell to put the scheme into effect.

He went about it with the remorseless brutality of the nickname, 'the bulldozer', which he had so aptly earned. Ostensibly, it was all done in the name of 'self-defence' and 'retaliation' against the terror which the Palestinians had initiated. In reality, however, it became clearer and clearer that, once he had got the war he needed, he himself was doing all in his power to fuel and perpetuate it.

True, Sharon constantly said that he wanted a ceasefire, and the resumption of the peace process that the ceasefire would bring in his wake. True, too, he even had a 'peace plan' of sorts. But his actions belied his words. Every time there was a period of calm, every time the Palestinians did observe the latest ceasefire call, every time Arafat did apparently get *Hamas* to rein in its suicide bombers, Sharon took fright. And, in his fright, he proceeded to violate the ceasefire himself, with precisely the kind of action, most typically and most frequently the so-called 'targeted killings' of Palestinian activists, which, he knew, would provoke precisely the kind of Palestinian terror he wanted. He did it again and again. It became so blatant as to make the whole pattern of cause and effect the very reverse of the one he and his government sought to sell to their public and the watching world: Israel became the clear aggressor, the Palestinians 'retaliated' in 'self-defence'. He did not want the ceasefire because he did not want a peace process, and he did not want the peace process because the 'peace plan' he had in mind would then be exposed for the total antithesis of both 'peace' and 'process' that it really was. Insofar as he ever spelt it out at all, it would have repudiated all the progress made, via the 1991 Madrid conference, Oslo, and subsequent accords and negotiations, since the peace-making began; it would have consecrated all existing Zionist 'facts on the ground' under yet another 'interim' agreement of indefinite duration during which Israel would be free to create ever more new ones. He hardly even bothered to pretend that he believed in it himself; the 'idea of making peace with the Palestinians is absurd,' he had said at the outset of the *Intifada.*[41]

The only thing Sharon actually wanted was to complete the real agenda—the destruction of Oslo—which lay behind his military campaign. In the guise of his war on a low-tech Palestinian terror, he unleashed a high-tech, state terror of his own. It was the Palestinians' random, hit-and-run, guerrilla-style attacks on soldiers and settlers, or civilians inside Israel proper, drive-by shootings, roadside bombs and home-made mortar volleys versus Israel's vast, conventional military might, its collective punishments, curfews, house-to-house searches, mass arrests, public stripping of civilians to their underwear or marking their arms with a number, re-occupation of major towns, savage pacifications of refugee camps, razing of houses and olive groves; it was suicide bombers versus tanks, helicopter gunships and F-16 fighters unleashed on densely populated areas; the deliberate mayhem of the one versus the inevitable mayhem of the other.

For Sharon it was two things intermingled. On the one hand, it was a personal, gladiatorial contest with an historic adversary who, like him, had reached the climax of his career; he repeatedly and publicly regretted that, in earlier phases of it, he had left the 'murderous' Arafat alive to fight another day. On the other hand, it was defeating what he regarded as the greatest threat to Israel since it came into being in 1948. He held Arafat and the PalestineAuthority directly responsible for every single terror attack, and constantly summoned them to end them. They were patently not responsible, and if there was anything that ensured that they were not, and could not, be, it was Sharon's own actions. He subjected Arafat himself to long, humiliating and wholly paralyzing sieges in his headquarters in Ramallah; in the last of them his army dynamited and bulldozed the entire compound, leaving only Arafat's office standing, an island amid mounds of rubble. Then he wrecked the very institutions, the security services and the police, without which Arafat was powerless to enforce his will. The terror went on, as he knew it must, because it simply wasn't Arafat's; in fact, hero one day as he withstood Sharon's sieges, virtual traitor the next, as he sought in vain to enforce his collaborationist role, it was *against* him. Yet even as he pronounced his historic foe 'irrelevant', Sharon still cast him as the terror's mastermind. It was a logical absurdity that merely betrayed his real purpose. So did the other tasks, far removed from any war on terror, which his soldiers performed. They rampaged through Palestinian ministries—of health, education or agriculture—destroying computers, the files and official records of Palestinian society, smashing furniture and ornaments, ransacking businesses and banks, looting public buildings and private residences; and, just as they had done on an even greater scale during Sharon's invasion of Lebanon twenty years before, they systematically defecated and urinated in any place but the lavatories at their disposal, on floors, carpets or children's paintings, in bottles, drawers or flowerpots, and even in an office photocopier.[42] They carved up the West Bank into countless separate and disconnected enclaves, making all traffic and communication between them impracticable, dangerous or enormously laborious. Routine journeys, to work or home, which might have taken five minutes now took five hours. They wrought havoc on the Palestinian economy; unemployment hit 60 per cent; 70 per cent of the population fell below the poverty line; nearly a third of the children suffered from malnutrition. Education, for the most educated community in the Middle East, was severely disrupted. In short they made life so generally impossible that, unless he had some very powerful reason to stay or nowhere else to go, any normal person would have left.

ANOTHER *NAKBA* IN THE MAKING?

LEAVE, INDEED, IS WHAT A great many Israelis had long devoutly wished the Palestinians would do. Down the years, as many a politician, from Israel's most famous defence minister, the late Moshe Dayan, to Sharon himself,[43] had confided, 'making life impossible'—by bureaucratic, economic and social harassment of one kind or another—became a surreptitious practice by which they sought to achieve it. It had not worked. But had the time now come to try more direct and forceful methods, to re-enact, indeed, something like the mass expulsions of 1948, or the lesser ones of 1967? Would this, another *Nakba*, another Catastrophe, be the *Intifada*'s final outcome? By the time of writing there had been no answer to such questions. But that they were being asked at all, and with such insistence, was suggestive in itself. Enough people in Israel and the world thought that a uniquely favourable set of circumstances—the unprecedented power and influence he had managed to concentrate in his own hands, the momentum of an implacable conflict, the impotence of the Arabs, the whole rightward shift of the Israeli body politic, the opportunities furnished by the American 'war on terror' and the onslaught on Iraq—might tempt Sharon, gambler extraordinary and promulgator of geo-political grand designs, to solve a problem that would never go away.

Their 'demographic problem'—that is what the Israelis now euphemistically called it. What was to be done about the non-Jews in their midst? The problem had of course been there since the Zionist enterprise began; it only found a partial and provisional answer in the expulsions of 1948. And ever since 1967, and the conquest of the remaining 22 per cent of historic Palestine, it had steadily re-asserted itself. From the left to right of the political spectrum, Israelis agreed that, with the Palestinians of the occupied territories added to Israel's own Palestinian citizens, the problem was a relentlessly growing one, a demographic 'time-bomb' in fact, that ultimately threatened the security, integrity and very identity of the Jewish state. A time would come, liberal thinkers warned, when, if Israel wished to preserve its essential nature, its very *raison d'être*, it would have to become an overtly discriminatory, indeed racist state, putting its Jewish character above its democratic one. For the left, broadly speaking, the solution lay in the 'separation' of the two peoples, to be accomplished, ideally, through a final settlement under which Israel would withdraw from most or all of the territories. But for most of the right, whose whole *Greater*-Israel ideology rejected withdrawal and the dismantling of settlements, the ideal, indeed the only feasible, solution lay in 'transfer', which—another euphemism—really meant expulsion and ethnic cleansing. They had long talked about it, and the forms, 'voluntary', by 'agreement' or 'persuasion', 'obligatory', it might take. Far right parties such as *Moledet*, with several seats in the Knesset, had openly inscribed it on their official programmes.[44] The *Likud* had not gone that far, but its public discourse reeked of it. As many as a third of Labour supporters were said to approve it. It was, in fact, a constant feature of the Israeli political landscape which only fluctuated in scale and prominence according to circumstances and the public temper. In 2002, a poll showed that 46 per cent of the population would like to see the 'transfer' of the inhabitants of the occupied territories, and 31 per cent (or a full 60 per cent when the question was posed in a more roundabout way) that of the Palestinians of Israel proper.[45]

The disturbing thing was that, since the *Intifada*, not only had the popularity of 'transfer' grown among its traditional advocates, it had increasingly entered into mainstream political discourse. In the old days this mainstream could take moral refuge in the myths of Israel's pure and miraculous birth. Now, thanks to the 'new historians', it could seriously do so no longer. But, fully apprized of Israel's 'original sin', the mainstream did not, by and large, consider Israel's responsibility for the *Nakba* to be a matter for regret, a wrong to be redressed; on the contrary, according to Ilan Pappé, one of those historians, 'although a very considerable number of Israeli politicians, journalists and academics have ceased to deny what happened in 1948, they have nonetheless also been willing to justify it publicly, not only in retrospect, but as a prescription for the future.' The *Nakba*

> now seems to many in the center of the political map an inevitable and justifiable consequence of the Zionist project in Palestine. If there is any lament it is that the expulsion was not complete. The fact that even an Israeli 'new historian' such as Benny Morris now subscribes to the view that the expulsion . . . should have been more comprehensive helps to legitimize future Israeli plans for further ethnic cleansing. Transfer is now the official moral option recommended by one of Israel's most prestigious academic centers, The Center for Inter-Disciplinary Studies in Herzeliya. It has appeared in policy proposals presented by senior Labour Party ministers to their government. It is openly advocated by university professors, media commentators, and very few now dare to condemn it. . . . The *Nakba* thus is no longer denied in Israel; on the contrary, it is cherished.[46]

After two years of *Intifada*, Sharon felt able to pronounce Oslo dead. But he had yet to achieve the complete subjugation of the Palestinians; yet to establish that puppet leadership, which, like the so-called 'Village Leagues' he had set up in the seventies and early eighties, would pacify and police the territories on Israel's behalf. His task was still incomplete. Pappé again: 'he senses that the public mood in Israel would allow him to go even further, should he wish to repeat the ethnic cleansing not only of the Palestinians in the occupied territories, but, if necessary, also that of the one million Palestinians within the pre-1967 borders.'

Should Israel, under Sharon or anyone else, ever attempt that fateful step, of all the factors, domestic, regional and international, which could thwart it, the United States, the world's only superpower and the metropolitan sponsor on which Israel ultimately depends for its very survival, is by far the most important. Would it summon up the will to do so, or, if it did, would Israel submit? That begs another question in its turn. There is an intrinsic conflict of interest between the two, always latent, sometimes apparent, ultimately as profound as the friendship required to mask or minimize it has to be strong. The more extreme and intransigent Israeli becomes, the more certain it is that, sooner or later, the conflict will get out of hand. And when it does, who, in this very special relationship, will prevail—America, or Israel and 'the friends of Israel' in America? Logically, given the immeasurable disparity of power, it can only be America—but there will be a mighty struggle before it does.

iii · ISRAEL AND THE 'FRIENDS OF ISRAEL' IN AMERICA

Who Is Master—George Bush or Ariel Sharon?

One American who learned about the conflict of interest between Israel and America the hard way is George Bush II. He is the most pro-Israeli president ever. Israeli commentators quipped that he could easily stand in for Sharon as keynote speaker at a *Likud* party convention.[47] But that did not mean that even he could ignore everything the Israeli leader did. In fact, there never was an occupant of the White House who, however sympathetic to the Jewish state, did not at some point feel obliged to exert 'pressure' on the protégé, when the damage its conduct was doing to the interests of its patron became simply more than the patron could bear.

Such an occasion came in April 2002, when, at the height of the second *Intifada*, Sharon launched Operation Defensive Shield. His most ferocious onslaught to date, it covered most of the West Bank, but it was the refugee camp of Jenin—along with the town of Nablus—that bore the brunt of it. The camp was a stronghold of *Hamas* militants, an arsenal of weapons of terror, a principal source of suicide bombers, and Sharon was determined to knock it out.

But his army encountered fierce resistance. There were well-founded fears that a massacre would take place, or already had, and, in an Arab world already aroused by the plight of their Palestinian brethren, hatred of the United States was at fever-pitch; distress signals were coming from key American allies, such as Jordan and Egypt, warning that if Sharon went unchecked, their regimes risked collapse, along with the whole structure of peace with Israel which they upheld; militants and outsiders—Saddam Hussein or Lebanon's fundamentalist, Iranian-backed militia, *Hizbullah*—were profiting from the helplessness of the mainstream; Crown Prince Abdullah, effective ruler of the world's largest oil-exporting country, was growing manifestly impatient. The matter was so serious that secretary of state Colin Powell was moved to tell Israel—albeit with the tact and deference which Israel usually inspires in American officials—that, 'as a friend, we have to take note of the long-term strategic consequences' of its actions and their 'effect on other nations in the region and the international climate'.

Finally, after long hesitation, Bush appeared to think better of his policy of 'disengagement'. This had really become a recipe for Sharon to prosecute, with growing ferocity, an Israeli 'war on terror' which, after 11 September, he likened to America's own. Bush launched yet another, if tepid, Middle East 'peace initiative' whose ultimate, now standard objective, was the creation of 'two states, Israel and Palestine, living side by side, in peace and security'. To be sure, and as ever, he reserved his main barbs for Arafat and the Palestinians. But at the same time—and here came the real pressure—he told Sharon to get his troops out of the West Bank 'without delay'. He made this demand in the manner of a leader expecting obedience. And he sent his secretary of state, less pre-disposed towards Israel than most of his Administration, to the region with a mandate to bring this about. When Sharon showed no sign of obliging, Bush grew more peremptory in tone. Yes, he told journalists, 'I meant what I said to the prime minister of Israel: I expect there to be withdrawal without delay.'

Before long, however, it became clear that if he ever did mean it—and there had been serious doubts about that—he didn't mean it any longer. And the reason why he didn't, or couldn't, lay right there, under his very nose, in Washington itself. There, Israel, and the 'friends of Israel' in America, were giving a spectacular, unprecedented demonstration of their ability to make the leader of the world's only superpower bend to the will of a faraway country of about the same size and population of one of the smallest of America's fifty states, New Jersey, say, or Connecticut. There they raised a hue and cry against this aberration from the most partisan of pro-Israeli norms. Sharon dispatched *his* envoy to Washington, in the person of his arch-rival the former prime minister Binyamin

Netanyahu. Formerly a resident of the United States, Netanyahu was a master of its politics and public relations, whom New York Representative Benjamin Gilman had once welcomed in Congress with the assurance that he was 'not only among friends', but 'among family', using the Hebrew expression for that.[48] He was, if anything, more extreme than Sharon himself. Senator Joe Lieberman, one of the most noted 'friends of Israel', asked him to address the chamber. 'I am concerned,' he told it, 'that when it comes to terror directed against Israel, the moral and strategic clarity that is so crucial for victory is being twisted beyond recognition. My concern deepened when, incredibly, Israel was asked to stop fighting terror and return to a negotiating table with a regime that is committed to the destruction of the Jewish state and openly embraces terror.' Thus was the plenipotentiary of America's most lavishly indulged of protégés invited to attack its patron from Capitol Hill itself.

Nor was he absent, a few days later, from a great pro-Israeli demonstration, outside Congress, in which the 'friends of Israel' showed their strength on the streets. On display was the newly potent triple alliance between the Jewish lobby, the so-called 'neo-conservatives' who dominated the Bush Administration and the 'Christian right.' These Evangelicals, or millenarian groups among them, believed that Israel and the 'ingathering of the exiles' were confirmation of biblical prophesy, prelude to Armageddon and the Second Coming of Christ. They used to be taxed with anti-Semitism; and certainly, their scenario for the End of Days is not at all kind to the Jews, who—while they themselves go straight to heaven without the pain of dying—will face a choice between conversion and annihilation of a very unpleasant kind. In 1994, the Anti-Defamation League, a Jewish organization officially dedicated to combating racial prejudice, published a scathing attack on them in a report entitled *The Religious Right: Assault on Pluralism and Tolerance in America*.

Eight years later, however, the League had entirely changed its views. 'Motives don't matter,' said Abraham Foxman, its director, 'as long as they don't make their support conditional on us accepting their motives'.[49] After all, in a country where the numbers of churchgoing Christians are far and away the highest in the Western world, where the interplay between religion and politics is intense, the Evangelicals were not an ally to be lightly spurned. Accounting for nearly 20 per cent of the electorate, they were a bulwark of the Republican party which Bush—said to share some of their beliefs—and other politicians took very seriously indeed. They were represented in the Administration and Congress, where one of them, James M. Inhofe, Senator from Oklahoma, opined that the occupied territories belonged to Israel because 'God said so.' They believed that Israel was beyond criticism because it was a vehicle of the divine purpose. They didn't believe in a peaceful settlement because the more Jews 'returned', settled and expanded, and the more hostilities which that provoked with the Arabs, the sooner the End of Days would come. They admired Sharon's martial ardour. They reportedly sent some 100,000 angry e-mails to the White House to protest the 'pressure' Bush was exerting on him.

In the face of this display of domestic political power, the President's resolve crumbled entirely. His secretary of state came home empty-handed: there was no Israeli withdrawal. And the defiant and bellicose Sharon, whom the Israelis themselves used to call 'a war waiting to happen',[50] he now called 'a man of peace'.

The Lobby

This abject climb-down was, at least in part, testimony to the power which Israel and the 'friends of Israel' had acquired in Washington. As *The Gun and The Olive Branch* recounts,[51] it was David Bengurion, the 'father' of Israel, who had first, and with brilliant, decisive effect, systematically targeted American Jewry—till then far from united behind, or even very interested in, ethnocentric political Zionism—as an instrument of leverage on the foreign policies of the newly emergent superpower. Since then, the nation's six million Jews, barely more than 2 per cent of the total population, have gone from strength to strength. In his book *Jewish Power*,[52] J. J. Goldberg called them 'the largest and most powerful Jewish community in history'. They are America's best-educated ethnic group, next to the much smaller Japanese American community its richest, and have achieved a strong, sometimes dominant, role in economic, cultural, and intellectual fields.[53]

And they have rallied overwhelmingly to the cause. 'Since the creation of Israel', wrote Seymour Martin Lipset and Earl Raab, 'the affinity of American Jews for Israel has been expressed on a dramatic and even heroic scale'.[54] For anti-assimilationist Jews in particular, Israel became a key factor in their sense of identity and achievement, an intrinsic part of their prestige and clout as an American community.

A great landmark in this evolution was Israel's smashing victory in the 1967 Arab-Israeli war, and the immense pride it bred. For many American Jews it was an event of even greater immediate and personal significance than the birth of the state had been, 'as though [Israel's] fate were literally their own'.[55] With time, however, the impulse to justify Israel's rule over a conquered people caused what some saw as a 'moral coarsening' of the community—increasingly removing it from those liberal, humane, multi-cultural and progressive ideals through which it had traditionally made so impressive a contribution to the welfare of American society at large—as well as an 'unapologetic tribalism' that was easily converted into raw political power in the nation's capital.[56]

Washington, then, became the all-important, metropolitan source of strength without which Israel could never, in the face of Palestinian and Arab hostility, have sustained and developed its strength at home. The two strengths became so complementary, so organically linked, that Israel and 'the friends of Israel' in America amounted, for all practical purposes, to one and the same thing. In whatever measure one deemed the friends to be mere extensions of Israel's will, or autonomous forces in their own right, the fact was that since this book was written, Israel's influence on America's Middle East policies, exerted by itself or through them, grew more formidable than ever, and (with the ironic exception of George Bush the father) each new president became more pro-Israeli than the last, a process that reached its apogee under George Bush the son.

The Jewish lobby, the organized expression of Israeli influence in Washington, was not merely the most powerful ethnic interest group to have emerged in recent American history, it is probably the most powerful of any kind. 'We no longer feel that we live in the Diaspora, the United States no longer has a government of Gentiles, but an administration in which the Jews are full partners in the decision-making at all levels';[57] 'never in our history has a foreign power had such a grip on our government';[58] 'its pervasive intimidation . . . seems to reach every government center and even house of worship and revered institution of high learning.'[59] Whether it comes, almost awestruck, from Israelis who have benefited from it, or, in disgust, from leading Americans who have suffered, hyperbole such as this is commonplace whenever 'the Lobby' comes under discussion.

The Lobby is a loose network of some fifty-odd organizations of which the two most influential are the American Israel Public Affairs Committee, or AIPAC, and the Conference of Presidents of Major American Jewish Organizations. Both, along with such bodies as the World Zionist Organization and the Anti-Defamation League, are more hawkish than many of the others and—though the Jewish community at large too has also shifted to the right—than it too. Both support *Likud* against Labour, sharing the Israeli right's distrust of, or outright opposition to, the Oslo accord. J. J. Goldberg describes AIPAC as 'an all-purpose pressure machine' with 'no agenda but Israel'; although it and the Conference have managed to get themselves recognized, in Washington's corridors of power, 'as the all but official voices of American Jewry', but they are more like an 'organ of *Likud* policy'.[60]

AIPAC first really came into its own in the early eighties when, under President Ronald Reagan, the United States connived in Sharon's disastrous invasion of Lebanon. It was—said a former AIPAC staffer—a 'revolution', 'so dramatically [had] American Middle East policy shifted in favor of Israel'. According to AIPAC executive director Thomas Dine, Reagan and his secretary of state George Shultz were going to 'leave a legacy that will be important to Israel's security for decades to come'. Shultz had told him that he would 'build institutional arrangement so that eight years from now, if there is a secretary of state who is not positive about Israel, he will not be able to overcome the bureaucratic relationship between Israel and the United States that we have established'.[61]

CONGRESS

AIPAC CONCENTRATES ITS PERSUASIVE POWERS mainly on the legislative branch of government. Money is its first instrument, in the vast amounts available to it from so prosperous a Jewish community. Exceptionally among ethnic interest groups—along, perhaps, with the much weaker example of the Cuban American lobby—it operates on a nationwide scale. Exploiting what many regard as the corruption of American laws on campaign finance, donors, via nearly a hundred pro-Israeli Political Action Committees, can exert a decisive influence on the fortunes of Congressional candidates anywhere in the land.

Fear and intimidation are AIPAC's second instrument. It keeps a close record of every Congressman's voting habits. It rewards the compliant—those, as an Israeli newspaper put it, who 'forever speechify about the right of Jews to settle anywhere in the Land of Israel, keep showing maps and charts demonstrating that nothing short of the Jordan River can be [Israel's] defensible border, and say that even this border may not be enough because no Arab can ever be trusted'.[62] And it ruthlessly punishes the recalcitrant. Every Congressman knows the names of those whom it has undone. An early victim was Paul Findley, a Republican senator from Illinois, who subsequently became an outspoken campaigner against it. 'Congress', he said, 'behaves as if it were a sub-section of the Israeli parliament.' Not in thirty-five years 'has a word been expressed . . . in either chamber . . . that deserves to be called a debate on Middle East policy;' for 'on Capitol Hill, criticism of Israel, even in private conversation, is all but forbidden, as downright unpatriotic, if not anti-Semitic'.[63] A recent victim was Earl Hillyard. AIPAC turned on this black Representative from Alabama after, interesting himself in foreign affairs, he had opposed a House resolution that gave *carte blanche* to Sharon's brutal pacification of the West Bank. It opened its coffers to a black opponent who was ready to mouth the correct sentiments about a distant country of almost zero interest to his potential voters. Israel's *Haaretz* newspaper noted that among the names of the contributors to the victor's election campaign were 'ten Cohens from New York and New Jersey; but before one gets to the

Cohens, there were Abrams, Ackerman, Adler, Amir, Asher, Baruch, Basok, Berger, Berman, Bergman, Bernstein and Blumenthal. All from the East Coast, Chicago and Los Angeles. It's highly unlikely that any of them have ever visited Alabama'.[64] The 'votes and bows', said former Senator James Abourezk, 'have nothing to do with love of Israel' but 'everything to do with the money that is fed into their campaigns' by the Lobby.[65] The result, according to William Quandt, a member of the National Security Council under Nixon and Carter, is that '70 per cent to 80 per cent of all members of Congress will go along with whatever they think AIPAC wants'.[66]

What AIPAC wants is basically two things. One is virtually unconditional American support for Israel wherever, in the United Nations and other forums, and whenever, in the latest twist of the peace process or a dispute with Arab governments, Israel itself wants it. There should be 'no daylight' between an American government, be it Republican or Democrat, and the Israeli government—especially if it is a hard-line *Likud* one. In the immediate aftermath of the Presidential humiliation at Sharon's hands, both chambers surpassed themselves in a grovelling exhibition of knee-jerk fealty to Israel. The Senate, in a 94–2 vote, passed a resolution effectively equating Israel with the United States in 'the war on terror'. Nary a hint of a suggestion that Sharon had any blameworthy part in the escalating violence. Within minutes, the House of Representatives passed an even stronger one by a 325-to-21 majority. 'Let every terrorist know, the American people will never abandon freedom, democracy or Israel,' said House majority whip Tom Delay; Palestinian attacks on Israel were 'attacks against liberty, and all free people must recognize that Israel's fight is our fight'. One of the dissenting minority, Nick Rahall, called it 'so unbalanced, so one-sided' that 'we've become the laughingstock of the world'. But there was soon even worse to come in this paroxysm of unquestioning bias, when the House majority leader Dick Armey, a Republican from Texas, told his astonished and disbelieving interviewer: 'I'm content to have Israel grab the entire West Bank. I happen to believe that the Palestinians should leave . . . to have those people who have been aggressors against Israel retired to some other area'.[67] Such ethnic cleansing is not even the official, openly declared agenda of Sharon himself.

The other thing AIPAC wants is an unceasing flow of aid to Israel. And it unfailingly gets it in the form of the annual payments which Congressional committees, almost all of whose members are recipients of huge AIPAC campaign donations, lay before the Senate and the House, which then proceed to vote them through with barely any debate, let alone demur. In earlier years the aid to Israel was relatively small; only in the sixties and seventies did America become its principal economic and military patron, in addition to the political and diplomatic one it already was. But, once it did, it did so with the unstinting excess that characterizes all its dealings with its foster-child extraordinary. In recent times the declared annual package, officially classified as 'economic' and 'military' aid, has hovered above the $3-billion-a-year mark, but, thanks to all manner of disguised subventions, special privileges, *ad hoc* extras, loans which—thanks to annual bouts of Congressional kind-heartedness—almost always end up as grants, the real amount is actually very much more than that, probably $5 billion or more. Thus has a country smaller in size than, say, Haiti or Hong Kong, become far and away the largest single recipient of American largesse. And long gone are the days when it might have qualified as a poor, or developing, country, those being the normal, indeed in principle the only, beneficiaries of this kind of assistance. By 1997, its *per capita* gross national product, at $16,180, equalled that of a prosperous European country such as Ireland, and had overtaken Spain's. By the turn of the century, according to one calculation, Israel had received over $91 billion in foreign aid. And that did not take into account more than $15 billion in loan guarantees of one kind or another, or the more than $20 billion in supposedly philanthropic, and therefore tax-exempt, contributions which American Jews have made to Israel since its foundation, contributions that are liable to end up in the coffers of such 'charitable' institutions as, say, LIBI—The Fund for Strengthening Israel's Defense. Official benefactions to Israel amount to no less than a third of the United States' entire annual aid allocations—and half if one factors in its indispensable concomitant, the money that goes to Egypt as a reward for keeping the peace with Israel. So it was that between 1949 and 1997 the $64 billion that went to the 1,410 million inhabitants of sub-Saharan Africa, Latin America and the Caribbean combined, was $7 billion less than what went to an Israeli population of (at the time) fewer than 6 million. That is to say, for every dollar the United States spent on an African, it spent $250.65 on an Israeli, and for every dollar on someone from the Western hemisphere outside the United States, $214 on an Israeli. But most American tax-payers are almost certainly blithely unaware of the supreme act of munificence, the *nec plus ultra* of financial altruism, that their government lends itself to in their name. Since Israel gets its whole annual aid appropriation during the first month of the fiscal year, instead of in the quarterly instalments that every other recipient has to be content with, it can promptly invest any surplus funds in American Treasury notes. And since, on the other hand, the American government has to borrow the money to finance these donations, it pays interest on the selfsame sums on which Israel earns it. Taking such factors into account, economist Thomas Stauffer calculates that, since 1973, the actual cost, to the American tax-payer, of American aid to Israel added up to a whopping $240 billion.[68]

The Administration

Another key measure of the Lobby's growing power is its influence over Administration appointments. It is in dealings with the executive branch that that other key agency, the Conference of Presidents of Major American Jewish Organizations, comes particularly into its own. The major breakthrough came with President Reagan—then even more dramatically with Bill Clinton. So dramatically in fact that, in 1994, the Israeli newspaper *Maariv*[69] carried a long article bearing the title 'The Jews Who Run Clinton's Court'. Its Washington correspondent, Avinoam Bar-Yosef, marvelled at the 'huge Jewish power' which his Democratic Administration embodied, at the extraordinary number of Jews who occupied some of its highest and most sensitive positions. Many of them were 'warm' Jews to boot. Some had lived in Israel, or had close personal and professional ties with it; others were graduates of the Lobby.

Seven out of eleven of the National Security Council's senior staff were Jews. Two 'warm' Jews, Martin Indyk and Dennis Ross, headed its Middle East peace-seeking team. And once, when Bar-Yosef telephoned the State Department, he thought for a moment that he had mistakenly called the Israeli Foreign Ministry; the voice at the other end of the line answered in such flawless Israeli Hebrew.

It represented a total rout of 'the Arabists'. Typically, according to the caricature often drawn of them by their pro-Israeli detractors, these were scions of the East Coast, White-Anglo-Saxon-Protestant establishment who, emotionally involved with the Arab world, had long dominated American Middle East policies from the State Department or the CIA. In truth, they had at most tried, from time to time and without much success, to limit the pro-Israeli bias of policies which, since Eisenhower's day, had been shaped more by domestic political considerations than any expertise they could bring to bear.

Under Bush, the 'friends of Israel' reached their apogee, measured by their numerical strength as well as their influence, within his Administration. They did so as the so-called 'neo-conservatives'. They had first made their mark as an identifiable group some thirty years before under the aegis of the Committee on the Present Danger. They were imbued with a Manichean, 'good-versus-evil' view of the world; their hallmarks were a crusading zeal against the Soviet Union, strident advocacy of larger military budgets and fanatical opposition to arms control. Central, if not pre-eminent, in their wider philosophy of action was their championship not simply of Israel, but of the right-wing Israel of Menachim Begin and Yitzhak Shamir, Netanyahu and Sharon. For them American and Israeli interests were one and the same. They had gone from the margins of power under Carter to its centre under Reagan. But it was only under Bush II that they came truly into their own: indeed, they became the chief shapers of his policy.

They had built themselves round two key organizations. One was the Jewish Institute for National Security Affairs, whose objective, according to its website, was to 'educate the American public about the role Israel can and does play in bolstering democratic interests in the Mediterranean and the Middle East'. The other was the Center for Security Policy, virtually identical with the first in aims and methods, and interlocking with it in membership.[70] The militant, far-right, almost messianic ideas which, under Bush, they were to translate into the actual policy of the world's only superpower had found their first authoritative formulation, appropriately enough, in a very Israeli setting. Middle Eastern components of that policy which were to come to full fruition in the aftermath of 11 September had been clearly foreshadowed in a document called *A Clean Break: A Strategy for Securing the Realm*, which Richard Perle and Douglas Feith, and four others, addressed in 1996 to Israeli premier-designate Netanyahu. Their virulently anti-Palestinian opinions were already well known. One of them, Feith, spelled them out in a succession of writings urging the reversal of all those inroads, theoretical ones at least, which, as the peace process unfolded, the Palestinians had made into official American thinking on the issue. The Palestinians, he argued, simply did not exist 'as a national group as such'; Jordan was the true 'Palestinian state'; the League of Nations mandate had granted Jews irrevocable settlement rights in the West Bank; Israel should re-occupy 'the areas under Palestine Authority control' even though 'the price in blood would be high'.[71]

In *A Clean Break* the authors proposed a hugely ambitious, region-wide, neo-imperial agenda, with Israel—'proud, wealthy, solid and strong'—as the cornerstone of a truly new and peaceful Middle East. It would no longer simply 'contain its foes, it [would] transcend them'. First, it should replace 'land for peace', the core principle of the Oslo accord, with 'peace for peace', or 'peace through strength'. Its claim to biblical Palestine was 'legitimate and noble'. The Arabs must be pressed into 'unconditional acceptance' of Israel's rights, 'especially in the territorial dimension'. Secondly, in 'strategic partnership' with the United States, it should embark on a grandiose scheme of geo-political engineering for the whole region. It would start by 'removing Saddam Hussein from power in Iraq'. Then—if successful in helping Jordan restore a fellow-Hashemite dynasty there—Iraq, Jordan and Turkey could combine in 'weakening, containing and even rolling back Syria', and, by extension, other 'agents of aggression', Iran and *Hizbullah*, that strike at Israel via Lebanese territory.

Under Bush, Perle, identified by Seymour Hersh in his biography of Henry Kissinger[72] as someone whom Kissinger discovered to have been passing classified material from the National Security Council to the Israeli embassy, became chairman of the Pentagon's Defense Policy Board, while Feith, identified by the Israeli newspaper *Haaretz* as closely linked to extremist Israeli settlers in the West Bank,[73] became deputy under secretary of defense for policy at the Pentagon. Dozens of kindred spirits, many of them graduates of the Lobby and its sub-groups entered the bureaucracy, from deputy secretary of defense Paul Wolfowitz, 'an over-the-top crazy when it comes to Israel',[74] to Frank Gaffney, chief executive officer of the Center for Security Policy, who once underwrote a TV and print advertising campaign, financed in part by the far-right, Ultra-Orthodox Californian bingo magnate Irving Moskowitz, designating the Palestinians as enemy Number One in the 'war on terror'.[75]

It was so very far-reaching, this penetration, that some Israelis began to wonder out loud whether the protégé had now turned the tables on the superpower patron; whether, in the words of novelist and celebrated jazz musician Gilad Atzmon, America was 'about to lose its sovereignty . . . becoming a remote colony of an apparently far greater state, the Jewish state . . . very small place in the eastern corner of the Mediterranean Sea' though it might be. 'We must remember', he went on, 'that this kind of strange scenario does happen. Last month I heard Israel Shamir's [an anti-Zionist Israeli historian and peace activist] observation regarding this very issue. In a very open manner he said that no one would be surprised to hear that during different phases of the British Empire the world was governed by a very close group of Eton graduates. "Sometimes", he added, "great empires are taken over by very marginal groups." We might have to acknowledge that this is the case with America. American foreign policy is dictated by a very marginal group of Zionist activists, even by the state of Israel itself'.[76]

The Media

Atzmon is, of course, overstating things—a hyperbole, however, that only serves to dramatize the paucity of this kind of talk in the nation where, logically, one would most expect to hear it. The disproportionate power of the Lobby, its grip on the Administration and Congress, is more discussed abroad, and especially in Israel, where the press is freer and more forthright on matters Israeli, Zionist and Jewish than it is in America itself. And that is testimony to the influence the Lobby also exerts on the media, academia and public opinion at large. Indeed, this influence constitutes its third main asset. Twenty five years ago, the Jewish anti-Zionist writer, Alfred Lilienthal, identified what he called 'Israel's stranglehold over the American media' as the most important of the three. However, given the Lobby's subsequent, spectacular achievements in relation to the other two, that is probably no longer the case.[77]

In the mainstream media at least, there is a kind of taboo over discussion of the very subject, so sensitive is it felt to be, among both Jews and non-Jews. 'Even the words 'Jewish lobby" stick in the throat', wrote Philip Weiss in the *New York Observer*.[78] People talk freely about black power, or the pressure tactics of other ethnic groups, but almost never about something called Jewish power, even though this power is obvious, understood by everyone in politics, and actually more important; in fact, it is 'too important *not* to talk about'. But 'you don't see the *New York Times* pussyfooting when it comes to the anti-Castro lobby or the National Rifle Association, two other powerful special-interest groups. When they muscle the system, we read faintly sinister accounts of the Arlington, Va., headquarters for the gun lobby . . . or hysterical interviews with nutso Castro-haters on Eighth Street in Miami . . . Talking about "Jewish influence" reminds people of the Nazis'.[79] Almost no one in the mainstream media raises the sensitive question of dual loyalty, of whether, in a potential clash of interests, American citizens, and for ethnic and religious, not moral, reasons, would place those of a foreign state above those of their own. The unfortunate result is that only at the periphery, in the 'alternative' media, is one liable to find a systematic critique. That periphery includes a left which, America having the generally conservative politics it does, is apt to be considered unrepresentative or outlandish, and a far right tainted by racism, religious bigotry and anti-Semitism. In the absence of the serious, responsible, centrist discussion of this topic for which the

Lobby itself is largely to blame, it becomes all too easy for it to brand any criticism at all as the product of extremist prejudice—or the kind of nonsense that Arab conspiracy theorists might peddle. Yet, given this lack of candour in one of the most open societies on earth, it is hardly surprising, Weiss points out, that such theories take root in the much less open ones of the Middle East. And they can only take deeper root when even so brilliant and generally liberal a performer as the *New York Times*'s foreign affairs columnist and old Middle East hand Thomas Friedman, told by a leading Saudi intellectual and anti-government critic that 'the Jews control America', simply walks out in indignation, rather than take issue with this admittedly provocative remark.[80]

Obviously, this failure to address such a key question of American domestic politics extends to the object of all the Lobby's solicitude, and the source of its occasional discomforts, Israel itself. It, too, is generally spared anything like the rigorous scrutiny it gets in the rest of the Western world. It is not so much the reporting of the Israel-Palestine conflict on the ground—though that is generally circumspect and more likely be slanted in Israel's favor rather than the Palestinians'—where the indulgence shows, but in the op-ed pages of daily newspapers and journals of opinion. Editorials are overwhelmingly, at times almost monolithically, pro-Israeli. Even the Lobby occasionally concedes that. At the outset of the second *Intifada*, one of its member-organizations, the Anti-Defamation League, conducted a survey of the editorials in forty three major American newspapers; its findings were that thirty six of them displayed either 'out-and-out support' for Israel or what it defined as 'even-handed commentary'.[81]

Most of the leading newspapers are replete with outright apologists for Israel, many of them Jewish, who are not remotely matched by any contrary opinion from the other side. Some leading pundits—and Jews—do criticize the Israeli right, or some of the less defensible forms of Israeli behaviour, severely enough to incur the virulent abuse of what one of them, Anthony Lewis of the *New York Times*, called 'Jewish McCarthyism'.[82] But it does not have to be very severe to incur it, and the fact is—says Michael Lind, senior fellow at the New America Foundation—that 'anything more than the mildest criticism of Israel is taboo in the mainstream media'.[83] Apparently even a magazine such as *Newsweek*, which is not one of the more dogmatically pro-Israeli of its kind, sometimes finds it hard to attain even a show of impartiality. Thus, early in the *Intifada*, it featured a sympathetic interview with Sharon, then in opposition, conducted by Lally Weymouth, a pro-Israeli columnist in the *Washington Post* whose family owns the magazine. The next week, by way of 'balance', Weymouth interviewed Sharon's political adversary, centre-left prime minister Barak, during which she asked such cosy questions as: 'You offered Arafat a generous deal. Why is he turning to violence?' There followed an interview with former *Likud* premier Netanyahu, then another Weymouth encounter with former Labour premier Shimon Peres. So altogether *Newsweek*'s attempt at editorial even-handedness amounted to offering readers the thoughts of two Israeli leaders from the right and two from the left. But what about the Palestinians? There was, it is true, one contribution from them, an essay by Azmi Bishara, the Knesset's most eloquent Palestinian deputy. But there was apparently no room for it in the magazine's American edition—where his point of view would have been novel and arresting—but only in its European one, where it was rather more commonplace.[84]

If America's coverage of Israel is set against Europe's, it sometimes looks more like a cover-up, or at least a rationalization, of Israel's excesses. When, at the beginning of the second *Intifada*, a French television cameraman caught on film the shooting by the Israeli army of twelve-year-old Muhammad al-Durra, as he cowered for protection behind his father, it galvanized world-wide indignation. Not many European newspapers had much doubt that this was a deliberate act. But the American media, characteristically evasive, 'revived one of the Middle East press corps more notorious clichés: the shop-worn euphemism "caught in the crossfire" often used to describe high-profile civilian killings by Israeli soldiers'.[85] A month later, in a report on the conclusion of his 'personal' investigation into the boy's death, the Israeli commander in Gaza not surprisingly absolved himself of all blame. 'It is hard to describe in mild terms the stupidity of this bizarre investigation'—such was the verdict of Israel's leading, liberal newspaper *Haaretz*. But while, among foreign newspapers, the Jerusalem correspondent of the London *Guardian* dismissed the enquiry with an unsparing report under the headline 'Israel Washes Its Hands of Boy's Death', the ever-protective *New York Times* played it straight, with the deadpan headline 'Israeli Army Says Palestinians May Have Shot Gaza Boy'.[86]

In the nature of things, however, it is usually the correspondents on the ground rather than the editorialists and commentators at home who are the first to breach the walls of Israel's irreproachability. For they are bound, if they are honest, to describe with at least a modicum of accuracy what they see with their own eyes. But whenever they do, whenever they begin, cautiously enough, to venture on to ground already occupied by their European counterparts, the Lobby goes into action. So it is that while this self-same American press is perceived abroad as being unambiguously, if not grotesquely, sympathetic to Israel, the most visible form of media criticism in the United States actually takes the opposite view—namely that American newspapers are constantly propagandizing for the Palestinian cause. When they took exception to some of the reporting on the siege of the Jenin refugee camp in April 2002, and other episodes in Sharon's onslaught on the West Bank, the Lobby and its ancillaries launched a campaign against leading American newspapers, even including—and not for the first time—the *New York Times.* A blizzard of e-mails told its pro-Israeli readers to boycott it for a day. They had no problem in mobilizing an army of individual protesters; as the *Forward*, a Jewish newspaper, observed, 'rooting out perceived anti-Israeli bias in the media has become for many American Jews the most direct and emotional outlet for connecting with the conflict 6,000 miles away'. The *Times* felt obliged to issue an abject apology after publishing two photographs of a pro-Israeli parade in Manhattan; its heinous crime had been to put a group of anti-Israeli protesters in the foreground. Similar protests hit the *Los Angeles Times*, the *Chicago Tribune*, the *Minneapolis Star Tribune*, the *Philadelphia Inquirer*, and the *Miami Herald.* On the East Coast, at least one local radio station lost $1 million from a Jewish philanthropist while other stations attempting to cover the Middle East with some degree of fairness were said to have lost even more.[87]

The Lobby boasts a plethora of organizations dedicated to the unmasking and correcting of anti-Israeli opinions wherever—in the media, academia, the entertainment industry, civil society in general—they can find it. In addition to AIPAC, the better known include the Zionist Organization of America, the Anti-Defamation League, and CAMERA, the Committee for Accuracy in Middle East Reporting.

AIPAC never simply confined itself to legitimate propaganda. In 1983, in a pamphlet called *The Campaign to Discredit Israel*, it published what was effectively a blacklist of twenty one organizations and thirty nine individuals 'who are active in the effort to weaken the bonds between the US and Israel, who seek to enhance US-Arab relations at the expense of Israel, or who perform paid services to Arab governments pursuing these goals'. Reactions to the blacklists were so negative that it took its activities underground. It continued to monitor 'anti-Israeli' individuals and groups, but disseminated the results secretly. According to a scholar who once worked as an AIPAC researcher, 'revelations about AIPAC's blacklisting and smear tactics have barely scratched the surface of the pro-Israel lobby's secret activities . . . AIPAC operates a covert section within its research department that monitors and keeps files on politicians, journalists, academics, Arab-American activists, Jewish liberals, and others it labels "anti-Jewish". AIPAC selects information from these files and secretly circulates lists of the 'guilty', together with their alleged political misdeeds, buttressed by their statements, often totally out of context'. Later it brought out a weekly publication called *Activities*, warning its selected readers—such as major Jewish leaders, pro-Israeli activists, the Israeli embassy—that they were free to make use of its material 'subject only to the proviso that AIPAC not be attributed as its source'.[88]

The Anti-Defamation League, which used to publish a similar blacklist called *Arab Propaganda in America: Vehicles and Voices*, has ventured into open criminality. Originally established with the laudable purpose of combating racial and religious prejudice, it degenerated into a conspiratorial and—with a $45 million budget—extremely well-funded vigilante group devoted primarily to identifying and discrediting critics of Israel. In the 1980s, during the tenure of Seymour Reich, who went on to become the chairman of the Conference of Presidents, it circulated two annual fund-raising letters warning Jewish parents against allegedly negative influences on their children arising from the increasing Arab presence on American university campuses. Later it was it was found to have been engaged in a massive espionage operation directed against American citizens opposed to the Israeli occupation of the West Bank and Gaza and the Apartheid regime in South Africa. Through the planting of informants in the meetings of Arab-American and other civil action organizations, and the bribery of corrupt officials, the League illegally compiled records on more than 1,000 citizens, mostly Arab-Americans, but including anti-Apartheid activists, environmentalists and members of such groups as the American Civil Liberties Union and the American Friends Service Committee. It spent millions of dollars trying to prevent the case from coming to trial. In 1994, it stumped up $75,000 for the County of San Francisco in return for the district attorney's dropping of criminal charges against it. Two years later it made an out-of-court payment of $175,000 in a civil rights lawsuit brought by the American-Arab Anti-Discrimination Committee and other plaintiffs.[89]

These pro-Israeli organizations have at their disposal that most potent of weapons, the charge of anti-Semitism. They probably use it most effectively as a pre-emptive threat: any would-be transgressor knows that he risks coming into the line of fire. But often enough they actually unsheath it, and often for the flimsiest of reasons. That makes for a crucial advantage over any other lobby, however rich and powerful. 'If', writes Andrew Hurley in his book *One Nation under Israel*, 'one disagrees with or opposes the Farm Lobby, for example, one is free to say so. No such freedom exists in America so far as opposition to the Israel lobby is concerned. It is simply taboo. To do so automatically exposes one to being branded anti-Semitic, a fascist, a Nazi, or part of the lunatic fringe.'[90]

Early in the second *Intifada*, CAMERA detected what it called 'blatant anti-Semitism on CNN'. The global television network is generally considered pro-Israeli in the Arab world, certainly much more partial to the Israeli point of view than, say, its British counterpart, the BBC. The trivial occasion for this accusation, to which CAMERA devoted an entire press release, was the manner in which

CNN reporter Fionnula Sweeny had paraphrased a Palestinian-American living in Ramallah as saying that 'she would have voted for George W. Bush because the Democratic vice presidential candidate, Joe Lieberman, is Jewish'. It did not allege that CNN's reporter agreed with this supposedly anti-Semitic comment, only that the comment was reported 'as if this were a perfectly normal sentiment'. About the same time, Israeli prime minister Barak, members of his staff and the foreign ministry, met with CNN representatives to express their concern over the network's 'slanted and one-sided reportage of violence in the territories', particularly that of its Palestinian correspondent Rula Amin. Earlier, discussing Israel's media strategy with a group of sixty Jewish American leaders and other prominent supporters of Israel, government spokesman Nachman Shai had revealed that 'we are putting real pressure on the heads of CNN to have [Amin and other reporters] replaced with more objective pro-Israeli reporters that are willing to tell our side of the story'. Amin had been the object of almost obsessive loathing by many of Israel's supporters in the media. Among them, Amos Perlmutter, in the *Washington Times*, called her 'a purveyor of Palestinian propaganda'. His only example was the claim that 'with no evidence, she reported the false Palestinian argument that two Israelis who were lynched in Ramallah were Mossad agents'. In fact, Amin had merely reported that the mob which attacked them had 'assumed that these were undercover units'.[91]

These campaigns, noisy, pervasive and indefatigable, take their toll. For editors and publishers who are already zealous in the Israeli cause, they are of course superfluous. And these are many. But those, less so, who want to do justice 'to the other side of the story' know what moral and material damage, through vilification, boycotts and the withdrawal of advertising, they are liable to suffer if they try too hard. Most are no more willing than Congressmen to step out of line. 'In today's world', writes Raff Ellis in *Yellow Times*,[92] 'there are a handful of sensitive topics such as abortion, gay rights and the death penalty that are guaranteed to bring out the strongest advocates, *pro* and *con*, to the front lines, guns blazing. But criticism of Israel, which is at the top of the sensitivity list, sends publishers and pundits alike into overdrive in favour of the latest AIPAC position. The *pro* positions way outnumber the *cons* because *con* is seldom permitted. Behind closed doors some news types will admit they firmly adhere to the pro-Israeli line because it is editorial policy. This issue has long ceased having anything to do with right and wrong, it has simply become policy'.

Many journalists privately admit that they fear the retribution of pro-Israeli publishers and editors, and 'generally understand critical words about Israel to be hazardous to careers'.[93] Here is one of several such episodes recounted by a young Coloradan, Mark Schneider, who said that, before he took up political activism on the Palestinians' behalf, 'I used to be sceptical about . . . allegations of censorship and self-censorship in the American media, but now I've seen it first-hand.' The newly installed George Bush II had just launched the first large-scale bombing raid of his presidency into Iraq's so-called 'no-fly zones'. Schneider went on:

> Knowing my group would protest this bombing one of the local TV stations called us for an interview. In the studio hours later, a spokesperson for our group, Rev. Bob Kinsey, was asked by one of the station's veteran reporters what he thought were the main reasons for the troubles in the Middle East. Rev. Kinsey spoke of the massive US military aid to Israel and the resulting instability it caused. The reporter's stunning reply: 'While I agree with you, if I say anything about US geopolitical interests with Israel, I might as well clean off my desk.' Of course, the interview was never aired.'[94]

The Stirrings of Jewish Dissent

There is dissent, of course, and, though embryonic and weak, it is growing. Arab-American, Palestinian and Muslim activists are developing their own community institutions, learning the ways of ethnic politics, becoming a factor in electoral politics. The black minority have transferred to the Palestinians some, at least, of the sympathies which they used to reserve for American Jewry in gratitude for its championship of their cause. The activists have their own, if so far relatively ineffectual, media watchdog organizations.

Since the outbreak of the second *Intifada*, the Middle East struggle has become an increasingly contentious issue on university campuses, with pro-Palestinian groups beginning to challenge the Zionists' hitherto unimpaired ascendancy. Scores of them have signed on for an anti-Israeli divestiture campaign reminiscent of the one that helped bring down Apartheid in South Africa.

Most important, perhaps, is the evolution of opinion within American Jewry, and the potential for rank-and-file disaffection from AIPAC and the other, often small, right-wing, but highly effective engines of the Lobby machine. These claim to speak for the whole community, but—in their hostility to the peace process, over whose virtual collapse and the rise of Sharon they openly rejoiced, and to any pressure on Israel to compromise for its sake—they clearly do not.[95] According to an opinion poll conducted in 2001, the peace process actually commanded the support of a full 50 per cent of the community; the poll also showed that Malcolm Hoenlein, vice chairman of the Conference of Presidents and top of the Jewish newspaper *Forward*'s annual list of America's fifty most influential Jews,[96] was mistaken in his claim that the community was united in its refusal to countenance any concessions over Jerusalem; in fact, 35 per cent of it was willing to see the city divided for the sake of a final peace agreement. An organization called Israel Policy Forum, founded in 1993, has forged ties with many influential Congressmen, and got 50 Jewish leaders to sign a statement praising the President for seeking new peace negotiations at a time when AIPAC was trying to prevent him from leaning too hard on Sharon.[97] Lower down the hierarchy, at the grassroots, Jewish 'peace groups', springing up in many places, are beginning to pose a challenge to the established leadership. The dissidents may still revere Israel, still passionately espouse its right to exist, but they also believe that, with its occupation, military brutalities and diplomatic intransigence, this is an Israel that has gone astray; and they have broken that taboo on public criticism of it that the leadership, and the ingrained tradition of communal solidarity, have always required.

'The only ones', said Dennis Bernstein, a Californian activist, 'who begin to open their mouths are the Jews in this country. You know, as a kid, I sent money to plant trees in Israel. But now we are horrified by a government representing a country that we grew up loving and cherishing. Israel's defenders have a special vengeance for Jews who don't fall in line because they give the lie to the charge that Israel's critics are simply anti-Semite'.[98] Michael Lerner, the founder and editor of the left-wing Jewish magazine *Tikkun*, knows all about that. He came under 'tremendous pressure' to alter the magazine's editorial line, which is that the Israeli occupation is the 'fundamental source of the problem'. Hundreds of readers cancelled their subscriptions. More sinister, however, were the fulminations of a far-right pro-Israeli website, which called him a 'self-hating Jewish worm' and opined that 'you subhuman leftist animals should all be exterminated'. The Anti-Defamation League, so eager to decry critics of Israel, did not consider him the victim of racist hatred; he was not being targeted 'solely because he's Jewish', but because of his pro-Palestinian views.[99] The editor of the Wisconsin *Jewish Chronicle* was forced to resign after fourteen years on the newspaper because in an editorial he called Netanyahu 'the most incompetent' prime minister in Israel's history.[100] When an editor of the Kansas City *Jewish Chronicle* commissioned an article by a pro-Palestinian Jewish activist, she was fired the next day.[101] Admittedly Adam Shapiro, from Brooklyn, took his dissidence to unusual lengths: as a volunteer with the International Solidarity Movement, he found himself trapped in Arafat's compound during one of Sharon's sieges of it. But the price he paid was commensurate. After telling CNN that Sharon's government was behaving like a terrorist organization and his troops were going 'from house to house, much like the Nazis did', a columnist in the *New York Post*—which employs a life-long Sharon intimate, Uri Dan, as its correspondent in Israel—called him the 'Jewish Taliban' and 'our latest traitor'. His family, harassed and threatened, had to flee their Brooklyn home and seek police protection. Shapiro's father, a New York public high school and part-time *yeshiva* teacher, lost his job. His brother received regular death threats.[102]

Given the United States' ever-growing importance as Zionism's metropolitan sponsor, it stands to reason that that other struggle, the propaganda one for the favour of American, and especially American-Jewish, public opinion, will vitally affect the course of the physical and military struggle in the Middle East itself. But it is only in its early stages. The Jewish dissidents' task will be hard, bitter—and perhaps ultimately unavailing. Though no doubt dented, the dominant orthodoxy which, a quarter of a century ago, could so deride, or ignore, books such as *The Gun and the Olive Branch* and, a few years later, heap such idolatry on the tissue of multi-layered mendacity that was Joan Peters' *From Time Immemorial*, still retains much of its ascendancy.[103] And, in consequence, so, essentially, does that purblindness which, as Palestinian scholar Walid Khalidi first pointed out, has shaped the attitudes of the United States ever since it became so decisive a factor in the modern Middle East. The abiding strength of both can be discerned in the partisanship, conscious or unconscious, which still informs the American position, official or unofficial, on almost any aspect, fundamental or derivative, of this most enduring and intractable of conflicts.

iv · NO END OF AMERICAN PARTISANSHIP

The Peace Process Breaks Down: Arafat to Blame

The most fundamental issue is the peace process over which, for three decades now, the United States has all but exclusively presided. It has been anything but successful. If there have been no full-scale recent Arab-Israeli wars—though the Israeli invasion of Lebanon all but qualified as one—the violence between the principal parties, Israelis and Palestinians, has grown very much worse, in scale, ferocity and political significance, reaching its apogee in the still unfinished business of the second *Intifada*.

The United States, like any peace-maker, was supposed, in principle at least, to be a neutral arbiter, but given the great, and growing, number of Jews, Zionists and pro-Israeli Gentiles in succeeding Administrations, this was a non-starter. In fact, they did not even consider themselves neutral; one of the most important and long-serving of them, Martin Indyk—director of Middle East affairs on President Clinton's National Security Council, ambassador to Israel, and then assistant secretary of state for Near East affairs—said that the idea of 'even-handedness' or 'pressure' were 'not in our lexicon'.[104] It remained essentially Israel's historical narrative, Israel's interests and point of view to which, in practice, the arbiter almost always deferred.

From the Palestinians' point of view, as we have seen, theirs was a struggle for de-colonization of a kind which, normally, the whole world, including America, recognizes as legitimate. Yet it was only their 'recognition' of the Jewish state, and its 'right to exist' on territory they considered rightfully theirs, only their renunciation, unique in contemporary history, of the usual objective of such struggles, sovereignty in their own land, which enabled the peace process to keep going at all, at least with any prospect of success.

Ever since they made that historic concession, in 1988, the Palestinians have had a unified, official, declared and—in territorial terms at least—very precise standpoint on what, at the end of the process, a final settlement should look like. They solemnified the concession with a revision of the Palestinian National Charter, the manifesto of their national struggle. Originally promulgated, in conjunction with the founding of the Palestinian Liberation Organization, in 1964 at the first session of the Palestine National Council, or parliament-in-exile, the Charter had called for the complete recovery, by armed struggle, of the lost homeland, and the consequent 'elimination of Zionism in Palestine'. It was no trivial matter to repudiate such a document. To do so, at least in the absence of any reciprocal gesture from the enemy, seemed, to many Palestinians, to dishonour and invalidate their history as an oppressed people, the injustice that had been done them and their natural right to redress it; it was almost, in effect, to accede to Israel's demand that fifty years of struggle be branded as mere 'terrorism' and irrational violence.[105] But, under Oslo, they were required to abolish all those parts of the Charter deemed 'inconsistent' with it; and in 1998 the Council, at a meeting attended by President Clinton himself, finally and overwhelmingly approved, by acclamation, the abrogation of a full 26 of its 33 articles. There was of course opposition, especially in the Palestinian Diaspora, to Oslo, and all that ensued; doubtless, too, there had always been a good measure of official negligence and incompetence in explaining the significance of the Palestinians' historic concession and combating Israel's portrayal of it as a sham. But the fact remains that it was the legally constituted, internationally recognized representative of the Palestinian people, Arafat and his Palestine Authority, successor to the PLO, which adopted this standpoint. It has adhered to it religiously ever since. It cannot but be regarded as the *authentic* Palestinian position. True, it did not include a formal renunciation of the refugees' right of return; but, to have yielded so much on land and sovereignty all but amounted, of itself, to an earnest of commensurate concessions to come on that most crucial of questions too.

If it had been truly neutral, the United States, taking the Palestinians' dispossession—and Israel's 'original sin'—as the starting-point and root cause of the conflict, would have acknowledged the momentous importance of the concession, and required the maximum possible reciprocity from the other side. This could never have approached, in generosity, what the Palestinians had given. But, by virtue of the concession itself, the Palestinians were indicating that they did not expect it to. What the United States should have demanded was a formal re-definition of the nature and purpose of the Jewish state, incorporating recognition of the existence and legitimate rights of a Palestinian people, equivalent to that which, with the revision of their Charter, the Palestinians themselves had undertaken; full and automatic withdrawal from all the occupied territories; the disbandment of all settlements whose residents were not ready to live under Palestinian sovereignty; the sharing of Jerusalem; the acceptance of a Palestinian state to which, rather than to the 78 per cent of original Palestine—now Israeli—from which they mostly came, the refugees would have the right of return; respect for all international jurisprudence, enshrined in United Nations resolutions, that could be invoked on behalf of such a settlement.

But what, since Oslo, has been the official, declared, *authentic* Israeli standpoint on a final settlement? It doesn't have one, certainly not as regards the one issue, its own physical dimensions, which, as the Palestinian Council had shown, did lend itself to precise definition. But how, indeed, could it, when it does not even have a constitution? For, despite a United Nations injunction for it to do so, it has never managed to determine, constitutionally, what kind of a polity it really is—or what its final boundaries should be. What Israel does have is a series of covenants, declarations and laws—from the 1897 Basle programme of the World Zionist Organization and the 1917 Balfour Declaration to the 1948 Declaration of the Establishment of the State of Israel and the 1950 Law of Return—which shaped its essential nature. These documents, which called for the 'colonization' of Palestine 'on suitable lines', the establishment there of 'a national home for the Jewish people' and 'the ingathering of the exiles', could only mean what they eventually did mean: the dispossession of the indigenous inhabitants. The Palestinian National Charter might have been an extreme, intolerant document, calling as it did for the violent dismantling of an established state and society.

But it was no more than a response to, and mirror-image of, its foregoing Zionist counterparts, which had already *accomplished* what the Palestinian Charter only *proposed* should be accomplished by way of redress; it was no less an essential element in Palestine's historical narrative than its counterparts were in Israel's. Most Palestinians had in any case long come to regard 'complete liberation' as a 'dream' that was no longer realistically attainable. But if the Israelis required that solemn assurance that they really had renounced the dream which the revision of the Charter furnished, why should not the Palestinians have expected a similar renunciation from the Israelis?

Were the Knesset, like the Palestine National Council, to have convened for that purpose, one wonders, in the absence of an agreed constitution, which of the accumulated ideological and operational principles of Zionism it would have been ready to revise. Would Labour, the embodiment of 'official' Zionism before the state came into being and for nearly thirty years thereafter, have subscribed to a formulation on boundaries less amorphous, less susceptible to expansionist interpretation, than the 'the historic homeland, the Land of Israel',[106] of which, under Israeli law, 'no area . . . can be legally ceded to the control of a foreign nation or entity.'[107] Would the *Likud* have formally renounced its claim that the East as well as the West Bank of the Jordan forms part of Zionism's inheritance? Or would former prime minister Yitzhak Shamir—not to mention a host of secular and religious figures whose beliefs are even more fantastic and extreme[108]—have foresworn the tenets of LEHI, or the 'Stern Gang', of which he had been a leading member: namely, 'eternal war against those who satanically stand in the way of the realization of our aims', chief among them the conquest of a 'Kingdom of Israel' stretching 'from the river of Egypt unto the great river, the river Euphrates'?[109]

No one, not even the Palestinians, seriously thought of asking the Knesset to do such a thing, so unimaginable was it that it would ever have agreed. But nor, for that matter, could anyone have extracted from Labour or *Likud* separately, let alone any coalition of the two, a definitive statement of what they meant by peace. In the end, it was what they did, as much as what they said, that showed what they ultimately wanted. The peace which, under Sharon, the *Likud* was working for would preserve Israeli sovereignty over a 'Land of Israel' defined as the whole of historic Palestine. Unlike *Likud*, Labour, always more discreet, did not shout its expansionist ambitions from the rooftops, but it was always obvious, from a settlement drive hardly less assiduous than the *Likud*'s, that, under its peace, Israel would retain a goodly portion of the Land too. For decades, the United States had always looked on the principle of 'land-for-peace' as the basis of a final settlement. There was great irony in that. For it meant that, in practice, Arafat and his Palestine Authority always showed a greater respect for the official position of America than an Israel—be it Labour's Israel or *Likud*'s—on which American politicians fell over themselves to heap such honorifics as 'our strongest ally and best friend, not only in the Middle East, but anywhere in the world'.[110]

Yet this won the Palestinians no particular moral credit with the American peace-maker, no particular fund of good will for the negotiations to come. True, with Oslo, the Americans had finally acknowledged their centrality in the Arab-Israeli struggle, their peoplehood, national aspirations and right to self-determination. But even so, they—and especially, of course, the Zionists who dominated Middle East policy-making—had done so with manifest reluctance. Basically, they did not consider that what Arafat had done to earn that breakthrough amounted to much more than the very minimum that he had to. For them, it was simply a renunciation of the unreasonable, extremist objectives and violent, terroristic methods over which he had presided for so long; these being objectives and methods that supposedly contrasted with the essentially reasonable, moderate, peace-seeking purposes of the Israelis, whose only warlike actions were motivated by legitimate self-defense and the dictates of national security. The American attitude was epitomized by the backhanded compliment which President Clinton paid Arafat when he thanked him 'for turning away from violence toward peace'.[111] For the Palestinians, their past, their *Nakba*, was the essence of their cause—and their readiness to remove it from the moral and political calculus of a final settlement should, they thought, have earned them great virtue in American eyes. But it didn't. Oslo became the starting point of a new calculus almost as much shaped by the old mind-set, and as replete with the old prejudices in Israel's favour, as the earlier one.

The result was that the peace process moved rather more slowly towards its intended goal than it did towards America's shedding of the very postures and policies, coming under the general head of 'land-for-peace', on which the Palestinian had presumed they could count to advance it. Instead of demanding the full 'land-for-peace' reciprocity from the Israelis that true neutrality would have required, America tried in effect to espouse a median position somewhere between the Palestinian offer and the Israeli rejection of it. Principles had little part in determining what that position might be. Only bargaining did, a bargaining in which, instead of throwing its weight behind the weaker and therefore more deserving, Palestinian party, the United States, in the guise of such pieties as 'even-handedness', not 'imposing' a solution, or not being able to 'want peace more than the parties themselves', in practice let its Israeli ally's superior strength prevail. The Palestinians' unilateral, historic compromise was to become the basis for yet further compromise at their expense.

America's shift was reflected in the evolution of its official positions on such a key question as the settlements. These, which, till President Carter's time, had been 'illegal' and were still considered 'obstacles to peace' by Reagan, had become merely 'complicating factors' for Clinton. His Administration refused to discuss them at the United Nations, because 'it [was] unproductive to debate the legalities of the issue', and, in more general terms, inappropriate for the UN to involve itself in matters that the two parties to the conflict would have to settle between themselves. These evolving positions fell within the broader framework of an attempt to undermine the whole corpus of international jurisprudence on the Arab-Israeli conflict, to 'eliminate' or 'improve' long-standing United Nations resolutions unfavourable to Israel—including General Assembly resolution 194, calling for the return of the refugees, which America itself had annually co-sponsored for over forty years—because they were 'contentious'.[112]

Similarly, the United States ceased to consider the territories 'occupied'. They were merely 'disputed'. And by the time of Bush

II they had become, in the words of secretary of defense Donald Rumsfeld, the 'so-called' occupied territories, in effect the legitimate spoils of a war which, as the victors, the Israelis had the right to keep. 'My feeling', he said, 'is that they've made some settlements in various parts of the so-called occupied area, which was the result of a war, which they won'.[113]

With positions such as these, it was inevitable that each new 'interim' agreement under Oslo was just another American-supported Israeli gain at the Palestinians' expense. In the last and most difficult of them, the Wye Agreement of 1998, the Israelis won American blessing for the notion that it was not they, but the Palestinians, who had been responsible for all the blockages in the peace process so far, that it was their 'acts of terrorism, crime and hostilities', their 'incitement', their 'unilateral acts' which would have to be reined in if the process was to continue—not Israel's disastrously counter-productive settlement policy, its systematic violation of its pledges to carry out incremental troop withdrawals, the anti-Arab violence and 'incitement' of its settlers, its land expropriations and home demolitions, its economic blockades, and what amounted to ethnic cleansing by stealth in Jerusalem. This partisanship, remarked a Palestinian scholar, this 'unprecedented, massive asymmetry not only in the details but in the entire conception' was built into the 'very structure' of the agreement.[114] In theory the United States would henceforth keep an eagle eye on the 'compliance' of both sides. But in practice it was all one way. There was never any indication that it seriously intended to attempt any curbs on Israel's settlement programme, let alone punish it with any diminution in that never-ending cornucopia of economic and military aid—running at about $13 million a day—which merely encouraged the likes of Sharon in their stubborn pursuit of policies and practices to which, officially at least, the United States itself had always been opposed.

Before long the Palestinians' fall from grace was complete. Not merely did they lose the last vestiges of what little moral credit their historic compromise had earned them in the first place, Israel garnered heaps of it in their stead. It happened with Barak's refusal to implement 'interim' agreements already entered into and his determination to launch a grandiose alternative scheme for the two sides, under American auspices, to settle both outstanding 'interim' issues and yet untouched 'permanent status' ones in a single, marathon, 'end-of-conflict' summit conference. Arafat was deeply reluctant to attend one, considering as he did that, without capitulation on his part, failure was all but certain; and the Americans were likewise dubious. But, deferential as ever to America's ever-importunate protégé, Clinton got him to come to Camp David in July 2000, pledging, as part of his persuasions, that he would not put the blame for an inglorious outcome on him. But that is precisely what, hard upon the conference's ignominious collapse, he did. And so did the mainstream American media. In fact, in an outpouring of hosannas for Israel, they far outdid him. They unhesitatingly and overwhelmingly adopted the Barak story of 'the most generous Israeli offer ever' and Arafat's contemptuous spurning of it. 'Extraordinary', 'unprecedented', the 'most far-reaching ever'—so, in unison, rang the praises for Barak's 'concessions' from the *Washington Post, Time* magazine and the *Chicago Tribune*. And 'Arafat did not even make a counter-offer'—thus did the *Chicago Sun-Times*, and many others in almost identical language, lay all the blame on an 'intransigent', 'rejectionist' Palestinian leader.[115] It was over a year before an American participant in Camp David, Robert Malley, and a Palestinian researcher with close ties to the Palestinian negotiators, Hussein Agha, jointly debunked this version for the almost ludicrously partisan myth it was. To be sure, the fact that it took so long exposed the incompetence of a Palestinian leadership which miserably neglected to tell its side of the story; but it was also an indictment of such weighty organs of news and opinion as the *New York Times*, which had failed to investigate the claim, or even to wonder whether there might possibly be something blatantly self-serving about it.[116] By then it was too late—for by then a no less partisan corollary to the myth had long established itself as the dominant new orthodoxy.

'Palestinians Attack, Israelis Defend'

This corollary was that, having failed to get what he wanted at the negotiating table, Yasser Arafat tried violence instead. 'The most pro-peace prime minister in the country's history and what', asked Charles Krauthammer in the *Washington Post*, 'does he get?' 'War', comes the sublimely confident reply to his own question.[117] Krauthammer is among the more extreme of America's army of pro-Israeli columnists. But most subscribed to the same basic thesis. In a front-page news analysis in the *Los Angeles Times*, Tracy Wilkinson wrote that 'by declining to stop his men who have seized the streets of the West Bank and Gaza . . . [Arafat] has solidified his reputation for favoring the use of violence as a negotiating tool'.[118]

Few paid much attention to evidence that suggested otherwise: that Yasser Arafat had begged Barak not to allow Sharon to make the provocative al-Aqsa walk-about which certainly triggered[119] even if it did not, in the deeper sense, cause the *Intifada*; that even if the Palestinians had started the violence, it was, in the early stages at least, essentially unarmed, a resumption of the first *Intifada*'s 'uprising of stones'; that the Israelis themselves turned it very lethal indeed with their swift and massive recourse to the firing of live ammunition against demonstrators; that in the first month the ratio of fatalities was twenty Palestinians to one Israeli, a disparity reduced to only ten to one by the end of the third month; that organizations such as Amnesty International, America's Human Rights Watch or Physicians for Human Rights amply documented the extra-judicial 'executions' that had so quickly got under way, the gratuitous brutality, the wanton and unnecessary shootings to kill or injure, the reckless disregard for standard methods of riot control.

No, the American punditocracy decided, if the Palestinians were dying in such large numbers it was largely their own—and especially their leadership's—fault, not that of the Israeli soldiers who were killing them. 'Arafat has encouraged his youth legions to write their refusal in a blood that is mostly their own.' Thus spake Jim Hoagland of the *Washington Post*. It was the standard view. Krauthammer was only offering a more extreme variant of it when he said that 'some telegenic massacre to rally the world to his side would be Arafat's fondest wish'.[120] A long-standing, but long discredited, Israeli perception of itself—as a nation wedded to 'self-restraint' and 'purity of arms' in battle—permeated American commentary. The *Washington Post* conceded that 'Israel's measures against the rioters are sometimes excessive', but it called its use of helicopter gunships and missiles against Palestinian towns and cities 'largely symbolic reprisal attack'.[121]

The real and wholly obvious explanation for this self-sacrificial Palestinian zeal, a portent of the suicide bombers to come, was what the Palestinian themselves said it was: their fury against the accursed occupation. Some American reporting did give that fundamental reality the prominence it deserved; so, even, did a tiny handful of commentators and editorial writers.[122] But, by and large, the very words 'occupation' and 'occupied territories' were fading from media coverage, sometimes even to the point of extinction. This was particularly blatant on television. In the first five weeks of the *Intifada*, the evening news shows of the three main television networks, ABC, CBS and NBC, aired 99 reports on the West Bank and Gaza, but only in four of them were viewers informed that these were Israeli-occupied territories. Some outlets went so far, in effect, as to refer to them as part of Israel itself. Tom Brokaw, of NBC's *Nightly News*, introduced a report about 'the ever-widening eruptions of violence in Israel'; his reporter on the spot then proceeded to explain that the Palestinians were 'storming an Israeli army outpost in Gaza' and 'setting siege to another army post in the West Bank'.[123]

For some, apparently, the occupation did not really exist any more: that, at least, seemed to be implied by the *Washington Post* when it said that the negotiations between Israelis and Palestinians simply had to go on 'because the possibility of reverting to the pre-Oslo days of occupation and violence is almost unthinkable'.[124] It was a line of argument that, characteristically, the redoubtable Krauthammer took to surrealist lengths. Demanding to know what the Palestinians were protesting about, he exclaimed: 'Israeli occupation? It ended years ago; 99 per cent of the Palestinians live under the rule of Yasser Arafat'.[125]

If, according to this dominant orthodoxy, Arafat had proved his unwillingness or inability to make peace with Israel, or even his unregenerate determination to destroy it, if there was no real occupation against which his people could exercise their internationally recognized right of resistance, it followed that, when fighting did break out, the Palestinians were always likely to be the aggressors, the Israelis merely reacting in self-defence. And so it duly appeared in most American news coverage. 'Palestinian (or Arab) violence'—as it came to be known—was met by Israeli 'retaliation'. 'The renewed Arab violence provoked a new wave of retaliation from Israel', ran a typical, *Newsweek* formulation,[126] with a built-in partisanship upstaged a week later by a *New York Times* headline: 'New Violence after Rocket Strikes on Palestinians'.[127] Since the Palestinian violence seemed to have no serious or legitimate purpose, it was the logical next step to describe it as an expression of hatred and nothing else; on his CBS *Evening News* programme Dan Rather took that step with his announcement, in a story about a Palestinian militia using firearms against Israeli troops, that 'hatred now has live ammunition'.[128] 'The Fires of Hate', 'Ancient Hatreds Re-ignited', 'At the Speed of Hate'—such titles became commonplace.[129] FAIR, or Fairness and Accuracy in Reporting, a media monitoring organization, calculated that, in a given period, out of the 150 occasions that the television networks used some variant of the word 'retaliate' they were referring to Israeli actions nine times more often than they were to Palestinian ones—and this long after it had become clear to every serious observer that if ever there was a lull in the 'Palestinian violence' Sharon deliberately set out to re-ignite it with an attack of his own.[130]

For the bulk of the American media, then, Arafat was well and truly 'the terrorist' again. So he was, of course, for Congress, where, within two weeks, ninety six out of a hundred senators urged President Clinton to 'condemn the Palestinian campaign of violence . . . and express solidarity with Israel in this critical moment'. As it happened, however, Clinton was about to make one last bid for a settlement in the dying days of his presidency; and that required at least an appearance of impartiality. At talks in the Egyptian town of Taba, in January 2001, Barak, himself about to be replaced by Sharon, submitted Clinton-inspired proposals that went way beyond what he had ever offered at Camp David six months before. Apparently he did it for propaganda purposes only: they were swiftly withdrawn. Still, the new proposals of themselves made a mockery of that earlier, 'unprecedented generosity' out of which American politicians and pundits had fashioned their whole new canon of self-evident Middle Eastern verities.

It was only with the coming of President Bush that the Administration fell in with the new orthodoxy. Even before 11 September, 'terrorism' had been, for him and the neo-conservatives who peopled his administration, a phenomenon—like communism in the past—of absolute evil, and whoever practiced it automatically de-legitimized himself and the cause in whose name he did so. These neo-conservatives themselves, in close association with rightwing Israelis such as the 'terrorism expert' Binyamin Netanyahu,[131] had played a key role in defining and identifying the terrorists. Not surprisingly, the PLO, and all its member-organizations, were foremost among them, eventually, of course, to be joined by such Muslim fundamentalist groups as *Hamas*, which Israel itself had originally tolerated as a counterweight to the secular-nationalist mainstream. It was not surprising either, therefore, that, as the cycle of violence intensified, the Administration increasingly shed any semblance of neutrality.

To be sure, the suicide bombings, when they finally came, some six months into the *Intifada*, were horrible. Yet so was the scarcely less random and even more destructive 'collateral' damage wrought by Israeli tanks, helicopter gunships and F-16s. To be sure, too, the suicide bombers, and other, 'legitimate' forms of resistance, significantly raised the Israeli death rate; yet still, by the end of 2002, it was 2,073 Palestinians killed to 683 Israelis.[132] And that is not to speak of underlying motives: Palestinian atrocities came, after all, in the service of what the world regards as a legitimate purpose, the ending of occupation, Israeli ones in the service of an illegitimate one, its perpetuation.

But that meant little to the new Republican administration. It found no moral equivalence between the two. It had assumed office spurning the activist, hands-on peace-making of its Democratic predecessor. It had been prepared to 'facilitate' negotiations, no more, and that only if both parties seriously wanted them. This so-called 'disengagement' could not but favour the stronger, Israeli party. But, in any case, there first had to be a ceasefire, and there was no doubt, from the outset, which side was expected to bear the main responsibility for that. 'The signal I'm sending the Palestinians', Bush said early into his presidency, 'is to stop the violence'. A different signal went to Sharon, who, in his judgement, had come to occupy the 'high moral ground' for his restraint in the face of that violence. There was to be no abatement of these remorseless double standards.

In August 2001, the eleventh month of the *Intifada*, Sharon chose a high-ranking political figure, Abu Ali Mustafa, the head of the left-wing, but no longer so radical Popular Front for the Liberation of Palestine, to be the 63rd victim of his 'targeted killings'; he died in a helicopter gunship attack on his Ramallah office. The American government refused to condemn this. The Front promised, and delivered, a 'qualitative' retaliation. Its choice of target—Rehavim Zeevi, the Israeli minister of tourism—could hardly have been more appropriate, not simply because Zeevi was a political figure of equivalent stature, but because he headed *Moledet*, an extreme right-wing party which had adopted the 'transfer' of the Palestinians as its official, publicly proclaimed policy, and because he had made a habit of describing those whom he wanted transferred as 'lice', 'vermin' and a 'cancer'. This time the American government was not silent; it called his assassination a 'shocking and despicable' act.

A year later, an Israeli F-16 dropped a one-ton bomb on a crowded apartment in Gaza; the air force commander said that he had 'not lost a minute's sleep'[133] over the fact that, in addition to the intended target, a top *Hamas* military commander, the bomb had—all but inevitably—killed seventeen others, nine of them children, and injured 140. The surreptitious but ill-concealed purpose was to sabotage the agreement on the cessation of suicide bombings which Arafat's *Fatah* and *Hamas* were on the point of announcing. The action did at least provoke the White House to one of its occasional, mild admonitions of Israel: it was 'a heavy–handed action that does not contribute to peace'. But when, in retaliation, *Hamas* killed seven students—five of them American—in a bomb blast at the Hebrew University in Jerusalem, there was no such emollient tone about the White House's condemnation of this 'horrific act of violence, this horrific act of terrorism'.

Nothing could stem Bush's growing 'disappointment' and 'dissatisfaction' with the Palestinian leader, who had done more to 'enhance' terror than to fight it, and generally 'betrayed the hopes of the people he's supposed to lead'. And finally, in a long-awaited policy speech in June 2002, he declared Arafat unfit to rule at all—as 'irrelevant', in other words, as Sharon had long said he was. It was time, he announced, for the Palestinians to establish 'a new constitutional framework', build a 'working democracy', develop a market economy, and elect new leaders untainted by 'corruption and terrorism'. Once they achieved all that, the United States would assist them to set up a 'provisional state'. This was a new concept, unknown to political science. But, for the Beirut's *al-Safir*, its implication was clear enough—'a provisional state to ensure a permanent occupation'. 'Sharonian in both letter and spirit', concluded another Beirut newspaper.[134] And, in truth, Bush's 'man of peace' had reason to be very pleased indeed.

Vile Words, Vile Ideologies—From Both Sides

As former CIA analyst Kathleen Christison has pointed out, the kind of 'hatred' that supposedly impelled the Palestinians is not usually singled out as a prime, or exclusive, motivating force behind other political, ethnic or religious conflicts around the world.[135] Yet the very idea, she went on, that, despite the existence of a peace process in which the United States had invested so much, the Palestinians could have had a really serious, legitimate grievance did not enter the calculations of most Americans, whether ordinary citizens, supposedly knowledgeable commentators or current or former public officials. So there had to be other explanations for the hatred. And indeed, for many, perhaps most, Americans, this otherwise seemingly motive-less Palestinian violence conformed all too easily with widespread and long-standing perceptions which they held about Arab and Muslim peoples: namely, that they were inherently prone to violence, fanaticism, intolerance and racial prejudice. Nothing, in fact, helped to sustain and deepen these perceptions more than the Arab-Israeli conflict. And since the Israelis, the 'good guys', had always enjoyed a prejudice in their favour, it was only to be expected that, with the help of the 'friends of Israel' in America, they should try to build on it by exposing the wickedness and malice that drove the 'bad guys'.

In 1998, an organization called MEMRI, the Middle East Media Research Institute, was established to do just that. Officially headquartered in Washington, but with offices in Jerusalem, it was an American-Israeli adjunct of the neo-conservative clan that later came to dominate the Bush Administration. Its method is clever, simple and effective. It monitors just about everything that is said or written—by government officials or opposition politicians, by newspaper commentators or preachers in mosques—in the length and breadth of the Arab world. In its selection of material, MEMRI tends to focus on the rabid and the outrageous. But, inevitably perhaps, that comes across as only the extreme expression of a general disposition, as symptomatic of an entire region apparently foaming with 'incitement'—an activity outlawed by Oslo—against Israel, America and the West, with anti-Semitism and with Holocaust-denial.

It is an Egyptian columnist, Ahmad Ragab, who give 'thanks to the late Hitler, who took revenge on the most vile criminals on earth—though we blame Hitler because his revenge was not quite enough'.[136] It is a call on the Almighty, from the Grand Mufti of Jerusalem, Ikrima Sabri, to 'destroy America—for she is ruled by Zionist Jews—and to take revenge against the colonialist settlers who are the sons of monkeys and pigs'.[137] It is 'the impossibility'—according to Saudi Arabia's Sheikh Muhammad al-Munajjid—'ever to make peace with the Jews . . . who are defiled creatures, satanic scum, the cause of the misery of the human race, together with the Infidels and other polytheists'.[138] It is the everlasting and vastly bemedalled Syrian minister of defence, Mustafa Tlass, promising that 'to every new reprint of his book, *The Matzah of Zion*, which presents the Damascus blood libel of 1840 as "historical fact", he will attach a document or a new chapter shedding light on the distortion of the Torah [by the Jews] and on the criminal Jewish religious rituals. He said he will do it on the basis of the belief in Allah's words, be He praised'.[139]

MEMRI distributes its translations by fax and e-mail to over 10,000 journalists, diplomats, politicians and activists around the world. Colonel Yigal Carmon, MEMRI's co-founder and a former adviser on terrorism to two Israeli prime ministers, said it had been an 'uphill battle' to get the press of democratic nations to report on the 'vile ideology' his organization had exposed; for the 'Western mind does not believe there's such a thing as undeserved hatred'.[140] But in due course its contributions began to appear regularly in American and Western newspapers. It was 'invaluable', said one columnist, a 'lifting of the veil, an antidote to darkness'. Thanks to MEMRI, said Congressman Brad Sherman, the United States could now 'hold Arab leaders accountable for failure to refute outrageous lies about America and Israel'.[141]

The Center for Monitoring the Impact of Peace is another such American-Israeli organization. Its research director lives in a West Bank settlement. It won international attention with its examination of post-Oslo Palestinian school textbooks. It had set itself the task of assessing whether, in the light of the textbooks' portrayal of Israelis and Jews, the Palestine Authority was making a serious effort to promote the values of peace and co-existence. It concluded emphatically that it was not, that the textbooks promoted a 'total de-legitimization of Israel', which was 'mentioned only in contexts that breed contempt, such as having expelled and massacred Palestinians'; they 'glorified' Palestinian terrorists; they propagated 'virulent anti-Semitism', a prime example of which was a title-page banner declaring that 'there is no alternative to destroying Israel'.[142]

These allegations were not merely misleading, they were for the most part wholly false. There was no such banner on any textbook. Their contents did reflect the Palestinian historical narrative, essentially that of an indigenous people in conflict with a colonial settler movement, and did refer to the creation of Israel as the Palestinians' *Nakba*, or Calamity. But, at the same time, far from questioning Israel's post-Oslo right to exist, they promoted the virtues of tolerance, openness and democracy, so much so, in fact, that Ruth Firer, member of a research team from the Truman Institute, wrote: 'we were surprised to find how moderate is the anger directed towards Israel in the Palestinian textbooks, compared to the Palestinian predicament and suffering. This surprise is doubled when you compare the Palestinian books to Israeli ones from the 1950s and 1960s, which mentioned Gentiles [only] in the context of pogroms and the Holocaust'.[143] Indeed, though there had been fitful and tentative improvements in Israeli textbooks, which portrayed Palestinians as violent, bloodthirsty, backward, unproductive and excitable, they still contained 'overt and covert fabrications', with little or no concession to the idea that the Palestinians constitute a people with national or civil rights.[144]

Despite their inaccuracy, the Center's allegations had a very considerable impact in the United States. They furnished the material for full-page newspaper advertisements, under the title 'There Is No Alternative to Destroying Israel', sponsored by a group called Jews for Truth Now. Then, even as the Palestinians were reeling beneath Sharon's military onslaught, the question of what their schoolchildren read became a new battle cry for American politicians. Just before he left office President Clinton called on Palestinians to 'change the culture of violence . . . and incitement that, since Oslo, has gone unchecked; young children still are being educated to believe in confrontation with Israel', And six months later his wife Hillary, now a New York senator, called a press conference to denounce the 'the hateful, anti-Israeli rhetoric in official Palestinian . . . schoolbooks'.[145]

Unlike the Center's findings, MEMRI's renditions of the wider Arab discourse are accurate enough. But its tendentious choice of material casts the Arab world in a much worse light than that discourse, taken as a whole, could reasonably justify. It is a game that two sides could play. If the Arabs were seriously to play it they would not have to peer into the darker and more disreputable corners of Israeli newspapers, or mine the more exotic seams of political and religious rhetoric, though they would find 'incitement' and 'vile ideology' in plenty if they did. They would barely have to look beyond the statements of high-ranking Israelis. Such statements have occasionally made it into Western, or even American, media, precisely because they did come from such exalted quarters. But there is no all-powerful Arab lobby exploiting them, no Arab MEMRI disseminating them in systematic compilations and analyses. And, even if there were, it is doubtful whether, given the dominant orthodoxy, American politicians and pundits would consider them to be as representative of a general Israeli disposition as their Arab counterparts are of an Arab one. Nonetheless, they *are* just as representative—and no less shocking.

Consider this one, from the most politically influential of Israel's spiritual leaders, whose party was the third largest in the Knesset and represented by a number of ministers in the cabinet:

> How can you make peace with a snake? They [the Arabs] are all accursed, wicked ones. They are all haters of Israel. It says in the Gemara that the Holy One, Blessed be He, is sorry he created these sons of Ishmael . . . It is forbidden to be merciful to them. You must give them missiles, with relish—and annihilate them. Evil ones, damnable ones.'—Rabbi Ovadia Yossef, former Chief Sephardi Rabbi of Israel.[146]

Or consider another one, from a chief of staff: 'When we have settled the land, all the Arabs will be able to do about it will be to scurry around like drugged cockroaches in a bottle'—Rafael Eitan.[147]

From a cabinet minister: 'A world without Jews is a world of robots, a dead world; and the State of Israel is the Noah's ark of the world's future, its task to show everyone the image of God'. [We are] 'in the place of Moses and King David'—Effi Eitam, leader of the National Religious Party, and minister of infrastructure.[148]

From a *Likud* MP: 'I would myself peck out the eyes and cut open the stomach of the saboteurs among Arabs'—Meir Cohen-Avidov, deputy speaker of the Knesset.[149]

From a *Likud* prime minister: 'The Palestinians would be crushed like grasshoppers . . . heads smashed against the boulders and walls'—Yitzhak Shamir.[150]

From a Labour prime minister: 'They [the Arabs] are the product of a culture in which to tell a lie creates no dissonance. They don't suffer from the problem of telling lies that exists in Judeo-Christian culture. Truth is seen as an irrelevant category'—Ehud Barak.[151]

From an unnamed army commander: 'An Armored Forces commander told how his company was the battalion's toughest in dealing with Arabs and got better results than other companies, and because of this the company was called "the Auschwitz company." It is a bad phenomenon of expressions and nicknames from the period of the Holocaust being used by Israeli soldiers who are putting down the *Intifada* in the territories'.[152]

Islamic Fundamentalism—But What about the Israeli-Jewish Variety?

The propensity to insert Palestinian resistance into a wider civilizational context finds sustenance in that phenomenon which, in the quarter century since *The Gun and the Olive Branch* was first written, has had such a tremendous impact on the region and the world. In the minds of many Westerners, Muslim fundamentalism, or 'political' Islam, has replaced communism as perhaps the greatest single 'threat' to the existing world order, a cultural, ideological and strategic challenge to which, wherever it manifests itself, be it in the Muslim world itself or in the Muslim immigrant communities of the West, politicians, academics and commentators have devoted enormous attention. For those who look at it from this perspective, the *Intifada* becomes just another episode in a so-called 'clash of civilizations'. For them, there is an intrinsic link between Palestinian 'terrorism' and, say, the al-Qaeda bombing of an American warship off Yemen; 'above all else', said a neo-conservative commentator in the *New York Times*, both are the 'violent expressions of the age-old confrontation between Islam and the West'.[153] Strikingly, almost totally absent from such arguments is any inclination to examine Jewish fundamentalism, or so much as to ask whether it, too, might be a factor in the conflict over Palestine, one of the reasons why it seems so insoluble.

There is, in fact, a great ignorance of, or indifference to, this whole subject in the outside world, and not least in the United States. This is due at least in part to that general reluctance of the mainstream American media to subject Israel to the same searching scrutiny to which it would other states and societies, and especially when the issue in question is as sensitive, as emotionally charged, as this one is. But, in the view of the late Israel Shahak, it reflects particularly badly on an American Jewry which, with its ingrained, institutionalized aversion to finding fault with Israel, turns a blind eye to what Israelis like himself viewed with disgust and alarm, and unceasingly said so.[154] Indeed, Shahak, childhood inmate of Belsen concentration camp, scholar, human rights activist, moralist and lover of Judaism in its high Prophetic form, was so affected by it that he devoted a portion of his later years to a study of the subject. In 1994 and 1999, this yielded two illuminating books, *Jewish History, Jewish Religion* and *Jewish Fundamentalism in Israel*, the second of which was co-authored with an American scholar, Norton Mezvinsky.[155]

When it comes to bigotry and fanaticism, there may not be much difference between American and Israeli branches of the same phenomenon. But while the American branch is insignificant in the totality of democratic American politics and society, it exerts from afar a very significant influence in the only place, Israel, where—self-evidently—Jewish fundamentalists could ever hope to achieve their ultimate purpose, which is not merely to shape the policies of a Jewish state, but to rule one, in just the same way as the Ayatollahs do in Iran, or the Taliban did in Afghanistan. American Jewry, especially those of the Orthodox persuasion, are generous financiers of the shock troops of fundamentalism, the religious settlers; indeed a good 10 per cent of these, and among the most extreme, violent and sometimes patently deranged, are actually immigrants from America. They are, says Shahak, one of the 'the absolutely worst phenomena' in Israeli society, and 'it is not by chance that they have their roots in the American-Jewish community'.[156] It was from his headquarters in New York that the '*Lubavitcher Rebbe*', the late Menachem Schneerson, seer of possibly the most rabid of Hassidic sects, the *Chabad*, gave guidance to his many followers in both Israel and the United States.[157] While the *New York Times*, perhaps a third of whose readership is Jewish, has published in-depth studies of Muslim or Christian fundamentalism, it has not done the same for Jewish fundamentalism; meanwhile the rightwing, Brooklyn-based *Jewish Press*, the Jewish community's largest-circulation weekly, is an open supporter and advocate of it.[158]

The ignorance or indifference is all the more remiss in that Jewish fundamentalism is not, and cannot be, just a domestic Israeli question. Israel was always a highly ideological society; it is also a vastly outsize military power, both nuclear and conventional. That is a combination which, when the ideology in question is Zionism in its most extreme, theocratic form, is fraught with possible consequences for the region and the world, and, of course, for the world's only, Israeli-supporting superpower.[159]

Like its Islamic counterpart, Jewish fundamentalism in Israel has grown enormously in political importance over the past quarter century. Its committed, hard-core adherents, as distinct from a larger body of the more traditionally religious, are thought to account for some 20 to 25 per cent of the population; that is probably higher than the proportion of *bona fide* Muslim fundamentalists in most countries of the region; it is certainly much higher than in Iran. They won twenty three out of the Knesset's 120 seats in the 1999 elections, compared with the merest handful in the early years of the state.[160] They, and more particularly the settlers among them, have acquired an influence, disproportionate to their numbers, over the whole Israeli political process, and especially in relation to the ultra-nationalist right which, beneath its secular exterior, actually shares much of their febrile, exalted outlook on the world. It is fundamentalism of a very special, ethnocentric and fiercely xenophobic kind, with beliefs and practices that are 'even more extremist', says Shahak, 'than those attributed to the extremes of Islamic fundamentalism', if not 'the most totalitarian system ever invented'.[161]

Like fundamentalism everywhere, the Jewish variety seeks to restore an ideal, imagined past. If it ever managed that, the Israel which the American 'friends of Israel' endlessly celebrate as a 'bastion of democracy in the Middle East' would, most assuredly, be no more. For, in its full and perfect form, the 'Jewish Kingdom' which arose in its place would elevate a stern and wrathful God's sovereignty over any new-fangled, heathen concepts of the people's will, civil liberties or human rights. It would be governed by the *Halacha*, or Jewish religious law, of which the rabbis would be the sole interpreters, and whose observance clerical commissars, installed in every public and private institution, would rigorously enforce, with the help of citizens legally obligated to report any offence to the authorities. A monarch, chosen by the rabbis, would rule[162] and the Knesset would be replaced by a Sanhedrin, or supreme judicial, ecclesiastic and administrative council. Men and women would be segregated in public, and 'modesty' in female dress and conduct would be enforced by law. Adultery would be a capital offense,[163] and anyone who drove on the Sabbath, or desecrated it in other ways, would be liable to death by stoning.[164] As for non-Jews, the *Halacha* would be an edifice of systematic discrimination against them, in which every possible crime or sin committed by a Gentile against a Jew, from murder or adultery to robbery or fraud, would be far more heavily punished than the same crime or sin committed by a Jew against a Gentile—if, indeed, it were considered to be a felony at all, which it often would not be.[165] All forms of 'idolatry or idol-worship', but especially Christian ones (for traditionally Muslims, who are not considered to be idolators, are held in less contempt than Christians), would be 'obliterated'.[166] Those Gentiles, or so-called 'Sons of Noah', permitted to remain in the Kingdom could only do so as 'resident aliens', obliged, under law, to accept the 'inferiority' in perpetuity which that status entails, to 'suffer the humiliation of servitude', and to be 'kept down and not raise their heads to the Jews.'[167] At weekday prayers, the faithful would intone the special curse: 'And may the apostates have no hope, and all the Christians perish instantly'.[168] One wonders what the Jerry Falwells and Pat Robertsons think of all this; for it is passing strange, this new adoration, by America's Evangelicals, of an Israel whose Jewish fundamentalists continue to harbour a doctrinal contempt for Christianity only rivalled by the contempt which the Christian fundamentalists reserve for the Jews themselves.

It is upon the coming of the Messiah that the Jewish Kingdom will arise, and the twice-destroyed Temple will be reconstructed on the site where the Dome of the Rock and al-Aqsa mosques now stand. Fundamentalists come in a multitude of sects, often fiercely disputatious with one another on the finest and most esoteric points of doctrine, but all are agreed on this basic eschatological truth. It is important, however, to distinguish between two conflicting attitudes towards it. One school of fundamentalists believes that the Messiah will appear in His own good time, that the millennium, the End of Days, will come by the grace of God alone. These are the *Haredim*, the more extreme in their uncompromising rejection of the sinful, secular modern world, who spend their time—and the state's money—in prayer and sacred study. The *Shas* party is their largest single political component. Their position has in it something of the traditional religious quietism which, historically, opposed the whole idea of Zionism, emigration to Palestine and the establishment of a Jewish state.

The other school, less extreme in outward religious observances, is more so, indeed breathtakingly revolutionary, on one crucial point of dogma: the belief that the coming of the Messiah can be accomplished, or hastened, by human agency, here and now, in the terrestrial realm. In fact, the 'messianic era' has already arrived.[169] This, the *messianic* fundamentalism, is represented by the National Religious Party, and its progeny, the settlers of the *Gush Emunim*, who eventually came to dominate it. Its adherents are ready to involve themselves in the world, sinful though it is, and, by so doing, they sanctify it. Except for the symbolic *yarmulke* skullcap, they have adopted conventional modern dress; they include secular subjects into the curricula of their seminaries.[170]

The *Gush*, which first emerged in 1974, only figured in the second, 1984 edition of *The Gun and the Olive Branch*. By then the religious settlers, *yarmulke* on head and Uzi in hand, were already well established as the new, most authentic and admired vanguard of the whole Zionist enterprise. This was deeply ironic. Settlement, the 'redeeming' of the land, had always been Zionism's central, defining task. But while the original pioneers had been secular-modernist rebels against the medieval, theocratic tyranny of Judaic Orthodoxy, now that Orthodoxy, or the *Gush*'s re-cycled, messianic version of it, had usurped the leadership of a movement that it once regarded as a heretical subversion of its own authority.

According to the teachings of their spiritual mentor, Rabbi Tzvi Yehuda Kook, the *Gush*, or at least the rabbis who lead it, are themselves the collective incarnation of the Messiah. Since, in biblical prophesy, the Messiah was to appear riding on an ass, he identified the ass as those errant, secular Jews who remain in stubborn ignorance of the exalted purpose of its divinely guided rider. In the shape of those early Zionists they had, it is true, performed the necessary task of carrying the Jews back to the Holy Land, settling it and founding a state there. But now they had served their historic purpose; now they had become obsolete in their failure to renounce their beastly, ass-like ways—and to perceive that Zionism has a divine, not merely a narrow national, purpose.[171]

The mainstream secular Zionist leadership had wanted the Jewish people to achieve 'normality', to be as other peoples with a nation-state of their own. The messianics—and indeed, though for emotional more than doctrinal reasons, much of the nationalist right—hold that that is impossible; the Jews' 'eternal uniqueness' stems from the covenant God made with them on Mount Sinai. So, as Rabbi Aviner, a *Gush* leader and head of a *yeshiva* which studies the ancient priestly rites that would be revived if and when the Temple were rebuilt, put it, 'while God requires other, normal nations to abide by abstract codes of "justice and righteousness" such laws do not apply to Jews'.[172] Since Zionism began, but especially since the 1967 war and Israel's conquest of the remainder of historic Palestine, the Jews have been living in a 'transcendental political reality', or a state of 'metaphysical transformation', one in which, through war and conquest, Israel liberates itself not only from its physical enemies, but from the 'satanic' power which these enemies incarnate. The command to conquer the Land, says Aviner, is 'above the moral, human considerations about the national rights of the Gentiles in our country'. What he calls 'messianic realism' dictates that. Israel has been instructed to 'be holy, not moral, and the general principles of morality, customary for all mankind, do not bind the people of Israel, because it has been chosen to be above them'.[173] It is not simply because the Arabs deem the land to be theirs—though, in truth, it is not theirs and they are simply 'thieves' who took what always belonged to the Jews[174]—that they resist this process, it is because, as Gentiles, they are inherently bound to do so. 'Arab hostility', says another *Gush* luminary, Rabbi Eliezer Waldmann, director of the Kiryat Arba settlement's main *yeshiva*, 'springs, like all anti-Semitism, from the world's recalcitrance' in the face of an Israel pursuing 'its divine mission to serve as the heart of the world'.[175]

So force is the only way to deal with the Palestinians. So long as they stay in the Land of Israel, they can only do so as 'resident aliens' without 'equality of human and civil rights', those being 'a foreign democratic principle' that does not apply to them.[176] But, in the end, they must leave. There are two ways in which that can happen. One is 'enforced emigration'. In that eventuality, the usual distinctions made in an enlightened state between civilian and combatant is forbidden, because both the civilian and the combatant belong to the category of a population for whom there is *a priori* no room in Israel, and both are considered its enemies.[177] The other way is based on the biblical injunction to 'annihilate the memory of Amalek'. In an article on 'The Command of Genocide in the Bible,'[178] Rabbi Israel Hess opined—without incurring any criticism from a state Rabbinate whose official duty it is to correct error wherever it finds it—that 'the day will come when we shall all be called upon to wage this war for the annihilation of Amalek'. He advanced two reasons for this. One was the need to ensure 'racial purity'. The other lay in 'the antagonism between Israel and Amalek as an expression of the antagonism between light and darkness, the pure and the unclean, between the people of God and the forces of evil, an antagonism that continues to exist in regard to the children of Amalek through all generations'—currently embodied by the Arab nations. Or, as a liberal Israeli commentator put it when, two years into the *Intifada, Gush* feelings were running high: 'transfer is not enough' for them; 'it is too weak, a leftist agenda; what they want is terrible revenge—transfer to the dead, not across the Jordan'.[179]

For the *Gush*, there is a dimension to the settlements beyond the merely strategic—the defending of the state—or the territorial—the expansion of the 'Land of Israel' till it reaches its full, biblically foretold borders, whatever those might be. Settlements are the citadels of their messianic ideology, the nucleus and inspiration of their theocratic state-in-the-making, the power-base from which to conduct an internal struggle that is inseparable from the external one—the *intra*-Jewish struggle against that other Israel, the secular-modernist one of original, mainstream Zionism, which stands in their path. The *Gush* must make good what Rabbi Kook taught: which is that the existing '*State* of Israel' carries within itself 'the *Kingdom* of Israel, the Kingdom of Heaven on Earth; consequently, total Holiness embraces every Jewish person, every deed, every phenomenon, including Jewish secularism, which will be one day swallowed by Holiness, by Redemption'.[180]

It goes without saying that the *Gush* consider any American-sponsored, Arab-Israeli peaceful settlement to be a virtual impossibility; but any attempt to achieve that impossible should be actively sabotaged. For them Oslo, and the prospect of the 're-division' of the 'Land of Israel', was a profound, an existential shock. It was, said Rabbi Yair Dreyfus, an 'apostasy' which, the day it came into effect, would mark 'the end of the Jewish-Zionist era [from 1948 to 1993] in the sacred history of the Land of Israel'.[181] The *Gush* and their allies declared a 'Jewish *Intifada*' against it. This was directed primarily against the Palestinians. Resolving to use 'the only language which the Arabs understand', armed settlers blocked their roads with stones and burning tires, ransacked property and fired on Palestinian stone-throwers. The grisly climax came when, in the Ramadan of February 1994, a doctor, Baruch Goldstein, Israeli but Brooklyn-born-and-bred, machine-gunned Muslim worshippers in Hebron's Ibrahimi Mosque, killing twenty nine of them before he was killed himself. This was no mere isolated act of a madman. Goldstein was a follower of New York's *Lubavitcher Rebbe*. But what he did reflected and exemplified the whole milieu from which he sprang, the religious settlers, and the National Religious Party behind them.[182] There was no more eloquent demonstration of that than the immediate, spontaneous responses to the mass murder; these yielded nothing, in breadth or intensity, to the Palestinians' responses to *their* fundamentalist suicide bombings, when these first got going in the wake of it. Many were the rabbis who praised this 'act', 'event' or 'occurrence', as they delicately called it, but none, perhaps, waxed so lyrical as another *Lubavitcher*, rabbi Yitzhak Ginsburg, who, originally from St Louis, Missouri, now headed the Joseph Tomb *yeshiva* in Nablus. In a pamphlet to honour the new 'martyr', he said that the death of any Arab was 'a fortunate event', but that Goldstein's deed was on another plane altogether; this was 'heroism so lofty that its source could only be located in a divine grace that emanated from the highest sphere'. It should inspire the Jews 'to possess the entire Land of Israel'.[183] The religious community at large did not hide its enthusiasm either; it had happened on Purim, a joyous feast, and many, in their merry-making, expressed the hope there would be more such Purim 'miracles'.[184] Within two days the walls of Jerusalem's religious neighbourhoods were covered with posters extolling Goldstein's virtues and lamenting that the toll of dead Palestinians had not been higher. In fact, the satisfaction extended well beyond the religious camp in general; polls said that 50 per cent of the Israeli people, and especially the young, more or less approved it. At a hugely attended funeral in Jerusalem, mourning onlookers murmured individual tributes like 'what a hero!', 'he did it for all of us', while, among the procession of rabbis who eulogized him, one, Israel Ariel, said that 'from now on the holy martyr, Baruch Goldstein, is our intercessor in heaven who did not act as an individual but heard the cry of the Land of Israel.'[185] The army guarded the funeral cortège on its way from Jerusalem to his tomb in Hebron. That in due course turned into a large and sumptuous memorial, and place of pilgrimage for Jews from all over Israel, Europe and the United States, who lit candles and sought the intercession of the 'holy saint and martyr'.[186] Shortly after the massacre, Yitzhak Rabin addressed an AIPAC convention in Washington. AIPAC, being far from happy about the Oslo accord, was also less than keen on its chief Israeli architect. The prime minister was politely received, and sometimes warmly applauded, but a correspondent of the Israeli newspaper *Maariv* could not help remarking, with some surprise, that the most rapturous plaudits were reserved for another speaker, Shlomo Diskin, rabbi of the West Bank settlement of Efrat, when he said that Goldstein was no more a murderer than a victim.[187]

The 'Jewish *Intifada*' also turned on other Jews. Yigal Amir, who assassinated Rabin in November 1995, was no less a product than Goldstein of the milieu from which he sprang. As in other religious traditions, the hatred which Jewish fundamentalists nurtured for Jewish 'traitors' and 'apostates' was perhaps even greater than it was for non-Jews. Rabin, and the 'left', were indeed traitors in their eyes; they were 'worshippers of the Golden Calf of a delusory peace'.[188] 'The Jews who lead us into that sin,' thundered Rabbi Dreyfus, 'no longer deserve any divine protection. We must fight those who cast themselves off from the community of true Israel. They have declared war against us, the bearers of the word of God'.[189] And in a clear example of their deep emotional kinship with the fundamentalists, Sharon and several other *Likud* and far-right secular nationalist leaders joined the hue and cry against Rabin and his government of 'criminals', 'Nazis' and 'Quislings'. Declaring that 'there are tyrants at the gate', Sharon likened Oslo to the collaboration between Marshall Pétain and Hitler and said that Rabin and his foreign minister Shimon Peres were both 'crazed' in their indifference to the slaughter of Jews.[190]

The struggle between the religious—in its fundamentalist form—and the secular, between ancient and modern, ethnocentric and universal, is a struggle for Israel's very soul. The *Gush* settlements are at the heart of it. The struggle is intensifying. But it is wholly unresolved. The fundamentalists can never win it; they are simply too backward and benighted for that. But, appeased, surreptitiously connived with, or unashamedly supported down the years by Labour as much as by *Likud*, they have now acquired such an ascendancy over the whole political process, such a penetration of the apparatus of the state, military and administrative, executive and legislative, that no elected government can win it either. Meanwhile, they grow increasingly defiant, lawless and hysterical in pursuit of the millennium. The Zionist-colonial enterprise has always had a built-in propensity to gravitate towards its most extreme expression. And what, with the rise of the Begins and Shamirs, the Sharons and now a new breed of super-Sharons, has been true of the whole is bound to be even more true of its fanatical, fundamentalist particular. Its latest manifestation is the so-called 'hill youth'; these sons and daughters of the original, post-1967 settlers, born and reared in the closed, homogenous, hothouse world of their West Bank and Gazan strongholds, surpass even their elders in militancy. In keeping with a time-honoured, Sharon-approved Zionist tradition, they have taken to seizing and staking out hill-tops as the sites of settlements to come, and, in every neighbourhood they claim as their own, they forcibly prevent the Palestinians from harvesting the fruit of their ancestral olive groves. In October 2002, they brought down Sharon's coalition government when its Labour partner resolved, at last, to do something about them. But it failed pathetically, and there is surely worse—much worse—to come, as the well-known columnist Ben Kaspit wrote in the newspaper *Maariv*:

> It is clear that the world is divided into two: the fundamentalist-messianic countries that are run by religious edicts, and the modern Western world, which operates with force against terror, but also rationally and according to the law. The question for us, therefore, is

> to which camp we belong . . . The peak was reached in the messianic character (where is his ass?) of Rabbi Mordechai Eliahu [a former Chief Sephardi Rabbi of Israel]. This is the person who is supposed to be a symbol and model for hundreds of thousands of skullcap-wearing youth, who leads national religious Judaism, who is the spiritual father of the National Religious Party. The man, with knitted cape and stylish turban, let the cat out of the bag. He made a public statement, on the record, shamelessly. Without giving a second thought, and with lots of arrogance. Arabs? Palestinians? It's all fiction. They are all our slaves. We are the masters of this land. Even their olive trees are ours. Therefore anyone who shoots a Palestinian olive-picker is to be praised. . . . We complain about extremist Islam . . . Later we are shocked at the sight of a young, good-looking man wearing a skullcap caught by a TV camera at Havat Gil'ad [a hill-top site] screaming at the top of his lungs at [Israeli] soldiers. 'Refuse to heed the order. Refuse. Refuse. Refuse to heed the order!' Later we are surprised at intelligent, thinking people, like Shmu'el Shoham of Ramat Gil'ad, who told me: 'Nothing will help. In the end they [the Palestinians] won't be here.' In this situation there is no certainty that *we* will be here, not as we dreamed we would be. This genie cannot be put back in the bottle by peaceful means. We are now struggling for Israel's character as a democratic state, for the chance of a peaceful solution in our region, to belong to the cultured, Western, peace-seeking world, to prevent us sliding into the status of a nuclear Afghanistan, militant Iran, or skinhead *Halachic* state.'[191]

YES, ISRAEL *IS* A RACIST STATE

'BY ANY STANDARD', SAYS ISRAEL Shahak, 'the State of Israel must be considered a racist state'.[192] For him, this has its roots in that narrow, ethnocentric interpretation of Jewish destiny, duly transposed into the modern political creed of Zionism, of which the Jewish fundamentalism just described is only the most extreme and malignant expression.

To level this charge is usually to provoke outrage in the United States, not merely from organized Jewry, but from any Administration,

Republican or Democrat, and from much of the mainstream media. It is generally dismissed as Arab propaganda, or ascribed to the extremist prejudice, the anti-Semitism, held to be rife in the Arab and Muslim worlds. Thus it was normal, part of his job, that Abraham Foxman, head of the Anti-Defamation League, should have decried as 'hideous' the very idea that Israel could be likened to the South Africa of the Apartheid era.[193] Normal, too, that the United States should have been so active in securing the annulment of the United Nations General Assembly's 'Zionism-is-Racism' resolution of 1975, a legacy of the times when, with Arab economic clout at its height and Third World solidarity still a force to be reckoned with, the Arabs could match their propaganda with real diplomatic achievement. At the World Conference Against Racism which took place in Durban, South Africa, in 2001, secretary of state Colin Powell led an American walk-out in protest against the fact that, as he put it, 'some delegates said that Apartheid exists in Israel'.

But so, like Shahak, do many Israelis, and not least, of course, those of them who, like some of South Africa's anti-Apartheid whites, chose exile over continued residence under such a repugnant regime. The fact that the Arabs turned it into a propaganda issue, or that Arab regimes themselves are, in their different way, at least as repressive as Israel does not impress them. Yes, Israel *is* a democracy, for its Jewish citizens at least; all the more reason, they say, for people like themselves to speak out, and agitate, against all those practices that make it anything but a democracy for its non-Jews.

Like Shahak, too, some, such as Michael Ben-Yair, Ilan Pappé and Neve Gordon, contend that Zionism, as an ideology, had racist propensities from the outset. Others, such as the former attorney general Ze'ev Sternhell, think that there was nothing intrinsically racist in a movement which only sought self-determination for the Jewish people in an independent state of their own. But both agree that, through its inevitable conflict with the Palestinians on whose land they sought it, it has become racist in practice.[194]

This is to be found at its sharpest in the occupied territories, in the treatment by Jewish settler fanatics of Palestinians now fanaticized in response. But, more instructively perhaps, it is to be found in the plight of what used to be called the 'forgotten' Palestinians. In 1948, instead of seeking to exploit the natives *in situ*, the new-born state of Israel drove most of them out; that ranks, historically, as the most extreme and fateful act of Zionist colonialism. Ironically, it would have been harder to accuse the Israelis of racism today if, at the time, they had been even more extreme, and expelled them all. For, in fact, classical racism of the kind the outside world most easily understands is that which Israel has practiced against the 160,000 Palestinians who, for one reason or another, were 'left behind' in 1948 and the community of more than a million into which they have subsequently grown. About 20 per cent of the total population, they are fully-fledged citizens of the Jewish state. They are supposedly equal before the law.

That, at least, is what one finds if one consults the literature of the Anti- Defamation League. 'Modern Israel', it proclaims, 'is an open, democratic, multi-racial society whose Arab citizens are afforded all the rights and privileges of Israeli citizenship'.[195] However, claims like that only go to show that the propaganda in which such Zionist organizations engage on Israel's behalf is steeped in precisely that mendacity they attribute to the propaganda of their enemies. It is not just that, at the popular level, anti-Arab prejudice is almost as intense, in Israeli society at large, as it is among the settlers and the fundamentalists. At that level, writes Israel Shamir, an immigrant from the Soviet Union, it could be said that 'Israel did, after all, fulfill at least one United Nations resolution, the one that called Zionism a form of racism. . . . What is upsetting is that the internationalist upbringing that we Russian Jews received in the Soviet Union could not withstand the poisonous Zionist propaganda of Jewish superiority'; and he cites the 'typical answers' of hundreds of Russian Jews who were asked about their feelings towards the Palestinians. 'I would kill all Arabs', said one; 'an Arab is an Arab,' said another, 'they all have to be eliminated'.[196] The fact is that, as any systematic perusal will reveal, the Israeli media are rife with sentiments of this kind. But although, according to its own publicity, the Israeli-American research organization MEMRI is supposed to spread enlightenment through translations from the Hebrew as well as the Arabic media, it never touches on these things; so not surprisingly they rarely get a mention in the Western, and least of all the American, media either.

The prejudice is also official, legal and institutionalized. In 1987, Uri Davis, an Israeli exile, published a book whose title—*Israel: An Apartheid State*—said it all.[197] In this analysis of the whole structure of Israeli law and practice, he pointed out that, unlike in South Africa, where racial discrimination was official policy, in Israel it was generally disguised. That was the only way to deal with a basic contradiction. On the one hand, Israel's whole *raison d'être* was to be 'the Jewish state', as 'Jewish' as England was 'English'. On the other, it was morally and materially imperative, from the outset, that it should present itself as an upholder of Western values, modern, progressive, democratic; it was also formally committed, under United Nations auspices, to enact a constitution 'guaranteeing all persons equal and non-discriminatory rights in civil, political, economic and religious matters and the enjoyment of human rights and fundamental freedoms'.[198] What Davis called 'a radical, legal apartheid of Jew versus non-Jew' came into being under 'cover' of 'seemingly non-discriminatory legal terms'.[199] For the only law that explicitly mentioned the word 'Jew' was the 1951 Law of Return, whereby any Jew, anywhere in the world, had that automatic right to Israeli citizenship which was automatically denied to all Palestinians driven from the land of their birth.

Israel never did manage to promulgate a constitution. Ostensibly, however, all laws, 'basic' or otherwise, passed by the Knesset applied, universally and impartially, to all Israeli citizens. The crucial, operational distinction between Jew and non-Jew came elsewhere—via the quasi-sovereign status which the Knesset granted to such formerly private, pre-state bodies as the World Zionist Organization, the Jewish Agency and the Jewish National Fund. These were constitutionally bound to confine themselves to a strictly Jewish agenda only. The World Zionist Organization/Jewish Agency promoted 'agricultural colonization based on Jewish labor', while the Jewish National Fund acquired real estate 'for the purpose of settling Jews on such lands and properties'. The basic, constitutional discrimination which, behind an irreproachable façade, this subterfuge embodied bred legal, administrative, financial, social and cultural discriminations against the Palestinians of every conceivable kind. This was the system, discussed at length in *The Gun and the*

Olive Branch,[200] that quickly spawned such Orwellian categories as the 'absent-presents'—the term devised to designate Palestinians whose lands and villages were subject to confiscation because, even though they themselves might be physically present, and fully-fledged citizens of the new-born state, legally speaking they were absent. It went on to construct a whole edifice of interlocking hypocrisies quite Byzantine in their complexity. Thus it was not, on the face of it, because they were Palestinians that their towns and villages did not benefit from the far greater budgetary allocations that went to Jewish ones; it was because *their* towns were not among the 'the localities whose name appear on the list of development towns drawn up by the Department of Revenue'. They were not among those localities because another such, outwardly unexceptionable, regulation ensured that no Arab town ever was. It was not *because* they were Palestinians that they did not, like Jews, qualify for all manner of special entitlements, such as more generous child allowances or house loans and grants, it was because they were not 'demobilized soldiers'. But they never *could* be 'demobilized soldiers', because no Palestinian[201] could serve in the army in the first place. That, in turn, was not because he was a Palestinian; of course not; it was simply because, under the Military Service Law, it fell to an 'enumerator' to 'authorize draftees and candidates for conscription to report' for duty—and it just so *happened* that no Palestinian ever earned the enumerator's authorization.[202]

The upshot of it all, at the most basic level, was that Palestinians have no right to live in areas reserved by law for Jews—now well over 90 per cent of a country that was formerly over 90 per cent Palestinian—in much the same way that blacks could not live in the similarly disproportionate 'white' areas of South Africa, or Jews in 'Gentile' areas of some countries of pre-modern Europe.[203] 'What', asks Israel Shahak,

> is the difference between prohibiting a Jew *qua* Jew from living in Saudi Arabia and prohibiting a non-Jew *qua* non-Jew from living in Carmiel [an Israeli town where Palestinians were trying, unsuccessfully, to take up residence]? Let us just compare it with how Jewish organizations in the United States react when they discover a club

> which refuses, or merely avoids accepting, Jewish members. It instantly becomes a target for a furious public protest campaign. Yet a club is only a private affair. By contrast, the Israeli policy of preventing non-Jews from living or doing business in specific Israeli cities is a public one. Isn't it much worse? In truth, the Zionists here and the anti-Semites there are on the same side of the fence. They achieve here what the anti-Semites try, usually without success, to achieve there.[204]

Nor can Arabs join *Kibbutzim*, those internationally admired, socialistic enterprises that are actually bastions of ethnic exclusivism, or lease—still less buy—land from Jews in order to cultivate it. In practice, under pressure of business interests, this last does happen. Indeed, it became prevalent enough to constitute a 'pestilence' which the government, and those quasi-sovereign Zionist bodies entrusted with the 'Judaization' of the land, felt obliged to stamp out. A campaign to that end opened with a statement from a minister of agriculture declaring that 'Arab labor in Jewish agricultural settlements amounts to a cancer racking our body'. 'Could you imagine', expostulated Shahak, 'a French minister labeling the Jewish merchants of France a cancer, and taking "appropriate" steps against its spread?'[205]

The Palestinian minority always were, and remain, dramatically under-represented in government, administration and public life. Their own affairs are almost exclusively handled by Jewish 'Arab experts' or 'advisers'. Only recently did they get their first cabinet minister in fifty years. They have no directors general, no Supreme Court judges, no ambassadors, no member on the board of Israel's most famous—and oh-so-liberal!—newspaper, *Haaretz*. They constitute only 4 per cent of government employees, mostly in jobs that only Palestinians can perform; most Jerusalem-based ministries do not staff them at all. Three out of the 641 managers of government-controlled companies are Palestinians. Their unemployment rates are more than a third higher than the national average. In 1998, only 8.8 per cent of local government budget allocations went to the 'Arab sector'. In the same year, 37.6 per cent of Palestinian families were below the poverty line, compared with the national average of

16.6 per cent. Some 53 per cent of Palestinian children live with more than two persons per room, compared with only 2.8 per cent of Jewish children. The mortality rate for premature Palestinian babies is 14.8 per cent compared with 8.2 per cent for Jewish ones. A community representing 20 per cent of the population is confined to municipal areas amounting to 2.5 per cent of the total. While 700 Jewish settlements were established since the state came into being, not a single new town or village has been built for a Palestinian population now over six times its original number. In 1998, despite a vastly greater need, out of 429 localities classified as 'priority areas', and therefore qualifying for special budgetary assistance, only four were Palestinian. Some 70,000 Palestinians live in over 100 villages which—in another Orwellian term—the government does not 'recognize', even though most of them pre-exist the state of Israel itself. Being 'unrecognized', they appear on no map, they are denied basic services such as mains water, electricity, sanitation and paved roads; though desperately overcrowded, they are forbidden to construct new houses, or even erect a tent; since they are also forbidden to repair existing houses—let alone add an extension, a lavatory or a bathroom—these fall into *dis*repair, whereupon the government, ruling them unsafe, orders their demolition. That, in fact, was the objective from the outset. For the real, if unavowed, reason for their 'non-recognition' is that they and the land that comes with them are destined to join that estimated 96 per cent of formerly Palestinian-owned territory which has already passed into Jewish hands.[206]

There have been improvements. When a Palestinian, Adel Qa'adan, applied in 1995 to buy a plot of land offered under a 'build-your-own-home' scheme in the Jewish community of Katzir, he was turned down because he was a non-Jew. All that this forty one-year-old surgical nurse wanted was something very ordinary, very human indeed: a better environment in which to raise his family than the squalor, dirt roads, defective sewers, dismal schooling and lack of any community institutions to which his own village, the nearby Baka al-Gharbiya, had been reduced by years of official neglect and discrimination. He petitioned the Supreme Court. Five years later, the court ruled in his favour; 'all people in Israel', it decreed, 'whatever their religion and nationality' must enjoy equal rights. On the face of it, this was a legal breakthrough for the Palestinians. Yet too much store could never be set by such seemingly progressive Court verdicts—and there had been others—or by new and high-sounding laws passed by the Knesset, because there was almost always that one little catch that negated their whole beneficent effect, that one little paragraph ensuring that the latest dispensation had no retroactive impact on earlier ones, and therefore on the whole structure of legalized discrimination to which these had given rise.[207]

Yet, restrictive though it was, the ruling infuriated the religious and nationalist right. The *Likud* party denounced it; Haim Druckman of the National Religious Party called it a 'black day for the Jewish people' and Meir Porush of the United Torah Judaism Party declared that 'they are destroying the state'. As for the Katzir Cooperative Association itself, it would have none of it. Court ruling or not, the Qa'adans could not have their plot: for it would set a precedent. Meanwhile, with the outbreak of the *Intifada*, and the intensified hostility towards the Palestinian minority which it engendered, the authorities went on the warpath again. The 'Judaization' of what remained of Palestinian land was resumed; the ministry of agriculture poison-sprayed 12,000 dunums of crops which the bedouins of the Negev had planted on their ancestral territories; the ministry of interior began stripping Palestinians of their citizenship for 'breach of allegiance to the state of Israel'. Under a new law against 'incitement to violence', the attorney general brought charges against Azmi Bishara, a Palestinian deputy, but none against a Jewish deputy, Michael Kleiner, who, in no less inflammatory fashion than Bishara, had said that people like him 'are routinely put in front of a firing squad in most countries'.[208] Finally, in the summer of 2002, the Sharon government effectively dispensed not merely with the very notion that the Palestinians should enjoy the same basic rights as their Jewish fellow-citizens, but, for the first time in Israel's history, with the whole, Orwellian pretence that they ever had or could. In a bid to by-pass the Qa'adan ruling, his coalition cabinet voted by 17 to 2 to endorse a bill, introduced into the Knesset by the National Religious Party, that would have permitted the allocation of 'state land' as residential areas for the exclusive use of Israel's Jewish citizens. Although the government retracted its support for the bill, nothing could wash its original, shocking intent away; it would, if passed, have enshrined racial discrimination as the official policy of the state. 'The advocates of this bill', wrote left-wing columnist B. Michael,

> have confirmed the most appalling of the accusations leveled at Israel—that it is an ethnically racist state. . . . So far, shame and our Jewish heritage have kept the phrase 'for Jews only' out of the statute books. But Rabbi Druckman and [education minister] Limor Livnat have no shame, and not much knowledge of Jewish heritage except perhaps for the Book of Joshua [the story of the Israelites slaughtering and driving out their enemies] and they have set about contaminating our legal system with concepts worthy of South Africa's Apartheid regime, Afghanistan's Taliban and Germany's Nuremburg laws.[209]

It was protest from such quarters that forced the cabinet retraction. Their ability to protest re-affirmed that, for the Jews at least, Israel was still a democracy. But there was no such protest, barely a squeak, from an American Jewry which is typically far more indulgent of Israel's shortcomings than Israelis themselves. The Anti-Defamation League was perhaps busy adjusting its time-honoured role—chastising the critics of Israel, never Israel itself—in accordance with the new guidelines laid down in Jerusalem the month before by the Congress of the World Zionist Organization. At its thirty-fourth session since its founding in Basel, in 1897, the Congress, which styles itself as 'the parliament of the Jewish people' but in practice is an overwhelmingly Israeli-American body, called for the establishment, in all countries, of 'working groups' who would collaborate with legislators to 'outlaw' not only anti-Semitism and Holocaust-denial, but even anti-Zionism too.[210]

And the American government? Not a word either. For George Bush and his neo-conservatives it was not Israel and its policies that stood in need of correction. It was the Arab and Muslim worlds. There had to be complete 'regime change' in the sickest and incurable cases, such as Iraq and 'Palestine', and, at the very least, far-reaching 'reform' of all those regimes which, through their own misrule, repression, encouragement or indulgence of Islamic extremism, anti-American and anti-Israeli propaganda, had nurtured the 'culture of violence' out of which grew Osama bin Laden and the apocalyptic atrocity of 9/11.

9/11—Never Ask Why

In the opening paragraph of their book *Why Do People Hate America?*[211] Ziauddin Sardar and Merryl Wyn Davies relate that 'as the dust cloud settled over Lower Manhattan on 11 September 2001, an unnamed, shell-shocked woman emerged from the swirling gloom around the Twin Towers. Her words to a waiting television reporter were not 'why', a simple expression of incomprehension, but a focused and pained question: 'Why do they hate us?' The question was instantly taken up by politicians and commentators, and, on the streets and in their homes, by ordinary people everywhere. The answer, from establishment America, was, in essence: 'American values'. On 20 September George Bush told a joint session of Congress: 'They hate our freedoms—our freedom of religion, our freedom of speech, our freedom to vote and assemble and disagree with each other. . . . America was targeted because we're the brightest beacon for freedom and opportunity in the world. And no one will keep that light from shining'. Similarly, for a lead analysis in the *New York Times*, 'the perpetrators acted out of hatred for the values cherished in the West as freedom, tolerance, prosperity, religious pluralism and universal suffrage'.[212]

But another distinguished American, Paul Findley, had a very different answer. 'Nine-eleven', said this former Congressman whom the Lobby had driven from office, 'would not have occurred if the US government had refused to help Israel humiliate and destroy Palestinian society'. In other words, it was not American values, but American policies, that were to blame. Although, he went on, 'many believe it is the truth . . . few express this publicly'. For it was impolitic to do so. '9/11 had its principal origin 35 years ago when Israel's US lobby began its unbroken success in stifling debate about the proper US role in the Arab-Israeli conflict'.[213]

To be sure, America's relentless, unthinking support for its Israeli protégé was not the only cause of the catastrophe. Ossama bin Laden and al-Qaeda did not come out of a void. They were a product of the Arab, and to some extent the wider Muslim, condition. And that condition was dismal. The Arab world was racked by all manner of social, economic, cultural and institutional sicknesses. There was no more compelling measure of that than the United Nation's Arab Human Development Report. Published in 2002, it described a Third World region which has fallen behind all others, including sub-Saharan Africa, in most of the main indices of progress and development; whose 280 million inhabitants, despite vast oil wealth, have a lower Gross National Product than Spain; whose annual translation of foreign books is one fifth of Greece's; 51 per cent of whose young people would emigrate if they could. A prime cause of this backwardness, said the Report's exclusively Arab authors, is that the Arab peoples are the world's least free, with the lowest levels of popular participation in government. 'Those who wonder why Afghanistan became a lure for some young Arabs and Muslims', wrote Jordanian columnist Yasser Abu-Hilalah, 'need only read this report, which explains the phenomenon of alienation in our societies and shows how those who feel they have no stake in them can turn to violence'.[214]

This was the explanation for 9/11—the purely internal, Arab and Muslim one—on which America focused. Indeed, within days, there arose a whole new Washington orthodoxy to which, it seemed, just about everyone, officials, congressmen, editorialists and academic specialists, subscribed. The Arabs and Muslims' deficiency in those American 'values' of freedom and democracy—therein the lay the root of the problem. And, the new orthodoxy proclaimed, the deficiency was by no means confined to countries where established American villains, such as Saddam Hussein's Iraq, or 'radical' regimes, such as President Asad's Syria, held sway; it also encompassed those, such as Saudi Arabia and Egypt, whose governments had hitherto been embraced as sound, reliable, 'moderate' friends of America and the West. 'In [Saudi Arabia's] closed political system'. now typically opined the *New York Times*,[215] 'the only available outlet for criticism of government policies and corruption is Islamic fundamentalism'. And the government itself was 'tolerant of terrorism'. President Mubarak, declared the *Washington Post*,[216] had a policy of 'deflecting frustration with the lack of political freedom or economic development' by 'encouraging state-controlled clerics and media to promote the anti-Western, anti-modern and anti-Jewish propaganda of the Islamic extremists'. There had to be root-and-branch reform and modernization, ushering in democracy, human rights, accountability.

Few Arab opinion-makers would by and large have disputed America's explanation—were it not for the fact that it was the only one that America advanced. It was, they said, but half of the matter, and you could not have one half without the other. That other was the part that America itself, and the West in general, had played in creating the Muslim, but more particularly Arab, condition of which bin Laden was the ultimate, evil fruit. In the Arabs' eyes this Western contribution had begun, in modern times at least, with the collapse of the Ottoman Empire during the First World War, the subsequent take-over and carve-up of most of its former Arab provinces by a Europe which had promised them their unity, freedom and independence, and, most cavalier and unconscionable of all, the hand-over of one of them, Palestine, in its entirety to another people. These betrayals and humiliations continued, after the Second World War, with the American-led support of repressive, corrupt or reactionary regimes enlisted as bulwarks against communism or accomplices in the quest for an impossible, because unjust, settlement of the Israeli-Palestinian conflict.

It is hard to exaggerate the importance that Palestine—virtual synonym for the most resonant and emblematic of contemporary world conflicts—had acquired in the politics and psyche of the Arabs and Muslim worlds. By the eve of 9/11, with the *Intifada* about to enter its second year, a survey revealed that some 60 per cent of the people in four rather disparate Arab countries—Saudi Arabia, Kuwait, the United Arab Emirates and Lebanon—regarded it as the 'single most important issue to them personally'; in Egypt, the most powerful and populous Arab country, that figure rose to a remarkable 79 per cent. 'The Palestinian issue remains an identity concern for most Arabs', said American academic Shibley Telhami; 'most Arabs are shamed by their inability to help the Palestinians'.[217]

It is hard to exaggerate, too, the level of resentment to which American purblindness and partisanship had by now given rise. Throughout the nineties—ever since the 1991 Gulf war and the subsequent 'containment' of Iraq which, in Arab minds, became a secondary source of grievance inextricably linked with, and reinforcing, the primary one—anti-Americanism had steadily, remorselessly grown. In the weeks before 9/11 no less a personage, and staunch friend of the West, than President Mubarak of Egypt was moved to complain, publicly, of 'the complete and blatant American bias in Israel's favour', while his confidant, Ibrahim Nafei, the editor of *al-Ahram*, the very sober mouthpiece of his regime, warned that 'hatred of America has reached unprecedented levels'. And yet another government newspaper, *al-Akhbar*, said that the Arab-Israeli conflict was being superseded by a 'broader and more dangerous Arab-American conflict'.[218]

Little did *al-Akhbar* foresee just how. But, when it came, the most spectacular terrorist exploit of all times relied, for its psychological impact, on this very climate of opinion which bin Laden himself had done nothing to create. To be sure, he had his own religious 'values', archaic and obscurantist, his messianic vision, his fundamentalist's ambition to establish Taliban-style theocracy throughout the Muslim world. But these were not the dominant values of the constituency to which he was making his appeal. It was only for very contemporary, very practical, political reasons, of which Palestine was unquestionably the chief, that his atrocious, apocalyptic deed had the resonance it did. Only for those reasons did those who would otherwise have dismissed him for the crazed fanatic he certainly was derive a certain *Schadenfreude* from the havoc and horror his kamikaze disciples wrought. And the man himself was shrewd enough to realize it. In an address to the Arabs and Muslims he did not labour his doctrines and beliefs, or dwell excessively on what he called this 'decisive war between the faith and global impiety'; rather, he enumerated the injustices and oppressions to which, be they secular or devout, the Arabs and Muslims felt they have been subjected in modern times at Western hands. And, first of all, he pointed out that 'Israeli tanks are wreaking havoc in Palestine—in Jenin, Ramallah, Rafah and Beit Jala and other parts of the Land of Islam, but no one raises his voice or bats an eyelid (in protest)'. It was shamelessly demagogic. But in linking his cause to Palestine he was only, like Saddam Hussein before him, doing what any politician does, which is to exploit the most profitable and emotive issue to hand.

To Arabs and Muslims, the inevitability of such 'linkage', and the American partisanship which makes it possible, is an obvious and fundamental reality—even if they simultaneously concede, as many of their opinion-makers do, that the sicknesses in their own societies are part of that reality too. And, for them, the very fact that it is so obvious explained why the 'other side', Israel and America, appeared so resolutely blind to it. Naturally, the Israelis were to the fore in this myopia. It was to be expected, for example, that the former Israel ambassador to Washington, Zalman Shoval, would contend that, in his opinion, there was 'no connection whatever' between fundamentalist terror and the 'Israeli occupation'.[219]

Some Americans, at least, apparently disagreed with him; like Paul Findley, they did see the connection. Thus, in a *Newsweek* poll conducted shortly after 9/11, 58 per cent of the respondents said that American ties to Israel and its policies towards the Palestinians were 'a major motivation behind the attacks on New York and Washington', and, more ominously, that the United States should 'consider changing its Middle East policies to reduce the violent backlash against it'.[220] What this seemed to suggest was that America's political classes—the Administration, Congress and the media—were at odds with a sizeable, and probably growing, portion of the public for which they reckoned to stand or speak, or at least they were when this public, without much help from them, managed to apprize itself of the real facts at issue. 'What shocked me', said Robert Fisk, Middle East correspondent of London's *Independent*, and an outspoken critic of American Middle East policies and compliant newspapers that endorse them, about his first American lecture tour after 9/11, 'was the growing angry awareness among Americans that they were being lied to and deceived. For the first time, it wasn't my lectures that they objected to, but the lectures they received from their president and the lectures they read in their press about Israel's "war on terror" and the need always, uncritically to support everything that America's little Middle Eastern ally says and does'.[221]

But, whatever the public might think, establishment America by and large refused—like ex-ambassador Shoval—to see the connection. What this meant, at its most bigoted and insulting, was what Rudolph Guliani, mayor of New York, did to Prince Walid bin Talal, billionaire Saudi tycoon. The two had stood side by side at 'Ground Zero'; there, the prince had presented the mayor with a $10-million check as a donation to the stricken city, and the mayor had graciously accepted it. But on his departure the prince issued a press release in which he urged America to 'address some of the issues that led to such a criminal attack'; it 'should adopt a more balanced stand towards the Palestinian cause'. The United Nations, he said, had for decades been passing clear resolutions calling for Israeli withdrawal from the West Bank and Gaza, but 'our Palestinian brethren continue to be slaughtered at the hands of Israelis while the world turns the other cheek'. Whereupon, the outraged mayor ostentatiously announced that he was returning the prince's check.

Meanwhile the media continued to lecture, not their own government, not Israel, but the Arabs and Muslims on their need to put their house in order. One searched almost in vain for any serious or systematic investigation of, or commentary on, the fact, a fact which seemed pretty obvious to the rest of the world, that there had been another, an American responsibility for what happened on that momentous day, and a consequent need to put America's house in order too. Insofar as the root causes were American, there was almost no disposition to look for them. And why of course should there be if, as establishment America had it, there *were* none in any case? If, in other words, it was only American 'values' that had been targeted.

But was it? James Abourezk, a former Congressman of Lebanese origin, is another distinguished American, like Paul Findley, who certainly did not think so. 'Anyone', he said, 'who knows anyone in the Arab world will tell you that they love our freedoms'.[222] That may not be much of an exaggeration. For, *pace* Ossama bin Laden and his messianic band, few Arabs and Muslims seem to have any serious quarrel with American values. Unquestionably, at least, it is what they see as deviations from those values, and the policies to which the deviations give rise, with which they overwhelmingly take issue; it is not the values themselves. Saudi Arabia, from which fifteen of the 9/11 suicide bombers came, must surely rank as the very heartland of bin Ladenism. Yet when Saudis were asked on what, specifically, they mainly based their attitude to the United States—its values or its policies—86 per cent said the second and a mere 6 per cent the first.[223]

It is hard to escape the conclusion that one key reason why Bush and establishment America saw only values, where most of the world saw policies too, was that any serious attempt to investigate the policies, and then, *a fortiori*, to act on what the investigation revealed, would have been far too radical and risky a venture for any American government, let alone the present one, to undertake. It would have led to the greatest, the most wrenching, parting of the ways between America and Israel—an Israel which is not only, of all the nations of the earth, among the very closest to America's heart, but, it is said, among the staunchest of allies and most valuable of 'strategic assets' too.

Is Israel an American Strategic Asset . . .

Between nations as between individuals, friendship and its obligations are a domain in which, understandably, subjective judgments tend to hold sway. But, objectively observed, friendship is often one thing, the friend's utility quite another. Getting America not merely to suspend its objectivity, but to trample it underfoot, has been one of the greatest triumphs of Israel and the 'friends of Israel' in America. Not merely, according to them, is there no contradiction between America's moral commitment to Israel and its higher national interests, there is no greater champion and defender of them than Israel itself.

It was in the early eighties that the 'strategic alliance' first came, formally proclaimed, into its own. But the notion had been around for a long time. Just as, in the earliest days, the Zionists had looked for very solid, practical reasons why Britain, at the height of its imperial power, should have deemed it profitable to sponsor their cause, and came up with the proposition that a Jewish presence in Palestine would help protect its vital imperial artery, the Suez Canal, so it made very good sense for them to persuade the world's only superpower of today that it was not just reciprocal affection and respect which bound it to the Jewish state, it was also, in *real-political* terms, a very good investment indeed. Under President Reagan, whose Administration was, till that time, the most pro-Israeli ever, America took to concluding 'strategic' agreements with its ally, and the Lobby to extolling the services which Israel had already rendered, and would be doing in the future.

The first, and most abiding, of these services supposedly stemmed from Israel's very nature as an exemplary, Western-style democracy in a region that lacked such a thing. In that capacity, it was also a sturdy rampart against such ideologies as communism and militant Arab nationalism, then the Islamic fundamentalism which came in their wake. It was America's regional 'gendarme', which, through deterrence or direct intervention, performed such tasks as keeping 'radical', Soviet-backed Syria in check, or saving Jordan's pro-Western monarchy from Syrian-sponsored, Palestinian overthrow in the civil war of 'Black September', 1970. In 1981, it destroyed the Osirak reactor, lynchpin of Saddam Hussein's nascent nuclear armaments programme; had it not done so, it might have been a nuclear-armed Iraq with which the United States and its allies would have had to contend when they drove it out of Kuwait in the Gulf War of 1991. On a wider front, Israel has served as a conduit for American arms to unsavoury regimes and movements, such as the Salvadoran junta or the Nicaraguan Contras, which it was too embarrassing for the United States to supply openly or directly itself.[224] In the technical field, it has furnished a very useful testing-ground for American weaponry, and for their further refinement and adaptation in ways from which America itself then profited.[225]

. . . or the Costliest of Liabilities?

Yet, could there have been a greater sophistry, a greater fallacy, than this: that the United States should have elevated Israel into a champion of its interests when Israel itself was the greatest single cause of all the threats to which those interests were exposed? For that, at bottom, is what it amounted to.

There is no historical evidence to suggest that the Palestinians, Arabs, or Muslims in general, had ever been more intrinsically hostile to American 'values', or, in consequence, to American national purposes, than any other peoples or religions on earth. Indeed, initially at least, the Arabs were in modern times probably better disposed towards them than most. After the First World War, President Wilson and his Fourteen Points, with their call for 'self-determination', 'justice' and 'fair dealing' for all peoples, the weak as well as the strong, and an end to 'force' and 'selfish aggression', inspired in them hope of an American counterweight to the designs of the traditional European colonial powers. At his insistence the Versailles Peace Conference dispatched a fact-finding mission to ascertain the wishes, not just of the Palestinians, but of all the newly liberated Arab inhabitants of the former Ottoman provinces. The 'King-Crane Commission', as it came to be known after the names of its exclusively American participants, concluded that, if the Zionist project were to go through, it would constitute 'a gross violation of the principle of self-determination and the peoples' rights'; furthermore, if they really did need to undergo a period of foreign tutelage to equip them for full independence, then, 'from the point of view of the people concerned, the mandate should certainly go to America'.[226] The residue of this Wilsonian idealism, the freedoms, the material progress and creative vitality, the opportunities for individual advancement and the good life, which America did seem so uniquely to embody, the activities in the region of American travellers, educators, philanthropists and missionaries in the late nineteenth and early twentieth centuries—all these filled up a reservoir of good will among the Arab peoples which only in 1948 began to drain away, and which, by now, has almost entirely evaporated.

In fact, Israel, the colonial enterprise, was bound to be a strategic liability—not an asset—for any outside power, not just America, which the Arabs perceived to be aiding and abetting it. That was something which the United States, or at least its specialized agencies such as the State Department, the CIA and the Pentagon, with their professional grasp of realities on the ground, perceived from the very outset. In 1947, as President Truman, in his zeal for Jewish votes, was pinning his colors to the Zionist mast, the CIA was reporting that the Zionist leadership was 'pursuing objectives without regard for the consequences', thereby 'endangering not only the Jews in Palestine but also the strategic interests of the Western powers in the Near and Middle East, since the Arabs now identify the United States and the United Kingdom with Zionism'.[227] The more powerful Israel became, in Washington as well as in Palestine itself, the less the foreign-policy and intelligence experts were listened to, and the more they risked identification with that failed and derided species, 'the Arabists'. For those who had routed the Arabists, those, in fact, whom one might just as well, if not—as a mark of single-minded devotion to another country's cause—far more aptly call the 'Israelists', the realities on the ground took second place to domestic concerns, to the imperious demands of the Lobby and all those politicians, which meant little short of all of them, who did the Lobby's bidding.

Israel-the-strategic-asset never had a serious basis. If the Arabs had wanted to learn about democracy they would rather have turned to America itself as their model than to an Israel whose chief impact on themselves, however democratic it might be for its own people, had been that of colonial usurper and military aggressor, endless source of conflict, turmoil and humiliation, bane of their domestic politics and their international relations, and vast drain on talents, energies and resources better devoted to other purposes. During the Cold War, Israel did nothing to check the advance of communism; on the contrary, it only furthered it, because Arab countries, despairing of the United States, turned to the Soviet Union for the arms, diplomatic backing and economic aid which most of them would have preferred to get from the West. Far from its furnishing any strategic assistance during Desert Storm, the war to liberate Kuwait, the Americans had to beg it to stay out—for fear that the least hint of Israeli involvement would destroy the Arab coalition ranged against Iraq—and then reward it to the tune $1,650 billion in military and economic aid for doing so.[228]

Indeed, the cost, political, psychological and economic, of Israel-the-strategic-liability is very great, and liable at any time to become catastrophic. It is hard to measure precisely. But there is no doubt that, insofar as 280 million Arabs, and more than a billion Muslims, a good sixth of the world's population, do 'hate' the United States, Israel, and its infinite complaisance towards it, is the single most important cause. If there is a danger to American interests in the region, it stems from the seemingly endemic political turbulence to which this Israeli-American complicity is the single most important, and continuous, contributor. And, of course, that, too, is what makes anti-Americanism such an ever-ready weapon in the hands of a bin Laden or a Saddam Hussein, or furnishes the Arab 'street' with a rallying cry to hurl at pro-American regimes.

Of all the reasons why, on the global stage, the United States has earned a general reputation for unilateral arrogance, hypocrisy and double standards, Israel again looms large. On its behalf, it has endlessly vetoed resolutions at the United Nations which even its closest European allies have supported; nor has it ever done anything serious to oblige Israel to implement those resolutions to which it itself has lent its name. Weapons of mass destruction is one of the matters on which, historically, the double standards have been particularly flagrant, and liable, in the end, to prove most dangerous to the peace of the world. On the one hand, the United States always expected the Arab states to sign up for the nuclear Non-Proliferation Treaty. On the other hand, Israel has long boasted a nuclear arsenal which—with perhaps 200 warheads, many times more powerful than those that were dropped on Hiroshima and Nagasaki, and long-range delivery systems—far exceeds any conceivable deterrent need. This came about not simply because the United States still connives in the ludicrous Israeli fiction that it 'will not be the first to introduce nuclear weapons into the region'—and, in theory, hasn't done so yet. It came about because, in earlier, less partisan days, when the United States still considered that weapons of mass destruction in Israeli hands would grievously impair the prospects of Arab-Israeli peace, Israel itself—setting an example that Saddam Hussein was later to follow—earnestly and repeatedly assured it that it was *not* developing them. It did so by systematically lying to it at the highest levels.[229] Under heavy pressure from the Kennedy Administration, it agreed to annual inspections by American scientists of its top-secret plant at Dimona in the Negev desert. Almost incredibly, however, the inspectors came away persuaded that the plant was entirely peaceful in purpose; perhaps they could not imagine that America's dear friend and ally would stoop to the brazen subterfuge it did—which was simply to brick off the plant's most sensitive area every time they visited. But still, American suspicions persisted and grew. And, as they did, the Israeli cover story chopped and changed. What at first had been a 'textile factory' suddenly became a 'pumping station'. And just after foreign minister Golda Meir solemnly assured the United Nations of Israel's 'special concern' about 'the growing nuclear arming' and its anxiety to 'remove [its] awful dangers to humanity', Dimona underwent yet a third transformation; it was now—according to Shimon Peres, original overseer of Israel's nuclear programme and a subsequent prime minister—a 'desalinization plant'.

In due course, exhibiting what had already become an ingrained habit where Israel was concerned, America resigned itself to what it had formerly opposed. And in the end it actively connived in it. There had been prolonged and active resistance, within the Clinton Administration, to a decision to supply Israeli universities with nine super-computers. These machines are used to simulate a nuclear weapon's launch, delivery and detonation, making it possible to complete its design without actual tests. George Bush I had rejected the sale. But his successor, the most pro-Israeli president yet, was more sympathetic. Even so, the internal critics had asked, was it wise to supply the computers to academic institutions involved in developing Israel's nuclear programme, just when the Non-Proliferation Treaty was due for renewal, and Egypt, the first Arab country to make peace with Israel, was threatening to withdraw from it if Israel persisted in its refusal to join it? In 1995, Clinton gave the go-ahead regardless.[230]

As for the economics of Israel-the-strategic-liability, it involves more, far more, than just the aid which the United States has heaped on it and—to underpin the evolving *Pax Americana* in the Middle East—on Egypt and Jordan too. This alone had cost the American taxpayer $379 billion by 2002.[231] It also includes the price the United States paid for great, Israeli-related emergencies down the years and for guarding against the eventuality of new ones. Economist Thomas Stauffer puts the cumulative cost of American policies in the region at over $1,500 billion, greater than the cost of the Vietnam war. Of that, some three quarters—about $1,200 billion—grew out of the American defence of Israel since the 1973 Arab-Israeli war. The rescue operation which President Nixon mounted on that occasion triggered an Arab oil embargo and an increase in the price of imported oil that cost the United States almost $900 billion in lost GDP.[232] Two other American economists, Norman Bailey, former special assistant to President Reagan, and Criton Zoakos argue that, since that war, the Americans 'have been paying, on the average, dramatically more than [they] like to believe [they] have' for their energy supplies. This is because the true cost of securing the Gulf as the prime source of 'cheap oil'—that key, politically contrived cornerstone of the global energy market—has to take into account all the administrative, technical, diplomatic and military expenditures that make it possible in the first place, and which come out of the Federal budget. These increased drastically after the first great, 1973 'oil shock'. Since then, and even by the most 'extravagantly conservative estimates', what, via taxation, the Americans actually end up paying per barrel of Arab oil has in any one year been two to five times higher than the benchmark price of Saudi light crude.[233] 'Trade follows the flag'—and deteriorating political relations have resulted in the loss of hundreds of thousands of American jobs. Some disappeared because of Arab trade boycotts, some because American companies forfeited big contracts to foreign competitors as a consequence of economic sanctions, mainly inspired by the Lobby, imposed on such countries as Iran, and others because of the dangerously growing trade-aid imbalance between the United States and Israel. They have also cost America some $5 billion a year in lost exports.[234]

To top it all, Israel is far from being the grateful, sensitive ally which the United States, in its munificence and almost saintly tolerance of troubles endured on its behalf, might legitimately expect it to be. It shows a fine disregard for American law. It has continuously violated the terms of the Arms Export Control Act—under which American-supplied military hardware can be used for defensive purposes only—be it in Lebanon for many a year, or more recently, during the second Intifada, in Palestine itself. It has illegally and repeatedly—if sometimes with official US complicity—re-transferred secret American military technology to third parties, including Ethiopia during the despotic, Soviet-backed rule of Mengistu Mariam and the Dergue, South Africa during Apartheid, the Chile of General Pinochet, or the communist China of today. By doing so, it has raked in yet further profits from American bounty, posed unfair competition to American defence industries, and bolstered regimes guilty of gross human rights abuses or actively working against American national interests. Few countries have spied more assiduously on the United States than its most favoured friend, eavesdropped on its political or economic secrets, or pilfered its materiel and technology. In 1986 the Jewish American, Jonathan Pollard, was sentenced to life imprisonment for the damage 'beyond calculation'[235] he did to his country by passing tens of thousands of pages of military and intelligence data to Israel, which then found their way to the Soviet Union, leading to the execution of Russian agents in American employ and putting the lives of thousands of American soldiers at risk. Among the resolutions of its 34th Congress, the World Zionist Organization, adding its voice to an already swelling chorus of Israeli and Jewish American pleas for clemency, formally 'call[ed] upon the President of the US, Mr George W. Bush, to pardon and free' this very mercenary spy—he had earned $50,000 by the time of his arrest and was expecting 'ten times that amount'—and upon 'all Jewish and Zionist activists in the world, and in particular in the United States, to participate in activities' to that end. During the 1967 war, Israeli warplanes made a deliberate and unprovoked attack on the intelligence-gathering ship the USS *Liberty*, killing thirty four of the crew. Till this day the survivors have failed to secure a Congressional enquiry into what amounted to an act of premeditated murder; the self-same legislators who regularly fete a foreign politician such as Binyamin Netanyahu as if he were one of their own have indefatigably blocked an investigation on behalf of their own, American constituents.

The 'Axis Of Evil': America Adopts Israel's Enemies as Its Own

Yet far from worrying about the doubtful company it might have been keeping, the America of George Bush II and his neo-conservative henchmen now keeps it more closely than ever before. Since 9/11 it has all but aligned itself with Sharon, Bush's 'man of peace', all but assimilated his war on Arafat and the Palestinians with its own, against the 'axis of evil,' al-Qaeda and international terror. There was, it is true, an uncertain, vacillating period in which it looked as though Bush might grasp that America's Middle East policies, not just its values, had something to do with the adversities it had suffered. It was a genuflection, probably, towards Colin Powell and the more balanced and reasonable, but weaker, side of his Administration which his secretary of state seemed to represent. It began with his declaration about the need for a Palestinian state. That had been long awaited and was hardly revolutionary. Even so it was quite enough for the Lobby and its Congressional claque to cry 'appeasement'. 'It means', said Mortimer Zuckerman, chairman of the Conference of Presidents of Major American Jewish Organizations, 'that if you attack America you'll get something.'[236] Sharon himself went further: for him, it smacked of Czechoslovakia, of Munich, 1938. But vacillation did not last very long. By the summer of 2002 Bush had firmly set his new course: 'regime change' and reform in the Muslim and Arab worlds, and, where necessary, American military intervention to achieve it.

So it was that the America which in the early twentieth century had insisted, much to the consternation of the European colonial powers, on consulting the freely, democratically expressed wishes of the Arab peoples was now about to impose 'democracy' on them by force of arms. This was the new, the Transatlantic, the twenty-first-century imperialism by another name. It started with Iraq: after Afghanistan, that was where the promised 'phase two' of the 'war on terror' took place, where the decisive battle between good and evil was joined. Hitherto, it had been assumed that 'linkage' would make this very difficult, if not impossible, that the United States just could not go to war in one of the two great zones of Middle East crisis, Iraq and the Gulf, before it had at least calmed things down in the other, older and more explosive one, Palestine. Conquering and occupying Iraq, while permitting Israel to pursue its depredations in Palestine, was to carry double standards to new and awesome lengths; it was seen as aggression against the whole Arab world. But the neo-conservatives had a very simple answer to that. They just turned the argument on its head. The road to war on Iraq no longer lay through peace in Palestine; peace in Palestine, or—to be more precise—the total subjugation of the Palestinians, lay through war on Baghdad. It was all set forth, in its most comprehensive, well-nigh megalomaniac form, by Norman Podhoretz, their veteran intellectual luminary, in the September 2002 issue of his magazine *Commentary*. Changes in regime, he proclaimed, were 'the *sine qua non* throughout the region'. And those that 'richly deserve to be overthrown and replaced are not confined' to the two officially designated Middle Eastern members of Bush's 'axis of evil'. 'At a minimum the axis should extend to Syria and Lebanon and Libya, as well as "friends" of America like the Saudi royal family and Egypt's Husni Mubarak, along with the Palestine Authority, whether headed by Arafat or one of his henchmen'. Such an all-encompassing purge, he said, might 'clear a path to the long-overdue internal reform and modernization of Islam'. On the other hand, it might not. 'There is no denying that the alternative to these regimes could easily turn out to be worse, even (or especially) if it comes into power through democratic elections', because 'very large numbers of people in the Muslim world sympathize with Osama bin Laden and would vote for radical Islamic candidates of his stripe if they were given the chance'. 'Nevertheless,' he dauntlessly continued, 'there is a policy that can head it off, provided that the US has the will to fight World War IV—the war against militant Islam—to a successful conclusion, and provided that we then have the stomach to impose a new political culture on the defeated parties'.

This, of course, was a full and final elaboration of that project, *A Clean Break*, which some of his kindred spirits had first laid before Israeli prime minister Binyamin Netanyahu back in 1996. It was the apotheosis of the 'strategic alliance', at least as much an Israeli grand design as it was an American one; indeed, it was probably more so. Under the guise of forcibly divesting Iraq of its weapons of mass destruction, the United States is seeking to 'reshape' the entire Middle East, with this most richly endowed and pivotal of countries as the lynchpin of a whole new, pro-American geopolitical order. Witnessing such an overwhelming display of American will and power, other regimes, such as *Hizbullah*-supporting Syria in particular, will either have to bend to American purposes or suffer the same fate.

With the assault on Iraq, the United States was not merely adopting Israel's long-established methods—of initiative, offense and pre-emption—it was also adopting Israel's adversaries as its own. Iraq had always ranked high among those; together with Iran, it was one of its so-called 'faraway' enemies. These had come to be seen as more menacing than the 'near' ones, the Palestinians and neighbouring Arab states, and especially since they had begun developing weapons of mass destruction. Israel had always advertised an implacable resolve to preserve its own monopoly in that field. It had entertained high hopes that George Bush I would destroy Saddam Hussein and his regime in Desert Storm. The hopes were dashed. But the prospect that George Bush II was now about to complete the job his father had left unfinished produced a rare consensus in Israel. It was not just Sharon, the *Likud* superhawk, who urged him to proceed without delay; it was Shimon Peres, his supposedly moderate, Labour foreign minister, too. The author of so many deceits and shameless strategems, at America's expense, in the early days of Israel's own nuclearization, he now solemnly warned a Washington audience that postponing a strike against Iraq would be 'taking maybe the same risk that was taken by Europe in 1939 in the face of the emergency of Hitler'.[237]

So excited was Sharon about this whole new Middle East order in the making that, he told the *Times* of London,[238] 'the day after' Iraq the United States and Britain should turn to that other 'faraway' enemy. For Israel, in fact, the Ayatollahs' Iran had always seemed the greater menace of the two, by virtue of its intrinsic weight, its fundamentalist, theologically anti-Zionist leadership, its more serious, diversified and supposedly Russian-assisted nuclear armaments programme, its ideological affinity with, or direct sponsorship of, such Islamist organizations as *Hamas* or *Hizbullah*. Nothing, in fact, better illustrated the ascendancy which Israel and the American 'friends of Israel' have acquired over American policy-making than did Iran. Quite simply, said Iran expert James Bill, the 'United States views Iran through spectacles manufactured in Israel'.[239] On any true reckoning, Israel was not merely the only beneficiary, it was the virtual sponsor of the trade sanctions, very damaging to American business interests, which President Clinton imposed on it in 1995, and which Bush, outmanoeuvred by the Lobby, reluctantly renewed in 2001. Such is the distorting effect of this influence that, according to the *Washington Post*,[240] Israel, with the help of Congress, was instrumental in getting the CIA, at the expense of its professional objectivity, to adopt an alarmist assessment of the missile threat posed to the United States by such 'rogue' states as Iran—an assessment which flew completely in the face of its own previous orthodoxy. Impressing on the United States the gravity of the Iranian threat has long been a foremost Israeli preoccupation. In the early nineties, the Labour MP and former minister Moshe Sneh told a symposium at the Yaffe Center for Strategic Studies that Israel 'cannot possibly put up with a nuclear bomb in Iranian hands'. Such a development could and should be collectively prevented, he said, 'since Iran threatens the interests of all rational states in the Middle East'. However, 'if the Western states don't do their duty Israel will find itself forced to act alone, and will accomplish its task by any [i.e., including nuclear] means.' The hint of anti-American blackmail in that remark was nothing exceptional; it has always been a *leitmotif* of Israeli discourse on the subject. Another expert, Daniel Lesham, urged Israel to play up Iran's terrorism and 'explain to the world' the urgency of provoking it into war. Yet others said that the United States should demonize and isolate Iran by blockading its coasts and 'stationing warships, especially nuclear submarines, threateningly close'.[241] The showdown with Iraq has only encouraged this kind of thinking, the more so in that, some reports have it, the Russian-built nuclear plant at Bushire, which the Iranians and Russians say is for peaceful purposes, but Israelis and Americans believe is for military ones, will go on stream before long. 'Within two years', said John Pike, director of Globalsecurity.org, 'either the US or Israel is going to attack Iran's [nuclear sites] or acquiesce in Iran being a nuclear state'.[242]

Before It Is Too Late: Save Israel from Its 'Nuclear-Crazy' Self

To where this Israeli-American, neo-conservative blueprint for the Middle East will lead is impossible to forecast. All that can be said for sure is that it could easily turn out to be as calamitous in its consequences, for the region, America and Israel itself, as it is preposterously partisan in motivation, fantastically ambitious in design and terribly risky in practice. Even if, to begin with, it achieves what, by its authors' estimate, is an outward, short-term measure of success, it will not end the *Violence in the Middle East*. Far more likely is that, in the medium or the long term, it (would) will make it very much worse. For the *violence* to truly end, its *roots* must be eradicated too, and the noxious soil that feeds them cleansed.

It is late, but perhaps not too late, for that to happen. The historic—and historically generous—compromise offer which Yasser Arafat, back in 1988, first put forward for the sharing of Palestine between its indigenous people and the Zionists who drove most of them out still officially stands. It is completely obvious by now that, without external persuasion, Israel will never accept it; that the persuasion can only come from Israel's last real friend in the world, the United States; that, for the persuasion to work, there has to be 'reform' or 'regime change' in Israel quite as far-reaching as any to be wrought on the other side; and, finally, that it is the only way, in the end, to save Israel from itself. This is something which some Israelis clearly understand, and strive to get America and, perhaps more to the point, the 'friends of Israel' in America to understand too. 'For decades', laments activist Gila Svirsky, 'we in the Israeli peace movement have been struggling to get Israelis to compromise on the issue that feeds the conflict with the Palestinians. And then our work for peace gets doused twice: once by a prime minister who believes brutality will convince the Palestinians to give up, and then by a US president who supports him on this. Bush has become a big part of the problem'.[243] Or, as Gideon Samet, a *Haaretz* columnist puts it, 'instead of calming things down, and balancing the pressure on Arafat with demands on Sharon . . . Uncle Sam is writing a script for a horrifying Western of the good guys against the bad—to the death'.[244]

Given the partisanship, it is, admittedly, highly unlikely to happen any time soon. And it would never be easy even in the very easiest of circumstances. Only the most resolute of presidents could pull it off. Capturing the White House for the cause was always one of Zionism's supreme objectives; one which, down the years, it has by and large brilliantly accomplished. The last time the incumbent of 1600 Pennsylvania Avenue took an absolutely unflinching stand against Israel was when President Eisenhower enforced its unconditional withdrawal from the Sinai it had invaded, in a deliberate act of unprovoked aggression, in the 1956 Suez War. Indeed—says Stephen Green in his book *Taking Sides*—'a strong case can be made that Eisenhower was the last American president actually to make US Middle East policy', rather than 'Israel and the friends of Israel in America'.[245] In the nearly half century since then, it was perhaps George Bush I who turned more strongly against Israel than any other president, in a dispute over a $10-billion loan guarantee in 1991; some believe that it cost him his re-election for a second term.

But if it doesn't happen in the reasonably foreseeable future, there may come a time when it can no longer happen at all. The Palestinian leadership may withdraw their offer, having concluded, like many of their people already have, that, however conciliatory they become, whatever fresh concessions they make, it will never be enough for an adversary that seems to want all. The *Hamas* rejectionists, and/or those, secular as well as religious, who think like them, may take over the leadership. The whole, broader, Arab-Israeli peace process which Anwar Sadat began, and which came to be seen as irreversible, may prove to be reversible after all; Camp David and the Wadi Araba (the Israel-Jordan treaty of 1994) may collapse. In which case the time may also, indeed almost certainly will, come when the cost, to the United States, of continuing to support its infinitely importunate protégé in a never-ending conflict against an ever-widening circle of adversaries is greater than its will and resources to sustain. That would very likely be a time when Israel itself is already in dire, even existentially terminal, peril. And if it were, then America would very likely discover something else: that the friend and ally it has succored all these years is not only a colonial state, not only extremist by temperament, racist in practice, and increasingly fundamentalist in the ideology that drives it, it is also eminently capable of becoming an 'irrational' state at America's expense as well as its own. For to be a 'strategic asset' is also to have the option of becoming, wilfully and deliberately, a 'strategic liability'. That is something of which Israeli leaders from time to time remind their American benefactor; it was, for example, the real meaning—or, as Israeli columnist Haim Baram put it, 'the naked blackmail'[246]—behind Sharon's 'Czechoslovakia' outburst and his warning that 'from this day on, we can rely only on ourselves'. In fact, the threatening of wild, irrational violence, in response to political pressure, has been an Israeli impulse from the very earliest days. It was first authoritatively documented, in the 1950s, by the dovish prime minister Moshe Sharett, who wrote of his defense minister Pinhas Lavon that he 'constantly preached for acts of madness' or 'going crazy' if ever Israel were crossed.[247] In his book *The Fateful Triangle*, Noam Chomsky argues that the real target of the Israeli nuclear bomb is the United States.[248] That Israel was indeed seeking this kind of leverage over the United States was also the presumption of the French, when, in a collaboration rigorously concealed from the Americans, they furnished the first, indispensable assistance for Israel's project to become a nuclear power. 'We thought', said Francis Perrin, High Commissioner of the French Atomic Energy Agency at the time, 'the Israeli bomb was aimed against the Americans, not to launch against America, but to say "if you don't want to help us in a critical situation we will require you to help us, otherwise we will use our nuclear bomb" '.[249] When, in the 1973 war, Israel did unsheathe its nuclear sword, it was not to frighten the Arabs, but to force the United States to come through with a massive, emergency supply of conventional weapons, or risk a catastrophic Israeli-inflicted blow to its wider interests in the region.[250]

Without a 'just, comprehensive and lasting' peace—that fruitless quest of over half a century of Middle East diplomacy—which only America can bring to pass, Israel will remain at least as likely a candidate as Iran, and a far more enduring one, for the role of 'nuclear-crazy' state. Iran can never be threatened in its very existence.

Israel can. Indeed, despite its enormous military superiority over the Palestinians and any combination of Arab states, such a threat could even grow out of the current *Intifada*. That, at least, is the pessimistic opinion of Martin van Creveld, the well-known professor of military history at the Hebrew University in Jerusalem. If it went on much longer, he said, 'the Israeli government [would] lose control of the people. . . . In campaigns like this the anti-terror forces lose, because they don't win, and the rebels win by not losing. I regard a total Israeli defeat as unavoidable. That will mean the collapse of the Israeli state and society. We'll destroy ourselves'. And in this situation, he went on, more and more Israelis were coming to regard the 'transfer' of the Palestinians as the only salvation; resort to it was therefore growing 'more probable . . . with each passing day'. Sharon 'wants to escalate the conflict and knows that nothing else will succeed'. But would the world permit such ethnic cleansing?

That depends on who does it and how quickly it happens. We possess several hundred atomic warheads and rockets and can launch them at targets in all directions, perhaps even at Rome. Most European capitals are targets for our air force . . . Let me quote General Moshe Dayan: 'Israel must be like a mad dog, too dangerous to bother'. I consider it all hopeless at this point. We shall have to try to prevent things from coming to that, if at all possible. Our armed forces, however, are not the thirtieth strongest in the world, but rather the second or third. We have the capability to take the world down with us. And I can assure you that that will happen, before Israel goes under.[251]

In its first edition, *The Gun and the Olive Branch* concluded with a quotation from the *Jerusalem Post* warning of the second 'Holocaust' that might one day encompass Israel's enemies as well as itself. Clearly, the quotation is just as relevant today, a quarter of a century on, as it was then. And the 'anthem of hope' whose 'opening chords'—according to the reviewer—Anwar Sadat, with his pilgrimage to Jerusalem, had just struck remains an anthem of hope unfulfilled. And it will continue so to do until the United States awakes, fully, from the kind of purblind infatuation which—ever since George Washington warned against 'excessive partiality' for 'one foreign nation', the 'imaginary common interest' to which it gives rise, and 'the facility' it offers to 'deluded citizens to betray or sacrifice the interests of their own country with the appearances of laudable zeal for the public good'—has been at odds with most of the 'values' for which it presumes itself to stand.

Notes

1. Letter to myself from Senior Editor Thomas Stewart.
2. *Washington Post*, 18 December 1977; only long after publication, and then only due to a personal intervention on my behalf, did a friend of mine, the late Joe Alex Morris of the *Los Angeles Times*, write the only other serious—and complimentary—review to appear in any of America's leading newspapers.
3. Pryce-Jones, David, *The Face of Defeat: Palestinian Refugees and Guerillas*, Weidenfeld and Nicolson, London, 1972; *New Republic*, 9 December 1981. The 'discussion' to which Pryce-Jones referred was actually an interview, published in the London *Guardian*, which I conducted with General Saaduddin al-Shazli, the former Egyptian Chief of Staff, who was the mastermind behind the Egyptian army's crossing of the Suez Canal in the opening offensive of the 1973 Arab-Israeli War. Subsequently disgraced by President Sadat, he was in exile at the time.
4. Littlefield, David, *Library Journal*, 1 December 1977.
5. I learned this from the late James Markham, then a Middle East correspondent of the *New York Times*, who had been instrumental in the commissioning. He expressed himself 'ashamed' of his own newspaper, but, evidently in the interests of his career, he asked that I keep not only the source of this information confidential, but the fact of the suppression as well. My surprise was all the milder in that I had already had personal experience of the lack of professionalism—some might call it plain stupidity or gross disservice to its readers—into which the *New York Times*'s Middle Eastern *parti pris* could lead it. In the summer of 1973, I had written a 3000-word piece for its Sunday *Magazine*; it was about President Anwar Sadat, and it tended to flatter the then widespread view of a leader whom America later all but canonized as the 'great Arab peace-maker': namely, that he was a clown and a war-monger. The *Times*'s editors liked it so much that they promptly asked for another article, assessing the chances that the Arabs might exploit the West's heavy dependence on their oil as a weapon in their conflict with Israel. I argued, emphatically, that they very well might. This was at odds with

the newspaper's editorial line, which was to belittle any connection between America's Middle East policies and the growing energy crisis of the time. The editors rejected my submission, with an evasive and disingenuous explanation why. I wrote to my intermediary, Heather Bradley, saying that if I had ever received such a response from my own newspaper, the London *Guardian*, I would have considered it 'most unsatisfactory', and expressing my belief that the editors had declined to publish the article because—although it contained no criticism of Israel as such—they regarded it as 'inimical to Israel's interests'; this, I said, lent 'some credence to what I have been so often told about the attitude of the *New York Times* and other American newspapers towards the Middle East'. Bradley wrote back: 'I quite agree with you. I will not forward your letter, though, since we are sensitive in these matters, and I very much want to see you again in the *Magazine*. It's a very great pity we are as we are, but there it is'. Two months later, with the outbreak of the fourth Arab-Israeli War, the Arab oil-producers did unsheath the oil weapon, and the West suffered its first great oil 'shock'. However, I was never asked to write for the *New York Times* again.

6. *I. F. Stone's Weekly*, 9 March 1978.
7. Christison, Kathleen, *Perceptions of Palestine: Their Influence on US Policy*, University of California Press, Berkeley, Los Angeles and London, 1999, pp. 2–3; 'US Policy and the Palestinians', *Journal of Palestine Studies*, Issue 104, Summer 1997.
8. Address to Israel's Fiftieth Anniversary Jubilee, 30 April 1998.
9. *From Haven to Conquest: Readings in Zionism and the Palestine Problem until 1948*, Institute for Palestine Studies, Beirut, 1971, pp.xxi–xxiv.
10. Harper and Row, New York, 1984.
11. *Blaming the Victims*, ed. Edward Said and Christopher Hitchens, Verso, London and New York, 1998, p. 24.
12. *Ibid*, pp. 23–5, 33.
13. *Ibid.*, pp. 33–4.
14. *Ibid.*, pp. 29–30.
15. *Ibid.*, pp. 27–8, 62.
16. *Ibid.*, pp. 33–69; see also Norman Finkelstein, *Image and Reality of the Israel-Palestine Conflict*, Verso, London and New York, 2001, pp. 25–50.
17. *Ibid.*, p. 62.
18. Morris, *Birth of the Palestinian Refugee Problem, 1947–1949*, Cambridge University Press, Cambridge and New York, 1988; Shlaim, *Collusion Across the Jordan: King Abdullah, the Zionist Movement and the Partition of Palestine*, Clarendon Press, Oxford, 1988; Pappé, *The Making of the Arab-Israeli Conflict, 1947–1951*, I. B.Tauris, London and New York, 1992.
19. Pappé, Ilan, 'Post-Zionist Critique on Israel and the Palestinians', *Journal of Palestine Studies*, Issue 102, Winter 1997; Gershon Shafir, 'Israeli Decolonization and Critical Sociology', *Journal of Palestine Studies*, Issue 99, Spring 1996.

20. Morris, 'The New Historiography: Israel Confronts its Past', *Tikkun*, November/December 1988.
21. Morris, *Birth of the Palestinian Refugee Problem*, p. 286.
22. Christison, *op. cit.*, pp. 1–15.
23. Kerr, Malcolm, *America's Middle East Policy: Kissinger, Carter and the Future*, IPS Papers 14 (E), Institute for Palestine Studies, 1980, pp. 8–9.
24. Sarid, Yossi, 'The Night of the Broken Clubs', *Haaretz*, 4 May 1989, *Translations from the Hebrew Press* (a monthly collection prepared for many years by the late Israel Shahak, and often accompanied by his own notes and comments; hereafter cited as Shahak, *Translations*).
25. *Jerusalem Post*, 3 February 1989, cited in Joost Hiltermann, 'Human Rights and the Mass Movement: The First Year of the *Intifada*', *Journal of Palestine Studies*, Issue 71, Spring 1999.
26. *Haaretz*, 1 October 1990, Shahak, *Translations*.
27. Shlaim, 'The Oslo Accord', *Journal of Palestine Studies*, Issue 91, Spring 1994.
28. Strictly speaking, it was not wholly reciprocal, in that while the PLO recognized Israel and its right to exist, Israel only recognized the PLO as the legitimate representative of the Palestinian people, not the Palestinians' right to self-determination.
29. Rabin, Yitzhak, 'Peace in the National Order of Priorities', *Israeli-Arab Negotiations: Political Positions and Conceptual Frameworks*, ed. Tamar Herman and Robin Twite, Tel Aviv, Papyrus, 1993 (Hebrew), cited in *Journal of Palestine Studies*, Issue 117, Autumn 2000.
30. *Israeli Settlements in the Occupied Territories: A Guide*, The Foundation for Middle East Peace, March 2002.
31. *Agence France Presse*, 15 November 1998.
32. Walid Khalidi, *The Prospects for Peace in the Middle East*, speech delivered in London, 8 October 2002.
33. See *The Gun and the Olive Branch*, p. 459.
34. *Maariv*, 21 November 2002.
35. *Ibid.*
36. Luft, Gal, 'The Palestinian H-Bomb', *Foreign Affairs*, July/August 2002.
37. Vidal, Dominique, *Le Monde Diplomatique*, January 2002.
38. Tanya Reinhart, 'Evil Unleashed', *Media Monitors Network*, 17 December 2001.
39. See *The Gun and the Olive Branch*, pp. 529–579.
40. Reinhart, *op. cit.*
41. Kapeliouk, Amon, *Le Monde Diplomatique*, May 2001.
42. Amira Hass, *Haaretz*, 6 May 2002; see Kathleen Christison, 'Israel, A Light Unto Nations?', *Counterpunch*, 11 May 2002.
43. Masalha, Nur, *Imperial Israel and the Palestinians: The Politics of Expansion*, Pluto Press, London, 2002, pp. 878.
44. *Ibid.*, pp. 105–95.
45. *Haaretz*, 12 March 2002.

46. *Al-Ahram Weekly*, 16–22 May 2002.
47. Shalom Yerushalmi, *Maariv*, 17 October 2002.
48. *Washington Report on Middle East Affairs*, July 1998.
49. Cited in *Mideast Reporter*, Beirut, 26 October 2002.
50. *The Gun and the Olive Branch*, p. 516.
51. *Ibid.*, pp. 111–23.
52. Goldberg, J. J., *Jewish Power: Inside the American Jewish Establishment*, Perseus Books, Reading, Massachusetts, 1996, pp. 8–9.
53. Ginsberg, Benjamin, *The Fatal Embrace: Jews and the State*, University of Chicago Press, Chicago and London, 1993, p. 2; see also Goldberg, *op cit*, pp. xxi, 14.
54. *Jews and the New American Scene*, Harvard University Press, Cambridge, Massachussetts, and London, 1995 p. 116.
55. Goldberg, *op. cit.*, p. 135.
56. Lind, Michael, 'The Israeli Lobby', *Prospect*, London, April 2002; *Maariv*, 28 July, 1997, Shahak, *Translations*.
57. Bar-Yosef, Avinoam, *Maariv*, 2 September 1994, Shahak, *Translations*.
58. Former Senator James Abou Rizk, *Al-Ahram Weekly*, Cairo, 20–26 June 2002.
59. Former Senator Paul Findley, *Daily Star*, Beirut, 16 October, 2002.
60. Goldberg, *op. cit.*, pp. 197–226.
61. Findley, Paul, *Deliberate Deceptions: Facing the Facts about the U.S.—Israeli Relationship*, Laurence Hill Books, New York, 1993, pp. 97–8.
62. *Al-Hamishmar*, 14 August 1991, Shahak, *Translations*.
63. *The Daily Star*, Beirut, 16 October 2002.
64. *Haaretz*, cited in Robert Fisk, *Independent*, 9 July 2002.
65. *Al-Ahram Weekly*, Cairo, 20–26 June 2002.
66. Massing, Michael, 'Deal Breakers', *American Prospect*, 11 March 2002.
67. Interview with Chris Mathews on MSNBC's *Hardball*, 1 May 2002.
68. *Christian Science Monitor*, 9 December 2002; Richard Curtiss, *Daily Star*, Beirut, 11 November 1999, *Washington Report on Middle East Affairs*, March 1997, September 1999, January 2001.
69. 2 September 1994.
70. Vest, Jason, 'The Men from JINSA and CSP', *Nation*, 16 August 2002.
71. 'A Dangerous Appointment: Profile of Douglas Feith, Under Secretary of Defense under Bush,' *Middle East Information Center*, 18 April 2001.
72. *The Price of Power: Kissinger in the Nixon White House*, Summit Books, New York, 1983, p. 322.
73. al-Tantawi, Sarah, Communications Director of the Muslim Public Affairs Council, *US Media Turns a Blind Eye to Israeli Occupation*, no date.
74. Christison, Kathleen, *Middle East International*, London, 8 March 2002.
75. Vest, *op. cit.*
76. 'The Zionist Lobby and American Foreign Policy', *Counterpunch*, 22 August 2002.

77. *The Zionist Connection: What Price Peace?*, Dodd Mead and Company, New York, 1978, p. 312.
78. 23 September 2002.
79. *New York Observer*, 23 September 2002.
80. *New York Times*, 27 March 2002.
81. Ackerman, Seth, 'Al-Aqsa Intifada and the US Media', *Journal of Palestine Studies*, Issue 118, Winter 2001.
82. *New York Times*, 13 January 1998.
83. *Prospect*, April 2002.
84. Ackerman, *op. cit.*
85. Fisk, Robert, *Independent*, London, 2 October 2000.
86. Ackerman, *op. cit.*
87. Massing, Michael, *Nation*, 10 June 2002; Robert Fisk, *Independent*, 9 July 2002.
88. Findley, Paul, *op. cit.*, pp. 101–4.
89. See *Washington Report on Middle East Affairs*, October 1996, January 1999, April 2002.
90. Truth Press, Scottsdale, Arizona, p. 104.
91. Ackerman, *op. cit.*
92. 15 September 2002.
93. Soloman, Norman, *Media Beat*, 19 April 2001; See Michael Lind, 'The Israeli Lobby', *Prospect*, London, April 2002.
94. Schneider, Mark, *Palestine Chronicle*, 19 March 2002.
95. *Washington Report on Middle East Affairs*, May/June 2001.
96. Massing, *op. cit.*
97. *Ibid.*
98. Fisk, Robert, *Independent*, 9 July 2002.
99. *Washington Report on Middle Eastern Affairs*, July/August 2001; Seth Ackerman, *op. cit.*
100. *Washington Report on Middle East Affairs*, March/April, 1998.
101. *Daily Star*, Beirut, 31 January 2001.
102. See Laura Flanders, *Tom Paine.com*, 5 April 2002.
103. It is worth noting that, despite the overwhelming critical disrepute into which it has fallen, *From Time Immemorial*, was re-published in 2000 and is apparently selling very well.
104. Christison, Kathleen, 'Bound by a Frame of Reference', *Journal of Palestine Studies*, Issue 108, Summer 1998.
105. Naseer Aruri, 'The Wye Memorandum: Netanyahu's Oslo and Unreciprocal Reciprocity', *Journal of Palestine Studies*, Issue 110, Winter 1999.
106. The formulation used after Israel's conquest of the West Bank and Gaza in the 1967 Arab-Israeli war; see Davis, Uri, *Israel: Utopia Incorporated*, Zed Press, London, 1987, p. 154.
107. The Areas of Jurisdiction and Powers Ordinance; originally passed in 1948, it was updated after the 1967 war.
108. The exact geographical definition of the 'Land of Israel' (*Eretz Israel*) is much disputed in Talmudic literature, and the debate has continued in modern times between various shades of Zionist opinion. According to

the maximalist view, it includes the whole of Sinai, Jordan, Lebanon and Syria and considerable parts of Turkey; the more prevalent, minimalist interpretation puts Israel's northern border 'only' about half-way through Syria and Lebanon, level with the central Syrian city of Homs. In all Talmudic interpretations, it includes the island of Cyprus. Rabbis belonging to the powerful *Gush Emunim* movement, the driving force behind the settlement of the West Bank and Gaza, often refer to such claims; see Israel Shahak and Norton Mezvinsky, *Jewish Fundamentalism in Israel*, Pluto Press, London and Sterling, Virginia, 1999, pp. 69–72; Shahak, *Jewish History, Jewish Religion: The Weight of Three Thousand Years*, Pluto Press, London and Boulder, Colorado, 1994, p. 90.

109. 'The Real Opinions and Ideology of Yitzhak Shamir', Shahak, *Translations*, February 1992.
110. Senator Al Gore, Democratic vice presidential candidate, 1992; see Findley, *op. cit.*, p. 220.
111. Aruri, *op.cit.*
112. See Christison, 'Bound by a Frame of Reference', *op. cit.*
113. See Tim Phelps, *Newsday*, 7 August 2002.
114. Aruri, *op. cit.*
115. See Seth Ackerman, 'The Myth of the Generous Offer', *Fairness and Accuracy in Reporting*, New York, 8 July 2002.
116. Malley, Robert, and Hussein Agha, 'Camp David Tragedy of Errors', *New York Review of Books*, August 2001; Kathleen Christison, 'Just How Much Does The New York Times Tilt Towards Israel; And How Much Does It Matter?', *Counterpunch*, 19 August 2002; see also Deborah Sontag, 'Quest for Middle East Peace', *New York Times*, 6 July 2001.
117. 23 October 2000, cited in Ackerman, 'Al-Aqsa Intifada and the US Media', *op. cit.*
118. 3 October 2000, cited in *Ibid.*
119. According to a detailed report published two years later, Muhammad Dahlan, Arafat's security chief in Gaza, did indeed plead desperately but unsuccessfully with Israeli foreign minister Shlomo ben Ami in the presence of American envoy Dennis Ross, who refused to take sides. Ben Kaspit, in *Maariv*, 13 September 2002.
120. *Washington Post*, 27 October 2002; cited in Ali Abunimah and Hussein Ibish, 'The US Media and the New Intifada', *The New Intifada: Resisting Israel's Apartheid*, Verso, London and New York, 2001, pp. 233–58.
121. 10 October 2002, cited in *Ibid.*
122. See *Ibid.*
123. Ackerman, Seth, 'Missing from Mideast Coverage: Occupied Territories No Longer "Occupied" on TV News', *Fairness and Accuracy in Reporting*, New York, 3 November 2000.
124. 11 October, cited in *The New Intifada, op. cit.*
125. 6 October 2000, cited in *Ibid.*
126. 23 October 2000; see Ackerman, 'Missing from Mideast Coverage', *op. cit.*
127. 1 November, cited in *Ibid.*

128. 14 October 2000; see *Ibid.*
129. See Kathleen Christison, *Washington Report on Middle East Affairs*, April 2001.
130. 'In US Media, Palestinians Attack, Israel Retaliates', *Fairness and Accuracy in Reporting*, 4 April 2002.
131. The former Israeli prime minister is the author of a book on the subject, *Fighting Terrorism: How Democracies Can Defeat Domestic and International Terrorists*, Noonday Press, New York, 1997.
132. *Le Monde*, 2 January 2003.
133. *Yediot Ahronot*, 27 August 2002.
134. Cited in the *Guardian*, 26 June 2002.
135. *Washington Report on Middle East Affairs*, April 2001.
136. MEMRI. 21 April 2001.
137. MEMRI. 10 October 2001.
138. MEMRI. *Friday Sermons in Saudi Mosques*, 26 September 2002.
139. MEMRI. *Inquiry and Analysis*, no. 99; citing *al-Hayat*, London, 21 October 2002.
140. *Koret Communications*, 8 February 2002.
141. See MEMRI website.
142. See Fouad Moughrabi, 'The Politics of Palestinian Textbooks', *Journal of Palestine Studies*, Issue 121, Autumn 2001.
143. *Ibid.*
144. Meehan, Maureen, 'Israeli Textbooks and Children's Literature Promote Racism and Hatred Toward Palestinians and Arabs', *Washington Report on Middle East Affairs*, September 1999.
145. Moughrabi, *op. cit.*
146. BBC, 10 April 2001, *Reuters*, 6 August, 2002.
147. *New York Times*, 14 April 1983.
148. *Haaretz*, 3 March 2002, cited in *Le Monde Diplomatique*, June 2002.
149. *Davar*, 7 January 1990, Shahak, *Translations*.
150. *New York Times*, 1 April 1988.
151. *New York Review of Books*, 13 June 2002.
152. *Haaretz*, 27 July, 1989, Shahak, *Translations*.
153. Reuel Marc Gerecht, 14 October 2000; cited in *The New Intifada*, p. 244.
154. Shahak, 'The American Connections of the Jewish Terror in the West Bank', *Translations*, November 1984; 'The Chauvinism of the American Jews and Its Political Influence on Israel, *Translations*, January 1985; Israel Shahak and Norton Mezvinsky, *Jewish Fundamentalism in Israel*, Pluto Press, London and Sterling, Virginia, 1999, pp. 151–63.
155. Shahak, *Jewish History, Jewish Religion: The Weight of Three Thousand Years*, Pluto Press, London and Boulder, Colorado, 1994; Shahak and Mezvinsky, *Jewish Fundamentalism in Israel.*
156. Shahak, 'The Chauvinism of American Jews and its Political Influence on Israel', *Translations, op. cit.*
157. Shahak, *Jewish History, Jewish Religion*, pp. 58ff.
158. Shahak and Mezvinsky, *op. cit.*, p. 159.
159. Shahak, 'The Jewish Religious Fanaticism', *Translations*, March 1985.

160. Shahak and Mezvinsky, *op. cit*., pp. 6–8; see also Ehud Sprinzak, *The Ascendance of Israel's Radical Right*, Oxford University Press, New York, 1991.
161. Shahak, 'The Ideology of Jewish Religious Fanaticism and the Opposition,' *Translation*, September 1984; Shahak, 'The Ideology of Jewish Messianism', *Race and Class*, February 1992.
162. *Haaretz*, 27 November 1991, Shahak, *Translations*.
163. Shahak, *Jewish History, Jewish Religion*, pp. 43, 87.
164. In an interview with *Hadashot* newspaper (8 March 1985) Rabbi Simon Ben Shlomo, of the ultra-Orthodox *Shas* party, MP and member of the Knesset's committee for foreign and security affairs, said that his role in the Knesset was to work for the re-instatement of the *Halacha*; since the *Halacha* 'lacks for nothing', and the 'Jewish people need no parliament', the Knesset itself would in due course become redundant; once that had come to pass, he would be ready to stone his own brother, if that were the sentence of a religious court; he would 'give him life by stoning him'; 'who has to be stoned, is stoned, whose verdict is fire, is burned, and who has to be choked, is choked'.
165. Shahak, *Jewish History, Jewish Religion*, pp. 75–98.
166. *Shas* party leader Rabbi Ovadia Yossef said in a public statement (*Yated Ne'eman*, 18 September, 1989) that 'while the Israeli government is obliged under international law to protect and guard the churches of the Christians in the Land of Israel, even though these are places of idolatry, we are obliged by our Torah to destroy all idolatry and idol-worship and to pursue it until we shall obliterate it from all of our country, and from all places which we shall conquer.' (*Haaretz*, 5 April 1990)
167. These conditions were laid down by Maimonides, the great thirteenth-century philosopher and Talmudic scholar, whose *Halacha* rulings are holy writ to the fundamentalists. Such views on the proper status of non-Jews in the Jewish Kingdom even found expression in an official publication of the World Zionist Organisation, *Kivunim* (August 1984), where Mordechai Nisan, a lecturer at the Hebrew University in Jerusalem, wrote that if they 'refuse to live a life of inferiority, then this signals their rebellion and the unavoidable necessity of Jewish warfare against their very presence in the Land of Israel'. (See Yehoshavat Harkabi, *Israel's Fateful Hour*, 1988, Harper and Row, New York, p. 153–6.)
168. Such passages in the standard prayerbooks used to be censored, or watered down, in the Diaspora and Israel, but they have been increasingly restored in recent years. (Shahak, *Jewish History, Jewish Religion*, pp. 92ff)
169. For an illuminating analysis of the theological reasoning behind this conclusion, see Uriel Tal, 'The Foundations of Political Messianism in Israel', *Haaretz*, 26 September 1984, Shahak, *Translations*. It should be noted that the *Gush Emunim* are not alone in these beliefs; Shlomo Goren, former Chief Rabbi of Israel, argues that 'the days of the Messiah are [in] this world as it is now', days of a 'political change that is taking place by force of Israel's weapons and with special Heavenly support'.

170. Shahak, *Race and Class, op. cit.*
171. See Shahak, *Jewish Fundamentalism in Israel*, pp. 66ff; Arthur Hertzberg, 'The End of the Dream of the Undivided Land of Israel', *Journal of Palestine Studies*, Issue 98, Winter 1996; Ilan Pappé, 'Israel at a Crossroads between Civil Democracy and Jewish Zealotocracy', *Journal of Palestine Studies*, Issue 115, Spring 2000.
172. Shahak, *Race and Class, op. cit.*
173. Tal, *op. cit.*
174. Shahak, *Race and Class, op. cit.*
175. *Ibid.*
176. Tal, *op.cit.*
177. *Ibid.*
178. *Bat Kol*, the student newspaper of Bar Ilan University, 26 February 1980, cited in Tal, *op cit.*
179. Meir Stieglitz, *Yediot Aharonot*, 23 October 2002.
180. Tal, *op. cit.*
181. Shahak, *Race and Class.*
182. See Shahak, *Jewish Fundamentalism in Israel*, pp. 96–111.
183. *Davar*, 11 March, 1994, Shahak, *Translations.*
184. *Haaretz*, 4, 9 September, 1994, Shahak, *Translations.*
185. Shahak, *Jewish Fundamentalism in Israel*, p. 102.
186. *Ibid.*, p. 111; in 1998, under pressure from secular Jews, the Knesset passed a law against the erection of monuments to mass murderers.
187. Khami Shalev, *Maariv*, 16 March 1994.
188. Rubinstein, Danny, *Haaretz*, 5 October 1992.
189. Shahak, *Jewish Fundamentalism in Israel*, p. 89.
190. See Benny Morris, 'After Rabin', *Journal of Palestine Studies*, Issue 98, Winter 1996.
191. *Maariv*, 28 October 2002.
192. Shahak, 'Racism and Discrimination in Israel', *Translations*, February 1992.
193. *International Herald Tribune*, 14 October 2002.
194. See Roane Carey and Jonathan Shainin, *The Other Israel: Voices of Refusal and Dissent,* The New Press, New York, 2002.
195. www.adl.org/Israel/Record/society.html . . . minorities.html.
196. Israel Shamir, 'The Handwriting on the Wall', *Russki Israiltyanin*, 23 January 2001, cited in *Journal of Palestine Studies*, Issue 119, Spring 2001.
197. Uri Davis, *Israel: An Apartheid State*, Zed Books, London and New Jersey, 1987.
198. United Nations General Assembly Resolution 181 of 29 November 1947, otherwise known as the UN 'Partition Plan', which, at the time, Israel regarded as the founding charter of its very existence.
199. Davis, *op. cit.*, p. 58.
200. *The Gun and the Olive Branch*, p. 319.
201. Unless—in accordance with the no less than ten different religious/ethnic classifications that define Israeli citizenship—he is a Druze or a Bedouin.

202. *Haaretz*, 29, 31 January, 17 May 1992, Shahak, *Translations*.
203. Shahak, 'Zionism Redux', *Journal of Palestine Studies*, Issue 87, Spring 1993.
204. Shahak, 'Racism and Discrimination in Israel', *Translations*, February 1992.
205. *Ibid.*
206. This 96 per cent has been acquired, through expropriation, by the state (76 per cent), the Jewish National Fund (17 per cent) or individuals (3 per cent); see Oren Yiftachel (a teacher of political geography at Bengurion University in Beersheva), MERIP, summer 2002. Other facts and figures in this section came from: 'The Unrecognized Villages', 'Land and Planning in Israel', *Factsheet*, Arab Association for Human Rights(AAHR), Nazareth; *Discrimination Diary*, AAHR, 26 December 1998, 29 December 1999, 21 June 2000; Arie Dayan, *Haaretz*, 27 December, 1991, cited in *Journal of Palestine Studies*, Issue 84, Spring 1993; Shamir, *op. cit.*
207. Shahak, *Washington Report on Middle East Affairs*, 15 November 1998.
208. MERIP, *op. cit.*
209. *Yediot Ahronot*, 10 July 2002.
210. See Walid Khalidi, *Journal of Palestine Studies*, Issue 125, Autumn 2002.
211. Icon Books, Cambridge, 2002.
212. Schememann, Serge, 16 September 2001.
213. *Daily Star*, Beirut, 16 October 2002.
214. *Al-Rai*, Amman, 5 July 2002.
215. 11 October 2001.
216. 11 October 2001.
217. *Washington Post*, 25 July 2001.
218. Cited in the *Guardian*, 25 September 2001.
219. *Yediot Aharonot*, 10 October 2001.
220. See *Middle East International*, 9 November 2001.
221. *Independent*, 16 April 2002; see also Stephen Zunes, *Middle East Policy*, September, 2002.
222. *Al-Ahram Weekly*, Cairo, 20–26 June 2002.
223. *Middle East Policy*, September 2002.
224. See Stephen Zunes, 'The Strategic Function of US Aid to Israel', *Middle East Policy*, October 1996.
225. *Ibid.*
226. See Robert John and Sami Hadawi, *Palestine Diary*, Vol. I, Palestine Research Centre, Beirut, 1968.
227. See Stephen Green, *Taking Sides: America's Secret Relations with a Militant Israel, 1948–1967*, Faber and Faber, London and Boston, 1984, p. 20.
228. Twing, Shawn, *Washington Report on Middle East Affairs*, April 1996.
229. See Honoré Catudal, *Israel's Nuclear Weaponry: A New Arms Race in the Middle East*, Grey Seal, London, 1991, pp. 13–42.
230. *Ibid.*; see Green, *op. cit.*, pp. 148–79; *Guardian*, 24 February 1995.

231. Stauffer, *Christian Science Monitor*, 9 December 2002.
232. Stauffer, 'Costs of US Middle East Policy: An Economic Overview', *Abstract*, 19–20 October 2002; *Christian Science Monitor, op. cit.*
233. *International Economy*, March/April 1992.
234. Stauffer, *op. cit.*
235. The words of Joseph di Genova, prosecutor in the case; see *Washington Report on Middle East Affairs*, September, October 1998, February 1999; Twing, *op. cit.*
236. See *Middle East International*, 12 October 2001, 25 January 2002.
237. See Ed Blanche, *Daily Star*, Beirut, 2 October 2002.
238. 5 November 2002.
239. *Middle East Policy*, September 2001.
240. 13, 14 January 2002.
241. Shahak, Israel, *Covert Action*, Fall 1993.
242. *Washington Post*, 29 July 2002.
243. Kathleen Christison, 'Who's Behind US Middle East Policy', *Middle East International*, 8 March 2002.
244. *Haaretz*, 2 February 2002.
245. Green, *op. cit.*, p. 92.
246. *Middle East International*, 12 October 2001.
247. Livia Rokach, *Israel's Sacred Terrorism: A Study Based on Moshe Sharett's 'Personal Diary' and Other Documents*, The Association of Arab-American University Graduates, Belmont, Massachusetts, 1980, p. 38.
248. See Noam Chomsky, *The Fateful Triangle: The United States, Israel and the Palestinians*, South End Press, Boston, 1983, p. 467.
249. Catudal, *op. cit.*, p. 12.
250. Amos Perlmutter, Michael Handel and Uri Bar-Joseph, *Two Minutes over Baghdad*, Vallentine, Mitchell, London, 1982, pp. 46–7.
251. http://www.de.indymedia.org/2003/01/39170.shtml, 20 January 2003.

The GUN and the OLIVE BRANCH

For my mother and father

PREFACE TO THE SECOND EDITION

In November 1974 Yasser Arafat, Chairman of the Palestinian Liberation Organization, stood on the rostrum of the United Nations General Assembly and told the world: 'I have come bearing an olive branch and a freedom fighter's gun. Do not let the olive branch fall from my hand.' The Israelis promptly hurled it to the ground; it was, they said, a grotesquely stunted foliage. Arafat's peace offer was made in unusually theatrical circumstances, but it got essentially the same reception as all those—from either side—which had preceded it. The gun, not the olive branch, rules in the Middle East. It always has.

There have been five full-scale wars between the Arabs and the Israelis—in 1948, when the Jewish State came into being, in 1956, 1967, 1973 and 1982—but the history of one of the world's most implacable and dangerous conflicts reaches way back into the 1880s, when the earliest Zionist pioneers began to settle in Palestine, and from the very outset it has been shot through with continuous violence. The full-scale wars, once they are under way, tend to have a mindless character of their own, in which the single obsession of achieving victory or avoiding defeat masters all else; the lesser forms of violence often furnish more interesting insights into the nature of the conflict and the minds and motives of the protagonists.

The forms which this violence have taken are diverse. It has been both Arab and Jewish. It has been individual and spontaneous, or large-scale and state-sponsored; a selective assassination or an indiscriminate massacre of innocents; a clumsy protest of illiterate peasants or the ruthless exploits of 'revolutionary' zealots; frontier raids and reprisals, mobs on the rampage, or the deliberate uprooting, through terror, of whole communities. It has included some very conventional uses of violence and some weirdly unexpected and ingenious ones.

Diverse though it has been, the violence has had its own internal logic and patterns, its characteristic phases and episodes, and these, though sometimes intertwined with the larger cataclysms of the last quarter century, are clearly distinguishable from them. *The Gun and the Olive Branch* is an attempt to identify them in a straightforward chronological narrative. There have been several books on aspects of the subject—and a spate of them on the Palestnian guerillas who are its most spectacular contemporary manifestation—but historical surveys of Jewish or Arab violence, let alone the two together, are rare. Thus a mere chronicle of the events as they have occurred can lay claim to a certain originality in itself. It does not, of course, claim to be comprehensive—that would make an interminable catalogue. Nor does it dwell exclusively on the events themselves—it also encompasses the moral, political and psychological climate in which they take place.

In the author's opinion, only by tracing it stage by stage from its origins is it possible to expose the true nature of a conflict which has been unusually prone to prejudice and propaganda. Doubtless the first impulse of many readers, friends of Israel, will be to cry that if ever there were prejudice and propaganda it is here. But upon maturer reflection they will, he hopes, come to another conclusion: that the literature hitherto available to them, particularly if they are Americans, has been overwhelmingly Zionist in sympathy or inspiration. It is therefore only right and proper that the balance be redressed, the other side of the story told. It is also very important. For the acts of violence here described are no more than episodes in an inexorably unfolding drama which, more than any other conflict of our times, raises passions among ordinary people—in the West, the Soviet bloc and Asia—far beyond the arena in which it is enacted; a drama, almost Lilliputian in origin, whose ever-widening dimensions could eventually plunge mankind into World War Three.

The Gun and the Olive Branch was first published in 1977. In this second, updated, edition three chapters have been added to the original nine, which remain unchanged.

D.H.
October 1983

1 · THE SEEDS OF CONFLICT, 1882–1920

Herzl Reassures the Arabs

'In the name of God, leave Palestine in peace.' The recipient of this plea was Zadoc Khan, Chief Rabbi of France. Its author was Yusuf Zia al-Khalidi, the Mayor of Jerusalem and former deputy in the Ottoman parliament. It was sent from Constantinople in March 1899. And it came at the end of a long and carefully argued letter which, the seventy-year-old scholar explained, a 'sacred call of conscience' had bade him write. Theoretically, he told his friend in Paris, the Zionist ideal was 'completely natural, fine and just'. 'Who can contest the rights of the Jews to Palestine? God knows, historically it is indeed your country!' In practice, however, the ideal was unworkable. The 'brutal force' of reality had to be taken into account. Al-Khalidi pointed out that Palestine was now an inseparable part of the Ottoman Empire; it was already inhabited; and he warned that if the Zionists persisted in their ambitions, they would face a popular uprising which even the Turks, however well disposed towards them, would not be able to put down. They should therefore look for a homeland elsewhere.[1]

Zadoc Khan immediately conveyed the letter to a personal friend of his, Theodor Herzl. Herzl, a Jewish journalist and playwright, was the father of Zionism as we know it today and his book, *The Jewish State*, is its bible. The 'political Zionism' he preached was to be the solution to the so-called Jewish Question which had bedevilled Christian civilization for centuries. It was his answer to the age-old curse of anti-Semitism, with which he had come face to face in all its ugliness in his native Hungary where pogroms and ritual-murder trials still persisted. Although things were not so bad in Vienna, the metropolis of the ailing

Austro–Hungarian empire where he began his career, to be a Jew was still a grave disadvantage for an ambitious and brilliant young man like Herzl. Had it not been for the offence to his father, he would gladly have converted to Christianity. But in 1891, after several years of struggle, he was appointed Paris correspondent of the famous Vienna newspaper *Neue Freie Presse*. In the French capital, he covered the notorious Dreyfus affair, the frame-up, rigged trial and conviction of the Jewish officer accused of passing secrets to the Germans, and he saw how deep was the prejudice still to be found even in the land of Liberty, Equality and Fraternity. He also knew that in those traditional bastions of anti-Semitism, Russia and Eastern Europe, the Jews were suffering renewed and terrible persecution. The Herzl who had previously toyed with the idea of complete assimilation into gentile society as the answer to the universal Jewish Question now reverted to the belief that anti-Semitism was an incurable gentile pathology. He determined to lead his people out of 'perpetual enemy territory'. The Jews should have a nation-state of their own.

Herzl himself would have been ready to contemplate any territory for this purpose, but most Zionists felt that Palestine was the only possible one. Palestine was the Land of Their Ancestors; the idea of the Return to Zion, of Next Year in Jerusalem, had been kept alive through long centuries of exile and suffering; only 'the mighty legend' of Palestine had the power to stir the Jewish masses. True, the idea of return had become essentially spiritual in significance; it meant redemption, a recovery of grace in God's sight; moreover, the ethnic connection between nineteenth-century European Jewry and the Ancient Hebrews was a myth. But Palestine was so deeply rooted in the Jewish cultural and sentimental heritage that it was not difficult for the 'political Zionists' to invest the return with a secular, physical meaning. So in 1897, at their first congress in Basle, they adopted a formal programme whose object was the 'establishment for the Jewish people of a home in Palestine secured by public law'. The first, and most important, item on the programme was to be the 'promotion, on suitable lines, of the colonization of Palestine by Jewish agricultural and industrial workers'.

It was a very meek and reassuring reply which al-Khalidi received from the founder of Zionism. There was 'absolutely nothing to fear' from Jewish immigration, he insisted, for 'the Jews have no belligerent Power behind them, neither are they themselves of a warlike nature. They are a completely peaceful element, and very content if they are left in peace.' As for the Arabs of Palestine, 'who would think of sending them away? It is their well-being, their individual wealth, which we will increase by bringing in our own. Do you think that an Arab who owns land will be very angry to see the price of his land rise in a short time, to see it rise five and ten times in value perhaps in a few months?' No, the Arabs would gain 'excellent brothers' in the Jews, and the Turkish Sultan 'faithful and good subjects'; Palestine, benefiting from Jewish intelligence, enterprise and financial acumen, would prosper for the good of all.[2] A few months later Herzl began to write a novel, *Altneuland* ('Old-Newland'), his vision of Palestine as it might be, through Zionist colonization, in a mere twenty years' time. At one point in the story, delighted visitors to this Jewish utopia are introduced to a distinguished Arab who, showing them round a prosperous and contented village, speaks of the love which his compatriots feel for the Jewish brethren to whom they owe so much.

Yet al-Khalidi was right, and Herzl knew it. One should remember, in looking for extenuating circumstances, that Herzl was a child of his age. It was the heyday of European imperialism; an advanced and dynamic continent competed in the conquest and penetration of backward lands. Force, in the service of civilization, did not seem as reprehensible as it does today. And what was Palestine, in Herzl's view, if not a 'plague-ridden, blighted corner of the Orient?' to which the Jews, 'as representatives of Western civilization', would 'bring cleanliness, order, and the well-distilled customs of the Occident'?[3] Yet, in adopting the Basle programme, Herzl knew that the 'brutal force' of reality would make nonsense of the *Altneuland* idyll and provoke the uprising of which al-Khalidi warned. He knew—indeed, he had written—that immigration into an already populated country would soon turn the natives against the newcomers, breeding, as he saw it, that very anti-Semitism which it was his purpose to combat. 'An infiltration is bound to end badly. It continues till the inevitable moment when the native population feels itself threatened, and forces the government to stop a further influx of Jews. Immigration is consequently futile unless based on an assured supremacy.' And that could only come through statehood.[4]

Violence, then, was implicit in Zionism from the outset. The prophet of Zionism foresaw that coercion and physical force were inevitable; they were not unfortunate necessities thrust, unforeseen, on his followers. To his diaries, not published until twenty-six years after his death in 1904, Herzl confided the beliefs which, in his public utterances, he had been careful to omit: that military power was an essential component of his strategy and that, ideally, the Zionists should acquire the land of their choice by armed conquest.[5] True, the Jews had had no military means of their own, but Herzl sought to enlist, among the imperial powers of the age, a sponsor which did. The methods which he recommended to achieve this include the trading of Jewish influence in press and finance, the promotion of antagonisms and the exploitation of rival colonial ambitions. He sought to instil in non-Jews fear of the Jews, their influence and particularly their revolutionary mentality. He portrayed his co-religionists as ten million secret agents. He tried to confront European statesmen with a dilemma: Zionism or Jew-fomented revolution. All who did not desire that 'the Jews corrupt everything' should support Zionism. A new European war, he contended, could not harm Zionism, but only urge it forward.

As for the natives of Palestine, the new settlers should 'gently' expropriate their property and 'try to spirit the penniless population across the border by procuring employment for it in the transit countries, while denying it any employment in our own country. The property-owners will come over to our side. Both the process of expropriation and the removal of the poor must be carried out discreetly and circumspectly. Let the owners of immovable property believe that they are cheating us, selling us things for more than they are worth. But we are not going to sell them anything back.'[6] Before they left, however, the natives should be put to work exterminating wild animals, such as snakes, to which the Jews were not accustomed. The settlers would pay 'high premiums for snake skins, etc., as well as their spawn.'[7]

In 1901, Herzl arrived in Constantinople in an unsuccessful

attempt to obtain a charter for the establishment of a Jewish-Ottoman Colonization Association in Palestine. Article Three of the draft charter would have granted the Jews the right to deport the native population.[8]

'Qui veut la fin, veut les moyens' ('he who desires the end desires the means') is a saying which Herzl cited with approval.[9] But in proposing such an end—a Jewish State in Palestine—and such means he was proposing a great deception, and laying open his whole movement to the subsequent charge that in any true historical perspective the Zionists were the original aggressors in the Middle East, the real pioneers of violence, and that Arab violence, however cruel and fanatical it might eventually become, was an inevitable reaction to theirs. Some, perhaps, of his followers really did not know what awaited them in Palestine, really did believe that it was more or less uninhabited, that—in the mischievous epigram of Israel Zangwill, a contemporary of Herzl's—it really was a 'land without a people, waiting for a people without a land'.[10] The truth, when they learned it, might at first have disconcerted them. When Max Nordau, one of Herzl's earliest disciples, did so, he came running to his master crying: 'I didn't know that—but then we are committing an injustice.' But it did not seem to disconcert them for long. Nordau himself helped develop two strains of Zionist thought—the need for physical force and dissimulation—which Herzl had first propounded. Doubtless he was reflecting the German *Zeitgeist*, in which many early Zionists were deeply steeped, when he called for a 'muscular Judaism' of the kind that had been lost through eighteen centuries of exile and wandering. Zionism, he taught, was to awaken Jewry to new life, 'morally through renewal of the National Ideal, materially through physical rearing'.[11] The modern Jewish youth should model themselves on Jewish heroes of old, on Bar Kokhba, the last incarnation of a Judaism that maintained itself by the sword—Bar Kokhba, 'who refused to accept defeat and, when victory deserted him, knew how to die'.[12] Nordau was echoed by other poets and theorists who, in their idealization of martial virtues, were rising in revolt against two millennia of Judaic pacifism.

Like Herzl, whom he survived by nineteen years, Nordau tried to reassure the natives of Palestine—while privately claiming credit for the systematic duplicity which this entailed. Instead of a Jewish

State, the Basle programme had introduced the expression 'a home secured by public law'. This expression was deliberately ambiguous. Twenty-three years later Nordau wrote that it was he who had thought up the term 'homeland' (*Heimstätte*):

> I did my best to persuade the advocates of the Jewish State in Palestine that we might find a circumlocution that would express all we meant, but would say it in a way that would avoid provoking the Turkish rulers of the coveted land. I suggested 'Heimstätte' as a synonym for 'state'. . . . this is the history of the much commented expression. It was equivocal but we all understood what it meant . . . to us it signified 'Judenstaat' (Jewish State) and it signifies the same now. . . .[13]

From Basle onwards, it became deliberate policy to deny that there was, or ever had been, any intention of establishing a Jewish State. For example, fourteen years later the President of the Zionist movement opened the tenth Congress with a speech in which he indignantly declared that 'only those suffering from gross ignorance, or actuated by malice, could accuse us of the desire of establishing an independent Jewish kingdom'.[14] And yet, on 3 September 1898, after that first congress, Herzl confided in his diary:

> Were I to sum up the Basle Congress in a word—which I shall guard against pronouncing publicly—it would be this: at Basle I founded the Jewish state. . . . If I said this out loud today, I would be answered by universal laughter. Perhaps in five years and certainly in fifty everyone will know it.[15]

It was hardly an inspired prophecy which al-Khalidi made. The omens of eventual revolt were already easily discernible. If it is possible to designate a year in which, on the earliest possible reckoning, the great Zionist adventure began it would be 1882. Obviously that antedates Herzl's political Zionism proper. But it is the year to which Zionist historians now assign the first *Aliyah*, the first 'going up', or wave of immigration, to the Land of Israel. At that time there were already about 24,000 Jews, mostly immigrants, in Palestine. For much of the nineteenth century the character of the *Yishuv*, as the community was called, had remained the same. They had come mainly to Jerusalem, as to Hebron, Safed and Tiberias, with a religious aim: to end their days in one of these holy cities. They were often old, and many spent their time in perpetual study of the Talmud. Most lived in great poverty. The newcomers were different; they called themselves the 'Lovers of Zion'; they emigrated to Palestine to establish agricultural settlements there. But their political ideas were still vague: they had no clearly formulated, Herzlian grand designs for Jewish statehood. They sought a refuge from East European and Russian anti-Semitism, the dignity of toil, cultural—as much as national—regeneration. Their numbers were small; in thirty-two years, by 1914, they—and their post-Herzl successors—raised the Jewish population to 85,000. As a result of World War I, the total fell to a mere 56,000 in 1918. By that time the immigrants had managed to acquire some 162,500 acres, or about 2 per cent of the land area of Palestine.[16]

Their numbers may have been small, and their political ambitions limited, but from the very beginning there was an Arab reaction commensurate with the threat which the Lovers of Zion did seem to represent. It came not so much from the élite, from the political leadership, as from the humblest segment of Palestinian society, the peasantry, who were the first really to feel the threat. At the time a good 75 per cent of the Palestinians were peasants, deeply attached to their land. Contemporary European travellers spoke of the skill and diligence with which, in spite of primitive resources and political and social oppression, they tended their fields and orchards.[17] The fame of the Jaffa orange had spread throughout Europe. The peasants were the first to lose land and livelihood to the settlers from overseas. They intuitively sensed the ultimate dimensions of the threat. 'Is it true that the Jews want to retake this country?' This naïve questioning of illiterate villagers was recorded by Albert Antebi, an official of the Jewish Colonial Association, before the turn of the century.[18]

The Peasants Resist

It was only a few years after the first *Aliyah* of 1882 that the peasants resorted to physical violence against the settlers. Their resistance, spontaneous and clumsy as it was, nevertheless followed a pattern. They did not resist the actual sale of the land from which they were to be expelled. That was frequently completed without their knowing anything about it, for they were tenants working plots whose owner they might never see. They did resist the ensuing takeover process. This happened in 1901 when peasants from villages near Tiberias fell upon the estate agents who had come to stake out land bought from the Sursock family of Beirut.[19] They naturally resisted the eviction itself. Sometimes Turkish troops had to be brought in to enforce it; this happened in 1910 when, in another Sursock sale, the dispossessed tenants from Lower Galilee were arrested and thrown into prison.[20] Then, defeated, they, or other threatened neighbours, might make a single planned assault on a new colony or keep up a sporadic harassment of it in a variety of ways, plundering cattle or produce, ambushing, robbing and occasionally killing farmers.[21]

Contemporary accounts of Jewish-Arab relations in these early pioneering days are rare, but one, which describes the founding of the Jewish township of Hadera, illustrates with piquant irony the disdain in which the newcomers frequently held the natives, and their indifference to any hardship which they inflicted upon them. The settlement dates from 1891, and the author of the account, Moshe Smilansky, a well-known Jewish orange-grower and writer, was one of the original settlers, being at the time a boy of sixteen. One day that winter, recalls Mr Smilansky, immigrants freshly disembarked at Jaffa learned that 30,000 dunums of land had been acquired in the north of the coastal plain. A group of enthusiasts, some middle-aged men with families, some still boys, volunteered to take part of this land. An experienced settler asked them if they knew why the village in the neighbourhood was called Hadera.

> Our host looked somewhat confused. 'Unless I err, it means green.' 'H'm a bad sign! Isn't there some connexion between the name and the blackwater fever which the Arabs claim prevails in that district?' 'Possibly, but surely we're not going to let ourselves be frightened off by Arab tales of fever? We're not Arabs, and we'll find some way of putting an end to malaria. . . .'

When the first settlers arrived at Hadera, their driver smiled wryly on observing their delight at the green appearance of their land.

> 'These green valleys are swamps. . . . That's where the malaria comes from. . . . Look around you. In all this broad valley you see not a single village! There's a Circassian village on the edge of your land, but almost all its inhabitants are dead. The few who are left are cripples!' 'We needn't take our cue from barbarians!' replied the settlers.

The pioneers set to work, planted a vineyard, and sowed wheat. With the summer came the fever, and soon the colonists were dying off. Sometimes an entire family, such as the Reverend Jacob Idelsohn, his wife and two sons, were wiped out. The enthusiasm of the settlers carried them through five years. But there came a moment when, defeated by disease, it seemed they must abandon the colony. At this moment, however, the millionaire philanthropist Baron de Rothschild intervened from Paris with a promise of funds for draining the swamps. Accordingly in the summer of 1896 'hundreds of black labourers came from Egypt to dig the broad and deep trenches required for the drainage'. These men also 'died in scores'. But in time the drainage was completed and Hadera eventually became a prosperous colony. Besides the Circassians, Smilansky recalls, there used to be bedouins living in the vicinity, who sometimes stole the settlers' horses. 'The Bedouin neighbours, the Damireh and the Infiat tribes, rose up in protest. . . . Where would they pasture their cattle and sheep? But the [Turkish] mudir came from Caesarea with a detachment of police and dispersed them. From that time on the work proceeded without disturbance.'[22]

Commenting on this account, the British historian Neville Barbour points out that while the enthusiasm of the colonists was admirable, their arrogance was at least equally conspicuous. The draining of the swamps was not accomplished through their superior skill, as compared with that of the native 'barbarians', but through the aid of superior funds. Characteristic, too, was the reliance of the settlers on the Turkish police for driving off neighbours whose livelihood they had put in jeopardy.[23]

It was about this time that Ahad Aham, the conscience of early

Zionism, first raised his stern and eloquent voice against the aberrations of a movement which he conceived of in a very different way from Herzl. Zionism, for this moralist cast in the prophetic mould, was to be a means for the Jews to recover their spiritual and cultural greatness, to become once again, in the noblest sense, 'a light unto the nations'. Zionism in its narrow political form, land-obsessed and predatory, the Zionism of force, diplomatic manipulation, the facile Messianic short-cut—this Zionism was anathema to him. There was no more fundamental and obvious test by which the Zionists should be judged than the way they treated their Palestinian neighbours—and no test, in his opinion, by which they failed so badly. Jewish history, he insisted, proved the need for the befriending and respecting of neighbours.

> Yet what do our brethren do in Palestine? Just the opposite! Servants they were in the land of their exile. Suddenly they find themselves in a state of freedom without limits, an unbridled freedom such as exists only in Turkey, and the sudden transformation has produced in them that inclination to despotism that always occurs when the servant becomes the master! They treat the Arabs with hostility and cruelty, unscrupulously deprive them of their rights, insult them without cause, and even boast of such deeds; and none opposes this despicable and dangerous inclination.[24]

That was in 1891. Already, in these earliest, embryonic days of Zionism, the settlers were earning harsh judgements from the man who, for the next thirty years, was to lament the misdeeds done in its name. Nevertheless, the settlers were less imbued with that myopic egoism of later, more doctrinaire Zionists, and on the surface at least they frequently managed to establish profitable and even friendly relations with their Arab neighbours. According to H. M. Kalvariski, Arabs and Jews

> . . . met both in their houses and in their fields and got to know each other intimately. When the Jewish colonies were first started there was a great demand for labour . . . and there were no Jewish labourers in the country. It was therefore necessary to engage Arab labour, and thus

> Jewish farmers and Arab labourers had an opportunity of knowing each other. The fellahin from neighbouring villages worked in the Jewish colonies, returning at night to their own homes. There they related that the 'Yahudi' (the Jew) and the 'Hawaja' (owner) were good men who paid well. At the same time close relations were gradually established between the Jewish colonists and the Arab landowners. Jewish farmers bought horses for breeding and riding in partnership with Arab Sheikhs and often owned flocks of sheep and cattle in common.[25]

Mr Kalvariski was a Jewish publicist and administrator of the Palestine Jewish Colonization Association, but his impressions, though doubtless too sanguine, seem to be basically honest ones. The newcomers did have much to offer. They used new methods and machinery, they could provide remunerative employment, a market for produce, medical care and the loan of equipment. Most colonies actually employed five to ten times as many Arabs as Jews. Naturally the peasants violently resented the initial intrusion by which they were ousted from their lands, but once they had come to the conclusion that a colony was permanent, a *modus vivendi* could often be struck up. This pattern—initial resentment, suppressed or open hostility giving way in time to resignation and outward reconciliation—repeated itself almost every time a colony was founded.[26]

The Conquest of Labour

With the turn of the century, Jewish attitudes hardened. The second *Aliyah* brought to Palestine a tougher breed of settlers armed with the ideological apparatus that Herzl and his disciples had developed. They were bent, in the words of Leviticus, on 'redeeming the land'; the Jewish National Fund, established in 1901, laid down that all land which it acquired was to remain inalienable Jewish property that could not be sold or leased to others. They were bent on the 'conquest of labour'; only Jews should work the land that Jews acquired. It was of course from the Arabs that the land was redeemed, from them the labour conquered. The Jews often took this ideology to absurd lengths. Zionist historians speak with great pride about what happened in 1908 at Ben Shemen near Lydda. A forest was founded there in memory of Theodor Herzl. But when they learned that the saplings had been planted by Arabs, Jewish labourers came and replanted them, and only then were they satisfied. Such purism was not always practicable. Dr Ruppin, the first head of the Zionist Bureau in Palestine, records in his memoirs that he tried to build Tel Aviv with 'Hebrew Labour' only, but he soon had to turn to the Arabs on account of their experience (and low wages); the first house built by Jewish labourers had collapsed under construction.[27] The settlers were socialists, deeply committed to the communal ideal, but the deeper their commitment the narrower its application seemed to be. Their socialism did not extend to their non-Jewish fellow-men. True, it repudiated conventional European colonialism, frequently regarded as morally reprehensible, but it was heavily impregnated with a colonial mentality which, in effect if not in intent, was worse. It did not deliberately set out to exploit the natives, but it blithely deprived them of their livelihood—and eventually of their country. 'The international brotherhood of workers', they would argue, 'applied only to workers who were already secure in their employment; it did not apply to a potential proletariat that had to struggle to find employment and could not refrain from conflict with workers whose places of work they must take for themselves.'[28] From this philosophy grew the celebrated *kibbutzim*, agricultural communes founded on exclusively Jewish labour; it also led to the expulsion of Arab labour, which one Zionist theoretician described as a 'painful leprosy',[29] from existing Jewish colonies, and eventually to the boycott of Arab goods as soon as the Jews could produce enough of their own.

The zealots of the second *Aliyah* were actually given to arguing that in the long run Arabs as well as Jews stood to benefit from Hebrew Labour. Some of them were doubtless quite sincere in this extraordinary belief, which was rooted in the Marxist theorizing of the period. Sophisticated European socialists were saying, on the eve of the biggest bloodletting in history, that war was becoming improbable because the workers of one nation would refuse to shoot at those of another. The Zionist pioneers, Marxists of a rugged and intellectually simplistic kind, contended that this must apply to Palestine too. They professed to see no contradiction between their proletarian enterprise and the interests of the local population. This was composed mainly of peasants and workers, exploited by a corrupt élite of feudal land-owners, who, they felt sure, would soon make common cause with their toiling Jewish brethren. If there were no 'exploitation' of Arab labour, Arab labour could not 'objectively' oppose the Zionists. There is a deep and tragic irony, writes the Israeli historian Amos Elon, in the fact that Hebrew Labour, advocated as a means of allaying conflict, actually led to that total cleavage between the two peoples which made it inevitable. It began a process of economic, political, cultural and psychological self-segregation, which the Arabs reciprocated with a vengeance. Since its foundation, the State of Israel has been trying to break out of the rigorous quarantine which the entire Arab world has thrown round it; the scale is immeasurably different, of course, but by all the laws of heredity the Arab blockade is but a lineal descendant of the first expulsion of an Arab labourer from a Jewish farm.

Militarization Begins

The 'conquest of labour', as the expression itself implies, could not be accomplished without violence. Indeed, a Zionist poet like Saul Tchernichowski could not conceive of one without the other: 'We shall put forth our hands in urging labour, the work that is holy, while grasping the sword. Raise the banners of Zion, warriors of Judah.'[30] By 1903, the more perceptive older immigrants had come to the conclusion that 'these Russian Jewish labourers together with the principle of exclusive Jewish Hebrew labour', constituted 'a major factor in arousing the hostility of the Palestinian Arabs'.[31] The process of militarization foreseen by Herzl gradually got underway. In 1907 an organization calling itself *Hashomer* ('The Guardian') came into being with the task of replacing Arab with Jewish guards on the ground that Jewish property must be protected by Jews. The name *Hashomer*, favoured by many Jewish youth organizations at this time, epitomized the pugnacious spirit in which they were formed. So too did the names which many of the new settlers, anxious to make a complete break with the abasements of their Diaspora past, took for themselves: Yariv ('antagonist'), Oz ('strength'), Tamir ('towering'), Hod ('splendour'), Barak ('lightning'), or Tsur ('rock').[32]

The *Hashomer* constituted the first nucleus of a military force. In 1909 a secret defence organization was created. Yitzhak Ben Zvi, a future President of Israel, was among the founders. His description of the organization's first meeting, which took place in his rooms, is full of forebodings about the future. 'Mats, spread out on the floor, and a few wooden crates served as arm-chairs and desks . . . one feeling seized all those present . . . they gathered up courage [and they knew] that not by word of mouth shall the nation be saved, nor shall a country be rebuilt by speeches. "In blood and fire Judea fell, in blood and fire it shall rise again".'[33] In the same year the Kaimakam (District Officer) of Tiberias authorized the formation of a Jewish armed guard for fear of a massacre.[34] The militarization had been preceded by a discussion between two young pioneers in the colony of Sejera. One of them, David, wished to establish a Jewish 'self-defence' organization. The other, Shlomo, opposed this. They had returned, he argued, to the Promised Land in order to lead a peaceful life. If they stirred up the Arabs, there would be no *shalom*, no peace, ever. David persisted. This was a world in which force and force alone won respect. Shlomo left for Paris. David—David Bengurion—remained.[35]

Arab attitudes were hardening too. It was a slow and halting process. For the Palestinian leaders had a less developed ideological propensity towards the use of force than their Zionist counterparts. It was alien to their whole outlook as the representatives of a subject people. When, in 1890, the Palestinian élite, in the shape of a group of Jerusalem 'notables', took their first formal initiative in the struggle that was beginning, they did the only lawful thing they could. They protested to their imperial masters, the Sublime Porte in Constantinople. They were thereby exhibiting a deferential instinct which remained with them in gradually diminishing strength, through the remaining years of Ottoman rule, thirty years of the British Mandate, and twenty-five years of their post-1948 diaspora. They protested at the appointment of a Turkish governor who manifestly favoured the Zionists. The next year, they submitted another petition which contained two demands: the ending of Jewish immigration and land purchases. Then, in 1898, Yusuf Zia al-Khalidi made his direct approach to the Zionists. Appeals of this kind had little effect. The Zionists only pretended to listen. The Turks listened—but only fitfully. The Porte would periodically impose restrictions on immigration, only to lift them again under European pressure, or to allow venal officials on the spot to turn a blind eye to the continued defiance of them.

Inevitably, therefore, as time passed and the Zionists continued to make slow, but steady, headway, the Palestinian élite gradually lost that popular respect which, for the conduct of a national struggle, a leadership must have. If more men of influence and authority had behaved as a Jewish observer described the Kaimakam of Tiberias as behaving things would have been different. Of the eviction of peasants from the estates in Lower Galilee he wrote:

> It was then that, for the first time, I came in contact with Arab nationalism. Rashid Bey the Vali (Governor), who was a Turk, cared very little whether the Tiberias District was inhabited by Arabs or Jews, and was thus prepared to order the eviction of the tenants. But Emir Amin Arslan, the Kaimakam of Tiberias, who was an Arab Druze, not only insisted on the payment of compensation to the evicted Arabs, but also as I was later informed, resisted the de-Arabization of the district. . . .[36]

The Landsellers

Few of the élite were like the Kaimakam of Tiberias. Their chief offence, in the eyes of their critics, was the readiness of too many of them, as individuals, to make their fortunes out of those very Zionist land acquisitions in which, as citizens, they perceived the omens of national calamity. The great bulk of the land that the Zionists acquired came from large, predominantly absentee, landowners. As resistance built up, the area relinquished by small farmers, 42.7 per cent of the total from 1891 to 1900, fell to a mere 4.3 per cent from 1900 to 1914.[37]

The name Sursock occupies an invidious and recurrent place in this story. The Sursocks were a Levantine family of high breeding and immense wealth who spent much of their time in Western Europe. They also owned some of the richest land in Palestine. In a series of transactions from 1891 to 1920 they sold it all to the Zionists, as unmoved by high appeals to their sense of Arab history as by workaday calls on their conscience. In 1910 they sold the region of Foule, with its Crusader castle made famous by Saladin, in the fertile Vale of Esdraelon; in 1920 they disposed of the rest of their holdings, along with 8,000 peasants in twenty-two villages who made a living from them. They had acquired the whole area in 1872 from corrupt Ottoman officials for the derisory sum of £18,000 to £20,000.[38] It brought in a revenue of £12,000 to £40,000 a year. They sold it for ten times the price they had paid for it, but sub-sequently complained bitterly that they had let it go so cheap—as indeed they had.[39] The fate of the 8,000 peasants was never determined; the tenants among them—but not the labourers—received 'compensation' of £28,000—precisely £3.5 per head for the lot. The Sursock sale was a famous and much-deplored transaction. But there were many others.

Patriotic voices soon began to rise in protest. *Carmel*, a newspaper published in Haifa, never ceased to reproach the *zaims* and *effendis* and their business agents.

> 'Today with your own hands, and your own seals, you are wasting your own substance, thinning your own ranks, increasing the substance of others and swelling their ranks . . . what are we to think of a people whose leaders, many of them champions of reform and self-styled guardians of the nation's security, sell out to the Zionists and act as their agents . . .'; leaders 'who sate their appetites and pursue their quarrels indifferent to the dangers that surround them', and 'enter the Zionists' service to fritter away the homeland.'[40]

Anti-Zionism Spreads

How should the Palestinian leaders—and everyone else—have behaved? Like the Zionists themselves, of course. It did not take the Palestinians long to feel that the Zionists were an enemy. And it did not take much longer for those who felt it most strongly to conclude that the best way to fight the enemy was to learn from him. Najib Nassar, the Christian from Haifa who established his newspaper *Carmel* to urge this idea on his countrymen, and other campaigners did not hide their admiration for the Zionists. It marked a striking change of attitude. For the Palestinians had tended to despise those Jews, mostly meek, devout and impoverished, who came to Palestine before the first *Aliyah* of 1882. They even taunted cowards among their own ranks with the insult *isiknag*, a distortion of Askenazi. 'The Jewish people', wrote Nassar, 'was scattered for two thousand years until Herzl appeared and convened the [Basle] conference; the Zionist Organization came into being with all its ramifications and in fifteen years it spread its doctrine to the whole nation, purchased the best land in Palestine, gave the Jews a united voice, and opened banks to finance the farmers; if we do likewise we shall succeed. . . .'[41] He and others found the Jews to be a 'purposeful people, hardworking, energetic . . . anyone who sees the villages they have colonized will realise that a struggle for existence lies before the people of this country . . . the people must be aroused to compete with the Jews . . . otherwise they will fall prey to their neighbours.'[42] They listed the manifold ways in which the Arabs could profit from the Zionist example: in holding conferences, organizing communal projects, helping peasants, education, social reform, and generally catching up with the modern world the Zionists brought with them. They even foreshadowed the famous claim of the Zionists that they, unlike the Arabs they displaced, at least 'made the desert bloom'. 'Let us be their equal in toil and devotion . . . it is a general law of civilization that the land is for him who works it.'[43]

By the eve of the Great War, anti-Zionism, from being the essentially non-political, spontaneous eruptions of the peasantry it was at the outset, had broadened into the central issue of Palestinian politics. After the peasants, it was the small class of urban traders and professional men who reacted most strongly against Jewish immigration. They were behind that first protest which, in 1891, the Jerusalem notables despatched to the Sublime Porte. They feared the economic competition that the continued growth of an alien community, as aggressive as it was ingrown, would indubitably bring. This class was largely Christian. In fact, the Zionists were at first inclined to believe that they had less to fear from Moslems than Christians; 'the one and only source of hatred of the Jews that raises its voice against Jewish immigration is the Christian establishment'.[44] The Christians' opposition was perhaps reinforced by a certain doctrinal prejudice and by the fact that, better educated and more widely travelled than their Moslem compatriots, they were influenced by typical European attitudes towards the Jews. Levantine minorities, second-class citizens themselves, had often derived satisfaction from the discomfiture of the Moslem majority, but—though this sentiment has not been entirely absent—an unusual degree of Moslem–Christian solidarity, engendered by the gravity of the 'Zionist peril', has been one of the permanent features of the Palestine struggle. Along with the traders and professional men, the intellectual élite, substantially Christian too, could not remain deaf to what European Zionists revealed of their plans in frequent indiscretions that were not intended for Arab ears. With the overthrow of Sultan Abdul Hamid in 1908 Palestinian publishers took advantage of the relative new freedoms. In *Carmel* Najib Nassar published a series of lengthy treatises, later reproduced as a book, entitled *Zionism: Its History, Aims and Importance*. It was rudimentary, evidently little more than a cleverly slanted translation from a section of the Jewish Encyclopaedia Nassar had acquired from an English friend. But it was the first of its kind in Arabic. After *Carmel*, other, more influential newspapers in Beirut and Damascus took up anti-Zionism. Arab leaders were invited to express their opinions. Gross caricatures of Jews began to appear in humorous weeklies. *Carmel* subscriptions were donated to school libraries in Haifa. Anti-Zionist societies were formed in several Palestinian towns, Constantinople, Cairo and Beirut. In Jaffa a political organization, 'The Homeland Party', made anti-Zionism its *raison d'être*. Anti-Zionism became an important vote-winning gambit in elections to the Ottoman parliament. All the while the peasants were growing more turbulent, and outsiders like Najib Nassar began to play a part in egging them on. He also formed a vigilante group to see that restrictions on Jewish immigrants were strictly applied at Haifa port. Zionist representatives would be molested on their way to official gatherings; they had to arm themselves with sticks and guns. By 1913, observed Albert Antebi, there was no Jerusalem notable who would dare compromise his political position by openly favouring Zionism.[45]

Abortive Attempts at Arab-Zionist Understanding

It was becoming clear that the Palestinians faced a basic choice; either to reach some kind of accommodation with the Zionists, who, in return for certain concessions, would be obliged to place definite limits on their ambitions, or to fight them tooth and nail. At all events, the failure of the leadership to demonstrate its ability, or even its desire, to contain the menace meant, in the end, that the people would try to do it for them—in their own way. Those first rural convulsions were harbingers of an inchoate, popular violence to come. In 1914, Rashid Rida, the leading Moslem thinker of his time, formulated the choice as follows:

> It is incumbent upon the leaders of the Arabs—the local population—to do one of two things. Either they must reach an agreement with leaders of the Zionists to settle the differences between the interests of both parties . . . or they must gather all their forces to oppose the Zionists in every way, first by forming societies and companies, and finally by forming armed gangs which oppose them by force. Some [Arabs] say this is the first thing to be done because cauterization is the only way—and cauterization is the ultimate remedy, as it is said [in an Arabic proverb].[46]

In 1913 and 1914 the Palestinians did attempt to reach an accommodation with the Zionists—although it is stretching a point to call it a representative Palestinian initiative at all. For its main impetus came from emergent Arab Nationalist parties of Syria who were seeking autonomy or independence for the Arab provinces of the moribund Ottoman empire. The Decentralization Party, *Fatah* and *al-Ahd* were numerically insignificant; according to one estimate, they numbered a mere ninety-six to 126 members all told, of whom a mere twelve or twenty-two were Palestinians.[47] As—for the most part—young, Western-oriented patriots, they were keen to profit from the capital, expertise and equipment which they thought the Zionists would inject into the Arab economy; as—for the most part—non-Palestinians, they had little direct experience of Zionism in practice. They did not realize how self-centred it was. Rashid Rida, a founder-member of the Decentralization Party, believed that, provided the Zionists could be induced to abandon their political ambitions, the Arabs should make a compact with them. In 1913 the party, through its Cairo Committee, did indeed reach an *entente verbale* with the Zionist representative in Constantinople. 'Being in principle favourable to Jewish immigration into Syria and Palestine,' the text of it read, 'the Cairo Committee undertakes to work for a rapprochement between the Arab and Jewish worlds, and, through the Arab press and by word of mouth, to dissipate the prejudices which prevail in the Arab world concerning Jewish immigration and which hinder Arab-Jewish rapprochement.'[48] The *entente verbale* was to be superseded by an *accord complet*. The First Arab Congress, held in Paris in June 1913, passed a resolution favouring such Jewish immigration as was capable of benefiting Syria economically.

In the end no final agreement was ever reached. In truth the Zionists did not really want one. For, though it offered them short-term tactical advantages, it would have involved grave strategic disadvantages: they were to be asked to come clean, to state what they really wanted in Palestine. This was the dilemma which confronted them when, in 1914, under the auspices of the Decentralization Party, Palestinians took a more representative part in renewed efforts to reach an accommodation. For a meeting they were to hold with Zionist representatives in Brummana, Lebanon, the Arab side submitted an agenda which read in part: 'The Zionists should explain, as far as possible by producing documentary evidence, the aims and methods of Zionism and of the colonization of Palestine connected therewith.'[49] The Zionists were loth to accept this agenda. For their aims were in fact unlimited; in the light of fundamental Zionist doctrine they could not have been otherwise. The Zionists were only too well aware that there was precious little room for compromise on precisely those points—immigration and land purchase—about which the Arabs wished to be reassured. They procrastinated. And in the event they never had to come clean. The Great War broke out. It rendered a meeting impossible.

This, for the Palestinians, was a historic opportunity lost. For, however obvious the Zionists' lack of interest in an agreement might be, the Palestinians have always stood to win an immense moral and political advantage by irrefutably proving it in the only way they could—by challenging them to reach one. Of course, they might not have taken the opportunity, even if great events had not snatched it from them, because the very idea of an agreement has always generated fierce resistance in their own ranks. And this was true, even in these early days, when the 'Zionist peril' was embryonic and the concessions they would have had to make in return for a clear delimitation of the settlers' rights and obligations, could hardly have been far-reaching. Thus, when the Decentralizationists reached their *entente verbale* with the Zionists they ran into fierce criticism from publicists like Nassar, who proposed the holding of another congress at Nablus, a traditional bastion of nationalist feeling, to discuss a harder line. And when, the following year, the Palestinian–Zionist meeting in Lebanon was mooted, its Decentralizationist sponsor had to include Nassar and four other well-known anti-Zionists among the ten Arab delegates. And after that it was not long before the Decentralizationists themselves began to have second thoughts. Taking issue with his colleagues who still favoured *entente*, Haqqi Bey al-Azm wrote to a friend:

> Understand, dear brother, that these people are moving towards their object at a rapid pace. . . . I am sure that if we do nothing to affect the status quo the Zionists will attain their object in a few years (in Palestine) where they will found a Jewish state. . . . But, by employing means of threats and persecutions—and it is this last method we must employ—by pushing the Arab population into destroying their farms and setting fire to their colonies, by forming gangs to execute these projects—then perhaps they will emigrate to save their skins.[50]

He had come to the conclusion that, an agreement being impossible, 'cauterization'—that is, violence—was the only answer.

Jewish Warriors

As for the Zionists, they now deemed that conciliation was unnecessary. War in Europe, as Herzl had foreseen, could be turned to their advantage. It opened up dazzling opportunities, both in Palestine itself and outside it. Early in the war, two young men, Joseph Trumpeldor and Vladimir Jabotinsky, created a Jewish fighting unit, the Zion Mule Corps, which served with British forces in Gallipoli. During the war, too, a third, Aaron Aaronsohn, organized an espionage network, the *Nili* (acronym for *Netzakh Israel Lo Yeshaker*—The Eternal Jewish Shall Not Fail), which collaborated with British intelligence. And as the war drew to a close, Jabotinsky succeeded in forming 'The Jewish Legion', four battalions of Royal Fusiliers, 5,000 men in all, who fought with the British under their own flag. The three men were celebrated militants. To Trumpeldor, said to have been the only Jewish officer in the Czarist army, is attributed this chilling description of the ideal Zionist:

> We need men prepared to do everything . . . we must raise a generation of men who have no interests and no habits. . . . Bars of iron, elastic but of iron. Metal that can be forged to whatever is needed for the national machine. A wheel? I am the wheel. If a nail or a flying wheel are needed—take me! Is there a need to dig earth? I dig. Is there need to shoot, to be a soldier? . . . I am a soldier. . . . I am the pure ideal of service prepared for everything.

For him, fighting against the Arabs demolished the gentile conception of the Jew:

> If only the Gogols, the Dostoevskis, and other Russian writers could have seen these brave, determined lads, their Jewish types would certainly have been portrayed differently . . . forty brave lads standing fearlessly at their post, facing an angry sea of [Arab] rebels.[51]

Trumpeldor furnished the *Yishuv*—and Zionists everywhere—with their first heroic legend. He fell in battle against Arab insurgents in Galilee. Of course, he was not the first to die this way. But he was the kind of awe-inspiring figure of whom national myths are made—and he rounded off a short life of blind dedication and unflinching valour with famous last words. These were: 'It is good to die for our country.' Some say, however, that this prosaic exit line was a jest, and that his last utterance was actually a hefty Russian curse.[52]

Aaron Aaronsohn took a seigneurial attitude towards the Arabs,[53] and no doubt shared this opinion of his brother, Alexander, with whom he lived: 'The Arab is a cunning fellow, whose only respect is for brute force. He exercises it himself for every possible victim and expects the same treatment from his superiors.'[54]

As for Jabotinsky, his aim—in the words of his biographer—was 'realistic and stern: the establishment of a Jewish majority in Palestine will have to be achieved *against the wish* of the country's present Arab majority; an "iron wall" of Jewish armed force would have to protect the process of achieving a majority.'[55] His Jewish Legion was formed with the avowed aim of occupying Palestine after its conquest by the British, and, in the minds of its founders, it was to serve as the military backbone of the future Jewish State. A contemporary historian noted the arrogance of the legionaries and the intoxicating effect which the sight of them had on certain Zionist leaders, one of whom 'came out with the fantastic idea of resettling Palestine Arabs back in the regions from which their forefathers had allegedly come to Palestine centuries ago'.[56]

It did seem fantastic and—officially at least—reprehensible too. The most influential Zionist of the time, Chaim Weizmann, disparagingly described Jabotinsky as 'our own D'Annunzio'.[57] And indeed, at this stage, he did believe that the main thrust of the struggle should be diplomatic; it would stand or fall by the leverage which it could exert in the contemporary centres of world power. It was there, more than in Palestine itself, that the European cataclysm furnished Zionism with its real opportunity—and there that this consummate diplomat seized the opportunity. What Weizmann needed was the kind of international charter for which, two decades before, Herzl had toured European chancelleries in vain. His skilful and untiring persuasions eventually conjured it out of the British wartime leaders in the shape of the Balfour Declaration. That famous document, which, from 1917 on, incorporated Zionism into the imperial designs of the dominant power of the age, revolutionized its prospects overnight and rendered agreement with the Arabs entirely superfluous.

The Balfour Declaration

The Balfour Declaration was one of the two key documents that have shaped the modern history of the Middle East. The other was the Sykes-Picot agreement of 1916. This secret deal was part of an understanding in which the three major allies, Britain, France and Czarist Russia, defined each other's interests in the post-war Middle East. Sir Mark Sykes, Secretary to the British Cabinet, and the French plenipotentiary, M. Georges Picot, agreed that, after the break-up of the Ottoman empire, Britain and France would divide its former Arab provinces between them. Ironically, the most backward parts of the Arab world—what is now Saudi Arabia and Yemen—were to be permitted independent statehood, while the more advanced and mature were to come under 'direct or indirect' foreign rule. France was to take over Lebanon and Syria, Britain would get Iraq and Transjordan. Palestine was to be placed under an 'international administration' of a kind to be decided on later. This document, made public, much to Britain's embarrassment, by the newly installed Bolshevik government, violated the promises which it had earlier made to the Arabs. In return for the Arab contribution to the allied war effort, it had undertaken to 'recognize and support' the independence of the Arabs in the Arabian Peninsula, Palestine, Transjordan, Syria and Iraq.

The Balfour Declaration grew out of Sykes-Picot, but, in retrospect, its importance far outweighs it. Indeed, it is difficult to recall a document which has so arbitrarily changed the course of history as this one. The Arab-Israeli struggle is the likeliest of contemporary world problems to precipitate the nuclear doomsday; if it does, surviving historians will surely record that it all began with the brief and seemingly innocuous letter, consisting of 117 words, which Arthur Balfour, the British Secretary of State for Foreign Affairs, addressed to Lord Rothschild on 2 November 1917. Poetic licence will enable them to point out that though Palestine, with which the letter dealt, seemed at the time a rather benighted patch of the earth's surface, hardly destined for such a cataclysmic role, it is a country steeped in poignant symbolism, at whose centre lie the barren hills of Armageddon. The letter ran as follows:

> Dear Lord Rothschild,
>
> I have much pleasure in conveying to you, on behalf of His Majesty's Government, the following declaration of sympathy with Jewish Zionist aspirations which has been submitted to, and approved by the Cabinet:
>
> 'His Majesty's Government view with favour the establishment in Palestine of a national home for the Jewish people, and will use their best endeavours to facilitate the achievement of this object, it being clearly understood that nothing shall be done which may prejudice the civil and religious rights of the existing non-Jewish communities in Palestine, or the rights and political status enjoyed by Jews in any other country.'
>
> I should be grateful if you would bring this declaration to the knowledge of the Zionist Federation.
>
> Yours sincerely,
> Arthur Balfour

It seemed, on the face of it, to be a purely British initiative, sprung wholly from the good will and wise purposes of His Majesty's Government. The Zionists certainly have reason to remember Balfour as one of the great benefactors of the Jewish people. But it was hardly love of the Jews that inspired a charity far from home. In the last years of the nineteenth century, Britain had been flooded with Jewish refugees from Eastern Europe; there were riots and demonstrations against them in the streets of London. An Aliens Act was passed which restricted Jewish immigration. None other than Balfour, Prime Minister at the time, defended the legislation in language which the Zionists denounced as 'open anti-Semitism against the whole Jewish people':

> A state of things could easily be imagined in which it would not be to the advantage of the civilization of the country that there should be an immense body of persons who, however patriotic, able and industrious, however much they threw themselves into the national life, still, by their own action, remained a people apart, and not merely held a religion differing from the vast majority of their fellow-countrymen, but only inter-married among themselves.[58]

The document bears Balfour's name, but in reality it was the Zionists themselves who, in very large measure, both inspired the Declaration and framed its text. It must be reckoned the finest flower of Zionist diplomacy at its most sophisticatedly ambivalent. A whole chapter would be required to do justice to the genesis and real import of those few words. Whole chapters have indeed been devoted to the task, and suffice it to say here, on the strength of others' researches, that the Zionists who framed the Declaration saw in it the charter of a future Jewish State and that, in appearing to care for the rights of the 'non-Jewish communities in Palestine', they were actually laying a legal foundation, through the ingenious deployment of the words 'civil', 'religious', and 'political', for taking these rights away.[59]

The Zionists were not entirely unmasked by their triumph. It was still too early for that. They continued to deny the ultimate ambition, Jewish statehood, which friends and enemies attributed to them. Weizmann warned more extreme Zionists than himself that 'Palestine must be built up without violating the legitimate rights of the Arabs—not a hair of their heads shall be touched'.[60] He went to Palestine to assure the Arabs that it was not 'our objective to seize control of the higher policy of the province of Palestine. Nor has it ever been our objective to turn anyone out of his property.'[61] Yet even as he was there, dispensing these assurances to the natives, he was conveying what he really thought about them in his correspondence with Balfour:

> The Arabs, who are superficially clever and quickwitted, worship one thing, and one thing only—power and success. . . . The British authorities . . . knowing as they do the treacherous nature of the Arab, have to watch carefully and constantly that nothing should happen which might give

> the Arabs the slightest grievance or lest they should stab the Army in the back. The Arab, quick as he is to gauge such a situation, tries to make the most of it. He screams as often as he can and blackmails as much as he can. The first scream was heard when your Declaration was announced. All sorts of misinterpretations and misconceptions were put on the declaration. The English, they said, are going to hand over the poor Arabs to the wealthy Jews, who are all waiting in the wake of General Allenby's army, ready to swoop down like vultures on an easy prey and to oust everybody from the land. . . .[62]

Yet even in public Weizmann could often only cloak his real hopes in the thinnest disguise of discretion and sweet reason. And occasionally this most eloquent of speakers seemed quite to forget himself, as when he told a London audience a mere two years after the Declaration:

> I trust to God that a Jewish state will come about; but it will come about not through political declarations, but by the sweat and blood of the Jewish people. . . . [The Balfour Declaration] is the golden key which unlocks the doors of Palestine and gives you the possibility to put all your efforts into the country. . . . We were asked to formulate our wishes. We said we desired to create in Palestine such conditions, political, economic and administrative, that as the country is developed, we can pour in a considerable number of immigrants, and finally establish such a society in Palestine that Palestine shall be as Jewish as England is English, or America is American . . . I hope that the Jewish frontiers of Palestine will be as great as Jewish energy for getting Palestine.[63]

It appears that Zionist historians have been more discreet than Weizmann. These revealing passages were omitted from later editions of the book in which they appear.

As for the mechanics of the thing, the *modus operandi*, Weizmann pioneered two basic concepts that have underlain Zionist policies ever since. One was the concept of the empty framework. As he subsequently explained in his autobiography, 'the Balfour Declaration was no more than a framework, which had to be filled in by our own efforts. It would mean exactly what we would make it mean—neither more nor less. On what we could make it mean through slow, costly and laborious work would depend whether and when we should deserve or attain statehood.'[64] The other was the concept of stages. In a speech to the English Zionist Union, a few months before the issue of the declaration, he put discretion aside to explain it.

> States must be built up slowly, gradually, systematically and patiently. We, therefore, say that while the creation of a Jewish Commonwealth in Palestine is our final ideal . . . the way to achieve it lies through a series of intermediary stages. And one of those intermediary stages, which I hope is going to come about as a result of the war, is that the fair country of Palestine will be protected by such a mighty and just Power as Great Britain. Under the wing of this Power, Jews will be able to develop, and to set up the administrative machinery which . . . would enable us to carry out the Zionist scheme.[65]

What the Zionists were to do in the fair land of Palestine they could only do in the teeth of increasingly vigorous opposition from the Arabs who lived there and in violation of those terms of the Balfour Declaration which, properly interpreted, would have safeguarded their interests. But that they could rely on mighty and just Britain to help them do it was not, for those in the know, a wildly optimistic interpretation of the British intent. Indeed, what more reassuring than the interpretation which the author of the famous declaration himself put upon it? Weizmann had been confidentially assured by the Prime Minister, in Balfour's presence, that 'national home' was a euphemism for Jewish State.[66] He may also have read a candid secret memorandum which Balfour submitted to the British cabinet. In this memorandum Balfour discussed the League of Nations Covenant, its championship of the principle of self-determination of peoples and its insistence that 'the wishes of these communities ("independent nations" like Syria and Palestine requiring administrative advice and assistance until they are able to "stand alone") must be a principal consideration in the selection of a mandatory.' Lord Balfour wrote:

> Do we mean, in the case of Syria, to consult principally the wishes of the inhabitants? We mean nothing of the kind. . . . The contradiction between the letter of the Covenant and the policy of the Allies is even more flagrant in the case of the 'independent nation' of Palestine than in that of the 'independent nation' of Syria. For in Palestine we do not propose even to go through the form of consulting the wishes of the present inhabitants of the country. . . . The Four Great Powers are committed to Zionism. And Zionism, be it right or wrong, good or bad, is rooted in age-long traditions, in present needs, in future hopes, of far profounder import than the desires and prejudices of the 700,000 Arabs who now inhabit that ancient land. . . . In short, so far as Palestine is concerned, the Powers have made no statement of fact which is not admittedly wrong, and no declaration of policy which, at least in the letter, they have not always intended to violate.[67]

NOTES

1. Central Zionist Archives, Jerusalem, H111 d 14, 1 March 1899; see Mandel, Neville, 'Turks, Arabs and Jewish Immigration into Palestine, 1882–1914', St Antony's Papers, *Middle Eastern Affairs*, ed. Hourani, Albert, Oxford University Press, 1965, p. 89.
2. UN General Assembly, 2nd Session, 9 September, 1947, *Report of the Special Committee on Palestine*, Vol. II, A/364, Add., I, pp. 39–40.
3. *The Complete Diaries of Theodor Herzl*, Herzl Press and Thomas Yoseloff, New York, 1960, Vol. I, p. 343.
4. Herzl, *The Jewish State*, Rita Searle, London, 1946, p. 29.
5. Herzl, *Besammelte Zionistische Schriften*, Jüdischer Verlag, Berlin, 1934–5, Vol. I, p. 114; Vol. II, pp. 50, 58, 78, 102; Vol. III, p. 526. This and the following list of Herzl's recommended techniques is largely taken from L.M.C. Van der Hoeven, 'Het Palestina-Vragstak in Zijn Ware gedaante', *Libertas* (Holland), Lustrum, 1960; republished in English in Khalidi, Walid, *From Haven to Conquest*, Institute for Palestine Studies, Beirut, 1971, p. 115.
6. *The Complete Diaries*, *op. cit.*, Vol. I, p. 88.
7. *Ibid.*, p. 98.
8. Böhm, Adolf, *Die Zionistische Bewegung*, Berlin, 1935, Vol. I, p. 706.
9. Herzl, *Besammelte Zioniste Schriften*, *op. cit.*, Vol. III, p. 77.
10. Zwangwill, Israel, 'The Return to Palestine', *New Liberal Review II*, December 1901, p. 627.
11. Nordau, Max, *Zionistische Schriften*, Jüdischer Verlag, Berlin, 1923, p. 72.
12. *Ibid.*, p. 425.

13. Sykes, Christopher, *Two Studies in Virtue*, Collins, London, 1953, p. 160.
14. Barbour, Neville, *Nisi Dominus*, Harrap, London, 1946, p. 52.
15. *The Complete Diaries*, *op. cit.*, Vol. II, p. 581.
16. Hadawi, Sami, *Bitter Harvest*, The New World Press, New York, 1967, p. 11.
17. Oliphant, L., *Haifa or Life in Modern Palestine*, William Blackwood, Edinburgh, 1887, p. 60; Newton, Frances E., *Fifty Years in Palestine*, Coldharbour Press, Wrotham, England, 1948, p. 97.
18. Mandel, *op. cit.*, p. 90.
19. Al-Kayyaii, Abdul al-Wahhab, *A History of Modern Palestine* (Arabic), Beirut, 1971, p. 50.
20. Barbour, *op. cit.*, p. 116.
21. Mandel, *op. cit.*, p. 85; see also Ro'i, Yaacov, 'The Zionist Attitude to the Arabs, 1908–14', *Middle Eastern Studies*, London, Vol. **4**, No. 3, April 1968, pp. 198–242.
22. *Hadera*, Jewish National Fund Library No. 2, Tel Aviv, 1935, cited in Barbour, *op. cit.*, pp. 115, 116.
23. Barbour, *op. cit.*, p. 116.
24. Aham, Ahad, *Am Scheideweg*, Berlin, 1923, Vol. I, p. 107.
25. *Jewish-Arab Affairs*, Jerusalem, 1931, p. 11, cited in Barbour, *op. cit.*, p. 124.
26. Mandel, *op. cit.*, p. 86.
27. Jiryis, Sabri, 'Recent Knesset Legislation', *Journal of Palestine Studies*, Institute for Palestine Studies, Beirut, Vol. I, No. 1, Autumn 1971, pp. 57–8.
28. Ro'i, *op. cit.*, p. 233.
29. Ussishkin, Menachim, see Avneri, Uri, *Israel Without Zionists: A Plea for Peace in the Middle East*, Macmillan, New York, 1968, p. 86.
30. Snowman, Leonard Victor, *Tchernichowski and his Poetry*, Hasefer Agency for Literature, London, 1929, p. 26. See Taylor, Alan R., *The Zionist Mind, The Origins and Development of Zionist Thought*, Institute for Palestine Studies, Beirut, 1974, pp. 47–80.
31. Ro'i, *op. cit.*, p. 223.
32. Elon, Amos, *The Israelis, Founders and Sons*, Sphere Books, London, 1972, p. 131.
33. *Ibid.*, p. 124.
34. Mandel, *op. cit.*, p. 93.
35. St John, Robert, *Bengurion*, New York, 1959, pp. 31–2.
36. Barbour, *op. cit.*, p. 117.
37. Grannott, Abraham, *The Land System in Palestine*, Eyre and Spottiswoode, London, 1952, p. 280.
38. *Ibid.*, p. 80.
39. Weizmann, Chaim, *Trial and Error*, Hamish Hamilton, London, 1949, p. 457.
40. Qasimiyah, Khairiyah, 'Najib Nassar and *Carmel* Newspaper, One of the Pioneer Opponents of Zionism', *Palestine Affairs* (Arabic), Beirut monthly, July 1973, p. 111, citing *Carmel*, 11 January, 22 and 26 August 1913.

41. *Ibid.*, p. 114, citing *Carmel*, 1 July 1914.
42. *Ibid.*, citing *al-Muqtabas* (Damascus newspaper), 11 January 1911.
43. *Ibid.*, citing *al-Muqattam* (Cairo newspaper), 1 May 1914, and *Carmel*, 5 May 1914.
44. Ro'i, *op. cit.*, p. 225.
45. Mandel, Neville, 'Attempts at an Arab-Zionist Entente: 1913–1914', *Middle Eastern Studies*, London, Vol. I, No. 3, April 1965, p. 263.
46. *Ibid.*, p. 256, citing *al-Manar* newspaper, Vol. 27, 1914, p. 320.
47. *Ibid.*, p. 340.
48. *Ibid.*, p. 246.
49. *Ibid.*, p. 260.
50. *Ibid.*, p. 265; translation from *Journal de Beyrouth* 413, 1 September 1915.
51. Elon, *op. cit.*, p. 143.
52. *Ibid.*, p. 143.
53. Tabenkin, Yitzhak, *Chemins et Détours de la Renaissance Juive*, Paris, 1948, pp. 120–3.
54. Aaronsohn, Alexander, *With the Turks in Palestine*, Constable, London, 1917, p. 25.
55. Schechtman, Joseph, *Fighter and Prophet, The Vladimir Jabotinsky Story*, Thomas Yoseloff, New York, 1961, p. 324.
56. Revusky, Abraham, *Jews in Palestine*, P. S. King, London, 1935, pp. 286 and 317–18.
57. Elon, *op. cit.*, p. 163.
58. See Rabinowicz, Oskar K., *Winston Churchill on Jewish Problems*, Thomas Yoseloff, New York, 1960, p. 167.
59. See Jeffreys, J. M. N., *Palestine: the Reality*, Longmans, Green and Co., London, 1939, Chapter II.
60. Speech to Fourteenth Zionist Congress, Vienna, 1925.
61. Khalidi, *op. cit.*, p. 189.
62. Ingrams, Doreen, *Palestine Papers 1917–1922, Seeds of Conflict*, John Murray, London, 1972, p. 31.
63. *Chaim Weizmann: Excerpts from his Historic Statements, Writings and Addresses*, The Jewish Agency for Palestine, New York, 1952, p. 48.
64. Weizmann, *op. cit.*, p. 302.
65. *Palestine, A Study of Jewish, Arab and British Policies*, ESCO Zionist Institute, Yale University Press, New Haven, Vol. I, pp. 98–9.
66. Ingrams, *op. cit.*, p. 146.
67. *Ibid.*, p. 73.

2 · NO PEACE IN ZION, 1921–1935

The Slaughter of 1921

In 1921 there was little to distinguish the town of Jaffa from the other seaports—Haifa, Tyre or Sidon—that lay along the eastern shores of the Mediterranean. It was a picturesque labyrinth of narrow alleys packed against the quay. Its dominant spirit was still conservative; it was touched, but not badly disrupted, by the intensifying contact with the modern world of Europe. Its merchant class was favourably disposed towards Britain, an important market for the famous orange to which Jaffa had given its name. It had its water-front world of boatmen, porters, artisans and labourers. They were sociable, credulous, excitable in the Levantine way and, when anything unusual occurred, they would quickly form a crowd. They included, as in any port, a number of toughs and bad characters. But in general the citizens of Jaffa were law-abiding and, if anything, more respectful of authority than vigorous Western societies would consider normal.

On 1 May of that year unprecedented violence erupted in Palestine. May Day traditionally raised uneasy expectations in many European countries. But the proletarian struggle meant very little to the Arabs of Palestine. There was little reason to expect trouble from them. Trouble came, however, and although it struck in a number of places, its focus was Jaffa. For the one thing which had, in recent years, distinguished this otherwise unexceptional Arab coastal town was a profoundly unsettling one. It had become the principal point of Jewish immigration into Palestine. It was there that the refugees from the ghettoes of Eastern Europe first set foot on the Promised Land. And just to the north the new city of Tel Aviv, the biggest concentration of Jews in the country, was taking shape.

The violence had small, indeed foolish, beginnings. The Jews came to Palestine armed with the social and political doctrines of their East European Diaspora, and since it was a time of revolutionary upheaval they naturally had their share of Bolshevik extremists. Since 1909 the Socialist Revolutionary Party—or *Mopsi*, the German for pug, as its rivals derisively called it—had been trying to win Jewish Labour groups to the principles of the Second International; but it never made much headway in these efforts to 'prepare the soil of Palestine for the Social Revolution'. In 1920 it was reinforced by newcomers from the Soviet Union; but at its height it never numbered more than 300 members. It was on May Day that *Mopsi*, in accordance with proletarian tradition, chose to make a show of its puny strength. Led mainly by illegal immigrants, it was determined to make up in noise and provocation for what it lacked in numbers. In the morning of 1 May, the militants assembled at their headquarters in the Borochoff Club in a mixed Arab-Jewish quarter of Jaffa. Then, in defiance of an official ban, they issued into the streets, eluded a police barrier and marched on Tel Aviv. They wore red rosettes and raised cardboard slogans stencilled in red: 'Long Live 1 May; Down with English Coercive Power; Long Live Socialist Revolution; Long Live Socialist Soviet Palestine.' In violent language they invited Jewish and Arab workers to join in overthrowing their oppressors and 'beating down the torturers and tyrants among you'. It was a clarion call to class warfare—but the very oppressed they were trying to save, their hapless co-religionists, were the main victims of the warfare, or, rather, the mindless slaughter which it provoked.

The violence began as an inter-Jewish clash. *Mopsi* ran into the much bigger, officially authorized demonstration staged by *Ahdot ha Avodah*, a social democratic party. The two sides came to blows; there were some injuries and one woman was knocked down with a bad head wound. Hitherto, Jewish labour disturbances had produced little more than Arab curiosity. This time, however, it was different. Quite suddenly the Arabs seemed to go berserk. Normally law-abiding citizens perpetrated acts of savagery that lasted a week and spread deep into the surrounding countryside. A crowd had gathered to watch the quarrelling Jewish demonstrators. British-controlled policemen stood between the two groups at opposite ends of a sandy open space. They glowered at each other. Tension rose. Neither side would disperse. Somebody began breaking Jewish shop windows in the adjoining quarter of Menshieh. The crowd deserted the sandy space and, armed with sticks, iron bars, knives and anything that came to hand, they began a general hunt of the Jews. The civil police, overcome by partisan emotions, were completely ineffectual. Three Arab notables offered their services to quieten the populace. In Menshieh they found the Jewish market entirely looted, and pillage in progress elsewhere. They stilled the tumult only where they were; it resumed as soon as their backs were turned. The army was called in, but the rioting kept breaking out afresh, and by the time it finally subsided nearly 200 Jews and 120 Arabs were dead or wounded. The Arabs had been the first to turn it into a racial conflict, but the Jews retaliated with equal savagery. After examining the dead bodies on this first day, Dr Beadles, the Medical Officer in Jaffa, recalled that he was 'struck most with the number of wounds on each body, and the ferocity of the wounds. I am speaking particularly of broken skulls. Some of the victims had dozens of wounds.'[1] Some of the worst atrocities were premeditated.

On the second day groups of Jews went out seeking cold-blooded vengeance. One of them, apparently led by a policeman from Tel Aviv, broke down the door of a house; they shot a man in the stomach and when his little daughter ran to her father her head was cleft with the blow of an axe. The Arabs were no less methodical. On the same day six Jews who lived in an isolated house were found dead nearby; five of them had been beaten or stabbed to death; the sixth, some distance apart from the others, had died with his hands tied behind his back. But the symbolic climax had already come on the first day, when the Arab mob stormed the Zionist immigration hostel in the middle of the town. Arab constables, caught up in the general frenzy, actually led the assault. The official British committee of inquiry, led by Sir Thomas Haycraft, concluded:

> We are satisfied from the evidence of the Reverend A. C. Martin, of the London Jews' Society, who saw much of what happened from a window on the opposite side of the main street, that the police in the

> street broke through the door and led a part of the mob into the yard. They broke into the ground floor of the main building and into the other buildings. Men who sought refuge by running into the street were beaten to death by the crowd. Others were killed inside the courtyard. The invaders came in from all the entrances when the defence had broken down. Only one woman was killed, namely by a shot fired through a window. Those women who escaped into the street were roughly handled by the crowd, but not killed. They were wounded, but not dangerously, and were sheltered from further harm by an Arab neighbour. Perhaps the most revolting incident was the conduct of one of the Arab policemen. He was at first regarded by the women as a protector, but he took advantage of the prevailing terror to rob them of their small possessions, and to two he made indecent advances, telling them that he was a Jew, with threats of violence if they refused to comply with his demands. They appear to have avoided this crowning act of brutality by escape. This man was convicted by a special court for the trial of offences committed during the riots, and was sentenced to 13 years' imprisonment. It must not be supposed that no resistance was made by the Jews. The toll of dead and wounded in the gruesome episode of the Immigration House was as follows: 13 Jews killed or mortally wounded and 24 wounded; one Arab killed and four wounded.[2]

Coming three years after the greatest carnage in history, what Bengurion called 'the slaughter of 1921' might seem an insignificant affair. But it was not so for the Jews. They might regard anti-Semitic outbreaks in Eastern Europe as a kind of seasonal misfortune, but that a pogrom could occur in Palestine, and under the enlightened rule of Great Britain, many of them found shocking and incomprehensible.

Haycraft Vindicates the Arabs

Yet the pogrom had a specific and a general cause, and Sir Thomas Haycraft had no difficulty in identifying them. The *Mopsi* demonstration, he concluded, was the specific cause, the immediate trigger of the Arab rampage, while the fear and hatred of the Jewish immigrant, and all he stood for, was the general one. *Mopsi* amounted to little in themselves; they were a complete failure, despised by most of their own community as much as by the Arabs. But, owing to the deeper inter-communal antagonisms, they produced an effect far out of proportion to their numbers. For the Arabs, they were not fundamentally different from their fellow-Zionists; they merely typified, at its most offensive, an alien invasion which, by its very nature, they found intolerable. Not only were the foreigners invading their country, here they were desecrating it with their repugnant, subversive creeds, their quarrels and their violence. Repudiated by their own people, here they were trying to convert them, the natives, and importing Communist literature in Arabic from Vienna for the purpose. The Arabs saw 'the beginnings of industrial strife, previously unknown in the country; they saw strikes and labour demonstrations, which filled their conservative minds with alarm; they read leaflets . . . in which the people were invited to participate in class war, and to promote anarchy and social upheaval.'[3]

Labour unrest was only part of a whole complex of alien and insulting ways. The Arabs felt that in all they did the newcomers were arrogant and aggressive. They also found them indecent. 'Several witnesses have referred to the manner in which strings of these young men and women, in free and easy attire, would perambulate the streets arm in arm, singing songs, holding up traffic and generally conducting themselves in a manner at variance with Arab ideas of decorum.'[4] Other contemporary reports speak of the shock which the straitlaced Arabs felt at such extremes of modernism as mixed bathing in the nude. The Jews had come, they felt, to corrupt their society and whole way of life.

The animosity was frequently reinforced by outright pre-judices. Through Westernization, the Arabs had acquired some of these. Communism, revolution and anarchy, they claimed, were rooted in the Jews' very being. In many countries they were 'sowers of controversy and ruin'. In their view Jews were like bacteria; if Britain and America were unable to contain them, how could Palestine? The Arabs also had some inherited prejudices of their own. Even a leading scholar wrote that it was forbidden to believe the Jews, who claimed that their intentions were good, since 'they are scoundrels and the Koran itself is full of stories of their fraudulent acts'.[5]

It was a favourite Zionist argument that in coming to Palestine the Jews would help to develop it for the benefit of all its inhabitants. The Arabs were never impressed, particularly when they saw what kind of people these would-be developers were. They were not, they said, the wealthy, the merchants, the men of property, but a disparate multitude, 'vagabonds and outcasts', from all over the world.[6]

It was a fundamental clash of culture, yet the Arabs would have absorbed it but for the one totally inadmissible premise that underlay the whole Zionist enterprise. The Jews were not only introducing an alien culture, they planned to make it the only one in the country. Nor was the takeover bid only cultural; it was political, economic and demographic too. To this deep-rooted fear the Haycraft Commission—like many that were to succeed it over the years—devoted much sympathetic attention:

> It is important that it should be realized that what is written on the subject of Zionism by Zionists and their sympathizers in Europe is read and discussed by Palestinian Arabs, not only in the towns but in the country districts. Thus a witness from Tulkaram . . . quoted as an instance of provocative writing the following passage from a book entitled 'England and Palestine', by H. Sidebotham: 'It is desired to encourage Jewish immigration by every means, and at the same time to discourage the immigration of Arabs. . . .' The book was published as far back as 1918; but our attention has been called to other not less provocative statements appearing in Zionist publications since the disturbances, whilst we were sitting. Thus the *Jewish Chronicle*, No. 2,720, of the 20th May, 1921, makes the following statement in the course of its leading article: 'Hence the real key to the Palestine situation is to be found in giving to Jews as such, those rights and privileges in Palestine which shall enable Jews to make it as Jewish as England is English, or as Canada is Canadian. That is the only reasonable or, indeed, feasible meaning of a Jewish National Home, and it is impossible for Jews to construct it without being accorded a National status for Jews.'
>
> Again, Palestine, the official organ of the British Palestine

> Committee in its issue of the 4th June, 1921, in discussing the question of Jewish immigration, describes Palestine as a 'deserted, derelict land'. This description hardly tallies with the fact that the density of the present population of Palestine, according to Zionist figures, is something like 75 to the square mile. On the 14th May there appeared in *The Times* a letter from Mr. V. Jabotinsky . . . in which he urged that, in view of the Jaffa disturbances, Jews alone should have the privilege of military service in Palestine, Arabs being excluded from the right to bear arms. . . .
>
> Until the Commission came to examine Dr. Eder, acting Chairman of the Zionist Commission, they were unaware to what extent such expressions of opinion as those we have quoted above were authorized by responsible Zionists. Dr. Eder was a most enlightening witness. He was quite unaggressive in manner and free from any desire to push forward opinions which might be offensive to the Arabs. But when questioned on certain vital matters he was perfectly frank in expressing his view of the Zionist ideal. He gave no quarter to the view of the National Home as put forward by the Secretary of State and the High Commissioner. In his opinion there can only be one National Home in Palestine, and that a Jewish one, and no equality in the partnership between Jews and Arabs, but a Jewish predominance as soon as the numbers of that race are sufficiently increased. . . . As acting Chairman of the Zionist Commission, Dr. Eder presumably expresses in all points the official Zionist creed, if such there be, and his statements are, therefore, most important. There is no sophistry about Dr. Eder; he was quite clear that the Jews should, and the Arabs should not, have the right to bear arms, and he stated his belief that this discrimination would tend to improve Arab-Jewish relations. . . .[7]

The Arabs were genuinely persuaded, Haycraft went on, that the Palestine government was under Zionist influence and therefore led to favour a minority at the expense of the vast majority of the population. And in the light of all this he exonerated Arab leaders:

> We are convinced that the charge constantly brought by Jews against the Arabs, that this outbreak had been planned by them, or by their leaders, and was pre-arranged for the 1st May, is unfounded. It

> appears in evidence that on more than one occasion Arabs in European dress incited the crowd; but the notables on both sides, whatever their feelings may have been, were always ready to help the authorities in their restoration of order, and we think that without their assistance the outbreak would have resulted in even worse excesses. A good deal has been alleged by Jewish witnesses about the instigation of the Arab mob to violence by their leaders. If this means no more than that while educated people talk and write, the mob acts, then there is truth in the allegation. But if it means that had it not been for incitement by the notables, effendis, and sheikhs, there would have been no riots, the allegation cannot be substantiated. . . . All that can be truly said in favour of the Jewish view is that the leaders of Arab opinion not only make no secret of what they think, but carry on a political campaign. In this campaign, however, the people participate with the leaders, because they feel that their political and material interests are identical. There is no evidence worth considering, to show that the outbreak was planned and organised. Had that been the case, we hesitate to conjecture what the consequences would have been.[8]

British government papers of the period are replete with similar opinions expressed by officials on the spot. The Jaffa location of the outbreak—said the monthly political report from Jerusalem—'can cause no surprise' because discontent is most acute in places 'where the irritant which causes it is most in evidence'.[9] And immigration, said the Chief Secretary of the Palestine government, is 'the tangible, visible evidence of Zionism. It is a measure which they [the Arabs] can judge by.'[10] For the temporary inmates of the immigration hostel, defenceless newcomers to the Promised Land, it was a cruelly ironic fate. But for those who cared to see it, the Arabs could scarcely have chosen a starker way of making their point: there would be no peace in such a Zion.

The Zionists Blame the Arab 'Politicians'

The Zionists did not care to see it. Dr Eder's opinions were standard. Jabotinsky's were merely an immoderate version of them. It is one of the many peculiarities of a movement born of resistance to injustice and persecution that it should have been so insensitive to the self-same resistance that it bred in others. Yet it is not very surprising. The Zionists came to Palestine with such a passionate determination to succeed that they could not bring themselves to acknowledge the seemingly insurmountable obstacles—both moral and physical—which they found in their way when they got there. They preferred to maintain the Diaspora illusion that the Promised Land, if not actually uninhabited, could easily accommodate them and all their aspirations. Or, finding that it could not, they preferred the deception—which was also a conscience-salving self-deception—that no harm would ever come to those all-too-numerous inhabitants.

In short, they invented a world of make-believe in which there could be no resistance for there was nothing to resist. From the turn of the century to this day, the Zionists, so sure of their own high motives, have resolutely blinded themselves to the motives of their enemies. It is scarcely going too far to say that, confronted with Arab resistance, they have found explanations for it which, to those who have unprejudiced eyes with which to see, are not merely wrong, but often quite the opposite of the real ones. And on the strength of their false diagnosis they have with unfailing perversity proceeded to advocate remedies which simply aggravate the malady which they were supposed to cure. The trouble, they almost invariably said, lay with the 'politicians' and not with the 'people'. In the Palestine of the Mandate, it was local notables, the *zaims* and the *effendis*, who supposedly incited the anti-Jewish riots—just as, after 1948, it was to be President Nasser and other 'revolutionary' leaders who supposedly spread hatred of the newly-born state of Israel throughout the Arab world. The best way to handle rabble-rousing politicians, they said, was implacably to oppose them—in other words, to press on, more resolutely than ever, with the great Zionist enterprise. Discrimination against the Arabs would improve the situation for everyone—including, of course, the Arabs themselves. And the more the Arabs disliked the discrimination, the more of it they should suffer.

True, there were a few Zionists for whom this was an extraordinary contortion of logic. In the opinion of Chaim Arlosoroff, 'the slaughter of 1921' meant that 'an Arab movement really exists and—

no matter what sort it is—it will be calamitous if we negate its importance or rely on bayonets, British or Jewish. Such support is valid for an hour but not for decades . . . the "strong-arm" policy never attained its aim.'[11] This was completely at odds with the usual diagnosis, of which Gershon Agronsky, founder of the *Jerusalem Post*, furnished a typical example: 'The Jaffa riots this year', he argued, 'and the Easter outbreak in Jerusalem last year were not the result of a popular uprising. They were caused by Arab politicians who, in their campaign against the announced British Zionist policy, have used the good-natured, uneducated Arab as a dupe. These politicians . . . are of two classes: there are the superior natives of Palestine, members of the landed class, who have had a much better time of it under the Turkish regime, and who feel that their interests are endangered by a Western government with Western ideas of justice. They also fear Jewish immigration because of the effect of the Jews' higher standard of living upon the exploited cultivator.' He concedes that the riots and other overt acts do seem to point to hostility on the part of a section of the native population towards Zionist immigration. But he goes on: 'It is based, however, on a misconception of the Zionist aims, and could be overcome. Those who have spent any time in the country know, as the Arabs directly affected by Zionist work know, that Palestine has much to gain and nothing to lose from a large Zionist immigration. Where Arab villages cluster about Jewish colonies, said Winston Churchill, "the Arab houses are tiled instead of being built of mud, so that the culture from this centre has been spread out into the surrounding district". Low as the standard of wages is in Palestine, it is infinitely higher where Arabs are employed by Jews. Jewish labour has given an impetus to the organization of Arab labour.' And then comes the paradoxical remedy. 'Peace will be secured when the League of Nations puts the formal stamp of approval on the mandate, and when the Zionist organization obtains the means for carrying out its program. Those earnestly wishing to see peace in Palestine . . . want the Mandate to be ratified, the Keren Hayesod (Jewish National Fund) to succeed, and, as a result of the two, the Arab to be reconciled.'[12]

If this Zionist journalist on the spot could perhaps be excused for failing to see the wood for the trees, what about the world-renowned

British scientist Redcliffe Salman? He was confident that 'the Jew and the Arab would get on perfectly well if the politicians would but leave them alone. There is more than enough room for both. The Arab is utterly incapable of developing the land alone. The Jew is the only one who will bring capital and the Arab knows it; even as one writes comes information of letters from village chiefs all over the country . . . praying for Jewish immigration.' He had no time for 'an Administration which has truckled to the noisy pan-Arabic party for the sake of peace and quiet, which has allowed party sedition to grow under its nose, which has removed the few arms from the hands of the voluntary Jewish police of the colonies and has suffered the wholesale pilfering of arms and ammunition by the Arabs.' And he too came to the unscientific conclusion that the more forcefully Britain adopted the Zionist programme—a programme which, he insisted, should lead to Jewish majority rule in Palestine—the happier the Arabs would be: 'As one writes one hears of conflicts and bloodshed in Jerusalem and a noisy Press campaign, which informs the world that the Arab *fellah* dreads the incoming rush of Jews. It would be idle to say that there is no opposition, but this much can be said without hesitation: had Britain assumed the Mandate immediately after the Armistice and carried out its promise contained in the Balfour Declaration, there would have been little or no opposition on the part of the *fellahin*.'[13]

It is of course questionable whether all those who expressed such unrealistic opinions sincerely believed them. There is no record of Bengurion stating publicly at the time what he was to write forty years later: 'I believed—and still do—that Jewish-Arab cooperation holds enormous benefit for both peoples. But at the same time I realized that the battle of Tel Hai in 1920, the slaughter of 1921, were as nothing compared to the blood-letting that was to come.'[14]

There is a tendency on the Arab side, especially among contemporary left-wing historians, to overstate the opposite thesis—namely, that the 'people', in their immediate and intuitive hostility to Zionism, were all irreproachable patriots, while the 'politicians' were quislings almost to a man. It is certain, however, that resistance derived its main impetus from the people; it was they who enforced it on the politicians, not the other way round.

The Arab Politicians Choose Non-Violence

The dilemma that the Palestinian leaders faced was a grave one. It was enshrined in the Balfour Declaration. It has been seen what this meant for the Zionists. They could rely on the British to help them fill in the 'framework' which—in Weizmann's phrase—it represented. They had not been disappointed. They secured sufficient imperial backing to tip an otherwise highly adverse balance of power in their favour. For the Arabs there had always been a choice between conciliation and resistance. In earlier pre-Balfour days, as we have seen, they had toyed with the idea of conciliation as a means of containing the embryonic 'Zionist peril'. But now that peril had assumed far more alarming proportions. Conciliation meant coming to terms with the British; resistance meant fighting them. It was a very difficult choice. It was, said the Palestinians, quite 'impossible to set up a Jewish homeland without prejudicing the civil and religious rights of the existing non-Jewish communities of Palestine'.[15] How, then, could they cooperate with an alien rule which, by its very nature, trampled the national interest underfoot? On the other hand, how could they take on the leading military power of the age? They chose conciliation.

Naturally, the Palestinians did not like their new quasi-colonial status. Like other Arabs they regarded it as a breach of faith. But their immediate concern was not to get rid of it—they would manage that in due course—it was to ensure that, before they eventually did, the national interest would not be damaged beyond repair. They did try to cooperate with their new masters in the hope of persuading them to drop the whole idea of establishing a Jewish National Home. In 1921, Musa Kazim al-Husseini, President of the Arab Executive, which represented the Palestine community in dealings with the British authorities, appealed to his compatriots 'to put their hope in the government of Great Britain, which is famous for its justice, its concern for the well-being of the inhabitants, its safeguarding of their rights, and consent to their lawful demands.'[16] Basically, they had two approaches. One, the direct one, was to work for a formal renunciation of the Balfour Declaration, or at least the quiet non-implementation of its operative provisions; the other, the indirect one, was to work for the establishment of representative government in Palestine, thereby enabling them, the vast majority, to block the designs of the Zionist minority. After all, in accordance with the Covenant of the League of Nations, Britain had assumed the Mandate as a 'sacred trust of civilization', and the development of self-governing institutions was one of its basic obligations. Had it not already granted self-rule to far more backward areas of the Middle East?

They did not get very far with either approach. When Winston Churchill, the Colonial Secretary, visited the Middle East in 1921, he effectively foreclosed both. A delegation of Palestinian leaders petitioned him to rescind the Balfour Declaration, end all Jewish immigration and agree to the formation of a national government answerable to a popularly elected assembly. 'You ask me', Churchill replied, 'to repudiate the Balfour Declaration and to stop immigration. This is not in my power, and it is not my wish.' After extolling the idea of a Jewish national centre in Palestine, he turned to the second, 'safeguard' clause in the Declaration and what he described as 'the sacredness of Arab and religious rights'. 'I am sorry', he told his petitioners, 'that you regard the second part as valueless. It is vital to you and you should hold and claim it firmly. If one promise stands so does the other. We shall faithfully fulfil both.' As for a Palestinian parliament, he was at least frank: 'The present form of government will continue for many years. Step by step we shall develop representative institutions leading to full self-government, but our children's children will have passed away before that is accomplished.'[17]

Here, in Churchill's reply, lay the dilemma that was to face the Palestinians for most of the Mandate. They were trapped in a constitutional blind alley. It was no good their going direct to the heart of the matter—the basic unworkability of the Mandate—for Britain had neither the 'wish' nor the 'power' to give it up. It did not wish to do so, for such was British policy, and it did not have the power because, it claimed, it was merely performing the 'sacred trust' which the League of Nations had conferred upon it. That august body had early ruled that 'the two obligations imposed on the Mandatory are in no sense irreconcilable'. Armed with this verdict,

Britain countered Arab assertions that they were. The Arabs could of course take their case over Britain's head to the League itself—only to find that the Permanent Mandates Commission was not competent to question the basic provisions of the Mandate.

They got no further with the indirect approach, for, even when due allowance was made for Churchillian rhetoric, it was clearly the British government's intention that they should wait a very long time for truly self-governing institutions. All they could do, then, was to put their faith in the safeguard clause and in Britain's promise that it would faithfully fulfil its obligations to both Jews and Arabs. Those obligations *were* irreconcilable, and in 1937 a British Royal Commission formally acknowledged it. But since, in the meantime, Britain had been consistently fulfilling the first obligation at the expense of the second, the Arabs had indeed come to regard the safeguard clause as 'valueless'.

It took sixteen years for the British officially to acknowledge it, but 'the slaughter of 1921' should have been warning enough: if a society has no means of expressing itself by legitimate constitutional means, it resorts to other means which, if it did have them, it would certainly condemn. Indeed, in the opinion of a British intelligence officer in Palestine, Churchill's visit and his outright insistence that he intended to deny to the Arabs the democratic privileges which he regarded as the birthright of every Englishman, lit the fuse of the Jaffa explosion. 'He upheld the Zionist cause and treated the Arab demands like those of a negligible opposition to be put off by a few polite phrases and treated like bad children . . . if policy is not modified the outbreak of today may become a revolution tomorrow.'[18]

In fact, Churchill appeared to have second thoughts. In June 1922, eight months after the Haycraft Commission published its findings, he laid before the Zionist and Palestinian representatives in London proposals for a legislative council. This, surely, would provide a constitutional alternative to violence. The proposals came in the form of a White Paper which made certain concessions to the Arab point of view. It reaffirmed the Balfour Declaration and insisted that a Jewish National Home would be founded in Palestine as of right and not of sufferance; it claimed that Arab apprehensions were 'partly' based on 'exaggerated interpretations' of the Declaration. But there was definitely to be no Jewish State. There was to be no subordination of the Arab population, language or culture. But what kind of legislative council was it to be? Clearly, the last thing the Zionists really wanted was that all the inhabitants of Palestine should have an equal say in running the country. This was embarrassing for them because they were supposedly coming to Palestine as the standard-bearers of Western civilization. To be sure, they did not reject self-governing institutions outright. They persuaded their imperial sponsor to offer a very limited form of them. With the backing of Lloyd George, the Prime Minister, and Lord Balfour, Weizmann had impressed on Churchill that representative government would have spelled the end of the National Home in Palestine. So, together with its twelve elected members—eight Moslems, two Christians and two Jews—the council was to include eleven appointed officials. The Palestinians rejected the offer. In their view—and leaving aside the fundamental objections of principle—this combination was likely to produce a permanent majority in favour of government policies which, in spite of the White Paper's reassurances, they considered completely unacceptable. All it would mean, they thought, was that the 'Zionist policy of the government will be carried out under a constitutional guise, whereas at present it is illegal, against the rights and wishes of the people and maintained by force of arms alone'.[19]

This was the first important instance of an attitude of mind which is often held, even by sympathetic outsiders, to have contributed more than anything else to the disasters that eventually overtook the Palestinian people. This standing on principle—however just the principle—this rejection of compromise, this forever saying 'no', has been judged the most purblind intransigence. 'Appalling blunder', says British historian Christopher Sykes, who argues that the Palestinians' 'pathetic obstinacy' ensured that they never got representative government even in a crude form and as a result could not avoid the evils of arbitrary rule.[20] A contemporary Israeli scholar, General Yehoshafat Harkabi, goes further. He believes that 'had the Arabs accepted what the Legislative Council offered in the 1920's Israel would not have existed. . . . Arab instransigence', he goes on, 'forced partition and Jewish statehood. It is an irony of history that the Arabs should be counted among the founding fathers of the Jewish state.'[21]

It is certainly arguable that had the Palestinian leadership accepted the Council they might have fared better; there was much hostility to Zionism in the ranks of the British administration, and some, at least, of the eleven officials might have taken the Arab part. The argument cannot be disproved. But, in its harsher forms, it is certainly unfair. The Palestinians were not to know at the time—though their intuitions were accurate enough—that subsequent events would furnish an impressive counter-argument. When, in 1935, the British government did offer a limited measure of self-government which, though by no means wholly impartial, was much less weighted in the Zionists' favour, it was they, not the Arabs, who rushed to bury this timid experiment in democracy. The Zionist Congress announced its 'categorical rejection'[22] of the offer, and when, at Westminster, the Mother of Parliaments rejected it too, the Zionist press hailed this as 'a great Jewish victory'.[23] The Arabs had at least been ready to consider the offer. In fact, the celebrated 'Arab refusal' has always been welcomed by the Zionists, for it has given them their most effective moral alibi—their *ein brera*, their 'no-choice' but to fight the Arabs, fight them again and again. And if, in the process, they gained more than they planned or hoped for, that was their good fortune. The Arabs, they contended, only had themselves to blame. General Harkabi seems to be hoist with his own petard when, fifty-two years after this early Arab rejection, and in the wake of the fourth Arab-Israeli war in a generation, he could still advise against a settlement of the ever-expanding Middle East conflict:

> We must define our position and lay down basic principles for a settlement. Our demands should be moderate and balanced, and appear to be reasonable. But in fact they must involve such conditions as to ensure that the enemy rejects them. Then we should manoeuvre and allow him to define his own position, and reject a settlement on the basis of a compromise solution. We should then publish his demands as embodying unreasonable extremism.[24]

In rejecting the council, the Palestinians were not rejecting conciliation. Resistance—merely civil disobedience or outright violence—did not seem to them to be a serious alternative. This is not to say that they had not considered it. The Palestinians never managed to throw up the kind of leadership in which they could place much confidence, but, before he became Mufti and the most influential of the leaders they did have, Haj Amin Husseini had in 1920 been sentenced by the British for incitement to violence. There were those who argued that violence did pay. Before the Jaffa riots, Shaikh Arslan, a Syrian leader in exile, wrote to his friends in the town to tell them that just such an eruption in Palestine would be far more effective than sending a delegation to the West.[25] The Arab Executive, semi-official spokesman for the Palestinian community, condemned the riots—but exploited them, for publicity purposes, as a manifestation of the hatred which Zionism inspired among the people. There was an attempt, albeit embryonic and short-lived, to set up a guerilla movement. The Palestinians were deeply impressed by Kemal Ataturk's triumphant repudiation—in so far as it affected Turkey—of the same post-war allied *diktat* under which they laboured: 'learn from Kemal, and follow in his footsteps', his admirers urged.[26] And it cannot have been lost on anyone that, though it was to be abused and unworkable in practice, an official policy of limiting immigration in accordance with so-called 'economic absorptive capacity' was a direct result of the Jaffa explosion.

At the Fourth Arab Congress in 1921, it was resolved that political, not violent, means should be used for pressing Palestinian demands. Young militants opposed this, but the Arab Executive and the traditional leadership called for law and order and promised the government that they would work for it. They listened to the advice, among others, of a group of pro-Arab British politicians who achieved prominence in 1921. Their advice, which commanded great influence, was that violence would make the Palestinians odious to the outside world and therefore unworthy of the self-rule they were asking Britain to grant them. Haj Amin, once he had become Mufti and President of the Supreme Moslem Council, completely changed his stand on violence. And on the whole, the rest of the ruling élite, for all their bitter rivalries and militant attitudinizing, put their faith in their own powers of persuasion, in their personal dealings with the Mandatory authorities. Their faith was misplaced. By 1923 they had ample evidence of that. Whenever resistance did manifest itself, they usually intervened in a bid to restrain it. The Jaffa riots were but the first of several occasions on which the notables went out with the security forces to appeal for calm. They also undermined various forms of organized passive resistance—strikes, the boycott of Jewish goods, the non-payment of taxes or a ban on accepting government employment—which the majority of the people tended to favour.[27] They would put their case to a sympathetic British quarter in what—according to the first High Commissioner—they saw as a calculated alternative to the violence favoured by the lower classes.[28] In 1923, Jamal Husseini, secretary of the Arab Executive, told a British official that there were two ways to secure Palestinian political rights: 'either by constitutional means or by revolution; that the first was to be preferred though the second would give them what they justly claimed in six months'.[29] Even in the growing tensions of the early thirties the High Commissioner, Sir Arthur Wauchope, warmly praised the Mufti for the moderation he showed in spite of his 'fears that the criticisms of his many opponents that he is too British may weaken his influence in the country'.[30]

Not only did they oppose violence, but—partly encouraged by the difficulties Zionism faced in the late twenties—they actually grew more conciliatory, and seemed ready to accept proposals for limited self-government of the kind which they had so firmly rejected in 1922. In early 1929, impressed by this moderation, the High Commissioner advised London that it would be difficult to resist demands for a legislative council. The Arabs, he said, were no longer demanding the abrogation of the Balfour Declaration and the Mandate, and their fear of Zionism had abated.[31] From a representational and democratic standpoint, the legislature he proposed was even less attractive than the 1922 version. But the Arab Executive acquiesced in it and, in protracted negotiations with him, discussed the delicate business of bringing it into being.

The People Choose Violence

VIOLENCE ERUPTED ALL THE SAME. It destroyed the negotiations. It came in August 1929 and, like the Jaffa explosion of eight years before, it was the sudden, blind fury of the mob. It erupted in spite of the politicians. It was the people's instinctive response to what they saw as the violence of the other side. For was not the Zionist programme, relentlessly pressed forward under the British régime, a form of violence? True, the Zionists did not rely on armed strength. They relied on the British; their persuasions worked where the Arabs' did not. Nevertheless, they were already developing military organizations. Jabotinsky's Jewish Legion had been disbanded by the British; but in the early Mandate years, he set up a militia for the defence of Jewish settlements; this was the *Haganah*, out of which the Israeli army eventually grew. The ideals of the *Betar* also flourished. The *Betar*—the name of the fortress in which Bar Kokhba made his last stand against the Romans—was another of Jabotinsky's creations. It was a youth organization intended to set an example of *hadar* (a Zionist concept of honour and chivalry) and it made a deep impression on the younger generation. One of its leaders wrote a newspaper column called 'Journal of a Fascist'.

But if, at this stage, there was no outright violence, no actual fighting, there was a ceaseless Judaization of Palestine by every other means. The classic techniques of earlier days were broadened, intensified and refined. Immigration, the cornerstone of the whole edifice, had in effect slipped out of control of the British administration and into the hands of the Zionist Labour Federation. The Federation represented 3 per cent of the people of Palestine—creating an anomaly of which a visiting British expert said that 'power has been, more or less completely, divorced from responsibility'.[32] At 156,000 in 1929, the *Yishuv* had doubled in ten years. A relatively crowded little country had the highest rate of population increase in the world, outstripping even pioneering countries like Australia and the Argentine. The 4 per cent, or thereabouts, of Palestine which the Jews had acquired represented about 14 per cent of its cultivable area.[33] It was not just the achievements of the newcomers that so alarmed the Arabs, it was the steadily unfolding evidence of the fully-fledged statehood they planned: their 'conquest' of land and labour, their insistence on Hebrew, their separate schools and hospitals, their self-segregation—residential, economic, social and cultural—and their expulsion of the Arabs from every institution they established. This is a veteran's vivid recollection of the atmosphere of the early Mandate years:

> I remember being one of the first of our comrades to go to London after the First World War. . . . There I became a socialist. . . . When I joined the socialist students—English, Irish, Jewish, Chinese, Indian, African—we found that we were all under English domination or rule. And even here, in these intimate surroundings, I had to fight my friends on the issue of Jewish socialism, to defend the fact that I would not accept Arabs in my trade union, the Histadrut; to defend preaching to housewives that they not buy at Arab stores; to defend the fact that we stood guard at orchards to prevent Arab workers from getting jobs there. . . . To pour kerosene on Arab tomatoes; to attack Jewish housewives in the markets and smash the Arab eggs they had bought; to praise to the skies the Keren Kayemet (Jewish National Fund) that sent Hankin to Beirut to buy land from absentee effendis and to throw the *fellahin* (peasants) off the land—to buy dozens of dunums from an Arab is permitted, but to sell, God forbid, one Jewish dunum to an Arab is prohibited; to take Rothschild, the incarnation of capitalism, as a socialist and to name him the 'benefactor'—to do all that was not easy. And despite the fact that we did it—maybe we had no choice—I wasn't happy about it.[34]

Such were the general, underlying causes of the violence that erupted. They were essentially the same as those which had produced 'the slaughter of 1921'. The specific cause, the immediate trigger, was different.

The Wailing Wall, the last remnant of the Temple, is the most sacred of Jewish shrines. But the Wall is a symbol for the Arabs too. It could not be otherwise, for the massive platform on which Herod raised the temple destroyed by the Romans in A.D. 70 is the same on which the two great mosques of al-Aqsa and the Dome of the Rock stand. The Wailing Wall is actually sacred to Moslems; they call it the Burak, the name of the Prophet's horse, and believe that it was from there that he embarked on his night journey to heaven. The whole Wailing Wall compound is also Moslem property.

Jewish devotional rights at the Wall had since time immemorial been governed by the so-called status quo, a repertoire of agreements and reciprocal adjustments between the three great faiths established in the city. The status quo had been supervised by the Moslem temporal authorities. As the Jewish population increased, there developed at the Wall devotions of a more formal and communal kind. The worshippers sought to chip away at the status quo. They introduced innovations there, bringing benches, chairs and other appurtenances, or tried to secure the right, suggestive of ownership, to pave the passageway below the Wall. But it was only with the rise of Zionism that they began to press, quite openly, for a complete takeover. For the Zionists, the Wall was to become less and less the reminder, essentially religious in significance, of past glories and past sufferings, and more and more the political symbol of the new Jewish nation-in-the-making—or, as the *Jewish Chronicle* put it, 'a gauge of Jewish prestige in Palestine'.[35] Inevitably, the Arabs came to vest in the preservation of the status quo all their passionate determination to keep Palestine for themselves, while the Jews saw in its erosion evidence of their progress in wresting it from them.

When British forces entered Palestine in 1917, General Allenby, their commander, solemnly declared that in matters of religion the status quo was all. But the Zionists were quick to challenge his proclamation. One of the first acts of a Jewish detachment with the British army was to hold a 'public service' at the Wall. Weizmann wrote to Lord Balfour asking for the 'handing over the Wailing Wall', asserting that 'our most sacred monument, in our most sacred city, is in the hands of some doubtful Maghreb religious community'.[36] But all the stepped-up efforts which the Zionists now made to acquire land and houses near the Wall came to nothing. No *Waqf* (religious foundation) property, let alone this one, linked as it was to the third most holy place in Islam, could be sold to the Jews, who had designs on the western wall of the Haram al-Sharif, the Noble Sanctuary. The Zionists were not deterred. On the first anniversary of the Balfour Declaration, they insisted on a public demonstration in Jerusalem. The Jewish detachment with the British army behaved so provocatively during its visit to the Wall that the British military authorities eventually forbade them entry. When some Jewish soldiers disobeyed the order and marched in the direction of the Wall, they were court-martialled and the entire detachment was disbanded. In April 1920 Arabs and Jews were killed in the first major clash in Jerusalem. Not long after that Sir Alfred Mond (later Lord Melchett) declared that he would 'concentrate the remainder of his energies on building a great edifice where once stood the Temple of Solomon'.[37] The statement gained notoriety among the Arabs, who found in it confirmation of their fears that, fantastic though it might seem, this really was the ultimate Zionist ambition. There followed an endless series of incidents, childish in themselves, with each side trying to assert itself in the Wailing Wall compound at the expense of the other. In general, the underlying issue was ownership. The Jews were essentially on the offensive, trying to establish the possession which they did not have; the Arabs retaliated with various initiatives, deeply annoying to the Jews, designed to emphasize that possession was, and would remain, theirs. Britain, faithful to the status quo, backed the Arabs and when, on the Day of Atonement, 1928, Jewish worshippers attempted to introduce a partition screen they did so in express defiance of the Mandatory authorities. After this incident, Jewish exasperation grew fast; the whole community was aroused, and, characteristically, it was from the unbelieving majority, especially the young, that the loudest clamour came. Jabotinsky and his right-wing militants led the field. Their mouthpiece, *Doar Hayom*, the Hebrew newspaper with the widest circulation, called for 'revolt and insubordination'.[38] The Arab press was just as inflammatory. Throughout the summer of 1929 the tension rose alarmingly. Vincent Sheehan, an American journalist living in the city at the time, said that 'you could stick your hand out in the air and feel it rising'. In his book, *Personal History*, he records what happened when it finally reached boiling-point. He begins with his diary entry for Thursday, 15 August:

> Yesterday was the Eve of Tisha ba'Av. . . . Today is the actual fast itself: commemoration of the destruction of the Temple. The day is particularly associated with the Wailing Wall; and with the new Jewish Agency just formed, all the Wailing Wall propaganda going full tilt, the Arabs in a rare state of anxiety, the situation was ripe for anything. Trouble, trouble, and more trouble. There will be plenty. I knew

nothing about it all—didn't even know Tisha ba'Av was so near—when Miss X (a young Jewish-American journalist) arrived at the Hospice at three in the afternoon. . . . Said she had to go to the Wailing Wall and write a telegram about it for *The Times* . . . would I go with her and help? I couldn't understand why, but she said there was going to be a 'bust-up'. . . . she said the word had been passed round and hundreds of Haluzim (rugged pioneer youth from the agricultural settlements) were coming in during the afternoon and evening from the colonies and Tel-Aviv, ready to fight. I simply couldn't believe all this. She said the Haluzim would be armed—'three quarters of them'—and it would be a good thing if there was a row at the Wall to 'show that we are here.' I didn't believe a damned word of it; too fantastic; but I told her I'd be ready to go along at five o'clock if she would come back. She was inconceivably cynical and flippant about the whole thing; said a row would be a very good thing for the Zionist cause, arouse world Jews and increase contributions to the new Agency. Before we reached the Wall it was evident that the police were well prepared. . . . There was no excitement whatever, only about half a dozen religious Jews and Jewesses (Oriental) praying and weeping against the Wall. Towards six, a little before, we went away to the Hotel St John for a glass of beer. Sat there a bit, talking; I couldn't understand her point of view at all, and tried to find out. When we returned to the Wall, a little before seven, everything had changed. There was a dense crowd, made up chiefly of Haluzim, in the little area in the front of the Wall. A Yemenite Jew was chanting the lamentations, from the Book, while four other Yemenites sat around him, weeping and rocking themselves back and forth. These seemed to be the most sincerely religious manifestants present—they paid no attention to their surroundings, but only to their lament. The rest of that crowd was spoiling for a fight. The crowd I was in, that is, farther off, at the end of the Wall before the Grand Mufti's house, the service was being read by a Cantor (Sephardic, I believe) who stopped and looked around angrily at the slightest noise. Since noises were continually being made, he was continually stopping, but always had to begin again, as he discovered that the sounds came from zealous but irreverent Haluzim. . . . All the people who choked the area seemed to be either people like myself, who had come out of curiosity or interest, and Haluzim who were—as Miss X said—'rarin' to go.' The Yemenites went on weeping and praying throughout; they noticed nobody and nobody noticed them. Strange scene.

Saw Halkin, the poet: very excited. So was everybody I spoke to (Warschawer was there, the most peaceful of people, and even he was angry). What seems to have upset them so is the new door in the Wall. I actually saw one revolver, but don't know who the man was who had it (hip pocket). There were only two actual 'incidents'. In the first a Christian Arab whom I did not see was accused of mocking at the services: I heard cries of 'Notzri!' (Nazarene) and saw the Haluzim shoving, but the police took the man out safely. Then there was an Arab in white clothes who walked through the place three times—did nothing, simply walked. I believe he was unmolested the first time, although there were angry murmurs. The second time he came through without difficulty. The third time he appeared, the police wouldn't let him go on—made him turn back. Very wise of them, for that crowd was in no mood to stand any kind of 'incident' without serious trouble. But in this incident the shouts of the Haluzim must certainly have been far more disturbing to the prayers of the religious Jews than the Arab's progress through the street would have been.

. . . Jews parading again today. Extreme provocation, but the Arabs are doing nothing. Small army of Haluzim—these precious Maccabees—passed half an hour ago, on their way to the Wall, with a flag, the Zionist national flag, I suppose, but I couldn't see it: it was furled. Shouts and cheers come from down there; the whole thing makes me very nervous. . . . The young heroes who passed a while ago were guarded heavily by the police; mounted police officers in front of them and behind them, with policemen on foot marching alongside them. The material for an awful three-cornered fight. What an exhibition of imbecility the whole thing is!

Saturday, Aug. 17th. The Jewish holy day passed off without disaster, but now we are in the midst of a Moslem one, the Prophet's Birthday. Yesterday a big crowd of Moslems came into the Wailing Wall area and tore up the sacred books, pulled petitions out of the stones of the Wall, etc. Might have been expected; was, in fact, inevitable. No Jews there; nobody hurt. Jews will be in terrible state of excitement, just the same.

Sunday, Aug 18th. Jewish boy hurt in a row between Jews and Arabs yesterday; feeling gets worse all the time. . . .

Wednesday, Aug. 21st. The Mizrachi boy . . . died yesterday. They are going to make a martyr of him, as sure as fate. . . .

Friday, Aug. 23rd. The situation here is awful. Everyday I expect the worst. It can't go on like this without an outbreak. The Mizrachi boy . . . who was stabbed by an Arab after a row in the football field (it seems to have been a row started by the Jewish boys, or so they tell me), died on Tuesday. Wednesday morning was the funeral. Of course, the precious Maccabees had to seize the opportunity; fine chance to link up everything with the Wailing Wall and the general agitation. Two or three thousand of these heroes gathered with flags and tried to head their march through the Jaffa Gate into the Arab city. Feeling has been running so high among the Arabs since these fools raised their flag at the wall of the mosque that anything might have happened. Police barred the way, therefore, and the Jews made a rush at their cordon. Police beat them back with clubs. About twenty-five Jews were injured, none very seriously.

After I had finished the last entry in my diary I went downstairs to lunch and heard a new crop of disquieting rumours. At about half-past one I went out to get some cigarettes, and the old Arab porter at the Hospice told me the Grand Mufti had passed a short time before, going out to speak to the crowds around the city walls. Since the Mufti was not given to public appearance—I had never once seen him, although I lived within five minutes' walk of the Haram and his house—this seemed serious. I ran back into the Hospice for my hat, found a friend of mine (a British official), and went out with him to see what was to be seen. We walked up the narrow street, through excited or terrified groups of people, to the Damascus Gate. There we found ourselves in the midst of a mob of country Arabs, who seemed to be in a frenzy of excitement. Long yells of 'Islamiya!' were going up. We got through these people without trouble—my companion spoke Arabic well—and reached the corner of the street called, I believe, the Street of the Prophet. The mob was gathering directly in front of us, and it was certain that somebody, somewhere, would soon be shedding blood. The houses on the other side of the mob, opposite us, belonged to a group of Georgian Jews, as I afterwards learned; the attention of the crowd was directed towards them. In front of the Jewish houses were ranged six policemen, armed only with short truncheons. The mob gathered with incredible speed—it could, not have taken more than two or three minutes for them to get dense in front of us. The long yells that filled the air were enough to curdle one's blood.

A man dressed as a city Arab noticed us standing there and thrust us almost by force into a doorway. 'Stand here, stand here for God's sake,' he said. 'These fellahin will kill you.' We stood in the doorway, and he took his place in front of us, shouting hoarsely at the mob, telling them to go back, that all was well. They paid no attention to him. They rushed towards the police, who laid about them valiantly with their truncheons; but what good were truncheons at such a time? The fellahin were flourishing sticks, clubs and knives, and, as is the way of mobs, they rushed on regardless of the efforts to stop them. Some rushed under horses' bellies, others squirmed through between the inadequate six; in another moment we heard smashing and a long scream. There was nothing we could do but run, which we did. . . .

I returned to the Damascus Gate about a quarter of an hour after I had left it. When I got there the Arab mob had vanished (so little time is required to accomplish the most irrevocable acts); there were shattered glass and torn-up wood, débris of all sorts in the street, and before the Georgian Jewish houses and on their stone doorsteps there was blood.

The Jews of Jerusalem outnumbered the Arabs two to one. It was a matter of common knowledge that the Jews possessed firearms; the Arabs did not. Under these conditions it seemed likely that the Jewish superiority in numbers and equipment, as well as their organization and centralization, would enable them to do great damage among the Arabs for a day or two if they so desired, and from what I had seen and heard the previous week I thought this was probably the wish of a good many among them. . . .

. . . The disorders of Friday resulted in many deaths among both Jews and Arabs . . . and the impulse of murder continued for a week. At the end of the terror the official roll for Jerusalem was: 29 Jews and 38 Arabs killed, 43 Jews and 51 Arabs wounded. Here, as in Haifa, the Arabs got considerably the worst of it, but it seems clear . . . that the casualties inflicted by Jews were chiefly in self-defence. . . .

The horrors of Friday in Jerusalem were followed by something much worse: the ghastly outbreak at Hebron, where sixty-four Jews of the old-fashioned religious community were slaughtered and fifty-four of them wounded. Hebron was one of the four holy cities of Judaism, and had had a small, constant Jewish population since medieval days. These were not Zionists at all; a more innocent and harmless group of people could not have been found in Palestine; many of them were Oriental Jews, and all were religious. They had had nothing to do with the Zionist excesses, and had lived in amity with their Arab neighbours up to that day. But when the Arabs of Hebron—an unruly lot, at best—heard that Arabs were being killed by Jews in Jerusalem, and that the Mosque of Omar was in danger, they went mad. The British police force at Hebron was inadequate—indeed, it could scarcely be said to have existed, for there was but one British officer there with a tiny native staff. In spite of the remarkable exertions and courage of this one officer (Mr. R. O. Cafferata), the Jewish houses were rushed by the mob, and there was an hour of slashing, killing, stabbing, burning and looting. Among the Jewish victims were some American boys who had arrived only a short time before to study at the rabbinical college. Eight or nine of them died at Hebron, and an equal number suffered severe wounds.

I cannot, at this late date, go through all the story of that week; it has been told over and over again. The horrors of Hebron were not repeated elsewhere, but an Arab mob attack on the religious Jews of Safad, on the following Thursday, was sufficiently terrible to be classified as another massacre. In Haifa, where the Jews were predominantly of the modern Zionist type and occupied an excellent strategic position at the top of the hill, the Arabs had much the worst of it. The same was true in some of the colonies; others were almost wiped out. At the end of the disturbances the official British casualty lists showed 207 dead and 279 wounded among the population of Palestine, of which the dead included 87 Arabs (Christian and Moslem) and 120 Jews, the wounded 181 Arabs and 198 Jews.

The effort to be an efficient, unemotional newspaper correspondent was difficult to the point of impossibility. Living as I did, without sleep and without rest, eating little, and that at the weirdest hours, I should probably have collapsed in time simply from physical exhaustion. But there was a great deal more to it than that. I was bitterly indignant with the Zionists for having, as I believed, brought on this disaster; I was shocked into hysteria by the ferocity of the Arab anger; and I was aghast at the inadequacy of the British government. I knew that the Moslem authorities were trying to quell the storm, and that the British officials were doing their best against appalling difficulties; I also assumed that the responsible Zionist leaders (none of whom were in Palestine then) had done what they could. But all around me were the visible evidences of their failure. Although I had spent a good part of my life amid scenes of violence and was no stranger to the sight of blood and dying men, I had never overcome my loathing for the spectacle even when it seemed, as in some of the conflicts I had witnessed, compelled by historical necessity. But here, in this miserable little country no bigger, in relation to the rest of the world, than the tip of your finger in relation to your body, I could see no historical necessity whatever. The country was tiny and was already inhabited; why couldn't the Zionists leave it alone? It would never hold enough Jews to make even a beginning towards the solution of the Jewish problem; it would always be a prey to such ghastly horrors as those I saw every day and every night: religion, the eternal intransigence of religion, ensured that the problem could never be solved. The Holy Land seemed as near an approximation of hell on earth as I had ever seen.[39]

Britain Surrenders to the Zionists

Britain reacted to the outbreak in the time-honoured way—with the despatch of a commission of inquiry. Sir Walter Shaw, like Sir Thomas Haycraft before him, ruled essentially in the Arabs' favour. There had been nothing planned or premeditated about the massacres. The Mufti had indeed rallied Arab and Moslem opinion in defence of the Wall. That was legitimate. True, he could and should have restrained some of the extremer forms of Arab emotionalism which accompanied his campaign, but it was not he who set the mob on the Jews. It was the custom for the peasants to come into Jerusalem every Friday and if, on that fatal 25 August, they came armed with clubs, knives and sticks, it had not been at his urging. There were agitators at work in the country, but they acted independently of him. One of them had delivered a message to the headmen of the village of Kabalan near Nablus. It read: 'Fighting will take place on Friday next, the 18 Rabia, between the Jews and Moslems. All who are of the Moslem religion should come to Jerusalem to help. Peace be on you and your young men.' The message bore the Mufti's signature—but it turned out to be a forgery. The bloodiest outbreaks occurred in just those parts of Palestine where his influence was the weakest. In Jerusalem itself, the speeches which he and other religious dignitaries made during and after the Friday prayers had a distinctly pacifying character—so much so, in fact, that some of their hearers felt moved to ascend the platform and exhort the crowd to take no notice of the speakers, who were unfaithful to the Moslem cause. 'An appeal by the Mufti,' Shaw averred, 'issued on this date to his co-religionists, to arm themselves "with mercy, wisdom and patience for verily God is with those who bear themselves in patience", was, in our view, having regard to the outbreaks which had already taken place, to the highly dangerous temper of the people, and to the rumours of designs upon the Holy Places which at that time were flying from lip to lip, a timely and courageous appeal and one which, on the whole, had its effect in checking further outbreaks.'[40]

If the Commission had to single out one immediate and specific cause of the violence, it said, that would be the Jewish demonstration at the Wailing Wall; as for the general causes, it concluded that, without the political and economic grievances of the Arabs against the Mandate as a whole, 'the outbreak would not have occurred, or had it occurred at all, would not have attained the proportions which in fact it did reach'.[41]

The Zionists were stunned by Shaw's findings. But nine months later the verdict of a second commission, led by Sir John Hope-Simpson, angered them even more. His task had been to investigate those deeper sources of Arab unrest, immigration and land settlement, and his opinion, even more forcefully expressed than Shaw's, was that they should be drastically curtailed. And a legislative council should be set up.

Arab violence did seem to pay. But there was uproar in the Zionist camp, on both sides of the Atlantic, and through the application of heavy pressure at the metropolitan centre of power it managed to induce the British government to repudiate everything which its two distinguished emissaries had urged upon it. In a letter to Dr Weizmann—the Black Letter, the Arabs called it—the Prime Minister, Ramsay MacDonald, surrendered to Zionist demands. Immigration and land settlement would continue unabated; negotiations for a legislative council, suspended with the riots, were not to be seriously resumed for years.

Weizmann's diplomacy was still Zionism's main weapon. Arab violence was no match for it after all. Yet, more systematically and purposefully used, it might have been. 'It is difficult to determine', writes the Israeli historian Yehoshua Porath of the Jaffa explosion, 'what would have happened had the violent outbreaks not ceased, but one cannot escape the impression that certain developments, favourable from the Arab point of view, might well have come about ten years earlier than they did.'[42] After 'the slaughter of 1921' the attempt to redress the balance of British policy in the Arabs' favour had failed, but at least the Zionists had been obliged to acquiesce in the attempt. After 1929 they were able to crush the attempt in embryo; for by then they had the strength and self-confidence to do it, and, through successive governments, British policy was increasingly taking on that sanctity of precedent and tradition which was so difficult to disavow.

In the 1920s, conciliation by the politicians got nowhere. The resistance of the people, fanatic but unsustained, massive but aimless, merely raised hopes that were quickly dashed. Germinating in the mind of an itinerant preacher was the idea that there should be new leaders, and radical new methods.

Notes

1. Haycraft, Sir Thomas, *Commission of Inquiry into the Palestine Disturbances of May 1921*, Cmd. 1540, p. 44. This whole account of the violence is drawn from the Haycraft report.
2. *Ibid.*, p. 27.
3. *Ibid.*, p. 54.
4. *Ibid.*, p. 53.
5. Porath, Yehoshua, *The Emergence of the Palestine-Arab National Movement 1918–1929*, Frank Cass, London, 1974.
6. *Ibid.*, p. 56.
7. *Ibid.*, pp. 56–7.
8. *Ibid.*, p. 45.
9. Ingrams, *Palestine Papers 1917–1922, Seeds of Conflict, op. cit.*, p. 122.
10. *Ibid.*, p. 122.
11. See Cohen, Aharon, *Israel and the Arab World*, Funk and Wagnalls, New York, 1970, p. 60.
12. *Current History*, New York, October 1921, Vol. XV.
13. *The Contemporary Review*, London, May 1920, No. 653.
14. *Jewish Observer and Middle East Review*, London, 8 May 1959.
15. See Porath, *op. cit.*, p. 53.
16. *Ibid.*, p. 125.
17. See Jeffreys, *Palestine: The Reality, op. cit.*, p. 456.
18. See Ingrams, *op. cit.*, pp. 123–4.
19. Barbour, *Nisi Dominus, op. cit.*, p. 111.
20. Sykes, Christopher, *Crossroads to Israel*, Collins, London, 1965, pp. 83, 124.
21. Harkabi, Yehoshafat, *Time Bomb in the Middle East*, Friendship Press, New York, 1969, p. 19.
22. *Report on the Conditions in Palestine, 1935*, H.M.S.O., London, 1935, p. 19.
23. Lord Peel, *Royal Commission Report*, 22 June 1937, Cmd. 5479, p. 92.
24. *Maariv* (Israeli newspaper), 2 November 1973.
25. Porath, *op. cit.*, p. 131.
26. *Ibid.*, p. 159.
27. Al-Kayyali, *A History of Modern Palestine* (Arabic), *op. cit.*, pp. 178, 195, 210, 273; Allush, Naji, *Arab Resistance in Palestine* (Arabic), Vanguard House, Beirut, 1969, p. 113.
28. Al-Kayyali, *op. cit.*, p. 195.
29. *Ibid.*, p. 208.
30. *Ibid.*, p. 285.
31. Porath, *op. cit.*, p. 255.
32. Campbell, Sir John, see Shaw, Sir Walter, *Commission on the Palestine Disturbances of August 1929*, Cmd. 3530, p. 104.
33. Hope-Simpson, Sir John, *Report to the British Government*, 20 October 1930, Cmd. 3686, p. 19.

34. Hacohen, David, *Haaretz* (Israeli newspaper), 15 November 1969.
35. See Sheehan, Vincent, *Personal History*, Doubleday, Doran and Co., Inc., New York, 1935, p. 390.
36. Tibawi, A. L., *Jerusalem, Its Place in Islam and Arab History*, Institute for Palestine Studies, Beirut, 1969, p. 32.
37. Porath, *op. cit.*, p. 259.
38. Shaw Commission, *op. cit.*, p. 45.
39. Sheehan, *op. cit.*, pp. 392–408.
40. Shaw Commission, *op. cit.*, p. 78.
41. *Ibid.*, pp. 96, 155.
42. Porath, *op. cit.*, p. 13.

3 · THE ARAB REBELLION, 1935–1939

Shaikh Izzeddin Qassam—the First *Fedayi*

On 12 November 1935 a grey-bearded sexagenarian, wearing the turban and cloak of the Moslem cleric, presided over a secret meeting in the old slum quarter of Haifa. Shaikh Izzeddin Qassam realized that he could delay no longer: his hour had come. The British had been in Palestine eighteen years; their rule, resented from the outset, had become quite intolerable in its disregard of Arab interests. Legal—not to mention illegal—Jewish immigration had reached the record figure of 61,844 a year. Land sales were increasing; in 1933 there had been 673 of them, 1,178 in 1934. More and more peasants were losing their livelihood; yet already, in 1931, it had been estimated that 30,000 peasant families, 22 per cent of the rural population, were landless.[1] Their average *per capita* income was £7 a year, compared with £34 for the Jewish farmers who replaced them. And the peasant family's average indebtedness—£25 to £30—was about the same as its average earnings.[2] Driven from the land, the peasants flocked to the rapidly growing cities in search of work. Many of them ended up as labourers building houses for the immigrants they loathed and feared. They lived in squalor. In old Haifa there were 11,000 of them crammed into hovels built of petrol-tins, which had neither water-supply nor rudimentary sanitation. Others, without families, slept in the open. Such conditions contrasted humiliatingly with the handsome dwellings the peasants were putting up for the well-to-do newcomers, or even with the Jewish working men's quarters furnished by Jewish building societies.[3] They earned half, or just a quarter, the wage of their Jewish counterparts, and Hebrew Labour exclusivism was gradually depriving them of even that. By 1935, an economic crisis, partly the result of uncontrolled immigration, produced Arab unemployment on a catastrophic scale. There could be no more fertile ground than this dispossessed urban peasantry for the ideals that Shaikh Qassam had assiduously sown—ideals for which, that November evening, he and his followers resolved to fight and die, and would do so within a week.

His whole life had seemed a preparation for this supreme self-sacrifice. A Syrian of devout and cultured parentage, he studied at al-Azhar, Cairo's great centre of Moslem learning; he sat at the feet of Muhammad Abdu, the famous scholar who preached that, through a reformed and reinvigorated Islam, the Arabs could rise to the challenge of the modern world. On his return to Syria, he did not confine himself only to teaching at the religious college of Ibrahim bin Adham, he also took part in various patriotic movements. He was a military leader in one of the uprisings against French rule in Syria. Condemned to death in that country, he fled to Haifa in 1922. There he taught, preached, did charitable work and set up a night school for the illiterate. Appointed 'marriage steward' for the Haifa Moslem court, he attended wedding festivals in the surrounding countryside. He moved easily among peasants and workers; he knew their intimate thoughts. Everywhere he warned of the gravity of the Zionist invasion, he urged a true spirit of patriotism, the ending of petty feuds and divisions, the emulation of the heroes of early Islam. Verses from the Koran, particularly those which called for struggle and sacrifice, were constantly on his lips. And everywhere, but especially in the mosques, he looked for disciples among the pious and God-fearing. Over the years, with great care and patience, he gathered about himself a band of followers. There were about 800 of them altogether; 200 of them received military training. They pledged to give their lives for Palestine. They were expected to supply their own arms, and to contribute all else they could to the cause. Their training was done by stealth at night.

After the meeting in Haifa, Qassam and a group of his closest comrades, almost all of them peasants, made their way inland to the wooded hills of Janin. They had sold their wives' jewellery and some of their household furnishings to buy rifles and ammunition. They spent the daytime in caves, near the village of Ya'id, praying and reciting the Koran. At night they attacked the Jews and the British.

At least that was their intention, for they barely had time for action. The authorities, perhaps tipped off by an informer, lost no time in sending out a mixed force of British and Arab troops, aided by reconnaissance planes, to hunt them down. Surprised and overwhelmed, Shaikh Qassam was forced into premature battle. Called upon to surrender, he shouted back: 'Never, this is a *jihad* for God and country.' He exhorted his followers to 'die as martyrs'. When he saw the Arab troops, he ordered his men to attack the British and to fire on their compatriots only in self-defence. After a battle lasting several hours, Qassam and three or four companions were killed, the rest were captured.

It had been a brief and—from a military point of view—futile rebellion. But it stirred up the Palestinian masses. It pointed the insurrectional way ahead. And that was all Shaikh Qassam had hoped for. The Jews failed to grasp its significance. For them Shaikh Quassam was a kind of freak, the product of unnatural fanaticism, a mad dervish. They could not see that, fifteen years after their own hero's exemplary death, the Palestinians in their turn now had the legend they needed, their own Joseph Trumpeldor. There had been a few who died, gun in hand, before Shaikh Qassam, and there would be many thousands who were to do so after him. But in his deep piety, in his unswerving sense of mission and the deliberateness of its death-seeking climax, he was the archetypal *fedayi*—'one who sacrifices himself'—of the Palestinian struggle. He placed himself in a tradition that began with an earlier Western invasion of Palestine. For it was the Crusaders who had faced the first *fedayeen*—the militants of the revolutionary Ismaili sect—who came down from their mountain strongholds in northern Syria to terrorize the Frankish chieftains or rival Moslem princes, the original 'assassins'—*hashishiin*—who are popularly believed to have carried out their suicidal missions under the influence of drugs. In the struggle against the twentieth-century invader, Shaikh Quassam is the outstanding example in a tradition of heroism, usually reckless, sometimes high-minded and purposeful, sometimes pointless and ignoble, but generally unavailing, which the Palestinians have been practising to this day. From a distance of forty years, during which the Palestinians have suffered defeat and dispersal on a scale that even Shaikh

Qassam could scarcely have imagined possible, his altruism has about it all the pathos of people who never quite give up the struggle, but have so far been doomed, through their own shortcomings as well as their enemy's superiority, always to lose, and subconsciously seem to know it.

A huge throng attended Shaikh Qassam's funeral in Haifa. He was buried ten kilometres away in the village of Yajour; the mourners bore his coffin all the way on foot. They shouted slogans against the British and the Jewish National Home; they stoned the police, and their procession was defiantly decked out in the flags of various Arab states. In Cairo, the newspaper *al-Ahram* wrote: 'Dear friend and martyr, I heard you preaching from pulpits, calling us to arms, but today, preaching from the Bosom of God, you were more eloquent in death than in life.'

It was a truly national event. But the nation's official leaders were absent. Their absence was characteristic. They were afraid of the passions Qassam had unleashed. In his martyrdom they sensed a reproach and a threat to themselves. They were right to do so, for although there have been many and often fortuitous circumstances to which the Zionists owe their astonishing success, by no means the least have been the incompetence and irresponsibility of the Arab leaders, the frivolity and egoism of the privileged classes. The frailties which the Haifa newspaper *Carmel* had first denounced a quarter of a century earlier were all the greater now. About nine-tenths of all land acquired by the Jews up to 1929 was sold by absentee landlords. But after that, the ever-growing 'Zionist peril' notwithstanding, the main culprits were resident landlords. It was at this time, too, that Arab usurers came most offensively into their own; smallholders were forced to borrow at interest rates of up to 50 per cent; they would cling desperately to their little plots of land, but in the end, under a crushing burden of debt, were forced to abandon them to the land-hungry Jews.[4] There were mouth-watering profits to be made: the price of a dunum near Rishon-le-Zion, originally eight shillings, had reached £10 to £25 by the early thirties.[5] Officially, of course, the willing squanderers of the Arab heritage were becoming the pariahs of society. They were ritually condemned on every suitable occasion—at conferences convened to consider the

'Zionist peril', in the campaign statements of rival political parties, in the anathemas issued by religious authorities. Thus in 1932, the Independence Party issued a proclamation declaring that 'there is no future for the nation unless the gates are closed on immigration, and the sale of land prohibited; the delegates reaffirm their dissatisfaction at the middlemen and the landsellers, and consider that the time has come to punish and oppose them. . . .'[6] In Palestinian vocabulary *simsar*—'middleman'—has established itself ever since as a word of abuse. In 1935, when immigration and land sales were surpassing all limits, Haj Amin Husseini, the Mufti, assembled some 400 men of God, imams, qadis, muftis, preachers and teachers, who issued a *fatwa*, or religious edict, outlawing the sale of land to Jewish immigrants and denouncing its perpetrators as apostates to be denied burial in Moslem cemeteries.

However—and here is the real measure of the Palestinian leadership—although the landsellers and agents might suffer all manner of verbal abuse, they rarely suffered much worse. Landselling, branded as 'treason', was a characteristic accusation which one faction of notables hurled at another. It made for an immense hypocrisy. There was no real social ostracism, let alone any condign punishment. The very people who most vociferously condemned the practice were not infrequently the ones who most indulged in it. In 1928, the delegates to the Seventh Palestine Congress were described by a contemporary as a very odd assortment who included 'spies and middlemen selling land to the Jews'.[7] In 1932, the newspaper *al-Arab* found it strange indeed that the Arab Executive should wax so indignant about the sale of Arab land when some of its own members were doing the selling. No wonder a British fact-finding team's efforts to uncover the full extent of these odious transactions met with resistance from the Arab as well as the Jewish leadership.[8] If, by 1948, the landsellers had only allowed some 6.6 per cent of physical Palestine to fall into Jewish hands—though that represented a much higher proportion of its cultivable area[9]—the damage they inflicted on the Palestinian psyche is less easy to calculate. But it was undoubtedly great. The landsellers typified the Palestinians' response to Zionism at its most self-destructive. They were the most unhealthy part of a body politic so diseased that, instead of achieving that self-renewal which, under strain, an even slightly healthier one might have achieved, it degenerated still further. It did not immunize itself against the sickness which the landsellers represented; it let the sickness spread. The disloyalty of a few, rather than fortifying the constructive patriotism of the majority, aggravated the factionalism, recrimination and mistrust which poisoned the whole Palestinian struggle, and the behaviour of the politicians in particular.

When Shaikh Qassam stirred the people with his martyr's death, the politicians were still opposing violence—but failing to provide any alternative. Instead of marching behind the coffin, they sent lukewarm messages of sympathy—and ran to the High Commissioner to tell him that if he did not grant them some timely concessions they would lose what influence they still possessed and the situation would get quite out of hand.[10]

The Rebellion Begins

That is precisely what happened. The events of 1936 to 1939 go down, in most Zionist history books, as mere 'disturbances'; but, for the Palestinians, Shaikh Qassam's self-immolation ushered in the Great Rebellion. One side saw an eruption of banditry, murder and robbery, a reversion to what Weizmann called the 'barbarism of the desert',[11] in which a primitive people, urged on by unscrupulous politicians, a fanatical clergy and international Fascism, hurled themselves against the higher civilization they did not want or understand. The other side saw a glorious patriotic struggle, which naturally sought outside help where it could find it, against the foreign invader.

There was indeed, in the 'disturbances', something of what the Zionists saw in them. But, as the British historian John Marlowe, by no means a partisan observer, suggests, their essential character was quite otherwise:

> Somehow or other, whether as a result of the propaganda of Haj Amin and his minions, or of more complex and less identifiable forces, the last dying embers of the spirit of jihad were being fanned into a flame

> which was, for a few short years, to grow brightly and heroically before being extinguished for ever. Although instigated, to some extent guided, and certainly used, by the political leaders of Arab Palestine, the Arab Rebellion was in fact a peasant revolt, drawing its enthusiasm, its heroism, its organization and its persistence from sources within itself which have never been properly understood and which will never be known. Like Faisal's revolt in the desert (the movement which, in alliance with Britain, liberated Arabia from Ottoman rule), it was one of the blind alleys of Arab nationalism doomed, like the desert revolt, to failure, and destined, unlike the desert revolt, to oblivion for lack of a Lawrence to immortalize it. One is reminded of G. M. Trevelyan's words about another peasant revolt: 'the readiness of the rural population to turn out and die for their faith was a new thing. . . . The record of this brief campaign is as the lifting of a curtain; behind it we can see for a moment into the old peasant life. In that one glance we see not rustic torpor, but faith, idealism, vigour, love of liberty, and scorn of death. Were the yeomen and farm servants in other parts of England like these men of Somerset or were they everywhere else of a lower type? The curtain falls and knowledge is hidden for ever.'[12]

The Palestinian leadership did not plan this revolt any more than it did the riots and massacres of the 1920s. Nevertheless, in order to maintain its own supremacy, it accepted an involvement—though just how much is controversial—which was thrust upon it. The revolt was largely spontaneous in origin; its main impetus came from below, from the largest, lowliest segment of the population, from the peasantry who had suffered most from the Zionist invasion. It was a people's war, though not in the modern ideological sense, for it did not have, as a principal or even incidental aim, the overthrow of the existing social order. It represented a new stage in the Arab resistance that had begun, with those clumsy localized outbreaks, some fifty years before: the use of armed violence, in a sustained, organized and purposeful way, not only against the Jews but against the British who had brought them there. After their politicians had for twenty years vainly tried, through constitutional means, to win a sympathetic hearing from an indifferent or hostile Britain, the people had been goaded—as one of them put it—into 'speaking with rifles instead of with their lips'.[13] It was the product of a mysterious, but thoroughly natural, evolution.

Such was its essential nature, though it was accompanied by other forms of resistance. On the side of violence, there were more urban riots carried over from the previous era—plus a new strain of delinquency which was directed at least as much against Arabs as Jews. On the side of non-violence, there was a six-month, country-wide strike. And with the despatch of money, arms and volunteers from neighbouring countries, the Palestinian struggle first acquired a truly pan-Arab dimension that would never cease to grow in the years to come.

The rebellion had two phases.

It all began incoherently enough. On 15 April 1936, Arabs held up a number of cars on the Tulkaram-Nablus road. They only robbed the Arabs and Europeans, but two Jewish travellers they shot, killing one outright and fatally wounding the other. The next night two Arabs living in a hut near a Jewish settlement met the same fate. Before dying, one of the victims described his attackers as Jews; in all probability the murder was a reprisal for the previous day's killing. The day after that, mourners turned the funeral of one of the murdered Jews into a demonstration. They stoned the police, made inflammatory speeches and shouted: 'We don't want this government, we want a Jewish army.' Meanwhile, Arabs were beaten up, stoned or otherwise molested. On 19 April, rumours spread in Jaffa that two Arabs had been killed in adjoining Tel Aviv. Arab mobs in the neighbourhood turned on Jews, several of whom were killed. Three more days of rioting followed. In all, sixteen Jews were done to death, and five Arabs were killed by the police.

On 20 April a National Committee was formed in Nablus, and before the end of the month similar bodies had sprung to life in all the towns and larger villages of Palestine. In origin, the committees were largely independent of the traditional leadership, which had been bitterly criticized for its apathy. 'Rise to rid yourself of Jewish and British slavery . . .', one newspaper had urged. 'The leaders in Egypt have awakened. Where are our leaders hiding?'[14] But now this leadership joined the Nablus militants in calling for a general strike. An Arab Higher Committee was established under the Mufti, and the entire non-Jewish population, Christian and Moslem, moderate and extremist, came together, with an unprecedented show of unity, in a firm resolve to continue the strike until the British government changed its policy 'in a fundamental manner, the beginning of which is the stoppage of Jewish immigration'. A few days later, the committees decreed a nation-wide non-payment of taxes. Then lorry, bus and taxi owners, most of whom were relying on their monthly earnings to pay their instalments, laid up their vehicles. In June, senior civil servants, the judiciary among them, submitted a memorandum to the High Commissioner which insisted that Arab mistrust of the government was justified. Although successive investigators had vindicated Arab grievances, they complained, little had been done to remedy them. 'The Arabs have been driven into a state verging on despair; and the present unrest is no more than an expression of that despair.' The memorandum, described as unique in the history of British colonial administration, seemed to impress the authorities with its note of deep conviction moderately expressed.

The government did not stop immigration. On the contrary, when the so-called 'economic absorptive capacity' for the next six months came up for review, it authorized the Jewish Agency to bring in 10 per cent more newcomers than in the previous six. It did not want to give the Zionists the chance to accuse it of 'yielding to violence and terror'. This munificence was balanced by one of those reassuring statements that were apt to accompany pro-Zionist acts: it was announced that another Commission of Inquiry would be sent to Palestine. Unimpressed by a repetition of what they had seen so often before, the Arabs reiterated that they would only call off their strike if immigration were suspended until the Commission had delivered its report. And other official actions reinforced their resolve. With the strike as a pretext, the administration sanctioned the creation of an all-Jewish port at Tel Aviv; although, given the existence of a port at Jaffa, a mere two miles down the coast, this project had no economic justification, it had been a Zionist ambition since the days of Herzl. It meant that for the Jaffa boatmen there was to be no going back to work—ever. The administration also blew up 237 houses in down-town Jaffa. Ostensibly, the object was the 'beautification' of the town; in reality it was a peculiarly harsh security measure. The 6,000 victims helped swell the shanty town of old petrol tins which—like the one in Haifa where Shaikh Qassam had recruited his followers—was taking shape in the vicinity.

In the strategy of the National Committees, the strike action was to be confined to passive resistance and civil disobedience on the Gandhi model. That the leadership was still exerting a moderating influence long after the strike began was emphasized in a report which the High Commissioner addressed to the Colonial Secretary: 'It is a remarkable fact that the religious cry has not been raised during the last six weeks, that the Friday sermons have been far more moderate than I could have hoped during a period when feelings of the people are so deeply stirred, and for this the Mufti is mainly responsible.'[15] But, as in India, unofficial violence did continue, and developed new forms. Its perpetrators burned crops and maimed trees, mined and barricaded roads, derailed trains, cut telegraph wires and sabotaged the pipeline that carried Iraqi oil across northern Palestine to the terminal at Haifa. Arson was rife, and there was much hooliganism, with youths roaming the towns, beating up strike-breakers and puncturing the tyres of blackleg drivers. Many Jews were killed, sometimes in brutal and cynical ways. So were Arabs; gunmen would visit prominent personalities suspected of lukewarm sympathy for the cause; they would extort contributions from businessmen or wealthy landowners; often they did not stop at mere intimidation. But the mainspring of unofficial violence and of the Great Rebellion into which it quickly grew, was the armed bands that began to operate in hilly regions of the country.

These bands were joined by volunteers from the rest of the Arab world. The best known of them was Fawzi al-Kawekji. He later married a German woman and, like many of his contemporaries, he had seen the rise of Hitler as a development from which the Arabs could profit in their struggle against Britain. But neither this, nor the pro-Arab propaganda emanating from Italy and Germany, meant, as Zionists and their Western sympathizers put it about, that the rebellion was merely an arm of international Fascism.

Foreign support the uprising may have had, but its heart lay firmly in Palestine—above all in that peasantry on whom, as it grew, British aeroplanes showered leaflets urging them to abandon violence and put their trust in the Royal Commission. They had their local leaders. The best known was Abdul Rahim al-Haj Muhammad, a merchant of solid yeomen stock. He lacked the professional skills or training of an al-Kawekji. But he was described, even by the men who hunted him down, as a straight-forward, home-grown patriot. He observed his own moral code, insisting that his followers show a proper consideration for the people on whose behalf they were fighting. Other leaders, like Shaikh Qassam, were religiously motivated; just as the Zionists took ancient Hebrew names, so they called themselves after the heroes of early, militant Islam. Others, in varying proportions, were part freedom-fighter, part-brigand, cloaking ill-gotten gains in the glamour of revolution. In the first phase of the rebellion there were about 5,000 altogether. Their organization was rudimentary. They operated without centralized control. They were divided, broadly speaking, into two kinds. There were the full-timers in the hills; these constituted the hard core which bore the brunt of the fighting. There were the part-time confederates; these would join up for short periods when reinforcements were needed, but most of the time they would stay in their villages, keeping the rebels supplied with food, as well as with information about the movements of the police and troops, and about villagers who worked against them. Their training was also primitive. When they took to the hills, many of them had never borne arms before. And their arms, when captured, proved to be a jumble of antiquated stock abandoned in the Middle East at the end of World War I; they boasted no such thing as mortar or artillery. But what they lacked in equipment and expertise they made up for in determination. According to a Palestinian participant, al-Kawekji was amazed at the 'heroism, gallantry and self-sacrifice' he found at his service; he would assign ten men to a mission and 'scores would present themselves as if they were being invited, not to risk their lives, but to attend a wedding or a banquet'.[16] A British observer records that they would often see their comrades killed, a dozen at a time, by machine-gun fire or aerial bombardment, and yet return to fight a day or two later.[17] A delegation of Moslem religious dignitaries told the High Commissioner that 'by attacking His Majesty's troops they commit suicide, but, as Your Excellency is aware, a desperate man often commits suicide'.[18]

Furthermore, the British authorities, or some of them, were well aware of these motives. Vice-Marshal Pierce wrote from Palestine: 'The bands were not out for loot. They were fighting what they believed to be a patriotic war in defence of their country against injustice and the threat of Jewish domination.'[19]

Nineteen years before, the peasants had been flogged or imprisoned by the Turkish authorities for picking up the proclamations dropped by British planes urging them to 'come and join us' who are fighting 'for the liberation of all Arabs from Turkish rule so that the Arab Kingdom may again become what it was during the time of your fathers'.[20] By now, however, they had grown tired of the unfulfilled pledges of their one-time ally and they wanted that positive demonstration of goodwill—the suspension of immigration during the Royal Commission's investigations—which the government was not prepared to give. There is little doubt that, with such a suspension, the disorders would have ended in twenty-four hours. During the summer, Arab rulers sought to mediate between the British and the Palestinians—but all to no avail until, in September, the government announced its intention of sending a fresh division of troops to Palestine. From then on the insurgents would obviously have had a much tougher time. Moreover, in the towns, the strain of the six-month strike was beginning to tell; and to have extended the stoppage into the citrus shipping season, thus depriving the country of its most important export earning, would have strained unanimity beyond breaking point. Once again, the Arab states intervened; three kings jointly appealed to the Palestinians to call off their protest and rely upon the good intentions of 'our friend' the British government. The Arab Higher Committee in its turn called on the people 'to put an end to the strike and disorders . . . and to ask all members of the nation to proceed, in the early morning, to their places of worship, in order to hold services for the martyrs and to thank God for the power of patience and fortitude with which he has endowed them'. The response was immediate; work was resumed throughout the country, and the violence ceased. The first phase of the rebellion was over. Some thirty-seven British had died, and sixty-nine Jews—for anything up to a thousand Arabs. The latter had achieved nothing more than they began with—the despatch of yet another Royal Commission. And the very day it left for Palestine, the government announced an unusually generous labour schedule for Jewish immigrants. Indignant, the Arabs decided to boycott the Commission—a boycott which they lifted only a week before the end of its three-month stay.

Britain Recommends Partition

In July 1937, the Commission published its findings. To the amazement of the Arabs, it recommended precisely the kind of solution which, for years, they had fought against, and which finally proved the 'safeguard' clause of the Balfour Declaration to be as valueless as they had always claimed it was. It recommended the vivisection of their native land, the partition of Palestine into a Jewish and an Arab state.

One might have expected an immediate resumption of violence. But this did not happen; for despite its recommendations there was much in the report's analysis of the workings of the Mandate that vindicated Arab claims. Here, for the first time, was authoritative acknowledgement that the Mandate was in effect *un*workable and that the achievement of Jewish aims was of necessity prejudicial to the rights of the natives. It roundly asserted that only through 'the dark path of repression' could the present policies be maintained. Yet since the alternative which the Commission proposed in its stead was, in the eyes of the Arabs, even less feasible, they were content, initially, to let the logic of facts do their fighting for them.

The partition was not being implemented, it is true, but all those things which had driven the Arabs to revolt in the first place—immigration, land sales and signal acts of favouritism like the creation of an all-Jewish port at Tel-Aviv—continued unabated. The peasants of relatively fertile and prosperous Galilee were particularly impatient. For under partition this district was to be allotted to the Jewish State, and partition was to be enforced, if necessary, by a 'compulsory' exchange of population.[21] The Galileans—reported local British officials—received the proposals with 'shock bordering on incredulity'. For they assumed that they would be the first to be dispossessed of their lands and—as they pictured it—'left to perish somewhere in the desert'.[22] Thus, when Mr L. Y. Andrews was appointed District Commissioner for Galilee, those familiar with the temper of the peasantry openly expressed anxiety for his life. Galilee was the home of some of those politico-religious secret societies that Shaikh Qassam had inspired. In Jewish eyes, Andrews, who had been closely associated with the Royal Commission, was the only official who administered the Mandate as it should be administered; not surprisingly, therefore, he was for the Arabs the very symbol of their impending misfortune. At the end of September he and two companions emerged from the Anglican church in Nazareth. As they ascended the steep narrow land that led from it, four armed men stepped out of the shadows. 'Run for your lives,' Andrews shouted. It would have been better had they attempted to fight their way out, for as they ran another group intercepted them from a side lane. Andrews was shot dead and a police constable was also mortally wounded.

The Rebellion Reaches Its Climax

The second phase of the rebellion had begun. This time, more clearly than before, the traditional leadership, or at least the Mufti, was embroiled in it from the outset. To what extent he chose this role himself, is a controversy best left to specialist historians, but certainly it was now much more difficult for him to advocate conciliation if he wished to retain his leadership of the Palestinian people. Moderation was no longer politically realistic; the moderates had been treated with contempt. Before the Royal Commission published its report, the conciliatory wing of the leadership, the Nashashibis, bitter rivals of the Mufti's Husseini clan, had seceded from the Arab Higher Committee, in order to take an independent line should the report prove acceptable to Arab opinion. It had proved so unacceptable that the moderates were totally eclipsed and their lives threatened by extremists' bullets. The administration had been under fierce pressure from the Zionists, the British press and parliament to hold the Arab Higher Committee, especially the

Mufti, responsible for the violence. It is true that while the politicians disclaimed any part in it, describing it as a spontaneous manifestation of popular discontent, they did not denounce or seek to curb it. Yet there was no reason to attribute the Andrews murder to the Arab Higher Committee—indeed, this was one occasion when it did deplore the crime—but it was followed, a few days later, by the arrest and detention of two or three hundred notables. The Committee was dissolved, its members deported to the Seychelles; it was held 'morally responsible' for the violence. The Mufti himself was officially deposed, but no attempt was made to arrest him—evidently for fear of bloodshed in the Holy Places where he had taken refuge—and he managed, perhaps with official connivance, to escape to Lebanon. This high-handed action was a provocation to the entire Arab community. The traditional leadership may not have enjoyed much respect, but it was the only leadership the Arabs had; deservedly or not, it was symbolic of their aspirations; there was a sullen determination everywhere, and large deputations flocked into Jerusalem from all over the country to lodge a protest with the administration.

On the night of 14 October 1937, disorders erupted throughout Palestine; obviously, in its second phase, the rebellion had acquired a greater degree of coordination; to say that the Mufti was the evil genius behind the disturbances was at long last becoming a credible assertion, for he had finally been driven, largely through the influence on British policies of those who most insistently said it, into a conspiratorial exile. By the summer of 1938 the rebellion had reached a new climax, far surpassing that of 1936. In a despatch from Palestine, the correspondent of the London *Times* painted a grim picture of the 'murder, guerrilla warfare, rapine, brigandage, theft and arson' that prevailed there.[23] He recalled what the Peel Commission had reported a year before: that it was 'ludicrous' to suppose that Britain had not the resources 'to deal with a rebellion on so small a scale or so ill-equipped for modern warfare'. But the way things were going, he said in another melancholy despatch, it would soon be necessary 'to reconquer Palestine'.[24]

At the height of their power, when they numbered anything up to 15,000 men, the rebels' writ ran in most of the central mountain area, in Galilee, Hebron, Beersheba and Gaza; there they reduced the Mandatory authority to a fiction. The rebel 'government' collected its own taxes and established its own courts, in which it tried brigands who exploited their cause or spies and 'agents' who worked against it. The rebels won—or enforced—the cooperation of community leaders, schoolteachers and the Arab constabulary. Their encounters with the British took two forms: their own small-scale offensives—ambushing, sniping, bomb-throwing, or the mining of roads—or, in the later stages, the pitched defensive battles against pursuing forces. Their tactics were much the same against the Jews, although in that other characteristic form of warfare, waged against the fruits of Jewish labour, they also scored some heartbreaking successes: a settlement would wake up one morning to find that raiders had cut down a thousand orange trees in a single night.

It was a conquest of the towns by the countryside. This time the rebels came down from the hills into the plains; they moved out of their local fiefs to secure a much broader, interlocking hegemony; they dominated not just the villages, sympathetic from the outset, but some of the principal cities of Palestine. And everywhere, they drove the townsman's tasselled tarbush from the streets, replacing it with the *kefiyyeh*, the countryman's flowing headdress. This was a camouflage—for it made rebel infiltrators harder to detect—but it was also a symbolic self-assertion. Young zealots engaged in campaigns of tarbush-smashing. Members of the upper class, top civil servants, took to wearing hats; Armenians and the religious minorities fell into line too. Underlying it all, in the Qassam tradition, there was an Islamically inspired intolerance of decadent, westernizing ways. Christian women had to abandon their fashionable European headgear in favour of the veil; church-goers would have offending apparel torn from their heads; short sleeves and lipstick were outlawed.

The rebels would physically invest the towns. Several hundred of them descended on Bethlehem, disarmed the police, sang patriotic songs and withdrew, before the arrival of security forces, in their own good time. In Nablus they twice raided Barclays Bank under the noses of British soldiers. In Beersheba they seized seventy-five rifles and 10,000 rounds of ammunition from the unresisting police station. They took their defiance to the temporal and spiritual heart of the conflict; within the walls of the Old City of Jerusalem, with its Islamo-Judaic complex of great mosques and the Wailing Wall, its medieval warren of twisting alleyways, their control was absolute. Even in Jaffa, down on the coast, the administration enjoyed only a semblance of authority. The 3,000 Jewish citizens had to be evacuated; Arab 'enemies' of the revolt were forced to flee. Police stations were raided. There were almost daily assassinations whose perpetrators, slipping back into the anonymous mass, were practically never caught. Stores were looted in broad daylight. The inhabitants were obliged to forego the use of electricity, because it was a Jewish company which supplied it; street lights were smashed, and oil lamps were selling at a premium.

Once, in Tiberias, the rebels came down to find and kill as many Jews as they could. This was retaliation for bombs—presumed Jewish—which had slaughtered scores of Arabs in various public places. At nine o'clock one October evening, a large band entered the town; they had earlier cut all its telephone communications with the rest of the country; five minutes later, on a whistled signal from the adjoining hills, the massacre began. As one group attacked British and Arab police barracks, others set fire to the synagogue and houses in the Jewish quarter and killed their inmates. In all, nineteen Jews, including three women and ten children, some of them mere babies, died. It took two hours for the police, eventually reinforced, to drive the raiders out. It was not the largest, but it was certainly the most deliberate massacre since Palestinian violence began.[25]

Britain 'Reconquers Palestine'

The British did, in effect, have to 'reconquer Palestine'. By the autumn of 1938, they had more than 20,000 troops in the country. They had already, a year earlier, introduced emergency regulations under which the discharge or the mere carrying of firearms became a capital offence. Military commanders took charge of several districts, with the civil authorities acting as political advisers. The rebels, till then the attackers, became the attacked; the tide turned relentlessly against them. It was old muskets against aeroplanes and armoured cars; tactics out of Robin Hood's day against the logistics, mobility and weaponry of one of the leading military powers of the age. The infiltrators might abandon the towns—such as the Old City of Jerusalem—almost as unobtrusively as they had entered them. But in the exposed countryside they sustained terrible losses. 'A British police officer was killed, two British soldiers were wounded and a number of Arabs—officially estimated at 40 but unofficially at 60—were killed during an engagement at Ramallah yesterday.' So ran the deadpan despatch from Jerusalem in *The Times* of 3 October 1938. It was typical of this unequal combat. The rebels suffered veritable massacres from the air. *The Times* again:

> About 150 casualties, it is believed, were inflicted on rebels by aircraft late yesterday in the most important engagement of the year. An R.A.F. aeroplane making a reconnaissance flight observed a large band near Deirghassana, a village in the foothills east of Jaffa. The machine summoned assistance from Ramleh, where four aeroplanes are always ready to start at two minutes' notice. Twelve additional aircraft arrived, and the force engaged the band until nightfall. The planes were hit a number of times but there were no casualties among R.A.F. personnel and all the machines returned safely. Today the Air Force and troops thoroughly searched the area, where they saw signs of the burning of bodies during the night. Fifteen dead horses were found, showing that the band were partly mounted. During the search various remnants of the band were discovered. The R.A.F. killed four, and the Irish Guards met a party, of which they killed three . . . and wounded several others. . . .[26]

The military courts set up to enforce the emergency regulations were as thorough and expeditious as the troops. Under Moslem tradition no man over the age of seventy is executed and no man is executed during Ramadan, the holy month of fasting. But the first death sentence passed violated tradition on both counts. Shaikh Farhan al-Saadi was found hiding in a barn following a local skirmish between British forces and the rebels. Asked whether he possessed any firearms, he replied that he did have an old rifle hanging on the wall of his home. After a three-hour trial, during which he calmly refused to answer any questions, he was summarily hanged. His judges evidently convicted him less for this specific offence than for worse crimes—such as the murder of Andrews—which he was alleged to have committed. It was Ramadan, and he was at least seventy-five years old. For the Arabs, his was a martyrdom equal to that of Shaikh Qassam. Altogether the British hanged 112 Arabs, as against one Jew, in a ritual which made one commander, Sir Alec Kirkbride, who had to witness it, feel 'guilty and mean'.[27] Condemned men were reported to have uttered patriotic slogans on the way to the scaffold, or to have tried to jump the queue.

Then there were the collective fines and demolitions. The fines were paid in cash or in kind—and they were frequently imposed without sufficient inquiry or proof of guilt. When one Squadron-Leader Alderton was murdered, troops concluded, with the help of tracker dogs, that the killers had found shelter in the village of Igzim. It underwent a 'search' by a detachment of the South Kents infantry. The British missionary Frances Newton visited Igzim two days later. She found two houses at the entrance of the village blown up and some sixty others where 'the havoc which had been wrought was indescribable, and, unless seen with one's own eyes, unbelievable'.[28] She found shutters and cupboards smashed in, mirrors shattered, upholstered armchairs gutted, sewing-machines battered to bits, clothing and beds soaked in olive oil, and even a Koran ripped apart. Individual soldiers had stolen money and jewellery. One unfortunate was shot when, escaping with £25 he wanted for himself, he broke the security cordon round the village. All sheep and goats were seized as security for the collective fine. Those who could afford to buy them back at the price of eight shillings a head did so; those who could not lost them. Then, just to complete the ordeal, the government forced the villagers to foot the bill—nearly £700—for billeting forty supernumerary police in their midst for three months. Aware that if they did not pay up, all their possessions would be seized, they preferred to emigrate *en masse*, taking their property with them. Some of them, of course, ended up in Shaikh Qassam's Haifa shanty town. 'True refugees,' commented Miss Newton, 'but from *British* barbarism.' And it turned out in the end that Squadron-Leader Alderton's killers actually came from another village altogether.

When an Arab was killed laying ambush to a military patrol, the authorities ordered the demolition 'without compensation' of the house of a big landowner from the village of Endor. Their justification was that the dead man had been seen 'recently serving coffee' in the house—a justification that took no account of the fact that, in accordance with Arab traditions of hospitality, a part of the rich man's establishment had been set aside as a more or less public meeting place open to villagers and strangers alike. When the airport at Lydda was damaged by sabotage, a row of houses in the vicinity was dynamited in reprisal.

In March 1939, Abdul Rahim al-Haj Muhammad, the rebellion's outstanding commander, was killed, after prayers in a mosque, amid general Palestinian grief—and reluctant tributes from the British. Most other commanders fled the country. The uprising was virtually at an end. As a military force, the Palestinians had been broken. Official British figures for the number of Arab casualties during the 1936–9 disturbances have never been made fully known, but, according to the careful calculations of the Palestinian scholar, Walid Khalidi, the dead must have exceeded 5,000 and the wounded 14,000. These figures, translated into contemporary British or American terms, would have meant some 200,000 British killed and 600,000 wounded, or 1,000,000 Americans killed and 3,000,000 wounded.[29] Some 101 British died, and 463 Jews.[30]

The rebellion had its own internal defects and these, under the British onslaught, accelerated its collapse. There is much debate among contemporary Palestinian historians, spurred by the new phase of armed resistance, about just what the defects were.[31] They are inclined to lay heavy blame on the *zaims* and *effendis*. It was in origin, they contend, a truly spontaneous uprising; its very spontaneity was a measure of its authenticity; but it found no leadership to channel that spontaneity into organized, truly purposeful revolution. It was only when the urban élite had no choice that they tried to bring it under their wing—or at least some of them, led by the Mufti, tried, while the more conciliatory ones, led by the Nashashibis, fell into deeper discredit than ever. Yet it never really worked; the gulf between politician and fighter, between town and country, was never bridged. While the rebellion, as the Palestinians' first attempt at general armed violence, represented a qualitative growth in resistance to the Zionist invasion, it was not matched by the comparable social, political and organizational aptitudes that were needed to sustain this high challenge. The fighters were not encouraged to transcend regional, religious or family loyalties; many refused to join bands in other areas; those who did might be turned back as intruders. *Faz'a*, 'rallying to one's neighbour'—and no one else—impeded rational strategy. Warlordism flourished. But worse still was the debilitating effect of inherited clan rivalries, of old blood-feuds mixed up with new and half-understood political controversies. These could not only set village against village, but could divide a single one upon itself; it would sometimes happen that because one influential personage supported the uprising his rival automatically collaborated with the authorities. And occasionally rebel courts were debased into instruments for the bloody settling of scores. What possible justification could there have been for the 'execution' not merely of the Mukhtar of the village of Deir al-Shaikh, but of his wife, three sons, aged fourteen, twelve and ten, and a servant too?[32] And even the hated enemy justice could be exploited for sordid vengeance. A firearm would be 'planted' in the family domain of the intended victim and word passed to the military authorities; thus a man could send his neighbour to the gallows.[33] It was the same with the urban political leadership. Fragmentation there meant open war between the Husseinis and the Nashashibis. For the Mufti, champion of the Husseinis, the personal ascendancy he had achieved was not enough: he had to exploit the rebellion to reinforce it. It was mainly to his pernicious influence, his lust for power, that the 'opposition' attributed the wave of terror that enveloped them. When Fakhri Bey Nashashibi survived, with serious wounds, an assassination attempt, his resentment was so great that—in the judgement of the High Commissioner—he began to collaborate with local Jewish politicians.[34] He and his followers set up 'peace squads' to revenge themselves on Haj Amin's supposed victims. Armed violence against the common enemy, far from extinguishing the sterile feuding of the *zaims* and *effendis*, ignited a minor civil war, in which the opponents of the Mufti were driven to oppose the Great Rebellion itself.

Britain Relents: The 1939 White Paper

Yet even as 20,000 British troops were 'reconquering Palestine', the politicians back home were beginning to have serious misgivings about the whole rationale of a policy that required such harsh and costly methods to sustain. The misgivings arose from the belated recognition, in some influential quarters, that so desperate a Palestinian resistance, even if ultimately unavailing, must have profounder causes than hitherto understood. Malcolm MacDonald, the Colonial Secretary, told the House of Commons that most of the rebels were inspired by patriotic motives and suggested that, had he been an Arab, he would have felt the same as they did. A 'strong' policy, he said, could restore order, but not peace. At the same time, Britain had a higher self-interest to consider. With war clouds gathering over Europe, it could spare neither troops nor funds on unnecessary colonial conflicts that diplomacy could end; nor could it antagonize the entire Arab and Moslem world, strategically vital areas increasingly exposed to the blandishments of the Axis powers, for the sake of its importunate Zionist protégé. In 1937, Lord Peel had declared the Mandate unworkable and proposed partition instead; but at the height of the rebellion, yet another commission of inquiry, headed by Sir John Woodward, reported that partition was not workable either. At the same time the government invited Arab and Jewish leaders to a round-table conference in London. All that this gathering did, in a month of reciprocal obstructionism, was to demonstrate the immensity of the gulf between the two sides. Representatives of the Arab states—who were also invited—did meet Weizmann, but the Palestinians did not. Whereas, in 1914, the fathers would have been ready—had not global war prevented it—to meet with the enemy over the the dimensions of the struggle were such that, to have done so, negotiating table,[35] the sons were not. After a quarter of a century would have been a conferring of legitimacy on the whole Zionist enterprise almost as unthinkable as 'recognizing' Israel was to be for the generation to come.

In a prefigurement of 'indirect negotiations', of 'proximity talks', of jet-age 'shuttle-diplomacy'—and all the procedural ingenuities that peace-makers of the future would dream up—the conference took the form of separate discussions between British and Arabs, then British and Jews. When the inevitable deadlock was reached, Britain issued a 'statement of policy', the MacDonald White Paper, on its own. The government now asserted that it was 'not part of their policy that Palestine should become a Jewish state'; that 75,000 Jewish immigrants should be admitted over the next five years, but no more after that without the approval of the Arabs; that land sales should be strictly regulated; and that self-governing institutions should be developed with a view to the establishment, within ten years, of an independent Palestine State. There were aspects of the White Paper which caused the Palestinian delegation, on the instructions of the Mufti, to reject it; nevertheless, Palestinian opinion was impressed by its main provisions. At last, it was felt, the Arabs were getting a measure of justice; so much so, in fact, that the Mufti's rivals, the Nashashibis, announced that they would cooperate with Britain in enforcing the White Paper. Arab violence, which British arms had first drastically curtailed, British diplomacy now stilled altogether.

Britain 'Betrays' the Zionists

The Zionists' response to the publication of the White Paper was instantaneous and violent. Indeed, in Palestine itself, it could not be formally proclaimed at the appointed hour because the transmission lines of the broadcasting station were cut and its studios bombed. The next day Dr Herzog, the Chief Rabbi, stood in the pulpit of the great Yeshurim Synagogue in Jerusalem and before the weeping congregation tore up a copy of the infamous document. The headquarters of the Department of Migration was set on fire, and government offices in Haifa and Tel Aviv were stormed by crowds bent on destroying all files on illegal Jewish immigration. In Jerusalem

Arab shops were looted. A British constable was shot dead during a demonstration. A general Jewish strike was proclaimed. Throughout the country, mass meetings of Jews took an oath declaring that Britain's new and 'treacherous' policy would not be tolerated, that 'the Jewish population will fight it to the uttermost, and will spare no sacrifice to defeat it'. A few days later, activists initiated a campaign of sabotage and terror, directed against both British and Arabs. They blew up the Rex Cinema in Jerusalem; five Arabs were killed and eighteen wounded; two days later, they killed five more in an attack on the village of Adas. David Bengurion, acknowledged leader of the *Yishuv*, wrote after a day of demonstrations that these marked 'the beginning of Jewish resistance to the disastrous policy now proposed by His Majesty's Government. The Jews will not be intimidated into surrender even if their blood be shed.'[36] Zionism had come in many forms; there had been 'spiritual', 'cultural', 'political' or 'practical' Zionism. But the MacDonald White Paper marked the official beginning—as the Israeli deputy Uri Avneri was to dub it many years later—of 'gun Zionism'.[37]

The Revisionists Abandon 'Self-Restraint'

The ideological roots of 'gun Zionism' reach back, as we have seen, to Theodor Herzl himself. It was inevitable, as he foresaw, that armed force would eventually come into its own as the principal instrument of a movement which, in its earlier and weaker phase, could only rely on the protection of an imperial sponsor. That phase was now drawing to a close. But long before it had done so, the proponents and strategists of armed force were preparing the way, in moral, political and practical terms, for its eventual use. The spirit of Vladimir Jabotinsky, founder of the Jewish Legion during World War I and later of the underground *Haganah* army, was permeating the *Yishuv*. It has become fashionable, particularly among Zionist historians, to play down the significance of Jabotinsky, who early broke away from the mainstream Zionist leadership. Revisionism, as his rebellious heresy came to be known, has been described as 'the lunatic fringe of Zionism as the various *Ikhwan* movements represent the lunatic fringe of Arab nationalism, or the Fifth Monarchy Men represent the lunatic fringe of English Puritanism, or the Irish Republican Army represent the lunatic fringe of Sinn Fein'.[38] But the man Weizmann called 'our d'Annunzio'[39] played a key role in that militarization of Zionism which everyone subsequently endorsed. If he was repudiated by his contemporaries it was largely because he was ahead of his time. He represented an embarrassingly aggressive militancy when Weizmann-style pragmatism and equivocation were still necessary as means of securing support for Zionism from the imperial sponsor and the assimilationist Jewry of the Diaspora. It was feared that he would give the world the 'notion that we Zionists intend to dominate the Arabs of Palestine by force of arms, thus offering our enemies a weapon against us'.[40] Although Zionists might frown on his visionary enthusiasms, and oppose him officially, some of them admired him in private. Bengurion saw him as the 'Zionist Trotsky',[41] whose purist fervour doomed him to failure. But each had a sneaking affection for the other. What divided them—and that only for the time being—was style and method rather than aim. Thus it has been truly said that 'the struggle for Palestine was fundamentally Jabotinskian. For Jabotinsky represents the most uninhibited expression of Zionism as a political movement, and in this regard he symbolized an ideological norm toward which much of Zionism's latent disposition naturally gravitated.'[42]

There is no better example of that disposition than the confidential letter which Chaim Arlosoroff, the Director of the Political Department of the Jewish Agency, wrote to Weizmann as early as 1932. Arlosoroff—it now seems hard to believe—was actually one of the most conciliatory of Zionist leaders. His very appointment was designed to allay Arab fears, for he was apparently serious, unlike others, in his attempts at Arab-Israeli understanding. Indeed, that may have been the motive for his mysterious assassination in 1933. His letter is a revolutionary adaptation of the great diplomat's own concept of dynamic stages. While he decries Revisionism as a 'madness' which merely excites the Arabs, this mild and scholarly theoretician ends up with a plan of action which, so dry and reassuringly moderate in presentation, is fundamentally Jabotinskian in spirit. In his view, the evolutionary policy of immigration and colonization, of 'goat by goat and dunum by dunum', was the only right one in the past. But it would not work for much longer. Future strategy should be developed in the light of 'the relationship of forces of the two peoples contending in the country'.

> The present stage, which we have attained by means of gradual development, may be defined approximately as follows: The Arabs are no longer strong enough to destroy our position but still consider themselves strong enough to establish an Arab state in Palestine without taking into consideration Jewish political demands, whereas the Jews are strong enough to preserve their present positions without possessing sufficient strength to assure the constant growth of the Jewish community through immigration, colonization, and the maintenance of peace and order in the country in the course of this development.
>
> The next 'stage' will be attained when the relationship of the real forces will be such as to preclude any possibility of the establishment of an Arab state in Palestine, i.e., when the Jews will acquire such additional strength as will automatically block the road for Arab domination. This will be followed by another 'stage' during which the Arabs will be unable to frustrate the constant growth of the Jewish community through immigration and constructive economic activity. The constantly growing strength of the Jews will influence the Arabs in the direction of seeking a negotiated accord. This will be followed by a 'stage' during which the equilibrium between the two peoples will be based on real forces and an agreed solution to the problem. The test of the evolutionary practices of Zionist policy within the framework of the British mandate consists in whether it will be possible to attain the next 'stage' by means of this policy. . . . Should that prove impossible . . . it would no longer be feasible to cling to the evolutionary practices of Zionist policy or to base on it the strength and endurance of the Zionist movement. I am inclined to think that it is not possible.

One reason for this, he goes on to explain, is the limits of the Mandatory Administration; it would be too much to expect the British government to assume such a burden for the sake of the colonizing enterprise of a 'foreign' people. He therefore concludes:

> Under present circumstances Zionism cannot be realized without a transition period during which the Jewish minority would exercise organized revolutionary rule . . . during which the state apparatus, the administration, and the military establishment would be in the hands of the minority, in order to eliminate the danger of domination by the non-Jewish majority and suppress rebellion against us. . . . Such a conception of the problem might shake the foundations of many beliefs which we have cherished for a great many years. It might even resemble dangerously certain political states of mind which we have always rejected. At first it might even appear as impractical, visionary, and contrary to the conditions in which we live under the British Mandate. . . . But there is one thing about which I feel very strongly—I will never become reconciled to the failure of Zionism before an attempt is made whose seriousness corresponds to the seriousness of the struggle for the revival of our national life and the sanctity of the mission entrusted to us by the Jewish people.
>
> I hope I do not have to stress the fact that my way of thinking is as alien today as it always has been to that which is called Revisionism. Now, too, I consider that the activities, the policies, and the educational principles of Revisionism are madness.[43]

Rarely can a man have so brilliantly advocated a thesis which he simultaneously condemns. At any rate, it is hardly surprising that less fastidious people than himself did indeed develop the dangerous states of mind that he deplores. Ideas of coexistence with the Arabs, of bi-nationalism, were increasingly dismissed as the utopian illusions of an unrepresentative minority; the 'safeguard' clauses of the Balfour Declaration were becoming a forgotten irrelevance. Along with the rise of Hitler and the darkening situation in Europe, the Arab rebellion—an event forecast by Arlosoroff—did not engender, but simply accelerated, the process of militarization that was inevitable from the outset. If 'gun Zionism' emerged, open and proclaimed, only after the rebellion, it was very much in the making during it.

When the disturbances broke out, the *Yishuv* was officially wedded to *Havlaga*—'self-restraint'—a concept rooted in traditional Jewish ethics. The Jews should not respond to Arab terrorism with their own. In a rather vague way it was argued that there were methods—whether useful or not—which had to be abjured if the Jewish community's feeling of moral superiority over its enemies was to be preserved. *Havlaga* also earned credit abroad. Weizmann described it as 'one of the great moral political acts of modern times', which had 'won the admiration of liberal opinion all over the world'.[44] The London *Times* once contrasted Jewish discipline with what it called attempts by the Arab leaders to give proof of Arab nobility by releasing three Jewish children—adding that this had not prevented Jews and Christians alike from asking pertinently what had happened to the children's parents.[45]

Havlaga may have been a Jewish virtue, but—Zionism being in large measure a revolt against Jewish tradition—it was certainly not a Zionist one. As Arab violence grew, it came under increasing strain until, in spring 1938, three young Revisionists fired at an Arab bus on the Acre-Safad highway. It was a hopelessly bungled and amateurish operation by teenage novices, a naïve and impulsive response to constant Arab raids on Safad, in the course of which several Jews had been killed and one girl stabbed to death in a ditch. Perhaps it is true, as the Jews claimed, that if he had been an Arab the ringleader might have been spared; perhaps his ill-directed volley did come as an opportunity for the administration, which had already executed dozens of Arabs, to demonstrate its impartiality. At all events in June of that year the young Polish Jew, Shlomo ben Yussif, became the first, and last, Jew to go to the gallows during the 'disturbances'—and Jabotinsky, who numbered him among 'the heroes of Israel',[46] abandoned *Havlaga*.

In the single month of July at least 100 Arabs died in the public places of Haifa, Jaffa and Jerusalem—more people, in some six incidents, than Arabs had killed Jews in the whole of that year so far.[47] The Arab Melon Market in Haifa saw the last and worst of the series. There a bomb, placed a mere ten metres from where another one had killed eighteen Arabs three weeks before, went off at seven in the morning of 26 July. The detonation was 'accompanied by the hurling of bodies, killed, maimed and injured, in all directions . . . among the blood-spattered human remains were the mangled bodies of three horses, several mules and donkeys which had brought the villagers' produce to the crowded market.'[48] Fifty-three Arabs died, and one Jew.

The official Zionist response was ambiguous. There was, to be sure, outright condemnation. The newspaper *Davar* said that any deviation from *Havlaga* was a 'disgrace, because the pure Jewish colours have been stained by the blood of innocent people'; *Haaretz* found it 'incredible . . . that these crimes can be part of a political system, unthinkable that by such means anyone can hope to attain a desirable political end'.[49] But the condemnation was very general; indeed, if an accusing finger was pointed at all, it was liable to be in the direction of Arab quite as much as Jewish extremists. 'Is there a Jew so insane', asked the *Palestine Post*, 'even if cunning-minded, as to venture to deposit or throw a bomb among the usually large crowds coming out of the Mosque? What surer way of spreading the seed of inter-racial war . . . than by manufacturing the type of crime which, in its sacrifice and resultant panic, makes the credulous Arab point to the Jew as its author?'[50] None of the perpetrators was ever caught. The Jewish police were just as much in collusion with their own community as the Arab police were with theirs. The outside world had precious little doubt that the culprits were Jewish, but there was much readiness to find extenuating circumstances. The *Manchester Guardian* concluded that continual terrorism 'organized from outside' had caused a breakdown in Jewish self-restraint, but this was 'slight . . . natural, and indeed inevitable'. 'Certainly not one of the turbulent peoples of these Islands would have endured without violent retaliation a hundredth part of what the Palestinian Jews have suffered for over two years.'[51]

The bombs *were* Jewish, of course, though no one claimed them at the time, and more specifically they were Revisionist. The denunciations of the official leadership which impressed outsiders seemed so much hypocrisy to the Arabs who, though right in their general intuitions, were apt to jump to some naïve conclusions; after the Haifa explosion a deputation of veiled women protested to the High Commissioner, and one of them told him that Dr Weizmann, whose fame as a scientist had apparently reached their uninstructed ears, was manufacturing the bombs in his laboratory at Rehovoth.

According to his biographer and disciple, Joseph Schechtman, Jabotinsky long struggled with his conscience over the morality of terrorism. He saw what he thought to be the political justification for retaliation but, at the same time, he was a 'typical nineteenth-century liberal who considered human life as sacrosanct'. He once told a colleague: 'I can't see much heroism and public good in shooting from the rear an Arab peasant on a donkey, carrying vegetables for sale in Tel Aviv.'[52] In time, however, he openly and fully endorsed the policy of wholesale retaliation. Everybody, he wrote, likes retaliations, provided they are immediately and exclusively directed against the bandits and not against the Arab population, however hostile. 'But it must be realized that the choice is not between retaliating against the bandits or retaliating against the hostile population. The choice is between . . . retaliating against the hostile population or not retaliating at all. . . . To the spilling of *ha'dam hamutar*, the permitted blood, on which there is no prohibition and for which nobody has to pay, an end had been put in Palestine. Amen.' By June 1939 he had come to the conclusion that 'it was not only difficult to punish only the guilty ones, in most cases it was impossible'.[53]

The Arabs had begun the 1936–9 'disturbances', but—as an Israeli historian was to concede many years later—the Jews later imitated and, with their much improved techniques, quite out-did them.[54] If, in their preference for hit-and-run guerilla tactics, the Arabs were spurred by folk-memories of the 'assassins' or the tribal *ghazzia*, the Jews introduced an urban, and far more effective, terrorism that was more in the tradition of Russian Nihilists or the Anarchists of Spain.[55] It had indeed been proved possible—*pace Haaretz*—that such methods could 'be used to attain a desirable political end'. As Schechtman put it, they had been of 'inestimable political and education value. They freed the *Yishuv* from the humiliating status of British *Schutzjuden*; they taught the Arab terrorist bands a healthy lesson; and they generated a new spirit of militancy and self-sacrifice in the Jewish youth.'[56]

Yet it was in the maintenance of *Havlaga*, rather than in its breach, that the Zionists profited most from the 'disturbances'. While the British were breaking Arab military power, demoralizing the population and further emasculating an already low-calibre leadership, they were enabling the high-calibre Jewish leadership to mould the eager *Yishuv* into a formidable fighting force. *Havlaga*, however genuine in some, was purely expedient in others. It was designed to win British support for the establishment of a Jewish militia. And it succeeded. In 1936, the administration authorized the recruitment of a first batch of 1,240 Jewish supernumerary police; later that year, it informed the Zionist leadership that a special force of constables would be permitted to remain in being, with their arms, provided the already existing *Haganah* was disbanded and its illegal weapons handed over. With the growth of Arab violence, however, it tacitly dropped this condition. And in the following two years the force was further expanded until, by 1939, it totalled some 14,500 men, 5 per cent of the *Yishuv*. Its training, transferred from the police to the regular army, had continually grown in scope and sophistication. The lessons learned had been passed on to thousands of others in secret. The British civil authorities objected, on political grounds, to this rapid development of Jewish military capability, but the army command, interested only in crushing the Arab rebellion, supported Jewish demands for increased enrolment and training.

It was in the guise of the Special Night Squads that the Jews benefited most from the collaboration with the British, and, in particular, from the military genius of one eccentric captain, Orde Wingate, who, with the Old Testament as his inspiration, adopted the Zionist cause heart and soul. He it was who first inculcated those principles of offensive daring, of surprise, deep penetration and high mobility which the Israeli army subsequently developed to the full. It was under him that some of Israel's best officers had their first taste of battle with the Arabs—among them Moshe Dayan.

The British journalist Leonard Mosley describes the climax of the first raid in which Wingate took a party of young pioneers right into the enemy camp.

> By three o'clock in the morning, at the conclusion of the most strenuous thirty-mile walk even these earthy, hardened Jews had ever experienced, Wingate brought his column to the edge of the Arab village. . . . He went off into the darkness (to reconnoitre), and they waited for his signal. Soon they heard a shot, and they moved into the positions Wingate had mapped out for them. From the outskirts of the

village there was another shot; after which there was a fusillade of fire, obviously from the Arabs, a firefly spray of lights in the distance, shouts, screams and wails. And then, straight into the trap which Wingate had laid for them, came the Arabs. Dayan and Brenna, nearest the village, let the Arabs pass; they had instructions to hold their fire until the Arabs could be surrounded. Only when the Jews farthest away opened fire did Brenna and Dayan begin to pick off their victims. They killed five and captured four.

Wingate came back, carrying a Turkish rifle over his shoulder. He looked calm and serene. 'Good work. You are fine boys and will make good soldiers,' he said.

He went up to the four Arab prisoners. He said in Arabic: 'You have arms in this village. Where have you hidden them?'

The Arabs shook their heads, and protested ignorance. Wingate reached down and took sand and grit from the ground; he thrust it into the mouth of the first Arab and pushed it down his throat until he choked and puked.

'Now,' he said, 'where have you hidden the arms?'

Still they shook their heads.

Wingate turned to one of the Jews and, pointing to the coughing and spluttering Arab, said, 'Shoot this man.'

The Jew looked at him questioningly and hesitated.

Wingate said, in a tense voice, 'Did you hear? Shoot him.'

The Jew shot the Arab. The others stared for a moment, in stupefaction, at the dead body at their feet. The boys from Hanita were watching in silence.

'Now speak', said Wingate. They spoke.[57]

In 1939, after the MacDonald White Paper, the Jewish community was preparing to fight the Mandate with the weapons the Mandate had given it. British rule had served its evolutionary purpose; it no longer helped, it held back, the Zionists' inexorably unfolding design. The new, self-reliant stage of 'organized revolutionary rule' by the Jewish minority had been reached. The Mandate had to go. But great events elsewhere gave it new life. With the outbreak of world war the *Yishuv* rallied to the democracies and anti-British violence all but ceased. As Weizmann foresaw,[58] the second cataclysm of the twentieth century was to furnish opportunities as sensational as the first. Those opportunities, of which he again took full advantage, were primarily international and diplomatic. But this time they were supplemented, and eventually quite overshadowed, by other opportunities, local and military, furnished by the new balance of power in Palestine itself. Zionism's centre of gravity was shifting from the Diaspora to the *Yishuv*. Weizmann, the intimate of Western statesmen, still shaped the higher strategies. But the real striking-force, the real instrument of 'gun Zionism', was in the hands of David Bengurion, the rugged pioneer. And the seeds of the real, essentially Jabotinskian triumph—the swift, sharp transition to Jewish statehood in a land without Arabs—had already been sown in the British defeat of the Great Rebellion.

Notes

1. Warriner, Doreen, *Land and Poverty in the Middle East*, Royal Institute of International Affairs, London, 1948, pp. 61–2.
2. *Ibid.*, p. 63.
3. Barbour, *Nisi Dominus*, *op. cit.*, p. 133.
4. Warriner, *op. cit.*, p. 126.
5. Weinstock, Nathan, *Le Zionisme contre Israel*, François Maspero, Paris, 1969, p. 168.
6. Allush, Naji, *Arab Resistance in Palestine* (Arabic), *op. cit.*, p. 91.
7. Darwaza, Muhammad Izzat, *On the Modern Arab Movement*, (Arabic) The Modern Press, Sidon and Beirut, p. 59.
8. *Palestine Royal Commission Report* (the Peel Commission), H.M.S.O., London, 1937, Cmd. 5479, p. 80.
9. See p. 63.
10. Al-Kayyali, *A History of Modern Palestine* (Arabic), *op. cit.*, p. 296.
11. *Ibid.*, p. 306.
12. Marlowe, John, *The Seat of Pilate*, Cresset Press, London, 1959, pp. 137–8.
13. Newton, Frances, *Fifty Years in Palestine*, *op. cit.*, p. 275.
14. Peel Commission, *op. cit.*, pp. 93–4.
15. Al-Kayyali, *op. cit.*, p. 311.
16. Darwaza, Muhammad Izzat, *The Palestine Cause* (Arabic), The Modern Press, Sidon and Beirut, Vol. I, p. 131.
17. Barbour, *op. cit.*, p. 192.
18. Al-Kayyali, *op. cit.*, p. 313.
19. *Ibid.*, p. 315.
20. Shaw Commission, *op. cit.*, p. 126.

21. Peel Commission, *op. cit.*, p. 391.
22. Al-Kayyali, *op. cit.*, p. 333.
23. 6 September 1938.
24. 3 October 1938.
25. *The Times*, 4 October 1938.
26. 17 September 1938.
27. Kirkbride, Sir Alec, *A Crackle of Thorns*, John Murray, London, 1956, p. 56.
28. Newton, Frances, *Searchlight on Palestine: Fair Play or Terrorist Methods?* The Arab Centre, London, 1938, pp. 16–18.
29. Khalidi, Walid, *From Heaven to Conquest*, *op. cit.*, pp. 846–9.
30. *The Times*, 21 July 1938; *A Survey of Palestine*, Jerusalem, 1946, pp. 38–49.
31. See, for example, Sharabi, Hisham, *Palestine and Israel, The Lethal Dilemma*, Pegasus, New York, 1969, pp. 184–92.
32. *The Times*, 9 September 1938.
33. John, Robert and Hadawi Sami, *The Palestine Diary*, The Palestine Research Centre, Beirut, Vol. I, p. 279.
34. Al-Kayyali, *op. cit.*, p. 350.
35. See pp. 33–4.
36. The ESCO Foundation, *Palestine: A Study of Jewish, Arab and British Policies*, Vol. II, p. 910.
37. Avneri, *Israel Without Zionists: A Plea for Peace in the Middle East*, *op. cit.*, p. 88.
38. Marlow, *op. cit.*, p. 133.
39. See p. 36.
40. Taylor, Alan R., *The Zionist Mind, the Origins and Development of Zionist Thought*, *op. cit.*, p. 89.
41. *Ibid.*, p. 89.
42. *Ibid.*, p. 91.
43. *Jewish Frontier*, October 1948, pp. 7–8.
44. Weizmann, *Trial and Error*, *op. cit.*, pp. 484, 488.
45. 15 September 1938.
46. Schechtman, *Fighter and Prophet, the Vladimir Jabotinsky Story*, *op. cit.*, p. 474.
47. *The Times*, 21 July 1938.
48. *Palestine Post*, 26 July 1938.
49. 5 July 1938.
50. 17 July 1938.
51. 15 July 1938.
52. Schechtman, *op. cit.*, pp. 449, 453.
53. *Ibid.*, p. 485.
54. Bauer, Yehuda, *New Outlook*, July–August, Vol. IX, No. 7, p. 26.
55. Marlowe, John, *Rebellion in Palestine*, Cresset Press, London 1946, p. 244.
56. Schechtman, *op. cit.*, p. 483.
57. Mosley, Leonard, *Gideon Goes to War*, Arthur Barker, London, 1955, pp. 57–8.
58. Meinertzhagen, Richard, *Middle East Diary: 1917–1956*, Cresset Press, London, 1959, pp. 191–2.

4 · GUN ZIONISM

Driving Out the British

In 1946, the King David was something more, in the eyes of the *Yishuv*, than Jerusalem's most famous hotel. An entire wing of it, housing both military and civilian headquarters, had become the nexus of British power in Palestine. Every conceivable human and technical device protected this fortress in the heart of the city. Soldiers continuously patrolled around it; others manned machine-gun nests on its roof. Its front was covered by wire netting to prevent the casual throwing of explosives. You approached it through a barbed-wire alley flanked by armed guards. When you finally reached the outer door it was barred by steel shutters which could only be opened by an electrically operated switch from inside. And only when you passed through yet another electrically operated door had you penetrated to the inner sanctum itself.

This was the nut which one Menachim Begin resolved to crack. Jabotinsky had died in 1940, and it was Begin who, as the leader of the underground terrorist organization *Irgun Zwei Leumi*, emerged as a worthy successor to the founder of Revisionism. Begin had emigrated to Palestine from Poland during the war. 'A smallish man in his late thirties, looking older because of his heavy glasses', he 'appeared to be the typical Jew engaged in a small way in business in any town east of the Elbe. There was nothing military about him, nothing commanding, nothing exceptionally impressive.'[1] Yet he became a legendary figure in Palestine. Begin had one outstanding quality. He was a planner, albeit on a small scale, and meticulous down to the tiniest detail. This was the quality which he had used to the full when, in spring of 1946, he put before the *Haganah* and the official Zionist leadership Operation Malonchik—a plan for blowing up the King David Hotel. They eventually approved it, and on 22 July, shortly before noon, a truck drew up at the hotel's kitchen entrance, which lay at the opposite end to the government wing, and men dressed as Arabs got out. No one took any notice as they began to unload a cargo of milk churns and rolled them into the Regence Café next to the kitchen. No one guessed that those innocent milk churns were packed with high explosives or that these Arabs were the Assault Unit of the *Irgun*. In the basement, Begin's scouts had discovered, there was a broad passageway running the entire length of the building, and despite all the refinements of security deployed above ground, there was almost none below it. The 'Arabs' held up the staff of the Regence Café, clashed with two British officers, left the milk churns in their appointed place and set them to explode in half an hour. As the Assault Unit made its getaway, it released the café staff, who were told to run for their lives. The government workers above got no such warning—or at least none, in spite of Begin's claims to the contrary, on which they had any time to act.

> It was now twelve fifteen. Gideon [the commander of the Assault Unit] was counting the minutes. So far, everything had gone according to plan, except for the casualties we had suffered in the unexpected clash. . . . Only one question bothered him: would the explosives go off? Might not some error have been made in the mechanism? Would the building really go up? Would the documents be destroyed?
>
> Each minute seemed like a day. Twelve thirty-one, thirty-two. Zero hour drew near. Gideon grew restless. The half-hour was almost up. Twelve thirty-seven. . . . Suddenly the whole town seemed to shudder. There had been no mistake. The force of the explosion was greater than had been expected. Yitsak Sadeh, of the *Haganah*, had doubted whether it would reach the third or even the second floor. Giddy had claimed that, though only about 500 lbs of explosives—a compound of T.N.T. and gelignite—had been put into the milk-cans, the confined space of the basement would heighten the force of the escaping gases, and the explosion would reach the roof. The milk-cans 'reached' the whole height of the building, from basement to roof, six storeys of stone, concrete and steel. As the B.B.C. put it—the entire wing of a huge building was cut off as with a knife.[2]

More than eighty-eight people perished in the rubble: British, Arab—and fifteen Jews.

The blowing up of the King David carried a message for the whole world. A new nation had arisen in Palestine; conceived in the Balfour Declaration, nurtured in the Mandatory womb, it was delivered in the just violence that historic events always engender. Many, including faint-hearted Jews, had thought it would be crushed in embryo. How little they understood the innate resources of the human spirit. In his book *The Revolt*, Menachim Begin initiates his readers into the metaphysics of Jewish national redemption.

> The revolt sprang from the earth. The ancient Greek story of Antaeus and the strength he drew from contact with Mother Earth is a legend. The renewed strength which came to us, and especially to our youth, from contact with the soil of our ancient land, is no legend but a fact. The officials of the British Foreign Office had no conception of this when they made their plans. What could they foresee of those hidden forces which Herzl used to speak of as the 'imponderables'? Their error was not mathematical; they were not wrong about the number of Jews wanting to come to Eretz Israel. They assumed that in Eretz Israel, too, the Jews would continue to be timid suppliants for protection. The conduct of the Jews—or rather the attitude of their official leaders, expressed in the well-known policy of self-restraint (Havlaga)—seemed to justify and confirm this assumption. But those unseen forces, which have ever saved the Jewish people from obliteration, demolished the British assumption. . . . A new generation grew up which turned its back on fear. It began to fight instead of to plead. For nearly two thousand years, the Jews, as Jews, had not borne arms, and it was on this complete disarmament, as much psychological as physical, that our oppressors calculated. They did not realize that the two phenomena were interdependent; we gave up our arms when we were exiled from our country. With our return to the land of our fathers our strength was restored. . . .[3]

When Descartes said: 'I think, therefore I am', he uttered a very profound thought. But there are times in the history of peoples when thought alone does not prove their existence. A people may 'think' and yet its sons, with their thoughts and in spite of them, may be turned

> into a herd of slaves—or into soap. There are times when everything in you cries out: your very self-respect as a human being lies in your resistance to evil.
>
> We fight, therefore we are.[4]

'Gun Zionism' had truly come into its own. Like the Arab Rebellion a decade earlier, it was directed against the British rulers of Palestine. With the outbreak of World War II, the official Zionist leadership, stifling their anger at the 1939 White Paper, had decided to offer their services to the Allies. The further development of their own military capability, through the enrollment of Jews in British forces, was the reward they expected and secured. The *Irgun* respected this truce too; only an *Irgun* splinter, the *Stern Gang*, refused to relent.

With the end of the war, and the defeat of Fascism, the Zionists immediately began to clamour for that Jewish statehood which now revealed itself as the manifest purpose, the only true fulfilment, of all their strivings. In May 1942, some 600 delegates from Palestine, Europe and America had assembled for a kind of extraordinary World Zionist Congress in New York. Weizmann, the elder statesman, was there, but it was David Bengurion who infused the conference with the pugnacious new spirit of Palestine Jewry. The Jewish Commonwealth which the so-called Biltmore Programme demanded was, in all but name, a Jewish State; the *Yishuv* should have its own army, fighting under its own flag; the gates of Palestine should be opened to unrestricted immigration under the control of the Jewish Agency, which should also be granted the authority to build up the country and develop its unoccupied and uncultivated lands. Biltmore captured almost the whole Zionist movement. It was a moral triumph for the Revisionists. Bengurion and the moderate majority had caught up with Begin and the extremist minority. After Biltmore, the jurists duly reinterpreted the Balfour Declaration. 'The Jewish people is to have not only a home in Palestine but a national home. "National" means pertaining to a nation. . . . Logically, therefore, a national home appears to be an equivalent for State.'[5] Only a tiny, nonconformist few, moralists in the tradition of Ahad Aham, refused to be carried away. Moshe Smilansky, a veteran immigrant of the 1890s, complained that

> . . . a certain royal atmosphere has begun to impose itself upon the *Yishuv*. The first in the Zionist camp to proclaim the state as a fundamental tenet were the Revisionists—they who until the Biltmore days were, rightly, like pariahs in the Zionist movement. Formerly only the Revisionist youth were brought up in the spirit of chauvinism and militarism, which crass ignorance and short-sightedness considered 'nationalism'. Today, however, most of our youth are brought up in this spirit. . . . The *Haganah* was a pure creation in the beginning, clean of purpose and pure of motive. But the promulgation of a 'state' and the preparations that led to it have turned the *Haganah*'s dish upside down, putting that organization in the same rank as the murderers of the *Irgun Zvai Leumi* and the *Stern* Group. Since the Biltmore days, freedom of thought and speech have been banned. Scribes have turned into 'shofars' [horns] trumpeting the slogans dictated from above. Anyone who dares to have an opinion of his own is considered a traitor. Writers of any independence have been forced to remain dumb. . . .[6]

A fortnight after the end of the war in Europe, the Zionists, with Biltmore as their new canon, demanded from Churchill's coalition cabinet an immediate decision to proclaim Palestine, 'undiminished and undivided', as a Jewish State. They were told that any Palestine settlement must await a general peace conference. Two months later the Labour Party defeated Churchill and the Conservatives in a landslide victory at the polls. The Zionists naturally felt that this augured well for them, because Labour's record of devotion to their cause was a long and unblemished one. Their hopes were quickly shattered. The responsibilities of office brought the Archimedean discovery that all the theoretical, Zionist-inspired formulations of successive party congresses were completely incompatible with the Arab-dominated realities of the land to which they were supposed to be applied. To Ernest Bevin, the Foreign Secretary, fell the unhappy task of giving the discovery practical expression; he was soon to be vilified for his pains as the anti-Semite which, judging by his past record,[7] he certainly was not.

Bevin tried, in the spirit of the 1939 White Paper, to win acceptance for an independent state of Palestine that was neither Jewish nor Arab, but a marriage, in conditions of mutual respect and equality, of both. For nearly two years he refused to bow to the *diktat* of either side. It was an attempt at impartiality to which the Zionists took furious exception, for it was they, rather than the Arabs, who were now on the offensive. Bevin rejected Biltmore—and he also rejected lesser, interim demands, departures from the White Paper, whose acceptance would have blasted his credit in Arab eyes. Chief of these was the immediate admission of 100,000 refuges from war-ravaged Europe. He despatched yet another Commission of Inquiry to Palestine. This time America, now leader of the West, was invited to join in the investigations. The Commission recommended the formation, after a prolonged period of UN trusteeship, of some kind of bi-national state. This was broadly in keeping with the White Paper: the Zionists consequently rejected the proposal. It also endorsed the admission of the 100,000. The Arabs would have none of that—but since, at the same time, the Zionists were called upon to disband their illegal militias, neither would they. A little later they sabotaged a proposal for Arab-Jewish provincial autonomy put forward by an Anglo-American team of experts. Bevin finally gave up the struggle. In April 1947, Britain threw the whole desperate muddle into the lap of the UN. Thereafter, the final dishonourable scuttle, behind a sanctimonious façade of reluctant compliance with international will, was only a matter of time.

It was bound to come to this. The world had changed since 1939, and Britain, victorious but enfeebled, no longer had the will or the resources to sustain the burden which Palestine had become. Of this the Zionists were well aware, and when Bevin emerged as an obstacle in their path, they determined to sweep him aside. They would enforce the end of the Mandate in their own way.

The way they chose was the quintessentially Revisionist one of violence. And just as, at Biltmore, moderates had joined extremists in proposing a common goal, so the entire Zionist movement, faced with British opposition, came together in achieving it. Violence was not, of course, the only way. Diplomacy, the speciality of Weizmann and the official leadership, was still crucial. The emergence of the American super-power was one of the new realities of the post-war world, and from now on it was in the United States rather than in

Britain, the old imperial power in rapid decline, that the Zionists exerted their main leverage. Weizmann achieved his apotheosis with a demonstration that he was just as much a master of his diplomatic art on one side of the Atlantic as he was on the other. America's Jewish community, electorally pivotal and far more numerous than Britain's, had finally rallied *en masse* to the cause. The Zionists now converted this leverage, via the American administration, into a pressure on Britain that supplemented and far outweighed that which they exerted from their local British constituency itself. President Truman played shamelessly for the Jewish vote. He told American ambassadors to the Arab world: 'I am sorry, gentlemen, but I have to answer to hundreds of thousands who are anxious for the success of Zionism; I do not have hundreds of thousands of Arabs among my constituents.'[8] Time and again, he threw an obliging spanner into the delicate machinery of Arab-Jewish conciliation which Bevin was so laboriously trying to set in motion. He pushed for the admission of the 100,000 immigrants—blithely ignoring the suggestion that, in that case, he should share responsibility, through the despatch of American troops to Palestine, for quelling the Arab disorders it would provoke. No sooner had the Anglo-American experts produced their painstaking plan for provincial autonomy than, endorsing the rival Zionist scheme, Truman drove a coach and horses through it. Nor were America's persuasions free from the taint of economic blackmail; its gallant war-ravaged ally could only count on its portion of American financial aid if it behaved itself in Palestine.[9]

Violence was also coordinated with propaganda. Never slow to make a propaganda point, the Zionists now staged one of the most successful of all time. Among the human wreckage of Hitler's war were some 300,000 Jewish survivors of the Holocaust. Few of them would, of free choice, have gone to Palestine rather than the United States or Western Europe. But they did not have that free choice. America, in particular, denied it to them. This vast and prosperous country, this nation of immigrants, demanded of little Palestine that it open its doors to some 100,000 deserving refugees. Yet, at the same time, it was only with extreme reluctance that Congress agreed to admit a mere 20,000 of these self-same remnants of the

Holocaust, and especially the Jews among them; three years were needed to persuade it to accept a bill which, in Truman's words, 'discriminates in callous fashion against displaced persons of the Jewish faith'.[10] No one did more to encourage the American denial than the Zionists themselves. Truman's predecessor had sent Morris Ernst, a Jewish lawyer, on a mission to explore the possibilities of an international effort, with every country taking a reasonable share of the burden, to settle the refugee problem. Ernst recalled: 'I was amazed and even felt insulted when active Jewish leaders decried, sneered and then attacked me as if I were a traitor. At one dinner party I was openly accused of furthering this plan for freer immigration in order to undermine political Zionism.' But that did not prevent Truman or the Zionists from demanding that the gates of Palestine be thrown open to the refugees on humanitarian grounds—Palestine which, in Truman's words, had become their 'only hope of survival'. Nor did it prevent them from reviling Britain for refusing them entry—'the small impoverished island of Great Britain' which, as Ernst testified, had 'received to date more refugees than all the other nations of the world combined'.[11]

What easier way to the hearts of ordinary, decent men and women everywhere—particularly in innocent America—than this dramatization of the immigrants' struggle to reach the Promised Land? The story of the ship *Exodus*, most famous of those cargoes of human misery finding their way to the shores of Palestine, has been glorified in book and film. When, in 1947, this creaking vessel arrived in Haifa, the British authorities refused to allow the 4,500 refugees aboard to land. The Zionists knew this would happen—for by this time the British were strictly enforcing their immigration controls—and they had everything ready to make sure the world would see it. The *Exodus* sailed back to Marseilles and, after various adventures rich in heartrending spectacle, the refugees ended up in the British zone of Germany. Newspaper readers and newsreel audiences throughout the United States followed every stage of this dismal odyssey; little did they realize that it had been deliberately provoked.

The blowing up of the King David was the high point of anti-British violence in Palestine—as devastating in its symbolic as its physical impact. It was a blow deliberately aimed at the very nerve-centre of British tyranny. It was, if not a pre-ordained, at least an eminently predictable *tour de force* of 'gun Zionism'. It was the kind of deed to which all Zionists, moderate no less than extremist, had long been ineluctably gravitating. The theorists had propounded—and justified—such courses long before the men of action had carried them out. After the 1939 White Paper, Jabotinsky had come to the conclusion that 'the only way to liberate the country is by the sword'.[12] He formulated a plan for a military rebellion to be staged by the *Irgun*. In October 1939 a boatload of 'illegal' immigrants, Jabotinsky among them, would land in the middle of the country, if possible Tel Aviv. The *Irgun* would secure the landing, if necessary by force. At the same time there would be an armed insurrection in which as many official buildings as possible—including Government House in Jerusalem—would be invested. The Jewish flag would be raised. The positions were to be held and Jabotinsky's capture resisted, whatever the sacrifices, for at least twenty-four hours. During the rebellion the Provisional Government of the Jewish State would be simultaneously proclaimed in the capitals of Western Europe and the United States; this would subsequently function as a government-in-exile, the embodiment of Jewish sovereignty in Palestine.[13] (The Jewish *coup d'état* was conceived in much the same madcap spirit as another enterprise for which Jabotinsky had been trying to win United States support: the achievement of 'a Jewish majority overnight'. He had argued that the Zionists should 'dump into Palestine about a million lads at once'.[14]) The *coup d'état*—so Jabotinsky's thinking ran—was bound to be suppressed, but before it was it would have placed the Jewish and non-Jewish world before the historic *fait accompli* of proclaimed Jewish statehood. The very fact that Jews had been able, even for twenty-four hours, to occupy the country's key administrative strongholds would have created a political reality that could never be erased. For Jewish sovereignty—perpetuated by the symbol of the Jewish government-in-exile—no sacrifice was too great.

At the same time, the Arlosoroff scheme for 'revolutionary minority rule'[15] showed that the moderate mainstream Zionist leaders, however hotly they denied it, were instinctively drawn towards Revisionist solutions for otherwise insoluble problems;

Arlosoroff had closely studied Curzio Malaparte's book on the theory of insurrections in the twentieth century and what he had in mind—to put it in that plain language which, unlike the Revisionists, the moderates characteristically eschewed—was 'a real putsch against the British'.[16]

The official leadership had approved of the King David operation. It may be true—as the Jewish Agency later claimed—that the *kind* of operation which they approved, designed to achieve a maximum physical destruction with a minimum loss of life, was very different from the one carried out, or—as Menachim Begin claimed—it may not. But, in accordance with the theory of 'connected struggle', they did approve the principle. This was the theory by which the advocates of *Havlaga* in the thirties justified a resort to violence in the forties. The violence was supposed to be limited and selective, confined to attacks on obstacles which stood in what they considered to be Zionism's legitimate path. If, for example, Haifa Radar Station were interfering with immigration, then Haifa Radar Station must be destroyed. Railway tracks carried the trains which brought the soldiers who hunted the immigrants; it was therefore right and proper to blow up the railway tracks. The same principle governed the law of retaliation. *Haganah* theorists sought to establish a kind of mathematical relationship between 'attack' and 'reprisal'. 'The scope of the reprisal', so the equation went, 'is equal to the magnitude of the attack.'[17]

Operation Malonchik was, in their view, a fitting reprisal to a British provocation. Troops had occupied the offices of the Jewish Agency. This had been done in the course of a massive security drive which mounting Jewish violence, likewise approved or condoned, had prompted. Nevertheless, the Jewish Agency was deemed to be the 'Jewish Headquarters'. So the Jews must repay the British in kind, and attack them in *their* headquarters at the King David.

The official leadership, after some hesitation, denounced the 'dissident outrage'. The death toll had been far higher than they expected. But their denunciations had little moral worth. For it had long been their standard practice to dissociate themselves from operations which, under the theory of 'connected struggle', they had approved or actually sponsored. Indeed, when British forces invaded the Jewish Agency offices, which were fondly imagined to enjoy some kind of protected 'international status', they were able to take out of the very typewriter a verbatim report on the speech which Moshe Sharett, the head of the Agency's Political Department, had delivered to the Zionist General Council (which is why, incidentally, the destruction of incriminating documents furnished another motive for blowing up the King David). In this speech Sharett had praised a multiple sabotage operation carried out jointly by the *Haganah*, *Irgun* and *Stern*—praise which was hard to reconcile with the Agency's repeated protest that it knew nothing of such things.[18] In fact, the Jewish Resistance Movement, a working alliance of moderates and extremists, had come into being soon after the end of World War II. Under questioning, Bengurion was forced to admit that the Agency did nothing to suppress terrorism. 'We cannot do it because, as I told you, it is futile, sir, it is futile.' Of this excuse, Richard Crossman, an influential British champion of Zionism, said that 'he seems to want to have it both ways, to remain within the letter of the law as chairman of the Agency, and to tolerate terror as a method of bringing pressure on the Administration'.[19] Weizmann himself occasionally seemed to perceive, and abhor, the aberrations of 'gun Zionism' in action: 'If you . . . wish to secure your redemption through means . . . which do not accord with Jewish morale, with Jewish ethics or Jewish history, I say to you that you are worshipping false gods. . . . Go and re-read Isaiah, Jeremiah and Ezekiel, and test that which we do and wish to do in the light of the teachings of our great prophets and wise men. They knew the nature and character of the Jewish people. Zion will be redeemed through righteousness; and not by any other means.'[20] Yet when Crossman taxed him in private on the blowing up of the King David, Weizmann said, with tears streaming down his cheeks, 'I can't help feeling proud of our boys.'[21]

Tolerance of Zionist violence was not confined to Palestine; it permeated the United States. There, public and politicians were subjected to a propaganda *blitzkrieg* which yielded nothing, in sound and fury, to the deeds it glorified. Its message was as simple as it was tendentious. The Hebrew fighters in Palestine, it said, were rising against the self-same cruel oppressor from whom, 170 years before, the American Revolutionaries had won their freedom. It was the same patriotic war that the Irish had fought, and the Boers of South Africa. Two New York Senators felt obliged to protest directly to the British Foreign Secretary. One of them called on the United States to dissociate itself from the 'crimes' and 'the brutal imperialisms' of the British. Forgotten, in this virulent campaign, were the inestimable services which, often at great cost to themselves, those British imperialists had rendered to Zionism—forgotten the three-year Arab Rebellion which they had put down on its behalf. British Tommies, it now seemed, were not much better than Hitler's Storm Troopers. It was a climate in which the Zionists and their American friends could openly applaud acts of violence and solicit funds for promoting more of them. In a 'Letter to the Terrorists of Palestine', published in the *New York Herald Tribune*, Ben Hecht, the Hollywood scriptwriter, assured them:

> The Jews of America are for you. You are their champion. You are the grin they wear. You are the feather in their hats. In the past fifteen hundred years, every nation of Europe has taken a crack at the Jews. This time the British are at bat. You are the first answer that makes sense—to the New World. Every time you blow up a British arsenal, or wreck a British jail, or send a British railroad train sky high, or rob a British bank, or let go with your guns and bombs at the British betrayers and invaders of your homeland, the Jews of America make a little holiday in their hearts. . . . Brave friends, we are working to help you. We are raising funds for you. . . .[22]

After every performance of Hecht's Zionist 'musical', *A Flag Is Born*, thousands of dollars were handed over to the *Irgun* representatives. Eleanor Roosevelt put herself in the forefront of the fund-raising campaign. American law prohibits the private furnishing of arms to a foreign country, but Hecht and his friends managed to pass off the money they raised for the terrorists as tax-free contributions to charity.[23] British protests to the State Department about what 'amounted to an incitement to murder British officials and soldiers in the Holy Land' achieved nothing.

America was but the most important of sixty-four countries in which the Zionists operated. In France, for example, they commanded sympathy, as in America, through the exploitation of a traditional strain of anti-British sentiment. Several editorial writers on famous newspapers like *Le Figaro* and *Combat* were members of the French League for a Free (Zionist) Palestine and even the judicious and serious *Le Monde* was said to discern 'the justice and strength of *Irgun*'s fight against Great Britain'.[24]

It was hardly surprising that the country which least appreciated Zionist violence was Britain. Since the beginning of the Mandate British soldiers and administrators arriving in Palestine with neutral or pro-Zionist sentiments tended, through direct contact with both sides, to acquire pro-Arab ones. 'Gun Zionism' naturally accelerated and deepened such conversions. There have been some grudging Zionist acknowledgements that, on the whole, British troops, rough and contemptuous though they often were, behaved with a discipline that few other armies would have managed in the circumstances. Nevertheless, there were disreputable episodes in which police and soldiers took private vengeance on the Jews. Mosleyite tendencies made themselves felt.[25] A court-martial was less than zealous in the prosecution of a Major Farran, acquitting him on a charge of beating to death a sixteen-year-old suspected *Stern Gang* member.

The sentiment communicated itself to the mother country. The Foreign Secretary, Ernest Bevin, had become passionately anti-Zionist. The press described Begin's 'Hebrew fighters' as terrorists and thugs. A proverbially tolerant society—wrote an American Jewish magazine[26]—was growing resentful not only of the Jews of Palestine, but also of the Jews of Britain, who were felt to be in some kind of sympathy with these foreigners who were shooting British Tommies in cold blood. There were anti-Jewish outbursts. Police had to guard synagogues. When Major Farran sailed into Liverpool a crowd of thousands thronged the docks to welcome him.

The first emotional response to Zionist violence was anger—and a natural desire to strike back. That should have been quite feasible. Britain had 100,000 troops in Palestine. The second, and eventually decisive, response was the desire to have done with the whole wretched business. 'Govern or Get Out', screamed a *Sunday Express* headline the morning after sixteen synchronized terrorist actions throughout Palestine had left a score of armoured vehicles destroyed and eighty soldiers dead and wounded. In the House of Commons, Winston Churchill, now the Leader of the Opposition, conceded that 'the claims and the desires of the Zionists latterly went beyond anything that was agreed upon by the Mandatory power', but the thing to do now was 'to lay our Mandate at the feet of the United Nations Organization and thereafter evacuate the country with which we have no connection or tradition and where we have no sovereignty as in India and no treaty as in Egypt. . . .'[27] He berated the government for 'keeping one hundred thousand Englishmen away' from home in a 'squalid' war 'at a cost of £30 to £40 million a year'. Britain's diminishing resources were being squandered on a 'vast apparatus of protraction and delay'.[28] This was the impulse on which the Zionists counted. Originating in public opinion, taken up by the Opposition, it was bound, before long, to animate the hard-pressed post-war Labour Government itself. The war-weary British deeply resented the loss of yet more young lives in a costly colonial war against an enemy as ruthless as he was ungrateful. Operation Malonchik was the Zionists' greatest coup. But they also blew up bridges, mined roads, derailed trains and sunk patrol boats. Day after day they attacked barracks and installations. They raided armouries and robbed pay vans. They blew up twenty warplanes on closely guarded airfields in a single night. They staged what the British press called the 'greatest jail-break in history'. *Irgun* and *Stern* were ready to do anything, anywhere. They blew up the British embassy in Rome. They despatched letter-bombs to British ministers, and one addressed to Major Farran killed his brother by mistake. They sent an assassination squad into Britain, with the mission—which was not accomplished—of executing the former commanding officer in Palestine, General Evelyn Barker; its members included Weizmann's own nephew, Ezer Weizmann, one of the architects of the Israeli air force. They planned to sink a British passenger ship in Shanghai and a destroyer in Portsmouth.[29] In Palestine they killed soldiers in their sleep. They captured and flogged officers; then they hanged two sergeants from a tree and booby-trapped their dangling corpses. It was too much.

British war-weariness meant that, faced with Jewish rebellion, the Mandatory authorities did quite the opposite of what they had done, ten years earlier, in response to an Arab rebellion. Field Marshal Montgomery, the Chief of the Imperial General Staff, bitterly reproached the government for tying the hands of his soldiers, for the 'completely gutless' tactics they were obliged to adopt. 'The only way the army could stamp out terrorism was to take the offensive against it, and this was not allowed.' It had surrendered the initiative to the terrorists. He, too, concluded that 'if we were not prepared to maintain law and order in Palestine it would be better to get out'.[30] Thus it came about that while, in the late thirties, 20,000 soldiers broke the military power of a million Arabs, in the late forties 600,000 Jews, admittedly an altogether more formidable force than the Arabs, enforced the humiliating withdrawal of 100,000 soldiers.

It was more than just fatigue, a loss of imperial will, more than just overwhelming American pressure that generated such a partisan spirit. This was also rooted in the pro-Zionist traditions of the ruling establishment—traditions that were nowhere stronger, in spite of Bevin, than in the Labour Party. Even now, as British troops did battle with 'gun Zionism', Weizmann and his friends continued to enjoy that easy access to the centres of power from which they had profited so handsomely in the twenties and thirties. One startling illustration will suffice. John Strachey was the Under-Secretary of State for Air in the Attlee Administration. His biographer records that

> Only on Palestine did Strachey have any serious dispute with the government. One day, Crossman, now in the House of Commons, came to see Strachey. The former was devoting his efforts to the Zionist cause. He had heard from his friends in the Jewish Agency that they were contemplating an act of sabotage, not only for its own purpose, but to demonstrate to the world their capacities. Should this be done, or should it not? Few would be killed. But would it help the Jews? Crossman asked Strachey for his advice, and Strachey, a member of the Defence Committee of the Cabinet, undertook to find out. The next day in the Smoking Room at the House of Commons, Strachey gave his approval to Crossman. The *Haganah* went ahead and blew up all the bridges over the Jordan. No one was killed, but the British army in Palestine were cut off from their lines of supply with Jordan.[31]

In the opinion of Christopher Mayhew, a former Labour MP, this was but a particularly flagrant example of a pattern of behaviour which would normally be considered scandalous, if not positively treasonable, and certainly inconceivable in any other context than that of Zionism.

> At a time when the hard-pressed British army in Palestine is struggling to uphold the policy of the British [Labour] Government against attacks mounted by Zionist terrorists, a [Labour] Member of Parliament who supports the Zionists feels free to approach a Minister and ask him whether to encourage a specific terrorist action *against the British army in Palestine*. Most astonishing of all is the fact that the Minister, who is actually a member of the government's Defence Committee, gives his 'approval' for the action, which mercifully (and against the expectations of those who had planned it, and presumably of the MP and the Minister as well) caused no loss of life, but which did aggravate the difficult and dangerous situation of the British army in Palestine.[32]

On 2 April 1947, Sir Alexander Cadogan, the British representative at the UN, requested that the question of Palestine be put before that year's session of the General Assembly, which Britain would then ask 'to make recommendations . . . concerning the future government of Palestine'. On 29 November, the Assembly voted for the creation, within a partitioned Palestine, of a Jewish State. Britain subsequently announced that it would terminate the Mandate on 15 May 1948, by which date all its forces in Palestine would have been withdrawn.

'Gun Zionism' had driven out the British. Begin had no doubt about it: it was the hanging of Sergeants Paice and Martin in a eucalyptus grove near Natanya which gave the final push. But for 'this grim act of retaliation' which the execution of two terrorists had 'forced upon' the *Irgun*, a foreign power would be ruling in Palestine to this day. And the moral argument is reinforced by a historical aphorism which is quintessential Begin: 'When a nation re-awakens, its finest sons are prepared to give their lives for its liberation. When Empires are threatened with collapse they are prepared to sacrifice their non-commissioned officers.'[33] 'Gun Zionism' had driven out the British—but there still remained the Arabs.

Driving Out the Arabs

Kfar Sha'ul is an outer suburb of modern Jerusalem, not far from the highway that sweeps down to Tel Aviv and the coastal plain. It is the site of the Government Hospital for Mental Diseases, but, apart from that, there is nothing remarkable about Kfar Sha'ul. Yet it once had a very different appearance. Indeed, in 1948, it was an Arab, not a Jewish community, which clung to that rocky promontory. Its 400 inhabitants had a particular way of life; they were masons who worked a nearby quarry. Otherwise, however, the village was as typical, with its honey-coloured stone houses, of Arab Palestine as Kfar Sha'ul is typical of Jewish Palestine today. The story of its metamorphosis is the story of 'gun Zionism' at its cruellest. The Arab village has vanished. No map records it. But it remains indelibly printed in a hundred million Arab minds as the most emotive slogan of an unending struggle. Its name was Deir Yassin.

In 1948 Deir Yassin had a particularly peaceable reputation. For months, as Arab-Jewish clashes intensified throughout the country, it had lived 'in a sort of agreement' with neighbouring Jewish settlements;[34] it was practically the only village in the Jerusalem area not to complain to the Arab authorities that it was in danger; it had on occasion collaborated with the Jewish Agency;[35] it was said by a Jewish newspaper to have driven out some Arab militants.[36] On the night of 9 April 1948, the villagers went to sleep, as usual, in the comforting knowledge that they were among the least likely of Jewish targets. Just as a precaution, however, and in accordance with ancient custom, the village elders had appointed a score of night watchmen. These sported a few old Mausers and Turkish muskets whose main function, till then, had been the shooting of rabbits and the furnishing of a noisy backdrop for village weddings and feasts.[37]

At 4.30 the following morning, a combined force of *Irgun* and *Stern*, 132 strong, descended on the sleeping village. By noon they had slaughtered two-thirds of the inhabitants. For this operation, as for the blowing up of the King David, the *Irgun* was acting in collaboration with the *Haganah* and the official Jewish leadership.

'I wish to point out that the capture of Deir Yassin and holding it is one stage in our general plan.' So ran the letter, quickly made public by the *Irgun*, in which the Jerusalem commander of the *Haganah* had outlined his interest in the affair. 'I have no objection to your carrying out the operation provided you are able to hold the village . . . if foreign forces enter the place this will upset our plans for establishing an airfield.'[38] The raiders called it 'Operation Unity', for not only had *Irgun* and *Stern* joined forces, *Haganah* had made its contribution too. It had furnished weapons, and a unit of the *Palmach*, the *Haganah*'s élite commando forces, was to play some part in the actual fighting—supplying covering fire according to its own account,[39] demolishing the Mukhtar's house with a two-inch mortar according to the *Irgun*.[40]

Although it took place on the very edge of Palestine's biggest city, very few people, apart from its perpetrators and surviving victims, actually witnessed the massacre or its immediate aftermath. The perpetrators did not consider it an atrocity at all; people who did had fallen for 'lying propaganda' designed to besmirch their name. According to Begin, his men had fought a clean fight against fierce resistance; they had sought 'to avoid a single unnecessary casualty'; and, by using a loudspeaker to warn all women, children and old men to take refuge in the hills they had deprived themselves, in a spirit of humanity, of the elements of complete surprise.[41]

It seems, however, that the loudspeaker was as ineffectual as the claimed half-hour advance warning to the occupants of the King David Hotel; the armoured car on which it was mounted fell into a ditch well short of the first houses, and only the car's crew could hear the message which it blared into the night.[42] The surviving victims certainly told a very different story, although, mostly women and children, they were apparently very reluctant to tell it at all to the British police who interrogated them. Twelve-year-old Fahimi Zidan survived the first mass killing of about thirty-five villagers. He recalled: 'The Jews ordered all our family to line up against the wall and they started shooting us. I was hit in the side, but most of us children were saved because we hid behind our parents. The bullets hit my sister Kadri (four) in the head, my sister Sameh (eight) in the cheek, my brother Mohammad (seven) in the chest. But all the others with us against the wall were killed: my father, my mother, my grandfather and grandmother, my uncles and aunts and some of their children.' Halim Eid saw 'a man shoot a bullet into the neck of my sister Salhiyeh who was nine months pregnant'. Then he cut her stomach open with a butcher's knife. She said that another woman, Aisha Radwan, was killed trying to extract the unborn infant from the dead mother's womb. In another house, Naaneh Khalil, sixteen, saw a man take 'a kind of sword and slash my neighbour Jamil Hish from head to toe then do the same thing on the steps to my house to my cousin Fathi'. The attackers killed, looted, and finally they raped. They dynamited the houses; and when the dynamite ran out they systematically worked through the remaining buildings with Sten guns and grenades. By noon they had despatched 254 people; as for their own casualties, what Begin described as 'murderous' fire from the old Mausers and muskets had cost them four dead. To one of his reports, the British interrogating officer, Assistant-Inspector General Richard Catling, appended this comment:

> On 14th April at 10 a.m. I visited Silwan village accompanied by a doctor and a nurse from the Government Hospital in Jerusalem and a member of the Arab Women's Union. We visited many houses in this village in which approximately some two to three hundred people from Deir Yassin are housed. I interviewed many of the womenfolk in order to glean some information on any atrocities committed in Deir Yassin but the majority of those women are very shy and reluctant to relate their experiences especially in matters concerning sexual assault and they need great coaxing before they will divulge any information. The recording of statements is hampered also by the hysterical state of of the women who often break down many times whilst the statement is being recorded. There is, however, no doubt that many sexual atrocities were committed by the attacking Jews. Many young school girls were raped and later slaughtered. Old women were also molested. One story is current concerning a case in which a young girl was literally torn in two. Many infants were also butchered and killed. I also saw one old

> woman who gave her age as one hundred and four who had been severely beaten about the head with rifle butts. Women had bracelets torn from their arms and rings from their fingers, and parts of some of the women's ears were severed in order to remove earrings.[43]

One of the outsiders who did witness this terrible event waited twenty-four years before he allowed the account he made of it to see the light of day. On 9 April Meir Pa'el, then a young *Palmach* commando, had 'set down what he saw with his own eyes and what he heard with his own ears in the report which he sent at the time to Israel Galili (subsequently Minister of State), the head of the *Haganah* command'.

> It was noon when the battle ended and the shooting stopped. Things had become quiet, but the village had not surrendered. The *Etzel* [*Irgun*] and *Lehi* [*Stern*] irregulars left the places in which they had been hiding and started carrying out cleaning up operations in the houses. They fired with all the arms they had, and threw explosives into the houses. They also shot everyone they saw in the houses, including women and children—indeed the commanders made no attempt to check the disgraceful acts of slaughter. I myself and a number of inhabitants begged the commanders to give orders to their men to stop shooting, but our efforts were unsuccessful. In the meantime some twenty-five men had been brought out of the houses: they were loaded into a freight truck and led in a 'victory parade', like a Roman triumph, through to Mhaneh Yahuda and Zakhron Yosef quarters [of Jerusalem]. At the end of the parade they were taken to a stone quarry between Giv'at Sha'ul and Deir Yassin and shot in cold blood. The fighters then put the women and children who were still alive on a truck and took them to the Mandelbaum Gate.[44]

The other witness risked his life to learn the truth about Deir Yassin. The Jewish Agency refused to render any assistance to Jacques de Reynier, head of the International Red Cross delegation in Palestine, in his efforts to investigate the massacre. They did not expect him, unassisted, to come back alive from *Irgun*-controlled territory. But, more through good luck than any precautions he took, this courageous man did come back—eventually to record the grisly experience in his memoirs of the war:

> . . . the Commander of the *Irgun* detachment did not seem willing to receive me. At last he arrived, young, distinguished, and perfectly correct, but there was a peculiar glitter in his eyes, cold and cruel. According to him the *Irgun* had arrived 24 hours earlier and ordered the inhabitants by loudspeaker to evacuate all houses and surrender: the time given to obey the order was a quarter of an hour. Some of these miserable people had come forward and were taken prisoners, to be released later in the direction of the Arab lines. The rest, not having obeyed the order, had met the fate they deserved. But there was no point in exaggerating things, there were only a few dead, and they would be buried as soon as the 'cleaning up' of the village was over. If I found any bodies, I could take them, but there were certainly no wounded. This account made my blood run cold.
>
> I went back to the Jerusalem road and got an ambulance and a truck that I had alerted through the Red Shield. . . . I reached the village with my convoy, and the Arab firing stopped. The gang was wearing country uniforms, with helmets. All of them were young, some even adolescents, men and women, armed to the teeth: revolvers, machine-guns, hand grenades, and also cutlasses in their hands, most of them still blood-stained. A beautiful young girl, with criminal eyes, showed me hers still dripping with blood; she displayed it like a trophy. This was the 'cleaning up' team, that was obviously performing its task very conscientiously.
>
> I tried to go into a house. A dozen soldiers surrounded me, their machine-guns aimed at my body, and their officer forbade me to move. The dead, if any, would be brought to me, he said. I then flew into one of the most towering rages of my life, telling these criminals what I thought of their conduct, threatening them with everything I could think of, and then pushed them aside and went into the house.
>
> The first room was dark, everything was in disorder, but there was no one. In the second, amid disembowelled furniture and covers and all sorts of debris, I found some bodies cold. Here, the 'cleaning up' had been done with machine-guns, then hand grenades. It had been finished off with knives, anyone could see that. The same thing in the next room, but as I

was about to leave, I heard something like a sigh. I looked everywhere, turned over all the bodies, and eventually found a little foot, still warm. It was a little girl of ten, mutilated by a hand grenade, but still alive . . . everywhere it was the same horrible sight . . . there had been 400 people in this village; about fifty of them had escaped and were still alive. All the rest had been deliberately massacred in cold blood for, as I observed for myself, this gang was admirably disciplined and only acted under orders.

After another visit to Deir Yassin I went back to my office where I was visited by two gentlemen, well-dressed in civilian clothes, who had been waiting for me for more than an hour. They were the commander of the *Irgun* detachment and his aide. They had prepared a paper that they wanted me to sign. It was a statement to the effect that I had been very courteously received by them, and obtained all the facilities I had requested, in the accomplishment of my mission, and thanking them for the help I had received. As I showed signs of hesitation and even started to argue with them, they said that if I valued my life, I had better sign immediately. The only course open to me was to convince them that I did not value my life in the least. . . .[45]

The 'victory' at Deir Yassin—as the Irgunists called it at a press conference[46]—had immense repercussions. Begin described them:

Arab headquarters at Ramallah broadcast a crude atrocity story, alleging indiscriminate massacre by *Irgun* troops of about 240 men, women and children in Deir Yassin. The official Zionist bodies, apprehensive of the *Irgun*'s growing strength and popular support, eagerly seized upon this Arab accusation and, without even trying to check their veracity, accepted them at their face value and bestirred themselves to denounce and smear the *Irgun*. This combined Arab-Zionist *Greuelpropaganda* produced, however, unexpected and momentous consequences. Arabs throughout the country, induced to believe wild tales of '*Irgun* butchery', were seized with limitless panic and started to flee for their lives. This mass flight soon developed into a maddened, uncontrollable stampede. Of the about 800,000 Arabs who lived on the present territory of the State of Israel, only some 165,000 are still there. The political and economic significance of this development can hardly be overestimated.[47]

It is true that, just as they did after the King David incident, the official Zionist leaders publicly denounced the 'dissidents'. They were genuinely upset. Bengurion even sent a message of apology to King Abdullah. The chief Rabbi of Jerusalem excommunicated the killers.

Yet the Jewish Agency did not go beyond condemnation. 'You are swine,' the local *Haganah* commander told the 'dissidents' as his men surrounded them in the village square. But when ordered to disarm them, he refused; 'David,' he begged his superior, 'you'll bloody your name for life. The Jewish people will never forgive you.' David Shaltiel relented.[48] Three days after the massacre, the official leadership entered into formal alliance with the *Irgun*, which, while retaining its separate military structure, would henceforward fall under overall *Haganah* command. Twelve days after that the two mounted a joint attack on Haifa.

Deir Yassin fell in with official Zionist purposes. It was Herzl himself, as we have seen, who first proposed that the problem of the Arabs should be solved by their physical removal from their homeland. This was intrinsic to the whole concept of a Jewish State in Palestine. It was not the Zionists' habit to talk about it in public—or, if they did, they tended to employ Weizmann-style rhetoric ('Palestine shall be as Jewish as England is English') which, though its ultimate significance was clear enough, fell short of a precise and incriminating formulation of intent. Indeed, in the early years of settlement, they would often insist that there was no such thing as an Arab problem at all; there was therefore no incompatibility between unfulfilled Zionist ambitions and pre-existing Arab rights. In reality, the idea of a 'population transfer' was never far from their thoughts. As early as 1911 local Zionist leaders were wondering out loud whether the Arabs of Palestine could be persuaded to settle in neighbouring countries; they could buy land on the proceeds of the land they had sold in Palestine; or the Zionists could even buy it for them.[49] Clearly, however, these were utopian notions. The Arabs would not budge. So the Zionists hardened their hearts. Theirs was an all-or-nothing creed. With time, and with the consolidation of the Jewish presence in Palestine and the sense of strength it gave, the inescapable logic of Herzl's solution began to force itself upon them.

Who better qualified to judge than Joseph Weitz? As the administrator responsible for Jewish colonization, he combined a dedication to the Zionist ideal with an intensely practical understanding of how it would be realized.

> Between ourselves it must be clear that there is no room for both peoples together in this country. . . . We shall not achieve our goal of being an independent people with the Arabs in this small country. The only solution is a Palestine, at least Western Palestine (west of the Jordan river) without Arabs. . . . And there is no other way than to transfer the Arabs from here to the neighbouring countries, to transfer all of them; not one village, not one tribe, should be left. . . . Only after this transfer will the country be able to absorb the millions of our own brethren. There is no other way out.

This is what Weitz confided to his diary in 1940.[50] His views were shared not merely by the Revisionists, but by the mainstream, socialist leadership. Already, in the thirties, they had begun pressing the case for a forcible transfer of the Arabs. The Peel Partition Plan recommended an 'exchange of land and population'.[51] This was at the urging of Weizmann, who had told the Colonial Secretary, William Ormsby-Gore, that 'the whole success of the scheme depended upon whether the Government genuinely did or did not wish to carry out this recommendation. The transfer could only be carried out by the British Government and not the Jews. I explained the reason why we considered the proposal of such importance.'[52] Zionist lobbying was eventually to prove so successful that, in 1944, the National Executive of the Labour Party officially adopted the idea at its annual conference. 'Palestine', it affirmed, 'surely is a case, on human grounds and to promote a stable settlement, for a transfer of population. Let the Arabs be encouraged to move out, as the Jews move in.' Indeed, the lobbying was so successful that it embarrassed the Zionists themselves. Conscious of the effect that such a frank and extreme espousal of what were still essentially surreptitious aims might have on liberal opinion, Weizmann was moved to record in his memoirs: 'I remember that my Labour friends were, like myself, greatly concerned about this proposal. We have never contemplated the removal of the Arabs, and the British Labourites, in their pro-Zionist enthusiasm, went far beyond our intentions.'[53] American Zionists, characteristically, were less reticent about a proposal from ex-President Hoover, who called for 'engineering' the transfer of the Palestinians to Iraq. The American Zionist Emergency Council declared that:

> The Zionist movement has never advocated the transfer of Palestine's Arab population . . . nevertheless when all long-accepted remedies seem to fail it is time to consider new approaches. The Hoover Plan . . . represents an important new approach in the realization of which Zionists would be happy to co-operate with the great powers and the Arabs.[54]

The late 1940s threw up precisely that 'revolutionary' situation which Chaim Arlosoroff had foreseen.[55] The United Nations, to which a despairing Britain had handed over the whole problem, ruled in favour of partition. That vote was a story of violence in itself—albeit diplomatic violence—in which the United States went to the most extraordinary lengths of backstage manipulation on behalf of its Zionist protégés. Partition went against the better judgement of many of those nations which cast their vote in favour of it. America too—at least its State Department officials who knew something about the Middle East—had grave misgivings. But the White House, which knew a good deal less, overruled them. It sanctioned what a deeply distressed James Forrestal, the Secretary of Defense, described as 'coercion and duress on other nations' which 'bordered on scandal'.[56] President Truman warned one of his secretaries that he would demand a full explanation if nations which normally lined up with the United States failed to do so on Palestine. Governments which opposed partition, governments which could not make up their minds, were swayed by the most unorthodox arguments. The Firestone Tyre and Rubber Company, with plantations in Liberia, brought pressure to bear on the Liberian Government. It was hinted to Latin American delegates that their vote for partition would greatly increase the chances of a pan-American road project. The Philippines, at first passionately opposed to partition, ended up ignominiously in favour of it: they had too much stake in seven bills awaiting the approval of Congress. Important Americans were persuaded to 'talk' to various governments which could not afford the loss of American good will.[57]

For the Zionists the Partition Plan ranked, as a charter of legitimacy, with the Balfour Declaration which, in their view, it superseded and fulfilled. Certainly, it was a no less partisan document. Palestine comprises some 10,000 square miles. Of this, the Arabs were to retain 4,300 square miles while the Jews, who represented one-third of the population and owned some 6 per cent of the land, were allotted 5,700 square miles. The Jews also got the better land; they were to have the fertile coastal belt while the Arabs were to make do, for the most part, with the hills. Yet it was not the size of the area allotted to the Jews which pleased them—indeed, they regarded it as the 'irreducible minimum' which they could accept—it was rather the fact of statehood itself. Conversely, it was not merely the size of the area they were to lose, it was the loss of land, sovereignty and an antique heritage that angered the Arabs. The Partition Plan legitimized what had been, on any but the most partisan interpretation of the Balfour Declaration and the Mandate, illegitimately acquired. The past was, as it were, wiped out. Overnight, the comity of nations solemnly laid the foundations of a new moral order by which the Jews, the great majority of whom had been in Palestine less than thirty years, were deemed to have claims equal, indeed superior, to those of the Arabs who had lived there from time immemorial.

The Zionists graciously acquiesced in the will of the international community. This did not mean, however, that, while they acknowledged the momentous importance of their UN triumph, they were not acutely aware of its shortcomings—and determined to remedy them. The Partition Plan not only had a very tricky birth; it was in itself, as most of its UN midwives plainly said, a very curious infant. The two states, Arab and Jewish, were a very odd shape—like fighting serpents, was the apt description of an earlier such scheme. Demographically, they were even odder, or at least the proposed Jewish State was; for, at the outset at any rate, it was to contain more Arabs—509,780—than Jews—499,020. If the frontiers of Israel were a strategist's nightmare, this Arab majority, a ready-made fifth column, was an even greater threat. Moreover, it was an affront to fundamental dogma; could such a hybrid be called a truly Jewish State—as Jewish as England was English? The Jews were to be confined to but a part of the Land of Their Ancestors; indeed, they were to enjoy only a fettered presence, or none at all, in those places, such as Jerusalem and Hebron, to which they were most sentimentally attached.

The UN had been illogical; the creature which it brought forth was vigorous, but the conditions imposed upon it almost denied it the means of survival. The creature was bound to grow, to throw off its crippling handicaps, to achieve its full Zionist stature. Israel, more than any other nation, is the child of the UN; it is therefore ironic, though in no way surprising, that it was to prove such a delinquent child, with a unique record of censure by the organization which gave it birth.

The Zionists acquiesced in the sure knowledge that the Arabs would not. The Arabs were bound to oppose their own dispossession. Had they not mounted a full-scale rebellion against the mini-partition of Peel? Besides, they were in no sense obliged to accept what after all was only a 'recommendation' of the UN General Assembly. Yet it was this latest manifestation of the celebrated 'Arab refusal' which furnished the Zionists with the opportunity to remedy the shortcomings of the Partition Plan—and to do it without incurring the world's displeasure. For; in the eyes of the world, attempts to oppose its will by the only remaining means—force—became 'Arab aggression' while the Jewish attempts to uphold it were legitimate self-defence. Who was to hold it against them if, in the course of defending themselves, the Zionists went a little beyond the limits of what the UN had assigned them?

It did not matter if the Arab threat was a serious one or not. For propaganda purposes, it was the appearance of a threat that counted. And the actual threat, as they well knew, was far less serious than it looked. The unpreparedness of the Palestinian community was pathetic. The British had smashed their military potential in the 1930s; they had kept them disarmed ever since. They had prevented the re-emergence of such effective political leadership as they had ever enjoyed; only in 1946 was the Arab Higher Committee legalized again; the Mufti was exiled to the end. At the beginning of 1948 the Palestinians could muster some 2,500 riflemen; not only was this derisory force poorly trained, it lacked logistical support, and operated as a collection of separate regional units without centralized command and subject to the vagaries of remote and often divided political control. In 1947 the total strength of the rural garrisons in the key area of Jerusalem was twenty-five rifles. If there was a threat it came from outside Palestine. The Arab Liberation Army, hastily put together after the partition vote, mustered 3,830 volunteers under the command of Fawzi al-Kawekji—at least 1,000 of them Palestinians—who began their gradual entry into Palestine in January 1948. The forces which five Arab states despatched to Palestine on 15 May 1948—after the proclamation of the State of Israel—numbered some 15,000 men; their heaviest armour consisted of twenty-two light tanks; they could put up ten Spitfires.[58]

By 15 May Zionist forces included some 30,000 fully mobilized regular troops, at least 32,000 second-line troops, who, normally confined to regional or static defence, could be attached to the regulars as occasion arose, some 15,000 Jewish settlement police, a home guard of 32,000—plus the well-armed and highly aggressive 'dissident' forces of *Irgun* (3,000 to 5,000 in 1946) and *Stern* (200 to 300). Not only was this force better trained, it was far better equipped than the combined Arab armies. If there were any doubts about the outcome of a struggle for Palestine, they were not shared in a quarter that was particularly well qualified to judge. The opinions expressed as early as 1946 by the commander of the British forces in Palestine, General J. C. D'Arcy, were soldierly, crisp and accurate.

> We discussed with him what could happen if British troops were withdrawn from Palestine. 'If you were to withdraw British troops, the *Haganah* would take over all Palestine to-morrow,' General D'Arcy replied flatly. 'But could the *Haganah* hold Palestine under such circumstances?' I asked. 'Certainly,' he said. 'They could hold it against the entire Arab world.'[59]

There was also the question of intent. Of course the Arab states would, if they could, have stifled the Jewish State in embryo. Indeed, much fatuous confidence was publicly expressed, though perhaps not felt, that they would do so. Musa Alami, a distinguished Palestinian, went on a tour of the Arab capitals to discover what kind of help his people were likely to get from their Arab brethren. He found that the Arab leadership, directly confronted with the ever-expanding 'Zionist peril', was no better equipped to cope with it than the Palestinian leadership had been when it was alone in the field.

His first stop, in Damascus, gave him a foretaste of what he was to find everywhere.

> 'I am happy to tell you', the Syrian President assured him, 'that our Army and its equipment are of the highest order and well able to deal with a few Jews, and I can tell you in confidence that we even have an atomic bomb'; and seeing Musa's expression of incredulity, he went on, 'yes, it was made locally; we fortunately found a very clever fellow, a tinsmith. . . . ' Elsewhere he found equal complacency, and ignorance which was little less crass. In Iraq he was told by the Prime Minister that all that was needed was 'a few brooms' to drive the Jews into the sea; by confidants of Ibn Saud in Cairo, that 'once we get the green light from the British we can easily throw out the Jews. . . .'[60]

The Arab peoples were led to believe that their armies would have a walkover in Palestine. 'If the Arabs do not win the war against the Jews in an outright offensive you may hang all their leaders and statesmen,'[61] said Azzam Pasha, the Secretary General of the Arab League. The outside world, ignorant of the realities on the ground, was understandably none too sanguine about the chances for 600,000 Jews, pitted against 40 million Arabs. Yet the truth was that—in so far as the Arab governments, jealous, divided and incompetent, had any common policies at all—they tended towards moderation. The country with the best army, Transjordan, had made it clear that it would scrupulously observe the UN Partition Plan; it would occupy and defend that part of Palestine assigned to the Arab State, but not a foot more. As for the others they were still fundamentally thinking in terms of diplomatic solutions. This is admitted by the Zionists themselves. Thus on 19 March, *Haganah* radio broadcast that the Arab governments had reached full agreement on a plan, believed to be a moderate one, providing for the establishment of some kind of Arab-Jewish federal system in Palestine. In the realm of practical planning, the Arab Chiefs of Staff had their first conference only at the end of April; the decision to send in regular armies was not taken until early May—and that was a decision which, as late as 12 May, Egypt was still hesitating to act upon. Thus it may have been the Arabs who cried havoc, but it was the Zionists who, their enemies aiding, systematically wrought it.

The rise of the State of Israel—in frontiers larger than those assigned to it under the Partition Plan—and the flight of the native population was a cataclysm so deeply distressing to the Arabs that to this day they call it, quite simply, *al-Nakba*, the Catastrophe. The Zionists subsequently contended that the Arabs brought this misfortune upon themselves, for it was they who chose to invade the newborn state in defiance of the international community. Moreover, when it comes to the all-important question of the Palestinian refugees, the Zionists profess that their consciences are equally clear, for it was not they who drove them out, but their own leaders who ordered them to flee.

The Zionist version of the Palestinian exodus is a myth manufactured after the cataclysm took place. If the Zionists could show that the refugees had really fled without cause, at the express instructions of their own politicians, they would greatly erode the world's sympathy for their plight—and, in consequence, the pressure on themselves to allow them to return. Thus in public speeches and scholarly-looking pamphlets they peddled this myth the world over. It was not until 1959 that the Palestinian scholar, Walid Khalidi, exposed it for what it is. His painstaking researches were independently corroborated by an Irish scholar, Erskine Childers, two years later. Together, they demonstrated that the myth was not just a gross misrepresentation of accepted or even plausible facts; the very 'facts' themselves had been invented. Orders for the evacuation of the civilian population had not simply been issued, the Zionists said, they had been broadcast over Arab radio stations. One had come from the Mufti himself. This was the cornerstone of the Zionist case.

Yet when these two scholars took the trouble to examine the record—to go through the specially opened archives of Arab governments, contemporary Arabic newspapers and the radio monitoring reports of both the BBC and the CIA—they found that no such orders had been issued, let alone broadcast, and that when challenged to produce chapter-and-verse evidence, the date and origin of just one such order, the Zionists, with all the apparatus of the State of Israel now at their disposal, were quite unable to do so. They found, on the contrary, that Arab and Palestinian authorities had repeatedly called on the people to stay put and that the Arab radio services had consistently belittled the true extent of Zionist atrocities. Indeed, it appears that, if anything, they expected of the civilian population, helpless before the Zionist onslaught, a much greater fortitude than they legitimately should have. Far from urging his people to flee, the Mufti was so alarmed at the incipient exodus that he sent this cable to one of his staff: 'The emigration of children and others from Palestine to Syria is detrimental to our interest. Contact the proper authorities in Damascus and Beirut to prevent it. . . .'[62] Arab governments took steps forcibly to repatriate able-bodied Palestinians who had left the country, and Arab newspapers grew positively insulting about them. All this was corroborated by the Zionist radio services themselves. From time to time they carried reports of Arab efforts to prevent an exodus; when the exodus took place they duly reported it without mention of evacuation orders, and even when they came to refuting Arab claims that the Palestinians had been physically driven from their homes, they used all manner of argument except the one in question.

It was only a year later, when the refugee problem was beginning to impinge upon the world's conscience, that the Zionists began to develop their whole *post facto* thesis. Professor Khalidi traces its first elaborate appearance to two mimeographed pamphlets—almost certainly the work of Joseph Schechtman, the *Irgun*-Revisionist biographer of Jabotinsky—which were disseminated by the Israeli Information Office in New York and subsequently incorporated in a memorandum submitted by nineteen prominent Americans, including the poet Macleish and Niebuhr the theologian, to the UN. What is truly remarkable about this edifice of deceit, which has profoundly influenced Western opinion, is not merely that the Zionists were able to construct it from such unpromising materials, but that it stood solid and four-square for so long. There is no better example of the way in which Western, particularly American, opinion, prejudiced and ill-informed, has automatically tended to accept the Zionist side of the story—and, it must also be said, no better example of the ineptitude with which the Arabs have presented their case. The edifice, though crumbling, has not yet collapsed. For Zionist propagandists, with all the perversity of flat-earthers but none of their innocent eccentricity, are struggling to prop it up till this day.[63]

Deir Yassin was, as Begin rightly claims, the most spectacular single contribution to the Catastrophe. In time, place and method it demonstrates the absurdity of the subsequently constructed myth. The British insisted on retaining juridical control of the country until the termination of their Mandate on 15 May; it was not until they left that the regular Arab armies contemplated coming in. But not only did Deir Yassin take place more than five weeks *before* that critical date, it also took place *outside* the area assigned to the Jewish State. It was in no sense a retaliatory action. There had been violence from the Palestinians, but neither in scale nor effectiveness had it matched that of the Zionists themselves. It was also true that the British had turned a semi-blind eye to the infiltration of Fawzi al-Kawekji's Arab Liberation Army, and it did score some initial successes. But by April, overstretched and wretchedly supplied, it was already falling back in disarray.

In reality, Deir Yassin was an integral part of *Plan Dalet*, the master-plan for the seizure of most or all of Palestine. In the first phase of the military campaign that followed the partition 'recommendation', the Zionists, their forces not yet fully mobilized, contented themselves with a holding operation in which they simultaneously 'softened up' the Palestinians, engaged such fighting men as they did possess, and undermined, through terror, the morale of the civilian population. That was the essence of *Plan Gimmel*. Nothing was officially disclosed about *Plan Dalet, Gimmel*'s successor, when it went into effect on 1 April, although Bengurion was certainly alluding to it in an address, six days later, to the Zionist

Executive: 'Let us resolve not to be content with merely defensive tactics, but at the right moment to attack all along the line and not just within the confines of the Jewish State and the borders of Palestine, but to seek out and crush the enemy where-ever he may be.'[64] This discretion has persisted long after the event. Zionist histories of the 'war of independence' abound. But most of them, especially those written for Western consumption, hardly even mentioned *Plan Dalet*, or, if they do, they fail to give it the central importance it deserves. Some Hebrew accounts are franker. We learn from them that as early as 1942—the year of the Biltmore Programme and the espousal of Jewish statehood as the official Zionist goal—the military planners were already working on the broad conception.[65] By 1947 they had mapped and catalogued information about every village, its strategic character and the quality of its inhabitants in Palestine.[66] According to *Qurvot* (*Battles*) *of 1948*,[67] a detailed history of the *Haganah* and the *Palmach*, the aim of *Plan Dalet* was 'control of the area given to us by the UN in addition to areas occupied by us which were outside these borders and the setting up of forces to counter the possible invasion of Arab armies'. It was also designed to 'cleanse' such areas of their Arab inhabitants. In this way the Zionists would expand the 'irreducible minimum' which the UN had granted them, and make their state as large and Jewish as possible before the Arab armies could stop them, and before it dawned on the UN that its Partition Plan was unworkable. They went over to the offensive because, in spite of the relentless harassments of *Plan Gimmel* as well as the setbacks inflicted on the Arab irregulars, the civilian population, or its great majority, was determined to stay put; and because the United States, moving spirit behind partition, was now going back on it in what Dr Silver of the Jewish Agency described as 'a shocking reversal'[68] and the American Jewish Congress as 'shameful tactics and duplicity'.[69] It was Operation Nachson, designed to carve out a corridor connecting Tel Aviv with Jerusalem, which inaugurated *Plan Dalet*. It entailed the destruction and evacuation of some twenty villages. One of them was Deir Yassin. Twelve other operations were due to follow in quick succession, eight of them outside the area allotted to the Jewish State. Some succeeded, some failed; some were delayed beyond 15 May. Even so, by that date, the Zionists were well on the way to overrunning the whole of Palestine. Operation Nachson, as conceived by the *Haganah* planners, did not require such a bloodbath. Yet it was not, in method, the isolated episode that it has subsequently been made out to have been. It was merely an extreme application of a general policy. Twenty-four years after the event, the Israeli historian Arie Yitzhaqi, author of a 1,200-page history of the war, wrote:

> If we assemble the facts, we realize that, to a great extent, the battle followed the familiar pattern of the occupation of an Arab village in 1948. In the first months of the 'War of Independence' *Haganah* and *Palmach* troops carried out dozens of operations of this kind, the method adopted being to raid an enemy village and blow up as many houses as possible in it. In the course of these operations many old people, women and children, were killed wherever there was resistance. In this connection I can mention several operations of this kind carried out by Pa'el's comrades in arms—the *Palmach* irregulars who were trained to be concerned for the 'purity of Hebrew arms'.[70]

It was a sophisticated combination of physical and psychological *blitz*, mounted by official and 'dissident' forces alike, which finally drove the Palestinians out. The *Haganah* and the *Irgun* would launch massive surprise attacks on towns and villages, bombarding them with mortars, rockets—and the celebrated Davidka. This was a home-made contraption that tossed 60 lb of TNT some 300 yards, very inaccurately, into densely populated areas.[71] There was also the 'barrel-bomb'. In an article entitled 'All's Fair . . .', written long after the event for the US Marine Corps professional magazine, an Israeli army reserve officer who fought in 1948 has given precise details of this device. It consisted of a barrel, cask or metal drum, filled with a mixture of explosives and petrol, and fitted with two old rubber tyres containing the detonating fuse. It was rolled down the sharply sloping alleys and stepped lanes of Arab urban quarters until it crashed into walls and doorways making 'an inferno of raging flames and endless explosions'.[72] At the same time, additional panic would be induced by Arabic broadcasts from the clandestine Zionist radio stations or loudspeakers mounted on armoured cars in the target areas. The broadcasts warned of the spread of dangerous epidemics, such as cholera and typhus, hinted at Arab collaboration with the enemy, threatened that 'innocent people' would pay the price for Palestinian attacks on Jews. But there was one particularly revealing theme, of which Harry Levin, a British Zionist author, furnishes an apt example: 'Nearby [in Jerusalem] a loudspeaker burst out in Arabic. *Haganah* broadcasting to civilian Arabs urging them to leave the district before 5.15 A.M. "Take pity on your wives and children and get out of this bloodbath. . . . Get out by the Jericho road, this is still open to you. If you stay you invite disaster."[73] The Israeli reserve-officer reveals just how deliberate this was. Amid barrel-bombs, he wrote,

> . . . as uncontrolled panic spread through all Arab quarters, the Israelis brought up jeeps with loudspeakers which broadcast recorded 'horror sounds'. These included shrieks, wails, and anguished moans of Arab women, the wail of sirens and the clang or fire-alarm bells, interrupted by a sepulchral voice calling out in Arabic: 'Save your souls, all ye faithful: The Jews are using poison gas and atomic weapons. Run for your lives in the name of Allah.'[74]

A series of Arab towns—Tiberias, Haifa, Acre, Jaffa and much of Arab Jerusalem—fell in quick succession before the irresistible march of 'gun Zionism'. Some three or four hundred thousand refugees, sometimes attacked and stripped of their remaining possessions on the way, streamed towards the neighbouring Arab countries. Those who were not driven into the desert suffered a fate which, according to the Zionists, the Arabs have had in store for them ever since; inhabitants of coastal towns were literally 'driven into the sea'; many drowned in the scramble for boats.

There is no better insight into the urgency and scope of *Plan Dalet*, as the Mandate drew to a close, than the one furnished by Yigal Allon, the principal hero of the 'War of Independence'. In the *Book of the Palmach*, he recalls:

> There were left before us only five days, before the threatening date, the 15th of May. We saw a need to clean the inner Galilee and to create

> a Jewish territorial succession in the entire area of the upper Galilee. The long battles had weakened our forces, and before us stood great duties of blocking the routes of the Arab invasion [literally *plisha* or expansion]. We therefore looked for means which did not force us into employing force, in order to cause the tens of thousands of sulky Arabs who remained in Galilee to flee, for in case of an Arab invasion these were likely to strike us from the rear. We tried to use a tactic which took advantage of the impression created by the fall of Safed and the [Arab] defeat in the area which was cleaned by Operation Metateh—a tactic which worked miraculously well.
>
> I gathered all of the Jewish Mukhtars, who have contact with Arabs in different villages, and asked them to whisper in the ears of some Arabs, that a great Jewish reinforcement has arrived in Galilee and that it is going to burn all of the villages of the Huleh. They should suggest to these Arabs, as their friends, to escape while there is still time. And the rumour spread in all the areas of the Huleh that it is time to flee. The flight numbered myriads. The tactic reached its goal completely. The building of the police station at Halsa fell into our hands without a shot. The wide areas were cleaned, the danger was taken away from the transportation routes and we could organise ourselves for the invaders along the borders, without worrying about the rear.[75]

For all the bluster, it was only the Catastrophe unfolding before the eyes of their peoples that finally induced the Arab governments, under irresistible pressure, to send in their armies and to salvage what they could. Belated and inept though it was, Allon conceded that without this intervention

> . . . there would have been no stop to the expansion of the forces of *Haganah* who could have, with the same drive, reached the natural borders of western Israel, because in this stage most of the local enemy forces were paralyzed.[76]

Although, in the war that ensued, the ideal of an exclusively Jewish State in all of Palestine eluded them, the Zionists further consolidated their position. The war was marked by a series of UN-sponsored truces, but they took as much advantage of them as they did of the actual fighting. Announcing his government's acceptance of the first ceasefire on 10 June, Bengurion declared that

> . . . our bounds are set wider, our forces multiply, we are administering public services and daily new multitudes arrive. . . . All that we have taken we shall hold. During the ceasefire, we shall organise administration with fiercer energy, strengthen our footing in town and country, speed up colonization and *Aliyah* [immigration] and look to the army.[77]

When the war ended, in early 1949, the Zionists, allotted 57 per cent of Palestine under the Partition Plan, had occupied 77 per cent of the country. Of the 1,300,000 Arab inhabitants, they had displaced nearly 900,000. They came into possession of entire cities, or entire quarters of them, and hundreds of villages. All that was in them—farms and factories, animals and machinery, fine houses and furniture, carpets, clothes and works of art, all the goods and chattels, all the treasured family heirlooms of an ancient people—was theirs for the taking. Ten thousand shops, businesses and stores and most of the rich Arab citrus holdings—half the country's total—fell into their hands.

Chaim Weizmann, the revered elder statesman became the first President of the State of Israel. It was fitting. To him, more than to anyone else, the Jewish State owed its existence. Yet if there could have been no Israel without Weizmann, assuredly there would not have been one without Bengurion and Begin, *Plan Dalet* and Deir Yassin either. Weizmann had sometimes deplored the excesses of 'gun Zionism'. 'In all humbleness', he told a UN committee of inquiry in 1947, '*thou shalt not kill* has been ingrained in us since Mount Sinai. It was inconceivable ten years ago that the Jews should break this commandment. Unfortunately, they are breaking it today, and nobody deplores it more than the vast majority of the Jews. I hang my head in shame when I have to speak of this fact before you.'[78] But now his scruples seemed to desert him. He who, just thirty years before, had assured the Arabs of Jaffa that it had never been anybody's intention 'to turn anyone out of his property' or 'to seize control of the higher policy of the province of Palestine', now returned, burdened with years and honour, to the Promised Land which 'gun Zionism' had made as Jewish, or almost, as England is English. 'It was', he piously declared, 'a miraculous clearing of the land: the miraculous simplification of Israel's task.'[79]

Notes

1. Kimche, John, *Seven Fallen Pillars: The Middle East, 1915–1950*, Secker and Warburg, London, 1950, p. 171.
2. Begin, Menachim, *The Revolt*, W. H. Allen, London, 1951, p. 220.
3. *Ibid.*, p. 40.
4. *Ibid.*, p. 46.
5. *The Jewish Yearbook of International Law*, Jerusalem, 1949, p. 28.
6. *Commentary*, New York, July 1946.
7. See Bullock, Alan, *The Life and Times of Ernest Bevin: Trade Union Leader, 1881–1940*, Heinemann, London, 1960, pp. 455–7.
8. Eddy, William, *F.D.R. Meets Ibn Saud*, American Friends of the Middle East, New York, 1954, p. 36.
9. Mayhew, Christopher, and Adams, Michael, *Publish It Not*, Longmans, London, 1975, p. 18.
10. Divine, Robert A., *American Immigration Policy, 1924–1952*, Oxford University Press, London, 1957, p. 128.
11. Ernst, Morris L., *So Far So Good*, Harper and Brothers, New York, 1948, cited in Khalidi, *From Haven to Conquest*, *op. cit.*, p. 492.
12. Schechtman, *Fighter and Prophet, the Vladimir Jabotinsky Story*, *op. cit.*, p. 479.
13. *Ibid.*, pp. 483–4.
14. *Ibid.*, p. 364.
15. See pp. 98–100.
16. Schechtman, *op. cit.*, p. 484.
17. Begin, *op. cit.*, pp. 212–15.
18. *Ibid.*, p. 215.
19. Crossman, Richard, *Palestine Mission: A Personal Record*, Hamish Hamilton, London, n.d., p. 139.
20. *New Judea*, December 1946–January 1947, pp. 65–7.
21. Crossman, Richard, *A Nation Reborn, the Israel of Weizmann, Bevin and Ben Gurion*, Hamish Hamilton, London, 1960, p. 89.
22. 15 May 1947.
23. Zaar, Isaac, *Rescue and Liberation: America's Part in the Birth of Israel*, Bloch, New York, 1954, pp. 193–4, 200–3.
24. *Ibid.*, pp. 215–16.
25. Oswald Mosley led a small British fascist organization.

26. *Commentary*, May 1948.
27. *The Times*, 1 August 1946.
28. *Ibid.*, 19 February 1947.
29. Katz, Samuel, *Days of Fire*, Doubleday, New York, pp. 120–2, 178.
30. Montgomery, Bernard, *Memoirs*, World Publishing House Co., Cleveland and New York, 1958, pp. 340–1.
31. Thomas, Hugh, *John Strachey*, Eyre Methuen, London, pp. 228–9.
32. Mayhew, *op. cit.*, p. 33.
33. Begin, *op. cit.*, p. 290.
34. *New York Times* and *New York Herald Tribune*, 12 April 1948.
35. Kimche, *op. cit.*, p. 227.
36. *New Judea*, cited by Polk, William, Staller, David, and Asfour, Edward, *Backdrop to Tragedy*, New York, 1957, p. 29.
37. Lapierre, Dominique, and Collins, Larry, *O Jerusalem*, Simon and Schuster, New York, 1972, p. 272.
38. Ha-Mashkif (*Irgun* newspaper), 11 April, 1948; Begin, *op. cit.*, pp. 162–3.
39. *Palestine Post*, 13 April 1948; see also *New York Times*, 13 April 1948.
40. Katz, *op. cit.*, p. 215.
41. Begin, *op. cit.*, pp. 163–4.
42. Lapierre, *op. cit.*, p. 273.
43. *Report of the Criminal Investigation Division*, Palestine Government, No. 179/110/17/GS, 13, 15, 16 April 1948. Cited in Lapierre, *op. cit.*, p. 276.
44. *Yediot Aharonot* (Israeli newspaper), 4 April 1972.
45. De Reynier, Jacques, *A Jérusalem un Drapeau Flottait sur la Ligne de Feu*, Editions de la Baconnière, Neuchâtel, 1950, pp. 71–6.
46. *Jewish Newsletter*, New York, 3 October 1960.
47. Begin, *op. cit.*, p. 164.
48. Lapierre, *op. cit.*, p. 280.
49. Laqueur, Walter, *A History of Zionism*, Weidenfeld and Nicolson, London, 1972, p. 231.
50. *Davar*, 29 September, 1967.
51. Peel Commission, *op. cit.*, p. 391.
52. *Jewish Chronicle*, 13 August 1937.
53. Weizmann, *Trial and Error*, *op. cit.*, p. 535.
54. *Palestine* (Zionist periodical), Vol. II, Nos. 9–10, November–December 1945, p. 16.
55. See pp. 98–100.
56. *The Forrestal Diaries*, ed. Millis, Walter, Viking Press, New York, 1952, p. 363.
57. Lilienthal, Alfred, *What Price Israel*, Henry Regnery, Chicago, 1953, pp. 60–6.
58. See Khalidi, *op. cit.*, pp. 858–60.
59. Crum, Bartley C., *Behind the Silken Curtain*, Simon and Schuster, New York, 1947, p. 220.
60. Furlonge, Geoffrey, *Palestine is my Country; the Story of Musa Alami*, John Murray, London, 1969, p. 152.

61. Public Statement, 14 May 1948.
62. Khalidi, *op. cit.*, p. 14.
63. See for example, Prittie, Terence, Dineen, Bernard, and Goodhart, Philip, *The Double Exodus*, Goodhart Press, London, 1975.
64. Bengurion, *Rebirth and Destiny*, *op. cit.*, p. 239.
65. Yadin, Yigal, Chief of Operations in the 1948 war, *Maariv* (Israeli newspaper), 6 May 1973.
66. Sacher, Harry, *Israel: The Establishment of a State*, William Clowes and Sons, 1952, p. 217.
67. See Khalidi, *op. cit.*, p. 39.
68. *New York Times*, 20 March 1948.
69. *Ibid.*, 21 March 1948.
70. *Yediot Aharonot*, 14 April 1972.
71. See Lorch, Natanel, The Edge of the Sword, G. P. Putnam's, New York, 1961, p. 103.
72. Heiman Leo, in *Marine Corps Gazette*, June 1964; cited in Childers, Erskine, *The Wordless Wish: from Citizens to Refugees*, in *The Palestinian Issue in Middle East Peace Efforts*, hearings before the Committee on International Relations, House of Representatives, September, October, November 1975, US Government Printing Office, 1976, p. 252.
73. Levin, Harry, *Jerusalem Embattled: A Diary of the City Under Siege, March 25th 1948, to July 18th, 1948*, Gollancz, London, 1950, p. 160.
74. Childers, *op. cit.*, p. 253.
75. *Ha Sepher Ha Palmach*, Vol. 2, p. 286; cited in Khalidi, *op. cit.*, p. 42.
76. *Ibid.*, p. 43.
77. Bengurion, *op. cit.*, p. 274.
78. *Report of the UN Special Committee on Palestine* (UNSCOP) Document A/364, 1947, p. 77.
79. McDonald, James, *My Mission to Israel*, Simon and Schuster, New York, 1952, p. 176.

5 · SPECIAL USES OF VIOLENCE

The Assassination of Count Bernadotte

Israel was the child of the UN. So, on 14 May 1948, the day before the British Mandate expired, the UN appointed a Mediator to watch over Israel's birth, 'to use his good offices with the local community and authorities in Palestine . . . to promote a peaceful adjustment of the future situation in Palestine'.[1] The Zionists could hardly complain of this initiative by a body which, in its partition resolution, had already demonstrated such a bias in their favour; nor could they complain about the person chosen to carry it out.

Count Folke Bernadotte was a member of the Swedish royal family, cousin to the King. He was an aristocrat in whom wealth and high station had bred the need to serve his fellow men. So had his deep Protestant convictions. And his sense of mission was allied with great practical experience. He had made his name as a representative of the International Red Cross in World War II. It was he who had organized the first exchange of disabled prisoners. Both sides had respected him for his integrity and impartiality; they always granted him free access.

Although he came to Palestine with a rigorous conception of his Mediator's role, determined to show neither fear nor favour, he was in reality predisposed towards the Zionists. This was only natural, for, appalled by the whole-scale Nazi massacres of Jews, he had, on his own personal initiative, succeeded in rescuing a surviving remnant of them—some 30,000—from the concentration camps.[2] Moreover, like most Europeans, he had an instinctive affinity with the Zionists, who were mainly Europeans themselves. A cultural gulf lay between him and the Arabs, whom he had never encountered before and who, he wrote, expressed themselves in the 'elaborate and somewhat ceremonial style characteristic of the east'.[3] Like many Europeans, too, he was steeped in that Old Testament sentimentality which saw the return of the Jews to the Land of Their Ancestors as a prophetic fulfilment. His knowledge of the Palestine problem came largely from Zionist sources. He was deeply impressed by the Zionist claim to be making the desert bloom; in his diary he remarked upon the 'amazing work the Jews had done in cultivating this desert-like countryside . . . and the very sharp lines of demarcation between the desert on the one hand and the fertile gardens and orange groves on the other.'[4] The entry was made during his first visit to Palestine; apparently he was unaware, as he drove along the coastal plain from Haifa to Tel Aviv, that this was the most fertile part of the country, and that more than half of it was still owned and cultivated by Arabs. Only too familiar with the plight of European Jewry, Bernadotte seemed to know little about the suffering which the Jews-as-Zionists were inflicting on others. He was briefed by advisers who were apt to dismiss the Palestinians as of little consequence. One such report, his diary records, informed him that:

> The Palestinian Arabs had at present no will of their own. Neither have they ever developed any specifically Palestinian nationalism. The demand for a separate Arab state in Palestine is consequently relatively weak. It would seem as though in existing circumstances most of the Palestinian Arabs would be quite content to be incorporated in Transjordan.[5]

Not surprisingly, Bernadotte was at first inclined to see not only the problem, but its solution, through Zionist eyes. He imagined that his new mission, like the one he had performed during the war, would be more humanitarian than political, involving the exchange of prisoners, the repatriation of refugees, helping the sick, the needy and the homeless. Peace, he thought, would eventually follow.

His arrival in Jerusalem must have come as a bewildering shock to this representative of the organization to which Israel owed its existence. Jeeps flying the banners of the 'Fighters for the Freedom of Israel' (*Stern Gang*) careered around the city, warning him that 'Stockholm is yours. Jerusalem is ours. You work in vain. We are here . . . so long as there is a single enemy of our cause, we shall have a bullet in a magazine for him.'[6] On 17 September the *Stern Gang* killed him. But in the preceding four months it had been the whole Zionist community, the official representatives of the infant State of Israel, who, blow by blow, shattered his vision of a Palestine at peace with itself.

The Mediator's first task was to arrange a month's truce during which he could formulate proposals for a peaceful settlement. On 11 June, after a week of gruelling effort, Bernadotte persuaded Jews and Arabs to accept an unconditional ceasefire.

On 28 June, after intensive consultations with both sides, he put forward what he called a 'possible basis for discussion'. This included specific territorial recommendations, most of them favourable to the Arabs, revising the boundaries envisaged by the UN Partition Plan. But Bernadotte's main concern was the hundreds of thousands of Arab refugees whose misery, in their makeshift camps, he had seen with his own eyes. Their plight, he later told the UN, was the greatest obstacle to peace.

> It is, however, undeniable that no settlement can be just and complete if recognition is not accorded to the rights of the Arab refugee to return to the home from which he has been dislodged by the hazards and strategy of the armed conflict between Arabs and Jews in Palestine. . . . It would be an offence against the principles of elemental justice if these innocent victims of the conflict were denied the right to return to their homes while Jewish immigrants flow into Palestine, and, indeed, at least offer the threat of permanent replacement of the Arab refugees who have been rooted in the land for centuries.[7]

On 1 July, he got word of the Israeli response from his representative in Tel Aviv, who reported that the Foreign Minister, Moshe Sharett, was ready to go to Rhodes to continue negotiations provided that the Arabs also accepted the Mediator's invitation.

A breakthrough? Bernadotte believed so, and wrote enthusiastically in his diary: 'It is perhaps not difficult to imagine my joy when I read Reedman's communication. . . . This was a wonderful piece of news. It meant that the Jews accepted my proposals in principle.'[8]

At first, the Arabs' response—collectively made through the Arab League—was less encouraging. From his sources in Cairo Bernadotte had learned that 'the Arab attitude was negative in the extreme'.[9] But on 3 July he flew to Cairo himself and came away somewhat reassured from meetings with Arab representatives. The Arabs, he realized, were not ready for direct negotiations with the Israelis in Rhodes; nevertheless, he 'did not feel in the least disappointed': he 'had a feeling that the door to further discussions was still open', that 'the confidence the Arab representatives had in me was in no way impaired' and that they 'were still willing to accept me as Mediator'.[10]

An unpleasant surprise awaited him when, on 5 July, he returned to Tel Aviv to get the official reply of the Israeli Provisional Government. Not only did this reject his specific recommendations, it challenged his authority to 'adjust' the term of the UN Partition Plan. He was 'bluntly told by Jewish circles that they were surprised that anyone who came from a Christian country could put forward such a proposal'.[11] At the same time, even as they were condemning his 'adjustments' of the UN Partition Plan, they officially proclaimed that the Jewish State would not be bound by certain of its provisions.

On 9 July the first truce collapsed. Hostilities were resumed, during which the Zionists carried out further 'adjustments' of their own; whole new areas of central Palestine were 'cleansed' of their native population.

In Amman, on 1 August, Bernadotte visited some of the uprooted victims. 'A preliminary examination which we carried out . . . in Amman showed that the refugee problem was vaster and more baffling than we had imagined. . . .'[12] The same day, the Israeli Provisional Government officially informed him that there could be no return of these, or any other, refugees. It argued that 'if we find ourselves unable to agree on their readmission to the Israeli-controlled area, it is because of over-riding considerations bearing on our immediate security, the outcome of the present war and the stability of the future peace settlement'. It went on to describe 'the Palestine Arab exodus of 1948' as 'one of those cataclysmic phenomena which, according to the experience of other countries, change the course of history'.[13]

Bernadotte tried again. Afterwards, he confided to his diary this bitter reflection on his meeting with Moshe Sharett, the man who was considered a dove to Bengurion's hawk.

> Nothing that I could propose aroused any response; I got nowhere. It was significant to read later in the Jewish newspaper *Palestine Post*: 'Count Bernadotte has had a fruitless meeting with the Foreign Minister of Israel.' That was evidently regarded as a great triumph. . . . For my part I regarded the Jewish reaction as confirmation of what I had said before, namely that their military success during the ten days' war had gone to their heads.[14]

Another encounter with the refugees, this time at Ramallah, a few miles east of Jerusalem, deepened his indignation:

> I have made the acquaintance of a great many refugee camps; but never have I seen a more ghastly sight than that which met my eye here, at Ramallah. The car was literally stormed by excited masses shouting with Oriental fervour that they wanted food and wanted to return to their homes. There were plenty of frightening faces in the sea of suffering humanity. I remember not least a group of scabby and helpless old men with tangled beards who thrust their emaciated faces into the car and held out scraps of bread that would certainly have been considered uneatable by ordinary people, but was their only food.[15]

Back in Tel Aviv, in another meeting with Sharett, he appealed yet again for a change of heart over the refugees—only to incur an 'adamant refusal'. His diary entry for the day shows the radical change that was being wrought in his view of the Jewish State. At lunch with Sharett:

> I began the conversation by saying that in my opinion the international position of the government of Israel was worse than it had been only a week before. It no longer enjoyed the good will it had previously. The reason was . . . that the government had expressed itself on various occasions in such a way that people could only draw the conclusion that it was well on the way towards losing its head. It seemed as though Jewish demands would never cease.[16]

It was his impression, he went on, that the Israelis behaved as if they had 'two enemies': the Arabs were still 'enemy number one', but the UN Observers now 'ran them a close second'. He told the Foreign Minister that 'the Arabs had given the Observers every possible help, particularly during the second truce, while the Israelis had tried to put spokes in the wheel and did everything in their power to make the Observers' work more difficult'.[17] Bernadotte informed Sharett that his Observers' Corps was to be strengthened by 300 new officers; he added: 'I knew from my own experience that these officers, when they first arrived, would be very sympathetic to the Jewish cause; but I also knew that they would soon find themselves compelled by force of circumstances to revise their attitude. I could not understand . . . why the Jewish Government should adopt an attitude of such arrogance and hostility towards the United Nations representative.'

The Mediator thought he had 'made a certain impression' on Sharett, but while they were discussing certain alternatives for the future of Palestine, the Foreign Minister gave a display of that very arrogance of which he complained. One alternative, Sharett hinted, might be that 'the whole of Palestine should belong to Israel'.[18]

By 12 August, Bernadotte, '. . . had a feeling that the negotiations had reached a deadlock. The Jews had shown a blatant unwillingness for real cooperation. . . .' This came as no surprise; for he had already come to the conclusion that 'with respect to the people of Palestine, the Provisional Government had had a very great opportunity. . . . It had missed that opportunity. It had shown nothing but hardness and obduracy towards the refugees. . . .' Because morals, not politics, were his guide, he had at first been baffled by this attitude of 'the Jewish people, which itself had suffered so much'.[19] But before long he grasped that what he had attributed to 'arrogance' and the exultation of military victory actually flowed from deliberate policy, and he told the Israeli leaders of his surprise that

> . . . the representatives of the Jewish people in particular should look at this problem from such a narrow point of view, that they should regard it purely as a political question without taking into account the humanitarian side of the matter.[20]

In the Arab governments, by contrast, he discerned a certain flexibility. As he talked to Azzam Pasha, the Secretary-General of the Arab League, he could not help saying to himself: 'This man realizes deep down that the Arab world cannot any longer hope for a Palestine in which there will not be any independent Jewish State.'[21]

What the Arab states did insist upon was that there could be no direct negotiations with Israel until the refugees were allowed home. And to this plea Bernadotte was very sympathetic. The return of the refugees, he urged the Security Council, should take place 'at the earliest practicable date'—a date which, in his view, should not be contingent upon the conclusion of a formal peace nor even upon the initiation of negotiations to that end.[22] By now Bernadotte had replaced the Arabs as 'enemy number one'.

On 17 September, the day after he submitted his report to the UN, the Mediator flew to Jerusalem to inspect the building to which he was thinking of transferring his headquarters. It seemed foolish to risk his life on a mere administrative chore. That there was indeed such a risk he was well aware. The Jerusalem front line was the scene of constant ceasefire violations; it was infested with snipers and assorted gunmen who subjected the UN Observers to hold-ups. Only the previous day Rhodes radio station had picked up a report about a policeman coming across Bernadotte's dead body in a Haifa street. As his aircraft approached Jerusalem, the radio operator received a message, purporting to come from Haifa, warning that all aircraft landing at the city's Kalendia airport would be fired upon.

They landed without incident, but when General Aage Landström, the Mediator's Personal Representative and Chief of Staff of the UN Observer Corps, suggested that they take a round-about route into the city so as to avoid the 'hot' area of the Mandelbaum Gate, Bernadotte demurred. 'I would not do that,' he said, 'I have to take the same risks as my Observers and, moreover, I think no one has the right to refuse me permission to pass through the line.'[23]

They were on their way back when the assassins struck. 'We drove rapidly through the Jewish lines without incident,' Lundström wrote.

> The barrier was up, but when the guard saw us, he let it down halfway,

> then drew it right up, and finally let it down completely. This forced us to stop. The Jewish liaison officer shouted something to the guard in Hebrew, after which he drew up the barrier completely and we were able to pass. It was suspected after the murder that this mysterious manipulation of the barrier must have been a signal to the murderers that we were on our way, possibly even indicating which car Folke Bernadotte was travelling in. That pre-supposes, however, that the Jewish soldiers at the road barrier were accomplices in the plot. . . . In the Qatamon Quarter we were held up by a Jewish army-type jeep, placed in a road block, and filled with men in Jewish army uniforms. At the same time I saw a man running from the jeep. I took little notice of this because I merely thought that it was another check-point. However, he put a tommy gun through the open window on my side of the car and fired point-blank at Count Bernadotte and Colonel Sérot. I also heard shots fired from other points and there was considerable confusion. . . . Colonel Sérot fell in the seat at the back of of it and I saw at once that he was dead. Count Bernadotte fell forward and I thought at the time he was trying to get cover. I asked him: 'Are you wounded?' He nodded and fell back. I helped him to lie down in the car. I now realized that he was severely wounded; there was a considerable amount of blood on his clothes mainly around the heart. . . . On reflection after the incident, I am convinced that this was a deliberate and carefully planned assassination. The spot where the cars were halted was carefully chosen, and the people who approached the cars quite obviously not only knew which car Count Bernadotte was in but also the exact position in the car which he occupied.[24]

Count Bernadotte died a few minutes after the shooting, and three days later the assassins identified themselves as *Hazit Hamoledeth* (Fatherland Front), a sub-group of the *Stern Gang*. In a letter to *Agence France Presse* in Tel Aviv, they declared that 'in our opinion all United Nations Observers in Palestine are members of foreign occupation forces which have no right to be in our territory'. They conceded, however, that the killing of Colonel Sérot was 'a fatal mistake. . . . Our men thought that the officer sitting beside Count Bernadotte was the British agent and anti-Semite General Lundström'.[25]

In a letter of protest, General Lundström described the assassinations as 'a breach of the truce of utmost gravity, and a black page in Palestine's history for which the United Nations will demand a full accounting'.[26]

There was to be no accounting, however, either to the UN or to any other authority. To the UN demand that the assassins be brought to justice, the Israelis at first replied that they could not find them. Then, after two months of international pressure, they arrested Nathan Yellin-Mor, the head of the *Stern Gang*, and Matitiahu Schmulevitz, both Polish Jews who had emigrated to Palestine a few years before. Another Polish Jew, Yitzhak Shamir, the organization's operational commander and future Prime Minister of Israel, went into hiding.

Yellin-Mor and Schmulevitz were tried by military court in Acre. They claimed that there was no case against them. Their organization was not a terrorist one, nor had they themselves been party to terrorist acts, since the prosecution furnished no proof. Yellin-Mor further objected to the trial of civilians by a military court.[27] As for Bernadotte, he denounced him, in a lengthy tirade, as an enemy of Israel. Among other things 'he stood in the way of Jewish absorption of the Kingdom of Transjordan as well as the whole of Palestine'.[28] The two men were sentenced to eight and five years. They were, however, to receive special treatment as political prisoners. Then, growing even more lenient, the court ordered that they and their witness be released altogether, since they had protested their sincere desire to be law-abiding citizens. . . .[29]

Twenty-seven years later, in July 1975, the perpetrators of the other famous *Stern Gang* assassination—that of Lord Moyne, the British Resident Minister in the Middle East—were accorded full military honours in Israel. Eliahu Hakim and Eliahu Bet-Zuri had been executed in Cairo in 1945. After lying in state in the Hall of Heroism, their bodies were buried in a section of Israel's military cemetery reserved for heroes and martyrs with the President, the Prime Minister and the Minister for Religious Affairs in attendance. They had been exhumed from their Cairo graves. As their flag-draped biers were conveyed from Egyptian to Israeli lines, Swedish troops of the UN forces in Sinai, unaware of their contents, furnished the honour guard.

'CRUEL ZIONISM'—OR THE 'INGATHERING' OF IRAQI JEWRY

IT WAS THE LAST DAY of Passover, April 1950. In Baghdad, the Jews had spent it strolling along the banks of the Tigris in celebration of the Sea Song. This was an old custom of the oldest Jewish community in the world; the 130,000 Jews of Iraq attributed their origins to Nebuchadnezzar, the destruction of the First Temple and the Babylonian exile. A good 50,000 of them thronged the esplanade. By nine o'clock in the evening the crowds were thinning out. But on Abu Nawwas street young Jewish intellectuals were still gathered in the Dar al-Beida coffee-shop.

Suddenly, the convivial atmosphere was shattered by an explosion. A small bomb, hurled from a passing car, had gone off on the pavement just outside. By chance no one was hurt. But the incident shook the Jewish community. They were convinced that Iraqi extremists wanted to kill them. The fainter-hearted began to murmur 'it is better to go to Israel'. The next day there was a rush to the offices where Jews wishing to renounce their Iraqi citizenship had to present themselves for registration. Their right to emigrate had been officially acknowledged by the government on the feast of Purim a month before. Its object was to prevent emigration by illegal means. As the newspapers had explained, 'the encounters between the police and the emigrant groups showed that some Iraqi Jews do not want to live in this country. Through their fleeing they give a bad name to Iraq. Those who do not wish to live among us have no place here. Let them go.'[30] There had been little response. Police officers had appeared at synagogues and explained that all Jews had to do in order to leave Iraq peacefully was to sign the necessary form. But the Jews were afraid that this was a trap to unmask the Zionists among them; and Zionism, under Iraqi law, was a grievous offence.

In all, about 10,000 Jews signed up to leave after the bomb; the big Ezra Daud synagogue had to be set aside as a registration office; police officers and volunteer clerks worked day and night to complete the task. A special kitchen was set up to feed them. Most of the would-be emigrants were poor, with little to lose. The panic did not last very long, however, and registration tapered off. Moreover, they were to leave by air—but only one aeroplane came to take 120 of them, via Cyprus, to Israel.

Then there was another explosion. This time it was at the US Information Centre, where many young Jews used to come and read. Again the theory was that an extremist Iraqi organization had planted the bomb, which only by chance failed to hurt anyone. Once again, therefore, there was a rush on the Ezra Daud synagogue; only this time the panic—and the number of would-be emigrants—was less than before.

The year ended, and March 1951, the time-limit set for the renunciation of citizenship, was approaching.

The third time there *were* victims. It happened outside the Mas'uda Shemtov synagogue, which served as an assembly point for emigrants. That day in January the synagogue was full of Kurdish Jews from the northern city of Suleimaniyyah. Outside a Jewish boy was distributing sweetmeats to curious onlookers. When the bomb went off he was killed instantly and a man standing behind him was badly wounded in the eyes.

And this time there was no longer any doubt in Jews' minds: an anti-Jewish organization was plotting against them. Better to leave Iraq while there was still time. The queues lengthened outside the Ezra Daud synagogue, and on the night before the time-limit expired some were paying as much as £200 to ensure that their names were on the list. A few days later the Iraqi parliament passed a law confiscating the property of all Jews who renounced their citizenship. No one was allowed to take more than £70 out of the country. The planes started arriving at a rate of three or four a day. At first the emigrants were flown to Nicosia accompanied by an Iraqi police officer. But after a while even that make-believe was dropped and they went directly to Israel's Lydda airport—the police officer returning alone in the empty plane. Before long all that was left of the 130,000 abandoning home, property and an ancient heritage was a mere 5,000 souls.

It was not long before a bombshell of a different kind hit the pathetic remnants of Iraqi Jewry. They learned that the three explosions were the work not of Arab extremists, but of the very people who sought to rescue them; of a clandestine organization called 'The Movement', whose leader, 'commander of the Jewish ghettoes in Iraq', had received this letter from Yigal Allon, chief of the *Palmach* commandos, and subsequently Foreign Minister of Israel:

> Ramadan my brother. . . . I was very satisfied in learning that you have succeeded in starting a group and that we were able to transfer at least some of the weapons intended for you. It is depressing to think that Jews may once again be slaughtered, our girls raped, that our nation's honour may again be smirched . . . should disturbances break out, you will be able to enlarge the choice of defenders and co-opt Jews who have as yet not been organized as members of the Underground. But be warned lest you do this prematurely, thereby endangering the security of your units which are, in fact, the only defence against a terrible pogrom.[31]

The astonishing truth—that the bombs which terrorized the Jewish community had been Zionist bombs—was revealed when, in the summer of 1950, an elegantly dressed man entered Uruzdi Beg, the largest general store in Baghdad. One of the salesmen, a Palestinian refugee, turned white when he saw him. He left the counter and ran out into the street, where he told two policemen: 'I recognize the face of an Israeli.' He had been a coffee-boy in Acre, and he knew Yehudah Tajjar from there. Arrested, Tajjar confessed that he was indeed an Israeli, but explained that he had come to Baghdad to marry an Iraqi Jewish girl. His revelations led to more arrests, some fifteen in all. Shalom Salih, a youngster in charge of *Haganah* arms caches, broke down during interrogation and took the police from synagogue to synagogue, showing them where the weapons, smuggled in since World War II, were hidden. During the trial, the prosecution charged that the accused were members of the Zionist underground. Their primary aim—to which the throwing of the three bombs had so devastatingly contributed—was to frighten the Jews into emigrating as soon as possible. Two were sentenced to death, the rest to long prison terms.

It was Tajjar himself who first broke Jewish silence about this affair. Sentenced by the Baghdad court to life imprisonment, he was released after ten years and found his way to Israel. On 29 May 1966 the campaigning weekly magazine *Ha'olam Hazeh* published an account of the emigration of Iraqi Jews based on Tajjar's testimony. Then on 9 November 1972, the *Black Panther* magazine, militant voice of Israel's Oriental Jews, published the full story. The *Black Panther* account includes the testimony of two Israeli citizens who were in Baghdad at the time. The first, Kaduri Salim

> . . . is 49 but looks 60. He is thin, almost hunch-backed, creased-face and with glass-eye: he lost his right eye at the door of the Mas'uda Shemtov synagogue. He recounts: 'I was standing there beside the synagogue door. I had already waived my Iraqi citizenship, and wanted to know what was new. Suddenly, I heard a sound like a gun report. Then a terrible noise. I felt a blow, as if a wall had fallen on me. Everything went black around me. I felt something cold running down my cheek, I touched it—it was blood. The right eye. I closed my left eye and didn't see a thing. The doctor told me: 'It's better to take it out.'
>
> He remained in Iraq for three months after leaving the hospital. Then his turn to leave for Israel arrived. The ex-clerk was sent to an immigration camp. Since then, all his efforts to receive compensations have been in vain. He claimed: 'I was hurt by the bomb. The Court of Law established that the bomb was thrown by "The Movement". The Israel Government has to give me compensations.' But the Israel Government does not recognize its responsibility for the Baghdad bombs and, anyhow, cannot recognize him as hurt in action. 'I am ready to be a victim for the State,' he said, 'but when the situation at home is bad, when my wife wants money and there isn't any, what is the self-sacrifice and goodwill worth?'

The second witness was an Iraqi lawyer, living in Tel Aviv. He told the *Black Panther* that

> After the first bomb was thrown at the Dar al-Bayda coffee-house, many rumours started running around about the responsible being communists. But the day after the explosion, at 4.00 AM, leaflets were already being distributed amongst the first worshippers at the synagogue. The leaflets warned of the dangers revealed by the throwing of the bomb and recommended the people to come to Israel.
>
> Someone who saw in it something strange was Salman al-Bayyati,

> Investigating Judge for South Baghdad. He declared that the distribution of the leaflet at such an early hour showed prior knowledge of the bombing. He therefore instructed the police to investigate in this direction, determining at the same time that those who threw the bomb were Jews trying to quicken the emigration. Indeed, two youngsters were arrested.
>
> Unexpectedly, the Ministry of Justice intervened. The two boys were set free. The case passed over to the hands of the Investigating Judge Kamal Shahin, from North Baghdad. In other words, at this stage, there was still a willingness not to see. For the whole emigration movement came as results of a willingness not to see—or perhaps even of a more active agreement between the Government, the Court and the Zionist representatives.
>
> But after two more bombs and after the arrest of the Israeli envoy—it was too much. The police started acting, and it was impossible to stop the wheels. There is only one more thing to add: in the objective conditions of the issue, the trial was made according to international law. The evidence was just such that it wasn't difficult at all to pronounce such sentences.[32]

When Bengurion made his impassioned pleas for immigrants to people the new-born State of Israel he was addressing 'European' Jews (from both the New and the Old Worlds) in particular. Not only had European Jewry fathered Zionism, it was the main source of that high-quality manpower, armed with the technical skills, the social and cultural attitudes which Israel needed. But with the Holocaust over, the source was tending to dry up. So the Zionists decided that 'Oriental' Jewry must be 'ingathered' as well. It is often forgotten that the 'safeguard' clause of the Balfour Declaration—'it being clearly understood that nothing shall be done which may prejudice the civil and religious rights of the existing non-Jewish communities in Palestine, or the rights and political status enjoyed by Jews in any other country'—was designed to cover Diaspora Jews as well as native Arabs. But the uprooting of a million 'Oriental' Jews showed that, for the Zionists, it was a clause to be ignored in both its parts. Everywhere they applied the same essential techniques, but nowhere, perhaps, with such thoroughness as they did in Iraq. 'Cruel Zionism', someone called it.[33]

If Zionism, as a historical phenomenon, was a reaction to

anti-Semitism, it follows that, in certain circumstances, the Zionists had an interest in provoking the very disease which, ultimately, they hoped to cure. Herzl himself was the first to note the usefulness of anti-Semitism as an incentive to Jewish immigration. 'Anti-Semitism has grown and continues to grow—and so do I.'[34] There were dedicated Zionists who considered that it was the duty of the Rabbinate, Jewish nationalists and community leaders to keep the prejudice alive.[35] In the early fifties the need for immigrants was such that a columnist in *Davar*, influential voice of the Israel trade union movement, wrote:

> I shall not be ashamed to confess that if I had the power, as I have the will, I would select a score of efficient young men—intelligent, decent, devoted to our ideal and burning with the desire to help redeem Jews—and I would send them to the countries where Jews are absorbed in sinful self-satisfaction. The task of these young men would be to disguise themselves as non-Jews, and plague Jews with anti-Semitic slogans such as 'Bloody Jew', 'Jews go to Palestine' and similar intimacies. I can vouch that the results in terms of a considerable immigration to Israel from these countries would be ten thousand times larger than the results brought by thousands of emissaries who have been preaching for decades to deaf ears.[36]

Zionism had much less appeal to Oriental than it did to European Jews. In the pre-State period only 10.4 per cent of Jewish immigrants came from 'Africa and Asia'.[37] In their vast majority, the Oriental Jews were actually Arab Jews, and the reason for their indifference was simply that, historically, they had not suffered anything like the persecution and discrimination of their brethren in European Christendom. Prejudice did exist, but their lives were on the whole comfortable, and their roots were deep. They were nowhere more at home than in Iraq, and a government official conceded—tongue in cheek—that their Mesopotamian pedigree was much superior to that of the Moslem majority:

> Many of us consider the Jews to be the original inhabitants of this country. We believe, according to the Koran, they are descendants of

> Abraham and that goes back nearly 4,000 years. Compared to them, therefore, we Muslims are interlopers because we have been here only about 1,500 years.[38]

At one time, Baghdad numbered more Jewish than Arab residents. In this century, as an already prosperous, educated community, they were particularly well placed to benefit from the rapid development and modernization of the country. They controlled many national institutions, most of the banks and big shops. The poorest Jews were better off than the average Iraqi.[39] Under the constitution, the Jews enjoyed equality with other citizens. They were represented in parliament, worked in the civil service, and from 1920 to 1925 a Jew was Minister of Finance.

On the rare occasions in Arab history when Moslems—or Christians, for that matter—turned against the Jews in their midst, it was not anti-Semitism, in its traditional European sense, that drove them, but fanaticism bred of a not unjustified resentment. For, like other minorities, the Jews had a tendency to associate themselves with, indeed to profit from, what the majority regarded as an alien and oppressive rule. In recent times, this meant that from Iraq to Morocco the local Jewish communities found varying degrees of special favour with the French or British masters of the Arab world. If Arab Jews must themselves take some of the blame for the prejudice which this behaviour generated against them, they deserve much less blame for that other cause of Arab hostility—Zionism—which was ultimately to prove infinitely more disruptive of their lives.

Zionist activities in Iraq and other Arab countries date from the beginning of the century. They were barely noticed at first. There was actually a time, in the early twenties, when the Iraqi government granted the local Zionist society an official licence, and even when the licence was not renewed, it continued to function, unofficially, for several years. At first it was the British, rather than local Jews, who bore the brunt of Arab animosity. In 1928, there were riots when the British Zionist Sir Alfred Mond visited Baghdad. The following year demonstrations in mosques and streets, a two-minute silence in Parliament, black-edged newspapers and telegrams to London marked 'Iraqi disapproval of the pro-Jewish policy of Great Britain'.[40] It was not until the mid-thirties, when the troubles of Palestine were reverberating round the world, that Arab Jews began to excite suspicion and resentment. In Iraq these emotions came to a head in 1941 when, in a two-day rampage, the mob killed some 170 to 180 Jews and injured several hundred more.[41] It was terrible. But it was the first pogrom in Iraqi history. Moreover, it occurred at a time of political chaos; the short-lived pro-Nazi revolt of Rashid Ali Kailani was collapsing, and most members of his administration had taken flight as a British expeditionary force arrived at the gates of the city.

There was no more such violence. On account of this, and their economic prosperity, the Jews felt a renewed sense of security.[42] Nevertheless, the Zionists were still active in their midst. In the mid-forties, they disseminated booklets entitled 'Don't Buy from the Moslems'. However, they did not have the field to themselves. Left-wing Jews, who considered themselves 'Jewish and Arab at the same time', set up the League for Combating Zionism.[43]

By the end of Israel's 'War of Independence', there were still 130,000 Jews in Iraq. The Movement organized the 'Persian underground railway' to smuggle Jews to Israel via Iran. There were occasional clashes between the police and the caravan guides. It was these which prompted the government to legalize Jewish emigration. But, whether by legal or illegal means, very few actually left. As the Chief Rabbi of Iraq, Sassoon Khedduri, explained a few years later:

> The Jews—and the Muslims—in Iraq just took it for granted that Judaism is a religion and Iraqi Jews are Iraqis. The Palestine problem was remote and there was no question about the Jews of Iraq following the Arab position. . . .[44]

But Bengurion and the Zionists would not give in so easily. Israel desperately needed manpower. Iraqi Jews must be 'ingathered'. As Khedduri recalled:

> By mid-1949 the big propaganda guns were already going off in the United States. American dollars were going to save the Iraqi Jews—whether Iraqi Jews needed saving or not. There were daily 'pogroms'—in the New York *Times* and under datelines which few

> noticed were from Tel Aviv. Why didn't someone come to see *us* instead of negotiating with Israel to take in Iraqi Jews? Why didn't someone point out that the solid, responsible leadership of Iraqi Jews believed this to be their country—in good times and bad—and we were convinced the trouble would pass.[45]

But it did not. Neither the Iraqi Jews themselves, nor the government of what, by Western standards, was still a backward country, could cope with the kind of pressures the Zionists brought to bear:

> Zionist agents began to appear in Iraq—among the youth—playing on a *general* uneasiness and indicating that American Jews were putting up large amounts of money to take them to Israel, where everything would be in applepie order. The emigration of children began to tear at the loyalties of families and as the adults in a family reluctantly decided to follow their children, the stress and strain of loyalties spread to brothers and sisters.
>
> Then a new technique was developed:
>
> Instead of the quiet individualized emigration, there began to appear public demands to legalize the emigration of Jews—*en masse* . . . in the United States the 'pogroms' were already underway and the Iraqi government was being accused of holding the Jews against their will . . . campaigning among Jews increased. . . . The government was whipsawed . . . accused of pogroms and violent action against Jews . . . . But if the government attempted to suppress Zionist agitation attempting to stampede the Iraqi Jews, it was again accused of discrimination.[46]
>
> Finally there came the bombs.

'Ingathered' for what? The Iraqi Jews soon learned; those of them, that is, who actually went to Israel, or, having gone, remained there. For by no means all of uprooted Oriental Jewry did so. A great many of them—particularly the ones with money, connections, education and initiative—succeeded in making their way to Europe or America. But what the irretrievably 'ingathered' learned was the cruellest and most enduring irony of all: Oriental Jewry was no more than despised cannon-fodder for the European creed of Zionism.

> What did you do, Bengurion?
> You smuggled in all of us!
> Because of the past, we waived our citizenship
> And came to Israel.
> Would that we had come riding on a donkey and we
> Hadn't arrived here yet!
> Woe, what a black hour it was!
> To hell with the plane that brought us here![47]

This was the song which the Iraqi Jews used to sing. Nothing the rulers of Israel could do quelled the bitterness which the newcomers nurtured against them. They were lectured, in their transit camps, by teams of Zionist educators. But, long after they left the camps, they continued to sing that song, even at weddings and festive occasions. It remained popular throughout the fifties. Then it eventually disappeared, but it can hardly be said that nostalgia for the 'old country' disappeared with it. For the contrast between what they once were, 'in exile', and what they became, and remain, in the Promised Land is too great. One of the 'most splendid and rich communities was destroyed, its members reduced to indigents'; a community that 'ruled over most of the resources of Iraq . . . was turned into a ruled group, discriminated against and oppressed in every aspect'. A community that prided itself on its scholarship subsequently produced fewer academics, in Israeli universities, than it brought with it from Iraq. A community sure of its own moral values and cultural integrity became in Israel a breeding ground 'for delinquents of all kinds'. A community which 'used to produce splendid sons could raise only "handicapped" sons in Israel'.[48]

THE LAVON AFFAIR

IN JULY 1954 EGYPT WAS plagued by a series of bomb outrages directed mainly against American and British property in Cairo and Alexandria. It was generally assumed that they were the work of the

Moslem Brothers, then the most dangerous challenge to the still uncertain authority of Colonel (later President) Nasser and his two-year-old revolution. Nasser was negotiating with Britain over the evacuation of its giant military bases in the Suez Canal Zone, and the Moslem Brothers, as zealous nationalists, were vigorously opposed to any Egyptian compromises.

It therefore came as a shock to world, and particularly Jewish, opinion, when on 5 October the Egyptian Minister of the Interior, Zakaria Muhieddin, announced the break-up of a thirteen-man Israeli sabotage network. An 'anti-Semitic' frame-up was suspected.

Indignation increased when, on 11 December, the group was brought to trial. In the Israeli parliament, Prime Minister Moshe Sharett denounced the 'wicked plot hatched in Alexandria . . . the show trial which is being organized there against a group of Jews who have fallen victims to false accusations and from whom it seems attempts are being made to extract confessions of imaginary crimes, by threats and torture. . . .'[49] The trade union newspaper *Davar* observed that the Egyptian régime 'seems to take its inspiration from the Nazis' and lamented the 'deterioration in the status of Egyptian Jews in general'.[50] For *Haaretz* the trial 'proved that the Egyptian rulers do not hesitate to invent the most fantastic accusations if it suits them'; it added that 'in the present state of affairs in Egypt the Junta certainly needs some diversion'.[51] And the next day the *Jerusalem Post* carried this headline: 'Egypt Show Trial Arouses Israel, Sharett Tells House. Sees Inquisition Practices Revived.'

The trial established that the bombings had indeed been carried out by an Israeli espionage and terrorist network. This was headed by Colonel Avraham Dar—alias John Darling—and a core of professionals who had set themselves up in Egypt under various guises. They had recruited a number of Egyptian Jews; one of them was a young woman, Marcelle Ninio, who worked in the offices of a British company.

Naturally, the activities of such an organization, if ever unmasked, would do nothing to improve the lot of the vast majority of Egyptian Jews who wanted nothing to do with Zionism. There were still at least 50,000 Jews in Egypt; there had been something over 60,000 in 1947, more than half of whom were actually foreign nationals. During the first

Arab-Israeli war of 1948, the populace had sometimes vented its frustration against them, and some were killed in mob violence or by terrorist bombs. In spite of this, and of the revolutionary upheaval which followed four years later, few Jews—including the foreign nationals—left the country, and fewer still went to Israel. A Jewish journalist insisted: 'We, Egyptian Jews, feel secure in our homeland, Egypt.'[52]

But the welfare of Oriental Jewry in their various homelands was, as we have seen, Israel's last concern. And in July 1954 it had other worries. It was feeling isolated and insecure. Its Western friends—let alone the rest of the world—were unhappy about its aggressive behaviour. The US Assistant Secretary of State advised it to 'drop the attitude of the conqueror'.[53] More alarming was the rapprochement under way between Egypt, on the one hand, and the United States and Britain on the other. President Eisenhower had urged Britain to give up her giant military base in the Suez Canal Zone; Bengurion had failed to dissuade her. It was to sabotage this rapprochement that the head of Israeli intelligence, Colonel Benyamin Givli, ordered his Egyptian intelligence ring to strike.

He did so without consulting or even informing his boss, Defence Minister Pinhas Lavon, or the Prime Minister, Moshe Sharett. For Givli was a member of a powerful Defence Ministry clique which often acted independently, or in outright defiance, of the cabinet. They were protégés of Bengurion and, although 'The Old Man' had left the Premiership for Sde Boker, his Negev desert retreat, a few months before, he was able, through them, to perpetuate the hardline 'activist' policies in which he believed. On Givli's instructions, the Egyptian network was to plant bombs in American and British cultural centres, British-owned cinemas and Egyptian public buildings. The Western powers, it was hoped, would conclude that there was fierce internal opposition to the rapprochement and that Nasser's young régime, faced with this challenge, was not one in which they could place much confidence.[54] Mysterious violence might therefore persuade both London and Washington that British troops should remain astride the Canal; the world had not forgotten Black Saturday, 28 January 1951, in the last year of King Farouk's reign, when mobs rampaged through downtown Cairo, setting fire to foreign-owned hotels and shops, in which scores of people, including thirteen Britons, died.

The first bomb went off, on 2 July, in the Alexandria post office. On 11 July, the Anglo-Egyptian Suez negotiations, which had been blocked for nine months, got under way again. The next day the Israeli embassy in London was assured that, upon the British evacuation from Suez, stock-piled arms would not be handed over to the Egyptians. But the Defence Ministry activists were unconvinced. On 14 July their agents, in clandestine radio contact with Tel Aviv, fire-bombed US Information Service libraries in Cairo and Alexandria.

That same day, however, a phosphorous bomb exploded prematurely in the pocket of one Philip Natanson, nearly burning him alive, as he was about to enter the British-owned Rio cinema in Alexandria. His arrest and subsequent confession led to the break-up of the whole ring—but not before the completion of another cycle of clandestine action and diplomatic failure. On 15 July President Eisenhower assured the Egyptians that 'simultaneously' with the signing of a Suez agreement the United States would enter into 'firm commitments' for economic aid to strengthen their armed forces.[55] On 23 July—anniversary of the 1952 revolution—the Israeli agents still at large had a final fling; they started fires in two Cairo cinemas, in the central post office and the railway station. On the same day, Britain announced that the War Secretary, Antony Head, was going to Cairo. And on 27 July he and the Egyptians initialled the 'Heads of Agreement' on the terms of Britain's evacuation.

The trial lasted from 11 December to 3 January. Not all the culprits were there, because Colonel Dar and an Israeli colleague managed to escape, and the third Israeli, Hungarian-born Max Bennett, committed suicide; but those who were present all pleaded guilty. Most of them, including Marcelle Ninio, were sentenced to various terms of imprisonment. But Dr Musa Lieto Marzuk, a Tunisian-born citizen of France who was a surgeon at the Jewish Hospital in Cairo, and Samuel Azar, an engineering professor from Alexandria, were condemned to death. In spite of representations from France, Britain and the United States the two men were hanged. Politically, it would have been very difficult for Nasser to spare them, for only seven weeks before six Moslem Brothers had been executed for complicity in an attempt on his life. Nevertheless, Israel reacted with a great show of grief and anger. So did some Western Jews. Marzuk and Azar 'died the death of martyrs', said Sharett in the Knesset, whose members stood in silent tribute. Beersheba and Ramat Gan named streets after the executed men. Israel went into official mourning the following day. Israeli delegates to the Egyptian-Israeli Mixed Armistice Commission refused to attend its meeting, declaring that they would not sit down with representatives of the Cairo junta. In New York there were bomb threats against the Egyptian consulate and a sniper fired four shots into its fourth-floor window.[56]

This whole episode, which was to poison Israeli political life for a decade and more, came to be known as the 'Lavon Affair', for it had been established in the Cairo trial that Lavon, as Minister of Defence, had approved the campaign of sabotage. So at least the available evidence made it appear. And so it had in Israel too. There at Lavon's request, Prime Minister Sharett ordered a secret enquiry into an affair of which the whole cabinet knew nothing. Under questioning, intelligence chief Givli insisted that the so-called 'security operation' had indeed been authorized by Lavon himself. Two other Bengurion protégés, Moshe Dayan and Shimon Peres, also testified against Lavon. Lavon denounced Givli's papers as forgeries and demanded the resignation of all three men. Instead, Sharett ordered Lavon himself to resign and invited Bengurion to come out of retirement and take over the Defence Ministry. It was a triumphant comeback for the 'activist' philosophy whose excesses Sharett had tried to modify. It was consummated, a week later, by an unprovoked raid on Gaza, which left thirty-nine Egyptians dead and led to the Suez War of 1956.[57]

When the truth about the Lavon Affair came to light, six years after the event, it confirmed that there had indeed been a frame-up—not, however, by the Egyptians, but by Bengurion and his young protégés. Exposure was fortuitous. Giving evidence in a forgery trial in September 1960, a witness divulged *en passant* that he had seen the faked signature of Lavon on a document relating to a 1954 'security mishap'.[58] Bengurion immediately announced that the three-year statute of limitations prohibited the opening of the case. But Lavon, now head of the powerful Histradut Trade Union Federation, seized upon this opportunity to demand a public inquiry. Bengurion did everything in his power to stop it, but his cabinet overruled him. The investigation revealed that the 'security operation' had been planned behind Lavon's back. His signature *had* been forged, and the bombing had actually begun long before his approval—which he withheld—had been sought. He was a scapegoat pure and simple. On Christmas Day 1960, the Israeli cabinet unanimously exonerated him of all guilt in the 'disastrous security adventure in Egypt'; the Attorney General had, in the meantime, found 'conclusive evidence of forgeries as well as false testimony in an earlier inquiry'.[59] Bengurion was enraged. He issued an ultimatum to the ruling Labour party to remove Lavon, stormed out of a cabinet meeting and resigned. In what one trade unionist described as 'an immoral and unjust submission to dictatorship', his diehard supporters in the Histradut swung the vote in favour of accepting Lavon's resignation. Lavon, however, won a moral victory over the man who twice forced him from office. In the streets of Tel Aviv and Jerusalem, students demonstrated in his favour. They carried placards reading: 'Bengurion Go to Sde Boker. Take Dayan and Peres with You. We do Not Accept Leaders with Elastic Consciences.'[60] The affair rocked the ruling establishment, split public opinion, forced new elections and contributed largely to Bengurion's eventual disappearance from public life.

But Lavon was not the only real victim. There were also those misguided Egyptian Jews who paid with their lives or long terms of imprisonment. It is true that when, in 1968, Marcelle Ninio and her colleagues were exchanged for Egyptian prisoners in Israel, they received a heroes' welcome. True, too, that when Miss Ninio got married Prime Minister Golda Meir, Defence Minister Dayan and Chief of Staff General Bar Lev all attended the wedding and Dayan told the bride 'the Six-Day War was success enough that it led to your freedom'.[61] However, after spending fourteen years in an Egyptian prison, the former terrorists did not share the leadership's enthusiasm. When Ninio and two of her colleagues appeared on Israel television a few years later, they all expressed the belief that the reason why they were not released earlier was because Israel made little effort to get them out. 'Maybe they didn't want us to come back,' said Robert Dassa. 'There was so much intrigue in Israel. We were instruments in the hands of the Egyptians and of others . . . and what is more painful after all that we went through is that this continues to be so.' In Ninio's opinion, 'the government didn't want to spoil its relations with the United States and didn't want the embarrassment of admitting it was behind our action'.[62]

But the real victims were the great mass of Egyptian Jewry. Episodes like the Lavon Affair tended to identify them, in the mind of ordinary Egyptians, with the Zionist movement. When, in 1956, Israeli invaded and occupied Sinai, feeling ran high against them. The government, playing into the Zionist hands, began ordering Jews to leave the country. Belatedly, reluctantly, 21,000 left in the following year; more were expelled later, and others, their livelihood gone, had nothing to stay for. But precious few went to Israel.

NOTES

1. Resolution 186 (S2), 14 May 1948.
2. Menuhin, Moshe, *The Decadence of Judaism in Our Time*, Institute for Palestine Studies, Beirut, 1968, p. 512.
3. Bernadotte, Folke, *To Jerusalem*, Hodder and Stoughton, London 1951, p. 42.
4. *Ibid.*, p. 37.
5. *Ibid.*, p. 113.
6. Menuhin, *op. cit.*, p. 513.
7. *Progress Report of the UN Mediator on Palestine*, General Assembly, *Official Records*, Third Session, Supplement No. 11 (A/648) Paris, 1948, p. 14.
8. Bernadotte, *op. cit.*, p. 137.
9. *Ibid.*, p. 143.
10. *Ibid.*, p. 145.
11. *Ibid.*, p. 145.
12. *Ibid.*, pp. 196–7.
13. *Progress Report of the UN Mediator on Palestine*, *op. cit.*, p. 28.
14. Bernadotte, *op. cit.*, p. 199.
15. *Ibid.*, p. 200.
16. *Ibid.*, p. 208.
17. *Ibid.*, p. 208.
18. *Ibid.*, p. 210.
19. *Ibid.*, p. 209.
20. *Ibid.*, p. 190.
21. *Ibid.*, p. 186.
22. *Progress Report of the UN Mediator on Palestine*, *op. cit.*, p. 13.
23. *Death of a Mediator*, The Institute for Palestine Studies, Beirut, 1968, p. 25.
24. *Ibid.*, pp. 19–26.

25. *Ibid.*, p. 22.
26. *Ibid.*, p. 33.
27. *Palestine Post*, 14 December 1948.
28. Menuhin, *op. cit.*, p. 516.
29. *Palestine Post*, 23 January 1948.
30. *Black Panther* (Hebrew journal), 9 November 1972, see *Documents from Israel*, Ithaca Press, London, 1975, p. 127.
31. Allon, Yigal, *The Making of Israel's Army*, Valentine, Mitchell and Co., London, 1970, pp. 233–4.
32. *Black Panther*, *op. cit.*, pp. 130–2.
33. *Ibid.*, p. 131.
34. Herzl, *The Complete Diaries*, *op. cit.*, Vol. I, p. 7.
35. Lilienthal, Alfred, *The Other Side of the Coin*, Devin-Adair, New York, p. 184.
36. *Ibid.*, p. 47.
37. Central Bureau of Statistics, *Statistical Abstract of Israel*, No. 16, p. 96.
38. Berger, Elmer, *Who Knows Better Must Say So*, Institute for Palestine Studies, Beirut, p. 34.
39. *Black Panther*, *op. cit.*, p. 132.
40. Longrigg, Stephen Helmsley, *Iraq, 1900 to 1950*, Oxford University Press, London, 1953, pp. 19–23.
41. Cohen, Hayyim, J., *The Jews of the Middle East 1860–1972*, John Wiley and Sons, New York and Toronto, 1973, p. 30.
42. *Ibid.*, p. 30.
43. 'The League for Combating Zionism in Iraq', *Palestine Affairs*, (Arabic, monthly), Beirut, November 1972, p. 162.
44. Berger, *op. cit.*, p. 30.
45. *Ibid.*, p. 30.
46. *Ibid.*, pp. 32–3.
47. *Black Panther*, *op. cit.*, p. 132.
48. *Ibid.*, p. 133.
49. *Jerusalem Post*, 12 December 1954.
50. 13 December 1954.
51. 13 December 1954.
52. Berger, *op. cit.*, p. 14.
53. Love, Kennett, *Suez: The Twice-Fought War*, McGraw-Hill, New York, 1969, p. 71.
54. *Ibid.*, p. 73.
55. *Ibid.*, p. 74.
56. Love, *op. cit.*, p. 77.
57. See p. 198.
58. *New York Times*, 10 February 1961.
59. *Ibid.*
60. *Jewish Chronicle*, London, 17 February 1971.
61. *Ha'olam Hazeh*, 1 December 1971.
62. Associated Press, 16 March 1975.

6 · THE ARAB-FIGHTERS

A Colonial Society in a Post-Colonial Age

> Let us not today fling accusations at the murderers. Who are we that we should argue against their hatred? For eight years now they sit in their refugee camps in Gaza, and before their very eyes, we turn into our homestead the land and the villages in which they and their forefathers have lived. We are a generation of settlers, and without the steel helmet and the cannon we cannot plant a tree and build a home. Let us not shrink back when we see the hatred fermenting and filling the lives of hundreds of thousands of Arabs, who sit all around us. Let us not avert our gaze, so that our hand shall not slip. This is the fate of our generation, the choice of our life—to be prepared and armed, strong and tough—or otherwise, the sword will slip from our fist, and our life will be snuffed out.[1]

We have met the speaker before. Moshe Dayan was one of those rugged young farmer-soldiers whom, during the Arab Rebellion, Orde Wingate took on a daring night raid against an Arab village.[2] Here, in 1953, he is delivering the funeral oration of a young pioneer killed by Arab marauders as he was harvesting grain near the Egyptian frontier. For Israeli deputy Uri Avneri—to whom we owe the expression 'gun Zionism'—the speech epitomizes the stark philosophy of the 'Arab-fighter'; that is to say, the Israeli equivalent of what the Americans used to call an Indian-fighter, a type common to the second generation of settlers in a land where the newcomers are forced into conflict with the native population. It was the towering figure of Bengurion who guided the Jewish State through its early years, but in time, from the shadow of the master his disciple, Moshe Dayan the 'Arab-fighter', gradually emerged to become the most typical and celebrated embodiment of the forces which shaped its first quarter-century.

It had been through an extraordinary combination of chance and blind devotion, political skulduggery and ruthless coercion, that the Zionists realized Herzl's dream. It was, naturally enough, in an exalted and resolute frame of mind that they set about 'up-building' the new State. There was, in Weizmann's phrase, a whole new empty framework to be filled in, a whole new stage to be completed in the emerging grand design. No more urgent task faced the builders than the peopling of the Promised Land, than the furnishing of manpower for its farms, its factories—and its army. With the interfering British gone, and the Arab enemy vanquished, they could throw open the gates of Palestine to unrestricted immigration. Under the Law of Return, every Jew, wherever he might be, automatically acquired the right to full and immediate Israel citizenship. Indeed, in Bengurion's view, it was not merely the Jews' right, it was their duty, to avail themselves of this privilege. 'A state of seven hundred, eight hundred thousand Jews cannot be the climax of a vigil kept unbroken through generations and down the patient centuries; nor could it last for long . . . the Arabs too will arm themselves in the course of time; they will not always lack learning and technical skill. . . . No! So empty a State would be little justified, for it would not change the destiny of Jewry, or fulfil our historic covenant. The duty of the State is to end Galut [Jewish dispersion] at last.'[3] Zionists everywhere had 'to see to it that the Zionist flag which has begun to fly over the State of Israel is hoisted over the entire Jewish people until we achieve the completion of the ingathering of the exiles'.[4] They should have a 'collective obligation' to aid Israel 'under all circumstances and conditions even if such an attitude clashes with their respective national authorities'.[5]

It was not enough to build the new State—it had to be protected too. And that was destined, from the outset, to be a daunting task. There were two basic courses open to the policy-makers. One was to win the acceptance of their Arab and Palestinian neighbours; the other was to fight them. A peaceful settlement or permanent hostility—there was never really much doubt which course Bengurion and his successors would take. They chose war. That is not to say, of course, that they did not offer peace. Indeed, they did so with monotonous regularity. But it was to be a peace on Israel's terms, a victor's peace. And it was completely at variance with the UN recommendation which the Arabs had rejected but which the Israelis had acclaimed as the founding charter of their very existence. It was simple enough; there were, in essence, two things which Israel required of the Arabs. First, there was to be no return of the refugees. As 'aggressors' they forfeited that right. Accordingly, only a month after Bengurion, announcing Israel's establishment to the world, had called on the Arabs to 'play their part in the development of the State' and even as his government was claiming that the Arab exodus had been neither desired nor expected, he resorted to this remarkable line of argument: 'We did not want the war. Tel Aviv did not attack Jaffa. It was Jaffa which attacked Tel Aviv and this should not occur again. Jaffa will be a Jewish town. The repatriation of the Arabs to Jaffa is not justice, but folly. Those who declared war on us have to bear the result after they have been defeated.'[6] And if the Arabs' own folly was not reason enough, others were easily found. By 1 August, the Israel government had come to the conclusion that, on economic grounds, 'the reintegration of the returning Arabs into normal life, and even their mere sustenance, would present an insuperable problem'.[7] As Bengurion spoke, Zionist emissaries were streaming into the Diaspora to 'ingather the exiles', so many of whom had to be cajoled, shamed or frightened into 'coming home'. But reasons thus advanced were necessary cant, for, as Bengurion said elsewhere, 'we must do everything to ensure that they never do return'.[8] Secondly, there was to be no return of territory. The principle which he had so succinctly enunciated at the first cease-fire—'all that we have taken we shall hold'—informed all Israel's subsequent dealings, via third parties, with its neighbours. 'Security' became the great shibboleth; Israel would not participate in its own 'destruction'. All that Israel asked, Foreign Minister Moshe Sharett disarmingly explained, was that the Arabs accept it 'as we are, with our territory, our population and our unrestricted sovereignty'.[9] As for the UN Partition Plan, that recommendation, pronounced 'unassailable' on 15 May, was dead and buried, in the words of Bengurion, by 16 June.[10]

The choice which the Zionists made was hardly a voluntary, or even a conscious, one. It grew out of their predicament. Israel was *doomed* to everlasting conflict with its neighbours. This is what Dayan, the 'Arab-fighter', instinctively understood; it has been the one consistent strain of his often mercurial temperament. That which came into being by violent and unnatural means could only survive and prosper by violent and unnatural means. The nation born by the sword must live by it. The National Home had been conceived as the answer to anti-Semitism and the ghetto, but anything more closely resembling a massive, armed ghetto than the fortress state of Israel it would be hard to find. The implacable logic of Zionism in action, held partially in check by the Mandate, now came completely into its own. There was no third party—unless one counted the fickle and ineffectual will of the international community—to hold the ring. If the Arabs had rejected the lesser Israel of the UN, with its Palestinian majority and its built-in constitutional guarantees, they naturally took even less kindly to this larger Israel, which had expelled most of the Palestinians and torn up those parts of its founding charter which it did not like. The Arabs resolved that sooner or later they would 'liberate' Palestine, and the Israelis, with enemies on all sides, were impelled further down the road they had already taken. In security's name they found justification for military exploits which only deepened the encircling hatred—hatred which, in turn, engendered still more such exploits, and necessitated more and more arms to carry them out.

There can be no question about Israel's military prowess, the skill and daring of its commanders, the courage of its soldiers. In twenty-five years it has waged four 'big wars'—all-out struggles with one or a combination of its neighbours—and an endless succession of 'little wars', those trans-frontier raids and counter-raids, by land, sea or air, which, in the absence of a peaceful settlement, inexorably lead on to the big ones. Its performance on the battlefield has already assured it of an honoured niche in history. Israel came into being in 1948, with the defeat of five Arab armies. In October 1956, with French and British assistance, it reached the Suez Canal in a five-day *blitzkrieg* against Nasser's Egypt. In June 1967 it required only six days singlehandedly to defeat three Arab countries, Egypt, Syria and

Jordan, and capture the whole of Sinai, the Golan Heights and that part of Palestine—East Jerusalem and the West Bank—which it had failed to take in 1948. In October 1973 it was the turn of the Arabs—Egypt and Syria, to be precise—to strike the first, devastating blow; stunned and reeling, Israel fought back and, after a fierce eighteen-day struggle, it threw back the Syrian army beyond the 1967 cease-fire lines, and crossed the Suez Canal into 'Africa'; some military experts found this recovery even more impressive than the pulverizing victories of 1956 and 1967.

The Western public watched Israel choose war, and then ceaselessly wage it, with remarkable complaisance, not to say admiration. It was not merely because sheer military, like sporting, prowess, became its own justification, although that had much to do with it. It was also because, Hitler and the Holocaust aiding, the Zionists continued to enjoy that special favour and influence among the powerful, which had brought Israel into being in the first place. Israel also benefited from a certain cultural and historical prejudice, reinforced by European colonial experience, against the Arabs. Nor, on the face of it, did Israel fit the Western experience of a militarist society. On the contrary, nothing seemed less regimented, less Prussian in appearance than its citizens' army, rakish and debonair, which went to war in taxis, ice-cream wagons, with long hair and wearing the most eccentric attire. Above all, perhaps, the Israelis found it all too easy to persuade Western opinion, impressed by misleading disparities in size, that here was a clear-cut struggle between the weak and the strong, in which an Israeli David always won a heartwarming victory against the Arab Goliath. 1948 set the pattern. In that war, as we have seen, the Zionists were unquestionably the real aggressors, yet they had a remarkable success in portraying the Arabs in that role. Having established this travesty of history—this extraordinary distortion of cause and effect—they built on it. The Arabs helped them do it, not only because they were as incompetent in propaganda as they were in war, but because, as losers, it was they who now had to take the initiative, to undo the *fait accompli* which the Zionists had achieved at their expense. All the Israelis had to do was to stand still, to 'hold what they had taken'. They called their army the Israeli Defence Forces, and all its actions were ostensibly defensive in nature. Its 'little wars' were to punish and deter; its 'big wars' were 'wars of survival'.

In outward manner Israel may not be a militarist society, but, to the very depth of its being, it is a military one. It may not be a totalitarian society, but, in their attitude to the Arabs and the rest of the world, its people, in their overwhelming majority, slavishly approve official deeds and dogma. The army *is* the people. The Israelis made of armed might not merely the instrument of their own preservation, but of Zionism's still unfinished mission as well. Force was not merely 'punitive', it was 'purposive' too. For Israel did not really intend to stand still. That was just a façade. Israel was an aggressive colonizing power in a post-colonial era. It is true that, for Jewish and other reasons, and unique among anachronisms of its kind, it operated in a climate of extraordinary Western tolerance. But it could not tax that tolerance beyond all limits, and wherever possible—for sometimes it simply was not possible—it virtuously subscribed to the anti-colonial and other moralities of the age. Meanwhile, behind the façade, it exploited Arab violence—or the Arab counter-violence which, in historical perspective, it really was—as the pretext for an opportunistic and far more effective violence of its own, disguising offence as defence, the 'purposive' as the 'punitive'. And for twenty-five years, under Moshe Dayan, the Arab-fighter, it achieved an astonishing success.

Frontier Raids and Reprisals

From 1948 onwards, of course, the Israelis had as enemies not just the Palestinians, but the entire Arab world as well. It is often hard to draw a clear distinction between the two, although for our present purposes we shall do so. We can also, again a little arbitrarily, make a further sub-distinction among the Palestinians themselves, and assume that, for the Israelis, these now fell into two kinds: the 'outsiders' and the 'insiders', the immense majority who had left and those, something less than 200,000, who had managed to stay behind, unwanted Arab citizens of the Jewish State.

It was in their dealings with the 'outsiders' that Dayan and the

Arab-fighters truly came into their own. Their aim was not simply to keep the outsiders out. It went deeper than that. It was to eradicate the very idea that, one day, they would return for good. The Palestinians did of course entertain that idea, and eventually, the Israelis feared, they might act upon it. They might organize their own irrendentist movement, or, more important, as a powerful and disruptive force in Arab politics, they might induce the Arab régimes to take up their cause in earnest. Thus it was that the Israelis reacted to any attempt at Palestinian self-assertion, however trivial or pathetic, with extreme, indeed neurotic, severity. The reaction was entirely punitive not purposive in nature, for the outsiders, driven from land and property, no longer represented a physical obstacle, *in situ*, to Zionism's long-term purposes.

What the outsiders could do was to make raids across the frontiers; indeed, as Moshe Dayan acknowledged, it was entirely natural that they should. The Palestinian 'infiltrators'—as they were called—came mostly from that part of Palestine, the West Bank, which had been absorbed by the Hashemite Kingdom of Jordan. For political and geographical reasons, incursions were easier from there than they were from Egypt, Syria or Lebanon, which also had refugee populations. To begin with, the infiltrators usually had little hostile intention at all. They were going back, many of them, simply to rescue some of their belongings, sneaking by night into deserted villages to recover the valuables they had buried before their flight. Some would go searching for missing relatives. Others might cross to pick a few oranges from their own orchards or even to plough a part of their fields which, though they might not know it, had suddenly become enemy territory. For such was the caprice of the armistice line that more than a hundred villages were cut off from the land their inhabitants had tilled with asses and yoked oxen for generations; there it lay before their very eyes, but strangers were tilling it with tractors and modern machinery in their stead. The plight of these border villagers was particularly distressing because, though cut off from their livelihood, they did not qualify for refugee assistance—a refugee, in the UN definition, being one who has lost both land *and* house. Moreover, it was in a mean and pettifogging spirit that the strangers insisted on their territorial 'rights'. In his memoirs, Commander Hutchison, a UN observer from America, recalled how a group of families working a patch of rocky soil on their side of the line depended, for irrigation, on a cistern that lay on the other side. The nearest Israeli settlement was a mile away, and the cistern was no use to it. When he asked if the Arabs could continue to take their water from there, Commander Hutchison was told that 'if they cross they will be shot'.[11] In fact border patrols, consisting mostly of locally recruited vigilantes, frequently did shoot on sight.[12] Infiltration fell off. But naturally there remained a determined few who kept it up, and by now some of those were bent not simply on recovering what they had lost, but on wreaking a private, if useless, vengeance on the people who had taken it from them. They would steal: horses, cows, goats, agricultural implements. And then they would kill.

Yet it was not until the summer of 1953 that organized terrorism, under the auspices of the ex-Mufti and various Arab régimes, began in earnest, and then only on a small scale. Moreover, the Israelis were getting the better of it: they were killing far more Arabs than Arabs were killing Israelis. It may have been natural, as Dayan said, for the refugees to raid, but it was equally natural, according to his uncompromising credo, that those who had displaced them should hit back a hundred-fold. The Israelis spurned peaceable alternatives. These were available. Most Arab governments would probably have tried to 'liberate' Palestine, if they thought they had a serious chance. But they knew they did not, and whatever their declared policies, their actual ones were generally restrained. At all events, they were not going to let a handful of Palestinian irregulars drag them into the full-scale war they did not want—or for which they were not prepared. Jordan, the most dangerously exposed of Israel's neighbours, strained every nerve on Israel's behalf. Legislation was introduced which made a mere crossing of the line punishable by six months' imprisonment, and at one time at least half the prisoners on the West Bank were serving terms for this offence. The Jordanians even went so far, in defiance of Arab public opinion, as to seek Israeli cooperation in tracking down offenders, and on one occasion they proposed a so-called Local Commanders' Agreement providing for joint Israeli-Jordanian patrols, direct telephone communications and frequent meetings between officers. The Israelis would have none of it and even when, under pressure from the UN peacekeeping forces, they acquiesced in one or other such measure they were denouncing it within two or three weeks. They insisted on blaming Jordan. Everybody who crossed the line—the real terrorist, the orange-stealer or just the man on a visit to his relatives—belonged to the 'paramilitary forces of Jordan'.[13]

Spurning peace, they needed a war machine equal, in spirit and technique, to the task that confronted them. During their 'little war' along the Jordanian frontier they developed one. The *Haganah* and *Palmach*, the official forces of the Jewish state-in-the-making, had subscribed to the military ethic they called 'purity of arms'; during the 'War of Independence', they proved themselves ruthless enough, but, on the whole, their methods were distinguishable from the uninhibited brutality of *Irgun* and the 'dissidents'. They would not cold-bloodedly plan a Deir Yassin. After independence *Haganah* and *Palmach* furnished the backbone of the Israeli Defence Forces, but before long, it was the spirit of the *Irgun* that animated their crack units. With Zionism, as we have seen, extremism has almost always won in the end; it is the norm to which, under pressure of foreseeable circumstance, its latent forces have always gravitated. The Israelis' kill rate, across the troubled frontier, may have been far higher than the Arabs' but it was not high enough. To remedy this, the army offered money for what an Israeli newspaper, many years later, described as 'acts of revenge at so much a piece'. The practice had to be discontinued because the mercenaries so employed used to claim more killings than they had actually performed.[14] Furthermore, the army was not happy with its own reprisal raids. Indeed, according to the *Paratroopers' Book*, the semi-official history of the Israeli Airborne Corps, it was positively smarting at its failures. What 'most infuriated General Moshe Dayan—chief of operations at the time—was the scandalous defeat of the *Givati* Brigade at the Jordanian village of Palma. An entire battalion, a shock battalion with a glorious name, set out to attack the village. There were only a dozen Jordanian frontier guards armed with rifles in the village. The Jordanians opened fire, the battalion halted at the village walls and retreated.'[15]

Profiting from setbacks of this kind, influential 'activists' began to agitate for the formation of a specialized reprisal unit. Their ascendancy was not achieved without a struggle. General Dayan threw his weight behind the idea, but opponents of it blocked a decision. The opposition came not merely from 'doves' on the civilian side—chief among them Foreign Minister Moshe Sharett—but from much of the military establishment, who feared the emergence of a new organization, Dayan's 'private army', liable to lead an aggressive, independent existence of its own. The activists forced the issue, and in the jingoistic atmosphere of a deliberately stepped-up violence, they succeeded in forming the celebrated Unit 101 under the command of the equally celebrated Ariel Sharon.

Unit 101 carried out its first major operation—a landmark in this history—on 14 October 1953. It was a reprisal for the killing, by a grenade, of a mother and two children in the village of Yahuda. Sharett's diary entry for 14 October records that the Mixed Armistice Commission (part of the UN peacekeeping machinery) had 'roundly condemned' the killing and 'even the Jordanian delegates voted in favour of the resolution. They took it upon themselves to prevent such atrocities in the future. Under such circumstances is it wise to retaliate? . . . If we retaliate, we only make the marauder bands' job easier and give the [Israeli] authorities an excuse to do something. I called Lavon [Defence Minister] and told him what I thought. He said he would consult B.G. [Prime Minister Bengurion].' The diary continued: 'In the afternoon, during a meeting with Lavon and others in connection with developments in the north, an army representative brought Lavon a note from the UNTSO Chief of Staff, Gen. Vagn Bennike, saying that the Commander of the Jordan Legion, Glubb Pasha, had asked for police bloodhounds to cross over from Israel to track down the Yahuda murderers.' After Lavon had read the note, Sharett records, the army man asked: 'Any change in plans?' Lavon replied: 'No change.'[16]

'No change', after Jordan had asked for Israeli bloodhounds to track down acknowledged Jordanian criminals, no change in the plans to massacre that night the sleeping inhabitants of the village of Qibya. As the *Paratroopers' Book* described it: 'The operation at Qibya was to be distinguished from other operations by its purposes and its effects. The dynamiting of dozens of houses in Qibya was an ambitious undertaking surpassing anything in the past. Once and for all, it washed away the stain of the defeats that Zahal [the Israel army] had suffered in its reprisal operations.'[17] As the UN military observers, who reached the village two hours after the soot-smeared Israeli commandos had left, described it: 'Bullet-riddled bodies near the doorways and multiple bullet hits on the doors of the demolished houses indicated that the inhabitants had been forced to remain inside until their homes were blown up over them. . . . Witnesses were uniform in describing their experience as a night of horror, during which Israeli soldiers moved about in their village blowing up buildings, firing into doorways and windows with automatic weapons and throwing hand grenades.'[18] Sixty-six men, women and children died in an operation which reminded even pro-Israeli newspapers like the *New York Post* of Lidice.[19]

The Israeli government did not admit responsibility for the reprisal raid. Public opinion still lagged behind the Arab-fighters; there were still too many people who could not reconcile such methods with 'purity of arms'. Bengurion announced in a special broadcast that 'the government of Israel emphatically denies the false and fantastic tale according to which 600 Zahal soldiers participated in an operation against the village of Qibya. We have examined the facts in detail, and we can state without hesitation that not a single unit, not even the smallest, was absent from its barracks on the night of the attack on Qibya.' It was frontier settlers who had done it, the Prime Minister insisted, 'mostly Jewish refugees from Arab countries or survivors of Nazi concentration camps'; it had been their impulsive response to the murder of a mother and her two children. Such became the official explanation for all the exploits of Unit 101.

In time, however, public opinion did catch up, and by March 1955 the government all but officially announced to the world that 'there has been nothing reckless or impulsive about the lethal raids across the borders. On the contrary, the policy of reprisals is the fruit of cold, unemotional political and psychological reasoning.'[20] Unit 101 was never a large force, and it was composed entirely of volunteers, but its example was to be lasting and profound. Established as an antidote to the *Palmach*, the virus it carried did meet with some resistance. Of one squeamish recruit the *Paratroopers' Book* records, 'As an ex-Palmach who believed in the purity of arms he refused to participate in an expedition directed not against enemy soldiers but against the civilian population. Arik [Sharon's nickname] did not force him to take part. In a heated discussion, Shlomo Baum [Sharon's adjutant] hurled a remark at him: "There are no pure or impure arms; there are only clean weapons that work when you need them and dirty weapons that jam the moment you fire." '[21] In spite of resistance, the virus quickly spread. Three months after Qibya, at Dayan's initiative, Unit 101 was merged with the newly formed paratroop corps. According to Sharon, who assumed command of the combined force, Dayan 'was aware of the decisive influence the small unit would have on the Airborne (paratroopers) and, later, on the whole Zahal. . . . One might say that the ideology of reprisal operations was, in all respects, crystallized among the Airborne units.'[22] The army did in fact fall increasingly under the influence and command of men of the 101 and the Airborne. The spirit and methods of the *Palmach*—and the *Palmach* was hardly gentle—gave way to the spirit and methods of the *Irgun*. Meanwhile, in the country as a whole, there developed around Unit 101 the aura of heroic legend. Its centrepiece was the Arab-fighter extraordinary, Meir Har-Zion. Two or three nights a week, for months on end, this young commando took part in reprisal raids, 'laconically killing Arab soldiers, peasants, and townspeople in a kind of fury without hatred'.[23] He would introduce variations into a monotonous routine. Once, he and his comrades crossed the frontier, seized six Arabs, killed five of them with a knife as the others watched, and left the sixth alive so that he could tell.[24] His private exploits revealed the same natural bent. On leave, and bored, he once made a daredevil foray deep into enemy territory; on his way back to Jerusalem he shot an Arab soldier on the main highway. Later his sister was killed by a bedouin on one of her own sorties into enemy territory. Har-Zion revenged her by killing two bedouins whom he deemed to be connected with her death. Eventually he was critically wounded in action; his life was saved by a battlefield tracheotomy performed with a penknife. His memoirs and numerous press interviews are the story of a man who can describe, with dry relish, what it is like to stab an Arab shepherd in the back—and who recommends that anyone who wishes for the 'marvellous, sublime feeling' of 'knowing that you are a male' should kill with a knife rather than a gun.[25]

The cult which surrounded Har-Zion was both official and popular. Ministers and generals would glorify him as a 'model' for Israeli youth, the 'fighting symbol' of the entire Israeli army. He was placed above the law; when he killed the two bedouins, he was arrested and could have been charged with murder, but, on Bengurion's personal intervention, he was released without trial.[26] Half-crippled and forced into retirement, he was presented with a large piece of confiscated Arab land on Mount Kaoukab high above Lake Galilee. In this desolate spot, not far from his old *kibbutz*, he set up his private cattle ranch and played host to the soldiers who came, as pilgrims, to see and admire him. 'A whole ceremony developed around Kaoukab,' he recalls in his memoirs; 'they arrived after a long march that lasted a day and a night. At the end of the march, the Unit's insignia were distributed to the soldiers. The goal of the march was the ranch. To ascend it has become a tradition; it is a summit one must reach.'[27]

The Arabs Who Stayed Behind

Keeping out the outsiders was almost exclusively punitive; keeping down the insiders was both punitive and purposive. For the Palestinians who stayed behind were not merely a security problem; their very presence stood in the way of Zionism's historic mission.

The military governed the lives of Israel's Arab minority. Outright armed violence, though by no means absent, was not its characteristic method; force and coercion sufficed. Nevertheless, there was a grave difficulty. Israel described itself as an outpost of the 'free world' on which it so heavily depended, a 'bastion of democracy' in an area which lacked such a thing. It was a nation ostentatiously founded on law, justice and humanity. Racial and religious persecution, the bitter cup from which the Jews had drunk so deep, could have no place in the Jewish State. In the Declaration of Independence it promised 'complete equality of social and political rights for all its citizens, without distinction of creed, race or sex'. So it looked on the surface. In practice, however, some citizens were more equal than others. The words Arab and Jew never actually appeared in the statute books, but in the enforcement of the law there was one set of principles for one kind of Israeli and another set of principles for the other. Among those who looked beneath the surface and then defended what they saw it generated a 'double-speak' and 'double-think' which an Israeli civil rights campaigner has called 'the Orwellian tax that Israel pays to the concept of democracy'.[28]

The legal foundations of the military rule under which the insiders fell were the Defence Regulations of 1945. It was the British who introduced them and the Jewish community, then in revolt against the Mandate, which first bore the brunt of them. Their introduction had raised a storm of protest. Dr Yaacov Shimson Shapira, a future Israeli Minister of Justice, described them as 'unparalleled in any civilized country; there were no such laws even in Nazi Germany. . . . There is indeed only one form of government which resembles the system in force here now—the case of an occupied country. They try to pacify us by saying that these laws are only directed against malefactors, not against honest citizens. But the Nazi Governor of Occupied Oslo also announced that no harm would come to citizens who minded their own business. It is our duty to tell the whole world that the Defence Laws passed by the British Mandatory Government of Palestine destroy the very foundations of justice in this land.'[29] After 1948 Israel did not abolish this system of 'officially licensed terrorism', as another future Justice Minister called the Defence Regulations. It enforced them with greater severity—against the Arabs. Under these laws, the army could uproot whole communities at will, deporting them or transferring them from one place to another; it could impose indefinite curfews and establish security zones which no Arab could enter without permission; seize land and destroy or requisition property; enter and search any place; imprison a man without trial or confine him to his home, quarter or village; prohibit or restrict his movement inside or outside Israel, or expel him without explanation from his native land. The only means of redress, through a military court, was wholly futile.

Armed with such Draconian powers, the military authorities lost no time in exploiting them. Outright violence, entirely punitive in intent, may not have been their characteristic method, but there is no more revealing example of the Arabs' plight than one notorious occasion when they did use it. The Arabs remember Kafr Qasem as the Deir Yassin of the established State. Less revealing, perhaps, than the event itself was the reaction it generated. On 29 October 1956, on the eve of Israel's invasion of Egypt, a detachment of Frontier Guards imposed a curfew on villages near the Jordanian frontier. Among them was Kafr Qasem. The Mukhtar was informed of the curfew just half an hour before it was due to go into effect. It was therefore quite impossible for him to pass the message on to the villagers who would be returning, as dusk fell, from their various places of work. Major Shmuel Melinki, the detachment commander, had foreseen this eventuality, and he asked his superior, Brigadier Yshishkhar Shadmi, what should be done about anyone coming home in ignorance of the curfew. The Brigadier had replied: 'I don't want any sentimentality . . . that's just too bad for him.'[30] And there was no sentimentality. In the first hour of the curfew, between five and six o'clock, the Frontier Guards killed forty-seven villagers. They had returned home individually or in batches. A few came on foot, but most travelled by bicycle, mule cart or lorry. They included women and children. But all the Frontier Guards wanted to know was whether they were from Kafr Qasem. For if they were, they were curfew-breakers, and once they had ascertained that they were, they shot them down at close range with automatic weapons. 'Of every group of returning workers, some were killed and others wounded; very few succeeded in escaping unhurt. The proportion of those killed increased, until, of the last group, which consisted of 14 women, a boy and 4 men, all were killed, except one girl, who was seriously wounded.'[31] The slaughter might have gone on like this had not Lieutenant Gavriel Dahan, the officer on the spot

> . . . informed the command several times over the radio apparatus in the jeep of the number killed. Opinions differ as to the figure he gave in his reports, but all are agreed that in his first report he said: 'one less', and in the next two reports: 'fifteen less' and 'many less—it is

> difficult to count them'. The last two reports, which followed each other in quick succession, were picked up by Captain Levy, who passed them on to Melinki. When he was informed that there were 'fifteen less' in Kafr Qasem, Melinki gave orders, which he was unable to transmit to Dahan before the report arrived of 'many less—it is difficult to count them', for the firing to stop and for a more moderate procedure to be adopted in the whole area. . . . This order finally ended the bloodshed at Kafr Qasem.[32]

All this was established in the trial which, as the scandal slowly leaked out, the government was obliged to hold. The trial was a *pro forma* affair. There was little moral outrage in the courtroom, and, apart from a few lone voices, very little outside it. During the proceedings the leading newspaper *Haaretz* reported that 'the eleven officers and soldiers who are on trial for the massacre in Kafr Qasem have all received a fifty per cent increase in their salaries. A special messenger was sent to Jerusalem to bring the cheques to the accused in time for Passover. A number of the accused had been given a vacation for the holiday. . . . The accused mingle freely with the spectators; the officers smile at them and pat them on the back; some of them shake hands with them. It is obvious that these people, whether they will be found innocent or guilty, are not treated as criminals, but as heroes.'[33] One Private David Goldfield reportedly resigned from the Security Police in protest against the trial. According to the *Jewish Newsletter*, his testimony merely reflected what most Israelis thought: 'I feel that the Arabs are the enemies of our State. . . . When I went to Kafr Qasem, I felt that I went against the enemy and I made no distinction between the Arabs in Israel and those outside its frontiers.' Asked what he would do if he met an Arab woman, in no sense a security threat, who was trying to reach her home, he replied: 'I would shoot her down, I would harbour no sentiments, because I received an order and I had to carry it out.'[34] The sentences were *pro forma* too. Melinki and Dahan got gaol terms of seventeen and fifteen years respectively, but it was a foregone conclusion that they would only serve a fraction of them. In response to appeals for a pardon, the Supreme Military Court decided to reduce the 'harsh' sentence; and, following this generous example, the Chief of Staff, then the Head of State, and finally a Committee for the Release of Prisoners all made contributions, so that within a year of their sentence Melinki and Dahan were free men. As for Brigadier Shadmi—the 'no sentimentality' senior officer—a Special Military Court found him guilty of a 'merely technical' error, reprimanded him and fined him one piastre. But the twist in the tail was yet to come. Nine months after his release from prison, Dahan, convicted of killing forty-three Arabs in an hour, was appointed 'officer responsible for Arab affairs' in the town of Ramleh.[35] And the last that has been heard of Major Melinki was that, through his influential connections in the army, he had secured a coveted permit, sought after by many an entrepreneur, to set up a tourist centre in southern Israel.[36]

Let us now turn to those other, more characteristic, uses to which the military authorities—aided and abetted by the civil administration—put their Draconian powers. Zionism's basic impulse has always been to take possession of the land. It goes without saying that the new state appropriated all the land which the outsiders left behind; but it also appropriated the insiders' land too—about a million dunums of it.[37] In 1948 perhaps 5 per cent of Israeli-controlled territory was still in Arab hands. By 1967—and the war which brought the remaining 20 per cent of Palestine under Israeli control—it had fallen to about 1 per cent.[38] It was here, perhaps, in the systematic harassment of the hapless vestige of a community they had destroyed and dispersed that the Zionists showed how far, in serving their own people, they could harden their hearts against others.

In the early years, with wartime techniques still fresh in their memories, the authorities would frequently 'cleanse' the land in the quick and easy way. They would send in the army to drive the inhabitants out—over the frontier or to other parts of Israel. Thus, as late as the summer of 1950, the village of Ashkelon was still Arab—at least it was until one morning when the soldiers arrived, put all the inhabitants on trucks, took them to the Gaza frontier and, with the help of some shooting in the air, told them to go and join the refugees who had passed that way two years before.[39] Under the Defence Regulations this kind of procedure was legal. However, it was not good for Israel's reputation; the world was sensitive about the refugee problem, and the

Arab states were exploiting it. So, being a country where the rule of law prevailed, Israel enacted legislation to furnish a sound juridical basis for expropriations which had already taken place and for those which were still to come. The first of a series of enactments—the 1950 Law for the Acquisition of Absentee Property—was a very ingenious, retroactive device. The absentees in question were for the most part the outsiders who could not return. Their property was acquired by a Custodian of Absentee Property, whose ostensible task was to look after it pending a solution of the whole refugee problem, his real one being to hand it over to the appropriate authorities for Jewish settlement in perpetuity. But insiders could become absentees too. They are known as 'absent-presents'; the precise number of these Orwellian beings is a well-kept military secret, but they run into tens of thousands.[40] It was very easy for the Custodian to classify a man as 'absent-present'. For under the new law any person who left his usual place of residence between 29 November 1947 and 1 September 1948 for any place outside Palestine, or any place inside Palestine but outside Jewish control, was considered to be an absentee—and never mind if he was actually present in Israel, a fully-fledged citizen of this 'bastion of democracy'. The simple villager of Galilee had not been vouchsafed the power to tell the future, and little did he realize that for this 'offence' committed two years before it actually became one, all his worldly possessions—his homes and fields—could be taken away from him and given to somebody else, a total stranger who came from across the seas. It did not matter how long he had been away; it could have been for one day only. No matter where he had gone; it could have been to the next village. No matter why he left; perhaps it was to buy some sheep. Moreover it was so much easier for the Custodian in that he was not expected to furnish proof of absence. His own investigations sufficed. When, on the strength of them, he 'declared' a man an absentee, he became an absentee and no one could gainsay him; for 'he may not be questioned about the information sources which led him to issue a decision by virtue of this law'. And just in case the Custodian, by his own admission, did make a mistake, the law took care of that too: 'No deal concluded spontaneously between the Custodian and another person in connection with property which the Custodian believes to be absentee property at the moment the deal is concluded may be invalidated, but shall remain in force even if it is later proved that such property was not absentee property at that time.'[41]

Thus it came about that whole communities of insiders, citizens of Israel, were no less refugees than their brethren beyond the borders. For during the nine months in question—an arbitrary time-span, dating from the UN Partition recommendation, well suited to Israel's purposes—a great many Palestinians had indeed left their normal places of residence, not simply for business or pleasure, but because they thought it was dangerous to remain where they were. They planned to return home when the fighting ended. But their new masters had other ideas. If they ever saw their homes again, it was with strangers living in them; if they ever tilled their fields again, it was in the service of those strangers. Townspeople were no better off. A frightened family might have moved for a few days to another quarter, or just across the street.[42] The Custodian declared them 'absent-presents' none the less. He was a man of principle. What was the difference between town and country, between ten metres or ten miles? It might seem hard, and he was sorry. But what could he do about it? The law, after all, was the law.

Another typical enactment—the Emergency Articles for the Exploitation of Uncultivated Areas—was particularly useful because it dovetailed so nicely with the Defence Regulations: a happy blend of the purposive and the punitive. On the face of it, this law had an entirely laudable purpose. It empowered the Minister of Agriculture to take possession of uncultivated land to ensure that it is cultivated when he 'is not satisfied that the owner of the land has begun, or is about to begin, to cultivate it, or is going to continue to cultivate it'.[43] However, it could also be turned to another purpose. The procedure was quite simple. The Minister of Defence, with laws of his own to draw upon, would declare some choice farmland a 'closed area', thereby making it a grave offence to enter the area without written permission from the Military Governor. The Military Governor finds himself unable, for security reasons, to grant such permits to farmers. Their fields quickly become 'uncultivated land'. Noting this, the Minister of Agriculture takes prompt action 'to ensure that it is cultivated'. He has this done either 'by labourers engaged by him' or by 'handing it over to another party to cultivate it'. This other party, of course, is always the neighbouring Jewish colony.

Clearly, in the enforcement of Israeli law, some people were more equal than others. Indeed, some people seemed to be above it altogether. At least that is what the inhabitants of Ghabisiya, Kafr Bar'am and Iqrit—to name only three villages—could legitimately conclude after they appealed to the Supreme Court. The Military Government had declared Ghabisiya a 'closed area' and expelled its inhabitants. The Supreme Court ruled that the Military Governor had been entitled to take this step, but that his decision was invalid because it had not been published in the Official Gazette. The Military Government found this ruling very hard to accept, and a few days later, while continuing to keep the villagers out, the necessary order was published in the gazette. The villagers went back to the Supreme Court. This time it ruled that since they had failed to return before publication of the order they could not do so after it. The inhabitants of the Christian, and notably docile, village of Kafr Bar'am, which had become a 'closed area' too, applied to the Supreme Court in their turn. It ruled in their favour: they should be permitted to return. The authorities were extremely angry. Aircraft of the Israeli Defence Forces attacked the village. The bombardment went on until Kafr Bar'am was reduced to rubble, whereupon the aircraft returned safely to their bases.[44] In July 1951 the Supreme Court ruled in favour of another Christian village, Iqrit, whose inhabitants had been ordered, three years earlier, to leave their homes 'for two weeks' until 'military operations in the area were concluded'. After this judgement the Military Government found another justification to prevent them from returning. The villagers once more appealed to the Supreme Court, which decided to consider the case on 6 February 1952. But a month and a half before that date, on Christmas Day to be precise, the Israeli Defence Forces took the Mukhtar of this Christian community to the top of a nearby hill and forced him to watch the show—the blowing up of every house in the village—which they had laid on for his benefit.[45]

It hardly needs to be demonstrated that, however democratic Israel was for the Jews, it was in every sense a tyranny for the Arabs. Tyranny, like freedom, is indivisible, and it was not to be expected that a government which could so persecute its citizens in one way—by plundering their land and property—should treat them any better in others. Israel has always claimed that it cares for its Arab as much as its Jewish citizens, indeed that they are far better off than they would have been under Arab rule. But the fact that Israel made this claim—and above all the fact that none but a 'lunatic fringe' of its freedom-loving Jewish citizens ever challenged it—merely confirmed a natural law: Orwellian 'double-think' will always be as pervasive as the evil it seeks to hide. Just what did happen, for example, to those dispossessed Arab farmers? Merely to ask the question is to open a Pandora's Box of ramifying iniquities, for the truth is that the Arabs were deliberately reduced to the *lumpenproletariat* of Israeli society or—in the biblical parlance which Zionists so often affect—they became the 'hewers of wood and the drawers of water'. If the Arabs continued to work what little land was left to them, they did so in the face of a whole series of obstructionist measures, designed to consolidate Jewish agriculture at their expense, which forced them to sell their produce at uneconomic prices and starved them of financial assistance, modern machinery and the beneWts of irrigation projects. If they gave up the struggle and worked for Jewish masters, they had to offer their services on a black market which grossly exploited them. And even that was eventually denied them. For by the sixties thousands of Arab farmers found themselves working what was once their own land on behalf of a new class of Jewish *effendis* whom time, and the weakening of the Zionist ideal, had brought into being. So in 1967, parliament passed a law which in reality—though not, God forbid, in appearance—was designed to prevent Israel's Arab citizens from working the 'Land of the Nation'—even if they worked it for Jews.[46] Not until 1962, and even then on a small scale, would the trade union federation accept Arabs in its ranks. The exclusivist dogmas of Hebrew Labour—or 'organized labour' as Orwellian 'double-think' renamed it—still held sway. Arab unemployment was rife. But Arabs who did find work were liable, not being 'organized', to dismissal at any time. They were usually reserved for the most menial and dirty jobs. Where they managed to rise above that, there was no such thing as equal pay for equal work. If, as an increasing number did, they found jobs in the cities, they could not—thanks to the Defence Regulations—live there. They became itinerant labourers, forced to travel huge distances every day to and from their villages—although, as a special favour, construction workers would be permitted to spend the night in unfinished buildings or makeshift accommodation of the kind. The Arab minority could not seek collective redress through Israel's democratic system, because there was no place in the system for representative Arab political parties, no opportunity for Arabs to achieve positions of real influence in government and administration; the 'Arab Department' of every institution was headed by a Jew. The Arabs could only vote as appendages of Jewish parties, and what the Israelis paraded in the outside world as the proof of their own enlightenment they occasionally admitted to themselves was a farce, 'a struggle in the name of the Arabs between the Jews themselves, for the sake of the Jews'.[47] Arab writers, intellectuals or community leaders who showed the least independence of spirit would be placed in 'administrative detention', confined to their place of residence, or exiled to some remote corner of the country. Nor could parents, miserable though their own plight might be, look forward to a brighter future for their children. The deliberate stunting of Arab education meant that there were about nine Jewish university graduates, *per capita*, for every one Arab.

Zionist apartheid, whatever one might think of its original motivation, quickly proved itself as harsh as South Africa's. It was rather strange therefore that whereas enlightened Western opinion condemned racial discrimination in one place it was apt to condone or even praise it in another. One key reason, of course, was the extraordinary built-in favour which the Zionist movement had always enjoyed. Another was that while South Africa's apartheid was open, even flaunted, Israel's was disguised. Moreover, Israel's was much *easier* to disguise; for the citizens it persecuted were a small minority, not a large majority. That in turn was because, in 1948 and after, the Arab-fighters simply drove the Arabs out. Ironically, therefore, it was the very extremism of that original and massive act of violence which subsequently helped Israel seem less extreme, less oppressive, in its treatment of the few who stayed behind. The Arab-fighters' most dazzling triumph still lay ahead—but this time it was destined to make Israeli apartheid much harder to hide.

Wars of Expansion

For Bengurion and his lieutenants, the 1948 'War of Independence' had left unfinished business. There is no need to exaggerate Zionism's inherent expansionist tendencies. Inevitably, being an exalted creed by any standards, it spawned its share of fantastic conceits. But, however seriously entertained at the time, visions of a Hebrew Kingdom stretching from the Nile to the Euphrates, or other far-flung boundaries of biblical inspiration, belonged essentially to the romantic early days of the movement. When an unlikely configuration of international circumstances suddenly brought Zionism into the realm of the possible, the politicians who exploited this opportunity had to set what they deemed to be realistic limits on Zionist ambitions. Although—to any but themselves—those ambitions must have seemed overweening enough, they were always distressed at any enforced curtailment of them. The politicians had seriously envisaged full-scale Jewish settlement on the East Bank of the River Jordan, and when, one afternoon in 1921, Winston Churchill, the Colonial Secretary, conferred British-protected but independent statehood on the Amirate of Transjordan, thereby severing the East Bank from Palestine, the Zionists considered this to be a grievous blow to the territorial integrity of the 'National Home'. In 1948, Bengurion proclaimed that the new state had only been established in 'a portion of the land of Israel' and there were subsequent expressions of regret that even fuller advantage had not been taken of the revolutionary opportunities, perhaps never to be repeated, which had then presented themselves. 'Israeli territory might have been greater', said Bengurion, 'if Moshe Dayan had been chief of staff during the war of 1948 against the Arabs in Palestine.'[48] On the other hand, Dayan's rival, Yigal Allon, commander of the *Palmach*, thought that Bengurion himself (bowing to international pressures) had been mainly to blame. When Bengurion 'ordered a halt in our army's advance, we had been on the crest of victory . . . from the Litani [a Lebanese river which, in Zionist thinking, would always have made an ideal frontier] in the north to the Sinai desert in the southwest. A few more days' fighting would have enabled us . . . to liberate the entire country.'[49] For Bengurion, it soon became clear, expansion followed as naturally on the 'War of Independence' as growth is a consequence of birth. 'To maintain the status quo', he declared, 'will not do. We have to set up a dynamic state bent upon expansion.'[50] Nor was it just a question of territorial aggrandizement. Military conquest would stimulate other forms of growth—in manpower and wealth, in prestige, self-confidence and ideological conviction. Growth, dynamism, the maintaining of a permanent sense of emergency, were all the more important, in Bengurion's view, because the Arabs would not make peace with Israel. The Arabs would not always remain as weak as they were; Israel must therefore either pre-empt their strength, and/or strengthen itself against the day when they felt able to fulfil their promise to 'liberate' Palestine.

For all his theatrical 'peace offers', which as often as not coincided with a bloody reprisal raid, peace was low in Bengurion's priorities, as his franker asides revealed: 'And if we cannot get real peace for ten years or twenty years, we can stand it, and there will be some blessing in it too.'[51] What those blessings were an Israeli scholar and diplomat has disclosed at greater length.

> Seen in retrospect, peace with the Arabs in the early stages of the State could have had disastrous effects. The half-million Jews from the Arab countries would not have been forced to immigrate to Israel. Had peace come, say, in 1952 or 1953, these immigrants, having arrived impoverished and despoiled in an unfamiliar, even hostile culture and facing hard social, economic and dietary adjustments, would in all probability either have gone back to their former homes, or, under the impact of free and peaceful association with the Arabs, maintained their old culture, which is incompatible with a modern, strong, and homogeneous Israeli nation capable of survival. There might be no-one speaking Hebrew today in Beersheba—perhaps not even in Jerusalem. The people would have lost their sense of crisis and purpose. We were fighting in those days, as we still are, for survival and the creation of one homogeneous nation—one culture, one language. Everything was subordinated to this.[52]

If Zionism's still unfinished business led to the kind of behaviour which, by contemporary civilized standards, represented a more or less permanent violation of international law and order, that troubled few consciences in Israel. The Israeli establishment constructed a morality of its own to which, characteristically, the highly politicized religious hierarchy contributed quite as much as the politicians, the press and the intelligentsia in general. Truculence, heavily tinged with self-righteousness, inevitably put down deep roots in a nation whose official conscience encouraged it. Only a few voices cried in the wilderness against rabbis who 'rave about the army and the military spirit, applaud the ways of armed violence' and 'certify that the doings of the Israeli army are in conformity with the teachings of the Jewish religion'.[53] For an impartial verdict, as to which side in the Middle East conflict has always been the more aggressive, there is surely no better place to look than the UN. Israel has been taken to task by the General Assembly and the Security Council more often than any other nation. Unabashed, it has long since had the answer to that: it simply denies the body which gave it birth any moral authority whatsoever. More impressive, however, than formal condemnations, so often spawned by an automatic bloc vote, have been the experiences of the UN's own devoted servants. We have already dealt with those of Count Bernadotte. Three soldiers who came after him also record theirs in books which they wrote on completing their tour of duty. Commander Hutchison, an American, General Burns, a Canadian, and General von Horn, a Swede, cover twelve consecutive years of UN peace-keeping from 1951 to 1963. Their task was to police the armistice agreements which marked the end of the 'War of Independence'. The territorial lines the agreements laid down were not supposed to be the definitive frontiers of the State of Israel, even if, with the passage of time, that is how the world tended increasingly to regard them. The observers' brief was a narrow legalistic one; they were to forget how they had come into being, that they represented in themselves a pure Israeli gain against a pure Arab loss, a status quo built on force of arms. If any verdict, therefore, can be taken as a cautious one, it is theirs. The verdict all three convey, on almost every page, is essentially the same; it amounts to a withering indictment of Israel—an Israel which, not content with what it had achieved by force of arms, ceaselessly, deliberately violated the new legality to which it had committed itself. Contrasting Arabs and Israelis, General von Horn said that from time to time his staff would incur a certain degree of animosity from the Arabs but never 'in the same implacable and frenetic way' that they did from the Israelis. 'The Arabs', he said, 'could be difficult, intolerant and indeed often impossible, but their code of behaviour was on an infinitely higher and more civilized level.' He said that everybody came to this conclusion, which was 'strange, because there was hardly a man among us who had not originally arrived in the Holy Land without the most positive and sympathetic attitude towards the Israelis and their ambitions for their country. . . . After two or three years in daily contact with officials, soldiers and private individuals on *both* sides, there had been a remarkable change in their attitude.' Whenever he asked them what they had liked least about their service, he almost always got the same reply: 'the consistent cheating and deception of the Israelis'.[54]

Israel has fought two 'big wars' for growth—a recourse to all-out 'purposive' violence which it presented as wars of survival, or wars for peace. Twice it scored devastating military victories. But the first war—against Egypt in 1956—yielded only minor long-term gains; Israel was forced to yield up all the territory it had captured. For opportunity was all, and Bengurion had misjudged the diplomatic circumstances. Although he had planned the whole adventure in collusion with Britain and France, which also attacked Egypt, he went beyond the limits of Western—in this case American—tolerance. But the long-term gains of Israel's next 'big war'—in June 1967—were to prove commensurate with its military victory. For the diplomatic circumstances were as ideal as they ever could be; this time Israel had waited for the perfect opportunity. Western public opinion overwhelmingly applauded the single-handed Israeli *blitzkrieg* against Egypt, Syria and Jordan; the American government did not hide its satisfaction. To this day Israel remains in possession of the Golan Heights, the West Bank and the vast bulk of Sinai, where, with expropriation and settlement, it is pressing on with the great Zionist enterprise.

Suez, 1956

In early 1955 Bengurion put war with Egypt on his agenda. This was a deliberate act of policy. 'It is today frankly admitted', according to the *Paratroopers' Book*, 'that if it had been up to David Bengurion, the Sinai war would have taken place a year earlier' than it did.[55] Bengurion deliberately sought a showdown with the country which, as the great power of the Arab world, could bring the most decisive influence to bear for war or peace in the Middle East. He did this at a time when the young President Nasser of Egypt, for all his revolutionary idealism, was manifestly doing his best to preserve the peace. What Bengurion needed was a pretext, for, as Dayan subsequently admitted, he and his friends had decided 'not to miss any politically favourable opportunity to strike at Egypt'.[56] He coolly set about manufacturing one. It grew naturally out of a 'little war', ceaseless reprisal raids Qibya-style, which had a far broader purpose than the discouragement of marauding Palestinians. In his article on 'Israel's Policy of Reprisals' Moshe Brilliant explained that the rationale behind them was deeply rooted in the Zionist experience. In British Mandate days, the Jews had won great praise with their *Havlaga*, their 'self-restraint', but they had courted disaster. They then turned to 'gunpowder and dynamite' and discovered that, although it earned them international censure, it also 'earned them . . . ultimately the coveted prize' of statehood. The Israelis had never forgotten that lesson. These bloody 'border incidents' were seldom accidental . . . they were 'part of a deliberate plan to force the Arabs to the peace table'. Since 1948 'each reluctant step the Arabs took from hot war toward peace was taken when they were held by the throat'.[57]

In February 1955, the Israeli army attacked Egyptian military outposts in Gaza. Thirty-nine Egyptians died. Until then this had been Israel's least troublesome frontier. That was no accident. Just as, in earlier days, the Zionists accused the Palestinian *zaims* and *effendis* of stirring up hatred against them, so now they levelled the same charge against the Arab leaders. President Nasser, the emergent pan-Arab champion, became the obvious candidate for Israeli bogeyman. The reputation was thoroughly undeserved: the real Arab militancy was to be found, as always, among the people rather than the politicians. For six years, in the last days of Farouk and the early ones of the revolution, Egyptian rulers studiously avoided militant attitudes. Israel, it was felt, should not distract them from problems nearer home. President Nasser persuaded Western visitors, even passionately pro-Israeli ones like British politician Richard Crossman, that he really was as pacific as he sounded. 'Driving back to Cairo that night, I could not help thinking that not only Egypt, but the whole Middle East, must pray that Nasser survives the assassin's bullet. I am certain that he is a man who means what he says; and that so long as he is in power directing his middle-class revolution, Egypt will remain a factor for peace and social development.'[58] One motive for that revolution had been the humiliation of Egypt's defeat in 1948; Egyptian officers, Nasser among them, attributed it in part to the poor and malfunctioning arms with which, owing to the corruptions of the old order, they had been sent into battle. Yet he made no serious attempt to narrow Israel's rapidly lengthening lead in armaments. He preferred to spend Egypt's meagre reserves of hard currency on the welfare of his backward and overpopulated country.

Not surprisingly perhaps, but disingenuously, Israeli leaders such as Bengurion and Dayan do not even mention the Gaza raid in their accounts of the period. Nasser called it a 'turning point' and all independent authorities agree with him. The raid brought him under intensified pressure not merely from the Arabs in general, but from quarters most directly involved—his own army and the refugees in the Gaza Strip. As a soldier, General Burns, the Chief of Staff of the UN forces, had a sympathetic grasp of Nasser's problem with the army.

> Shortly before the raid, he had visited Gaza and told the troops that there was no danger of war; that the Gaza Armistice Demarcation Line was not going to be a battlefront. After that many of them had been shot in their beds. Never again could he risk telling the troops they had no attack to fear; never again could he let them believe they could relax their vigilance. It was for this reason that he could not issue and enforce strict orders against the opening of fire on the Israel patrols which marched along the demarcation line, a hundred metres or less from the Egyptian positions. These positions were held by the friends and perhaps the relatives of the men who had perished in the Israeli ambush of that bloody night.[59]

There was only one way to still his commanders' clamour for arms: to furnish them. He took that decision during the confused and sleepless night of the raid, even before the last explosions had died away.[60] At first he sought Western, especially American, arms, and in such small quantities that when President Eisenhower saw his shopping list he exclaimed: 'Why, this is peanuts.'[61] Western intelligence was convinced that he had no intention of attacking—even if he were sure of quick and easy victory. Nor was this conviction shaken when, rebuffed by the blundering and short-sighted Americans, he negotiated the famous Czech arms deal which marked the Soviet Union's first great breakthrough in the struggle to undermine Western influence in the Middle East.[62]

As for the refugees, there were more than 300,000 of them, living in poverty, idleness and a festering hatred for Israel, who shared the temptation of their brethren in Jordan. Hemmed in upon themselves by the sea, the desert and the armistice lines, they only had to look east to see the broad fields, once theirs, which the Israelis cultivated from a chain of *kibbutzim* guarding the heights of the area beyond. They too were 'infiltrators'; and so were the 7,000 bedouins whom the Israelis had driven across the border since 1948.[63] They too had crossed the lines in defiance of the official policy of the Arab country in whose territory they had found themselves. For years they had been demanding arms and the establishment of a militia. The Egyptians had done no more than make encouraging noises. The Gaza raid changed all that. For three days the Palestinians vented their indignation in riots and demonstrations which threatened the stability of a still young and none-too-secure régime. As the sun rose over the battered town of Gaza, two hundred youths stormed Egyptian and UN installations, smashing windows, burning vehicles and trampling on flags. The next day mob violence spread to Khan Yunis and Rafah, where refugees burned down the warehouse for the UN rations off which they lived. They greeted truckloads of Egyptian soldiers with stones and shouted abuse. 'Arms,' was the universal cry, 'give us arms, we shall defend ourselves.'[64]

The other decision which Nasser took in the wake of the Gaza raid was to turn the hitherto discouraged, freelance 'infiltration' into an instrument of Egyptian policy. It was in August 1955 that the world first heard of the world *fedayeen*—'those who sacrifice themselves'—applied to Palestinians sent on raids into Israel. On their first raid—which began on the same day that Nasser finally committed himself to the purchase of Soviet arms—they penetrated as far as twenty-seven miles inside enemy territory on a week-long spree of ambushes, mine-laying and assaults on persons, vehicles and buildings in which five soldiers and ten civilians died.[65] But even then, and subsequently, Nasser had only unleashed the *fedayeen* under pressure from his own public opinion in the wake of further provocations from Israel—provocations which he had at first met with conciliatory gestures such as the pull-back of front-line soldiers.[66]

The raids, and Russian weapons for Egypt, were just what Bengurion needed. The 'hosts of Amalek' were re-arming in Egypt, he said;[67] the 'grave and dangerous' Czech arms deal which he had virtually forced on Nasser had been concluded for 'one reason and one reason only—to destroy the State of Israel and the people of Israel.'[68] The least sign of Egyptian activism, at a time when border skirmishing was costing five times as many Arab as Israelis lives,[69] was 'a vile and nefarious conspiracy . . . which would encounter a Jewish force capable of . . . striking any aggressor or enemy so that they shall not rise again, as in Operation Joab [against Egypt] in 1948 and the Gaza operation a month ago.'[70] In outright defiance of all the evidence he forecast that, if there were no peaceful settlement, Egypt would attack Israel within five or six months.[71]

The road from the 'hidden war' of border skirmishing to the 'open war' of Suez was, as the *Paratroopers' Book* later said, a short one.[72] In October 1955, Bengurion ordered his Chief of Staff, General Dayan, to prepare for the capture of the Straits of Tiran. Shortly afterwards, in the Knesset, he denounced Egypt's violations of the armistice agreements. He named three forms which these took; *fedayeen* marauding certainly was a violation, but there was nothing in the armistice which specifically forbade Egypt from blocking the Straits or closing the Suez Canal to Israeli shipping. 'This one-sided war will have to stop', he declared, 'for it cannot remain one-sided for ever.'[73] According to the faithful Dayan, this was an appeal for war within a short time; he himself urged action within a month. 'It may be, of course, that one of these days a situation will be created which makes military action possible. But this will be the fruit of chance and not the planned result of postponing it to a specific "time" and "place".'[74] Nevertheless, Bengurion had still not overcome the resistance of the 'doves' within the government who, apprised of the war plans, decided that 'the moment was not propitious'.[75]

In June 1956, after a long and bitter dispute, Foreign Minister Moshe Sharett, the leading 'dove', was driven from office. He was replaced by Golda Meir and, in the words of the *Paratroopers' Book*, 'Israeli foreign policy was adjusted to the hard and energetic line of the Minister of Defence.'[76] A month later came the final, fortuitous bonus, the event which persuaded two Western powers, Britain and France, to throw in their lot with the Israelis. 'On July 27', recorded the *Paratroopers' Book*, 'Nasser announced the nationalization of the Suez Canal before an enthusiastic crowd in Alexandria. Without knowing it, he thereby kicked off the Suez campaign.'[77] On 29 October, with the secret backing of Anglo-French accomplices, the Israeli army invaded Sinai and captured the whole of it, including the island of Tiran in the Gulf of Aqaba, in four days. The British and French governments issued a hypocritical ultimatum to both sides, calling on them to withdraw from the banks of the Canal, and then sent in their own forces, ostensibly to occupy and secure the waterway for international shipping, but really in the hope of overthrowing the man who had nationalized it. If, in laying the diplomatic groundwork for his all-out assault on Egypt, Bengurion had implicitly confined his aims to the ending of Egypt's armistice 'violations' and the achievement of peace, Menachim Begin and his rightwing *Herut* (ex-*Irgun*) opposition, a hotbed of extremist pressures, had no such inhibitions. More than a year before Begin had urged on parliament a 'preventive war against the Arab states without further hesitation. By doing so we will achieve two targets: firstly the annihilation of Arab power and secondly the expansion of our territory.'[78] After such an overwhelming victory, however, Bengurion and his ruling Labour party lost no time, characteristically, in 'catching up' with the extremists, whose leader now said that he supported the government 'with all my heart and soul'.[79] Even the most 'dovish' parties, such as the left-wing *Mapam*, were not far behind either. All, in greater or lesser degree, developed expansionist appetites. And when the United States called on Israel to withdraw, Bengurion was outraged. 'Up to the middle of the sixth century

Jewish independence was maintained on the island of Yotvan [as the victors promptly renamed Tiran] south of the Gulf of Eilat, which was liberated yesterday by the Israeli army. . . . Israel terms Gaza an integral part of the nation. No force, whatever it is called, was going to make Israel evacuate Sinai. And the words of Isaiah the Prophet were fulfilled.'[80]

Unfortunately for Bengurion, the pretext he had so carefully manufactured was simply not good enough for the Americans. President Eisenhower quickly secured the withdrawal of the chastened British and French by withholding oil supplies from them, but it took six months to prise Israel out of all Egyptian territory. It was only by raising the threat of economic sanctions, to be applied by all members of the UN, that he managed it. 'Should a nation', he asked in a special television broadcast, 'which attacks and occupies foreign territory in the face of UN disapproval be allowed to impose conditions on its own withdrawal? If we agree that armed attack can properly achieve the purpose of the assailant, then I fear we will have turned back the clock of international order. . . .'

One condition, of sorts, Israel did get away with, the lifting of the Egyptian blockade on Israeli shipping in the Straits of Tiran, and this was to furnish the Arab-fighters with the pretext for the next 'big war'.

Notes

1. Avneri, *Israel Without Zionists: A Plea for Peace in the Middle East*, *op. cit.*, p. 134.
2. See pp. 104–5.
3. Bengurion, *Rebirth and Destiny*, *op. cit.*, pp. 276–7.
4. Lilienthal, Alfred, *What Price Israel*, *op. cit.*, pp. 210–11.
5. *Ibid.*, p. 210.
6. Gabbay, Rony, *A Political History of the Arab-Jewish Conflict, The Arab Refugee Problem*, Droz, Geneva, 1959, p. 109.
7. Israeli Foreign Minister Moshe Sharett to the UN.
8. See Bar-Zohar, Michael, *The Armed Prophet*, Prentice-Hall, London, 1967, p. 157.
9. See Weinstock, *Le Zionisme contre Israel*, *op. cit.*, p. 411.
10. Gabbay, *op. cit.*, p. 109.
11. Hutchison, E. H., *Violent Truce*, Devin-Adair, New York, 1956, pp. 120–1.

12. Glubb, Sir John Bagot, *A Soldier with the Arabs*, Hodder and Stoughton, London, 1957, p. 245.
13. *Ibid.*, p. 304.
14. *Haaretz*, 22 September 1968; see Ben-Yosa, Amitay, *Arab American University Graduate Bulletin* No. 2, reproduced in The Arab Women's Information Committee, Beirut, Supplement, June 1971.
15. *The Paratroopers' Book* (Hebrew), Tel Aviv, 1969, p. 60; cited in *The Other Israel*, Doubleday, ed. Bober, Arie, New York, 1972, p. 68.
16. *Jerusalem Post*, 31 October 1965.
17. See *The Other Israel*, *op. cit.*, p. 77.
18. Hutchison, *op. cit.*, pp. 152–8.
19. Love, *Suez: The Twice-Fought War*, *op. cit.*, p. 54.
20. In an article in *Harper's* magazine entitled 'Israel's policy of Reprisals' by Moshe Brilliant, an American resident of Israel and a correspondent of both the *New York Times* and the *Jerusalem Post*, the English-language mouthpiece of Bengurion's ruling Labour party. The article which amounted to an official and public apologia for reprisals had been cleared by the military censor.
21. See *The Other Israel*, *op. cit.*, p. 72.
22. Sharon, Ariel, 'Introduction' to Meir Har-Zion, *Chapters from a Diary*, Tel Aviv, 1969, p. 16, cited in *The Other Israel*, *op. cit.*, p. 68.
23. Elon, *The Israelis, Founders and Sons*, *op. cit.*, p. 241.
24. Diary of Moshe Sharett, *Maariv*, 28 June 1974; see Shahak, Israel, *Middle East International*, January 1975.
25. *Haaretz*, 9 November 1965; see Shahak, Israel, and Davis, Uri, *Journal of Palestine Studies*, Vol. IV, No. 2, 1975, p. 155.
26. Elon, *op. cit.*, p. 242.
27. *The Other Israel*, *op. cit.*, p. 72.
28. Ben-Yosa, Amitay, *op. cit.*, p. 2.
29. Jiryis Sabri, *The Arabs in Israel*, Institute for Palestine Studies, Beirut, 1968, p. 4.
30. Judgements of the District Court attached to the Israeli Defence Army Military Court; see Jiryis, *op. cit.*, p. 98.
31. *Ibid.*, p. 102.
32. *Ibid.*
33. 11 April 1957.
34. *Jewish Newsletter*, 8 July 1957.
35. Jiryis, *op. cit.*, p. 111.
36. *Ha'olam Hazeh*, 11 February 1970.
37. Jiryis, *op. cit.*, p. 81.
38. Cattan, Henry, *Palestine, the Arabs and Israel*, Longmans, Green and Co., London, 1969, p. 85; see *Le Monde*, 3 March 1976.
39. Ben-Yosa, Amitay, *op. cit.*, p. 3.
40. *Ibid.*, p. 1.
41. Jiryis, *op. cit.*, p. 61.

42. Ben-Yosa, Amitay, *op. cit.*, p. 2.
43. Jiryis, *op. cit.*, p. 72.
44. *Ibid.*, p. 67.
45. *Ibid.*, p. 70.
46. Jiryis, Sabri, 'Recent Knesset Legislation and the Arabs in Israel', *Journal of Palestine Studies*, Beirut, Vol. I, No. 1, 1971.
47. *Haaretz*, 14 January 1966.
48. Bengurion, *op. cit.*, p. 466.
49. *New York Times*, 9 March 1964.
50. Bengurion, *op. cit.*, p. 419.
51. Alsop, Joseph, *San Jose Mercury*, 16 June 1956.
52. Love, *op. cit.*, p. 52.
53. *Ner*, January 1956, cited in Ibrahim al-Abid, *Violence et Paix*, Palestine Research Centre, Beirut, 1970, p. 34.
54. Horn, General Karl von, *Soldiering for Peace*, Cassell, London, 1966, pp. 282–3.
55. See *The Other Israel*, *op. cit.*, p. 70.
56. Dayan, Moshe, *Diary of the Sinai Campaign*, Weidenfeld and Nicolson, London, 1966, p. 37.
57. *Harper's* magazine, March 1955, see pp. 180–2.
58. *The New Statesman and Nation*, London, 22 January 1955.
59. Burns, General E. L. N., *Between Arab and Israeli*, Harrap, London, 1962, p. 18.
60. Love, *op. cit.*, p. 20.
61. *Ibid.*, p. 88.
62. *Ibid.*, p. 100.
63. *Ibid.*, p. 61.
64. *Ibid.*, p. 83.
65. *Ibid.*, p. 95.
66. *Ibid.*, pp. 99, 107.
67. *Ibid.*, p. 121.
68. *Ibid.*, p. 102.
69. *Ibid.*, p. 68.
70. *Ibid.*, p. 89.
71. *Ibid.*, p. 115.
72. See *The Other Israel*, *op. cit.*, p. 71.
73. Love, *op. cit.*, p. 106.
74. Dayan, *op. cit.*, p. 14.
75. Love, *op. cit.*, p. 106.
76. See *The Other Israel*, *op. cit.*, p. 71.
77. *Ibid.*, p. 71.
78. 12 October 1955.
79. Menuhin, *The Decadence of Judaism in Our Time*, *op. cit.*, p. 181.
80. *Ibid.*, p. 180.

7 · GREATER ISRAEL

The Six-Day War, 1967

The 'Arab-fighters' were bound to try again. According to Kennett Love, the former *New York Times* correspondent who has written the definitive history of the Suez War,

> . . . from the moment Israel realized that she would have to withdraw, Sinai was recognized as a campaign that would sooner or later be refought. Plans for the new war were drawn up immediately after the old . . . the 1956 war served as a rehearsal for 1967. The plans for the earlier war were only a year old when they were tested in action. Long before 1967 they had matured to near perfection, and, as in 1956, required only favourable circumstances and a political decision to be put into action.[1]

In early 1967 Israel's congenital militancy was pushing it towards such a decision. In a sense it needed the war. It was suffering the severest economic crisis of its existence; unemployment stood at 10 per cent; the growth rate had plummeted; subventions from the Diaspora were drying up; worst of all, emigration was beginning to exceed immigration—a yardstick which of course indicated, more than any other, that the economic crisis was a crisis of Zionism itself. What this portended General Burns, a soldier whose shrewd judgements ranged far beyond the arts of war, forecast in 1962. 'Israel's leaders have the habit of putting down her economic difficulties to the boycott of all trade and economic relations maintained by the Arab states, and the pressure they exercise on other countries to limit trade with Israel. In such circumstances there seems to me to be a great temptation to find some excuse to go to war and thus to break out of the blockade and boycott—to force peace on Israel's terms.'[2] He believed that if Israel should ever feel a need to expand beyond its present borders, 'the Israeli armed forces, supremely confident of their ability to defeat any and all of the Arab countries surrounding Israel with ease and speed, would take on such a task with alacrity'.[3]

As the *Paratroopers' Book* explained, the Israeli fighting man had matured:

> The reprisal actions of 1965–66 differed from those which preceded the Sinai campaign. . . . The operations were no longer acts of vengeance, savage and nervous, of a small state fighting for its independence. Rather they were blows struck by a state strong and sure of itself, and which did not fear the army it confronted.[4]

The ideal held up to the youth was not hatred of the enemy, but contempt. The flyer, particularly the bombardier, took the place of the paratrooper or the infantryman. It was typical that the bedside reading of Israeli officers in the 1950s included books like Alexander Beck's *The Men of Panfilov*, a Soviet work of World War II, which recounts the training of an assault unit, while in the 1960s their reading turned to the exploits of bombardiers 'for whom war became a hobby, something secondary that one calmly accepted'.[5]

All that was needed for the unleashing of the Israeli war machine was the 'favourable circumstances', and on 23 May they presented themselves. It was at four o'clock in the morning of that day that the Israeli Chief of Staff, General Yitzhak Rabin, woke up Prime Minister Levi Eshkol to tell him that President Nasser had decided to reimpose the Aqaba blockade. A few hours later the cabinet went into emergency session. In Israeli eyes Nasser had in effect declared war.

The challenge was indeed an intolerable one. This was not because Israel faced economic strangulation. Economically, the closure of the Straits of Tiran to all Israeli ships, and ships of other nations bound for Eilat with strategic materials, would have had little immediate impact. Only 5 per cent of Israel's foreign trade went through Eilat; oil from Iran was the main strategic material, but Israel could easily get that through Haifa. What damage the closure might have done would have been offset by President Johnson's reported offer—designed to stay Israel's hand—to maintain its economic viability. The long-term implications were certainly serious, for it was through Eilat that Israel intended to take advantage of new or expanding markets in Africa and Asia. But the really intolerable thing lay elsewhere. For the first time the Arabs were turning the tables on Israel. For the first time it was they who were administering the *fait accompli*. (Although the precise scope and strictness of the blockade are a matter of controversy. What the Egyptian leaders were saying in public was very different from what they were doing in private. Field Marshal Abdul Hakim Amer apparently instructed his troops not to interfere with any Israeli ships, or any naval vessels or ships escorted by naval vessels.[6]) If they could get away with one they could get away with another, and the Jewish State, that accumulation of a thousand such accomplished facts, would begin to wither away. It would be the beginning of Zionism in reverse. The Israelis did not need Nasser to tell them that. But he did so all the same. It was no more a question of the Gulf of Aqaba or the Straits of Tiran; it was a 'question of the Arabs having been driven from Palestine and robbed of their rights and their possessions . . . of the neglect of all UN resolutions in favour of the people of Palestine'. The whole Palestine cause had been resurrected, the confidence of every Arab revived; and 'just as we have been able to restore the pre-1956 situation, we shall certainly, with God's help, be able to restore the pre-1948 situation'.[7]

The re-imposition of the blockade was at the same time, however, the perfect opportunity. The Egyptian *fait accompli*, though arbitrary, was not illegal. After 1956, the Egyptians had continued to insist that the Straits fell in Egyptian territorial waters. The Israelis' claim to right of passage through those territorial waters was indeed an exceedingly dubious one; it was based on possession of a thin sliver of coastline, and this itself had been secured, on the Israelis' own admission, by 'one of those calculated violations [of the ceasefire] which we had to carefully weigh against the political risks'.[8] That was in 1949, during the final stages of the 'War of Independence', when, in defiance of a UN-sponsored ceasefire, an Israeli patrol thrust southward to the Arab hamlet and police post of Um Rashrash, expelling its inhabitants and founding the port of Eilat in its place.

The trouble was, however, that, while asserting a legal right, the Egyptians had acquiesced in Israel's political *fait accompli*; Israeli ships were allowed through under the symbolic protection of a handful of UN forces which had replaced the Egyptians at the garrison of Sharm al-Shaikh. True, the Americans had insisted that the Israeli withdrawal should be an unconditional one, but the Israelis had put up such a fierce resistance that Washington was obliged to affirm its belief that, once this ostensibly unconditional withdrawal was complete, Israeli ships would enjoy 'free and innocent passage' through straits which, in its view, 'comprehend international waters'.[9] This was less than a cast-iron guarantee that America would keep the Straits open. But it turned out, in the changed international circumstances of a decade later, to be quite enough to ensure that next time the Egyptians closed them the Americans would not object if Israel went to war to reopen them. Under President Johnson, who, as a Senator, had led Democratic congressional opposition to Eisenhower's threat of sanctions, the pro-Israeli bias of American policy was flagrant; dislike of President Nasser, and other Soviet-oriented 'revolutionary' régimes in the Arab world, was scarcely less so.

David versus Goliath

Western public opinion was no less partisan, particularly when, in the wake of Nasser's *fait accompli*, Arab armies began, or so it appeared, to converge on Israel from all sides amid a terrible clamour of boastful rhetoric. Genocide, Munich, the Arab Nazis, Nasser-the-new-Hitler—these, the most emotive and virulent slogans in Western political vocabulary, rang round Europe and America in late May and early June of 1967. Never in history had the passions of so many people been engaged by a conflict in which they had no part—and engaged with such unanimity on behalf of one of the combatants. The war in Vietnam, then becoming one of the great moral issues of the sixties, was drowned in the tidal wave of emotion which swept the Western world on Israel's behalf. Vietnam divided, the Middle East united. It was the Arab threat to annihilate their enemy, or what seemed to be their threat to do so, which really turned the world against them. Nor was their enemy just a people like any other. They were Jews. What the Arabs were setting out to do was all the more 'wicked, mad and insupportable'—as one British intellectual described it—in that their intended victims belonged to the same people who, a generation earlier, had lost six million in the Nazi Holocaust.[10] A crime against the Jews was worse than a crime against anyone else. Hitler's gas chambers still haunted the conscience of the West.

Great, then, were the fears of the outside world for little Israel on the eve of war. So they were, too, among the general public in Israel itself. It was only to be expected that the Israeli government, Zionists and sympathizers everywhere, should foster the world's alarm. None of them, at the time, would have challenged the Israeli Premier when he told the Knesset just after the war that 'the existence of the Israeli state hung on a thread, but the hopes of the Arab leaders to exterminate Israel were brought to nought'.[11] But there were those, the generals, who knew that the real situation was the exact reverse of the apparent one, that David was not merely a match for Goliath, but hopelessly outclassed him. They knew that, whatever the politicians might say and the people believe, Israel's survival was never at stake, that even if Nasser actually intended to go to war he had no chance of winning it. General Mordecai Hod had a profound confidence in the air force which he commanded. He and its real architect, General Ezer Weizmann, unruly nephew of Chaim Weizmann, had for a decade or more been perfecting their master-plan for the destruction of Arab air power. Their men were trained for every eventuality. They had pored over scale models of every possible target; it was with astonishing precision that in the first few hours of the 1967 War the pilot of a Mirage fighter machine-gunned, at close range, what he knew to be King Hussein's study at the Basman Palace in Amman. . . .[12] It was not until five years had passed, when the Israelis were basking in an unprecedented sense of their own strength, security and achievement, that General Matitiahu Peled, one of the architects of the Israeli victory, committed what, to an outraged public, seemed nothing less than blasphemy. But in the so-called 'annihilation controversy' which followed, and in spite of pleas to keep silent for the sake of Israel's reputation in the world, none of his military colleagues seriously contested his central thesis. 'There is no reason', he said, 'to hide the fact that since 1949 no one dared, or more precisely, no one was able, to threaten the very existence of Israel. In spite of that, we have continued to foster a sense of our own inferiority, as if we were a weak and insignificant people, which, in the midst of an anguished struggle for its existence, could be exterminated at any moment.' 'True,' General Peled went on, Arab leaders may have sounded menacing, 'but it is notorious that the Arab leaders themselves, thoroughly aware of their own impotence, did not believe in their own threats. . . . I am sure that our General Staff never told the government that the Egyptian military threat represented any danger to Israel or that we were unable to crush Nasser's army, which, with unheard-of foolishness, had exposed itself to the devastating might of our army. . . . To claim that the Egyptian forces concentrated on our borders were capable of threatening Israel's existence not only insults the intelligence of anyone capable of analysing this kind of situation, but is an insult to *Tsahal* [the Israeli army].'[13] Not only did Nasser lack the means to take on Israel, he did not have the intention either. The generals were well aware of that too. Yitzhak Rabin, the Chief of Staff, was frank about it: 'I do not believe that Nasser wanted war. The two divisions he sent into Sinai on May 14 would not have been enough to unleash an offensive against Israel. He knew it and we knew it.'[14]

The Myth of the Golan Heights

The seeds of the Six-Day War were sown on the Syrian front. This is universally accepted. It is also more or less taken for granted that the Syrians sowed those seeds. The Golan Heights appear to sum up, in a peculiarly stark and affecting way, the image of David versus Goliath. But it would be nearer the truth to say that the Golan Heights represent one of the most successful of Zionist myths. A post-war visit to the windswept, battle-scarred plateau was a moving experience—at least it was for those of this writer's fellow-tourists, probably all of them, who accepted what our guide told us. He told us, of course, about the Syrian guns which used to rain destruction on the farmers peacefully tilling their fields in the valley below and how finally, on the last day of the war, some of Israel's finest troops had given their lives scaling those mine-infested heights to silence the guns for ever. It was a partisan account. That was to be expected. It also included one or two untruths, not unexpected either, like the allegation that the Arabs, in trying to divert the headwaters of the Jordan, intended to send them to waste in the Mediterranean. However, the guide did, with an air of complicity, tell one unexpected truth. 'We are now entering what used to be the demilitarized zone,' he said, 'regular soldiers were forbidden to enter it. Of course, we got round that by sending them in disguised as police. But that's another story.' It *is* another story, a long one, and naturally he did not tell it.

Among the many complications of the 1949 armistice agreements were the demilitarized zones. They were sources of conflict everywhere, but particularly on the Syrian frontier, where, strips of fertile soil ranging from a few hundred metres to a few kilometres wide, they ran nearly half its length. They represented bits of Palestinian territory which the Syrian army managed to hold during the fighting of 1948 and from which it only agreed to withdraw, behind the old frontier, under the provisions of the armistice agreements. These laid down that neither side should send military forces into any part of them; Arab and Israeli villages and settlements in the zones should each recruit their own police forces on a local basis. Neither side showed a scrupulous regard for these provisions, but it was the Israelis who, from the outset, showed less. They began by staking an illegal claim to sovereignty over the zone and then proceeded, as opportunity offered, to encroach on all the specific provisions against introducing armed forces and fortifications. They repeatedly obstructed the operations of the UN observers, on one occasion even threatening to kill them.[15] They refused to cooperate with the Mixed Armistice Commission, and when it suited them they simply rejected the rulings and requests of the observers.[16] They expelled, or otherwise forced out, Arab inhabitants, and razed their villages to the ground.[17] They transplanted trees as a strategem to advance the frontier to their own advantage.[18] They built roads against the advice of the UN.[19] They carried out excavations on Arab land for their own drainage schemes.[20] But most serious of all was what General von

Horn described as 'part of a premeditated Israeli policy to edge east through the Demilitarized Zone towards the old Palestine border (as shown on their maps) and to get all the Arabs out of the way by fair means or foul.' 'The Jews', he explained, 'developed a habit of irrigating and ploughing in stretches of Arab-owned land nearby, for the ground was so fertile that every square foot was a gold mine in grain. Gradually, beneath the glowering eyes of the Syrians, who held the high ground overlooking the Zone, the area had become a network of Israeli canals and irrigation channels edging up against and always encroaching on Arab-owned property.'[21] It is unlikely, in his opinion, that those Syrian guns on the Golan Heights would ever have gone into action but for Israeli provocations.[22]

There was always tension on the frontier, and incidents without number, but it flared into the dimensions of a 'little war' only when the Israelis, apparently for reasons of higher strategy, decided to visit upon the Syrians their familiar technique of massive punishment to fit a menial crime. They did that in the build-up to the Suez War. In December 1955, as part of the aggressive strategy which had begun with the Gaza raid ten months before, they attacked positions on the north-eastern shore of Lake Tiberias, killing more than fifty soldiers and civilians. The alleged pretext—that the Syrians had opened fire on fishing and police boats—was a singularly inadequate one, even if it had been an authentic one. But in the opinion of two UN observers who subsequently recorded their experience it was not even that. The most charitable interpretation was that, although the Syrians may have opened fire, the Israelis had done their best to provoke them into doing so. 'It was', said one of them, 'a premeditated raid of intimidation motivated by Israel's desire . . . to bait the Arab states into some overt act of aggression that would offer them the opportunity to overrun additional territory without censor. . . .'[23] Eleven months later Israel did overrun the whole of Sinai, but not, as we have seen, without censure. They were to be more successful next time.

Every year brought its shooting season; naturally enough, it began, in a fertile valley like this, with the ploughing, and went on through the sowing and harvesting.[24] It was then that the Israeli farmers ventured forth with their armour-plated tractors to plough a few more furrows of Arab-owned land. On 3 April 1967 it was reported in the Israeli press that the government had decided to cultivate all areas of the demilitarized zone, specifically lots 51 and 52, which, the Syrians insisted, belonged to Arab farmers.[25] At eight o'clock on the morning of 7 April a tractor began work on a little strip of Arab land south of Tiberias. The Israelis waited for the Syrians to open up with mortars as they knew they would—and then struck back with artillery, tanks and aircraft. Seventy jet fighters pounded the enemy with napalm and high explosives. The Syrians took a bloody nose: six planes shot down, one over Damascus, some thirty fortified positions hit and perhaps a hundred people killed. The Israelis, for their part, lost one tank commander; he had got down to observe the results of his shooting. Chief of Staff Rabin expressed the hope that the Syrians had learned their lesson.

In reality, the 'lesson' was the curtain-raiser to the June War. Nasser could not afford to stand idly by again. Syria, he could see, was now the target of the kind of military activism to which Egypt had been exposed before Suez. For the 'Arab-fighters' it represented just the kind of plausible external peril they needed. After all, Syria *did* bombard settlements from the Golan Heights. It *was* apparently going ahead with its part of a scheme to divert the headwaters of the river Jordan and thereby sabotage Israel's own scheme, unilaterally undertaken, to channel water south to the Negev desert. It *was* giving aid and comfort to *Fatah*, the Palestinian guerilla organization which, since January 1965, had been sending its men into enemy territory to lay mines and blow up installations. And since February 1966, when an extreme faction of the ruling Baath party seized power, Syria had officially adopted, with bellicose rhetoric to match, the *Fatah* doctrine of a 'popular liberation war'. Obviously, the Arab-fighters did not shout their intentions from the roof-tops, but it was none the less apparent, from the indiscretions which did escape them, that what Dayan and his men had in mind was to engineer a general preventive war—to deliver a crippling blow at the Arabs' growing military strength, to do as soon as possible, at lesser cost, what they would be forced to do, probably at much greater cost, some time in the future. It was this search for a pretext which the Chief of Staff was getting at, in a duly circumspect way, when he told the army magazine *Bamahane* in May 1965 that the Israelis could upset any Arab military timetable at a moment's notice if they knew 'how to exploit the moment when the Arabs are preparing to reach a certain level of military strength'.[26]

For anyone who cared to look closely the external peril was plausible in the extreme. Of course it must have been uncomfortable and sometimes dangerous living in a frontier *kibbutz* under the shadow of Syrian guns, but how many people actually got killed? Between January and June 1967, apparently not one. In the same period, how many Israelis died at the hands of the *Fatah* guerrillas? One. As for the Jordan diversion scheme, this was a vain enterprise, whatever Arab propaganda might proclaim, and the Israelis knew it. Even if the Arabs had the means and the will to carry out their plans to the full—and this was doubted in official Israeli quarters—they would have deprived the Israelis of a mere 5 or 6 per cent of the share which they were taking for themselves.[27] As for the 'popular liberation war', the Israelis knew more than anyone else about the gulf between the Baathist words and Baathist deeds.

Unfortunately not many people did look very closely, and President Nasser was very afraid that, Syrian verbal excesses and irresponsible brinkmanship aiding, the Arab-fighters would lead him into a trap. Replying to the taunts of his Arab opponents, he told a Palestinian audience as early as 1965: 'They say "drive out UNEF". Suppose that we do. Is it not essential to have a plan? If Israeli aggression takes place against Syria, do I attack Israel? That would mean that Israel is the one to determine the battle for me. It hits a tractor or two to force me to move, is this a wise way? It is we who must determine the battle.'[28]

Nasser Falls into the Trap

But withdraw UNEF he eventually did. When, on 8 May 1967, two highly agitated Syrian emissaries arrived secretly in Cairo to announce that Israel was about to attack their country, Nasser could look back on at least two years of growing Israeli pugnacity, and what he felt to be American connivance with it, as good reason for taking the news very seriously indeed. He sought confirmation from other sources, including the Russians, and they provided it. Forces had indeed been concentrating on the front. The Israelis hotly denied it at the time, and unchallenged by any impartial arbiter such as the UN observers, their denial was convincing enough; it has served since as vital evidence for their contention that, in the build-up to the June War, the real provocations came from the Arabs, not from them. But five years later, during the 'annihilation controversy', General Ezer Weizmann, one of Israel's bluntest soldiers, conceded: 'Don't forget that we did move tanks to the north after the downing of the aircraft.'[29] UN observers also saw them, but for various reasons their observations were—and remain to this day—a closely guarded secret. (This is one of the conclusions of what is probably the most accurate account of the origins of the June War. By Godfrey Jansen, an Indian journalist, it argues that from early in 1967 the small inner group of politicians and generals who are the real rulers of Israel felt the need for another attack on the Arabs.[30]) The tank concentrations were followed by a verbal threat and a taunt which were almost guaranteed to make Nasser react the way he did. The threat, an officially enunciated one, portended a full-scale invasion of Syria and the overthrow of the regime. The taunt was a prediction that, when that happened, Nasser would not go to Syria's aid. Both were made in such a way as to reach their target, but without being officially recorded so that Israel could not be called to account later. And just as all the pro-Israeli, and indeed the relatively impartial, accounts of the June War dismiss the allegation of Israeli tank concentrations, so they make out that there was no real threat either. Thus in his widely read book *The Road to War* Walter Laqueur says: 'There had been, to repeat again, no Israeli threat to overthrow the Damascus government.'[31] But there had been. On 11 May, General Yitzhak Rabin said on Israel Radio: 'The moment is coming when we will march on Damascus to overthrow the Syrian Government, because it seems that only military operations can discourage the plans for a people's war with which they threaten us.'[32] This crude provocation was picked up by Arab listening posts but not one word of it was printed in the Israeli press. Somehow a monitoring report does not carry the same weight as a printed statement, and it can be that much more easily denied. The taunt came the very next day. General Aharon Yariv, Director of Military Intelligence, gave a background briefing for forty foreign correspondents in which, after repeating Rabin's threats against Syria, he harped on one insistent theme: Egypt was weak, and Nasser, 'the all-Arab leader', would not intervene. 'I would say that as long as there is not an Israeli invasion into Syria extended in area and time, I think the Egyptians will not come in seriously . . . they will do so only if there is no other alternative. And to my eyes no alternative means that we are creating such a situation that it is impossible for the Egyptians not to act because the strain on their prestige will be unbearable.'[33] By saying these words he deliberately put that very strain on the prestige of the 'all-Arab leader', who was already the butt of similarly exasperating jibes from his Arab adversaries.

Israel's 'impertinence', Nasser said later, was such that 'every Arab had to react'.[34] He sent his army into Sinai. At the same time he ordered the removal of UN forces. He had to do that to lend his move conviction. UNEF's role was a purely symbolic one. It was in Sinai strictly by Egypt's consent; Israel had steadfastly rejected any UN presence on its side of the frontier; what it symbolized was Nasser's self-imposed restraint. Its removal would therefore symbolize the end of that restraint. That was the last thing Nasser wanted; he therefore aimed at a partial withdrawal. The Egyptian Chief of Staff sent a cryptic message to the UNEF commander; he asked him to withdraw his men from the Israeli-Egyptian frontier to their bases in Gaza, but not from Sharm al-Shaikh, the lonely outpost at the mouth of the Gulf of Aqaba, which furnished symbolic protection for the passage of Israeli ships. The stratagem backfired. The UN Secretary General clumsily insisted that it had to be all or nothing. Nasser had no way out; he made it all. But of course that was not enough either. Logic—and the taunts of both Arab and Jew—required that he complete what he had begun. He imposed the blockade. He did not *really* impose it, as we have seen,[35] since he had no intention of fighting, but that did not deprive the Israelis of the ostensible *casus belli* they needed.

There would now be a war, which Israel felt certain of winning, against Egypt and Syria. Could the Israelis also exploit this unique opportunity to lay their hands on the rest of Palestine—East Jerusalem and the West Bank—which had eluded them in 1948? One wonders whether the open letter which the celebrated columnist, Ephraim Kishon, addressed to King Hussein is quite as ironic as it sounds:

> Frankly, you were not the only one to fall for our little trick. Veteran statesmen of world calibre stepped dazedly into the fiendish trap we prepared over the years in order to fool both our enemies and our friends. . . . Or did you imagine even for a second that all this was not planned? You silly man! Today it can be told, poor Hussi! Six or seven years ago we decided to take the Old City. But, we said to ourselves, we won't be able to pull it off unless the Arabs attack us first. Yes, but how could they be coaxed into doing that? As long as the Old Man [Bengurion] was at the helm, it was to be assumed that they would have cold feet. The Old Man therefore had to be removed. So we invented the Lavon Affair. We had a few spins on the Committee of Seven, published the brief of the Legal Adviser and played around with other odd-ball gimmicks. I hardly remember what, then we started building up Eshkol as a compromiser and waverer. It came off beautifully. He cooperated, so did Abba Eban. In short within a few years we succeeded in implanting in Gamal's mind that the time was ripe to attack us. The only thing that hampered our plans was the UN force in the Strip. How to get rid of it, how? In this matter we put our trust in U Thant and he did not let us down. Gamal innocently moved into Sinai and closed the Straits of Tiran. All this was exactly according to our plans. When would they at last conclude a pact, we asked ourselves anxiously, when? For long days we waited tensely—nothing, you wouldn't budge. We shamelessly tempted you, begged the naval powers to defend us, asked the Prime Minister to make a radio speech (a stammering performance which did anything but boost Israeli morale), pressed de Gaulle to drop us, what didn't we do to bring you nearer to Nasser? In the end our efforts were successful, you flew to Cairo and signed a mutual defence agreement. We sighed, relieved. Next day we brought in Dayan, and the rest is history. Sorry, Hussi, maybe they didn't teach you such tricks at Harrow but we had no choice, we wanted all of Jerusalem so badly.[36]

Israel Acquires an Empire

'The triumph of the civilized'—that was how one leading Western newspaper described the Israeli victory. It was indeed an extraordinary feat of arms. Israel had destroyed three Arab armies and acquired territory several times its own size in the space of six days. But history will perhaps record that greater than the military was the public relations triumph. Here was a people which had conquered another's land and expelled its inhabitants—here it was winning ecstatic international approval for yet more conquests and more expulsions. In 1917, Lord Balfour had proclaimed that nothing should be done to prejudice the civil and religious rights of the non-Jewish inhabitants of Palestine; if anyone had prophesied that exactly fifty years later the Arabs would attempt to restore by force merely a portion of those rights which had been taken away by force and then be universally condemned for doing so—such a prophet would surely have been dismissed as mad. Of course, not everyone went as far as the London *Daily Telegraph*, whose pro-Zionist enthusiasms were always extravagant, but very few questioned whether, in this case, might had indeed been right.[37] But the 'civilization' of which Israel is the foster-child had its reasons, not the least of which was eloquently summed up in the Paris newspaper *Le Monde*:

> In the past few days Europe has in a sense rid itself of the guilt it incurred in the drama of the Second World War and, before that, in the persecutions which, from the Russian pogroms to the Dreyfus Affair, accompanied the birth of Zionism. In the continent of Europe the Jews were at last avenged—but alas, on the backs of the Arabs—for the tragic and stupid accusation: 'they went like sheep to the slaughter.'[38]

It was immensely valuable, this international goodwill which Israel had accumulated—a rich fund of credit upon which it drew as it launched into the next stage of the great Zionist enterprise. For, historically speaking, this was a third great breakthrough. Like the Balfour Declaration and the 'War of Independence' it created a whole new empty 'framework' to be filled in. Zionism had been reborn; their pre-war depression behind them, the modern Israelis rediscovered overnight something of the zeal and vision which had moved the early pioneers. It all gushed forth, this Zionist renewal, in a torrent of biblico-strategic, clerico-military antics and imagery. It was atheists talking about the 'God of the armies'. It was paratroopers taking their oaths of allegiance, a Bible in one hand and a rifle in the other, at the Wailing Wall. It was a spate of biblical poems and hymns set to jazz on the weekly hit parade. It was the indefatigable parachuting warrior-priest, Rabbi Shlomo Goren, resplendent in all his military decorations, planting the Israeli flag on Mount Sinai. It was all, of course, at the expense of the Arabs.

The Zionists needed, as before, to hold the land they had acquired, to people and develop it, and to expel, or otherwise keep down, the Arabs who might oppose them. It was first a question of how much land should be held. There were those who, from the outset, insisted that Israel should annex all the occupied territory. Typically, the Rabbinate was to the forefront. According to the Chief Rabbi, the occupied territories belonged to Israel anyway. The land had been promised to the Jews by the Almighty and all the prophets foretold its return to them. Therefore, 'it is forbidden by the Torah for all Jews, including the Israeli government, to return even one inch of the territory of Eretz [Greater] Israel in our hands'.[39] Another member of the Supreme Rabbinical Council argued that, since Israel's conquest meant the liberation of the Holy Land from Satan's possession, any withdrawal would increase Satan's power.[40] Greater Israel movements proliferated. They cut across party lines. Enthusiastic meetings were held up and down the country. Generals and cabinet ministers addressed them. Menachim Begin's Revisionists—or the *Gahal* as the party was now known—furnished expansionism with its organized political backbone. *Gahal*'s basic position was 'no evacuation—even with peace'. The Israelis should settle the occupied territories, not just with colonies in uninhabited or rural areas but with 'suburbs' in all its towns—'Ramallah, Jenin, Nablus, Tulkaram, Qalqilia, Gaza, Rafah and elsewhere'.[41] It would not countenance the return of 'one inch of the Land of Israel to any foreign government', nor any official declaration, helpful to the peacemaking process, which suggested that Israel might make such territorial concessions.

General Dayan the Arab-fighter, appointed Defence Minister on the eve of the war, was the most famous and typical embodiment of Israel's post-1967 expansionism. In essence he shared the opinion of *Gahal*; he professed the same basic drive and vision. But he was more subtle, more politic than they. For him, the June War was not just another victory against the enemy. It woke in him new and unexpected feelings:

> For twenty years, from the War of Liberation to the Six-Day War we had the feeling we were living at the summit, breathing pure air. We had fought to reach the summit; we were content with what we had achieved . . . but in our heart of hearts, deep down, we were not really happy and content. We made ourselves accept Eilat as our southern frontier, a State of Israel which from Qalqilia to the sea was less than fifteen kilometres broad. Old Jerusalem stood outside its frontiers—this was Israel. In our daily life we made our own private peace with all this. The source of the great disturbance we feel today lies in our understanding of the fact that we were wrong. We have to acknowledge this. We thought we had reached the summit, but it became clear to us that we were still on the way up the mountain. The summit is higher up.[42]

What, in practice, would Zionist self-renewal mean? Dayan felt it necessary to remind his compatriots of what they perhaps forgot—or what some of them, the younger generation, never really knew:

> Jewish villages were built in the place of Arab villages. You don't even know the names of these Arab villages, and I don't blame you, because these geography books no longer exist. Not only do the books not exist, the Arab villages are not there either. Nahalal [Dayan's own village] arose in the place of Mahlul, Gvat [a *kibbutz*] in the place of Jibta, Sarid [another *kibbutz*] in the place of Haneifa, and Kfar-Yehoshua in the place of Tel-Shaman. There is not one single place built in this country that did not have a former Arab population.[43]

Given this unflinching perception of the past, Dayan paints this grim picture of the future:

> We are doomed to live in a constant state of war with the Arabs and there is no escape from sacrifice and bloodshed. This is perhaps an undesirable situation, but it is a fact. If we are to proceed with our work against the wishes of the Arabs we shall have to expect such sacrifices.

And in Dayan's view, they must continue their work:

> This is what used to be called 'Jew after Jew', *Aliyah* (wave of immigration) after *Aliyah*, or 'acre by acre', 'goat by goat'. It meant expansion, more Jews, more villages, more settlement. Twenty years ago we were 600,000; today we are near three million. There should be no Jew who says 'that's enough', no-one who says 'we are nearing the end of the road.' . . . It is the same with the land. There are no complaints against my generation that we did not begin the process . . . but there will be complaints against you [Dayan is addressing the Kibbutz Youth Federation on the Golan Heights] if you come and say: 'up to here.' Your duty is not to stop; it is to keep your sword unsheathed, to have faith, to keep the flag flying. You must not call a halt—heaven forbid—and say 'that's all; up to here, up to Degania, to Mufallasim, to Nahal Oz!' For that is not all.[44]

It was therefore not only as a devout Zionist, but as a hard-headed strategist, that Dayan believed in expansionism. In Dayan the strategist there was a heavy streak of fatalism. Israel was 'doomed' by its own past to perpetual conflict with the Arabs—doomed, therefore, to expand the better to prosecute the conflict. But Dayan was also, some of the time at least, a politician. As a politician he sometimes assumed the plumage of a dove. He did not resign from the government, like *Gahal*, over Israel's acceptance of the 1970 peace proposals of US Secretary of State William Rogers. Yet in his true, his hawk's plumage, he had previously insisted, like *Gahal*, that he 'strongly opposed' the Security Council resolution 242 on which the Rogers proposals were based.[45] He was only waiting for a telephone call from King Hussein to begin negotiations. Yet, in his real self, he did not want them. 'It is perhaps possible to conclude peace treaties between ourselves and our Arab neighbours, but the Arabs are asking too high a price and I pray heaven that the day never comes.'[46] And in fact, he could be very confident that it never would. As a politician, and a clever one, he knew that he could rely on the mechanisms of the conflict to ensure that, in practice, the Israelis would never be called upon to make the territorial concessions which the *Gahal* super-hawks found it necessary to reject in advance. He was waiting for his telephone call from Hussein—but it would be 'the surprise of [his] life' if the King were to accept the kind of terms he would be offered.[47] Why therefore, like *Gahal*, flaunt an insatiable expansionism before a potentially disapproving world? He knew that the Arabs were bound to reject such terms as even the Israeli doves proposed, and he knew that, spurned, the doves would join the hawks in insisting that, until the final peace settlement, the Israelis should hold what they had.

It was the apogee of the ideology of force. In earlier, weaker days, the Zionists, while never losing sight of their long-term goal, had tempered force with a certain political realism, a readiness for tactical compromise. But now the conviction took root that the existence and defence of Israel depended exclusively on its own strong right arm, that Israel was master not merely of its own destiny but of that of the entire Middle East. The ideology of force broke down into a number of axioms which, by dint of almost unchallenged repetition, acquired a sacrosanct character. Amon Kapeliouk, a brilliant critic of Zionist orthodoxy, has listed them: 'We shall maintain the status quo in the region for as long as we like; security frontiers deter the Arabs from attacking; the Bar Lev Line (along the east bank of the Suez Canal) is impregnable; our intelligence services are infallible; the Arabs only understand the language of force; war is not for the Arabs; the Arab world is divided and without military options; the oil weapon is a mere propaganda tool; the Palestinians of the occupied territories will resign themselves to their fate; time is on our side; it does not matter what the Gentiles say, but what the Jews do.'[48] The vast majority of Israelis saw in this, and its principal exponent, the incarnation of political wisdom. From there to the massive settlement of Greater Israel was only a short step. It was quickly taken, and Dayan the 'Arab-fighter' acquired a new title, 'emperor of the occupied territories'.

'Come and build Jerusalem.' 'Send your son to Jerusalem.' 'Have a second home and a first child in Jerusalem.' The slogans were addressed not to the Arabs who might once have lived there, and would like to return, not to the Israelis who had already been 'ingathered', but to the five-sixths of the world's Jews who lived outside the frontiers of Israel, above all to the prosperous Jews of the West who, bringing with them money and skills, would make desirable inhabitants of the Holy City. Immigration, a fresh wave of *Aliyah*, was one of the first things the Israelis thought of in the wake of their victory. There had to be a reversal of the disastrous pre-war situation when more people were 'going down' than 'coming up'. Not surprisingly, the Israelis exploited their possession of Jerusalem, unified and whole, to revive it—Jerusalem, the symbolic prize and strategic fulcrum of an implacable conflict. But not only Jerusalem, for the rest of occupied territories were also part of the Jewish heritage. Israel did not formally annex them, in defiance of world opinion, as it did Jerusalem. From the very outset, however, the message went out to world Jewry, to the would-be immigrants, that it intended to hold these too. It is unmistakably, if furtively, embodied in this grandiloquent appeal, put out by the Israeli government and the World Zionist Executive to 'arise, come up and build the land'. In a language reminiscent—according to the *Jerusalem Post*—of a proclamation issued in the time of Ezra and Nehemiah, it declares:

> The Israeli army, a people's army, daringly overcame and vanquished vast hostile forces, who had gathered to exterminate Israel. The enemy siege was broken, our ancestral heritage liberated and Jerusalem redeemed to become once more a city that is one. In the hour of deliverance . . . new vistas have been opened and immense challenges present themselves. A sacred duty to up-build the country speedily and to ensure the future of the Jewish state now faces the Jewish people. The inevitable call of the hour is for Aliyah—the Aliyah of the entire people, young and old; a return to Zion of the House of Israel. In its homeland the Jewish people has risen to full stature.[49]

Twice in a Lifetime: Another Arab Exodus

The immigrants did come—though in nothing like the numbers expected—and, once again, bringing in the Jews meant driving the Arabs out. The immediate aftermath of the war, with its fast-changing confusion, and especially a war in which the whole world applauds the victory, was an ideal opportunity which the Israelis had no scruples about taking. Jerusalem ranked first in their ambitions; they immediately began the process of turning it into what one minister subsequently described as 'an emphatically Jewish city'.[50] The main, and only substantial, relic of Jerusalem's Jewishness is the Wailing Wall. For Zionists everywhere, God-fearing or not, there could be no more fitting way of commemorating the deliverance of the Holy City than to dignify the remnants of the Temple with a proper, spacious foreground, making them into a national-religious shrine worthy of the name. Thus would they celebrate, with a monument, the gratification of their age-old yearning for 'Next Year in Jerusalem'. 'Jerusalem has been the Jewish capital for 3,000 years since King David. Jerusalem is more Jewish than Paris is French or London English,' said David Ben-gurion.[51] This is historical nonsense. But to the devout Zionist it makes bedrock emotional sense. As another Israeli leader explained it, less fancifully, to the city's Moslems: 'For the Jewish people there is only Jerusalem. Other religions have places in the city which we deeply respect, but they also have other places in the world.'[52] Only through Jerusalem does Israel feel itself a nation. And no one, neither Mandatory Power nor United Nations, was now going to stop Israel from bringing the physical appearance of the city into harmony with this spiritual reality. What, nearly fifty years before, Weizmann had called the 'doubtful Maghreb community'[53] would have to go. And, in a single night of bulldozing, go it did. On 11 June, the inhabitants of the quarter, beneficiaries of an endowment which Saladin's son had founded seven hundred years before, were turned out of their homes at a few minutes' notice. Of their possessions many rescued only what they could carry. A thousand people, or 129 families, were scattered in the adjacent lanes and streets, in a nearby market, an unfinished school or any other spot they could find.

The Israelis could not hide what they had begun to do in Jerusalem. They could only count it as a drawing, the first of many, on their immense new fund of international goodwill. Nor could they hide for very long what they were doing in less accessible parts of their newly conquered territory. But they could, and did, try. As they were driving bulldozers through the Magharibah quarter of Jerusalem, they were simultaneously wiping whole villages off the face of the earth. Among the first to go were Beit Nuba, Imwas and Yalu, situated close to the 1967 frontier in the strategic Latroun salient north of Jerusalem. Their 10,000 inhabitants were scattered to the four winds. In 1967 other villages, such as Beit Marsam, Beit Awa, Habla and Jifliq, met a similar fate.

There were not many foreign observers about with the determination and local knowledge to discover and document these acts, and the authorities tried hard to impede the few there were. Among them was Sister Marie-Thérèse, a French nun, who recorded in her diary that, after meeting all sorts of official obstructions, she and others from the order of Companions of Jesus decided to fight to get to Latroun. They succeeded . . . 'and there was what the Israelis did not want us to see: three villages systematically destroyed by dynamite and bulldozer. Alone in a deathly silence donkeys wandered about in the ruins. Here and there a crushed piece of furniture, or a torn pillow stuck out of the mass of plaster, stones and concrete. A cooking pan and its lid abandoned in the middle of the road. They were not given enough time to take anything away.'[54]

Amos Kenan, an Israeli journalist who participated in the war, tells the story of Beit Nuba:

> We were ordered to block the entrances of the village and prevent inhabitants returning to the village from their hideouts after they had heard Israeli broadcasts urging them to go back to their homes. The order was to shoot over their heads and tell them not to enter the village. Beit Nuba is built of fine quarry stones; some of the houses are magnificent. Every house is surrounded by an orchard, olive trees, apricots, vines and presses. They are well kept. Among the trees there are carefully tended vegetable beds. In the houses we found one wounded Egyptian commando officer and some very old people. At noon the first bulldozer arrived and pulled down the first house at the edge of the village. Within ten minutes the house was turned into rubble, including its entire contents; the olive trees, cypresses were all uprooted. . . . After the destruction of three houses the first column arrived from the direction of Ramallah. We did not fire into the air but took cover, some Arabic-speaking soldiers went over to notify them of the warning. There were old people who could hardly walk, murmuring

old women, mothers carrying babies, small children. The children wept and asked for water. They all carried white flags.

We told them to go to Beit Sura. They told us that they were driven out everywhere, forbidden to enter any village, that they were wandering like this for four days, without food, without water, some dying on the road. They asked to return to the village, and said we had better kill them.

Some had a goat, a lamb, a donkey or camel. A father ground wheat by hand to feed his four children. On the horizon we could see the next group arriving. A man carrying 100 lbs of flour in a sack—he had walked like that, mile after mile. More old people, more women, more babies. They dropped down exhausted where we told them to sit. Some had a cow or two, a calf; all their property on earth. We did not allow them to enter the village and take anything.

The children cried. Some of our soldiers started crying too. We went to fetch the Arabs some water. We stopped a car with a major, two captains and a woman. We took a jerrican of water and distributed it to the refugees. We also handed out cigarettes and candy. More soldiers burst into tears. We asked the officers why those refugees were sent from one place to another and driven out of everywhere. They told us that this was good for them, they should go. 'Moreover', said the officers, 'why do we care about the Arabs anyway . . .?'

More and more columns of refugees arrived, until there were hundreds of them. They failed to understand why they had been asked to return, yet not permitted to enter. We could not stand their pleading. One asked why we destroyed their houses instead of taking them over ourselves.

The platoon commander decided to go to headquarters and find out if there were any orders about what to do with them, where to send them, and whether it was possible to arrange transport for the women and food for the children. He returned saying that there were no orders in writing, simply that they were to be driven out.

We drove them out. They go on wandering in the south like lost cattle. The weak die. In the evening we found that they had been taken in, for in Beit Sura too bulldozers had begun to destroy the place and they were not allowed to enter. We found out that not only in our sector was the border straightened out for security reasons but in all other sectors too. The promise on the radio was not kept; the declared policy was never carried out.[55]

How magnanimous the Israeli victors must have seemed, if one judged by their radio alone, with its announcers calling on enemy civilians to return to their homes without fear. But how Machiavellian they must have seemed to anyone, like Sister Marie-Thérèse, who saw Israeli soldiers driving round Bethlehem with loudspeakers to warn the populace: 'You have two hours to leave your homes and flee to Jericho and Amman. If you don't, your houses will be shelled.' The razed villages and the loudspeakers spoke for themselves. But the general behaviour of the victorious soldiery also contributed to the same end. 'It is necessary', she writes,

> To state unambiguously that the first wave of Israeli soldiers were decent, humane, and courageous, doing as little damage as possible, the second wave was made up of thieves, looters and sometimes killers, and the third was more disturbing still since it seemed to act from a resolute desire for systematic destruction.

She recorded a distressing encounter:

> An Israeli addressed Father Paul who could not recognize him for the look of anguish that appeared on his face: 'But I am your friend from Haifa.' 'Oh, but you look so tired,' replied Father Paul. 'No, disheartened by these Jewish bandits, who have robbed and sacked like vandals. In the region of G—— our soldiers killed two women to steal their jewels. I have so much to tell you, but I have to go with these disgusting characters.' He pointed to his road companions. 'They do not understand French. Good-bye, come and see me. I want to tell you. . . .' Their car started; one of them had time to ask in Hebrew: 'Have all the Arabs left yet?'[56]

They had not. But in that first great post-war exodus, about a fifth of the population of the West Bank, something over 200,000, crossed the Jordan river. For some it was for the second time in a lifetime. The Israelis could not be directly blamed for all the things that made the Arabs go, but, as Sister Marie-Thérèse discovered when she went down to the Allenby bridge, they were very pleased when they did.

> It was there that the fleeing refugees had to go, most of them once before refugees from that other war. With their children and their parcels they had to clamber down the smashed bridge and wade through the water with the help of ropes. The Israeli soldiers, seated in armchairs, had been watching them pass for a fortnight. If it had been necessary for tanks to cross during the war, the bridge would have been rebuilt in a few hours. Why should human beings be so humiliated? From below, glances of hatred, from above, glances of contempt; but it is the glances of the frightened children in front of the broken bridge that hurt most. A woman carrying her sewing machine moaned and mumbled something. Another replied to her groans: 'May their houses collapse upon them.' As we were leaving, a weeping woman approached me; she told me that she had just crossed the river to help some relatives who were leaving, but that she herself had to return to Bethlehem where her children were; for the soldiers had said that, according to the law, she had to go to Amman since she had crossed the bridge. We thought this little business could easily be settled by speaking to the officer. The officer, who remained seated in his armchair, said: 'This woman has signed at the first station and they all know that once they have signed they never go back. . . .'[57]

The Arabs then had to be *kept* out too. The Israelis had two ways of doing that. They made it illegal for anyone to return without authorization from themselves, an authorization which (with very few exceptions) they then withheld, and they shot those who tried to return illegally. Under Order No. 125, issued by the Commander of the Israeli Defence Forces in the West Bank, any person who was absent from the West Bank or any other occupied territory as of 7 June 1967 and attempted to return without Israeli permission was to be considered an 'infiltrator' and, as such, liable to anything up to life imprisonment. This could make infiltrators not merely of the refugees who had fled from the fighting and Israeli intimidation, but of the many thousands who, say, had their places of work on the East Bank or Kuwait, who simply happened to be away, on business or on holiday, when the war broke out. It was 1948 all over again.[58]

The 'infiltrators' would try to wade across the Jordan under cover of darkness. At one time as many as 300 to 500 were crossing every night. But the risks were considerable, and they were the same whether the infiltrator was an armed guerilla or a woman rejoining her family—just as they had been the same, after 1948, for anyone who crossed the armistice line, whether he was in search of missing relatives or picking some oranges from his own orchard. The Israelis laid ambushes and shot everything that moved. The result—according to the exile publication *Imperial News*—was that 'every morning bodies litter the Jordan, men, women, children, whole families, massacred during their attempt to return home without the coveted Israeli permit'.[59]

The New Jerusalem

With the war, and its unique opportunities, passed, the Israelis proceeded with greater caution—but an undiminished sense of long-term purpose. In Jerusalem, under the urgings of the powerful Rabbinate, they pressed on with the Judaization of the holy places which the demolition of the 'doubtful Maghreb community' had begun. Immediate post-war fantasies about the construction of a synagogue between the mosques of al-Aqsa and Dome of the Rock, or even the restoration of the Temple itself, subsided, but the men of God regularly proclaimed no less an ambition than to expose two full sides of the Haram al-Sharif, the great platform on which the two mosques stand, from the south-west corner, near the existing Wailing Wall, all the way to the Gate of the Tribes in the north-east. Along this entire three-quarters of a kilometre length are the religious endowments, schools, courts, hospices—not to mention hundreds of Arabs living in them—which any great place of worship and pilgrimage gathers about itself. They are the accretions of centuries, an organic growth, one with the Noble Sanctuary itself. To remove them is a maiming, a severance of the mosques from their natural environment. No sooner had the authorities inserted an item in the *Jerusalem Post* about the need to 'clear' 82 metres of Wailing Wall, than, ignoring all the protests of the Moslem Council, they began archaeological excavations to investigate the Wall's southern reaches. Cracks appeared in historic buildings—the Fakhriyah Hospice, ancient residence of the Mufti of the Shafi sect, and an adjoining mosque—together with fourteen houses traditionally reserved for Haram officials. The inhabitants were ordered out, and the Fakhriyah went the way of the Magharibah two months before. Shortly afterwards, the Israelis turned their attention northwards. They used the pretext of bombs discovered in the vicinity of the Chain Gate—bombs which, local Arabs believe, the Israelis planted themselves—to confiscate all the property, including the ancient al-Tankiziyah School, on the northern side of the Wailing Wall compound.

Meanwhile, the Ministry of Religious Affairs was burrowing northwards under Arab buildings, tracing the extension of the Wailing Wall. Their ultimate and undisguised purpose—and that of the anything-but-religious nationalist extremists who joined forces with them—was not archaeological. They were at work on a two-fold undermining—of the buildings themselves and the resistance of the 'moderates' in the Municipality and the Ministry of Foreign Affairs, who were worried about Israel's reputation in the world and even (a few of them, and in a strictly limited sense) about the welfare of their Arab citizens. By May 1972, after they had covered about 180 metres, leaving another 160 to reach the north-west corner, what the extremists really wanted began to happen. Just beyond the Iron Gate a Mamluk structure, rent by great fissures, threatened to collapse and its inhabitants were evacuated. The Municipality buttressed it with a temporary scaffolding and began making four small holes in the Haram Wall, exposed at this point, as sockets for permanent props. Outraged religious leaders rushed to stop this desecration; they collected the chippings, wrapped them in silk, and, with the Minister of Religious Affairs at their head, paraded round the town with them. The government was obliged to issue a decree affirming that the Wall could not be defiled to support the threatened building. But the resistance of the 'moderates' was not yet undermined. The Municipality did not go along with this pretext for demolition, as it had with the Fakhriyah; it devised awkward and expensive means for preserving the building instead.

But in Israel extremists usually win in the end. Devout Jews went and prayed there among the rubble and scaffolding. Menachim Begin's right-wing expansionists supported them. And the Chief Rabbi of the Sephardi Sect, Itzhak Nissim, issued a bigoted, an un-Judaic, proclamation from there:

> City contractors . . . where are your bulldozers and machines which went to work as they should on the first night to clear the ground before the Wailing Wall [i.e. to demolish the Magharibah Quarter] . . . the Municipality decided to do away with the slums and ruins and the decision must be carried out without fear or shame . . . the hundreds of people living in them must be given their marching orders . . . we shall not cease our clamour, nor desist from the struggle, until the Wall is exposed, from summit to base, from its southern extremity to its northern one near the Gate of the Tribes.[60]

The Israelis did not, of course, confine themselves to creating religious facts, although it was with quasi-religious fervour that they set about creating the secular ones that were destined to make Jerusalem, in its daily living fabric, 'more Jewish than Paris is French, more Jewish than London is English'. The first secular *fait accompli* was the formal annexation of the city. The enlargement of the Israeli Municipality—under the Interior Minister's Ordinance No. 5727 of 28 June 1967—brought it up to, and where that suited him, a little beyond the boundaries of the Jordanian Municipality. A whole series of supporting laws followed in rapid succession. They Judaized the Jerusalem administration. On 29 June the Assistant Military Commander of Jerusalem had 'the honour to inform' the Mayor of East Jerusalem, Ruhi Khatib, that his municipal council was dissolved. Municipal property and records were seized, and all government departments were brought under Israeli jurisdiction. They Judaized the Jerusalem economy. Arab banks were closed down and their funds appropriated, the Israeli taxation system was introduced along with the Israeli currency, and West Bank products were banished from the city, which Israeli suppliers had largely to themselves. They Judaized the Jerusalem citizens. All businessmen, craftsmen and professional men had to obtain Israeli licences, state schools had to follow the Israeli curricula, civil courts had to work under the Israeli judiciary, and the ordinary citizen was expected to vote in Israeli municipal elections. They Judaized Arab land and property.

'We take the land first and the law comes after.' With remarkable candour Yehoshafat Palmon, adviser to the Mayor on Arab affairs, thus put in a nutshell for me his government's strategy for taking what did not belong to it. Taking the land has always been Zionism's basic impulse. Taking it in Jerusalem was a sacred compulsion. The Israelis applied to the Holy City essentially the same methods they had learned in the pioneering frontier days. It was the tower-and-stockade technique adapted to a unique urban environment. In a frantic programme of expropriation and construction, immigration and settlement, they sought to obliterate, as quickly as possible and by sheer physical presence, the remaining Arab claim to Jerusalem, which was built not only on sentiment and centuries of sovereignty, but on the abstract legality of immemorial possession of the land. During the Mandate, as a result of Zionist efforts to pack the city, the Jews had retained their majority in the city proper; however, if Jerusalem had been internationalized—as a UN General Assembly resolution of November 1947 recommended—the boundaries prescribed by the UN plan would have incorporated 100,000 Jews as against 105,000 Arabs and others.[61] As for the land, only about 5,000 dunums, or some 18 per cent of the area of Jerusalem, had been Jewish-owned.[62] On the eastern, subsequently Jordanian, side the Jews had represented a much smaller proportion of the population and they had owned the merest fraction—perhaps 0.6 per cent[63]—of the land.

'We take the land. . . .' Between 1948 and 1967, the Israelis had used their Absentees' Property Law to take some 20,000 dunums of it,[64] along with a rich haul of movable and immovable property, belonging to the Arabs on the western side of the city. Since 1967 they have taken more than 15,000 dunums on the eastern side.[65] This included, of course, the tiny particle of Jewish land abandoned in 1948. To their surprise, it seems, the Israelis found it juridically intact. For there was a Jordanian Custodian of Absentees' Property too, and he—said Israeli lawyer Chaim Aron Valero—had been 'quite fair. . . . I don't know about all the properties, but I know quite a number of properties remained registered to this day in Jewish names as in Mandate times. They were not expropriated and their ownership did not pass to the Jordanian government.'[66] It goes without saying that it was a one-way process. The Arabs of unified Jerusalem who put in a claim for property they had abandoned on the Israeli side in 1948 got short shrift. For the job of the Israeli Custodian, unlike his Jordanian counterpart, was not to preserve property for its rightful owner, but to deprive him of it.

'The law comes after. . . .' In fact, for most Arabs it did not come at all. There might have been a few exceptions—propaganda exceptions—but they knew that it was futile to take their cases to the courts. 'When your enemy is your judge, to whom do you complain?' goes an Arab saying, much in vogue in Jerusalem. Besides, it was for the higher good of the whole community that they were forfeiting their land. For this time it was not its own Absentees' Property Law, but another of those British laws—the Land Acquisition for Public Purposes Ordinance of 1943—which the Israeli government resurrected for the occasion. How useful that much-maligned, but never quite abandoned, British legislation was continuing to prove! The beauty of this law—though not, of course, its framers' intention—was that it could be put to any 'purpose' the Israelis saw fit, such as turning Jerusalem into an 'emphatically Jewish city'. The British had decreed that there should be compensation for the owner of the expropriated land or property—and the Israelis duly offered it. But they practically never paid it. As they well knew, the Arabs could not take their money anyway; that would be 'selling Palestine'. But in any case what was the point of taking their money when all they were offered, as the Arabs scornfully put it, was 'the ear of a camel'?

By 1972, land values in fashionable parts of the city, such as Qatamon, were reaching £30,000 a dunum and more. Few of the 15,000 dunums could have been worth less than £3,000 a dunum. But almost every Arab would tell you that, in so far as the Israelis talked business at all, they were offering a tenth, twentieth or thirtieth of that. The Israelis have always been extremely reticent about the whole subject, but their offer to compensate Jerusalemites—the minority of them who could still reside there—for property they lost anywhere in Israel after 1948 was a measure of their intentions. The Custodian of Absentees' Property had of course irrevocably deprived them of every good and chattel they owned, but in 1971 the Ministry of Justice suddenly decided that justice of sorts should be done. The sum of $150,000,000 was set aside for the purpose. The compensation was to be paid at 1948 prices, plus 25 per cent in Israeli bonds, over a period of twenty years. What this meant in practice was explained by a leading businessman who, taking me on a sentimental journey round West Jerusalem, and showing me the house in which he and his father were born, came finally to a commercial property which his family had bought in 1944. 'If it were mine now,' he said, 'I wouldn't sell it for £450,000. But I reckon that if I accepted Israeli compensation I would get about £6,000 for it.' That is to say, he would receive less than one seventy-fifth of its true value.

Although the municipal booklets—which seem to be designed for readers who never ask questions—asserted that the Arabs were compensated, officials, when confronted by the unaccustomed questioners with evidence to the contrary, admitted that they were not, and took refuge in the alternative argument that the Arabs, insisting on retaining their rights of ownership, refused to come forward to take the compensation they were due. 'We have not yet reached the stage of talking about the price of land,' Mr Palmon conceded. It was difficult to measure these things in terms of cold cash but did he mean, assuming—on a conservative estimate—an average value of £3,000 per dunum, that the Israelis were in the process of acquiring land in East Jerusalem to the value of £45,000,000 for almost nothing? 'Yes,' he replied, 'it's not very much. It may seem strange to you coming from Beirut. But everything is done according to the law, a detailed law, the law for the public benefit. The law is greater than me, greater than Golda Meir. We can't leave Jerusalem a desert, with donkeys in the streets.'

The lack of charity in Mr Palmon's words was even more forcefully reflected in the acts of his Municipality. Israel's smallest single expropriation—the 116 dunums of the Jewish Quarter—became a poignant paradigm of them all. For nowhere more than here, a stone's throw from the most sacred of Jewish shrines, was true religion, a true spirit of reconciliation, more strikingly absent. Here Yigal Allon, the Deputy Prime Minister, was quick to move into a fine new house. It has a magnificent view to the front, high above the plunging Kidron Valley, but for a long while it had an unsightly one to the rear, where Arab householders, refusing to leave, clung to islands of habitation amid the desolation wrought by the bulldozers and demolition squads. Before 1948, the Jewish Quarter was not more than 20 per cent Jewish-owned.[67] After 1967, the Israelis took over the lot. They relentlessly forced out the 5,500 people who lived there.[68] They described them as 'squatters'. A few squatters—that is to say, Israeli-created refugees—had found makeshift homes in the quarter. But most of the inhabitants were old Jerusalem families who had lived there from generation to generation.[69]

Ostensibly, the 5,500 left of their own free will with what the municipal booklets described as 'handsome' compensation. When I suggested to an official responsible for 'reconstruction' that this was untrue, he came close to losing his temper. 'Do we shoot them?' he asked. 'Do we drive them across the river, do we deny them work?' They didn't. What they did, when they could not persuade some obstinate tenant (the property is mostly *Waqf* religious endowments leased to tenants who did not feel, in taking money, that they were 'selling Palestine') to accept the inadequate compensation they offered, was to make his life unbearable by demolishing everything around him, even part of the house itself, the entrance steps or an outside lavatory. The walls cracked, the roof leaked, water got cut off, the rooms were choked with dust. They used intimidation. The hatchet man for the higher authorities, Ezra ben Simon—plain Ezra as the Arabs called him—decorated his room in a rather unusual way for a municipal office: beneath a full-colour picture of General Dayan were shelves bearing an array of upright bullets of different sizes, a grenade and what appeared to be a bayonet. Municipal regulations were cynically exploited. A housewife showed me the order she had received to evacuate her house for her own safety's sake. If her house was unsafe, it was, of course, because the Municipality, bulldozing all round it, had made it so. They used ignoble subterfuges. One girl recounted how, when a squad of soldiers and workmen came to her family's house with orders to demolish it, they told her father, in answer to his protests, to go and see Mayor, Teddy Kollek. He left them carrying out the furniture, but by the time he got back, bearing a stay of execution from Kollek, they had already pulled the house down, with a chain attached to a bulldozer, before his family's eyes.

It was the same with the much larger areas outside the Old City walls: the women from the village of Lifta, a twice-expropriated community, who told me they spent an unpleasant night in prison, one of them in a cell with prostitutes, after trying to resist the tractors ploughing up their land; the orphan boy from Aisawia village who showed me where his uncle gathered thirty members of his family to rebuild his humble home each time the Israelis knocked it down, only giving up after the third attempt; the woman who took me to a large patch of rubble near the Mount of Olives, the remains of a fine, uninhabited house, owned by an absentee Palestinian American, which the Israelis bulldozed with a subsequent explanation to the inquiring American consul that the house had never existed. These were just a few individual instances of the systematic spoliation which the Israelis tried to hide from prying eyes, just a few indications of what it really meant when an Israeli newspaper carried a report like this: 'The security forces yesterday sealed off the entrance to the village of Nabi Samuel and demolished some old buildings which were a danger to the public. . . . Journalists, including foreign correspondents and television crews, were denied access to the area.[70]

'Never forcibly evicted', 'handsomely compensated', the Arabs—the municipal booklet went on—were 'assured of alternative accommodation'. And officials told me brightly about the new housing estate at Wadi Joz. That sounded encouraging. Arabs building for Arabs, I learned from contractors, was at a very low ebb; costs had nearly quadrupled since the 1967 War; the risk of expropriation was ever-present; the Israelis were in no hurry to issue building licences. But perhaps, after all, I would find clinching rebuttal of Arab complaints at Wadi Joz. What I found was twenty-eight diminutive apartments. Twenty-six of them were shuttered and bolted. Only two were occupied. Salim Namari, the first to move in to one of the two, told me his story.

> I used to live in the Jewish Quarter. They knocked down so much of my house that I was all but living in the open air. I refused to move till I found another house. I couldn't find one. So they offered me one at Wadi Joz. First they said they wanted £1,500 down payment, then £2,300. I could not find the difference. I went to the Municipality about four days a week for six months. I was turned away every time. I only got them down to £1,500 again when I contacted a journalist on the *Jerusalem Post*, known for his opposition to the Municipality, and he threatened to write about me. Then it was the same business getting credit instalments. Only when I barged my way into the manager's

> office did I get what I wanted. It is going to cost me £7,000 all told. It took me twenty months to get here. The Israelis never lose a chance to make propaganda. They had the nerve at the end of it to hold a ceremony on my account. I was on television and in the papers.

And he showed me a picture of himself being presented with a bouquet of flowers before a seated audience of Arabs and Jews. 'I had certain advantages, I speak fluent Hebrew. My wife is Jewish. I have a lawyer friend in Tel Aviv. Imagine what it's like for the others.'

Taking the land was the main thing, but it was inseparable from a host of other unlawful actions which, by eroding Palestinian society, facilitated the taking. The severest of these—more severe, in fact, than expropriation itself—was the permanent exiling of Jerusalem's Arabs. The former Mayor, Ruhi Khatib, estimated at 100,000 the number of people, Jerusalemites by birth, background or property rights, who could not return to their city. A few, like himself, were banished for their anti-Israeli activities; but the vast majority were simply absentees who were not allowed back. They included 60,000 Jerusalemites who left Palestine in 1948, the 5,000 who happened to be away in 1967—because they fled, because they were studying abroad, taking a holiday, travelling on business or simply because they were taxi-drivers on errands to Amman or Damascus—and the 35,000 children born and bred in exile.[71] The Israelis never made any secret of it: they were bent on 'thinning out' the population of Jerusalem more effectively than anywhere else. After the 1967 War, there were many Jerusalemites who, unable to face the rigours and uncertainties of occupation, helped them by taking the emigrant's way out. The Christian Arabs, more educated and adaptable than their Muslim compatriots, were in the forefront of this 'distressing stampede without hope or joy',[72] as Archbishop Raya of Galilee described it. And in the words of another prelate, the Archbishop of Anchorage, emigration threatened to reduce the role of Christians in the Holy Land to 'no more than keepers of museums and curators of shrines'.[73]

It was the more vigorous elements of Palestinian society—the economic, cultural and intellectual élite—who fared worst in Jerusalem. The young, the students, faced the most serious problems. After

1967, they fell under the same disabilities that Israeli Arabs had suffered since 1948. In Israel's Arab schools, children have always had to see their own Arab culture, history and religion through Israeli eyes; they saw it deliberately mocked and falsified. Arab history became little more than a series of revolutions, murders, feuds and plunderings, while everything in the Jewish past was ennobled and glorified. It was always the Arabs in decline they learned about, never in their greatness; the heroes of the past, the Prophet, the Caliph Harun al-Rashid and Saladin, got perfunctory mention. In four years of secondary education Arab children had 384 periods of Jewish history as against only 32 of their own. The study of the Old Testament was compulsory, while the Muslim and Christian religions were not taught at all. The overall quality of education was extremely low; so much so that in 1966, the Arabs, who represented one-tenth of the population, boasted 171 university students compared with 14,000 Jews.[74] When, therefore, the Israelis extended their own syllabus to the Arab public schools of East Jerusalem, the result was immediate and dramatic. It meant that students had to forego their hopes of a university education. Places for Arabs at the Hebrew University—if not actually regulated by quota—were in practice extremely limited, and only the most brilliant of students, suddenly plunged into an alien language, culture and educational system could hope to pass the Israeli metriculation or *bagrut*, in order to qualify for one of them; but in making the attempt students would be denying themselves the chance of passing the Arab equivalent, or *taujihi*, to secure a place in an Arab university. Several well-known schools became ghosts of their former selves. The Rashidiya College, which had thrived since Ottoman times, boasted 800 students before the Six-Day War. By 1972 it had fourteen. Pupils and teachers transferred to private schools, and even to orphanages, which remained unaffected by Israeli legislation. But the invasion caused standards to fall sharply. There was a dramatic slump in the number of British General Certificate passes. There was only a slight improvement in the situation when the Israelis came up with an inspired compromise; public school pupils could work for the *bagrut* and *taujihi* at the same time.

Something else which the Israelis applied wholesale to East Jerusalem was their taxation system. They did not bother to ascertain whether it was truly applicable or not. And of course it was not. Israel, unlike Jordan, has a high-taxation economy—high wages with a high rate of fiscal recovery. Were the librarian in Saladin Street, the little grocer in the Old City, the civil servant from Shaikh Jarrah really the same, for tax purposes, as their counterparts in Western Jerusalem? Could the Arab citizen who had no assistance for educating his children or building his house on an instalment plan be put on the same footing as the Israeli who enjoyed welfare services from the cradle to the grave? Similarly, if municipal rates were assessed largely on the surface area a property occupied, should a prime residential or commercial quarter in East Jerusalem, where properties are spacious, be assessed on the same basis as its equivalent in the West, where they are cramped? The choice facing the Jerusalem property-owner was to submit to the new order, a burden which it was difficult, and sometimes impossible, to bear, or to cut his losses and leave. And imagine the feelings of the Jerusalemite, a non-citizen liable to expulsion at any time, when, in addition to the regular taxes, he had to make his contribution to periodic 'Defence Loans'—in other words, to the purchase of Phantoms for bombing his fellow-Arabs.

The Israelis also blessed the Arabs with what, in the Western world, is often hailed as their main achievement in an area which lacks such a thing—their democracy. The Arabs of Jerusalem were privileged to vote in municipal elections. The first time they were held some 4,000 out of 37,000 potential voters went to the polls. One official described this as an 'embarrassment' to Arab leaders. Indeed, not only did they go to the polls, they showed great enthusiasm to exercise their democratic rights; the booths were crowded with hundreds of Arabs pushing, shoving and literally begging to vote. They went there in buses decorated with slogans like 'We Want Teddy Kollek', and Arabs whose names were not on the electoral rolls would not leave without written confirmation that they had come to vote. It quickly turned out, however, that the whole operation had been organized, like a military campaign, by Kollek's own supporters, who violently drove out activists of other parties trying to corner the Arab vote for themselves. What made the Arabs so enthusiastic was the fear, deliberately inculcated, that if they did not vote for him they would lose their jobs. All this was exposed in the

Israeli press, not out of any concern for democracy, but because rival parties were jealous. A Dr Rosenberg summed it up in *Yediot Aharonot*: 'the circumstances in which they voted are well known, but we shall not deal with them here—for patriotic reasons'.[75]

Into the cruder fabric of obvious discrimination was woven the finer texture of subtle irritations that a conquered people, in daily contact with their conquerors, inevitably experience. It might be arrogant policemen or discourteous bureaucrats, unpleasant anywhere, but doubly so as the agents of an occupying power. It might be the partisan verdict of authority: if there was a traffic accident involving an Arab and a Jew, who was to prevent the law from taking the Jew's side? It might be the pedantic application of municipal regulations: an East Jerusalem school was told that its windows were six inches smaller than they should be; but one has only to go to schools in the slum areas of West Jerusalem to see—even if the windows are the regulation size—how unhygienic they are. It might be some trivial but maddening experience; Arabs often failed their driving tests for silly, petty reasons; one was asked what he would do if a woman with a dog asked him for a lift and he replied, 'I would take her if she was pretty.' 'Failed; you check to see if she has a dog licence first.' It might be Hebrew memorials to the Jewish dead in the battle for Jerusalem, as against the virtual absence of Arab ones; and one in English which records that 'on this spot, seventy-eight nurses, researchers and doctors were ambushed and massacred by Arab marauders on their way to work at the Hadassa Hospital one morning in 1948.' The Land of Israel Movement which went around expunging Arabic wall signs. The changing of street names—from Suleiman the Magnificent Street to Paratroop Street and Allenby Square to Zahal (Israeli Defence Forces) Square. The coming of prostitution to East Jerusalem with teenage girls assembling in droves at Jaffa Gate or bargaining with their customers outside the newly established bars of al-Zahra Street. The growing number of burglaries . . . the hooligans. . . . In themselves these things were often petty or accidental enough but, taken together, they made up, in a hundred little ways, the climate of the New Jerusalem.

Of all the occupied territories, only Jerusalem was formally annexed. Nevertheless throughout the new domains, the West Bank, the Golan

Heights, Gaza and Sinai, no time was lost with the 'creation of facts'—facts which, in the expansionist tradition, could never be undone. The old slogans were revived: where the Jews settled, there they would remain. The 'emperor of the occupied territories' never ceased to affirm that the new colonies were not mere flowerpots that could be moved from one place to another, but trees rooted in the soil. By the October 1973 War, some forty-two settlements dotted the face of Greater Israel, and many more were planned. Some lay well within the biblically defined frontiers of the Promised Land—like those on the West Bank, a third of which, under the so-called Allon Plan, was all but officially earmarked for annexation. Others lay beyond them—like those on the Golan Heights, or at Sharm al-Shaikh, renamed Ophir, deep inside Egyptian territory at the southernmost tip of the Gulf of Aqaba. The settlements were industrial as well as agricultural; and one, called Yamit, in north-east Sinai, was eventually destined to grow into a coastal township of some 250,000 people. Vast tracts of land went with them. Almost all of Golan, cleared of its Syrian inhabitants, was the victors' for the taking. On the West Bank, the Land Administration appropriated nearly a million and a half dunums of Jordanian state domain, as well as abandoned or absentee property. It helped itself to almost a third—some 120,000 dunums—of the entire Gaza Strip.[76] Ostensibly—and to make the colonization more acceptable to world opinion—the settlements had military as well as other purposes; they were portrayed as vital new assets in Israel's unending struggle for survival. But the officials concerned were not always too discreet about the real motives: 'We have to use the pretext of security needs and the authority of the military governor as there is no way of driving out the Arabs from their land so long as they refuse to go and accept our compensation.'[77] Sometimes it was necessary to uproot an entire village—though not necessarily all at once. For years the impoverished inhabitants of Beit Askariyah watched in impotent dismay as the great cantonments of the Kfar Etzion settlement went up around them, relentlessly encroaching on their agricultural and grazing lands before swallowing up their homes too.[78] In January 1972, the army expelled 6,000 bedouins from Rafah in north-east Sinai. It demolished their houses, poisoned their wells, and kept them at bay with a barbed-wire fence. The bedouins were eventually employed as night watchmen or labourers—on their own property and in the service of those who had taken it from them. But it was the villagers of Akraba who were taught the most original lesson. The military government had requisitioned some of their land for use as a shooting range. They objected. So their fields were sprayed from the air with a poisonous chemical which destroyed the entire harvest. In due course the fields were handed over to the nearby settlement of Nahal Gitit.[79]

Apartheid Israeli-Style

Expulsions and expropriations notwithstanding, most of the Palestinians managed to stay behind. The Israelis were not as thorough, in driving them out, as they had been in 1948. There were, after all, limits to Western tolerance. It remained, however, a frequently expressed desire that the Palestinians would eventually be persuaded to leave. Meanwhile, here they were, some 2,800,000 Jews, ruling over nearly 1,500,000 Arabs, composed of Israel's own rapidly growing minority, plus the newly conquered inhabitants of Greater Israel.

It was a new situation, and it troubled the Zionist soul, torn as it was between the two primal impulses of expansionism and exclusivism. The ruling élite were anxious to absorb as much territory as possible; but at the same time they were afraid, many of them, of having to absorb the Palestinians along with it. Not merely would that run counter to the whole idea of the Jewish State, it threatened to turn Israel into a typical colonial power in which the Jews would be to their Palestinians as the whites of South Africa are to their blacks. The most pungent expression of this fear came, as so often, from the Prime Minister, Golda Meir, herself. The Palestinians' birth-rate was so much higher than the Jews' that her sleep was often disturbed, she would say, at the thought of how many Arab babies had been born in the night. It was during her administration that the Israeli parliament passed a law which deputy Uri Avneri described as 'infamous, shameful and scandalous' in its discriminatory intent. It was designed—beneath its Orwellian disguise—to encourage child-bearing among Israeli Jews, but to discourage it among Israeli Arabs, 'to pay grants to the hungry children of one part of the population and withhold them from the hungry children of another part, the distinction—it is obscure but quite obvious to anyone who knows the facts—being an ethnic one. . . .'[80]

For all their anxieties, however, the leadership quickly adapted themselves to the new realities. The threat to the integrity of Zionism was a long-term one. Meanwhile, there were alluring opportunities to be seized. General Dayan, the hard-headed pragmatist, did his best to ensure that they were. For him the occupied territories were a market for Israeli products and a source of cheap labour; they should therefore be 'integrated' into the Israeli economy. By 1973, they had in fact become Israel's largest market (except for polished diamonds) after the United States. The exports were mainly manufactured goods—commodities which the Palestinians were not allowed to acquire from any other quarter. It was Dayan's hope that, via the West Bank and its 'open bridges' across the Jordan, Israel would eventually penetrate those vast 'natural' markets which, because of the rigorous Arab quarantine, it had been denied since its foundation. By 1973, some 70,000 workers from the West Bank and Gaza were employed in Israel. That meant that Israel was furnishing jobs for about half the employed men of the West Bank; their wages accounted for about a third of its gross product. Some twenty employment bureaux opened in the West Bank with the sole purpose of channelling workers into the Israeli economy. Like the Israeli Arabs before them, the West Bankers and Gazans were concentrated in construction and agriculture. Altogether, Arabs now accounted for about one-third of the jobs in these two sectors.[81]

Economic 'integration' injected a new strain into Zionist attitudes towards the natives, or rather it intensified one which had always been there, among the less doctrinaire, from the beginning. The exclusivist dogma of Hebrew Labour and its ruthless denial of jobs to Arabs, which had held sway since the early years of the century, was now being challenged by the notion that Arabs were particularly suited to work that was inappropriate for the Jews. In a letter to *Haaretz*, which supported Dayan's policies, a reader told Mrs Meir that if she wanted to see 'Hebrew workers sweating away on hot summer days, if it gives her pleasure, this is her own business. But it cannot be a national criterion on which to convince the public that we should not integrate the economy of the West Bank. . . . I would like to say that in many countries with developed national sensitivity there are millions of foreign workers carrying out most of the dirty work, and no one cares or is frightened about it.'[82] Joseph Chuba, a farmer, was more explicit: 'If Arabs exist, let them work. Why shouldn't Jews be the bosses? The Arab workers are naturally built for it. I have one who is fifty years old and works bent double for eight hours a day. Show me a Jew like him!'[83]

Although Dayan's pragmatism won the day, it never ceased to worry the keepers of the Zionist conscience. The Secretary General of the Trade Union Federation shocked an audience when he declared: 'I do not know whether the territories that we are holding are bargaining cards or perhaps embers burning away our foundations. . . . I must say it is very sweet building Zionism with Arab labour, to build cities of the economy and enjoy it. We shall soon hear that anyone who says he does not want to get rich on the work of the Arabs from the territories questions the realization of Zionism and holds back redemption and development.'[84] For the wife of a cooperative farmer, the old pre-war days of honest toil had obviously become an Arcadian memory:

> Until the Six-Day War we had lived in peace, we worked hard but were relatively prosperous. But since then the situation has changed. My husband, who is an able man, became a contractor for agricultural labour. We had the advantages of cheap sources of labour and a big market. Today we have five Arab workers and a situation where we do nothing for ourselves on our farm. My eldest son now even refuses to cut the grass saying: 'Let Muhammad do it.' And of course it is no good talking of any real hard work. All the children of the *Moshav* as well as my own children are changing in front of my eyes into the kind of rich children who have everything done for them by their servants. Nobody knows how to drive the tractor which stands in the yard or is interested in agriculture. Until about a week ago the Arab workers lived in the citrus warehouses where they were working but now it

> seems more labour has been brought in to work in the hothouses and the citrus warehouses are full. Therefore my husband has built them a hut in the yard. When I protested he sent me to look around the village and I realized that any man with ability had become a contractor. The village is full of hothouses in which only Arab workers are employed. The Arabs live mostly in mud houses some distance from the improved villas of the Jewish farmers who have adopted the style of *effendi*. Another point: the attitude towards our workers and the conditions in which they live are even worse than for the *Fatah* prisoners in jail.[85]

And for the Minister of Agriculture the phenomenon was obviously quite as repugnant as the 'painful leprosy' which so upset a Zionist pioneer more than half a century before.[86] 'The domination of Jewish agriculture by Arab workers', he lamented, 'is a cancer in our body.'[87] *Plus ça change. . . .*

Dayan's answer, in effect, was that such pragmatism does not, or should not, endanger the Zionist ideal. It was possible to have both expansionism *and* exclusivism. If there were a threat to the national fibre, to the traditional Zionist ethic of hard work and self-reliance, the Israelis should depend on their 'inner force' to meet it.[88] But there were also certain practical measures that could be taken to keep the Palestinians in their place. For it was not as if the inhabitants of the occupied territories had any political or civil rights. They might live under Israeli military rule; but juridically they were Jordanians, like the West Bankers, or just refugees, like the Gazans. It was really quite straightforward. 'When they are not Israeli citizens, they do not vote in parliamentary elections. The whole question of our demographic character, in the sense that the inhabitants of the territories would affect our way of life, *does not exist*.'[89] If the Palestinians did not like this, Dayan insinuated, then all they had to do was to leave for places where they felt more at home.[90] Thus it was that an 'Apartheid Israeli-style'—as Israeli civil libertarian Shulamit Aloni called it[91]—came quite openly into being. No longer was it the surreptitious thing it had to be for those, Israel's own Arab minority, who were supposed to be equal in the eyes of the law. The West Bankers and the Gazans could work in Israel, but there was no question of their living there. Some would try. So inspection teams went around preventing them from squatting near their places of work. For the squatters were liable to bring their wives and families along, and before you knew where you were you had a whole Arab village on your hands.[92] Of course, there were always exceptions; it might require a bribe from an employer or a middleman, but the authorities could often be induced to turn a blind eye to the squalid tents or hutments that went up on building sites on the outskirts of cities.[93] The Palestinians went automatically into the most menial of jobs. Their wages averaged about 40 per cent of those of their Israeli counterparts.[94] They could be dismissed overnight. There were thousands of 'illegal' workers too; they were favoured by employers seeking to evade the tax that was supposed to be paid on every immigrant worker; their conditions were even worse. Workers who had no regular employment had to present themselves at the 'open markets' in various towns. Israel's Arabic-language Communist Party newspaper describes the one at Jaffa:

> In this market foremen get rich by exploiting the labour of children and young men from the occupied areas. Every morning at 4. A.M. cars from Gaza and the Strip start arriving there, bringing dozens of Arab workers who line up in the street in a long queue. A little later at 4.30. A.M. Arab boys who work in restaurants in the town begin to arrive. These boys work in restaurants for a month on end, including Saturdays. . . . Dozens, indeed hundreds, of boys who should be at school come from Gaza to work in Israel. The cars can be seen coming and going from earliest dawn. At about 6. A.M. Israeli labour brokers start arriving to choose 'working donkeys' as they call them. They take great care over their choice, actually feeling the 'donkeys'' muscles (though fortunately they do not examine their teeth!). Those who are unlucky and do not get work await 'God's mercy' under the trees in a neighbouring garden.[95]

Under the Heel of the Conqueror

It hardly needs to be said that the upbuilding of Greater Israel could only be accomplished through the permanent, institutional use of violence to which Zionism was irretrievably wedded. There was the systematic torture of prisoners. This has been documented by the Israeli lawyer Felicia Langer, one of the very few who tried to secure real justice for the Palestinians before Israeli courts, in her book *With My Own Eyes*.[96] Earlier, a UN Investigating Committee, denied access to the occupied territories, heard what it considered to be convincing evidence of the vicious and occasionally lethal agonies which Palestinians suffered at the hands of skilled Israel torturers. It found the testimony of one Ahmad Khalifa 'particularly impressive' because 'he did not give the impression that he was moved by rancour towards his former captors'. More hurtful to his fellow-prisoners than the physical torture, Khalifa said, was the abuse and insults to which they were subjected as individuals or members of the Palestinian resistance movement. He tried to reason with his captors.

> I knew, I said, that the Israelis tortured prisoners brutally, and I could say a great deal about conditions even there, in the Russian Compound Prison. But I wanted to tell him something else. Physical torture was not important; sooner or later physical scars heal but psychological scars never heal. There had been intelligence services that had tried to destroy the self-respect and humanity of their enemies, and believed that they had succeeded. But in fact they had turned their victims into extremists full of hatred. 'What concerns us,' I said, 'is not the question of information and security; it is the question of the relations between two peoples. We are fighting now, and it may well be that we shall fight for a long time. But if you are concerned for the future of your children and ours, you should behave in such a way as to prevent extremism and hatred. This is your opportunity.'
>
> I stopped and the officer was silent, while Ghuwaili (a particularly brutal torturer) spoke. I shall never forget his words. He said: 'You Arabs are cowards. You wanted to annihilate us and you were "——" in the war. Now you must accept the facts. We shall not return Golan, nor the West Bank, nor the Gaza Strip. We want to live. If you don't like it, fight us if you are men, and may the best man win.'
>
> After what I had said, these words came as a shock, and all I could find to say was: 'You are right; we shall see.' The officer then spoke a few words to him in Hebrew, then rose and, putting his hand

> on my shoulder, said: 'Ahmad, I understand you very well. Believe me, we shall not try to break you.' Then with a greeting he left the room. I never saw him again, but I am sorry to say that his promise was not kept.[97]

There was the 'administrative detention'. This imprisonment of politically-minded intellectuals, who were the natural leaders of Israel's Arab minority, had been a time-honoured practice. It found a much harsher, less selective application in the occupied territories. At its worst it meant the establishment of veritable concentration camps buried in remote corners of the Sinai desert. Nakhl, Abu Zu'aiman, Kusseimah were the names of places where whole families were confined in total isolation from the outside world. They were there because relatives of theirs were suspected, no more, of working for the resistance. Crowded into tents surrounded by barbed wire, they were denied radios, newspapers or the most basic amenities from their homes, which were frequently destroyed during their captivity. Women and children would be put in one camp, male relatives of 'wanted persons'—brother, nephews, cousins—in another. It was decreed that at least one man must be confined along with the rest of the family, 'so that it might not be said that we desecrate the honour of Arab women'.[98]

There were the 'collective punishments', which at one time were an almost daily routine. Curfews, often imposed on the slightest pretext, could last for days. There was a standard procedure with local variations. The whole male population of a village or refugee camp, from fourteen to seventy years of age, would be driven to some deserted spot or herded into a stockade. There they would be divided into two groups, the young and the less young, so that fathers and children should not be together. Both groups would be made to kneel, squat on their haunches or adopt some humiliating posture. Thus they would remain for two or three days, and the soldiers who guarded them would keep firing in the air above their heads. Meanwhile the womenfolk would be confined to their houses, which frequently lacked water or sanitation. Mothers with small children would often be reduced to a state of hysteria. The women could go out for half an hour or so to bring food and water. The public latrines in refugee camps were not built for mass utilization in a half-hour period, and, occasionally, among the women killed or wounded were those who, being unable to contain themselves, made a dash for the lavatories.[99] The village of Beit Sahur, from which Katiusha rockets were fired on Jerusalem, held the record: a month-long, twenty-two-hour-a-day curfew during which the inhabitants, half-starved, could not open their doors, go out into the garden or even open the windows and stand beside them.[100]

Curfews and 'searches' were often carried out with great brutality and violence. In the middle of the night people had to leave their homes until the searches were completed. To spread panic soldiers would fire their machine-guns as they went. Sometimes people were killed or wounded; later the Israel press would report that they were 'shot while attempting to run away'.[101] It was a regular practice, during night-time raids, to carry men off to prison without any good reason, beat them up and torture them. The Israelis sometimes called in the notorious Green Berets, the Druze troops who seemed to take a special pleasure in hurting their fellow-Arabs. These might go into action with clubs and whips. They beat their victims savagely in order to scare them. Bones would be broken. They stripped women naked in the streets, stealing their jewellery and smashing their pathetic belongings.[102] Some Israeli soldiers privately expressed the opinion that 'the best way to combat terrorism was to bind suspects tightly with electric wire on arms and legs, and leave them in the sun. . . .'[103]

There was the demolition of houses. More than 7,000 had been blown up within two years of the 1967 War. This happened mainly—and in the immediate aftermath of the fighting—for strategic, Zionist purposes. There was no pretence of punishment or reprisal. But when there was it was often of the flimsiest kind. Suspicion, not proof, was all the occupying power required. The suspects might be released—for lack of evidence—but there was no redress for their demolished homes. An unsuspecting hotelier who happened to let a room to a guerilla would have his hotel wrecked.[104] And often a house, in Israeli parlance, meant a multi-storey apartment building, or a whole row of adjacent dwellings. Thirty-one houses might be blown up in this way, and they might turn out to contain 200 families, as they did in the village of Uga, near Jericho, half of which was reduced to rubble.[105] General Dayan made no bones about it: it was collective or, as he put it, 'neighbourhood' punishment in which the whole community was made to suffer for the hostile activities of one of its members. That is how he described the destruction of some seventy houses in the village of Halhul in the wake of a guerilla attack on Israeli soldiers. He told the villagers 'today we demolished twenty homes [sic]. If this is not enough we will demolish the whole town, and if you don't like this policy, the bridges are open before you for departure.'[106]

There were the deportations, which took both a public and a surreptitious form. The number of public deportees, a couple of hundred or so, has been relatively small; but their prominent position as the civic, religious or intellectual leaders of Palestinian society, made up for the small number. 'Non-cooperation'—a form of protest authorized by the Geneva Conventions—brought the expulsion of those who led it. It was a cheap and effective policy leaving no middle ground between resigned acceptance of Israeli rule or the total opposition of armed resistance. Ruhi Khatib, the Mayor of Jordanian Jerusalem, who opposed the illegal annexation of his city, and Shaikh Abdul Hamid Sayigh, head of the Supreme Moslem Council, who opposed the blatant interference in self-governing religious institutions, were two leading citizens who suffered this fate. Surreptitious deportation, by contrast, befell thousands of ordinary Palestinians. There developed a familiar sequence of which deportation would be the final stage. A bomb might go off near a man's house or land; he would be arrested in the curfew, search or campaign of intimidation that ensued; in prison he would be beaten up or tortured, but, manifestly innocent, or yielding no worthwhile information, he would be despatched across the Jordan. Thus deportation came as a kind of escape—provided the deportee survived this last and most hazardous stage in the sequence. Here is how one deportee concluded his story:

> They took us out of prison to the King Hussein Bridge. They made us sign some blank papers, hit us and said: 'get out of here to the East Bank'. Then they started shooting at us, and we made for the East Bank as fast as we could. As soon as I had crossed the bridge I fell into

> a faint, and when I came to myself some time later I saw the face of a public security soldier looking down at me. When I saw him I thought my time had come, for I didn't realize that I was in Arab territory, and I said: 'Don't kill me, sir.' He replied: 'Don't be frightened; I'm an Arab like you.'[107]

It was not enough, of course, to break the spirit of the Arabs within the frontiers of Greater Israel. They had to be cowed, along with the countries that gave them refuge, beyond those frontiers too. Palestinians, 'insiders' or 'outsiders', had to be kept down at all costs. So beyond the occupied territories, where the outsiders, recruited to the ranks of the guerilla movement, carried on the struggle, lay the Israelis' 'free-fire zones', those areas where, like the Americans in Vietnam, they deployed all their modern know-how, all their sophisticated weaponry, to pulverize an opposition which, in skill and fire power, was still rudimentary in comparison. Here the concept of 'neighbourhood punishment' took on an altogether more murderous form. For the Israelis directed their artillery and their all-conquering air-force not only against the guerillas themselves, but against the refugee camps which spawned them, the villages in whose vicinity they operated and the vital economic installations of the countries which, willy-nilly, backed them. They threw a *cordon sanitaire* of devastation round their new perimeter. And, in addition to the Palestinian refugees, they created Syrian, Jordanian, Egyptian and Lebanese refugees too.

It was during the 1967 War itself that the Israelis drove more than 100,000 Syrians from the Golan Heights—they have joined Palestinians in refugee camps near Damascus—and razed the towns and villages they left behind. After the war, they made periodic air raids over Syria. When Palestinian terrorists killed eleven Israeli athletes at the Munich Olympics of 1972, Syria bore the brunt of Israel's eye-for-eye reprisals. It was, of course, more like twenty eyes for one. For at least 200 people,[108] many of them women and children, and possibly as many as 500,[109] died in simultaneous air attacks on nine separate targets. The Phantoms and Skyhawks swooped on the suburban Damascus resort of al-Hama; the bombs fell indiscriminately on Palestinians in their hillside dwellings and on Syrians, in their cars or strolling by the river Barada on their weekend outing. Survivors recounted how they were machine-gunned as they ran for cover.[110]

Jordan took heavy punishment, for there the Palestinian guerillas, who emerged in strength after the defeat of the regular Arab armies, were at their most active. King Hussein had done his best to thwart them, just as he had tried to stop 'infiltrators' of the earlier post-1948 vintage. But he could not cope. So the Israelis did it for him in their own uninhibited way. Thus one afternoon in November 1967, as children from the Karameh refugee camp down in the Jordan Valley were coming out of school, they were caught in the splintering fire of Israeli mortars. 'Right down the main street, hitting the police post, the ration centre, the girls' school, came heavyweight high-fragmentation anti-personnel bombs. Western military attachés attest to this and to the scientific accuracy of the attack.'[111] Some miles up the river a Jordanian army post had given covering fire for returning guerillas. The Israelis knew that for every one given cover several others were prevented from crossing at all; but it was not good enough, and the children died as punishment for this failure. The Israelis went on to devastate frontier towns like North Shuneh with air and artillery bombardments; they shelled Jordan's second city of Irbid. Many more civilians died. Favourite among their economic targets was the East Ghor Canal, the newly constructed waterway, serving 80,000 farmers in the Jordan Valley, which has done so much for Jordanian agriculture. They knocked it out, and no sooner was it repaired than they knocked it out again. The bananas died off, and the fruit trees began to wither away. Snipers took random potshots at labourers driving tractors or harvesters too close to the river or surreptitiously trying to water their groves. Some 70,000 Jordanians took refuge in the hills.

On their Western front, the Israelis countered the Egyptian 'war of attrition' with massive retribution. They reduced the Canal Zone cities—Port Said, Suez and Ismailia—to a ghostly shambles, blitzed and rubble-strewn. Hundreds of civilians died, before they were almost all evacuated, a million of them, and absorbed at great economic and social cost into the teeming cities of the Delta. The canal silted up, and the longer it remained closed the less chance it was to have, with the coming of the supertanker, of regaining its old glory.

In early 1970, with their newly acquired Phantom bombers, the Israelis reached out beyond the canal to strike at the Egyptian heartland; seventy workers died in a direct hit on a scrap-metal plant at Abu Zaabal twelve miles north of Cairo. According to General Dayan, there had been a 'technical error'. A few weeks later, forty-six children died in a primary school at Bahr al-Baqr. This time the Phantoms had hit only 'military targets'.

As for Lebanon, least warlike of countries, Dayan warned in 1970 that if it failed to stop guerilla operations from its territory the same destruction that befell towns along the Suez Canal and the East Bank of the River Jordan would also befall the other side of the Lebanese border. Sure enough, in the month that followed, some 50,000 inhabitants of southern towns and villages fled northward as Dayan's soldiers began to put his threat into practice. Many ventured back, in periods of calm, only to flee again at the next raid. The Israelis went deeper into Lebanon than any other country. For what resistance could this little country, dedicated to money-making and the good life, offer? It was against Lebanon that the Israelis mounted one of those spectacular *tours de force* for which, in a Western world still fascinated by the bizarre and heroic exploits of two world wars, they are not surprisingly famous. In December 1968 two Palestinians, one of whom (like 300,000 others) happened to live in Lebanon, machine-gunned an Israeli Boeing 707 at Athens airport, killing a marine engineer; two nights later helicopter-borne Israeli commandos landed at Beirut airport and coolly, clinically, in the sure knowledge that the Lebanese would not resist, blew up thirteen passenger jets worth about £11 million.

The military parade marking Israel's twenty-fifth anniversary on 15 May 1973 was the most grandiose ever staged. A few weeks before it Dayan opened his heart to an assembly of parachuters: 'Until very recently, I was not sure of it, but now it seems to me that we are nearing the apogee of the return to Zion.'[112] Israeli leaders imbued their people with an extraordinary sense of power and achievement. Resistance in the occupied territories was at its lowest ebb. Calm reigned along the frontiers. Peace was assured for another decade, or even a generation. No one should take President Sadat's threats seriously. He surely was not mad enough to attempt the impossible, a crossing of the Suez Canal which, fortified by the Bar Lev line, was the 'best line of defence any King or president has ever had in the history of the Jewish people'. At all events, if he did, the Egyptians 'would take such a trouncing, inside Egypt proper, in their own homes, that the Six-Day War would seem like an agreeable memory in comparison'. Those were the words of General Ezer Weizmann, former airforce commander.[113] Soldiers and politicians vied with one another in eulogies of Israel's might and invincibility. Dayan said that for Egypt another war would be 'suicide'.[114] As for General Sharon, it was his opinion that it would entail Egypt's 'final destruction'. This was because Israel was 'today a power equal to France and Great Britain'; he did not think there was 'any military or civilian objective between Baghdad and Khartoum, including Libyan territory, which the Israeli army cannot conquer'.[115] The jokes people told exuded the same boundless arrogance. 'What does the Israeli army need to occupy Damascus, Moscow and Vladivostok?' 'To receive the order.' Generals Dayan and Elazar, very bored, are having their morning coffee. 'There is nothing to do,' said Dayan, with a sigh. 'How about invading another Arab country?' asked Elazar. 'What do you think?' 'Oh! that's no good', Dayan replied, 'what would we do in the afternoon?'[116]

Rare were the voices raised against this self-deluding folly and those that were went unheeded. Arie Eliav, deputy, writer and well-known 'dove', summed it up in a brief allegory. A ship is sailing on a perfectly calm sea; the captain and his officers are on the bridge, drunk with glory, bursting with self-confidence. Overhead a gull is circling. It sees the reef on which the ship is bearing down. It careers about, alights on the bridge, uttering ceaseless, piercing cries in an attempt to warn the men of the danger that faces them. But 'its language is not their language, its eyes not theirs, its horizon not theirs'. The night falls, the ship's passengers prepare for the great banquet to be held that evening, while the gull, impotent, continues to sound its incomprehensible cries of alarm.[117]

Davar, the newspaper for which the allegory was written, declined to publish it.

NOTES

1. Love, *Suez: The Twice-Fought War*, *op. cit.*, p. 677.
2. Burns, *Between Arab and Israeli*, *op. cit.*, p. 290.
3. *Ibid.*, p. 283.
4. *The Other Israel*, *op. cit.*, p. 74.
5. *Ibid.*, p. 74.
6. See Jansen, Godfrey, 'New Light on the 1967 War', *Daily Star*, Beirut, 15, 22, 26 November 1973.
7. 29 May 1967.
8. Kirk, George E., 'The Middle East 1945–1950', *Survey of International Affairs, 1939–1946*, Oxford University Press, 1954, p. 29.
9. Aide-memoire handed to Israeli ambassador Abba Eban by Secretary of State Foster Dulles, 11 February 1957.
10. Toynbee, Philip, *The Times*, 8 June 1967.
11. Kapeliouk, Amnon, *Le Monde*, 3 June 1972.
12. Vance, Vick, and Lauer, Pierre, *Hussein de Jordanie: Ma Guerre avec Israel*, Editions Albin Michel, Paris, 1968, p. 85.
13. *Maariv*, 24 March 1972.
14. *Le Monde*, 29 February 1968.
15. Report by Colonel de Ridder, Acting Chief of Staff, UN Document S/2084, 10 April 1951.
16. Horn, *Soldiering for Peace*, *op. cit.*, pp. 123–4.
17. Burns, *op. cit.*, p. 114.
18. Horn, *op. cit.*, p. 79.
19. Khouri, Fred. J., 'The Policy of Retaliations in Arab-Israeli Relations', *Middle East Journal*, Washington, Vol. 20, No. 4, 1966. p. 447.
20. Burns, *op. cit.*, p. 113.
21. Horn, *op. cit.*, p. 78.
22. *Ibid.*, p. 117.
23. Hutchison, *Violent Truce*, *op. cit.*, p. 110.
24. Horn, *op. cit.*, p. 69.
25. Syrian Complaint to Security Council, S/7845, 9 April 1967.
26. 2 May 1965.
27. Nimrod, Yoram, 'L'Eau, l'Atome et le Conflit', *Les Temps Modernes*, Paris, 1967, p. 893.
28. *Al-Ahram*, 1 June 1965.
29. *Ot* (Israeli weekly), 1 June 1972.
30. See *Daily Star*, Beirut, 15, 22 and 26 November 1973.
31. Laqueur, Walter, *The Road to War*, Weidenfeld and Nicolson, London, 1968, p. 75.
32. Jansen, *op. cit.*
33. *Ibid.*
34. *Ibid.*
35. See p. 208.
36. *Jerusalem Post*, 16 June 1967.
37. *Daily Telegraph*, 12 June 1967.

38. Vidal-Naquet, P., *Le Monde*, 11–12 June 1967.
39. Menuhin, *The Decadence of Judaism in Our Time*, *op. cit.*, p. 500.
40. *Noam* (annual publication of Jewish religious law), 1968, pp. 183–4.
41. Begin, Tel Aviv, 16 June 1967.
42. *Publications of the Israeli Ministry of Defence*, No. 204, January 1970, p. 23.
43. *Haaretz*, 4 April 1969.
44. *Ha'olam Hazeh*, 8 July 1968.
45. *Maariv*, 19 June 1968.
46. *Maariv*, 30 April 1968.
47. *Le Monde*, 6–7 July 1969.
48. Kapeliouk, Amnon, *Israel: La Fin Des Mythes*, Editions Albin Michel, Paris, 1975, pp. 28, 183–222.
49. *Jerusalem Post*, 13 July 1967.
50. Zeev Sharif, Housing Minister, *Time*, 1 March 1971.
51. *Lui*, Paris, March 1972.
52. Yigal Allon, *al-Quds*, Jerusalem, 13 April 1972.
53. See p. 65.
54. *Lés Cahiers du Témoignage Chrétien*, 5 October 1967, p. 47.
55. *Israel Imperial News*, London, March, 1968.
56. *Les Cahiers du Témoignage Chrétien*, *op. cit.*, p. 27.
57. *Ibid.*, p. 20.
58. *Ibid.*, p. 41.
59. March 1968.
60. *Maariv*, 8 February 1972.
61. UN, *Report to the General Assembly by the United Nations Special Committee on Palestine*, 31 August 1947, Chapt. VI, Part II, Justification 5.
62. Khatib, Ruhi, *The Judaization of Jerusalem*, Amman, 1971, p. 13.
63. Khalidi, Walid, Speech in the UN General Assembly, Doc. A/PV 1553, July 14 1967.
64. Khatib, *op. cit.*, p. 13.
65. *The Guardian*, 26 April 1972.
66. Israel Radio, 1 July 1971.
67. Khatib, Ruhi, *Jerusalem-Israeli Annexation*, Amman, 1968, p. 7.
68. *Al-Hamishmar*, 7 April 1971.
69. *Bulletin of the Institute for Palestine Studies* (Arabic), Beirut, Supplement, 1 June 1972.
70. *Maariv*, 23 March 1971.
71. Khatib, *The Judaization of Jerusalem*, *op. cit.*, p. 78.
72. Ryan, Joseph (Archbishop of Anchorage), 'Some Thoughts on Jerusalem', *The Link*, New York, September-October 1972.
73. *Ibid.*
74. Jiryis, *The Arabs in Israel*, *op. cit.*, pp. 151–5.
75. 31 October 1969.
76. *Jerusalem Post*, 13 April 1973.
77. *Haaretz*, 23 October 1969.
78. *The Guardian*, 28 December 1969.

79. Kapeliouk, *op. cit.*, p. 24.
80. Jiryis, 'Recent Knesset Legislation and the Arabs in Israel', *op. cit.*, p. 66.
81. See Ryan, Sheila, 'Israeli Economic Policy in the Occupied Areas: Foundations of a New Imperialism', *MERIP Reports*, No. 24, January 1974.
82. 15 May 1969.
83. *Davar*, 8 November 1972.
84. *Maariv*, 2 February 1973.
85. *Middle East International*, London, December 1972, p. 22.
86. See p. 26.
87. *Haaretz*, 13 December 1974.
88. *Middle East International*, *op. cit.*, p. 22.
89. *Maariv*, 17 April 1969.
90. Kapeliouk, *op. cit.*, p. 31.
91. *Yediot Aharonot*, 29 September 1972.
92. *Daily Telegraph*, 31 October 1972.
93. *Al-Ittihad*, Haifa, 30 April 1973.
94. Ryan, Sheila, *op. cit.*
95. *Al-Ittihad*, 30 April 1973.
96. Ithaca Press, London, 1975.
97. *Israel's Violations of Human Rights in the Occupied Territories*, Institute for Palestine Studies, Beirut, 1970, p. 147.
98. Statement by the Israeli League for Human and Civil Rights, 23 January 1971.
99. *The Guardian*, 26 January 1968; *The Observer*, 28 January 1968; Ben-Yosa, Amitay, *Arab American University Graduate Bulletin* No. 2, *op. cit.*
100. Reuters, 25 September 1969.
101. Agency reports, 18 December 1967.
102. *Israeli League*, *op. cit.*
103. *Sunday Times*, 23 November 1969.
104. *Ha'olam Hazeh*, No. 54, April 1969.
105. *Haaretz*, 12 February 1970; Ben-Yosa, Amitay, *op. cit.*
106. Israel Radio Broadcast, cited by *al-Ittihad*, 31 October 1969.
107. *Israel's Violation of Human Rights in the Occupied Territories*, Institute for Palestine Studies, Beirut, April 1970.
108. *L'Orient Le Jour*, 10 September 1972.
109. *Al-Nahar Arab Report*, 18 September 1972.
110. *Daily Star*, Beirut, 10 September 1972.
111. *The Economist*, 9 September 1967.
112. *Maariv*, 30 March 1973.
113. *Maariv*, 5 June 1973.
114. *Al Hamishmar*, 10 May 1973.
115. *Maariv*, 20 July 1973; *Haaretz*, 20 September 1973.
116. Kapeliouk, *op. cit.*, p. 68.
117. *Ibid.*, p. 49.

8 · THE ARAB ZIONISTS

The Earthquake, October 1973

'We shall turn your days into nights and show you the stars at high noon. We shall put your faces and noses in the mud. We shall make the enemy leaders pay dearly for this. We shall break your bones.'

In its bellicose hyperbole it sounded just like those Arab radio commentators who, in June 1967, had the Arab armies bearing down on Tel Aviv when in reality they were falling back in utter confusion before an enemy already assured of victory. It was actually an Arabic broadcast on Israeli radio in the early days of the Arab-Israeli war of October 1973.[1] 'Break their bones' was what General David Elazar, the Chief of Staff, pledged himself to do in a press conference on the third day of the war. The press took up the theme. Under the title 'Breaking Them', an editor of *Maariv* wrote: 'Our counter attack must be so fierce, so crushing, so pitiless and cruel that it causes a veritable national trauma in the collective consciousness of the Arabs; their Yom Kippur adventure must cost the Arabs so dear that the mere thought of a new adventure makes them tremble with fear. . . . We must strike a blow that exceeds all reason, so that the Arab people's instinct of self-preservation makes them accept Israel.'[2] These were violent reactions, but one could hardly expect less from a leadership which, over the past six years, had demonstrated such an overweening confidence in its own omnipotence. It was also what most of the Israeli public, who trusted their leaders, expected to hear. The Arabs had asked for it. Apparently even now they had not learned the lesson which three 'big wars' and countless little ones should have taught them. Here were two Arab countries—Egypt and Syria—mounting an all-out surprise attack, a fullscale *blitzkrieg* in the Israeli manner, and, as if to add sacrilege to brazen folly, they were doing it on the holiest day in the Jewish year.

At first, the Israelis really were persuaded that this was just a variant on 1967. On Tuesday, four days after the war began, the *Jerusalem Post* titled a report from the northern front: 'Golan Troops Hope to be Home for Sabbath'. Cartoons were similarly optimistic; one showed President Sadat rushing frantically back to the other side of the Suez Canal, shedding his shoes on the way. But as the struggle wore on, the commanders began to murmur that this was no 'express war', that no 'early and elegant victory' could be expected.[3] In the end, it was three weeks before the Israelis really got the upper hand, drove the Syrians back beyond the 1967 ceasefire lines and, crossing the Suez Canal into 'Africa', threatened Egypt's encircled Third Army with destruction. But still they had scored nothing like the kind of overwhelming victory to which they had grown accustomed. This in itself was a grievous setback to their whole security philosophy. The Arabs had not merely dared to challenge their 'invincibility' —that was bad enough—but, in breaking through the Bar Lev line, they had dealt it a shattering blow, along with the whole gamut of cocksure assumptions on which it was based. The October War was like an earthquake; it marked a fundamental shift, at Israel's expense, in the Middle East balance of power. For the first time in the history of Zionism, the Arabs had attempted, and partially succeeded in imposing a *fait accompli* by force of arms. The setback was not just military; it affected all those factors, psychological, ideological, diplomatic and economic, which make up the strength and vigour of a nation. The Israelis had paid a heavy price for merely holding their attackers to an inconclusive draw. In three weeks, according to the official count, they lost 2,523 men, two and a half times as many, proportionally speaking, as the Americans lost in the ten years of the Vietnam war. Earlier wars had produced a flood of glossy albums commemorating the victory; the first book to appear this time was entitled *Hamahdal* ('The Shortcoming'). In 1967 the Israeli generals, comrades all, lectured an admiring public on their various campaigns. Hardly had the 1973 War begun than they were exchanging accusations and the most vicious insults in the local and international press; later, bereaved mothers and wives were to greet the fallen idol, Moshe Dayan, with cries of 'assassin'. Earlier wars had been followed, on Independence Day, by grandiose military parades and the display of enemy booty; there was none this time. On the contrary, the Israelis were soon to learn that a big exhibition of captured hardware had opened in Cairo. For the first time, too, the Israelis witnessed the humiliating spectacle of Israeli prisoners, heads bowed, paraded on Arab television.

Whereas the 1967 War had reinvigorated Israel's flagging economy, this time it nearly broke it. 'We, our children, our grandchildren and our great grandchildren will have to pay for this war,' lamented the Minister of Finance,[4] and his forecast was followed by a series of savage austerity measures, drastically reducing living standards, which made an ominous contrast with the soaring revenues of the oil-rich Arabs. Israel's economic dependence on the United States, now financing it to the tune of $2,500 million a year, was complete. Its diplomatic isolation, again with America as its only real friend, was frightening too. Contrary to Israeli expectations, the Arabs really had made the oil weapon work; they had quickly discovered that when they reinforced their moral and political arguments with material threats the industrial nations of Europe and Japan lent them an altogether more sympathetic ear.

Most disturbing of all, however, the war generated deep, and no doubt enduring, anxieties about the whole future of Zionism and the Jewish State. It was mainly the young, especially the returning soldiers, who publicly aired their forebodings. Does this country really have a future, they asked? Must Israel be our only choice? Zionism was supposed to secure the existence of the Jewish people in its own homeland, but is not the existence of Jews living in Israel, literally and physically, in greater danger than anywhere else in the world? After the ceasefire a soldier wrote to *Haaretz*:

> I celebrated my birthday in the Sinai desert, alone, underground. . . . I thought of the three sons whom I am struggling to bring up—for future wars—of my wife racked by anxiety, of my deserted office . . . my head span with the wildest thoughts. Thought number one: When will this end? Thought number two: Why? Why has this happened? Thought number three: Could this not have been prevented, *at any price*? I am trying to fathom the thoughts of all those propagandists, those bleak pessimists for

> whom—what tragic purblindness—the force of arms was the only thing that counted. Why don't *they* try to fathom the thoughts of the enemy? Why can't they understand that he was pushed into battle, into the slaughter-house, because that was his only way out, because he had no other choice . . .? What have we seriously done, on our side, to exorcise murderous intentions from the minds of our adversaries during the six years that have passed since their terrible and shameful rout in the Six-Day War?[5]

A university professor went back much farther than that:

> The mistake was not made in the past six years, but in the last twenty-five, ever since the signing of the Rhodes Agreements. The guideline of our policy has always been the idea that a permanent situation of no peace and of a latent war is the best situation for us, and that it must be maintained at all costs. . . . As regards foreign and security policy, this has been that we are becoming stronger year by year in a situation of impending conflict where it is possible that actual fighting may break out from time to time. Such wars will usually be short and the results guaranteed in advance, since the gap between us and the Arabs is increasing. In this way we shall move on from occupation to further occupation. As its authors anticipated, this criminally mischievous policy has prevailed for twenty-five years. It has led us into the crisis we are living through today now that all the assumptions of that policy have collapsed. . . . We have not been seeking peace for twenty-five years—all declarations to that effect have been no more than coloured statements or deliberate lies. There is of course no assurance that we could have made peace with the Arabs if we had wanted to. However, it has to be heavily emphasized that we have not only made no attempts to seek peace, but have deliberately and with premeditation, sabotaged every possibility of doing so.[6]

Opinions of this kind worried the leadership. The Ministry of Education concluded that it was necessary 'to deepen patriotic consciousness' in schools.[7] But they remained the opinions of a minority. The majority, where they did not veer towards Menachim Begin and his Revisionist extremism, took refuge in the hoary old Zionist slogan of *Ein Brera*, 'No Choice'. Golda Meir, the Prime Minister, was characteristically unrepentant: 'We have done everything to avoid war. It is with a clear conscience that I can say that we neglected no opportunity for peace.'[8] When an official committee of inquiry was set up under popular pressure it was only empowered to look into 'shortcomings' in the actual conduct of the war. What the apprehensions of a thoughtful few should have prompted was precisely that which the government avoided: a look into the real, the *political*, short-comings that caused the war in the first place. But that would have been too much to expect. For to ask what 'pushed the enemy into battle' would have been to probe deeply into Israel's past, beyond the Six-Day War, beyond even the Rhodes Agreement, and to raise those moral issues which a small minority of Zionists have grappled with since Herzl's day, but which the majority, like Golda Meir, have simply thrust into a presumably guilty subconscious. To pose truly relevant questions about what drove the Egyptians and the Syrians, whose countries remain essentially intact, leads inexorably to another, and far more difficult question: what drives the Palestinians, who have lost everything they possess?

'No Such Things as Palestinians'

The October War was not the Palestinians' war. Their military organizations—the *fedayeen* or the Palestine Liberation Army—played only a very minor, if enthusiastic, part in it. It was to be followed, however, by the most remarkable upsurge in the Palestinians' fortunes since they were driven from their homes in the Catastrophe of 1948.

As we have seen,[9] the Israelis did everything they could, after 1948, to suppress a Palestinian sense of identity, to eradicate any ideas of Palestinian irredentism. They oppressed their own Palestinian citizens, the 'insiders' who had stayed behind, and, through their policy of reprisals, they intimidated the 'outsiders' who had taken refuge in neighbouring Arab states.

The thinking behind this strategy was quite simply that the Palestinians would eventually cease to exist. That is to say, the armistice agreements would eventually be superseded by a final settlement in which the Palestinians as a people—enjoying the attributes, historical, cultural and territorial, of peoplehood—could have no place.

For another people had taken that place. Over the years the Israelis won increasing international support for such a settlement. Everything hinged on the question of the Palestinian refugees. Their return would mean their reconstitution as a people, their resettlement elsewhere, their disappearance as a people. The history of the refugee problem, as inscribed in the annals of the UN, is an eloquent yardstick of Israel's fortunes. As we have seen,[10] Count Bernadotte, the murdered UN Mediator who was the first to come to grips with the problem, had no doubts about its proper solution. It lay in the refugees' unconditional right to return. That was a necessary part of 'any reasonable settlement', and he was persuaded that, given 'firm political decisions' from the UN, both sides would 'acquiesce' in it.[11] But there were to be no such firm decisions. After his assassination, the UN debated his proposals; during the debate, that same American-led coalition which had railroaded Partition through a reluctant Assembly a year before again went into battle on Israel's behalf. True, it was decreed—in Resolution No. 194 (III) of 11 December 1948—that 'the refugees wishing to return to their homes and live at peace with their neighbours should be permitted to do so at the earliest practicable date'. But, compared with what Bernadotte had sought, the resolution was weak and imprecise; its enforcement was made contingent upon Israel's goodwill; and it failed to specify by what agency the refugees would return.

Ineffectual though the resolution was, Israel did, at least to begin with, pay lip-service to it. Expediency required this. As a creation of the UN, the only one of its kind, Israel, by definition, was not sovereign in the sense that the United States, Britain or Egypt is sovereign. Certain limitations on its sovereignty were built into the very charter of its existence. When pressed, it formally acknowledged this. Only after the new State—in the person of Abba Eban, its UN representative—had in effect recognized the built-in obligations of its right to exist did it win admittance, hitherto denied, to the world body. Asked whether, upon admission, it would cooperate with the General Assembly in settling such outstanding problems as the refugees or whether, on the contrary, it would invoke that article of the UN Charter which deals with sovereign rights of independent states, Eban said that it would cooperate with the Assembly. 'My own feeling,' he went on, 'is that it would be a mistake for any of the governments concerned to take refuge, with regard to the refugee problem, in their legal right to exclude people from their territories.'[12] Summing up the debate, the Cuban representative said that Israel had given an assurance that it would regard the refugee problem as falling outside its domestic jurisdiction.

But the lip-service did not last a UN session longer than necessary. The reaffirmation of Resolution 194 became one of the hardiest of General Assembly perennials. Every year it came round, it left Israel unmoved—and jealously guarding its 'sovereignty' and 'domestic jurisdiction'. From the outset, the United States and other Western powers were hardly more respectful of Resolution 194 than Israel itself. They strove diligently to secure the integration of the refugees in their host countries. Throughout the fifties and early sixties mission after fruitless mission visited the Middle East and put forward schemes which, however diverse in some respects, all had one underlying assumption in common. This was that given the necessary material inducements—compensation, financial aid and regional development projects—the refugees could be prevailed upon to accept resettlement outside the Palestine they considered their own. In 1952, Israel achieved another important success at the UN. The 'Palestine Question'—as it had hitherto been formally inscribed on the General Assembly agenda—was downgraded into the 'Annual Report of the Commissioner-General of the United Nations Relief and Works Agency (UNRWA)'. The 'Palestine Question' lasted longer in the Security Council; everything relating to the Arab-Israeli conflict continued to be discussed under that heading. It was only in the wake of the 1967 War, the last and most spectacular of Zionism's great break-throughs, that Israel gave the *coup de grâce* to the 'Palestine Question' there too; it thereafter became the 'Middle East Situation'. The famous British-sponsored Security Council Resolution 242 of November 1967, holy writ for the peacemakers, was in keeping with this change, reducing the 'Palestine Question' to the achieving of 'a just settlement of the refugee problem'.[13]

The extinction of the Palestinians was by now almost complete. So, at least, it seemed to an Israeli leadership intoxicated by their own triumphs. The Palestinians, some of them now asserted, never *had* existed. In 1969, Prime Minister Golda Meir actually said it in those very words. 'It was not as though there was a Palestinian people and in Palestine considering itself as a Palestinian people and we came and threw them out and took their country away from them. They did not exist.'[14] Her predecessor, Levi Eshkol, though generally regarded as a moderate, was hardly less contemptuous: 'What are Palestinians? When I came here there were 250,000 non-Jews, mainly Arabs and bedouins.'[15] Prime ministers can make impetuous, ill-judged remarks like anyone else, but these extraordinary pronouncements were far from that. They reflected the congenital Zionist need to rewrite history; they were of a piece with the guidelines which a Minister of Education, in all seriousness, could lay down for the benefit of Israeli schoolteachers: 'It is important that our youth should know that when we returned to this country we did not find any other nation here and certainly no nation which had lived here for hundreds of years. Such Arabs as we did find here arrived only a few decades before us in the 1830s and 1840s as refugees from the oppression of Muhammad Ali in Egypt.'[16]

The Vision of The Return

The Palestinians were not extinct, of course, and the Meir-Eshkol pronouncements, in their very purblind extremism, no doubt disguised an anxious awareness of the fact—the ironic fact —that just as Zionism was reaching the zenith of its power and self-esteem it was beginning to be threatened by a Zionism in reverse. It had been a long time in gestation. But it was always foreseeable. No sooner had they left Palestine than the Palestinians resolved that they would return. That is why American-sponsored efforts to resettle the refugees were so fruitless. It is sometimes said that the mystique of The Return was artificially inculcated and sustained by unscrupulous politicians, that the refugee camps were deliberately perpetuated as hotbeds of hatred for Israel. It may be true that the Palestinians have suffered more than most people from unscrupulous politicians, their own included; but even if it is, the corollary—that, left to themselves, the ordinary people would have abandoned hopes of return—is not. It can just as well be argued that, if anything, the politicians, in exploiting The Return, debased and weakened it in the minds of the people. What was true of the Palestinian cause before the Catastrophe was equally true after it: its essential impetus came from the people, not from the politicians.

The Catastrophe left nearly a million Palestinians leaderless, fragmented, prostrate. For most of them, in those desperate first months of exile, their immediate concern was to keep body and soul together. Those with means and skills, mainly the urban middle classes, tried to rebuild their lives wherever they could. The destitute majority, mainly peasants, remained more or less where they had fetched up in their panic flight from Palestine; they were herded into the camps which—set up under UN auspices, in Lebanon, Syria, Jordan and Gaza—hugged the perimeter of the new-born State. The Palestinians had not, and in such circumstances could not have, a collective will of their own. Not surprisingly, the politics of exile were at first negative in character. Most of the refugees had fled their homes in the belief that, the fighting over, they would soon go back to them. Faced with the obduracy of a victorious Israel, they evolved a cantankerous counter-logic of their own. All right, they said, perhaps we cannot go home now, but let no one get the idea that we shall accept another. This did not mean that they elected to stay in the camps when employment and a better life presented themselves—which they did for about 20 per cent of Palestinian society.[17] But it did mean fierce opposition to schemes that were transparently promoted in Israel's interests; the 'Organization for Shattering Refugee Settlement Programmes' was a typical product of this era. It also meant opposition of a more irrational kind. Suspicious to the point of paranoia, the refugees tended automatically to reject anything, however innocuous or desirable in itself, that smacked of permanent residence. At the slightest provocation they found themselves staging demonstrations against the alleviation of their own misery. As late as 1958 they might still be protesting, say, against the planting of trees which, they well knew, would have furnished a welcome shade against hot summer sun.

There quickly developed a whole mystique of The Return. The inmates of the camps, particularly, thought and spoke of little else.

They made it an obsession. Just how they would return was not at all clear in their minds. But of one thing they were sure; one thing was self-evident, not worthy of discussion; this was that they could only recover by force what had been taken by force. The Return dominated everything, but violence, a just and necessary violence, was an inevitable sub-theme. The Return shaped camp rituals and regalia; children were steeped in it from birth. Schools were decorated with pictures of Palestine and of 'martyrs' who had fallen in the struggle to preserve it. Classrooms or scout groups would be named after famous Palestinian towns. A much-displayed map of the lost homeland was framed in black; it was surmounted by pictures of mosques, and refugees in their camps; and right across the Negev desert there ran a bold caption 'Verily, We are Returning', with the words superimposed on a background of infantry, tanks and planes. The refugees' schoolday would begin with the children standing to attention and taking the oath:

> Palestine is our country,
> Our aim is to return
> Death does not frighten us,
> Palestine is ours,
> We shall never forget her.
> Another homeland we shall never accept!
> Our Palestine, witness, O God and History
> We Promise to shed our blood for you![18]

The Return suffused Palestinian poetry, of which there was a prolific output. Kemal Nasr, a Christian, justified in his own way the future violence of which, as the Palestinian Liberation Organization spokesman assassinated by the Israelis, he was later to be a 'martyr'.

> The refugees are ever kindling
> In their camps, in that world of darkness,
> The embers of revolt,
> Gathering force, for the return,
> They have lost their faith in the doctrine of love,
> Even here in this land of love and peace

Their stolen rights cry in their hearts,
Inflamed by misery and hunger.
Dismayed by the persistent throng,
The enemy spreads poison and hatred abroad:
'They are Communists', he says, 'Their hopes are false,
Let us kill their hopes to return!'

He explains his Christian reasoning for repudiating love and peace in a *Hymn of Hate*: 'I do so because of the present suffering of humanity in my native land.'

If Jesus could see it now,
He would preach 'jihad' with the sword!
The land in which he grew
Has given birth to a million slaves.
Why does not He revolt,
Settle this account, tooth for tooth and eye for eye?
In despite of all His teachings
The West's dagger is red with blood . . .
O apostle of forgiveness! In our misfortune
Neither forgiveness nor love avail!'[19]

The Return was a passionate ideal in its own right; but it was reinforced by something else. The Arab régimes vied with one another in their devotion to the Palestinian cause. The air waves reverberated with their militant rhetoric. Cairo's Voice of the Arabs began its daily Palestinian programme with the song 'We Are Returning'. But the régimes' actions did not live up to their words. Indeed, the Palestinians were often made to feel despised and unwanted in lands which called them brothers. In his book *The Disinherited*, Fawaz Turki describes what it was like to grow up in a refugee camp on the outskirts of Beirut:

The irony of my plight was that as I grew up my bogeyman was not the Jew (despite the incessant propaganda that Cairo radio subjected us to), nor was he the Zionist (if indeed I recognized the distinction), nor was he for that matter the imperialist or the Western supporters and

> protectors of the state of Israel, but he was the Arab. The Arab in the street who asked you if you'd ever heard the one about the Palestinian who. . . . The Arab at the Aliens' Section who wanted you to wait obsequiously for your work permit, the Arab at the police station who felt he possessed a carte blanche to mistreat you, the Arab who rejected you and, most crucially, took away from you your sense of hope and sense of direction. He was the bogeyman you saw every morning and every night and every new year of every decade tormenting you, reducing you, dehumanizing you, and confirming your servitude. To the Palestinian, the young Palestinian, living and growing up in Arab society, the Israeli was the enemy in the mathematical matrix; we never saw him, lived under his yoke, or, for many of us, remembered him. Living in a refugee camp and going hungry, we felt that the causes of our problem were abstract, the causes of its perpetuation were real.[20]

The squalid new tensions of exile exacerbated an old rancour, the feeling that the Arab governments, in their bungling incompetence and hypocrisy, had been largely responsible for that exile in the first place. As the poet said about the League of Arab States:

> On foreign lands they fell
> Like stars, my brethren the refugees.
> Would that they had stayed in the battlefield
> In Palestine, unaided, for their strife.
> Had they borne their own burden,
> Disbelieved in the League of Shadows,
> They would have attained glory
> With their swords, under their own banners . . .[21]

In that first decade or more of exile, The Return found no more purposeful expression than the masochistic obstructionism of the camp-dwellers, solemn rituals and poetic fancy. It had precious little political, let alone military, substance. The troubadours of The Return sounded hopelessly unrealistic; they were flying in the face of the facts. Yet were they really? At least, were they any more unrealistic than the Zionists themselves when they began to propagate their ideas in the face of some very hard facts indeed? That was the question which the Palestinian scholar, A. L. Tibawi, asked in 1963, when, examining the growing literature of The Return, he concluded that such feelings were no less intense than those of the Psalmist: 'Should I forget thee, O Jerusalem. . . .'[22] It was after all from such powerful emotions, seemingly visionary at first, that great upheavals spring. For Tibawi, an Arab Zionism was now in the making.

The Rise of *Fatah*

No one paid much attention to an obscure, crudely produced magazine, published monthly in Beirut, which began to find its way around the Arab world in late 1959. *Our Palestine* always addressed its readers as 'The Children of the Catastrophe'. Consisting of some thirty pages, it carried no advertising, so small was its circulation. Its contents—editorials, articles, reports, poems, letters and slogans—were exclusively devoted to Palestinian affairs. Only in the middle of 1964 did the Israelis realize that, behind this mysterious publication, was much more than met the eye.[23]

Our Palestine—or, to give it its full title, *Our Palestine—the Call to Life*—was the mouthpiece of an organization which had set out to translate the dream of The Return into a reality. The organization was the Harakah al-Tahrir (al-Watani) al-Falastini, the Palestine (National) Liberation Movement; its initial letters in reverse gave the name which has now become a household word around the world: *Fatah*. It means 'Opening' or 'Conquest', but, as the title of the 48th Surah of the Koran, it is also resonant with deeper meanings to the Arabic ear. Every month *Fatah* contributed a column, 'Our Opinion', to the new publication. Though anonymous, it was usually written by Khalil al-Wazir, who, with Yasser Arafat, was one of the founder-members of the organization and who, to this day, remains one of the most elusive, but influential, of its leaders.

Our Palestine was the fruit of profound frustrations. Its language was angry, bitter, making up in impetuous uncouth vigour for what it lacked in sophistication. Its first aim—as its name indicated—was simply to 'call to life' the Palestinians, to restore their common identity and purpose. For, in effect, the Palestinians, if not dead, had been politically dormant since the Catastrophe. Ironically, they had found themselves further removed from their own struggle than other Arabs.

> Where are you, dispersed people . . . sons of the Catastrophe? Where? Are you just flotsam, just jetsam strewn around . . .? How do you live? What's become of you? Are you living with your kith and kin, or are you scattered far and wide? Have you grown rich, children of the Catastrophe, or are you still dragging out the years in the shadow of hunger and sickness? Sons of the Catastrophe, you cannot forget that terrible Catastrophe, having lived through it, whether you are rich and living a life of ease, or wretched in the camps. The loss of land and honour moulds you in the crucible of the Catastrophe. . . .[24]
>
> Our destiny is being shaped, but our voice is not heard. No one asks our opinion, no one cares if anyone of us is there. Has none of you asked why . . .? We tell you that our voice, the voice of the Palestinian people, will not be heard until the sons of Palestine stand together in one rank, the rank of 'life or death', solid and compact. Then you will find the world attentive to your merest whisper . . . yes, just a whisper.[25]

Never mind that they were 'the sons of the Catastrophe, provided that they become its destroyers'.[26] And that could only mean the complete recovery of Palestine—not partition, not resettlement, not emigration—but all of Palestine, 'one and Arab'.[27]

> There is one primordial, immutable reality: our fundamental desire is for the land, the land which was ours, whose loss we deem not merely material, but, above all else, a national dishonour, a badge of ignominy and shame. Our land is therefore our freedom, the land is our honour . . . the land—that is our right . . . that our wellbeing, that our peace. We made it what it was. If that goes, if that is taken from us, then everything goes, everything is taken from us, our very being, our humanity, our name. The quest of honour is to return to our usurped earth. Right—it is everything that hastens the disappearance of Israel: the good—the only good is that which leads to the collapse of the usurper state; and peace—peace is vengeance; vengeance against the butchers of Deir Yassin, the criminals of Qibya and Nahalin.
>
> Such is the psychological state in which we live, we the children of

> the Catastrophe; thus do we measure morals and ideals; in this scale do we weigh events. So strong have these feelings become that we only desire life insofar as life enables us to begin the battle for our land, our earth, our freedom and our dignity.[28]

The return of Palestine 'One and Arab' seemed to mean that its present inhabitants must leave. *Our Palestine* did not adopt a clear, authoritative position on this matter. It was so preoccupied with 'liberation' that it did not devote much thought to what might come after. But its various contributors just seemed to take the removal of the Jews for granted—that was the safe, unchallenged consensus; much of the time it was merely implicit—in such constantly recurring expressions as 'uprooting the Zionist entity' or 'destroying the Jewish presence'. But occasionally it became explicit. 'What shall we do with the Jews—two million Jewish usurpers? We shall say to them what Saladin said to the Crusaders. Go back to the lands you came from. Unless you can prove that you were in Palestine before the iniquitous Balfour Declaration of 1917, in which case you are our neighbours and brethren in the country, with your land and property. And then you are welcome, truly welcome. For the crime was not yours, not the work of your hands but of wicked Zionism and imperialism.'[29]

How was The Return to be accomplished? It was no good relying on others. Not on the world community which, year after year, passed pious resolutions upon which it did not act. The world's sympathy 'goes to revolutionaries more than it does to beggars'.[30]

> We cannot just sob and wail . . . we cannot just recite our woes and reiterate our complaints. We must gird ourselves—we alone—to solve our problem in our own way. We cannot just run to the United Nations, dominated by America and the imperialist states under its influence. We cannot rely on the world conscience as represented by the UN, which speaks for the hateful pair—Zionism and imperialism.[31]

Nor was it any good relying on the Arab states, which had:

> . . . contented themselves . . . with hysterical or anaesthetizing broadcasts and rousing speeches, the contents of which we all know in advance. . . .

> The Arab governments have stopped the Palestinians' mouths, tied their hands, deprived them of their freedom of action in what is left of their country, resisted the idea of their regroupment, turned them into a theatrical claque which applauds this and reviles that. . . .[32]
>
> You went with many parties, and fought for many causes . . . what was the result? Did you restore your honour? Or one inch of your land? Did any of the slogans relieve your distress? You remained scattered, without honour, or personal or collective identity. Let us raise the banner of our own unity, of revolution in Palestine, and put this aim above any other.[33]

In the first years of their diaspora, the Palestinians had, of course, relied very much on the Arab states. Lacking any organization of their own, they had given their main allegiance to a variety of Arab causes—left-wing, right-wing, Marxist, Moslem Brother—as an indirect means of promoting their own. This was a time of surging pan-Arabism, when the ideal of unity was still at its untarnished height, when 'regionalism'—the preserving of the artificial divisions in the Arab world—was held to be the outlook of reactionaries. Unity meant strength—strength to fight Israel. 'Unity', said a contemporary slogan, 'is the road to the liberation of Palestine.' President Nasser was the all-Arab champion upon whom these aspirations focused. Naturally, the Palestinians, without a 'region' they could call their own, were at first among the most fervent unionists of all. Nasser was their great hope too. Yet they were among the first to rebel against the Nasserist orthodoxy. A decade had passed, and their cause had advanced not an inch. Israel was consolidating its grip on Palestine; its population had passed the two million mark; Nasser had opened the Gulf of Aqaba to Israel shipping. Time was not on the Arabs' side; to believe so was a dangerous illusion. It was true that Arab governments had made gestures in the right direction. Both Syria and Iraq had incorporated special Palestinian units in their armed forces. In 1959 President Nasser had proposed that each host country encourage its Palestinian guests to establish a 'popular representative organization' which would be merged into a single body, the 'Palestine Entity', to be granted quasi-governmental status by the Arab League. Then, at a summit conference in January 1964, the Arab leaders agreed to set up a Palestinian Liberation Organization with the object of 'organizing the Palestinian people to enable them to carry out their role in liberating their homeland and determining their destiny'. But for the Palestinian activists all such gestures were suspect. For them the PLO was not what it proclaimed itself to be at all; on the contrary, it was designed by its creators, Nasser and leaders of other Arab régimes, as a means of restoring that 'tutelage' over the Palestinian cause which, as refugee impatience grew, they were in danger of losing.

Palestinians who rebelled against Nasserist orthodoxy were accused, even by some of their compatriots, of reverting to 'regionalist' heresies. But two events helped the heresies take root. One was the break-up in 1961 of the Egyptian-Syrian union; the other was the triumph in 1962 of the Algerian uprising against the French, a source of great inspiration for the Palestinians, who believed that they should do likewise without waiting upon the uncertain patronage of the Arab world. For *Our Palestine* the great shibboleths of unity and revolutionary change had become the pretexts for endless protraction and delay. It therefore reversed the slogans. They now became: 'Liberation of Palestine is the road to unity'; 'Through loyalty to my revolution, the Palestinian revolution, the revolution of the dispersed people, I shall free Palestine and unite my Arab nation.'[34] It scorned conventional political debate; it was neither right nor left; it had no official views on the ordering of society. That was a question to be tackled after 'liberation'. Till then the Palestinians' only concern was 'to be or not to be'.

Impatience with Arab tergivisation leapt from every page:

> The days pass; the conferences are held; the Arab military experts' conference, the Arab resources conference; the Arab Foreign Ministers' conference; the Arab Information Ministers' conference; the Jerusalem conference. But, for all that, the River Jordan is being diverted; the Negev is awaiting the coming of water, to be followed by Israel's third million of immigrants, and after that by its fourth million of usurping Jews. If we Palestinians take a look at ourselves, we find that we are going round in an empty circle of inter-Arab rivalries . . . the situation is reminiscent of the children's story Who Will Hang the Bell? It concerns a family of mice plagued by a cat. They took counsel among themselves how to get rid of the accursed cat. After a long

> discussion, they decided that they should put a bell around its neck, which would ring every time it moved. They would thus have warning of its approach and escape the danger. Their great problem, however, was who would hang the bell. And that is our problem too. The tragicomic thing is that we are thirteen cats represented in the Arab League, and not one of them comes forward to hang the bell on the Israeli mouse. Can this situation be allowed to endure . . .? No one will hang that bell but the Palestinian *fedayeen*. . . .[35]

Fedayeen—'the men who sacrificed themselves'. Armed violence. A popular liberation war. This was the only way. 'Our people, the people of the Catastrophe, know by instinct that Israel will not disappear by a natural disaster, not by persuasion, not by the decisions of Arab or international bodies, or vain and sterile politics.'[36] Indeed, Israel itself had taught the way. 'Israel says, "I am here by the sword." We must complete the saying—"and only by the sword shall Israel be driven out".'[37] In becoming *fedayeen*, the young men of this generation were merely proving themselves worthy of earlier ones:

> O heroes!
> Where are the revolutionaries of yesterday?
> Where are the companions of the *mujahideen*?
> Where the sons of Shaikh Qassam,
> The brethren of Abdul Qadir. . .?[38]

All that *Fatah* asked of the Arab governments was that they put no obstacles in the Palestinians' way—and that they throw a belt of defences around Israel's frontiers to guard against inevitable reprisals. But *Fatah* had little trust in the Arab governments, their willingness to fight, or their ability to win the kind of conventional war for which they were ostensibly preparing. It was therefore *Fatah*'s aim to draw the Arab peoples, rather than their governments, into the kind of 'popular liberation war' which they *could* win. It believed that *fedayeen* operations, of steadily increasing scale and intensity, conducted from bases inside and outside occupied territory, would win the backing of Arabs everywhere. The man in the street could not but take a simple black-and-white view of guerilla operations; he would regard it as patriotism to support them and treachery to oppose them—and judge his government accordingly. A 'supporting Arab front' would automatically spring into being; all patriots, including soldiers and government servants, would join it; so *Fatah* pledged itself not to raise arms against any Arab soldier or ruler, leaving it to the Arab peoples themselves to deal with anyone who stood in the way of armed revolution.

By 1964, Arafat and his men had gathered about themselves the nucleus of a guerilla organization. Partly for ideological reasons, but mainly in order to embarrass Nasser, the staunch opponent of military adventurism, Syria's radical Baathist régime agreed to give *Fatah* a secure base, and, in a small way, the operational support it needed to get going. The military strike force was backed by an embryonic network of collaborators and sympathizers that spanned the Palestinian diaspora. In the oil-rich shaikhdoms of the Persian Gulf, where Arafat had worked as an engineer, successful Palestinian businessmen were ready to devote some of their new wealth to the cause, or even to join it fulltime. In the more advanced and populous Arab countries, in Europe—especially West Germany—and in America, Palestinian student groups were a recruiting ground for youthful brain power and enthusiasm; the refugee camps were the main source of rank-and-file fighters. As the year passed and disillusionment with Nasser and the Arab governments grew, so did *Fatah*'s determination to act. All the leaders agreed that operations must begin as soon as possible. The question was when. To strike prematurely would be to risk hounding and suppression by Arab régimes for little in return. For *Fatah* was still a puny thing; its training—conducted mainly in Algeria—was inadequate; it was very short of money, arms and cadres. But Arafat, who favoured immediate action, carried the majority with him. The Palestinians had had enough of talk. Had not the Algerians launched their rebellion on the eve of All Saints Day with just such a penury of means? In September 1964 *Our Palestine* wrote:

> Our people asks 'when shall we begin?' It feels that the time has come for it to do something, to throw itself—with all the fury boiling up inside it, with all the fighting strength its sinews can muster, with all the anger that it feels to the depths of its being—to throw itself into battle. . . . Our slogan today is: let the revolution begin.

Fedayeen Operations Begin

On New Year's Day 1965 leaflets were unobtrusively slipped into the offices of various Beirut newspapers. After a rather grandiloquent preamble, Military Communiqué No. 1 of the General Command of the *Asifah* (Storm) Forces went on: 'On the night of Friday 31 December 1964–1 January 1965, detachments of our strike forces went into action, performing all the tasks assigned to them, in the occupied territories and returning safely to their bases.' It then addressed the Israelis, warning them not to take any action against 'peaceful Arab civilians, wherever they might be, because our forces, deeming such action war crimes, will reply in kind'. It also warned all (i.e., Arab) states against interfering on the enemy's behalf in any way, 'because, whichever they are, their interests will be exposed to damaging reprisals by our forces'. If—as was certainly the case—*Asifah*'s identity was a mystery to newspaper editors that day, such was precisely the intention. For the minority opposed to immediate action had succeeded in ensuring one precaution: the first operations should be carried out under a different name so that, should they fail, *Fatah*'s prestige would not be impaired from the outset.

It is hardly surprising that *Fatah*'s inaugural exploit has been shrouded in a certain romantic obscurity. For it appears to have been an ignominious failure. Military Communiqué No. 1 described a raid which never even took place.[39] The Lebanese security services got wind of the planned operation and arrested the would-be raiders before they set out. That was to be typical of *Fatah*'s predicament; the enemies in the rear—the Arab régimes—would prove hardly less troublesome than Israel itself. In another of these earliest raids the point was even more forcefully made. The new movement suffered its first 'martyr'. But Ahmad Musa, a veteran 'infiltrator', did not fall to Israeli bullets: the Jordanian army shot him on his way out of enemy territory.[40] On the completion of one of these earliest expeditions, Yasser Arafat himself had a spell in a Lebanese gaol.

Subsequent operations were more successful. They were necessarily limited in scope—confined mainly to the sabotage of isolated installations, water conduits and the like. *Fatah* did not have the resources for more. It was not merely a question of the manpower available to an infant organization that was obliged to operate in clandestine isolation from the mass of its people. Unlike the peasants of the 1936–9 rebellion, the *fedayeen* of this generation were unfamiliar with the terrain in which they moved; they had to hire men with local knowledge—such as smugglers—to serve as guides. And according to later accounts, the first captive, Mahmud Hijazi, fell into enemy hands 'because his gun was rusty and of no use to him'.[41]

The understandable modesty of *Fatah*'s early performance was, however, hardly discernible from the communiqués which it issued at the time. On the contrary, judging by them, it proved itself from the outset a master of guerilla warfare. Its units were bold, versatile and ubiquitous. From the Negev to Galilee, they attacked Israeli patrols, mined military vehicles and blew up arms dumps, dams, pipelines and canals. Their missions were almost always a complete success. Rare, it seems, were the occasions when the *Asifah* 'strike forces', in direct clashes with enemy troops, did not inflict losses of five to twenty dead and wounded; rare the occasions when they did not 'return safely to their bases'. It is natural, and often profitable, for armies to embellish their exploits; but a boastful exaggeration that defies all probability is eventually counter-productive. The external difficulties, both Arab and Israeli, which *Fatah* faced, as it launched this latest phase of the Palestinian struggle, were certainly daunting enough; but this habit of gross exaggeration showed that, from the beginning, internal difficulties of *Fatah*'s own making were by no means absent either.

Nevertheless, exaggeration notwithstanding, *Fatah*'s activities, or perhaps what they portended, were substantial enough to provoke an Israeli response—warnings to neighbouring Arab governments, protests to the United Nations, and, eventually, massive reprisal. This Israeli response meant more, for *Fatah*'s prestige, than anything it did, or said about what it did, itself. It impressed Palestinian and Arab public opinion. That public was not a very discerning one. For years it had been fed extravagant propaganda about the coming 'battle of destiny' with Israel. Yet the battle never seemed to come. Indeed, the Arab states could not even agree on a collective strategy to deter the Israelis from going ahead with their plans to divert the headwaters of the River Jordan. In this atmosphere, anyone who actually did something against Israel, however trifling, won immense prestige. *Fatah*'s attempts to sabotage Israel's Jordan diversion project might be mere pinpricks, but at least, in contrast with the Arab states, it was making the attempt. *Fatah* therefore became the catalyst it intended to be—though not quite, judging by its theoretical texts, in the *way* it intended to be. That is to say, it did not precipitate an ever-growing Arab involvement in a 'popular liberation war' of which it deemed itself to be the vanguard. There was no significant increase in the scale and effectiveness of guerilla raids in the two and a half years that preceded the June 1967 War and the radical new circumstances it ushered in. According to the Israelis, who were predisposed to dramatize the raids for their own belligerent purposes, they caused the death of only eleven people, and the injury of sixty-two, in the same period. The Israelis also claimed to have killed a mere seven *fedayeen* and to have captured two. They put *Fatah*'s manpower in June 1967 at a mere 200. But *Fatah* did present a formidable challenge to the champions of rival formulae for the liberation of Palestine. Essentially, this meant a challenge to President Nasser and all those, including Palestinians, who subscribed to the Nasserist orthodoxy of liberation *after* Arab unity and the completion of the socialist revolution.[42]

The challenge was instantaneously recognized. On 2 January, upon receipt of that first military communiqué, the Beirut newspaper *al-Anwar*, then a leading Nasserist mouthpiece, jumped to one of the most opportunistic—and, one presumes, most embarrassing—conclusions of its opportunistic career. It denounced *Fatah* as the instrument of a 'conspiracy . . . hatched by imperialist, CENTO and Zionist quarters'. *Fatah*—or *Hataf*, as *al-Anwar* and others in their ignorance at first called it—was a 'very small group of Palestinians' who were embarking on 'very small, individual' operations designed to furnish Israel with a pretext to attack its neighbours and foil their scheme for a counter-diversion of the Jordan waters. This was more royalist than the king: for at first Cairo newspapers simply reported *Fatah*'s activities without comment. But it foreshadowed a prolonged struggle between the Nasserist and the *Fatah* schools of thought. Declaring that 'we shall not put down our arms until victory', *Fatah* virtuously claimed that there was no contradiction between the two.[43]

But clearly there was. For other Beirut newspapers reacted in quite the opposite way. The weekly *al-Usbu'al-Arabi*, for example, came down wholeheartedly on *Fatah*'s side. The Palestinians should at least be allowed to 'die standing up', it said, and advised the Nasserists to take a leaf from the Zionists' book:

> He who gives his blood for his country does not ask permission. If the Arab states do not wish to appear as aggressors then they can allow the *fedayeen* to provoke Israel first. Or, if they are not ready yet, they can dissociate themselves completely from them, assigning them the same role that the *Irgun* and the *Stern* played. The Jewish Agency condemned [terrorist action] in diplomatic memoranda, but blessed them—indeed coordinated with them—in practice.[44]

It was a rearguard action which the Nasserists were fighting. President Nasser did not beat about the bush. He deliberately chose a Palestinian forum to make one of the franker speeches of his career: 'If we are today not ready for defence, how can we talk about an offensive? . . . We must provide Arab defence and then prepare to carry out our ultimate goal. That can only be fulfilled by revolutionary action.'[45] But neither Nasser personally, nor the more direct forms of dissuasion he brought to bear, could stop *Fatah*. The powerful Egyptian propaganda machine imposed a virtual news blackout on *fedayeen* activities. The Unified Arab Military Command (which had been set up to cope with Israel's Jordan waters diversion scheme) instructed Arab governments to prevent guerilla incursions into Israel. Jordan and Lebanon certainly needed no prompting to comply. In Lebanon would-be infiltrators were put on trial for illegal possession of arms; one apparently died under torture. Even the Syrians, *Fatah*'s only sponsors, did not scruple to impose unwelcome constraints, provoking quarrels 'which sometimes reached the point of bloody personal liquidations'.[46]

It was, of course, Palestinian Nasserists who suffered the most agonizing conflict between heart and head. Their 'official', institutional expression was the Palestinian Liberation Organization. The PLO chairman was a deferential, if demagogic, professional politician called Ahmad Shuqairi; well-behaved notables, more than half of them from Jordan, dominated its legislature. It may sound somewhat improbable today, for, as the head of the left-wing Popular Front for the Liberation of Palestine, Dr George Habash has come to symbolize revolutionary violence at its most uncompromising, but in those days he was actually one of the most influential critics of go-it-alone *fedayeen* raids. Habash was then the head of the Arab Nationalist Movement (from which the PFLP later grew), a radical organization with branches in many Arab countries which saw in Nasser the instrument of Arab unity and the liberation of Palestine through a conventional war he would fight in his own good time. Habash had no time for Shuqairi and his bombastic school of politics, but the two men had a common interest in containing *Fatah*'s excess of zeal. Shuqairi said that *Fatah* was doing very well, but that its timing was wrong and he would try to bring it under the PLO's wing. One of his officials reportedly told a Beirut newspaper that war was not 'a pastime to be indulged in by certain *fedayeen* . . . to satisfy a feeling of vengeance'.[47] The Palestinian branch of the ANM helped found a 'Preparatory Committee for Unified Palestinian Action'; its weekly journal *Palestine* insisted that 'to entangle Arab forces disposing of *real* military power, with all the risks and consequences which that entailed, is absolutely unacceptable'.[48] *Fatah* was contemptuous; the PLO 'talked but did not act'—and collected money for holding 'demagogic rallies'.[49] As for unified action, the only unity it ever believed in was 'unity on the battlefield'. The battle 'must be today not tomorrow'.[50]

Neither Shuqairi nor Habash could ignore popular sentiment, and before long these ill-matched allies, privately cursing one another and collaborating at the same time, were hurriedly improvising their own guerilla movements. Apparently they had the reluctant blessing of President Nasser, who no doubt calculated that, by allowing his protégés to compete for popular favour, he stood a better chance of restoring his weakened grip on Palestinian irredentism than if he gave them no leeway at all. Essentially, 'The Heroes of the Return', which first saw action in October 1966, was the creation of the Arab Nationalist Movement, while the PLO furnished it with financial and propaganda backing. On 31 November Shuqairi, in the uniform he now regularly affected, told a mass rally in Gaza that 'bullets and blood will now be the only exchange between us and the enemy'. Still other Palestinian groupings—and this period of ferment had thrown up no less than forty of them—announced that they too were putting their fighters into the field.

But President Nasser had miscalculated. He *was* stampeded into war. And if, before the second Catastrophe of June 1967, guerilla warfare commanded great appeal, it became quite irresistible after it. For Arabs and Palestinians alike it was an indispensable balm for their terribly wounded pride. *Fatah* soon announced that it was transferring its headquarters to the newly occupied territories; Arafat and some of his lieutenants crossed the River Jordan to mastermind the bold new strategy which they had adopted. Hitherto the *fedayeen* had largely confined themselves to hit-and-run incursions across the armistice lines, but now Arafat had the opportunity to forge a self-sustaining guerilla movement out of that segment of his people, well over a million, who had fallen under direct Israeli rule. In accordance with Chairman Mao Tse-tung's famous dictum, the *fedayeen* would now be fish with a revolutionary sea in which to swim; they would be well on the way to developing a full-scale 'popular liberation war'. Young men, graduates of training courses in Syria, followed their leaders, making the hazardous Jordan crossing with the help of local guides. Arms and explosives were ferried across too, and hidden in caves, wells, and the homes of *Fatah* sympathizers. Arafat stayed in the West Bank till the end of the year. Although he sometimes moved around under the Israelis' noses, he hid out much of the time in the warren of old lanes that make up the Kasbah of Nablus. From there he recruited personnel, organized networks, laid down tactics, set targets and planned operations. His agents went into the villages to try to arouse the peasantry. A clandestine leaflet which fell into Israeli hands conveys something of the measure and the spirit of Arafat's ambitions:

> To the heroes of the Arab people in the occupied land.We call upon you in the name of the Arab heroes Omar and Saladin to rise against the foreign occupation and prohibit the Zionist occupiers from treading on our sacred Arab land. The legendary resistance of Algeria, which had suffered more than a million casualties, will guide us on our way. . . . The Zionist occupation is nothing but the rise of a new

> Crusade. We shall continue to rebel until the final victory. We must boycott all economic, cultural and legal institutions of the Zionists. . . . We must set up secret resistance cells in every street, village and neighbourhood. For even one fighting cell, operating in any region, has the power to inflict great losses upon the enemy. Roll down great stones from the mountain slopes to block communication lines for the enemy's movements. If you happen to stand by an enemy's car, fill its gas tank with sand or sugar to put it out of action. Try to produce fires in the enemy's cars with oil and other means. . . .[51]

After a short breathing space, *Fatah* renewed its operations on a larger scale than before the war. It claimed ninety-two of them before the end of the year—some of which, deep inside the pre-1948 borders, the Israelis described as the boldest it had ever attempted.[52]

December saw the formation of *Fatah*'s left-wing rival, Dr Habash's Popular Front for the Liberation of Palestine, which, in its inaugural statement, declared that 'the only language which the enemy understands is that of revolutionary violence' and that the 'historic task' of the hour was to open a fierce struggle against it, 'thereby turning the occupied territories into an inferno whose fires consume the usurpers'.[53] The Front was to put down strongest roots in the festering, tightly-packed squalor of the Gaza Strip.

The *fedayeen* began to draw enthusiastic applause in the Arab world, not least from such Nasserist newspapers as *al-Anwar* which, forgetting *Fatah*'s alleged links with 'imperialist, CENTO and Zionist quarters', now concluded that the Palestinian resistance was a 'voice that could make itself heard in the Arab and international fields'.[54] Inevitably, the guerillas soon felt strong and bold enough to take over the PLO, the institution through which the régimes had tried to keep them under control. They demanded the resignation of Shuqairi, Nasser's protégé, who was denounced by a Palestinian official in Cairo as a 'selfish, ruthless, impetuous lover of propaganda'.[55] Seven members of the Executive Committee asked Shuqairi to step down 'because of the way you run the organization'.[56] In February, the guerillas secured effective control of the National Council—and it was only a matter of time before Arafat became the PLO Chairman.

The Battle of Karameh

It was not, however, until the Battle of Karameh that the *fedayeen* achieved their real breakthrough. Karameh means 'dignity', and, for the Palestinians, there could be no more fitting name to commemorate the biggest 'little' battle the Israelis had ever fought against them. It had been growing increasingly clear, in the months which preceded it, that Arafat and his men were developing Jordan as the main platform for their liberation war. Syria would always remain their ultimate mainstay—but under the strictest of official controls; in Jordan, however, half of whose population was Palestinian, they were acquiring a political and military presence which quite escaped the jurisdiction of King Hussein's war-weakened government and army. He had done his best to check the alarming growth of guerilla power. The June 1967 War had not changed him. The despatch of 'so-called *fedayeen*' into enemy-held territory was still an 'unparalleled crime'.[57] In February he announced that he had taken 'firm and forceful' measures to thwart them; they had nothing to do with the Arab nation.[58] But three days later the Prime Minister, Bahjat al-Talhouni, had to dissociate himself from these policies and announce that a 'popular resistance' was to be organized. After that there was another bout of heavy exchanges, precipitated by *fedayeen* raids, in which the Israelis used tanks, artillery and aircraft against Jordanian positions. Many civilians were killed. Some 70,000 inhabitants of the Jordan Valley fled to the relative security of the hills. On 18 March an Israeli schoolbus ran over a mine, killing a doctor and wounding several children. This, said the Israelis, was the climax of some thirty-seven acts of 'sabotage and murder' in which six people had been killed and forty-four wounded. It was obvious, to the *fedayeen* in the valley, that a massive reprisal was imminent. As they watched the enemy prepare for it, they debated what to do. By all the rules of guerilla warfare, there was only one possible course; they should withdraw to the hills and harass the vastly superior attacking forces from there. This is what the diminutive PFLP contingent, some thirty-odd strong, urged. *Fatah* may have been equally well versed in their Che Guevara, their Mao Tse-tung and Ho Chi Minh, but they none the less insisted on the opposite course. The *fedayeen* would stay where they were—in and around Karameh refugee camp—and confront the enemy head-on. There were a mere three or four hundred of them altogether; this was more or less the entire guerilla strength at the time; they were armed with light and medium machine-guns, RBJ anti-tank guns and grenades.[59] *Fatah*'s reasoning was essentially political, not military. 'There is a basic fact of which all have become aware; in all our encounters with him over the years, it has been the enemy who always advanced and we who retreated. If we must retreat, let it be to Amman or Damascus. But that we refuse. The Arab nation is watching us. We must shoulder our responsibility like men, with courage and dignity. We must plant the notion of steadfastness in this nation. We must shatter the myth of the invincible army.'[60] *Fatah* turned a deaf ear to advice proffered by the Jordanians, as well as by Iraqi forces stationed in the country. They were, they said, determined to 'convince the Arab nation that there are among them people who do not retreat and run away. Let us die under the tank tracks. We shall change the course of history in this area; and no one will blame us for that.'[61]

At dawn on 21 March the Israelis struck across the Jordan River. Some 15,000 men, and an armada of tanks, took part in this biggest reprisal raid in Israel's history. Although the attack came on a wide, fifty-mile front, the main force headed up the arid slopes to Karameh, as helicopter-borne paratroopers converged on it from the rear. A parachuter said later that Karameh was like a ghost town:

> On loudspeakers we called on the inhabitants to come out with raised hands to the square in front of the mosque, but we seemed to be talking to the walls. . . . We surrounded a building which we knew to be the barracks of the terrorists. Suddenly we came under heavy firing. We laid explosives under the gates and stormed the place. Inside we found about twenty guerillas in camouflage with al-Asifah insignia. They were armed with sub-machine guns and tried to shoot their way out, but were all shot dead.[62]

The Palestinians suffered heavy losses; anything up to half their fighting forces were wiped out.[63] The Jordanian army, which had joined in the fighting, put its own losses at 128 killed and wounded.

Nevertheless, from *Fatah*'s standpoint, Karameh was a great triumph, a turning point in their fortunes. For the first time, the Israelis, accustomed to easy, almost painless victories, got a bloody nose. They had met fierce resistance all the way. They had suffered what for them, a small embattled country that could ill afford them, were very heavy casualties, at least twenty-eight killed and ninety wounded.[64] They left several knocked-out tanks and other vehicles in the field. Moreover, they had achieved nothing. On the contrary, *Fatah*'s romantic 'martyrdom decision' had succeeded beyond its wildest dreams. The *fedayeen* had put on the mantle of heroism. General Mashhur Haditha, the commander who had brought in the Jordanian troops, paid a professional soldier's tribute: 'The *fedayeen* did their duty in Karameh right until the final stage of hand-to-hand fighting. Our estimate of their martyrs is 150. Having seen them, having seen that all their wounds are chest wounds, inflicted from the front, I must, for history's sake, record that they fought like heroes.'[65] Foreign correspondents who visited Karameh two days after the battle found the *fedayeen* there again in strength—more defiant, more self-confident than before. Israel, one of them concluded, had committed a 'massive strategic blunder'.[66] The guerillas' precarious foothold on Israel's eastern frontier had now become a virtual state within a state. If King Hussein had thought to crush them, he now gave up the idea; his subjects would not stand for it. Unable to beat them, he made as if to join them. In a famous press conference he said that 'maybe we are all becoming *fedayeen*'. Refugee camps throughout the Arab world 'celebrated the resurrection of the Palestinian people'.[67] There were huge funerals for the 'martyrs'. Volunteers began to flock to *Fatah* recruitment centres. They were not just Palestinians; by May, 20,000 Egyptians had offered their services; and 1,500 Iraqis within the space of a week.[68] In Lebanon, the *fedayeen* appeared to be a great unifying force. The press of this least Arab of Arab countries ran riot with accounts of young men determined to enlist—like nineteen-year-old Wahib Jawad, who, opposed by his family, held up a shop to raise money for his fare to Amman, taking only twenty-five out of a proffered 300 Lebanese pounds. A month after Karameh, Moslems and Christians turned out in their tens of thousands for the funeral of the first Lebanese 'martyr'. When the funeral procession reached the village of Kahhaleh, a stronghold of the right-wing Christian Phalangists on the main Damascus-Beirut highway, the inhabitants insisted on carrying the coffin themselves as church bells tolled; Beirut newspapers called this a 'plebiscite', the 'real face of Lebanon' carrying no 'stains of confessional fanaticism'.[69] Back in Jordan, a few months later, Wasfi al-Tal, a former Prime Minister and redoubtable scion of an influential Transjordanian family, urged the King to turn his kingdom into a latter-day 'Carthage'. The whole country should be fully mobilized behind the guerillas, who should step up their operations 'a hundred-fold' to become a real torment to the enemy. Jordan should develop its own defences to the point where it could positively welcome reprisals as a means of exhausting the enemy: the more Battles of Karameh the better.[70] It all began to look as though *Fatah* theory really was working out in practice, as if the revolutionary 'vanguards', through a process of spontaneous combustion, really were rallying the Arab masses behind them, bringing into being that 'supporting Arab front' which would strike down any ruler who stood in their way.

The impact of Karameh was not confined to the Arabs. The outside world began to take note of a new force emerging in the Middle East. It was apparent—*The Palestine Yearbook* for 1968 records—

> . . . in the enlistment into the ranks of the movement of foreign volunteers, such as the Frenchman, Roger Corday, who was martyred in June . . . in the pro-Arab demonstrations and scuffles that greeted Israeli Foreign Minister Abba Eban on his visit to Norway on 7 May, in the shouts of 'long live *Fatah*' hurled at him in Stockholm, and in the letters which the London *Times* published five days after Karameh under the signature of three British personalities, including Lady Fisher, wife of the Archbishop of Canterbury, who said that the Arabs were 'surely . . . only doing what brave men always do, whose country lies under the heel of a conqueror.'[71]

Notes

1. *Newsweek*, 22 October 1973.
2. 9 October 1973.
3. *Newsweek*, 22 October 1973.
4. *Davar*, 8 February 1974.
5. *Haaretz*, 11 November 1973.
6. Leibovitch, Yeshayahu, 30 November 1973.

7. Kapeliouk, *La Fin Des Mythes*, *op. cit.*, p. 106.
8. Israel Radio, 1 December 1973.
9. pp. 173–93.
10. p. 149.
11. *Progress Report of the UN Mediator on Palestine*, *op. cit.*, p. 4.
12. Official Records of the 3rd Session of the General Assembly, Part II, Ad Hoc Political Committee 1949, pp. 286–7.
13. See Tomeh, George, 'When the UN Dropped the Palestine Question', *Journal of Palestine Studies*, Beirut, Vol. IV, No. 1, 1974, pp. 15–30.
14. *Sunday Times*, 15 June 1969.
15. *Newsweek*, February 1969.
16. *Haaretz*, 9 September 1974.
17. Davis, John, *The Evasive Peace*, John Murray, London, 1968, p. 62.
18. See Tibawi, 'Visions of the Return: The Palestine Arab Refugees in Arabic Poetry and Art', *Mideast Journal*, XVII, 1963, p. 523.
19. 'Nasr, Kemal, *Jirah Tughanni*, Beirut, 1960; see Tibawi, *op. cit.*, p. 516.
20. Turki, Fawaz, *The Disinherited, Journal of a Palestinian Exile*, Monthly Review Press, 1972, p. 53.
21. See Tibawi, *op. cit.* 514.
22. *Ibid.*, p. 508.
23. Yaari, Ehud, *Strike Terror, the Story of Fatah*, Sabra Books, New York, 1970, p. 49.
24. *Our Palestine* (*Falastinuna*), January 1964, p. 7.
25. *Ibid.*, January 1964, p. 3.
26. *Ibid.*, January 1964, p. 3.
27. *Ibid.*, January 1961, p. 27.
28. *Ibid.*, September 1964. p. 3.
29. *Ibid.*, November 1959, p. 30.
30. *Ibid.*, April 1964, p. 3.
31. *Ibid.*, June 1959, p. 26.
32. *Ibid.*, May 1961, p. 5.
33. *Ibid.*, March 1961, p. 5.
34. *Ibid.*, August 1963, p. 24.
35. *Ibid.*, August 1964, p. 3.
36. *Ibid.*, September 1964, p. 3.
37. *Ibid.*, September 1964, p. 3.
38. *Ibid.*, March 1961, p. 9.
39. *Al-Anwar*, 2 January 1965.
40. *Revolutionary Studies and Practices* (Arabic), *Fatah* publication, p. 42.
41. *Ibid.*, p. 42.
42. Yaari, *op. cit.*, pp. 108, 112.
43. *Torches of the Revolution on the Way of Return* (Arabic), *Fatah* publication, 1965–6, p. 10.
44. 25 January 1965.
45. Speech to Palestine National Council, 31 June 1965.
46. Al-Sharqawi, Fawwaz, *Fatah—1965–1971*, Master's Thesis (Arabic, unpublished) Cairo University, 1974, p. 169.

47. *Al-Sayyad*, 4 June 1965.
48. 24 February 1966.
49. *Al-Jaridah*, Beirut, 5 June 1965.
50. Message to the Third Arab Summit Conference, 7 September 1965.
51. Yaari, *op. cit.*, pp. 133–5.
52. *Jewish Observer*, London, 12 August 1967.
53. 11 December 1967.
54. 10 October 1967.
55. *Al-Anwar*, 21 January 1967.
56. *Al-Muharrir*, 19 December 1967.
57. Jordanian News Agency, 5 September 1967.
58. *The Guardian*, 18 February, 5 September 1967.
59. Al-Sharqawi, *op. cit.*, pp. 346–7.
60. *Four Big Battles of Asifah Forces* (Arabic), *Fatah* publication, cited in Shafiq, Munir, *Palestine Affairs*, Beirut, March 1973, p. 107.
61. Hassan, Hani, 'The Fourth Anniversary of the Karameh Battle', *Palestine Affairs*, April 1972, p. 56.
62. *The Times*, 23 March 1968.
63. Al-Sharqawi, *op. cit.*, p. 347.
64. Harkabi, Yehoshafat, *Fedayeen Action and Arab Strategy*, Adelphi Papers, No. 53, Institute for Strategic Studies, London, 1968, p. 28.
65. Abu Aswan, Hadi, 'Testimonies from the Battle of Karameh', *Palestine Affairs*, Beirut, April 1972, p. 210.
66. Morris, Joe Alex, *New York Herald Tribune*, 25 March 1968.
67. *Le Monde*, 23 March 1968.
68. *The Palestine Yearbook* (Arabic), Institute for Palestine Studies, Beirut, 1968, p. 109.
69. *Al-Anwar*, *al-Nida*, 28 April, 1968.
70. *Al-Jadid* (Beirut weekly), 16 August 1968.
71. *Op. cit.*, p. 81.

9 · THE GUN AND THE OLIVE BRANCH

The Democratic State of Palestine

For all their undoubted achievements, the *fedayeen* were still a long way from the liberation of Palestine—indeed, a good deal further than they themselves thought—but success and recognition brought far-reaching changes of outlook, and, in particular, a much needed attempt to define what they meant by 'liberation'. Till then 'Shuqairism'—as it came to be known—had held sway. The former President of the PLO strenuously repudiated the notorious declaration—'I don't expect any of them [Israelis] to stay alive'—which news agencies attributed to him on the eve of the 1967 War.[1] But whether he actually said this or not is not really very important, for the ferocious rhetoric associated with his name had already done its work. Shuqairi was certainly not the only offender. Christopher Mayhew, the British MP, challenged supporters of Israel to produce any statement by an Arab leader which could be described as 'genocidal' in intent. He offered a £5,000 reward. No statement was produced, even though one persistent challenger had to lose a court case before he conceded defeat. In general, however, the language the Arabs used was very intemperate, and the man in the street could hardly be blamed for concluding that they really did intend to 'drive the Jews into the sea'.

The concept of 'liberation', wrote the Syrian scholar Sadiq al-Azm, was

> . . . held in such awe and reverence that it was forbidden to discuss it seriously, to subject it to objective criticism, or even to explain what it would eventually mean in actual practice. I had the impression that 'liberation', for the vast majority of Palestinians, meant some kind of literal and mechanical return to the situation which prevailed

round about 1948. By which I mean that, in people's minds, there was a picture of conquering Arab armies returning to Palestine; whereupon every Palestinian dusts off his documents and papers, presents himself to the Arab conqueror, shows him the title-deeds that prove his ownership of this or that piece of land, and the conqueror restores everything to its true owner, as if nothing had happened. That is to say, liberation would mean that the landowner returns to his estate, the *grand bourgeois* to his commerce and industry, the *petit bourgeois* to his shop, the worker to his toil, and the poor and destitute to his poverty and destitution.

The endless reiteration of the slogan, without any deeper analysis of it was

> . . . demagogy pure and simple . . . it was accompanied by a fearful official silence about the future of the Jewish masses in Palestine. The slogan of liberation, as presented, offered them no clear alternative to death and dispersal, no solid guarantee for their future as a large human community in a certain region of the Arab world. They, and world opinion, had no other criterion by which to assess the meaning of liberation than Arab information media of evil memory, our orators of Shuqairi's ilk, so much so that for the outside world (Jews and non-Jews) it became nothing but a great massacre.[2]

In the wave of official 'self-criticism' which swept the Arab world in the wake of the second Catastrophe of 1967, it was generally agreed that 'Shuqairism' and all such verbal excesses should be banished. But the Palestinians themselves went further; not only 'Shuqairism', but some of the ideas which Shuqairi—and many others—had held should be discarded too. In early 1968, *Fatah* began to formulate a new concept of 'liberation'.

Vengeance, it came to be understood, could not serve as the motive for a people's war; liberation had to be built on a vision of tomorrow, not on the nightmare of the past. It was natural, though regrettable, that in the first years of exile the Palestinians should have behaved in the way they did—that they had come to hate Jews and everything Jewish. For, although a distinction was usually made between Jews and Zionists, most refugees were either too bitter—or too simple—to take it seriously. They were inclined to accept Zionist propaganda at face value—and that propaganda insisted that all Jews were Zionists and potential Israelis. Had they not been driven out to make way for the *Jewish* National Home? Was it not *Jewish* money, *Jewish* pressure in the United States, that was perpetuating their misery and exile? Their hatred of Israel, and that of the Arabs in general, took on an anti-Semitic coloration. With the Protocols of the Elders of Zion and other classics of European racism as their inspiration, they fitted Israel and the Catastrophe into an updated demonology of their own. Indeed, there were influential, educated Palestinians who preached that it was a matter of the utmost importance *not* to distinguish between Zionism and Judaism. As the head of the PFLP, and a devout Marxist-Leninist, George Habash is now wedded to the internationalism of 'world revolution'; but in the early years of exile, as the moving spirit behind the Arab Nationalist Movement, he held that the real enemy was not Western imperialism but International Judaism, 'all Jews from the far left to the extreme right'; there was no choice for the Arabs but to meet the Zionist challenge on the same terms laid down by the Jews: expulsion or extermination. His slogan, which came in for a good deal of criticism even at the time, was 'Unity, Freedom, Vengeance'.[3]

With time, however, and especially with the growth of the *fedayeen*, new attitudes came into being. The distinction between Jews and Zionists really acquired meaning:

> Revolutionary leaders engaged in a serious study and discussion around the topic . . . old truths emerged. Jews suffered persecution at the hands of racist criminals under Nazism, so did 'we' under Zionism. Several revealing parallels were discovered. 'How could we hate the Jews *qua* Jews?' the revolutionaries were saying. How could we fall in the same racist trap? A study of Jewish history and thought was conducted. Jewish contributions as well as dilemmas were identified. The majority of those who came over to Palestine were fleeing German concentration camps and were told that they were a people without land—going to a land without people. Once they were there, they were told that the Palestinians left Palestine of their own wish,

> following orders from Arab leaders in a treacherous move to perpetrate a massacre of the remaining Jews.
>
> Further, it was discovered, new Jewish immigrants as well as old settlers were told by the Zionist machine that they had to fight to survive, that the only alternative to a safe 'Israel' was a massacre or at best a little sinking boat on the Mediterranean sea. Even Arab Jews—called Oriental by the Zionists—who were discriminated against in 'Israel' by the European Zionist oligarchy had to accept the argument and fight for what they considered to be their very survival. Fighting the Zionist revealed the strengths and limitations of the 'Jewish' character. Jews were not monsters, supermen or pigmies. Martin Buber, Isaac Deutscher, Elmer Berger and Moshe Menuhin, all spiritual, human Jewish thinkers, were read and re-read. . . .[4]

Fatah's vision of tomorrow was the 'Democratic State of Palestine'. The Jew-as-Zionist was still the enemy, of course, and against him and all he stood for *Fatah* would pursue its 'Revolution Till Victory'. Complete liberation was still the aim. And complete liberation still meant 'liquidating the Zionist aggressor-state—politically, militarily, socially and ideologically'.[5] There was no question of accepting some kind of mini-state to be set up in such territories as Israel, under a general settlement, might be induced to evacuate; together, the West Bank and Gaza represented no more than 22 per cent of original Palestine; it would, the *Fatah* theorist said, be a mere puppet—Israel's Bantustan. Only through complete liberation could the Palestinians fulfil their inalienable right to return; only thus could they assure themselves, as a people, of a free and decent life. But it was no longer a call for a literal and absolute justice, a restoration, pure and simple, of the *status quo ante*. If it did not acknowledge the Zionist *fait accompli* itself, it acknowledged the fundamental consequence of it, a physical Jewish presence in Palestine. It was a great leap forward in their thinking; a few years ago even 'discussing this proposal would have been considered as a complete sell-out or high treason'.[6] It happened 'because people who fight can afford to be more tolerant'.[7] The 'Palestine of tomorrow' was to be 'a progressive, democratic, non-sectarian Palestine in which Christian, Moslem and Jew will worship, live peacefully and enjoy equal rights'. The Palestine revolution stretched 'its welcoming hand to all human beings who want to fight for, and live, in a democratic, tolerant Palestine irrespective of race, colour or religion'. This was 'no utopian dream or false promise, for we have always lived in peace, Moslems, Christians and Jews in the Holy Land. The Palestine Arabs gave refuge, a warm shelter and a helping hand to Jews fleeing persecution in Christian Europe, and to the Christian Armenians fleeing persecution in Moslem Turkey; as well as to Greeks, Caucasians and Maltese among others.' What was new, its proponents said, was that those very Arabs who had been driven from their homes by the Jews-as-Zionists could still—while fighting to return—call for a society in which the ex-aggressors and persecutors, Jews as Jews once more, would have an equal place. Just what system of government the Democratic State of Palestine would adopt, and to what socio-economic philosophy it would subscribe, were matters to be decided after liberation; but, as to the higher ideals of human brotherhood on which it was based, *Fatah* would permit no doubts. All Jews now in Palestine, not just those who were already there before 1917, 1948, or whenever the Palestinians deemed the 'Zionist invasion' to have begun, would be entitled to stay there. Naturally they would have to foreswear their Zionist beliefs. The Palestine of tomorrow could not be a bi-national state, not just another Lebanon, with its confessional system which, rather than eroding contradictory loyalties, perpetuates them within a framework of precarious co-existence that is subject to frequent and bloody breakdowns. That would simply encourage the Jews, like the Maronite Christians of Lebanon, to go their own separatist way. There would, of course, be many diehards, the Begins, the Dayans and the Golda Meirs, who could not possibly adapt themselves to such a radical new order—they would have to leave; but it should be remembered that what the Israelis called Oriental Jews are, for the most part, Arab Jews, and they make up at least half the population; for them, adjustment would not be very difficult. Once they had made it, they would find themselves the victims of no discrimination whatever. A Jew could even be elected President just as well as an Arab. Reciprocal accommodations, transitional or permanent, could be made between the Arab and Jewish components of the Democratic State. These would be mainly cultural and linguistic; both Hebrew and Arabic would be official languages in government schools. But they could also embrace the higher policies of the state. Thus, in the transitional phase, immigration would be restricted to Palestinians wishing to return. Thereafter, however, and subject to agreed estimates of the country's absorptive capacity, it would be open to all without discrimination.

As *Fatah* conceived it, in fact, the Democratic State would offer liberation not merely for the Palestinians, but for the Jews too—for those of them, that is, whom it considered fellow-victims of a creed which professed to help them. It offered them an open, safe and tolerant Palestine in place of the insecurity of a Jewish State ever threatened by its neighbours. There would eventually come a time, it was hoped, when Jews would be fighting side by side with Palestinians in the liberation struggle.

The Democratic State won neither immediate nor universal acceptance from Palestinians. Some were totally opposed to the whole idea; it was an intolerable concession to the enemy. Some considered it no more than a tactical propaganda move designed to impress international opinion. Some objected to the creation of yet another Arab state; they preferred to talk of a 'democratic society' that would merge with the greater Arab world. Some were afraid that in such a state the Palestinians would be outnumbered by the technologically more advanced Jews, who would exploit their position to dominate the Arab world and destroy its unity. Some were critical of the religious classification — Moslem, Christian, Jew—of the citizens of the future state. Some said that the proposal was premature in that the Middle Eastern balance of power was still tipped heavily in the Israelis' favour. Some said that it would weaken the Palestinians' fighting spirit. In general, however, the Palestinians came to accept the principle, while deferring any precise definition of it, and in 1970, it was formally endorsed by the PLO's National Council, the 'parliament' of the Palestinian people.

No Uprising in the Occupied Territories

Karameh was the Palestinians' finest hour. But their very success contained the seeds of future failure. Indeed, the fact that Karameh took place at all was at least in part the consequence of an earlier failure, for which, however, it furnished a spectacular, if ultimately unavailing, cover. *Fatah* had failed, in that first six months after the 1967 War to set off the 'popular liberation war', *inside* the occupied territories, on which it had counted. The *fedayeen* failed to become fish in a revolutionary sea. True, there was great enthusiasm, especially in the countryside, for the new breed of fighting Palestinians and it was hoped that, inspired by their example, West Bankers and Gazans would in due course take to armed struggle themselves. But it became clear, during those first six months, that this was not going to happen. Gaza did have a considerable tradition of militancy, but in general the West Bankers were not ready for great self-sacrifice in a cause whose success they doubted. The *fedayeen* were the product of a refugee society which had lost all; but *they* still had something to lose. They were therefore more immediately interested in the evacuation of newly occupied territories than in the liberation of all Palestine, and they hoped that, by political or military means, the Arab states would achieve that for them. On the whole the local leadership—the mayors, the urban notables and the village *mukhtars*—discouraged the resort to arms. Thus, unlike those of the Great Rebellion of 1936–9, the fighters, though Palestinians, were in large measure outsiders. They found it hard to hide among the local population. It was to prove an embittering experience. The exhilaration which they felt on crossing the Jordan eventually gave way to demoralization in the inhospitable caves and hide-outs in the hills of Judea and Samaria.

Fatah itself was partly to blame, too, with its hasty and slipshod methods of organization, undiscriminating recruitment and poor security. Israel's efficiency, and the severity of its reprisals against the local population, did the rest. In the first three months of its efforts to establish a 'secure base' in the occupied territories it put its losses at forty-six—including twenty-six officers—of its best men.[8] And by early March 1968 the Israelis were claiming that they had wrecked *Fatah*'s hopes of promoting a 'serious' resistance movement. According to General Dayan, they had killed ninety *fedayeen* since the June War, fifty of them in the previous two months, and had captured a thousand. In January Arafat himself, roused from sleep in a sympathizer's house in Ramallah, had made a hair-breadth's escape from Israeli troops[9] and crossed the River Jordan for the last time. And only a few months after it had been decided to transfer guerilla headquarters to the occupied territories, they were transferred back again—to Karameh.

Fatah Makes Political Headway

THE GLORIOUS COVER OF KARAMEH held firm for a while, for who, confronted with the outward façade of *Fatah*'s rapidly growing power, paid much attention to the 'inner sickness' of which that rapid growth was itself a principal cause?[10] If the losses of Karameh were heavy, they were before long replaced a hundred-fold.[11] New recruits flocked to the training camps which dotted the countryside west of Amman; the tranquil hills and valleys echoed to the unaccustomed sound of gunfire. Advanced and specialized training was to be had in Algeria and Egypt, China and North Vietnam. The fighting forces of *Fatah*—some 300 before Karameh—and lesser, left-wing organizations had swollen to more than 30,000 two years later. There was also the Palestinian militia, the community self-defence organization, which supplemented the fulltime guerillas. There were the *Ashbal*, the Lion Cubs, ten- to fifteen-year-old youngsters who were being moulded as the *fedayeen* of the future. Women, too, found an emancipating place in the revolution. As for funds and arms, they registered an explosive increase in the order of 300 per cent.[12] A whole range of ancillary services—clinics, hospitals, schools and orphanages for the children of 'martyrs'—sprang into being. The civil servants of the revolution moved into offices in the respectable residential or business quarters of Amman and other Arab capitals. Militant posters and slogans decorated the walls of middle-class homes in the vicinity. Guerilla vehicles, bristling with armed men, plied as casually as taxis through the streets. The sudden emergence from a persecuted obscurity to international fame engendered a string of public relations departments devoted to the publishing of guerilla literature in many languages, the reception and guidance of foreign politicians, journalists, the curious and the sympathetic. In all the leading hotels, restaurants and bars, you would find the usual clientèle of businessmen and high society; but among them, and often hardly distinguishable from them, there would usually be a sprinkling of guerilla officials entertaining their foreign visitors.[13]

As the *fedayeen* movement grew in size and in the number of its competing organizations, so did the frequency of its operations. Most of them—61.5 per cent—were mounted by *Fatah*; they increased, according to its own estimate, from a mere twelve a month in 1967 to fifty-two in 1968, 199 in 1969, and 279 in the first eight months of 1970.[14] The small-scale mine-laying and sabotaging of the embryonic pre-1967 days developed into altogether bolder and more ambitious enterprises which—in spite of the failure on the West Bank—the movement's vastly expanded manpower and resources put within its grasp.

They put bombs in supermarkets in Jerusalem and bus stops in Tel Aviv; they lobbed rockets on Kiryat Shmona in the north and Eilat in the south. They mounted frontal assaults on border outposts, sometimes several at once, and raised the Palestinian flag for a few symbolic hours on patches of territory they seized.

It was disturbing for the Israelis. 'I have never underestimated this matter from the very beginning,' said Defence Minister Moshe Dayan,[15] and Prime Minister Levi Eshkol believed that in many respects the campaign against the guerillas was more violent than the 1967 War. But the really worrying thing was the political implications of the *fedayeen*, not their military effectiveness, although the former were partly a result of the latter. Politically, the *fedayeen* continued to build on what they had achieved at Karameh. Not, of course, that their ultimate goal, the Democratic State of Palestine, looked much less utopian than hitherto. Internationally, they won a certain credit for what was seen as a more civilized, if still hopelessly unrealistic, presentation of their case. But in Israel itself few indeed were those who showed any inclination to live in Arafat's 'Palestine of tomorrow'. That was hardly surprising since, by definition, Israel was a state for the Jews; the Jews-as-Zionists had driven out the Arabs to create it in the first place and now, to consolidate it, they were multiplying *faits accomplis* in the newly occupied territories. There were, of course, 'doves' of various feathers.

But they were still Zionists; they called for a return of the occupied territories—and, usually, not even all of them—in exchange for Arab recognition of Jewish statehood in all its essential Zionist attributes. Some accepted the need for a kind of 'Palestine entity'. The most 'dovish' among them, like Deputy Uri Avneri, urged a federation between a Jewish and an Arab State in Palestine. There were others who fought the occupation on moral and spiritual rather than political grounds. Men like Israel Shahak, former inmate of a Nazi concentration camp, were persuaded that Israel was now an oppressor which, in its treatment of the Arabs of the occupied territories and of Israel proper, was violating not only civilized international standards but the higher teachings of Judaism. As President of the Israeli League for Civil and Human Rights, he and a like-minded few, such as lawyer Felicia Langer, braved the abuse and hostility of fellow-citizens as they campaigned against the wrong done in Israel's name. But only outright anti-Zionists, wedded to the dismantling of the Jewish State, could so much as consider the Palestinians' vision of what would replace it; and anti-Zionists, as an organized political force, were a tiny handful, the merest *groupuscule* as the French say. *Matzpen*, or the Israeli Socialist Organization, stood on the lunatic fringe of the Israeli political spectrum, denounced as traitors even by those, such as Avneri, who came anywhere near them. Unlike the conventional 'doves' they did not draw an arbitrary distinction between Israel proper and the occupied territories; they considered that what was wrong in Hebron or Nablus must be wrong in Tel Aviv too, the original injustice committed in 1948 and before no less deserving of redress than a subsidiary injustice committed in 1967 and after. Only de-Zionization and the establishment of a society in which Jews and repatriated Arabs lived together without discrimination could bring peace to the Middle East. Socialist revolutionaries, *Matzpen* believed that, for the Israelis, the overthrow of Zionism should take precedence over the classical proletarian struggle; Arabs and Jews, inside and outside Israel, should join forces to bring this about. They recognized 'the right and duty of every conquered and oppressed people to resist occupation and struggle for its freedom . . . in our opinion resistance to occupation is natural and legitimate . . . as for the means used in the struggle—even when we do not approve of them—they do not constitute the main criterion by which we determine our position'.[16] *Matzpen* leaders, some of whom lived in exile, entered into direct communication with the *fedayeen*. They attended Palestinian conferences. Resistance publications disseminated their views in the Arab world. Even *Matzpen*, however, did not go quite far enough for the Palestinians, who tended to balk at its insistence that the Jews of Palestine, like the Arabs, had a national identity, preserving which, within the framework of a bi-national state, was not incompatible with the restoration of Arab rights. 'Despite the fact that it was created by Zionism,' *Matzpen* insisted, 'a Hebrew nation in the full sense of the term now exists in Palestine. And as such it has the right to self-determination, not certainly in the Zionist sense, but within the context of a socialist federation of the Middle East.'[17]

But the great majority of Israelis accepted the official vilification of the *fedayeen*, and the PLO under whose auspices they operated, as no more than 'terrorist gangs', 'murderers' and 'saboteurs'. How could they have the nerve to proclaim their desire for a peaceful coexistence in the 'Palestine of tomorrow' with their victims of today? The idea of a Democratic State, or even some kind of 'Palestine entity', should be as ruthlessly combated as the terrorists themselves. This emotional rejection of Palestinian aspirations was rationalized, at its most articulate and uncompromising, by General Yehoshavat Harkabi, the former military intelligence chief, who argued that the Democratic State was no more than a propaganda device to lend respectability to a struggle which was still 'genocidal' in intent.[18] In this he was helped by the Palestinians themselves, who, as one of their leading theoreticians concedes, furnished the Zionists with a 'rare opportunity' to question their sincerity, and to present the Democratic State as a tactical manoeuvre which caught them 'saying one thing in English and another in Arabic'.[19] For, as a result of doctrinal quarrels over the precise nature of this state, especially its relation to the rest of the Arab world, the Palestine National Council was unable to introduce an important promised amendment in the Palestine National Charter which would have endorsed *Fatah* doctrine that all Jews, not just those who arrived in Palestine before a certain date (1917 or 1948), would be entitled to Palestinian citizenship.

For all their disappointments, however, the Palestinians had established themselves once and for all as a political force, champions of their own cause, which they promoted not only in defiance of Israel, but, where necessary, of the Arab régimes. They had made nonsense of Golda Meir's claim that they did not exist. Never again was the conflict to be just an Arab-Israeli one. In the Third World they were recognized as an authentic liberation movement; ideologically opposed at first, the Soviet bloc eventually felt obliged, on political grounds, to bestow its favours on them; in the West they continued to make steady, if modest, inroads into a public opinion that was predisposed to see Israel as an outpost of civilization and a bastion of democracy in the Middle East. 'What we have done,' said Yasser Arafat, 'is to make the world . . . realize that the Palestinian is no longer refugee number so and so, but the member of a people who hold the reins of their own destiny and are in a position to determine their own future. As long as the world saw the Palestinians as no more than a people standing in a queue for UN rations, it was not likely to respect them. Now that they carry rifles the situation has changed.'[20] They were not strong enough to impose their will on anyone. But they had acquired a considerable power of veto. The least sign that an Arab régime was ready to foist some 'surrender settlement' on them and they reacted with strident indignation. A balloon which various Western quarters regularly floated at this time was the establishment of a mini-state of Palestine, co-existent with Israel. That it was floated at all was an encouraging measure of their success, but none the less they just as regularly shot it down.

Military Failure and the 'Inner Sickness'

Militarily, the *fedayeen* were never to be much more than a serious nuisance. They had a negative effect, certainly, in many fields. Israeli soldiers and civilians died. Counter-insurgency cost money and manpower. The less adventurous would-be immigrants, tourists and pilgrims were frightened off. But a 'popular liberation war' could not just stand still; it had to escalate. And that, beyond a rather low level, *Fatah* could not achieve. Indeed, at the height of their success, the *fedayeen* were already in decline.

Consciously or unconsciously, they sought to disguise this fact from the world and from themselves. True, the number of operations increased, but that was more than offset by the simultaneous Israeli success in driving the *fedayeen* even further east. For the increase was not to be found in operations inside Israel proper, nor even in the occupied territories. It was to be found in what can hardly be described as guerilla warfare, in the true sense, at all—in sniping and shelling across the ceasefire lines, and down in the Jordan Valley in particular. An Arab news agency reported that a mere 2.1 per cent of operations were taking place in Israel proper (excluding Upper Galilee), 3.4 per cent in Upper Galilee, 3.5 per cent in the West Bank, 7 per cent in the Negev desert, 7 per cent in the Golan Heights, 10 per cent in Gaza—as compared with a full 67 per cent in the Jordan Valley.[21] The prime yardstick of military effectiveness is casualties. The Israelis' figures were demonstrably confusing and contradictory.[22] But if they minimized their losses from *fedayeen* action—and they never admitted more than a hundred killed a year—this was not as flagrant as the way in which the *fedayeen* exaggerated them. In reality, as a Palestinian scholar later pointed out, Israel's casualties on all fronts, let alone from the *fedayeen*, never even approached the 'critical level' that might have pushed it into full-scale war.[23] Yet it was not unusual for *Fatah* to announce that, in a single operation, it had killed and wounded fifty, sixty or even seventy enemy soldiers for the most paltry losses of its own. 'Oriental fantasy,'[24] scoffed the Israelis; and clearly the spirit of Shuqairi, that contemptible symbol of a past which the Palestinians had supposedly put behind them, was far from dead. The extravagance of their claims was occasionally outdone by their efforts to prove them. Once, insisting that it had shot down six Israeli war planes over Jordan, *Fatah* exhibited a few twisted hunks of machinery as 'evidence'. Time and again, rival organizations would claim the same exploit. And if something quite ordinary or accidental happened—like the fatal heart attack of Premier Levi Eshkol or the injury of Moshe Dayan on an archaeological dig—they would rush in with silly assertions that nothing was beyond the long arm of the Palestinian revolution. And as if their own claims were not extravagant enough, the Arab propagandists who, before the June War, had derided the *fedayeen* now made amends with crass glorification and the raising of grandiose expectations. It frightened some of their sympathizers:

> I am afraid for the Palestinian revolution. I am afraid not from its enemies . . . but from some of its friends, dedicated to the 'true path' and committed to revolutions in the Arab world. . . . But the road is long. It is not paved with victories as the stalwarts of revolution imagine. The picture of the *fedayi* training to cross the enemy lines does not mean that he has already crossed that line and reached Haifa. It simply means that a new Arab has been born whose brother—should he perish—must follow him into the caravan of *fedayeen* and perhaps into the martyrs' grave—until one of them, crossing the enemy line, does reach Haifa, and another Askelon. . . .[25]

Exaggeration, as we have noted, was from the beginning one of the symptoms of the resistance movement's 'inner sickness'. Another, partly engendered by this embarrassing gulf between the real and the proclaimed performance, was an increasing readiness to compromise the ethical code by which they professed to fight. In its communiqué of 1 January 1965, announcing the completion of its first operation, *Fatah* warned the enemy not to retaliate against 'peaceful Arab civilians'. Thereafter, *Fatah* regularly insisted that the army and 'Zionist institutions' were its target, not civilians, 'particularly women and children';[26] if it did attack them, it was essentially in reply to Israeli attacks on Arab civilians, and it was selectively done. 'Whenever a civilian target is chosen, every effort is made to minimize loss of civilian life—though one would find it hard to distinguish civilians and non-civilians in this modern Spartan militaristic society where every adult is mobilized for the war. Hitting quasi-civilian areas aims at the psychological effect of shocking the Israelis into realization that the racist-militaristic state cannot provide them with security when it is conducting genocide against the exiled and oppressed Palestinian masses.'[27] The doctrine was not rigorously implemented. True, the Israelis, with their greater means, killed far more Arab civilians than the *fedayeen* killed Israeli civilians, and that furnished the justification. But there is little doubt that, even without it, the ineffectualness of day-to-day harassment of the

Israeli soldiery, the scant publicity it brought, was pushing *Fatah* into straightforward terrorism designed, by shock tactics, to achieve a maximum of impact with a minimum of resources. Besides, the doctrine, loftily enunciated, was not deeply inculcated in daily living practice. Thus in January 1968 the old, officially discredited idea of revenge seemed to win approval, as a motive for killing civilians, in the *Fatah* monthly *The Palestine Revolution* when it recounted what a captive *fedayi*, responsible for the death of a three-year-old boy, had told an Israeli court. His orders, he explained, had been to engage in patrols and sabotage everything he could. Asked whether that meant the killing of children too, he replied: 'Yes, to destroy everything, because we haven't forgotten Deir Yassin.'[28] A few months later an article in *The Palestine Revolution* dismissed the need for too much discrimination in the selection of targets:

> If military action in well-known guerilla wars concentrated on the armed forces of the enemy and spared the people whom the revolution wanted to win over, the Palestine revolution, owing to the nature of Zionist society, does not recognize this distinction between the enemy's armed forces and people. The colonialist Zionist society is a military society root and branch and there can be no distinction between military and civilian. . . .[29]

The great bulk of *fedayeen* operations were directed against the military proper, but when civilians were killed, the communiqués which announced it included few expressions of regret about this unfortunate necessity.

Hijackings and the Popular Front for the Liberation of Palestine

Fatah did at least try to confine the Palestine struggle to the land of Palestine itself. Its left-wing rival, the Popular Front for the Liberation of Palestine, did not. A former opponent of guerilla activism, Dr George Habash now became its most extreme practitioner. The ideologues of the PFLP saw themselves in the front line of a global struggle between the two great forces of the age. For them, the enemy—in the shape of Zionists, imperialists and local reactionaries—was one and omnipresent. Almost anything was therefore a fair target. It was legitimate to hijack not just Israeli civil aircraft, but American, British and even Swiss ones too. It was a contribution to the cause to blow up a pipeline transporting Arab oil—revenues from which helped finance the Arab war effort—because the oil was extracted by an American company, Aramco, on behalf of a 'feudal' Arab monarchy, the House of Saud. The planting of firebombs in Marks and Spencer's, a British chain store and big fundraiser for Israel, fitted without difficulty into the same Manichaean scheme of things. As for the ethics of hijacking, and the charge that it put the lives of uninvolved, non-Israeli civilians at risk, the PFLP had a prompt retort to that: don't blame us, blame the wicked Israeli crew who try to foil our irreproachable form of warfare. When the PFLP's Leila Khalid, the world's most celebrated aerial terrorist, was asked at a press conference what advice she would have for an Arab pilot confronted by Israeli hijackers, her only answer was a demure smile. The PFLP justified the machine-gunning of an Israeli airliner at Athens airport—and the killing and wounding of two aboard—on the ground the El Al was an integral part of the enemy war machine. When the Israelis replied by blowing up thirteen aircraft at Beirut airport and—for once—killing no one, the PFLP called this 'barbarous aggression' and 'unprincipled cowardly piracy'. Nor did the PFLP heed *Fatah*'s warnings about the obvious dangers to the whole guerilla movement of making unnecessary, above all Arab, enemies.

There is no doubt that 'foreign operations' of the kind that George Habash pioneered did bring publicity to the Palestinian cause, and, beneath the veneer of exalted ideology, that was one of his purposes:

> When we hijack a plane it has more effect than if we killed a hundred Israelis in battle. For decades world public opinion has been neither for nor against the Palestinians. It simply ignored us. At least the world is talking about us now.[30]

Probably, however, the underlying motive for a form of terrorism of which *Fatah* disapproved was the PFLP's military weakness, which, in the nature of things, pushed it into a series of spectacular, daring, but essentially facile exploits far removed from the real battlefield.

THE ENEMY IN THE REAR

THE 'INNER SICKNESS' WAS MORE than just military. It was organizational and political. Some of its symptoms were relatively concealed, obvious only to insiders, one of whom recalls that, both in theory and practice, the movement's

> . . . bungling was beyond all imagining; from a glance at the minutes of the PLO Central Committee's sessions, for example, with their muddle, their repetition, clashes and contradictions, one would hardly guess that they came from a common organization with a common purpose; there was nothing consistent or constructive in decision-making; rarely did one decision supplement or complete an earlier one; every session started from scratch. . . .[31]

Other symptoms were plain to all. The rise of the *fedayeen* had been an act of Palestinian self-assertion, against Arabs as well as Israelis, but, ironically, no sooner had one form of Arab 'tutelage' been thrown off than another took its place. Instead of opposing guerilla action altogether, the régimes now vied with one another in their support of it. Not content with their courtship of the mainstream *Fatch*, or of its PFLP rival, they spawned whole new organizations of their own. The Syrian Baathists had their own *protégé*—Vanguards of the Popular Liberation War (Saiqa)—so naturally the Iraqi Baathists, implacable rivals, had to have theirs too—the Arab Liberation Front—and, although both were punctilious about their own ideological *raison d'être*, they were really no more than extensions, in Palestinian guise, of the régimes which sponsored them. Palestinian politics were an Arab world in microcosm; much more democratic, it is true, but rent by the same splits, mergers and shifting alliances. No wonder Arafat was to exclaim that, in spite of the absence of real ideological differences, 'I feel that the difficulties of working for complete unity are greater than fighting itself.'[32]

It was gravely debilitating for the movement as a whole, however manfully *Fatah* strove to maintain its independence. It was a travesty of that spontaneous, popular-based 'supporting Arab front'—the scourge of aberrant governments—of which it had dreamed. For all their initial popularity, the guerillas failed to translate it into the organized backing which alone, in the end, could preserve them against official machinations. Indeed, even in their most sympathetic environment, East Jordan, where half the population were Palestinians, they began to lose rather than gain support, and their state-within-a-state, ever more powerful in external appearance, was in reality being eroded from within. Why was it that many a Jordanian village, which might once have offered food and hospitality to nearby guerillas without being asked, would now fire on them if they so much as entered it? How could things go so wrong in Lebanon that the Nasserists of Sidon engaged in street warfare against guerillas from a nearby refugee camp; or that the Christian village of Kahhaleh, which in 1968 paid such splendid tribute to the first Lebanese 'martyr', in 1970 laid a murderous ambush for a Palestinian funeral cavalcade?

The causes of the alienation were manifold. An immediately obvious one was the hooligan fringe of pseudo-guerillas which many people took to represent the whole. Another was the offence to the *amour-propre* of the regular armies. These were problems which the more responsible leaders, especially in *Fatah*, always recognized, but only half-heartedly corrected. But there were other problems, much more complex ones, stemming from the whole nature of the Arab environment. *Fatah*, hard though it often tried to cultivate the local population, fell into the trap one way, and its left-wing rivals in another. For *Fatah*, political pragmatism in the service of the military struggle was the supreme virtue, and it was inclined to believe that simple good behaviour and the distribution of largesse—like more guns for the tribes—would suffice. But all the Jordanian government, far more experienced in these time-honoured practices, had to do was counter with more and better. The left-wingers, on the other hand, naturally saw themselves in an educative, emancipating role. But they could take this to foolish extremes. Nayif Hawatmeh's Popular Democratic Front for the Liberation of Palestine, intoxicated by its own originality, grievously offended against those two sanctities of traditional Arab society: religion and woman's honour. The Front did what it did on a very small scale, but news of *fedayeen* paying nocturnal visits to the tents of *fedayaat*, and the broadcasting of Marxist slogans from a minaret to commemorate the 100th anniversary of Lenin's birth were the kind of things which the Hashemite régime could, and did, exploit to the full. It did not take much to shock the peasants and tribes of Jordan, but it was with the help of calculated indoctrination that they learned, some of them, to hate the *fedayeen*, as blasphemers and degenerates, in the way they did.[33]

The 'inner sickness' was not the only reason for the guerillas' military shortcomings. There were external ones too. Not the least of them was the continuing severity and efficiency of the enemy. The Israelis learned the lesson of Karameh. From then on they made relentless use of their complete aerial supremacy; the *fedayeen*, mercilessly pounded—along with a great many civilians—in their Transjordanian redoubts, bitterly complained about the absence of Arab anti-aircraft defences. At the same time the Israelis threw around their new frontiers a *cordon sanitaire*— minefields, electronic detection devices, highly mobile patrols—of formidable sophistication and complexity. As early as March 1968 they were claiming to have captured or killed thirty-five out of fifty *fedayeen* who had forged the River Jordan in the previous ten days[34]—and that was only a beginning. There were other inescapable obstacles too. The Palestinians had been greatly influenced by the Algerian struggle against the French—but if motivation was similar, geographic and demographic conditions were not. Palestine, unlike Algeria, was not good guerilla country. Moreover, in Algeria, not only did the *indigènes* far outnumber the *colons*, they lived all amongst them. In Palestine, by contrast, Israelis not only outnumbered Arabs, but, for the most part, lived in their own segregated, easily policed areas. Without the 'inner sickness', however, the resistance movement might have triumphed over the external problems—or at least avoided the calamity of 'Black September', 1970.

Civil War in Jordan

The story goes that, inspecting a tank regiment in early September 1970, King Hussein spotted an incongruous pennant suspended from a radio antenna. It was a brassière, and by it his loyalist bedouin troops were signalling that they could not be expected to behave 'like women' much longer. They had had enough of these so-called freedom-fighters who, instead of 'liberating Palestine', swaggered around the streets of the royal capital, or what they chose to call the 'Arab Hanoi', and, with variants on the Bolshevik slogan of 'All Power to the People', openly proclaimed their ambition of replacing the Hashemite kingdom with their own revolutionary order. The King's patience, too, was running out. It only required the PFLP's last great *tour de force*, a multiple hijacking, to exhaust it altogether. Leila Khalid, in her second such exploit, had failed to seize control of an Israeli airliner; she had been taken into custody at London airport. But the spectacle of three other airliners—American, British and Swiss—brought down in the desert wastes of eastern Jordan, the PFLP's threats to blow them up with all aboard unless Leila and other comrades were released, camels wandering by, hectic international negotiations as deadlines came and went, the final ceremonial destruction of the aircraft—all that was exotic and riveting drama enough.

And yet a larger drama overtook it when, on 17 September, King Hussein, after long hesitation—but also long preparation—unleashed his impatient bedouins. In ten days of fratricidal struggle, they broke the back of guerilla power in Jordan. In their hour of desperate need, the *fedayeen* were betrayed by the quarter which had most loudly trumpeted its solidarity with them: Iraqi forces in Jordan left them to fight alone. The Syrian régime despatched armoured forces of the Palestine Liberation Army to their assistance, but General Hafiz Asad, the Defence Minister and future President, fearing Israeli or American intervention, refused to give them air cover, and they were routed. Contrary to guerilla hopes, the Jordanian army, though substantially Palestinian, failed to disintegrate in a conflict of loyalties. Within a year of 'Black September', as the *fedayeen* called this disaster, they were expelled from Jordan altogether. Prime Minister Wasfi al-Tal, the very man who, three years earlier, had urged the King to turn his kingdom into a latter-day 'Carthage', conducted the final ruthless drive against their last bases in the north of the country. It was so ruthless that scores of *fedayeen*, in the last extremities of exhaustion and despair, crossed the River Jordan rather than fall into the hands of the King's vengeful troops. One of them told his jubilant Israeli captors: 'I am ready to join the Israeli army and fight against Jordan and Syria—because these are worse enemies of the Palestinians.'[35] Arafat had lost his most important political and military base. It had been an Arab army, not the Israelis, which, in 1965, claimed the first Palestinian 'martyr'; it was the same army which, characteristically, had now dealt the whole resistance movement the hardest blow of its career. For Arafat, it was the ultimate betrayal, by the Arabs, of their most sacred cause; Jordan was but the spearhead of 'an Arab plot'[36]—a plot whose full, astonishing and treacherous dimensions only the future would reveal.

Black September

The Jordanian civil war ushered in a whole new phase of Palestinian violence—pure, unbridled terrorism. Wasfi al-Tal was its first victim. On 28 November 1971 four young men shot him down on the steps of the Sheraton Hotel in Cairo, where he had been attending an Arab League conference. Although they belonged to something calling itself the Black September Organization, they had, they made out, acted largely on their own initiative. One said that he had sold his car to raise money for the operation; another that he had paid 300 Lebanese pounds for his false Syrian passport. They had been brought together in a common desire for revenge. One claimed to have seen King Hussein's bedouin troops rape his sister and cut her child's throat. The body of Ali Abu Iyyad, a *Fatah* commander, had—or so Palestinians believed—been dragged in triumph behind Centurion tanks. The four assassins made no attempt to resist arrest.

As grief and anger swept Jordan, or rather the loyalist Transjordanian half of the population, and as Arab kings and presidents despatched the obligatory messages of condolences, the Palestinian masses did not hide their feelings in those places—outside Jordan—where they could freely express them. In Lebanon the refugee camps reverberated with joyful salvos. The same day the Palestine Students' Union, and other popular organizations, appealed to President Sadat to release the four men 'because they did their national duty'. Three days later *Hisad al-Asifah*, mouthpiece of *Fatah*, said that 'the four heroes who executed the Palestinian people's sentence on Wasfi al-Tal are sons of the Palestinian people and represent the will of the Palestine revolution'.[37] Many Arabs shared the Palestinians' feelings, and scores of lawyers volunteered to defend the assassins when they went on trial. But they never did. They were released on bail by the Cairo State Security Court: a leading lawyer cited gun tests to prove that a fifth man, who escaped arrest, had actually fired the fatal shot, and added that 'even if they were responsible, their act is no crime but a commando action. The four were in a state of legitimate defence of themselves and their land.'[38] They eventually left Egypt scot-free.

Black September, in contrast to *Fatah*, shrouded itself in secrecy of an extreme, cloak-and-dagger kind. However, the Jordanians promptly denounced it as no more than a clandestine arm of *Fatah*, and there is no doubt that, from the outset, *Fatah* was deeply involved in the new-style violence. Discovering who, among its leaders, was the real *éminence grise* behind it became a rather futile guessing game of the international press and intelligence community. *Fatah*, or those of its leaders who were involved, could not, of course, acknowledge a connection. That would have run counter to its official policies. It had always opposed the kind of 'foreign operations' which the Popular Front had pioneered. It was the backbone of the Palestinian Liberation Organization, which, aspiring to be the internationally recognized representative of the Palestinian people, had to maintain a respectable façade. Nor could it embarrass Arab and other governments whose friendship it needed. On the other hand it could no more stifle the impulse Black September represented than, in the 1940s, the Jewish Agency and *Haganah* could stop their own extremists. And it was to those that some Arabs were to liken them. 'In their struggle against Zionist colonialism', commented the Beirut daily *L'Orient-Le-Jour*, 'the Palestinians have taken 27 years to come round to the methods of *Irgun* and *Stern*. Can we blame them for seeking to avenge Deir Yassin?'[39] Twenty-seven years was felt to be a long time. Most outsiders familiar with the cause, wrote one Palestinian scholar, were given to expressing their surprise—some as a commendation, others as a reproach—at the relative absence of this kind of violence.[40]

The classic definition of Black September, at the time, was that it was less an organization than a state of mind. 'It cannot be pinpointed, tracked down or crushed. It has no name, no flag, no slogans, headquarters or base. It requires only men who have the determination to fight and succeed and the courage to die.'[41] So one ardent youth described it. An arm of *Fatah*, it was at the same time a grassroots phenomenon, spontaneous and self-generating. It was a popular response to the mistakes and declining moral authority of the official guerilla leadership. It was a compensation for the slump—from some 300 a month before the Jordanian civil war to about fifty after it[42]—in the number of conventional guerilla operations. Above all, it was a product of extreme frustration and despair, the feeling that only by shocking the world could the Palestinians get it to redress the injustice it had done, or even to consider it as such. Black September required of its adherents a readiness to take suicidal risks. Martyrdom, however, did not merely advertise the Palestinian cause to the world in the most dramatic way possible, it was intended to regalvanize the Palestinians themselves, to trigger mass emotional reflexes, which, channelled in more constructive directions, would eventually revive the struggle where *Fatah* had begun it, in Palestine itself.

Munich, 1972

The most famous Black September operation—public relations terrorism at its most sensational—was the one which disrupted the Olympic Games at Munich in September 1972. A Palestinian spokesman was hardly exaggerating when he claimed that:

> A bomb in the White House, a mine in the Vatican, the death of Mao Tse-Tung, an earthquake in Paris could not have echoed through the consciousness of every man in the world like the operation at Munich. . . . It was like painting the name of Palestine on the top of a mountain that can be seen from the four corners of the earth.[43]

The Munich games were covered by 6,000 newsmen and the most

sophisticated electronic television set-up ever assembled. Apart from the guaranteed publicity of the world's most grandiose sporting occasion, the terrorists had another, fortuitous bonus. For the West, particularly for the German hosts, these were the Games which should, as it were, have formally buried the unsavoury past. Berlin, 1936, was the last time the Olympiad had been held on German soil. Hitler had turned it into a festival of his Nazi rule, of the militarism and racist, anti-Semitic doctrines which it exalted. Munich, by contrast, was to be remembered as the 'carefree games'; if there was a touch of the Mediterranean holiday resort about them, that was no accident; no one was forbidden to walk on the grass; *verboten* was *verboten*.

Munich, of course, was the city that set Hitler on the road to absolute power; and Dachau concentration camp had not been far away. But that, too, was forgotten—until, on the morning of the eleventh day, the camera atop the television tower, switching from the Olympic arena, zeroed in on Block No. 31 in the athletes' village, and, as if transfixed, remained on that 'shot' until the ensuing drama was over.

At 4.30 A.M. on 5 September post office engineers saw a group of men in track suits clambering over the eight-foot wire-mesh fence; they did nothing about it: that was how many athletes got home after a night on the town. Armed with Kalashnikov assault rifles and hand grenades, the group, eight Black September terrorists, entered the Israeli pavilion, in Block No. 31, through an unlocked door. They ran into Moshe Weinberg, a weight-lifter, and Joseph Romano, a wrestling trainer, who attempted to resist them. Weinberg was killed, Romano wounded. In the confusion, several Israeli athletes escaped, but nine others were captured. Romano, denied medical attention, died.

Shortly after 5 A.M. the terrorists throw a list of their demands out of a first-floor window. They want the release, by 9 A.M., of two hundred of their comrades held in Israeli prisons. If the demands are met, the hostages will be freed; if not, they will be shot. At 8 A.M. the German police start preparations to rescue the hostages by force. In negotiations with the authorities, the terrorists refuse to exchange the hostages for German volunteers but agree to extend their deadline till midday. Sharpshooters are summoned. At 11 A.M. the Israeli ambassador informs the Germans that his government rejects the

Palestinians' ultimatum, or any kind of negotiations with them: 'If we once give way to blackmail, hijackings and kidnappings will multiply infernally. Our citizens know and accept this. Every one of us has been explicitly warned: in no case can we serve as bargaining counters. After all, we are at war. Every kidnapping, every commando attack is regarded as a military engagement in which we Israelis, soldiers or civilians, risk losing our lives. We do not bargain, but we must defend ourselves. That means, in this case, that there must be an immediate counter-attack. My government will accept nothing else.'[44] Israeli security men, despatched from Tel Aviv, later join the ambassador to 'advise' the German police. They too insist: no bargaining. So the Germans have no choice but to buy time, and to complete their plans for a showdown. They offer the kidnappers free passage out of the country, a large sum of money, even a night with 'beautiful Munich blondes'.[45] Arab ambassadors, unaware of the Germans' real intentions, also act as go-betweens. But the eight men remain unmoved. 'Money means nothing to us,' they say, 'our lives mean nothing to us.' All they will countenance is fresh extensions of their deadlines. 1 P.M., 3 P.M., 5 P.M., 7 P.M.—still they do not execute any hostages; and they seem ready to walk into the trap which the police are preparing for them. They are willing to fly to Cairo, with their captives, aboard a German airliner. This is a trick; contacted by Chancellor Willi Brandt, the Egyptian Prime Minister has already turned down a proposal that, on arrival in Cairo, the Egyptians would see to it that the hostages are sent back to Munich, or on to Tel Aviv. The real purpose is to get the terrorists to leave the Israeli pavilion, which does not lend itself to armed assault. The terrorists suspect as much, but they take the plunge, and at 10.06 P.M. they and their hostages, bound one to another, leave Block 31. They board two helicopters which, twenty minutes later, land at Fürstenfeldbrück military airport. Five marksmen are in position; floodlights ensure excellent visibility at thirty metres' range. They are reinforced by police with sub-machine guns, and 600 men of the Frontier Guards surround the perimeter. The two helicopter pilots jump down—and so do two terrorists, who keep them covered at point-blank range. Two other terrorists, one from each helicopter, walk over to inspect the Boeing airliner which is waiting, all lit up and apparently ready for take-off, on the tarmac 150 metres away. But there is no crew aboard, and as the two walk back, the marksmen open fire. The two men guarding the pilots slump to the ground. The other two run. One is hit. A second, probably the leader, manages to hide beneath a helicopter. His comrades, still on board, shoot back, killing one of the marksmen. At 10.50, the police, using a loud-speaker, call on the surviving terrorists to surrender. They address them in German and English; an Israeli security man addresses them in Arabic. There is no reply; just the silence of impending disaster. The end comes at 1.05 A.M. The police open fire again. A terrorist jumps from one helicopter, and lobs in a grenade. Another shoots into the other helicopter. As armoured cars close in, all the hostages and two more terrorists die.

At first, through some ghastly blunder, it was announced to the world that the ambush had been a complete success; the hostages were safe. Altogether, it had been a day of error and misjudgements. Among other things, the German authorities had underestimated the number of terrorists; their five marksmen were not nearly enough for the job. They had also underestimated the skill and, above all, the determination of men who did not make a single tactical mistake themselves and were ready to die for their cause.

The three survivors were taken to prison; another Black September exploit secured their release a few weeks later. In their 'will', published by the Palestine News Agency in Damascus, their five dead comrades apologized to the world's sportsmen. 'But we want them to know of the existence of a people whose country has been occupied for twenty-four years, and their honour trampled underfoot. . . . There is no harm if the youth of the world understand their tragedy for a few hours . . . so let the Games stop for a few hours.' To their own people, the Palestinians, they appealed 'not to abandon your guns, in spite of the difficulties and conspiracies that beset the struggle. Our land will be liberated by blood, and blood alone. The world only respects the strong. We shall not be strong through words alone, but only by acting on them. We care not where we are buried for, as our ancestors said, it does not hurt the goat to be skinned after it is slain. We want Arab youth to know how to die for their people and their country . . . when one martyr falls from us, he is replaced by a thousand men . . .' Their bodies were flown to Libya, where they had a heroes' funeral which the official news agency described as a 'majestic spectacle'.

Three days later the Israeli airforce made one of its massive reprisal raids, over Syria and Lebanon, in which anything between 200 and 500 people, mostly civilians, died.[46]

Munich shocked the world. And, naturally enough, no people, apart from the Israelis themselves, were more outraged than the German hosts. In its cruder forms their outrage again stirred remembrance of unpleasant things past—though this time, of course, the man the popular cartoonists gave a hooked nose, swarthy complexion and shifty eyes was not a Jew, as he used to be in Göebbels' *Völkischer Beobachter*, he was an Arab. You were unlikely to overhear the world *Untermenschen* (subhumans), but the banner carried by a crowd of demonstrators asked: 'Are These People Human?' In cafés signs went up saying 'Arabs not wanted'. In the weeks to come, hundreds of Arab residents were summarily expelled from Germany; and Arabs trying to enter the country complained of their unfriendly reception at airports and border posts. Munich was denounced, with unusual severity, throughout the Western world. Readers' letters of rare virulence appeared in leading newspapers, like this one in *Time* magazine:[47]

> For this thing that they have done in Munich the Black September mob are truly the scum of the earth. On the battlefields they are nowhere to be found, yet these 'martyrs', these degenerate 'heroes of the sewers' shriek their hysterical victories over unarmed innocents, over women and children and airborne passengers, and then scuttle back to the dungheaps from where they came.

Munich was seen as a particularly odious example of a kind of violence, barbarous, random, pointless, that was becoming a worldwide plague. The Arabian Assassins, declared another letter in *Time*, have joined the Belfast Bombers and the Pakistani Predators. This breaking of the 'Olympic peace' was in addition a kind of sacrilege, the intrusion of human conflict on one of those universal rites of modern man which, by sublimating it, supposedly helped to prevent it. Attitudes towards Munich were held to distinguish the civilized from the uncivilized. President Nixon sought UN backing for a world-wide campaign against 'international terrorism.'

Yet there was clearly a counter-current of opinion which, in spite, or perhaps because, of the barbarism of Munich, argued that desperate men must have desperate reasons for doing what they do. That was the kind of response for which the Black Septembrists hoped. It was far from being a majority view which another letter in *Time* magazine expressed,[48] but at least the letter appeared. That, for the Palestinians, was progress.

> Must retaliation always follow atrocity in the awful agony of the Middle East? Harsh retaliation has only forged patriots into terrorists and forced them out into the world to destroy peace. Oh, Israel, let these people return to the land of their fathers. Show the world your great goodness. Destroy the cause of which terror is a symptom.

The only forthright condemnation in the Arab world came from King Hussein, who described Munich as a 'crime engineered by sick minds who have nothing in common with humanity'. That was to be expected; an implacable foe of the resistance movement, he himself was very high on Black September's list of targets. In the Palestinian refugee camps, by contrast, there was cheering when the final news from Munich came through, not so much because of the death of the hostages, but because eight Black Septembrists had acquitted themselves so well, foiling the German 'double-cross'—as one of the three survivors later called it—and demonstrating so conclusively that death really did mean nothing to them. In the rest of the Arab world, it was widely acknowledged—though without much conviction—that the massacre was unfortunate. The real thrust of Arab censure was not directed against the terrorists; it was reserved for the German authorities whose 'deceit' and 'trickery' were held mainly responsible for the tragic outcome. The Arab press and radio tended to endorse Black September's arguments that its men had been more than ready to negotiate with the German authorities, that they had treated the hostages 'humanely' and repeatedly refrained from executing them as the deadlines came and went. The last thing they wanted was a massacre of innocents, or, if it occurred, it was the other party's fault—this was familiar terrorist logic. It was all the more disingenuous in that, as every Palestinian knew, Israel could not compromise. Its whole security philosophy—indeed, as the Israelis themselves saw it, its very survival—was founded on the no-compromise of its strong right arm.

It was more honest to argue, as some apologists did, that terrorism was the weapon of the weak and the oppressed, of people who had no other means of fighting. The Arabs, like Mr Nixon, thought that terrorism was bad, but it was necessary to take into account not just the acts themselves but their underlying causes; that was the case which, with Third World support, they argued at the UN. But in any case, it was not for Israel, or its Western supporters, to wax indignant about a form of warfare which Israel itself had pioneered. 'After the creation of the State of Israel, classical terrorism gave way to the outwardly more respectable terrorism, designed to cow and subjugate the Palestinians and their Arab sympathizers, which the state, with all its resources, can mount. Palestinian violence, by contrast, is reactive, small-scale but more easily branded as barbaric. We may, indeed some of us do, have misgivings about this kind of terrorism but we also condemn that of an Israel which was built on terrorism and continues to glorify its terrorists to this day. Look at the former terrorist leaders who enjoy respected places in public life. Look at Marcelle Ninio.'[49]

But the more honest arguments were not those most frequently heard. The Black Septembrists wanted it both ways. On the one hand, by blaming their enemy for the unhappy endings of violent deeds which they initiated, they were paying lipservice to the conventional ethics of war: you don't slaughter unarmed civilians in cold blood. On the other hand, their operations depended, for their whole effect, on the flouting of conventional ethics, and each operation more flagrantly than the last. Palestinian terror and Israeli counter-terror were locked into an inexorable spiral of evergrowing ruthlessness. Thus, if the Munich hostages died, it was at least in part because earlier ones had lived.

Three and a half months before, four Black Septembrists had hijacked a Belgian airliner to Israel's Lydda airport. It was the most daring operation of its kind so far, the first time hijackers—two men and two women—had ventured right into the lions' den. They demanded the release of 106 Palestinian prisoners in Israeli prisons; otherwise they would blow up the aircraft and all aboard. After twenty-one hours of tergivisation and suspense, Israeli commandos stormed the plane, killing the two men and capturing the women. Six of the hundred passengers were wounded; one of them later died. Red Cross officials had been involved in the negotiations, and, in a breach of good faith, the commandos had exploited their presence to achieve complete surprise for their assault. According to a Black September communiqué, the four hijackers had received strict instructions not to blow up the plane; they had also agreed to let food and water aboard. It was, therefore, 'humanitarian' scruples which caused the operation to fail; next time, it warned, there would be no such mistakes.

The next occasion did not involve Black September, but George Habash's Popular Front. This left-wing organization prided itself on its world revolutionary role and, through its international connections, it had enlisted the services of three young members of the Japanese 'Red Army'. On 30 May, after training in Lebanon, the trio arrived at Lydda airport on an Air France flight from Rome, and, with the other passengers, they went into the customs hall to await their luggage. As soon as it arrived they whipped out their Kalashnikovs and grenades, and opened up on the crowd. They killed twenty-five people and wounded seventy-eight, many of them Christian pilgrims from Puerto Rico. Two of the *kamikazis* apparently committed suicide while a third, Kozo Okamoto, was overwhelmed before he could do likewise. The Puerto Rican pilgrims were not the planned target; it was their misfortune to get in the way. The planned target was passengers disembarking from an El Al flight and friends and relatives who had come to greet them; over and above that, the general idea was to 'kill as many people as possible at the airport, Israelis, of course, but anyone else who was there'.[50] The PFLP described its 'Deir Yassin Operation' as a 'revolutionary retaliation' to the 'cheap trick' by which the 'butcher' Moshe Dayan and his men had foiled the Black September hijacking three weeks before. It was a more than adequate revenge, but it did have a flaw. It was a 'struggle by proxy'[51] which naturally provoked the jibe that, when it came to the supreme self-sacrifice, the Palestinians had to enlist foreigners to make it. It tended to reinforce the belief—apparently dear to General Dayan—that an Arab's nerve usually cracks in the end.

That was the background against which the Munich terrorists, tricked by the Germans, were bound to kill their hostages and, if necessary, themselves in the process.

Terror Unlimited

After Munich, nothing Black September did could achieve the same impact. The law of diminishing returns began to operate; Black September went on trying all the same. The next major operation was a fiasco; this time, apparently, the Arabs' nerve did crack. On 28 December Black Septembrists seized six diplomats at the Israeli embassy in Bangkok, demanding the release of thirty-six Palestinian prisoners. But within a few hours two Thai ministers and the Egyptian ambassador had talked them out of it; the diplomats were released and the terrorists were flown to Cairo. A Beirut newspaper reported that a 'revolutionary court' might be set up to try the men for disobeying orders.

Ignominious failure in Bangkok meant cold-blooded murder in Khartoum. The world must be taught—a Black September source told a Beirut newspaper—to 'take us seriously'.[52] On 1 March eight armed men took over the Saudi embassy in the Sudanese capital. They seized Curtis Moore, the American *chargé d'affaires*, for whom a farewell reception was being held, his ambassador, Cleo Noel, the Belgian *chargé d'affaires*, Guy Eid, the Saudi ambassador and the Jordanian *chargé d'affaires*. They demanded the release, among others, of Abu Daoud, a *Fatah* leader, and sixteen comrades under sentence of death in Jordan. Abu Daoud had been convicted for subversive activities against the régime, and on Jordanian radio was later to confess—without much exaggeration—that 'there is no such thing as Black September'; its operations, he said, were masterminded by three men: Abu Iyyad, generally regarded as the *Fatah* second-in-command, Abu Yusuf, chief of intelligence, and Abu

Hassan, his assistant. After two extensions of their deadline, the Black Septembrists took Moore, Noel and Eid into the basement of the embassy, ignoring the impassioned pleas of a 'voluntary' hostage, the Saudi ambassador's wife. There were several bursts of machine-gun fire; when the terrorists re-emerged, said the ambassador's wife, they did not 'look like men who had killed before'.

They eventually gave themselves up to the Sudanese authorities, raising their arms in victory signs as they left the building. President Numairi of the Sudan was outraged. He saw 'no heroism in seizing defenceless men, when you yourself are armed to the teeth, bargaining with their lives for impossible demands, slaughtering them like sheep, and keeping their corpses for 24 hours to rot.' Many of his people agreed with him. A wall poster at Khartoum University denounced the exploit: 'Can any sane mind justify it? Does Israel's inhumanity justify the abandonment of all human values?'[53] It was inept and ungrateful too. A Libyan-backed branch of *Fatah* was behind the killing, or so it seemed to Numairi, and he produced much evidence to support his claim. It was apparently a coded message (*al-Nahr al-Barid*—Cold River—the name of a refugee camp in north Lebanon, which the Israelis had raided a fortnight before, killing forty people, mainly women and children) broadcast from a Palestinian radio station, probably in Tripoli, which instructed the Black Septembrists to despatch their victims.[54] And there seemed to be no doubt at all that the head and deputy head of the *Fatah* bureau in Khartoum had done all the local planning. This was an intolerable abuse of Sudanese hospitality—and all the more so in that it was Numairi who, in the Jordanian civil war of Black September 1970, had gone to Amman, at considerable personal risk, and reported back to the Arab leaders that King Hussein was out to crush the guerillas.

After the killing, there came the justification. Their operation had been 'in no way aimed at bloodshed', a communiqué said, 'but only to bring about the release of our heroes', who were being 'tortured and terrorized in violation of all human values'. As a diplomat in Amman, it claimed, Curtis Moore had helped King Hussein to make war on the Palestinians. In fact, Moore had never been in Amman. Why the Belgian diplomat, Guy Eid, deserved the same fate the communiqué did not say. When King Hussein confirmed the death sentence on Abu Daoud and his sixteen comrades, and then said that he would only reprieve them if the resistance movement would give up all subversive activity against his régime, the PLO accused him of 'blackmail'. It certainly was—but why, in that case, Black September's exploits did not also rank as blackmail of the most cruel kind is something which the PLO never cared to explain.

In Khartoum, not only did Palestinian terrorists go further, in their contempt for conventional ethics, than ever before, they did so one week after Israel, in shooting down a Libyan airliner that had strayed over Sinai, had demonstrated a capacity for the same thing. At a stroke they wiped out the debit which their enemy had incurred in the balance-sheet of world opinion. They also played into the hands of the enemy in the rear. *Fatah*, King Hussein and others could plausibly argue, was a menace to every Arab régime.

So it went on, this terrorism that fed upon itself. It was not, strictly speaking, Black September any more. It was a host of imitators. The *fedayeen* had always been faction-ridden and undisciplined, but, with the genie out of the bottle, they surpassed themselves, all but spawning a new organization for every exploit. They grew more and more capricious in their choice of targets, ever more remote from the real, the Palestinian, battlefield, ever more incoherent, not to say incomprehensible, in what they hoped to achieve. In July the 'Sons of the Occupied Lands' took a Japanese airliner on a ninety-hour odyssey round the Middle East; as 140 exhausted passengers made their getaway it finally went up in flames at Benghazi airport. The purpose—according to a mimeographed statement slipped under the doors of Beirut newspaper offices—was to punish the Japanese government, which had paid Israel six million dollars in compensation for the Lydda airport massacre a year before. In August, two members of the 'Seventh Suicide Squad' attacked passengers in the transit lounge of Athens airport with machine-guns and grenades, killing three and wounding fifty-five. The victims were about to board a Trans World Airways flight to New York. In its communiqué, the Seventh Suicide Squad crossed a new threshold in the logic of Palestinian violence: 'We have finally come to the conclusion that in order to make you understand us and appreciate our right to live . . . we must adopt your criminal methods . . . no sooner had we reached this conviction than we mounted our operations against you, the American people, against your men, women and children. These are not our usual ways, but it is you who forced them upon us.' Hostile crowds surged round the two gunmen on their way to an Athens court; they shouted 'death to the murderers'. In September it was the turn of the 'Punishment Organization' to deal a blow at Arab 'reactionaries'; its men seized the Saudi embassy in Paris and demanded the release of Abu Daoud, who, after a reprieve by King Hussein, was serving a life sentence instead. After a hectic two-day siege of the embassy, the terrorists secured a Syrian airliner to take them to Kuwait, then a Kuwait one to Saudi Arabia; their final flourish was a threat, not carried out, to hurl their four Saudi hostages from the aeroplane as it flew over the desert. In November the 'Organization of Arab Nationalist Youth' hijacked a Dutch airliner; during a two-day peregrination round the Middle East and the Mediterranean, they landed at five different airports and were denied access to three others; they demanded, among other things, the closure of transit camps which had been set up in Holland to receive Soviet Jews emigrating to Israel. In December, five Arabs shot their way out of the Rome airport terminal, killing two people as they went; threw incendiary bombs into a Pan American Boeing 707, burning to death twenty-nine people, including four Moroccan officials; seized seven Italian policemen as hostages, forced their way aboard a nearby Lufthansa Boeing 737 and ordered the crew to fly to Athens; demanded the release, on arrival in Athens, of the two gunmen of the Seventh Suicide Squad, shot one of their hostages and threw his body from the plane; flew off, empty-handed, to Damascus and Kuwait, where they released their hostages and surrendered. Apart from two obscure statements signed by 'the Palestinian people', this, the bloodiest hijack of them all, had no claimants. But perhaps the final extravagance, the *reductio ad absurdum* of the hijackers' reasoning, was reached eleven months later when the 'Martyr Abu Mahmud Group' seized control of a British Airways VC 10 and called on the British government to 'declare its responsibility for the greatest crime in history, which was the establishment of the Zionist entity, and foreswear the accursed Balfour Declaration, which brought tragedies and calamities to our region'.

The British Airways hijack was the last straw for Yasser Arafat and the mainstream *Fatah* leadership. With a fanfare of publicity, they mounted what was described as an all-out drive against the hijackers, the 'renegades' and 'mercenaries', in their midst. In Beirut the PLO announced that twenty-six people had been arrested and would face public trial. If the trial did take place, it was certainly not held in public. However, the PLO subsequently claimed that the British Airways hijackers had been tried and sentenced. Journalists were shown round a 'correction centre' in Damascus; its inmates were convicted of acting 'against the interests of the revolution'. They were also shown the PLO's newly amended code of criminal law; hijacking that resulted in loss of life had been made into a capital offence.

Accepters and Rejectionists

It was far from a routine purge. Higher policy, indeed the very *raison d'être* of the resistance movement, was ultimately at stake.

The *Fatah* leadership had, of course, always disapproved of hijackings and 'foreign operations' of that kind. Not that they were dogmatic about it. They did not condemn Munich or Khartoum; indeed, if *Fatah*, or a wing of it, did not actually sponsor those two exploits, there was an implicit blessing in the absence of serious criticisms. Although they took place outside the land of Palestine, their targets were at least Israeli in one case and (if one overlooks the unfortunate Guy Eid) official representatives of the arch-villain, America, standing behind Israel in the other. The leadership also appeared to feel that, in certain circumstances of which they themselves were the judge, such operations could, if not overdone, further the cause. However, if the wild, anarchic excesses that followed in Munich's wake had any public relations value it was heavily outweighed by the disgust they also engendered. Moreover, attacks on Arab targets, such as the Saudi embassy in Paris, were flagrant violations of the sacred *Fatah* principle of non-interference in Arab affairs. Above all, however, the hijackings were becoming a challenge from a new quarter: from the enemy within.

This was apparent before the October 1973 War, but it came right into the open after it. That war, as we have seen, was a great turning point in the history of the Arab-Israeli conflict, an earthquake which, overnight, produced a massive shift, in the Arabs' favour, of the Middle East balance of power. The Arabs have always been painfully aware that, politically and militarily, their potentialities—inherent in a large population, vast and strategically located territories and, of late, oil wealth beyond the dreams of avarice—far outstrip their actual power. If they could only mobilize the resources at their disposal, they would quickly bring Israel to its knees. But they never could; internecine conflict, endless upheavals and *coups d'état* frustrated them; their régimes were incompetent or corrupt, their societies backward and ill-adapted to the modern world; they lacked an institutional system of collective decision-making. And yet that potential was indeed *so* vast that it required only a minimal community of purpose to convert it into an awesome force. And that is what, in the unplanned *élan* of the October War, President Sadat achieved.

The Egyptian leader decided to exploit the new balance of power, not to pursue the struggle but to end it. This was a revolutionary step. For all Arabs, not just the Palestinians, Palestine is as much theirs as Oxfordshire is English, Pennsylvania American. That is axiomatic, not worthy of discussion. They had been deprived of it, in times of weakness and division, by alien invaders who were no more entitled to it than the Crusaders centuries before them; like the Crusaders, the Zionists would eventually be driven out. Yet here was President Sadat expressing a readiness to make peace with Israel and, with the weight of Egypt behind him, calling on the rest of the Arab world to do likewise. Egypt, Syria, Jordan and the Palestinians—all should now face the Israelis across the conference table in Geneva. Obviously this peace would require Israeli concessions, territorial and of other kinds, but, in the true historical perspective, it would be the Arabs, not the Israelis, who were making the real, the fundamental concession: the formal renunciation of the 'liberation' of Palestine as a national aim. They would be acknowledging Israel's existence as an independent state, consecrating a pure Zionist gain against a pure Arab loss; it would be an act of historic magnanimity. To sell this peace to the Arabs, the very least that Sadat needed in return was that Israel should surrender all the occupied territories. And there could be nothing like the full 'economic peace' which the Israelis apparently wanted. The idea, Sadat once said, that Mrs Golda Meir could drive down to Cairo on a shopping expedition was a pipedream. Nor could there be Israeli embassies in Arab countries, or anything like that. Such things might come in the end, but, after decades of hatred and bitterness, the Israelis could not expect so much so soon. Future generations would decide; what he had done was to take the all-important first step in that direction.

Selling this peace to the Palestinians was naturally Sadat's most difficult task. Almost all Palestinians believed that the tide had now turned against the Zionist intruders, the menace had been contained, the endless *faits accomplis* at their expense checked. Zionism had reached its zenith in 1967. But after the October 1973 War articles with titles like 'The Beginning of the Zionist Decline' began to appear in Palestinian journals. In one, Sabri Jiryis, a respected scholar who had lived most of his life in Israel and knew the country intimately, forecast the drastic repercussions, ideological, political, economic and psychological, which the war would have on an enemy that once seemed well-nigh invincible. But Palestinians reacted differently to this new and encouraging reality. Some accepted, some rejected a peaceful settlement. Those who accepted it—or at least did not strenuously oppose it—could be said, with a good deal of oversimplification, to fall into two schools of thought. One held that the more complete the peace the better. For it was in conditions of complete security that, paradoxical as that might seem to the uninitiate, the inherent unviability of the whole Zionist enterprise would be exposed. Thus in a second article, entitled 'Israel in Danger of Peace', Jiryis argued that both in the short and the long term the Arabs, not the Israelis, would come out 'winners' from a settlement. In effect, he said, the Jewish State—or at least the one they knew, exclusivist, expansionist, aggressive—would simply wither away. A revolution would break the hold of the old-guard activists—whether from Menachim Begin's Revisionist right, the religious parties, or the ruling Labour government—on the country's political life; social conflict, particularly between European and Oriental Jews, would intensify; immigration would fall off; normal relations with the Arabs would undermine the self-segregating instincts which had put down such deep roots among the people. Jiryis even went so far as to suggest that the Arabs would have nothing to fear from an 'economic peace' with Israel. The idea of Israeli economic domination was far-fetched. Owing to its scarcity of manpower and economic resources, Israel would have more need of the Arabs than they of it. In recent years, he pointed out, talk of a peaceful settlement had always raised the question of what guarantees the Arabs should give the Israelis in return for their withdrawal from the occupied territories. 'But now it seems that, in the event of negotiations or a peace with Israel, it is Israel which must give guarantees to the Arabs, not the other way round. . . . And if Israel were obliged to abolish all those peculiarities which perpetuate its Zionist character, would that not lead, in the end, to the disappearance of that character and the rise of a secular democratic state in its place?'[55]

The other school of thought, espoused by much of the resistance leadership, held that the Palestinians should adopt a 'provisional programme', seeking what 'immediate gains' they could from a settlement without forfeiting their 'historical' rights to the whole of Palestine. Ideologically, it was impossible for the *fedayeen* to renounce their official goal of complete liberation, of Revolution Till Victory. Yet it was also exceedingly difficult for them to boycott the peace-making. True, they now felt stronger, in relation to Israel, than they ever had before; but the new strength was essentially Arab, not Palestinian, and all the more so as the *fedayeen*, after their setback in Jordan, were simultaneously weaker, in relation to other Arabs, than they had ever been before. The Arabs, as represented by the two states which had done most of the fighting, wanted to exploit that strength to achieve peace. If they succeeded, the occupied territories would have to revert to someone, and there was a grave danger, unless the PLO came forward to claim Jerusalem and the West Bank, that the someone would once again be King Hussein. That would be almost as bad as not getting them back at all. Thus it was that a man like Abu Iyyad, who, through his links with Black September, had been widely regarded as one of the most uncompromising *Fatah* leaders, began to play a key role in preparing rank and file opinion for a new strategy that seemed to have much in common with President Bourguiba's 'doctrine of stages'. When, from a

Palestinian refugee camp in 1965, the Tunisian leader had first propounded that infamous doctrine, arguing that the Arabs should recognize Israel and seek to restore their lost rights by negotiation rather than by an eventual war which they would probably lose, he was burned in effigy round the Arab world. 'Absolute rejection', said Abu Iyyad, 'is sometimes a form of escapism. . . . How long can we go on saying no? . . . Is it not a provisional gain to get back part of our land, 22 per cent of Palestine?'[56] A 'national authority' should be established, under PLO control, on the liberated territory. What this really seemed to imply was a fully-fledged mini-state of Palestine, co-existent with Israel; but 'Palestine State' were two heretical words which Abu Iyyad, and like-minded comrades, would not utter (not yet at least, for they were to do so later); for they signified permanence, finality, the abandonment of historic rights. Even one of the most ardent advocates of the 'provisional programme', Nayif Hawatmeh, leader of the Popular Democratic Front for the Liberation of Palestine, insisted that the 'national authority' would indeed be able to 'retain its guns and pursue the struggle in all its forms'.[57] Popular support for the new strategy was strongest in the occupied territories, especially the West Bank, now the stronghold of Palestinian moderation. As 'insiders', the West Bankers had a greater interest than the 'outsiders', mainly refugees of 1948 vintage, in achieving the 'immediate gain' of throwing off enemy rule. For they were still living, most of them, on their own land, in their own homes. In the inevitable upheavals of Revolution Till Victory they would still have a lot to lose. And, in any case, was victory assured? An organization calling itself the National Front for the Occupied Lands urged the PLO to join the international peacemaking because 'it is clear that under the present circumstances the realization of our full strategic goal is impossible'.[58] What all this amounted to was the semi-official espousal of a new, and altogether more moderate form of Zionism-in-reverse. 'Remember', said a delegate to the Palestine National Council, 'remember what Bengurion told the 22nd Zionist Congress at Basle in 1946: that the Zionists would accept a state in a reasonable part of Palestine without foregoing their historic rights to it all.'[59] The 'provisional programme' was formally adopted by the twelfth session of the Palestine

National Council, or Palestinian parliament, in June 1974. It was a greater contribution towards Arab-Israeli conciliation than the concept of the Democratic State which had emerged six years before.

The 'rejectionists', as they came to be known, would have none of it. They were Arab as well as Palestinian. 'The Arab nation', proclaimed the Beirut newspaper *al-Muharrir*,

> . . . today stands at the crossroads. Either it acquiesces in a surrender solution, which consecrates the imperialist-Zionist entity in its heartland, consolidates and strengthens it, enabling it to carry out fresh expansionist aggressions against the Arab world and put it at its mercy for ever. Or it rejects such proffered solutions, looks to its own devices, summons up all its resources, all its human, financial, economic and military capability—a capability which, as the October War showed, is much greater than we imagined—and renews the fight on all fronts, however much that might upset the calculations of the great powers. Let us have done with the play-acting at Geneva. . . .'[60]

The 'rejectionists' were very disappointed when President Sadat, reluctantly followed two days later by President Asad of Syria, accepted the ceasefire that ended the October War. It was their conviction that, had Egypt and Syria gone on, they would, by a process of spontaneous combustion that was already far advanced, have forced the entire Arab world to throw ever more resources into the fray. Israel would eventually have been overwhelmed. Why 'rescue' an enemy which could now so easily be finished off? They rejected Geneva and all it stood for. If the Arab world was emerging as a powerful force on the world stage, it should act like one. It was not in the nature of the strong to forget what they lost in times of weakness; France waited forty-eight years to get back Alsace-Lorraine. They believed that the fabulous Arab oil riches should be spent on arms, and yet more arms. The most prominent of Arab 'rejectionists' was that *exalté* and *enfant terrible*, Colonel Gadafi of Libya, who fired off a message to Sadat, telling him: 'You would have been greater, Mr President, if you had led us in a war with swords only and if, during it, we had lived in mountains, jungles and barren land, without oil or electricity, without towns or night-clubs, without politics, but with honour and dignity, with religion and Arabism. Let the land and buildings fall, but not the honour.'[61] The ruling Iraqi Baathists officially adopted the same viewpoint, and in many an Arab 'accepter' there lurked a suppressed 'rejectionist'.

Among the Palestinians, it was Dr George Habash's Popular Front which led the opposition to the interim programme. There must be no deviation from Revolution Till Victory, from the stand their fathers and grandfathers had maintained since the Balfour Declaration of 1917—'total rejection of the Zionist presence and fighting it to the end'. Habash held that, in its refusal to take any clear-cut position, the *Fatah* leadership was simply 'burying its head in the sand'. The 'doctrine of stages' was so much wishful thinking, for the 'present balance of Palestinian, Arab and international power make it impossible to create a national, democratic state or authority which our masses could rely upon to continue the struggle'.[62] He was saying what the *Fatah* leaders were not brave or honest enough to admit, that an integral part of any settlement would be the once-for-all suppression of Palestinian belligerency. In the wake of the October War, Habash and the 'rejectionists' kept up a relentless harassment which threatened, if the international peace-making ever got seriously under way, to tear the whole resistance movement violently apart. They accused *Fatah* of pusillanimously following in the 'capitulationist' course charted by Egypt; they hinted darkly at secret contacts between Arafat and Dr Kissinger; the Popular Front walked out of the Executive Committee of the PLO amid threatened moves to set up a rival, and truly revolutionary body of its own. For the extremists among them, international terrorism was the only answer to Arafat and his interim programme, the only way of sabotaging that respectability which he now felt he needed. The main culprit, in *Fatah*'s view, was less George Habash than Abu Nidal, leader of a Baghdad-based *Fatah* splinter group. For his part, Abu Nidal, suspected sponsor of the British Airways and previous hijackings, warned of a 'Palestinian civil war'.

Suicide Missions: Qiryat Shmona and Ma'alot

The civil war did not come. For one thing, the peace-making never did grow serious enough for a cornered Arafat to make the critical choice—such as going to the Geneva peace conference—which might have provoked it. For another, he had not given up the armed struggle. He was ready for a showdown with the 'rejectionists' over international terrorism; and in fact it did decline. But he had no objection to operations which borrowed the essential techniques of international terrorism—hostage-taking and blackmail—provided only that they took place on the soil of Palestine proper. The spring and summer of 1974 saw a series of spectacular 'suicide missions' staged by 'accepters' and 'rejectionists' alike. In April, three young men belonging to Ahmad Jibril's Popular Front for the Liberation of Palestine (General Command), a small but militarily competent outfit, struck for the 'rejectionists'. They and eighteen Israelis, eight of them children, died in an apartment block in the northern town of Kiryat Shmona. According to the Israelis, the three terrorists systematically killed everyone they could find before they were killed themselves. According to the Popular Front, they seized hostages and demanded the release of a hundred Palestinian prisoners; when the Israeli soldiers stormed the building, they blew themselves and their hostages up. In a posthumous letter to Arafat, they told him that 'we have given our lives in confidence that, through you, our sacrifice, and that of all our martyrs, will not be sold for surrender solutions.'

A month later it was the turn of the 'accepters'. In the forefront of these was the Popular Democratic Front for the Liberation of Palestine. Its leader, Nayif Hawatmeh, often seemed to act as Arafat's trailblazer in post-October 'moderation'. His latest 'first' was an interview, carried in a Tel Aviv newspaper, directly addressed to the Israeli people. He assured them that what the Front wanted was 'peaceful relations between Palestinians and Israelis'; for the time being, the official Palestinian ideal, the democratic, de-Zionized state for Arab and Jew in all of Palestine, was unattainable; meanwhile, the fulfilment of certain Palestinian rights—the establishment of an 'independent national authority' in the West Bank and Gaza and the return of the refugees—would open the way to a dialogue between 'progressive and democratic' Palestinians and Israelis 'opposed to imperialism and Zionism'.[63] On the night of 13 May, seven weeks after the interview, three of Hawatmeh's men slipped across the heavily guarded Lebanese frontier; the next evening they killed two Arab women in the back of a pick-up truck; at 3 A.M. on the 15th, Israel's Independence Day, they broke into an apartment in the village of Ma'alot, shooting three of its occupants. Then they seized about ninety teenagers in a nearby school. The choice of children as hostages was apparently deliberate;[64] that they happened to be a party of *Gadna*—Israel's school cadets—was hardly a mitigating circumstance. The terrorists demanded the release of twenty-six prisoners—one for each year of Israel's existence—and, among them, two Israeli Jews convicted of working for the *fedayeen*. Equally deliberate, apparently, was Israel's failure to negotiate with the terrorists for the lives of the schoolchildren.[65] It was the climactic collision of two implacable logics and it ended in catastrophe. The terrorists would release their hostages upon receipt of a codeword, transmitted from Damascus, indicating that twenty-six prisoners had arrived in the Syrian capital. The codeword never reached them. The Israeli government's apparent readiness, for once, to bow to terrorist blackmail was no more than an outward show of compassion to impress an anguished public. It planned to storm the school all along, and shortly before night fell the assault force went in; twenty children and three terrorists died in the carnage, and some seventy were wounded.

At first, the Israelis thought that the same 'rejectionist' organization which had mounted the Kiryat Shmona raid a month before was behind this one too. It therefore came as an additional shock to learn that if, in the persons of Hawatmeh and Arafat, the Palestinians now had 'moderate' aims, their methods were still as 'extreme' as ever. *Fatah* had indeed come a long way from the early innocence of—officially at least—military targets only. 'It is sad and I dislike it,' said a PLO official, 'the Israelis have indoctrinated us and we are now fighting like them. It is the Israelis who have taught us, by bloody experience, that there can be no differentiation between the soldier and the civilian.'[66]

The efficacy of the 'suicide mission' seemed beyond dispute. To put it, as some guerillas did, in cold economic terms, it was very cost-effective. The difference between a conventional high-risk and a *kamikaze* operation was a quantum leap in one's kill rate. Hitherto, that had generally been in the Israelis' favour, but in the two most 'successful' of a series of 'suicide missions'—Kiryat Shmona and Ma'alot—it was forty-eight dead Israelis against six dead Palestinians. Only with the bombardment of the refugee camps did the Israelis restore the balance in their favour. For the Israelis, the guerillas believed, such losses were hard to bear, while their own people, who had little to lose but their camps, could absorb death and destruction with what, by contrast, looked like fatalistic serenity. The implication of the 'suicide mission', they believed, must also be deeply disturbing to the Israelis, who could not but see in it a measure of Palestinian determination never to give up the struggle. In fact, they did not have to look far for evidence of the 'hysteria' which—even the enemy press admitted—was permeating Israeli society. They heard about hostile crowds, in the bereaved frontier townships, mobbing General Dayan, who had to be protected by his soldiers; about an opinion poll indicating that 68.6 per cent of the Israeli people disapproved of his hard-line, 'no compromise' policies; about the demoralization of Oriental Jews who, already resentful of their second-class status, were the main victims of the new terror; about anxiety over renascent nationalism among Hebrew-speaking Israeli Arabs and their recruitment to the *fedayeen*; about the old man in Ma'alot who murmured: 'there will never be peace in this cursed land'.

Arafat Addresses the United Nations

Yet the new terror appeared, on the whole, to make the Israelis more, not less, intransigent. Israel's little band of 'doves', who had found encouragement in Hawatmeh's conciliatory overtures, now seemed to command less influence than ever. Where was his dialogue now? 'We have been set back ten years', sighed Uri Avneri, 'the left has lost all the ground it won. That Hawatmeh should play into the hands of Golda Meir and Menachim Begin is quite beyond me.'[67] Under its new Prime Minister, Yitzhak Rabin, the Israeli government found all the hard-line pretexts it needed. Ma'alot proved that, for all his humanist posturing, Arafat's aim was still as wicked as ever: to destroy Israel. There was therefore no need for Israel to change its policies either. It would not recognize that there was such a thing as a 'Palestinian people', still less that the PLO had a right to represent it. A Palestine state would be a 'time-bomb'. No less than 70.8 per cent of the Israeli people agreed with him; they were opposed to such a state even within the framework of a general peace.

The Israeli intransigence seemed increasingly unrealistic. The doves continued to point that out. Few Israelis, one said, would still contend that there was no such thing as a 'Palestine problem'. 'Yet the majority still hope that, by not thinking about it, it will simply go away, that the earth will magically open and swallow all the Palestinians.' Time, he warned, was not on Israel's side; one day it would 'wake up and find the Palestinians at the negotiating table whether it liked it or not'.[68] The outside world pointed it out too.

Indeed, it was there, in the international diplomatic arena, that Arafat was about to score a run of spectacular successes which reinforced, and quite overshadowed, the military ones—and pushed Abu Nidal's threatened civil war still further into the background. The key forum was the UN. In 1947, with the General Assembly's vote for partition, the Zionists had won a famous victory. They claimed it as the charter of Israel's legitimacy; yet, even though it was already a verdict grotesquely weighted in their favour, they systematically flouted those of its provisions which did attempt to safeguard the rights of the Palestinians. Thus, if there were any international legitimacy by which the Palestinians could buttress their cause and strengthen their hand in the peace-making, it was the UN that should furnish it. They had been seeking a definition of their rights—and making considerable headway. In 1947 the UN, a much smaller, Western-dominated body than it later became, was prejudiced in the Zionists' favour; the boot was now on the other foot; the Palestinian cause became an automatic beneficiary of Afro-Asian bloc voting. The Palestinians' main objective was to achieve recognition for themselves not merely as refugees deserving of help on humanitarian grounds, but as a people with political aspirations. Thus, in 1969, the General Assembly first affirmed the right of 'the people of Palestine' to 'self-determination'; the denial of that right, it said, was at the root of the whole refugee problem. This was reiterated, with growing emphasis, in succeeding years until, in 1973, the Assembly established a clear link between self-determination and the right of return, the latter being an 'indispensable' prerequisite of the former. Recognition of the 'rights' was accompanied by recognition of the right to 'struggle' for their attainment. Accordingly, in a resolution of 1970, the Palestinians had been classified with various peoples of Southern Africa as victims of 'colonial and alien domination', and, as such, entitled to restore their rights 'by any means at their disposal'.[69]

The climax was still to come. The UN General Assembly decided, for the first time since 1952, on a full-dress debate of the 'Palestine Question' and invited the PLO, as the representative of the Palestinian people, to take part in it. The climax was appropriately ushered in. In 1947, France had voted for partition, to become one of the staunchest friends of Israel's early years. But when, in October 1974, her Foreign Minister Jean Sauvagnargues paid an official visit to Lebanon he made a point of taking breakfast with Yasser Arafat. Afterwards, he reportedly confided that Arafat was acquiring 'the stature of a statesman'; he was a 'moderate' who 'represents, embodies, the aspirations of the Palestinians.'[70] The intimate repast, in the French ambassador's residence, began and ended to the accompaniment of loud sonic booms from overflying Israeli warplanes—apparently a gesture of displeasure at what amounted to the first official recognition of the PLO by a major Western power. A few days later came 'a wedding feast for the Palestinians.' That is how Arafat described the Arab summit conference in Rabat. In his eyes, the Hashemite throne ranked second only to Israel as an instrument of Palestinian misfortunes. At Rabat, King Hussein bowed to overwhelming Arab pressure and gave away half his kingdom—ceding, juridically, to the PLO the West Bank and Jerusalem which he had lost, physically, to the Israelis in 1967. It was a diplomatic victory that avenged the military defeat of Black September 1970.

Arafat's apotheosis—a fortnight later on the rostrum of the UN General Assembly—was savoured by all Palestinians, 'accepters' and 'rejectionists' alike, as a moment of truly sweet revenge. Not only—*pace* Golda Meir—did the Palestinians exist, here was their leader getting the kind of passionate attention, as he addressed the world, that no visiting statesmen, however illustrious or controversial, had ever quite commanded before him. Arab journalists reported from

New York that the man who, ten years before, began slipping across Israel's frontiers on almost unnoticed sabotage missions, was now mounting the most spectacular commando operation of his career. For New York, which contained more Jews than Israel itself, was definitely enemy territory. Arafat, said one Jewish leader, was regarded there with the kind of hatred once reserved for Hitler; the atmosphere, before his arrival, generated 'the same sort of solidarity as when a war breaks out'.[71] A huge demonstration preceded him. Tens of thousands gathered in Hammarskjöld Plaza in the shadow of the UN building to hear Israeli leaders denounce the outrage that was about to be perpetrated. They were led by Senators and Congressmen from New York and half a dozen other states, city councillors, the mayor, state officials, trade union leaders and most of the candidates in the forthcoming New York elections: such is the importance of Israel in domestic American politics. The demonstrators, Jewish and gentile, white and black, carried placards reading: 'UN Becomes a Forum of Terrorism'; 'PLO is Murder International'; 'We Refuse to Shake the Bloody Hand of the PLO'. Among the speakers, Senator Henry Jackson, champion of Soviet Jewry, earned the warmest applause. The UN decision to recognize the PLO, he declared, 'threatens the already pale prospect of peace. The United Nations reeks with the smell of blackmail.' On behalf of the AFL-CIO labour federation, another speaker called for an American embargo of 'poisoned Arab oil'. He claimed that America's European allies had already 'surrendered' to the Arabs. Protest took a violent turn too. Militants of Rabbi Meir Kahan's Jewish Defence League invaded the mid-town offices of the PLO on Park Avenue and clubbed the assistant director with a lead pipe. Russell Kellner, the League's 'operations officer', called a press conference, and with a pistol on the table in front of him, announced that the PLO 'murderers' had no place in New York and that 'trained men' would 'make sure that Arafat and his lieutenants do not leave New York alive'.[72]

Normally, on a sunny autumn weekend, the UN building is packed with four or five thousand visitors. New Yorkers stroll through the gardens of its eighteen-acre premises on the East River, enjoying the chrysanthemums or the last roses of summer. Suburban families descend on the gift shops in the basements and sightseers take the guided tour. But not on 11 and 12 November 1974—on that weekend the whole place was hermetically sealed off from the outside world. For Arafat was due to address the General Assembly on Monday, the thirteenth, and he was being guarded by the tightest security in UN history. Two US Army helicopters brought him and his party from the airport; as they deposited him in the compound, other helicopters patrolled overhead, launches cruised in the East River, sharp-shooters kept watch from high buildings and hundreds of specially assigned New York police and Federal Guards manned wooden barricades in the streets below.

Shortly before noon, Arafat entered the General Assembly to a standing ovation. Only the American delegation remained seated. The chamber was crammed to capacity; only two groups of seats were empty, those of the Israelis, who could not face this Palestinian triumph, and the South Africans, who had been suspended from the Assembly the night before. Arafat was escorted to the rostrum by the Chief of Protocol and seated in the white leather chair reserved for heads of state. Under a procedure which had been invoked only once before—and that for no less a personage than the Pope—he became the first leader of a 'national liberation movement' to receive such an honour. But he, in return, did little to affect the demeanour of a head of state. He was, as always, wearing his chequered *kefiyyah* headdress, his baggy trousers, open-necked shirt and ill-fitting jacket. And when, acknowledging the applause, he raised his arms in a revolutionary salute, he exposed the holster at his side. But for once, apparently, he had at least had a proper shave and, it was claimed, the holster was empty.

Figuratively speaking, however, he and the people he represented had certainly not disarmed—although they were eagerly awaiting the day when they could. 'I have come bearing an olive branch and a freedom fighter's gun. Do not let the olive branch fall from my hand.' With this appeal, he ended his 100-minute address. In the course of it he had dwelt lovingly on his 'Palestine of tomorrow', on his Democratic State for Moslem, Christian and Jew. He called it his 'dream' and invited the Jews now living in Palestine, all of them, to turn away from Zionist ideology, which only offered them perpetual bloodshed, and to share his dream.

The speech—and subsequent UN resolutions in favour of the PLO—met with much the same dark fury, among Israel and its supporters, as partition had, among the Arabs, twenty-seven years before. From the Israeli ambassador there came a tirade of rare violence not merely against Arafat's band of 'murderers and cutthroats' who had plunged the UN into a 'Sodom and Gomorrah of ideals and values' but against the international community which, in 'days of degradation and disgrace, of surrender and humiliation', had let them do it. For the Foreign Minister, 'the voice of Arafat was, and remains, the voice of indiscriminate terror, the voice of the gun, with nothing in it of the olive branch of peace'. The Minister was not to be deceived by gracious rhetoric. Nor was the Israeli press. It was obvious, the commentators said, that any Palestine State in the West Bank or Gaza would be no more than a platform for renewing warfare against an Israel conveniently reduced to its earlier, more vulnerable dimensions. 'No reasonable person—if there are any left in a world thirsty for oil—can ask us to hand over these regions to the PLO, unless it expects Israel to commit suicide.'[73]

But where the Israelis saw only the reiteration, in beguiling form, of an intransigent orthodoxy, the Palestinians, and particularly the West Bankers, saw more of the post-October moderation. Arafat's 'dream' was the only thing the Israelis noticed; the practical, immediate goal he put forward, the 'national authority', was what mattered to them. The Israelis only saw the gun; the Palestinians saw the olive branch. For most Palestinians, the 'dream' was mere lip-service to the goal of complete liberation. It was self-evident that Arafat had to pay it, for he had to appease those, the 'rejectionists', who believed that Revolution Till Victory, continuous armed struggle, was the only way to change the nature of Israel, the only way to achieve that goal which the newly 'moderate' Arafat and the unyielding George Habash still officially had in common. In reality, however, the establishment of a Palestine State could only mean that the struggle, if it continued at all, would be a peaceful and political one. The final Middle East settlement would outlaw violence. Iron-clad guarantees would have to come from all parties—and not least from the *fedayeen*, who, for the past ten years, had fought and died in the conviction that violence, or revolutionary counter-violence as they considered it, was their people's only salvation. Many Palestinians, especially West Bankers, understood and accepted that. 'For us', said the editor of Jerusalem's militant *al-Fajr* newspaper, 'the democratic Palestine is a dream too, but we believe that only by a gradual political process can the Arab and Jewish states in Palestine merge into one'.[74] It was also widely understood that that might be as far as Zionism-in-reverse would ever get, that what Arafat postulated as a transitional stage of indefinite duration would really be the final one. 'Deep down', said a professor from Bir Zeit University, '80 per cent of us realize this. It is very difficult for us to say goodbye to what is ours—Haifa, Jaffa and most of Jerusalem—but we are in effect telling the Israelis that we are ready to do so. We are saying that we no longer want to drive them out of the land from which they drove us. Some of us still want to do so, but they are not the dominant voice. But in return the Israelis must withdraw from at least all the territories occupied in 1967. Nothing less is feasible. They must grasp this.'[75]

They did not grasp it. Moreover, the professor did not really expect them to do so. If the Israelis saw no change in the Palestinians, he, like most of his compatriots, certainly saw very little change in them. In theory, Arafat was still holding his olive branch, but it quickly withered with neglect. The Israelis, the Arabs understood, were congenitally incapable of abandoning the policy of force upon which they had always relied. The more obvious the renaissance of the Palestinians became the more obdurately they refused to recognize it. The cartoonists now portrayed Israel as the man who put his fingers in his ears and refused to listen. Its 'refusal to accept realities', its 'perseverance in the absurd' became dominant themes of the editorialists. It was a defiant posture which they found all the more remarkable in that, as they saw it, Israel simply did not command the resources to sustain it. All the signs were, they said, that, whatever the strictly military situation, the underlying balance of power was continuing to shift in the Arabs' favour. Since the October War, said one Beirut news-paper, 'the whole Zionist entity has been in a state of permanent crisis which is now all but out of control'. Israel, said another, could no more expect to live as a 'foreign body' in its region than Rhodesia or South Africa in theirs.[76] But they warned that Israel would probably try to turn the tables on the Arabs in the one field, the military one, where it still had a chance of doing so. Such an attempt would be irrational, they pointed out, in so far as the main reason for its present plight was the economic, diplomatic and psychological consequence of the last war. But then the picture of a near-hysterical enemy, of an Israel on the run, an embattled, fortress Israel girding itself to die by the sword by which it was created was also taking root in the Arab mind.

In the immediate aftermath of the October War, it did not seem to be a wildly unrealistic view of changing fortunes in the Middle East. But so, before long, it turned out to be. To be sure, there were symptoms enough of decline in Israel and the forces that sustained it, a decline which, unchecked, would ultimately prove fatal to the whole Zionist enterprise. For the time being, however, Israel was able not merely to restore its fortunes, *vis-à-vis* Palestinians and Arabs, but to raise them to a higher degree of mastery over its environment than it had ever achieved before. For this view left out of account the deplorable condition, temporarily obscured by the October War, into which the Arabs themselves had sunk.

Notes

1. *Palestine Documents, 1967* (Arabic), Institute for Palestine Studies, Beirut, 1968, pp. 264, 1084.
2. Al-Azm, Sadiq, *Left Studies on the Palestine Problem* (Arabic), Dar al-Tali'ah, Beirut, 1970, pp. 53, 55.
3. See Kazziha, Walid, *Revolutionary Transformation in the Arab World*, Charles Knight, London, 1975, pp. 52–3.
4. Rashid, Muhammad (Nabil Shaath), *Towards a Democratic State in Palestine*, PLO Research Centre, Beirut, 1970, p. 16.
5. Al-Sharqawi, *Fatah—1965–1971*, *op. cit.*, p. 181.
6. Rashid, *op. cit.*, p. 15.
7. *Ibid.*, p. 48.
8. Al-Sharqawi, *op. cit.*, p. 321.
9. Yaari, *Strike Terror, The Story of Fatah*, *op. cit.*, p. 150.
10. Khatib, Husam, 'Whither the Palestinian Revolution?', *Palestine Affairs* (Arabic), Beirut, October 1971, pp. 5–7.
11. *Ibid.*, p. 7.
12. *Ibid.*, p. 7.
13. Al-sharqawi, *op. cit.*, p. 318.
14. *Ibid.*, p. 317.

15. *Haaretz*, 20 October 1968.
16. Orr, A., and machover, Moshe, *ISRAC*, March 1970.
17. *The Other Israel*, *op. cit.*, p. 176.
18. Harkabi, Yehoshafat, *Palestinians and Israel*, Keter Publishing House, Jerusalem, 1974, pp. 70–126.
19. Shaath, Nabil, 'Palestine of Tomorrow', *Palestine Affairs* (Arabic), Beirut, May 1971, p. 9.
20. *Al- Muharrir*, 19 November 1968.
21. Al-Sharqawi, *op. cit.*, p. 318.
22. *Ibid.*, pp. 313–15.
23. Sayigh, Yusif, *The Attrition of Israel as a Result of the Military Struggle, Palestine Affairs* (Arabic), Beirut, September 1971, p. 58.
24. Military spokesman, 8 August 1968.
25. Sulh, Alia, *al-Nahar*, 4 June 1968.
26. Yasar Arafat, to *Rose el- Youssef* (Cairo weekly), 11 November 1969.
27. Rashid, *op. cit.*, p. 33.
28. *Filastin Al-Thaurah*, January 1968, p. 25.
29. *Ibid.*, September 1968, p. 29.
30. *Der Stern*, 16 September 1970.
31. Khatib, *op. cit.*, p. 8.
32. *Al-Anwar*, 12 February 1969.
33. See *The Guardian*, 29 December 1970.
34. Yaari, *op. cit.*, p. 353.
35. *The Guardian*, 20 July 1971.
36. *Africasie*, Paris, 24 January 1972.
37. 1 December 1971.
38. *Arab Report and Record*, London, Issue No. 4, 1972, p. 104.
39. 7 September 1972.
40. Khatib, Husam, 'Thoughts on Palestinian Violence', *Palestine Affairs*, March 1972, p. 23.
41. *Observer* Foreign News Service, 15 September 1972.
42. Al-Sharqawi, *op. cit.*, p. 317.
43. *Al-Sayyad*, 13 September 1972.
44. *Le Nouvel Observateur*, 11 September 1972.
45. *Al-Nahar*, 24 November 1972.
46. See p. 251.
47. *Time*, 2 October 1972.
48. *Ibid.*
49. *The Guardian*, 3 October 1972; see pp. 164–70.
50. *Ibid.*, 1 June 1972.
51. Haikal, Muhammad, *al-Ahram*, 9 June 1972.
52. *Al-Muharrir*, 3 March 1973.
53. *The Guardian*, 22 March 1973.
54. *Sunday Times*, 29 April 1973.
55. *Al-Nahar*, 7, 8, 9 November 1973.
56. *The Guardian*, 17 January 1974.
57. *Ibid.*

58. *Ibid.*
59. *Ibid.*, 10 June 1974.
60. 5 January 1974.
61. *The Guardian*, 18 January 1974.
62. *Ibid.*
63. *Le Monde*, 23 March 1974.
64. *Sunday Times*, 19 May 1974.
65. *The Times*, 29 May 1974.
66. *Daily Star*, Beirut, 19 May 1974.
67. *Le Nouvel Observateur*, 21 May 1974.
68. *Davar*, 30 June 1974.
69. See Armanazi, Ghayth, 'The Rights of the Palestinians—the International Definition', *Journal of Palestine Studies*, Beirut, Vol. III, No. 3, 1974.
70. *The Guardian*, 22 October 1974M
71. *International Herald Tribune*, 11 November 1974.
72. *The Times*, 13 November 1974.
73. *Yediot Aharonot*, 14 November 1974.
74. *The Guardian*, 27 December 1974.
75. *Ibid.*
76. *Ibid.*, 14 November 1974.

10 · PEACE WITH EGYPT

Prime Minister Menachim Begin

In May 1977 Menachim Begin became Prime Minister of Israel. In the general elections his right-wing *Likud* coalition trounced the Labour party, which had ruled the country since its creation. Thus democratically did the fanatical, openly expansionist wing of the Zionist movement come triumphantly into its own. The man who, as chief of the *Irgun* terrorists, had blown up the King David Hotel and perpetrated the massacre of Deir Yassin, took charge of the awesome military machine into which the pre-independence militias had grown during his twenty-nine years in the political wilderness.

Begin and his followers had shed few of the romantic, ultranationalist beliefs imparted by their spiritual father Vladimir Jabotinsky. The *Herut* party, the main component of the *Likud*, had never formally abandoned the Revisionist slogan: 'The Jordan has Two Banks, One is Ours and so is the Other'. Begin was still, in the words of a distinguished Israeli critic, 'a nationalist fanatic who lives in a universe of historic symbols and mysticism.'[1]

The Labour party had not been slothful in the settling and 'upbuilding' of Greater Israel. Theirs had been the time-honoured policy of creeping annexation, of the *fait accompli* that could not be undone. Since the 1967 War it had set up eighty-five settlements of one kind or another in the occupied territories, most of them outside the main centres of Arab population in the so-called Allon Belt that ran the length of the Jordan Valley. They had also permitted the expansionist zealots of the *Gush Emunim* (The Bloc of the Faithful) to establish 'illegal' settlements, including one at Kaddoum in the hitherto exclusively Arab neighbourhood of Nablus. In principle at least—though in practice their settlement policy rendered the principle all but meaningless—they were ready for a partial withdrawal from the occupied territories within the framework of a general peace. But here came the *Likud*, with Jehovah as its authority, proclaiming openly what Labour had done surreptitiously.

Two days after his election Begin paid a triumphant visit to the 'illegal' settlement of Kaddoum and announced that there would be many more Kaddoums in the length and breadth of the land. These 'liberated' territories, as he termed them, would never be given up to the Arabs in the peace agreement which, in the same breath, he urged upon the people. They were 'an inseparable part of the State of Israel', and that was something the Arab states would 'have to understand'. He warned the world that the appellation 'West Bank' had no meaning: 'it is Judea and Samaria, which are Israeli lands and the property of the Jewish people'. These territories could not be annexed 'because you do not annex your own country'.[2] Drawing on that venerable strain of extremist Zionist logic—that the harder you hit the Arabs the more reasonable they become—he propounded that 'retaining Judea and Samaria would ensure the possibility of peace'.[3]

As for the Palestinians, they were an artificial invention. Henceforth they would be known as 'the Arabs of Eretz Israel'. There would never be a 'so-called Palestinian state on our land'. Nor could there be any question of negotiating with the Palestinians, who 'are the most implacable enemy since the Nazis. What do we have to negotiate with them? Our self-destruction?'

The change of régime was the greatest upheaval in domestic Israeli politics since the creation of the State. A key element in Begin's triumph was the massive support which he, an Ashkenazi Jew of European origin, had won from the Sephardi Jews of Oriental, mainly Arab origin. After suffering long years of neglect and disdain at the hands of the Ashkenazi Labour establishment, the Sephardim—who, with their higher birth rate, now constituted more than half the population—had come to see Begin as something of an 'outsider' like themselves and they loved his demagogy and intemperance. The upheaval took much of the world, and indeed many Israelis, by surprise. It should not have done. Like embattled colonial societies elsewhere, historically Israel has always gravitated towards the most extreme expression of nationhood.

The Arabs, 'accepters' among them at least, were dismayed. For the 'rejectionists' it confirmed that armed struggle, Revolution Till Victory, was the only possible course. Guerilla leaders forecast the fifth Arab-Israeli war.

Many Israelis could hardly believe it either. The Labour leadership had always held Begin in disdain. His triumph had grown out of the pre-independence struggle and the deep-seated antagonism between the mainstream leadership and the 'dissidents', between the *Haganah* and the *Irgun*. In 1948 Bengurion had forcibly disarmed the 'dissidents', going so far as to sink the *Irgun* arms ship *Altalena* at a cost of forty lives. He could never even bring himself to pronounce Begin's name in the Knesset. 'I have no doubt', Bengurion once said of him, 'that Begin hates Hitler—but this hatred does not prove that he is different from him. When for the first time I heard Begin on the radio, I heard the voice and screeching of Hitler. . . . If, one day, he comes to power, with his political adventures, he will lead the State of Israel to its destruction.'[4] Zionist historians have understated the key role which terrorists played in the creation of the State, generations of schoolchildren being taught that such methods were incompatible with 'purity of arms'. There was not a little self-deception and hypocrisy in this, in that the difference between the *Haganah* and *Irgun* was one of degree rather than kind. None the less, even though Begin and his followers entered the Knesset and for a while joined a Labour-dominated government coalition, they never achieved full respectability. There could now, however, no longer be any doubt about it: the whole of Israeli society was shifting to the right, into mystical chauvinism, religious obscurantism, and the cult of force. For the prominent 'dove', Arie Eliav, Begin's triumph was a 'national catastrophe'.

Nowhere was the confusion and consternation greater than in the United States. The little the Americans knew of Begin they found it expedient not to like. They had first been introduced to him in 1948 when he was a candidate for Prime Minister. His American supporters in the League for a Free Palestine spared no effort to promote the fortunes of 'the man who defied empire and gained glory for Israel'. They assembled a Reception Committee which included eleven Senators, twelve Governors, seventy-odd Congressmen, seventeen justices and judges along with educationists, public officials and mayors by the score. It required only a public warning by three prominent clergymen, one of them a rabbi, however, and the Reception Committee disintegrated. All the duped politicians—among them Congressman John F. Kennedy of Massachusetts—suddenly discovered that either they had been ignorant of the true nature of Begin's activities or they had no idea how they had got on the list. Albert Einstein joined other distinguished citizens in chiding these 'Americans of national repute' for honouring a man whose party was 'closely akin in its organization, methods, political philosophy and social appeal to the Nazi and Fascist parties'.[5]

Even before Begin came to power, Israel's reputation in the United States, though still very high, had been suffering a steady decline. For a doting American public, the 'bastion of democracy in the Middle East' was no longer quite the paragon of virtue it had been. Fulfilling its every wish was no longer quite so pressing a necessity for American governments. Administration officials were critical of Israel's colonization of the occupied territories. In the first half of 1976 there was serious Arab rioting, not only in the West Bank but in Israel itself. A primary cause was the renewed manifestation of the insatiable Zionist appetite for Arab land. It shattered the carefully fostered illusion that Israel's Arabs, if not content with their lot, were at least resigned to it and showed that the diplomatic successes of the PLO had deeply affected not only the West Bankers but also the 'forgotten' Palestinians of Israel proper. It also caused Israel to exhibit that ugly, oppressive side of its nature which it usually managed to hide from the world. Palestinians were now 'news'—another sign of the times—and although investigative zeal had never been the hallmark of Western newsmen based in Israel, they showed enough of it on this occasion to exasperate a government unaccustomed to such persistently unflattering scrutiny.

As if the riots had not been damaging enough, the Israeli government chose this time to dramatize one of the most significant, if hitherto little publicized, contemporary inter-national friendships. The official visit to Israel of John Vorster, Prime Minister of South Africa, and the warm welcome he received, consecrated the deepening alliance between two states whose predicament and method of dealing with it had long been remarkably similar. Shortly after came the embarrassing leak of the 'Koenig Memorandum'. In this top-secret document a high-ranking official in the Ministry of the Interior put forward proposals, overtly racist in tone, for 'thinning out' the Arab population of northern Israel. By the end of 1976 well over half the Soviet Jews who had secured exist visas for Israel were heading straight for the United States and other Western countries instead. Jewish charitable organizations in the United States came under heavy Israeli pressure to cut off aid to all such undeserving drop-outs. If Israel had its way, a group of émigrés protested, that would produce a situation in which 'the Jews of the Free World help the KGB stop Soviet Jews leaving the USSR'.[6]

Official American strictures were no longer so strenuously contested inside America itself as they had once been. For many years Israel's hold over American Jewry, that most potent and energetic of lobbies, had been all but complete. For the main Jewish organizations, official Israeli attitudes—regarding the Palestinians, the Arab world and the road to peace—were theirs too. But when Arie Eliav visited America in early 1976 he observed that the American Jewish scene was changing. 'It's deceptive,' he said, 'it's like a frozen river: the surface is quiet, but underneath, watch out.'[7] In 1976, the Social Action Unit of Reform Judaism adopted a formal resolution criticizing Israel's 'provocative' actions on the West Bank. In early 1977 Rabbi Albert Vorspan, Vice-President of the Union of American Hebrew Congregations, warned that, 'if it turns out that Israel cannot pull herself together to respond fast enough or creatively enough to a true prospect for peace, then millions of us—in Israel and in the Diaspora, especially America—will raise royal hell and put Israeli leadership's feet to the fire'.[8]

So, when Begin went to Kaddoum and spoke about the 'liberation' of the Land of his Ancestors, it wrought a last-minute change in the commencement speech which President Carter delivered at Notre Dame University. 'Disaster' lay ahead, he said, if any of the Middle East antagonists tried to block a peace settlement. If the Kaddoum pronouncement had annoyed the White House, the one that followed two days later provoked outright anger. There was no conflict, Begin contended, between the President and himself over the

West Bank. 'Why should there be a conflict?' he asked. 'I will try and explain it to Mr Carter. He knows perfectly well the Bible. I understand that he knows the Bible by heart.' There was shock and disbelief in the American Jewish community. Begin's policies, forecast a member of the non-conformist Jewish organization *Breira*, 'will lead to confrontation not only with the US but with the entire international community', threatening Israel with 'total isolation' and posing 'the greatest danger to her survival since the creation of the State in 1948'.[9] But in the event they did not—thanks, above all, to Anwar Sadat.

Arab Civil War by Proxy

The Egyptian leader was outwardly undismayed at the change of régime in Israel. There were 'no hawks and no doves' among the Israeli leaders, he said, and Begin was 'no different from Rabin or Peres'. That was that. For an autocrat like Sadat such smooth adjustments were easily made. The Americans, for all their misgivings, managed one too. Begin despatched Shmuel Katz, his old *Irgun* comrade, on a public relations mission to present him 'as a man of humane principle and reason, and to demand for him the same unswerving support that Israeli leaders have been accustomed to receive from American Jews'.[10] Rabbi Alexander Schindler, Chairman of the Conference of the Presidents of Major Jewish Organizations, returned from a fact-finding visit to Jerusalem apparently satisfied that Begin would be an entirely different person from the man of Deir Yassin and the King David Hotel. He told officials in the White House that he was 'not a raving extremist' but a 'sensitive patriot'. Setting the example for most of the US media, the *New York Times* dwelt at length on the *new* Begin, this 'courtly, baldish figure who kisses women on the hand or cheek on introduction and is particular about his attire'.[11]

By the time Begin arrived on his first Prime Ministerial visit the *New York Times* was able to report that the Jewish community, having discarded its doubts, was solidly behind him and that at a banquet given by the Israeli Bond Organization he had been hailed as 'the symbol of heroic leadership in the struggle for independence', now transformed into 'the spokesman for a new destiny for the Jewish people'. Begin seemed to hit it off with President Carter, whose National Security Adviser, Zbigniew Brzezinski, commented that he had 'a good chance of leading Israel to peace'.

Neither Sadat nor the Americans, Sadat especially, had much choice but to accept the verdict of the Israeli electorate. For in concert with the Palestinians and other Arab states, he was in the thick of a great new 'peace offensive'. 'We are headed for Geneva and a final settlement,' he had proclaimed at the beginning of the year. Geneva would be the 'final battle of the Arab-Israel conflict'. At the outset of his Presidency Carter had called 1977 'the brightest hope for peace that I can recall'. He had inspired Arab hopes of an American administration which might, at long last, hold its own against the all-powerful Zionist lobby. Acknowledging the Arabs' 'moderation', he had led them to believe that it would earn the response that it seemed to deserve, in the shape of real pressure on Israel. He had outlined his conception of a final peace. But for 'a few minor adjustments', he said, Israel should relinquish all the occupied territories. A 'homeland' must be found for the Palestinian refugees, 'who have suffered for many, many years'. 'If this is true,' exclaimed Yasser Arafat, in an unprecedented tribute to an American President, 'he has touched the core of the problem without which there can be no settlement.' Sadat was not going to throw away this new opportunity. He was in dire need of progress towards that 'just and lasting' peace which, four years after the October 1973 War, seemed almost as remote as ever.

The trouble was that the October War had not been the 'glorious' victory which he claimed. Although, for reasons we have described,[12] the war was an earthquake that shook Israel to its foundations, in the end its army came close to winning it. After the triumphant crossing of the Suez Canal, General Ariel Sharon, founder of the notorious Unit 101 and subsequently Israel's most reckless, controversial and insubordinate commander, led an almost suicidally dangerous counter-crossing of his own. Sadat turned to the superpowers, which, half in concert, half in competition, rescued him *in extremis*. He was obliged to end the fighting on terms for which he might almost not have fought at all. In Resolution 338 the Security Council called on all parties to cease fire in the positions they occupied and then to begin 'the implementation of Security Council resolution 242 in all its parts'. The situation was more or less back to square one. For it had been precisely to break the intolerable impasse of 242—a resolution so vague that Israel, battening on its territorial conquests, had rejected all friendly, let alone Soviet or Arab, interpretations of it—that Egypt had gone to war in the first place.

A victory of the dimensions Sadat claimed should automatically and quickly have yielded the victor's spoils in the shape of the just and lasting peace as the Arabs, by a broad consensus, defined it. From the outset Sadat swore to uphold his pan-Arab obligations. He was solemnly bound to a collective Arab strategy, the be-all and end-all of which was a 'comprehensive' settlement of the Palestine problem. The only alternative, he said, 'to Arab coordination is an Arab civil war that will put Israel's mind at ease and relieve it of the trouble of confrontation'.[13]

In practice he found himself throwing away the Arabs' assets one by one. The position of relative strength which, in spite of the Israeli counter-crossing, he had enjoyed on the morrow of the war, was reduced as time passed to one of abject weakness and desperation. The Egyptians, suffering from poverty and overpopulation, yearned for an end to the conflict as no other Arabs did. For their part the Israelis did have something to offer them in return. For, unlike the West Bank, Sinai was not, in their view, an inalienable, God-given part of the Jewish homeland. They did not consider it vital to their security as they did the Golan Heights. In order to recover Sinai for Egypt Sadat embarked on a stealthy, go-it-alone diplomacy, the effect of which was to make it even harder for everyone else, Syrians, Jordanians and Palestinians, to recover *their* territories. He acquiesced in the two Sinai disengagement agreements negotiated by his 'friend' Henry Kissinger in prodigious feats of shuttle diplomacy. The Israelis did yield territory, but not much and their concessions were richly rewarded.

The first disengagement in January 1974 was followed five months later by a similar one on the Golan Heights, but the second, in September 1975, drew the fierce reproaches of Syria, and charges on all sides that Sadat was selling out the Arab cause. To deal separately with its neighbours had always been a guiding purpose of Israeli foreign policy, and here was Sadat, the leader of the most powerful Arab country, giving Israel the non-belligerency it sought together with a secret promise that if Syria attacked Israel Egypt would keep out of it.[14]

The Palestinians paid the price of the first open schism in Arab ranks since the October War. It was profoundly ironic that, just as they were scoring brilliant victories against the main, Israeli enemy in the international diplomatic arena, they should be struck with devastating force by the enemy in the rear. It was another, scarcely credible twist in what Arafat had once called 'an Arab plot'.[15]

It was in Lebanon that the schism took its most virulent form. After Black September, 1970, Yasser Arafat and his guerillas had moved in strength to that small country. The autonomous politico-military power base which they established there was an encroachment on their sovereignty which the Lebanese, or at least the traditionally militant Maronite Christian minority, deeply resented. In April 1975 the right-wing Maronite militias, the Phalangists and the Chamounists, took up arms against the guerillas and their Moslem-leftist Lebanese allies. Sporadic and small-scale at first, after the second Sinai disengagement agreement the fighting grew in scope and intensity to become, if not the Arab civil war of which Sadat had warned, at least an Arab civil war by proxy. In Arabic commentaries on the war one word, *tahjim*, occurred again and again. It means 'cutting down to size' and furnishes a key insight into a uniquely complicated and savage conflict. They all wanted to cut the Palestinians down to size. Tactically divided, however, some of them wanted to cut each other down to size too. President Asad and his ruling Baathists were striving to establish a *Greater*-Syrian power base which they could use in the wake of Sadat's sell-out for a counter-strategy of their own.

If Egypt was to be the gateway for *Pax Americana* in the Middle East, Asad was determined that Syria should be the key that unlocked the gate. To this end he had already allied himself with King Hussein's Jordan on one flank. A few years before that would have been judged a most unnatural alliance because Hussein—whom Asad used to describe as 'an asset to the gangster-state [of Israel]'[16]—was a miraculous survival from that 'reactionary', pre-1967 order which 'revolutionaries' like the Baathists had tried so hard to destroy. Asad now sought to bring the Palestinian resistance movement—once destined, in his own words, to help 'blast the Zionist presence out of the Arab homeland'[17]—firmly under his wing in their last, Lebanese refuge on the other flank.

During the first half of the war, when the Egyptians were encouraging the right-wing Christians, Asad threw most of his weight, albeit cautiously, behind the Palestinians and their local Moslem-leftist allies. In the second half he rounded on his former allies. For all of a sudden the Palestinian resistance movement seemed about to achieve a destiny-shaping freedom of action that would undermine his *Greater*-Syrian designs. His was an almost unthinkable volte-face. Syria, the so-called 'beating heart' of Arabism, had always been militant for Palestine. So to turn against the Palestinian guerillas, however imperfect an embodiment of the supreme Arab cause they might be, was the worst heresy a Syrian ruler could commit. The Syrian army gave assistance to the Christian militias' siege and conquest of the refugee camp of Tal al-Zaatar, the greatest atrocity yet a war rich in gratuitous barbarism.

If, in achieving this, Asad had cut the Palestinians down to size, he had been cut down to size in his turn. For, having gone to such lengths to oppose the Sinai disengagement agreement, he now acquiesced in it. In fact, Arabs everywhere were diminished. For the Lebanese civil war was the most virulent outbreak of a malady, a crisis of civilization, that afflicted them all. It was therefore a thoroughly decadent order over which Sadat re-established Egypt's leadership. Moreover, that leadership was no longer rooted, as it had once been, in Egypt's manifest qualifications for the role, still less in those of the man who ruled it. It was a leadership in which, *faute de mieux*, the Arabs grudgingly acquiesced. And no sooner had Sadat re-established it than it was challenged, not by the Arabs but by the hungry, downtrodden masses of Egypt, and their great food riots of January 1977. Not since 1919, when the Egyptians had revolted against British rule, had there been such a commotion. Assuredly, President Sadat was in no position to meet the challenge of Menachim Begin, embodiment of Zionism at its most expansionist and extreme, with a new belligerency of his own.

Sadat in Jerusalem

On 20 November 1977 President Sadat made his historic pilgrimage to Jerusalem. No one had quite believed him when, as he neared the end of a routine speech to mark the annual opening of the Egyptian parliament, he appeared to depart from the prepared text and informed his audience that he was ready 'to go to the ends of the earth if this will prevent one soldier, one officer, among my sons from being wounded—not being killed, just wounded. I say now that I am ready to go to the ends of the earth. Israel will be astonished when it hears me say now, before you, that I am ready to go to their own house, the Knesset itself, to talk to them.' Yet with those words President Sadat had launched a gamble for peace which made his October Crossing pale into insignificance. Within eleven days, after a brief flight from Abu Sweir airbase, a Boeing 707, code-signed Egypt 01, touched down at Bengurion airport, not far from Tel Aviv. A few moments later something indescribable must have tugged at the hearts of countless millions, in Israel, Egypt and the world, as a flourish of trumpets greeted the arrival of Muhammad Anwar Sadat, President of Egypt, in the Land of Israel.

The climax of the visit, where the ceremonial merged with its momentous political import came the following afternoon in the Knesset Sadat mounted a rostrum beneath a portrait of Theodor Herzl, the founder of Zionism. The Speaker, Yitzhak Shamir, a former leader of the *Stern Gang*, introduced Sadat to the house and sat on one side as he delivered his speech. Begin sat on his other side.

Sadat's speech was in keeping with his lofty purpose. All war was vanity, he began, and the only thing vanquished was mankind itself. He harboured no ill-will towards those who had greeted his historic 'initiative' with 'surprise and amazement. No one had ever imagined that the President of the greatest Arab state . . . which bears the responsibility pertaining to the cause of war and peace in the Middle East could declare his readiness to go to the enemy with which we are still in a state of war.' He had consulted none of his 'colleagues or Arab brethren'. He had taken his decision after long thought, knowing that, although it constituted a grave risk, it was his responsibility before God 'to exhaust every means in a bid to save my Arab people and the entire Arab nation the horrors of new, shocking and terrible wars, the dimensions of which only God himself can foresee'. His mission could be 'a turning-point in the history of this part of the world, if not the history of the world as a whole'. He had not, he insisted, come for a 'separate peace' between Egypt and Israel, nor for a 'partial peace'—one that, in merely terminating the state of war, indefinitely deferred a final settlement.

He conceded that there had been fault on the Arab side. 'Yet today I tell you, and I declare it to the whole world, that we accept to live with you in permanent peace based on justice.' One barrier—Israel's alleged invincibility and the ability of its long arm to 'reach and strike anywhere'—had collapsed in 1973. Yet there remained another, 'a psychological barrier between us. A barrier of suspicion. A barrier of rejection. A barrier of fear and deception. A barrier of hallucination around any deed and decision.' This psychological barrier constituted '70 per cent of the problem'. The time had come to break it down. The Israelis would have to 'give up, once and for all, the dreams of conquest, and give up the belief that force is the best method of dealing with the Arabs'. There had to be complete withdrawal from all the occupied territories. Furthermore, the Israelis had to recognize what the entire world, even America, its foremost ally, recognized: namely, that the Palestinian cause was the crux of the whole problem. 'If you have found the legal and moral justification to set up a national home on a land that did not belong to you, it is incumbent upon you to show understanding of the Palestinian people's insistence on establishing once again a state on their land.'

President Sadat ended his address on the exalted plane which he had begun it, quoting a Koranic text to the effect that all 'people of the Book'—Jews, Christians and Moslems—were equal in God's sight. He had done his part for the peace of the world. In going to the Knesset he had 'set aside all precedents and traditions known by warring countries'. He now awaited a commensurate response. 'May God guide the steps of Premier Begin and the Knesset', he told a final press conference, 'because there is a great need for hard and drastic decisions.'

Just forty-four emotion-filled hours after it had touched down in the Land of Israel Egypt 01 took off home with an escort of four Kfir jet fighters. Sadat returned to a triumphant welcome, one of those characteristic Cairo carnivals, part spontaneous, part contrived, with lorry- and bus-loads of workers and peasants pouring into the capital to swell the welcoming multitudes. He rode, upright and radiant, in an open limousine through the human colonnade that lined the thirteen-mile, flag-draped route from the airport to his house in the suburb of Giza. But if he had really brought with him any hope for the 'hard and drastic' decisions which he had gone to extract from Menachim Begin, he was soon to be disappointed.

Camp David

With his descent upon Jerusalem, Sadat, the Arab leader whom the West, especially the United States, had once depicted as a warmonger, was now hailed as a hero of peace. What he called his 'psychological' crossing was a sublime gesture, a masterstroke, a watershed in history. It inspired wonder, reverence and piety and in no one more than President Carter who, before watching the Knesset encounter on television with his family, had offered a prayer for Middle East peace from the pulpit of Washington's First Baptist Church.

There was outrage and stupefaction in the Arab world and calls for vengeance. Syria went into national mourning. Offices were closed, traffic stopped for five minutes, muezzins and church bells sounded all day. A few hours after his war-time ally had prayed in al-Aqsa Mosque in Jerusalem, President Asad went to the Ommayyad Mosque in the heart of Damascus and heard the preacher condemn Sadat as 'a traitor who has plunged a dagger in the back of the Arab nation'. In Iraq the celebration of *Id al-Adha* (The Feast of the Sacrifice) was cancelled. Libyan envoys ceremonially burned the Libyan flag (still the same as Egypt's) because it had been flown alongside the Star of David. In Beirut the leading left-wing newspaper *al-Safir* commented:

> Sadat has entered history. As of today, his name will be remembered along with those of Herzl, Balfour, Weizmann, Bengurion, Golda Meir and Moshe Dayan as one of the founders of the State of Israel, the consolidators of its existence, the champions of its imperialist dreams. Sadat has entered history—but will he enter it again? The decision rests with the Arab people of Egypt, the Egyptian army, or indeed with any Arab. For he is now the enemy of them all, and it is the right of any one to pass judgement and carry it out.[18]

Yet Sadat did strike an authentic chord of popular approval in the Arab world, barely audible though that might have been against the clamour of denunciation orchestrated by party-cum-military dictatorships which monopolized the means of communication. It goes without saying that the approval was strongest in Egypt, for in addition to a genuine yearning for peace and the 'prosperity' that it was promised would follow, Sadat was exploiting a deepening strain of Egyptian nationalism that took an anti-Arab form. There was great daring and imagination in what Sadat was doing and many Arabs realized this. He wanted, as a Beirut newspaper put it,

> to show the Israelis that their 'extermination complex' is out of date, that the Jewish State can no longer exploit the Arab rejection of its existence to annex new territories in the name of secure frontiers. What more spectacular proof of that than the presence in Jerusalem, within the walls of the Knesset, of the leader of the most powerful Arab nation?[19]

In general, however, the genuine shock and consternation at least equalled the furtive satisfaction. The outrage may have come insincerely from governments such as Syria's, which had done their share of mischief at the Palestinians' expense. There was none the less good reason for the gravest misgivings. After all, it was not for nothing that the West had hailed the Jerusalem pilgrimage as the spectacular gesture it was. At a stroke it had shattered the most sacred of Arab taboos. The 'psychological' barrier which Sadat claimed to have breached was indeed formidable. Since the earliest days, when the Zionist 'peril' was merely embryonic, the Palestinians had refused to confer upon it the legitimacy of direct negotiations. If their fathers and grandfathers had refused to recognize the Zionism of their day—before it had even grown to statehood on the debris of the Palestinian community—how much more shocking for their sons to witness an Arab leader dealing with contemporary Zionism. And what a Zionism! A Zionism led, as a prominent Palestinian scholar observed, 'by the last Israeli to be worthy of shaking hands with the head of the largest Arab state'.[20]

It was not merely the symbolism of what Sadat was doing—

though that was troubling enough—it was the context in which he was doing it. Obviously, if the Arabs were ever to make peace with Israel all their leaders would have to do what he had done, but—and here was the vital point of difference—it should have come at the end of the peace-making process, not at the beginning. It would thereby have constituted that full recognition of the State of Israel which the Arabs, formally renouncing a territory they deemed their own, could only confer in exchange for the return of the occupied territories and the establishment of a Palestinian state. It was this that would have marked the consummation of a 'just and lasting' peace in the Middle East.

Sadat, however, had gone to Jerusalem not—as he and his publicists claimed—from strength, but from a position of abject weakness. In effect he had already come close to publicly admitting it. Only a month before he had threatened to go to war. 'If Israel wants to test us,' he told a rally at Suez, 'we shall teach her a crueller lesson than before. . . . We want peace, but if it is not realized then fighting will become imperative.' And a few weeks before that he had told Israel that he had the capability to wipe out a third of its population. He was in possession of

> definite information that the Israelis have nuclear weapons. . . . They put this about from time to time in the hope of weakening the Arab bargaining position. . . . If Israel uses the atom bomb against us, we may lose a million people, but there would still remain thirty-nine million Egyptians. . . . My plan is that we work to destroy one million of them in return for the million Egyptians, and in my opinion that would finish off Israel.[21]

For Sadat thus to have fallen back on the so-called 'language of no war and no peace'—language which the October War had supposedly banished for ever—was tantamount to admitting that his 'victory' had been no victory at all. It was, purely and simply, the language of desperation. A full four years had elapsed and nine-tenths of Sinai, not to mention the Golan, the West Bank and Jerusalem, still lay in enemy hands, and Sadat certainly did not have the means to carry out his threats. According to the *Washington Post* the Israelis were ready to use the overwhelming superiority which America had conferred upon them as a reward for the Sinai disengagements. If pushed into a corner they were ready to fight a war of 'annihilation', whether America liked it or not. Sadat publicly contradicted himself. Even as he sprang his plan to visit Jerusalem upon an astonished world and warned of the 'horrible' consequences he could inflict on Israel if it came to nothing,[22] he was telling American Congressmen a very different tale. Israel was the real threat to peace, 'the real threat to the Arab world in its entirety, not just to a Palestine state, but to all Arabs'.[23] 'Thanks to you, to your committee [The House Armed Services Committee] and what you have given Israel in the way of the most modern and sophisticated weapons—thanks to this, I fear that one day you will discover that they [the Israelis] are a threat to you, because they can get anything they ask for. They can start a war and . . . they can carry it on for six months without needing anything new from you.'[24]

As for Egypt's nuclear capabilities, they were a figment of Sadat's imagination. Muhammad Heikal, former editor of *al-Ahram*, said that it was time the Arab leaders stopped making idle threats about what they would do 'if' Israel introduced nuclear weapons into the area and, during the visit to Israel, one of Sadat's closest confidants, Mustafa Khalil, reportedly told the Israelis just how hollow the threats were. 'We know,' he said, 'that we would have no chance of winning a war and we also know that you have the atom bomb. Egypt doesn't have a military alternative and we have to seek a different solution.'[25]

There is little doubt that it was the rise of Menachim Begin which, in some measure, sent Sadat to Jerusalem. Begin had been proved right: extremism did pay. Officially, of course, Sadat was still wedded to Geneva and a 'comprehensive' peace. The Americans were behind him in this endeavour. Getting the Palestinians to Geneva in some guise or other that would satisfy the PLO without incurring the inevitable veto of the Israelis was the seemingly insuperable task to which Carter and his peripatetic Secretary of State, Cyrus Vance, had devoted Kissinger-like energies throughout the summer and autumn. It had carried them into an amazing labyrinth of proposals and counter-proposals, each more ingenious and sophisticated than the last, until finally, devising one of those procedural formulae not too suggestive of substance and which all parties could interpret as they pleased, it began to look as though they might fight their way out of the maze. Perhaps the Geneva conference would reconvene after all.

But if, before meeting Begin, Sadat had been profoundly sceptical of the prospects of Geneva—owing to inter-Arab wrangling as well as Israeli obduracy—he must have been even more so afterwards. Indeed, with his Jerusalem pilgrimage he had, in effect, sabotaged Geneva at the very moment when, according to him (though both Israel and the Palestinians contested this), he had finally solved the problem of PLO representation through an American professor of Palestinian origin. For the fact was that if, in his desperate weakness, he had any bargaining power, it lay in his readiness to take Egypt further along the road down which (with the Sinai disengagements) he had already taken it. It lay in the completion of that go-it-alone diplomacy whose premise was that the more Egypt detached itself from the Arab world, the more it could expect to get for itself. When he told the Knesset that he had consulted no one about his 'initiative' he was telling the truth. For Arab leaders the implications of Sadat's public confession of his own duplicity were shattering. For the consultation of colleagues lay at the heart of the concept of Arab solidarity by which he had formerly set such store. To an Arab world all-too-familiar with Sadat's backslidings the mere failure to consult meant that he was up to no good, but his *announced* failure to do so, and on so momentous an issue, meant that he was up to no good on a momentous scale. It was not what he said in the Knesset that mattered—for that, by and large, was an unimpeachable presentation of the standard Arab case—it was the circumstances in which he said it. Sadat had set in motion a process which neither he, the Arabs nor the Americans—whose more far-sighted policy-makers did not want a separate Israeli-Egyptian peace any more than the Arabs—could stop.

No sooner had Sadat returned from Jerusalem than he invited 'all parties to the conflict' to attend a conference in Cairo to prepare for Geneva. Apart from Israel, which promptly accepted, a lukewarm United Nations and a hesitant United States, everyone else turned down the invitation. If there was ever a remote possibility that his

Arab adversaries would show up in Cairo, he ensured that they would not by launching violent tirades against the very people he was inviting. President Asad and the ruling Baathists bore the brunt of them. As for the Palestinians, the prime objects of his solicitude, there were now good ones and bad ones—those who understood that salvation lay with him and those who danced attendance on their Syrian and Soviet masters. In the past no one had pushed harder for Arab and international recognition of the PLO. Spurned by it he now sought to exclude it from the peace-making process altogether or at least to frighten it with the spectre of an alternative Palestinian leadership. This he hoped to conjure out of the occupied territories, traditionally more moderate than the Palestinian diaspora. But, with one exception, all the mayors of the West Bank and Gaza expressed solidarity with the PLO and rejected the invitation to Cairo for consultation. In the end no one of any stature went at all. Those who had been ready to go did not, in the words of the Mayor of Ramallah, 'even represent their wives'. When this tactic failed Sadat tried another. He sought to re-assign to King Hussein the role which he had persuaded the other Arab leaders to divest him of at the Rabat summit conference in 1974, suggesting that the Palestinians should transfer their loyalty from Arafat to the King. But the Palestinians would not. Nor was the King going to make any attempt to persuade them to do so.

So Sadat was on his own. And he could no longer turn back. The 'hard and drastic decisions' he had pleaded for in Jerusalem failed to materialize. For Begin had not been taken in. He knew that 'weakness, even desperation' drove Sadat.[26] He remained what he had always been, the embodiment of Zionism at its most extreme and expansionist. And why not, asked one of the most irreverent critics of Zionist orthodoxy? 'For him', wrote Uri Avneri, 'this visit was a gift from Heaven. It was handed to him free, on a silver platter. It was Sadat who initiated it and paid the full price for it, endangering his life and his regime, and gave Israel an invaluable prize—full recognition of her existence and her legitimacy. What did Begin pay? Nothing at all, not even a piastre with a hole in it.'[27] Begin and his ruling establishment were well aware that Sadat had opened up the most alluring possibilities. A columnist was frank where the politicians tended to be discreet. 'Everyone is avoiding the word "separate peace" as if it was something shocking. For myself, with all respect for the politicians who took part in this, I disagree. A separate peace is a legitimate expression, not a dirty word: the wedge we have promised not to drive into the Arab world exists, and it would be a pity to ignore its existence.'[28] The Israelis knew that, at the very least, they were now in a position to eliminate or reduce the role of those powers—Russians or Americans, 'radical' or 'moderate' Arab states—who could influence the negotiations on the PLO's behalf.

The Cairo conference was a side-show which Begin turned into an irrelevance when, even as it was meeting, he suddenly took off for Washington to win approval for his plan for Palestinian 'autonomy' or 'self-rule'. He realized that he had to give something in return for Sadat's gesture and this was it. It was a *Likud* formula which, for all practical purposes, ensured that control of all the 'liberated' territories of Greater Israel was retained without their formal annexation, a so-called 'functional' solution which preserved the essential gains of occupation—military bases, immigration, settlement and economic domination—while passing the burdens of civil administration to the local inhabitants or, in part, to Jordan. The occupation would acquire permanent *de facto* legitimacy. It was hoped that with immigration and settlement the Jews would eventually become a majority. The West Bank and Gaza would be markets for Israeli products and springboards for economic penetration of the Arab hinterland. Arab manpower would furnish Israel with cheap labour. With time and economic neglect, educated Palestinians, finding no livelihood, would gradually be forced to emigrate. There would be no right of return for the Palestinian diaspora. In short, as Israelis put it, 'autonomy' would enable the Palestinians 'to determine the placing of sewage pipes in Hebron'. As Arafat put it, it was Israel's Bantustan. In private even Dr Zbigniew Brzezinski, President Carter's National Security Adviser, exclaimed to an outraged Begin, 'That's like South Africa. You are taking away the right to vote from the people.'[29]

Sadat owed it to himself and to Egypt to maintain his composure in the face of Begin's obstinacy. He did so for a while, but then, all of a sudden, he threw the first of his tantrums and found himself agreeing with those of his Arab adversaries who had ridiculed his 'initiative' from the outset. 'Begin has offered nothing,' he now protested. 'It is I who have given him everything. I offered him security and legitimacy and got nothing in return. This peace initiative is not the King David Hotel which Begin blew up when he was young. He cannot blow up the initiative without destroying himself and others for hundreds of years.'[30]

Sadat turned to the United States for the support he needed. Although he was already an American hero, he needed more than accolades. He needed practical assistance for promoting the kind of 'comprehensive' peace he was still trying to sell the Arab world. His Jerusalem pilgrimage had been calculated to engender a historic shift in Western, especially American, perceptions of the Arab-Israeli conflict, to transform the climate of opinion in such a way that the public sympathy gained for the Arab point of view would eventually be converted, by due political process, into governmental pressures for the commensurate Israeli response. Certainly there were signs that he was getting results. Those instant guides to the nation's mood, the public opinion surveys, recorded them. In February 1978 a *Newsweek*-Gallup poll which asked, 'Which country has been the more willing to compromise?' produced an astonishing 45–25 response in favour of Egypt. In the personality contest Sadat also trounced Begin. It was not merely the American public at large. The Jewish community itself was showing signs of division and disenchantment; for the first time since the State of Israel was founded, many Jews spoke out openly against its policies. President Carter was angry with Begin, there was no doubt about that, and the question of Jewish settlements in the occupied territories was the one on which both he and his advisers were least prepared to hide their irritation. Was true 'even-handedness'—which had provoked such an uproar when first proposed, ten years before, by Senator William Scranton—finally in the offing?

It was not. The Zionist lobby was still too strong for that. Carter and his Administration took the easy course which the Sadat 'initiative' had opened up. For them, after the first, stunned hesitation, the Jerusalem pilgrimage had become a godsend to be exploited, the opportunity for a facile foreign policy triumph that could reverse the rapid decline in their own popularity. Like Sadat himself, the United States was still wedded to a 'comprehensive' peace. Warnings from its Arab friends that this was impossible tended to fall on deaf ears in circumstances where realism in foreign affairs took second place to the electoral imperatives of domestic politics. The Administration profited from Sadat's descent on Jerusalem to vindicate the retreats from stated policy which, even before it, the Zionist lobby had managed to enforce. Zbigniew Brzezinski set the seal on this with a flippancy that seemed unbecoming in a man of his stature. The United States, he told *Paris Match*, had failed to persuade the PLO to 'moderate' its policy; so it was 'bye-bye PLO'.[31]

The climax came at Camp David. It gave its name to what Begin could justly regard as his greatest triumph. Throughout the spring and summer of 1978 peace-seeking diplomacy had continued in a climate of rock-like Israeli inflexibility, deepening American pessimism and a President Sadat alternating between moods of despairing frustration and brave assertions that, in spite of everything, he was not giving up his 'sacred mission'. Finally, on 5 September Begin and Sadat joined President Carter at Camp David, Maryland, 'to seek a framework for peace in the Middle East'. The idea was that they would remain closeted in the sylvan seclusion of the Presidential retreat until something was achieved. After all the stratagems—from 'indirect negotiations' to 'proximity talks', and from 'shuttle diplomacy' to the 'electric shock' of Sadat's Jerusalem visit—that had been applied to the world's most dangerous and intractable conflict, this summit of summits was surely the ultimate procedural resource. President Sadat accepted Carter's invitation in the hope that he would exert more pressure on Egypt's behalf than he had ever done before, that America's obvious exasperation with Begin's intransigence would at last find practical expression. Camp David, he said, would, 'determine the fate of the region for many generations, either by peace or endless struggle'.[32] For his part Begin was determined to give nothing away. 'Our nation has existed thousands of years before Camp David and it will continue to exist for thousands of years after it. . . . What is Sadat's alternative—war? Will he drop the Americans and return to the Soviets? Who will save him—Asad, Brezhnev, Gadafi?'[33]

From the moment it began Camp David seemed to hover on the

brink of calamity. But no one really knew for sure, because none of the world's press, milling about in the little town of Thurmont six miles away, got anywhere near that clearing in the chestnut, oak and hickory trees where the three leaders were closeted for thirteen days. Only the Egyptian press, notably Moussa Sabri of *al-Akhbar*, conveyed any idea of how things were going, and as the summit grew into the longest of its kind since Potsdam in 1945, Sabri's despatches grew gloomier and gloomier. Then suddenly, after days of unrelieved despondency, Sabri changed his tone entirely. 'Conference Saved from Collapse', ran the bold red headline of *al-Akhbar* on the morning of 17 September. There had been a 'surprising development', he enigmatically explained, narrowing the differences to four points which, while 'procedural' in nature, were 'substantive' too. Sure enough, that evening, a tired but triumphant Jimmy Carter announced the Camp David agreements to the world. They consisted of two parts, the Framework for Peace in the Middle East and the Framework for the Conclusion of a Peace Treaty between Egypt and Israel. The next day he told Congress that 'today we are privileged to see the chance of one of the sometimes rare, bright moments in human history.' The summit, he said, had exceeded his expectations. It certainly had—and the worst fears of almost the entire Arab world.

The circumstances of Sadat's cave-in remain something of a mystery. But there was no doubt that it was one. A leading Washington commentator drew a startling contrast between an 'almost recklessly confident Begin' and a Sadat so exhausted that at one point in a news conference he referred to the US Senate as 'the Knesset' and—causing reporters to gasp with astonishment—to Camp David as 'Waterloo'.

> The peace agreement which Israel is to negotiate with Egypt within three months looks like a separate Israeli-Egyptian peace, feels like a separate Israeli-Egyptian peace, and smells like a separate Israeli-Egyptian peace, but is not a separate Israeli-Egyptian peace. At least that is what Prime Minister Begin does not want the Israeli press to call it because 'it would weaken and embarrass President Sadat'.

This was the opening passage of a report in the *Jewish Week* on Begin's meeting with Hebrew-language newspapers the day after the summit ended.[34] Camp David was the consummation of a bargain that had been implicit in Sadat's go-it-alone diplomacy from the outset: Israel gives up Sinai in return for retaining the West Bank, Gaza and the Golan. The territorial bargain was, of course, reinforced by all the juridical guarantees—'normalization', exchange of ambassadors, United Nations forces, demilitarization of the Sinai, and so on—of the Israeli-Egyptian peace treaty. There was no 'linkage'. The implementation of the treaty, so desirable to Israel, was not contingent upon progress towards a 'comprehensive' peace, so vital to the Arabs.

Naturally there was an attempt to furnish the 'comprehensive' cover. In all essentials, however, the Framework for Peace in the Middle East was just an elaboration of the 'autonomy' plan which Begin had put forward nine months before. A 'self-governing authority' was to be established for a five-year 'transitional' period, by the third year of which negotiations would begin 'to determine the final status of the West Bank and Gaza and to conclude a peace treaty between Israel and Jordan'. But the supposed timetable for 'autonomy' was not really one at all. Within a month of the exchange of instruments of ratification, Egypt and Israel would begin negotiations for setting up the 'elected self-governing authority' in the West Bank and Gaza. They 'set themselves the goal' of completing them within one year so that elections could be held 'as expeditiously as possible' thereafter. Thus Israel was under no *obligation* to complete the negotiations on time, while 'as expeditiously as possible' was at the mercy of its interpretation of the possible. The autonomy formula bristled with conditions, and neither Begin—disobeying his own injunction—nor the Hebrew press had many inhibitions in elucidating them. They made for an 'autonomy devoid of meaning', which would 'add nothing to what [the inhabitants of the West Bank and Gaza] already had'. Autonomy would never signify sovereignty, and 'if one day the administrative council of the autonomous region declares the creation of an independent Palestinian state, it will be its first and last proclamation. We shall go in and dissolve it.'[35] The Israeli army would remain essentially where it was and the programme of immigration to and settlement on expropriated Arab land would continue unabated. As for East Jerusalem, Israel could press ahead with the Judaization of its 'capital city' as it pleased. The exchange of letters on the subject, with Sadat and Begin each informing Carter of their respective official positions and Carter informing them of his, out-Kissingered Kissinger in the boldness of its sophistry. It was left to Moshe Dayan, with his habitual candour, to size up the whole Camp David transaction. It would not be advisable, he said, to hold a public debate on Palestinian 'autonomy' because 'if the Egyptians understand Israel's real intentions on this matter they would not sign the peace treaty'.[36]

It was not quite over yet; there were last-minute hitches. Before he would sign the treaty, Begin, obdurate to the end, was insisting on his interpretation of disputed clauses in the Camp David agreement. The deadline for signing came and went without the deed being done, which made Begin's collection of his Nobel Peace Prize, just a week beforehand, rather more ironic than it already was. At the ceremony in Akershus Castle in Oslo, he accepted his share of the award—$40,000. It was rather more than the price the British authorities had put on his head thirty years before as the most wanted terrorist in Palestine. Once again, Begin said, the talks were in 'deep crisis'. He was going to conclude no 'sham treaty'. The deadlock was complete. The one great triumph of Carter's Presidential career was about to collapse in ruins about him. He no longer disguised an exasperation which was directed squarely at Begin and the Israelis. Something had to be done and on 4 March it was. Carter laid before Begin proposals which Begin instantly acknowledged to be 'different' from earlier ones, and expressed the opinion that if they were accepted by Egypt then 'we shall be on our way to signing a peace treaty'.

Carter announced that he would go to the Middle East in person to clinch the deal. The Arab world instantly saw this as the last, despairing attempt to salvage a fundamentally bankrupt policy from the collapse it deserved. To sustain this 'moveable Camp David'—as one Beirut columnist promptly dubbed it—he was clearly counting on President Sadat and another eleventh-hour cave-in of the kind which had saved the original one.

He got it. After the five most hectic days of Carter's career, and among the most critical for the future of the Middle East and perhaps the world, he announced that Begin and Sadat had accepted all the latest American proposals. 'I am confident that now we have defined all of the main ingredients of a peace treaty between Egypt and Israel and which will be the cornerstone of a comprehensive peace in the Middle East.' Peace treaty it may have been. The *Washington Post*, normally a sober journal, called it 'an extraordinary—a humbling—achievement reached by Carter's transcendent vision and steadiness'. But cornerstone of comprehensive peace in the Middle East it definitely was not. Through sheer willpower and fixity of purpose Begin had stripped it of every ingredient that might have made it one.

On a wan, wintry afternoon on Monday, 26 March 1979, Anwar Sadat and Menachim Begin met on the White House lawn to sign the historic treaty. President Carter appended his signature as witness. For some reason President Sadat failed to read page seven of his prepared address. It contained a passage that called for justice for the Palestinians. It was an appropriate omission. The betrayal of the Palestinians lay at the heart of this separate peace which he had sworn he would never sign.

Notes

1. Kapeliouk, Amnon, *Le Monde Diplomatique*, June 1977.
2. *Time* magazine, 30 May 1977.
3. *Haaretz*, 22 May 1977.
4. Letter from Bengurion to Haim Guri, 15 May 1963, cited in Michael Bar Zohar, *Ben Gurion*, Vol. III, p. 1,547; see *Middle East International*, August 1977; Kapeliouk, Amnon, *Le Monde Diplomatique*, June 1977.
5. Lilienthal, Alfred M., *The Zionist Connection, What Price Peace?*, Dodd, Mead and Company, New York, 1978, pp. 350–3.
6. *The Guardian*, 10 November 1976.
7. *Middle East International*, London, June 1976.
8. *Ibid.*, July 1977.
9. *Ibid.*, September 1977.
10. See *Middle East International*, October 1977.
11. *New York Times*, 19 May 1977.
12. See p. 258 ff.
13. *Al-Ahram*, 24 July 1974.
14. Sheehan, Edward, *The Arabs, Israelis and Kissinger*, Reader's Digest Press, New York, 1976, p. 194.
15. See p. 308.
16. *Al-Thaurah* (Damascus daily), 14 February 1967.
17. *Al-Baath* (Damascus daily), 21 May 1967.
18. *Al-Safir*, 20 November 1977.

19. *L'Orient-Le Jour*, 18 November 1977.
20. Jiryis, Sabri, 'The Arab World at the Crossroads', *Journal of Palestine Studies*, Beirut, No. 26, 1978, p. 39.
21. *The Guardian*, 8 July 1977.
22. See Carpozi, George, *Anwar Sadat, A Man of Peace*, Manor Books, New York, 1977.
23. *Al-Akhbar* (Cairo daily), 16 November 1977.
24. *Ibid.*, 13 November 1977.
25. Haber, Eitan, Zeev Schiff and Ehud Yaar, *The Year of the Dove*, Bantam Books, New York, 1976, p. 73.
26. Haber, *ibid.*, p. 42.
27. *Ha'olem Hazeh* (Israeli weekly), 23 November 1977.
28. Schnitzer, Shmuel, *Davar*, 25 November 1977.
29. Haber, *et al.*, *op. cit.*, p. 110.
30. *October* (Cairo weekly), 15 January 1977.
31. *Paris Match*, 28 December 1977.
32. *Al-Ahram*, 4 September 1978.
33. Haber, *et al.*, *op. cit.*, p. 218.
34. See Sayegh, Fayez, 'The Camp David Agreement and the Palestine Problem', *Journal of Palestine Studies*, Beirut, No. 30, 1979.
35. Kapeliouk, Amnon, *Le Monde Diplomatique*, January 1979.
36. *Ibid.*

11 · THE RAPE OF THE WEST BANK

'Demographic Lunacy' in Judea and Samaria

According to President Sadat, of course, the Camp David agreement was not a separate peace. Almost the entire Arab world, however, concluded that it was. It was perceived as a historic calamity, the lineal descendant of those earlier ones—the Balfour Declaration, the rise of Israel and the 1967 War—which had befallen the Arabs in the twentieth century. It consecrated the moral and political bankruptcy of the whole existing Arab order. In February 1949 the Egypt of King Farouk had been the first of the four defeated 'front-line' states to conclude armistice agreements with the new-born State of Israel. Within six months of this much-condemned defection, the three others, Lebanon, Jordan and Syria, had all followed suit. These armistice agreements set off a wave of violent upheaval in the Arab world. President Nasser and the 'revolutionaries' of his generation attributed the Catastrophe to the rottenness of the old order—the monarchies, the régimes of the *beys* and the *pashas*, the great landowners and feudalists, selfish, frivolous, reactionary and subservient to the Western creators of Israel—and, ostensibly at least, their central mission was to expunge the shame of defeat. But first they were to transform and modernize their own societies. While the transformation lasted Israel would enjoy a respite; once it had been completed the 'liberation' of Palestine would come, so to speak, as the crowning proof of their success. By any but the most partisan assessment, however, the 'revolutionary' order which the Catastrophe threw up proved a failure. The Arab world—to take the most famous slogans of the past quarter century—enjoyed neither Unity, Freedom nor Socialism. As for Palestine, far from liberating it the 'revolutionaries' succeeded only in losing more of it. President Nasser called the 1967 defeat the *Naksa* (the Setback), but in reality it was another *Nakba* (Catastrophe) and, since it was very difficult to blame it entirely on the imperialist foreigner, it was a worse one than before.

In October 1973 the Arabs had made a partial recovery. But this was achieved in spite as much as because of the régimes. It meant that they had finally succeeded, and scandalously late, in achieving a minimal mobilization of that vast potential which their countries' strategic location, manpower and immense wealth had bestowed upon them. But here, twelve years after the second Catastrophe, was the leader of the 'revolutionary' camp, Nasser's heir, making a full and final peace with Israel—with an Israel, moreover, which under Begin had crossed yet another threshold in its arrogance and its contempt for Arab rights. Here was the great power of the Arab world in effect opting out of it altogether, allying itself with the Zionist intruder and enormously enhancing its ability to disrupt what was left of the existing Arab order.

Having failed to deter Sadat from taking the fateful, final step, the Arabs now sought to punish him for having done so. A score of Arab states, 'radicals' and 'moderates', ranging from the Marxist-Leninists of South Yemen to the arch-conservatives of Saudi Arabia, came together at a summit conference in Baghdad, where they excommunicated the heretic and, with a judicious mixture of economic and political sanctions, sought to reconcile maximum damage to his régime with minimum hardship for the Egyptian people. Hitherto it had been Palestine itself—the more or less permanent emergency of Palestine—which had generated and perpetuated the theory and practice of collective Arab action, with Egypt as its mainstay. But with Egypt's defection the priority for everyone else was no longer the recuperation of Palestine—however the Arab consensus of the moment might define that evolving concept—it was the recuperation of Egypt itself. The unanimity of Baghdad could not endure, so divided were the Arabs states among themselves, so wracked by domestic disorders. Every Arab convulsion had its local causes, but if there was one great upheaval which now added to and exacerbated them all, it was the separate peace with Israel. No one felt it more keenly than Sadat's war-time ally, now his most implacable enemy.

Afflicted by terrorism and insurgency at home, bogged down as 'peace-keepers' in the morass of Lebanon, President Asad's was a régime besieged. The overthrow of the Shah of Iran, the rise of Ayatollah Khomeini sent tremors of alarm through a string of neighbouring, oil-rich Arab régimes, modernist as well as traditionalist; and the House of Saud itself, the last great pro-Western bastion in the Gulf, was shaken to its foundations when, in November 1979, religious fanatics staged a sensational, twenty-two-day siege of the Grand Mosque in Mecca. In September 1980 the Gulf War broke out dealing the *coup de grâce* to the anti-Egyptian coalition. Iraq, potentially a formidable enemy of Israel, had now in a sense defected from the Arab world in Egypt's wake. The eleventh Arab plenary summit conference that convened in Amman in November 1980 brought the Arabs to new depth of disunity. Along with Syria and other 'radical' Arab states the PLO—which symbolized the very *raison d'être* of Arab summitry—failed to attend. Eventually, President Sadat himself fell victim to that moral and political bankruptcy to which, by trying to escape from it, he had contributed so much. The 'hero of peace' died at a celebration of war. On 6 October 1981, as he attended a grandiose military parade to mark the eighth anniversary of the Egyptian army's crossing of the Suez Canal, he was shot at point-blank range. In the view of his assassin, Lieutenant Khalid Islambouli, he had deserved to die as a 'traitor to Islam'.

For Sadat, of course, Camp David would have remained incomplete until the second of its two components, the Framework for Peace in the Middle East, had been concluded to the satisfaction of Arabs and Palestinians. That it would have been, provided everyone showed the necessary good will and common sense, he had doggedly insisted. That it could not be was a possibility he had refused to admit. So Egypt entered into negotiations to attain the unattainable, a Palestinian autonomy which, with wonderful sophistry, Camp David had taken away even as it conferred it. To no one's surprise the Palestinians, in whose name the talks were conducted, and King Hussein, who was invited, if necessary, to participate in their stead, stayed away. So, with the United States as their 'partner' the Israelis and the Egyptians negotiated alone. The talks limped along, staggered, fell, picked themselves up again. The 'target date' for their completion, 26 May 1980, passed with no discernible progress. Finally, in the dying days of the Carter Administration they broke off altogether, never to be resumed. The fiction which they had provided—that a true, 'comprehensive' peace was really in the making—the Egyptians were no longer prepared to sustain. Begin did not really care.

In the next two years, Begin was to take, or solemnly propose, critical decisions which, certainly in spirit and many would contend in letter too, violated all that Camp David stood for. In July 1980 the Knesset passed a 'fundamental law' which declared Jerusalem to be Israel's united and indivisible capital. In December 1980 it effectively annexed the Golan Heights. Re-installed as Prime Minister in the summer of 1981, Begin formed a new coalition government which laid down that, if Palestinian autonomy ever did run its preordained, five-year course, Israel would then claim full sovereignty over the West Bank and Gaza. In the meantime, although the settlement and colonization of 'Judea and Samaria' had always been an integral part of Begin's Zionist mission, this had now acquired a special urgency for the clear, if not always so clearly enunciated, purpose of foiling the very autonomy which he had agreed to grant the 'Arabs of Eretz Israel'.

The 'conquest of the land' has always been Zionism's central task and the means of achieving it the central issue of its politics. So it was natural, after so momentous an event as Camp David, that a great debate should take place about the new 'framework'—as Chaim Weizmann once had it—which had to be filled in. General Ariel Sharon, as Begin's Minister of Agriculture and Chairman of the Ministerial Committee on Settlement, was at the heart of it. After warfare the main interest of this hero of the 1973 War was farming. For him the two merged in the higher cause of Zionism. There was little modesty in his opinions about the opportunities which the Israeli-Egyptian peace treaty opened up and he showed no reticence in his public expression of them. It was a pity, he had said to President Carter, that the Israelis would no longer be able to settle in Sinai, but:

> I told him that a million Jews shall live in Judea and Samaria together with the Arabs. Carter said: 'When Mr. Sharon talks about a million Jews in Judea and Samaria he arouses anger and resistance among the

> Arabs.' One of the Israeli ministers hurried to say: 'We are not at all sure that there will be a million Jews there.' And I said: 'Not sure? Maybe there will be two million Jews there. Not all of them at once. Not fast. It takes time. It will take years. But it will be so. I can definitely say so, Mr. President.'[1]

Sharon's grandiose schemes could not just be dismissed as the irrelevant expression of a wild, romantic strain inherent in Zionism from the outset. The 1967 War had spawned a similar outbreak of fantastic conceits. But rhetoric had remained one thing, government policy another. To be sure the rhetoric had influenced the policy, but it had never entirely dictated and moulded it. Nor did it now. None the less, eleven years later, the things which men like Sharon said they could do and the things which they actually set out to do had drawn much closer together.

The settlers, those who actually 'conquer the land', have always had a disproportionate impact on the official settlement policies of the state, and that has been so even, or indeed especially, when the settlers have acted independently, or in actual defiance of the state. This phenomenon had become more and more pronounced under Labour and it took new and daring forms under *Likud*. By 1979 the pioneering role in the colonization of the occupied territories had been usurped by that very unofficial, very obstreperous, but very determined movement known as the *Gush Emunim*, the Bloc of the Faithful. Formally established in 1974, the *Gush Emunim* had developed as an organized force from the National Religious Party, a partner in ruling coalitions of both Labour and *Likud*, and in particular from the party youth, who had been taught an explosive mixture of Zionist territorial expansionism and Jewish religious orthodoxy in their religious seminaries. These were young men imbued with a world outlook which, in its theocratic dogmatism, yielded nothing to the fundamentalist beliefs of an Ayatollah Khomeini or a Lieutenant Islambouli. Perhaps their single most influential ideologue was Rabbi Tzvi Yehuda Kook, whose politics, in the words of an Israeli journalist, are:

> consistent, extremist, uncompromising and concentrated on a single issue: the right of the Jewish people to sovereignty over every foot of

> the Land of Israel. Absolute sovereignty, with no imposed limitations. 'From a perspective of national sovereignty', he says, 'the country belongs to us.' . . . In his judgement, Transjordan, the Golan, the Basham (the Jebel Druze region of Syria), are all part of the Land of Israel. . . . In a public statement he defined the right as follows: 'the entire country is ours—there is no Arab land here, only Jewish lands, the eternal lands of our forefathers—and that land, in its original Biblical borders, belongs to the sovereignty of the Jewish people.'[2]

Like religious crackpots elsewhere the *Gush Emunim* could be severely practical, dogged and methodical in pursuit of their exalted goals. It was they who, in real or sometimes ostensible defiance of the Labour government, had pioneered settlement policies which, under *Likud*, were to become officially authorized. In general, practising the surreptitious gradualism of the *fait accompli*, Labour had confined settlement to the predominantly uninhabited areas of the West Bank, particularly the so-called Allon 'security belt' that ran the length of the Jordan Valley, as well as to the Golan Heights—although it should be noted that the inhabitants were so few there because most of them had been driven out in the 1967 War. In general, too, Labour invoked 'security' as the motive for this new phase of Zionist expansionism. Only in Jerusalem and its outskirts had they reinforced the security argument with that of Jewish historic right. Apart from the cantonments of Kfar Etzion between Bethlehem and Hebron they made few inroads into the densely populated, fertile hill areas of Judea and Samaria. That was a constraint, however, which the *Gush Emunim* and its forerunners had succeeded in breaking in three places, not without the complicity of certain ministers and army commanders. In 1972, after an epic four-year sit-in at a hotel and then at a nearby army camp, Rabbi Moshe Levinger and his followers secured official recognition for what was to become the big residential-industrial complex of Kiryat Arba, a suburb of the Jewish holy city of Hebron in the Judean hills at the southern end of the West Bank. Flushed with this success another band of zealots set up a colony at Ofra in the populated heart of Samaria. Finally, in March 1979 after Begin's rise to power, the *Gush Emunim* scored their most sensational coup by winning official recognition for their settlement of Alon Moreh just outside Nablus. With this the last vestiges of geographical constraint had been swept away. To all intents and purposes the policies of the zealots and the state had become one and the same.

They converged in the person of General Sharon. Small wonder, perhaps, that he seemed to spend more of his time with the *Gush* or with his old cronies of Unit 101 than he did with his fellow-ministers. Sharon believed that the *Blitzkrieg* strategies he had used on the battlefield could be applied to the complex political, geographic and demographic problems of the West Bank. Force was the answer to everything. Skill and daring made up for the shortage of resources. For him the religious bigots of the *Gush*, with their single-minded fanaticism, were the ideal shock troops of his settlement campaign. Besides, by the 1980s they were not so short of resources. The *Jerusalem Post* described them as a 'powerful, professional and well-financed operation', whose wage bill alone came to around 5 million shekels a year. 'Add to this the Amana [the body in charge of thirty settlements in Judea, Samaria and Gaza], and its staff, the offices, the emissaries abroad, the expensively-produced literature, and it can be seen that the *Gush Emunim* is very big business.'[3] People dubbed them Sharon's 'private army'.

In Israel the centre almost always catches up with the periphery. And in October 1978, just one month after Camp David, the settlement strategies pioneered by the *Gush* had already been substantially enshrined in an official manifesto of the World Zionist Organization, a *Master Plan for the Development of Settlement in Judea and Samaria*. In its opening paragraph, the Drobles Plan—as it came to be known after its principal author—baldly asserted that: 'settlement throughout the entire land of Israel is for security and by right . . . our right to Eretz Israel.'[4] Two years later in September 1980 Drobles issued an amended version of his plan which explicitly acknowledged the emergency to which Camp David had given rise.

> In the light of the current negotiations on the future of Judea and Samaria, it will become necessary for us to conduct a race against time. . . . It is therefore significant to stress today, by means of actions, that autonomy does not and will not apply to the territories but only to

> the Arab population thereof. This should mainly find expression by establishing facts on the ground. Therefore, the state-owned lands and the uncultivated barren lands in Judea and Samaria ought to be seized right away . . . so as to reduce to the minimum the danger of an additional Arab state being established in these territories. . . . There mustn't be even the shadow of a doubt about our intention to keep the territories of Judea and Samaria for good.[5]

Other zones of Jewish settlement, such as the Golan, were still very important, primarily for security reasons, but for the time being they enjoyed a lesser priority. The colonization of the Golan did expand rapidly and the number of settlers rose from less than 4,000, achieved under ten years of Labour rule, to nearly 7,000 under the first two and a half years of *Likud*. It goes without saying, too, that Begin pressed relentlessly ahead with the Judaization of Jerusalem. It was calculated that, in the fifteen years since the annexation of the Jerusalem Municipality in 1967, some 90,000 Jews had taken up residence in land and property expropriated from the native Arabs, be it in the 'Jewish Quarter' of the Old City or in the surrounding hills.[6] All this, however, constituted merely the core of a megalopolis in the making. A crash programme got under way to enclose Jerusalem in a ring of urban satellites, north, east and south, which, though conceived as an integral part of the city, lay well beyond its then outer suburbs. Once these urban settlements were in place, at least provisionally, they, together with all the land between them and the city proper, would be annexed to it and hence to Israel.[7] The main thrust of the new settlement drive, was however, directed where it was bound to run into the stiffest resistance—Palestinian, Arab and international—at the heartlands of 'Judea and Samaria', whose 800,000 inhabitants were the last major body of Palestinians, out of a total of some 4 million, who still lived in their own homes and till their own fields.

The purpose of the Drobles Plan was to seize as much Arab land as possible in as short a time as possible. The process by which this was to be achieved was expressly modelled on the techniques which, since 1948, had been applied to the organized remnants of the Palestinian community in the original Israel, despoiling yet more of their land and villages, fragmenting them geographically, paralysing them politically and reducing them to a condition of abject dependence on the Jewish economy. 'The disposition of the settlements must be carried out not only *around* the settlements of the minorities [this Orwellian usage, characteristic of official Zionist literature, was intended to designate the overwhelming Arab *majority* of the occupied territories], but also *in between* them, this in accordance with the settlement policy adopted in Galilee and other parts of the country.'[8] To this end the Israeli administrators of the West Bank brought to bear that whole panoply of means, brute force and physical coercion, material and economic obstructionism, and, above all, pseudo–legal subterfuges, which have already been described in earlier parts of this book. However, there was a difference. In Israel proper, the authorities had been dealing with a territory which, apart from parts of Galilee, they had virtually emptied of its inhabitants, while in the West Bank they were dealing with land on which the inhabitants still remained very much *in situ*.

To cope with this situation, they now developed to the full a legal skullduggery which had already occupied pride of place after 1948. It rested on the nature of land tenure in Palestine. When Israel came into being it automatically (though, under international law, quite illegally) assumed, as the self-styled sovereign authority in Palestine, that it inherited all the 'state' land which the Mandatory authority left behind. Everything depended, of course, on the definition of the public as opposed to the private domain.

Under Ottoman, British and Jordanian rule, land ownership (leaving aside minuscule localities which really did belong to the state) had fallen into three broad categories. The first, *mulk*, denoted property to which the owners could produce clear, registered title in the modern sense. This represented a small proportion of the whole. The second, by far the largest portion, was known as *miri*. This was land to which the owners, usually whole families, clans or villages, could produce no such clear title, but which, since they had exploited it for cultivation or pasture from generation to generation, was considered by custom and usage to be no less theirs. A third category of land, *jiftlik*, enjoyed much the same status as *miri*. Objectively speaking both *miri* and *jiftlik* were as 'private' as *mulk* and recognized as such by successive state authorities. The situation was, however, tailor-made for an Orwellian legal subterfuge of the kind to which the Israelis had so often had recourse in the past. It came in the disarming assurance of the Drobles Plan that 'new settlements will be established only on state-owned land, and not on private Arab-owned land which is duly registered'. So along with the physical scheme for settlement and development, the authorities armed themselves with a legal mechanism to 'maximize' the amount of 'state' land that could be expropriated. And maximized it was. As the settlers moved in with their bulldozers, their barbed-wire fences and their prefabricated homes, the bureaucrats served notice on the Arab owners of the land that unless they could furnish proof that it was really theirs—*mulk* in the duly registered, modern sense of the term—then it belonged to the 'state' and, *ipso facto*, to the Jews who were now taking physical possession of it. Naturally, in the overwhelming majority of cases, the Arabs could not furnish that proof, but in case they tried, as they often did, they faced a whole battery of subsidiary provisions designed to thwart them. Since, for higher reasons of state, Israel had not yet formally annexed the territories which it had 'liberated', it continued to administer them in accordance with Jordanian law. That, however, was just an internationally respectable *de jure* façade behind which it could engineer any *de facto* change in the law which it pleased. For the military authorities were empowered, ostensibly on a provisional basis, to 'amend' the law at will. In practice they enjoyed unfettered legislative power and, judging by the number of military orders passed by 1983—at least a thousand—they used it to the full. One of the earliest laws to be 'amended' dealt with 'Expropriation of Land for Public Purposes'. In its revised form it was entirely shorn of the elaborate safeguards to ensure the protection of the individual which the original had contained and, in its application, the military authorities were answerable to no one but themselves. Another means of 'creating' state land was by the simple expedient of announcing that a specific piece of territory was 'already' in state ownership, thus placing the burden of proving that it was not on the Arab owners who knew in advance that their cause was virtually lost. Similarly, under another decree, land with 'no ownership claim' was considered state land. Finally, Israel has took to expropriating land for roads, with very wide rights-of-way, designed to connect each and every settlement with all the others in a complex web of 'highways' that were yet to be built.[9] These new systems, supplementing earlier ones, furnished opportunities for land-grabbing on such a scale that even *Haaretz*, Israel's leading newspaper, termed it a 'mockery and a robbery', while a retiring Supreme Court judge said that what the Israelis were doing was 'stealing in one of the ugliest of ways'.[10]

Just how much of the West Bank was incorporated into the 'state', *ergo* Jewish-owned category, and thereby placed beyond the scope of Palestinian autonomy, it is obviously impossible, at any given moment, to say. What is sure is that, under *Likud*, the process of Judaization underwent a change, both quantitative and qualitative, which few would have deemed possible when the Drobles Plan was first unveiled. One commentator was moved to call the plan a form of 'demographic lunacy'.[11] In its first 1978 version the plan called for the establishment of forty-six new settlements to be inhabited by 16,000 families and the thickening of existing settlements through the addition of 11,000 families—all within a period of five years. The cost of this was put at no less than 54 billion Israeli pounds (*circa* $7 billion), compared with an estimated 2.6 billion which Labour had spent on settlements in *all* the occupied territories between 1967 and 1976.[12] Neglected Israeli slum-dwellers staged unavailing protests against a grotesque diversion of resources of which they—after the Arabs themselves—were the principal victims. In its second, even more ambitious, 1980 version, the Drobles Plan raised its goal for the following five years to the establishment of sixty to seventy-five new settlements, with a total population of between 120,000 and 150,000 people. 'Demographic lunacy' it may have seemed, but under the combined impact of *Gush Emunim*, the *Likud* government and the threat of autonomy, the number of Jews living in the West Bank (excluding Jerusalem) rose from some 3,000 in 1977 to some 25,000 in the middle of 1981 and the number of settlements from some twenty-five, most of them in the Allon 'security belt', to eighty-five, most of them in the central, densely populated hill areas of 'Judea and Samaria'.

No stratagem was too outrageous for the Begin-Sharon team in their race against the clock. One of them could hardly have been further removed from the pioneering ethic of the earliest Zionist settlers, with their communal living and their dignity of toil, or from the religious bigotry of the *Gush Emunim*, who, for all the difference in ideology, became their spiritual heirs of today. At the World Zionist Congress in December 1982 it was announced that the number of Israeli residents in the West Bank would double to 50,000 in the space of three months. This sudden, dramatic increase was to be made possible because 6,000 apartments in dormitory estates within easy commuting distance of Tel Aviv and other Israeli towns were nearing completion. The forecast was a considerable, but by no means a wild, exaggeration, for the trend it represented was real enough.

In the previous two years the whole character of land development and settlement in the West Bank had been undergoing a remarkable change. Under the *laisser-faire* economics of the Begin era, the private sector was flourishing as never before and consequently private contractors were encouraged to supplement the messianic exertions of the *Gush Emunim* in the 'upbuilding' of Greater Israel. Tracts of 'state' land were confiscated by the army and sold off to the profit-hungry entrepreneurs at a mere 5 per cent of their true value.[13] Ordinary middle-class families were able to acquire a 'dream home' in the country for a third or even a quarter of the price of its equivalent within the 1967 borders. In April 1983 eager crowds thronged a convention centre in Tel Aviv where eighteen private construction companies advertised thousands of new villas for sale in 'Judea and Samaria'. Some would be linked by private computer to neighbourhood banks and supermarkets. It was all a far cry from the rugged, isolated outposts of the *Gush Emunim*. One American firm was even offering to ship complete, luxuriously fitted log cabins direct from the United States.[14]

By 1986, at this rate of construction, there were to be 100,000 Israelis living in the West Bank.[15]

Yet, however grave the damage it inflicted in other ways, numerically even 100,000 settlers did no more than dent the Arab majority. Which was no doubt why the settlement department of the World Zionist Organization was already working on yet another, long-term scheme which, within a period of thirty years, would bring the Jewish population of the West Bank up to parity with the Arabs.[16] Fantasy or realistic intent? It remained to be seen. For the time being at least, however, official settlement policy could not be to outnumber the Arabs merely for the purpose of acquiring their land. According to some estimates, Israel, by its own criteria, already disposeed of a full 55–60 per cent of the West Bank.[17] Clearly, if it could take that much it could take it all. Indeed, a Ministry of Defence report conceded as much. According to its calculations, there is hardly any land which *really* belonged to the Palestinians. Of the West Bank's 5 million dunums—itself a mere 19 per cent of original Palestine—the Arabs could produce clear, registered title to a mere 200,000.[18] By the time one of Begin's successors was ready to annex the West Bank, he should have no difficulty in proving that, by his criteria at least, it all belonged to the Jews in any case. But what about the 800,000 Palestinians who, though they no longer owned it, still inhabited it?

The Dissidents' Revenge

The *Gush Emunim* had an answer to that too. If they had been able to enforce their land settlement policy—the logical prelude to expulsion—why not, eventually, expulsion itself? They were, after all, very practical people. In an article entitled 'The Realpolitik of Our Sages', published by the movement's Department of Information, Israel Eldad argued that the Palestinians faced the same predicament as the Canaanites of old. He pointed out that the choice which he himself would prefer them to make—that they abandon their native land—was by no means new to political Zionism: 'Israel Zangwill suggested it in 1920, the British put it forward in the Peel Report of 1937 as did Avraham Sharon and Avraham Stern in the 1940s. Official Zionists opposed the plan due to moral hesitations (not a Jewish morality but one influenced by liberal emancipation).' According to him, 'Jewish morality' prohibited expulsion except in times of war, so the best course of action would be to bring about large-scale emigration through the deliberate creation of economic distress in the West Bank and Gaza. At every *Gush* settlement rank-and-file members would express similar views. Elyakim Haetzni, of Kiryat Arba, said that it was 'not necessary to throw bombs into the casbah or expel the Arabs. There is nothing wrong, however, with making their life difficult in the hope that they will emigrate.'[19] At Ofra in Samaria Rachel Cohen, echoing the famous aphorism of the late Prime Minister Golda Meir, said that, 'after all there are no Palestinian people. We invented them, but they don't exist.'[20]

In reality, although it did not come up to the extreme expectations of the *Gush Emunim*, economic discrimination against the Arab inhabitants of the West Bank had long been deliberate, flagrant and systematic, and growing ever worse. More than 100,000 people had emigrated from the West Bank since 1967.[21] Expulsion, however, had never been public policy. Begin and Sharon said, in effect, that it was not necessary. There was room enough for both Arabs and Jews. 'Seizure of Arab land does not increase friction with the Arab population,' Sharon contended, 'it will prevent such friction in the future.'[22] But if, in the past, the 'official' Zionists had always acquiesced in the *faits accomplis* for which the 'dissidents' were mainly responsible, they could do so again, especially since the former 'dissidents' were now the officials, and the former officials, or their ideological successors, were in the opposition. It was a kind of historic revenge. After the 'War of Independence' *Irgun* and *Stern* had rejected the armistice agreements which left the Jews in possession of 'only' three-quarters of the West Bank (not to mention the East Bank of the Jordan River, which the *Irgun* also coveted, and the *Gush Emunim* still does).[23] As we have seen, Bengurion had decided that the new-born state's monopoly of force should be upheld at all costs and the dissident organizations had been ruthlessly dismantled. Now that Begin was Prime Minister and a former *Sternist*, Yitzhak Shamir, became Speaker of the Knesset and then Foreign Minister, they and like-minded colleagues were neither psychologically prepared nor perhaps even physically able to curb *their* dissidents, who were hardly more extreme than themselves.

It was public knowledge that the *Gush Emunim* enjoyed the personal support of Begin, Sharon and the Chief of Staff, General Rafael Eitan.[24] Their first task was to defend the country's borders; they were equipped, said Sharon, with everything, including 'highly advanced anti-tank weapons', they needed for that.[25] At the same time, the settlers were incorporated into a guard system with the authority to police their own particular areas. It was still the army which furnished the backbone of security operations, but it was the settlers who increasingly dictated the course these took. In Hebron, as in many other places, *Gush Emunim* vigilantes were an integral part of the army's security network. They walked the streets armed. The Ramallah area was policed mainly by settlers from nearby Ofra. A security official said that 'they are the best soldiers for this task'. They had strong discipline and, most important, motivation. For them a 'roadblock is a roadblock and a search a search'. They were so confident of favour in high places that when the Governor of Ramallah asked them to hand back the arms they had been given they refused.[26] In the opinion of the Chief of Staff there would be 'nothing particularly worrisome' if the settlers became a private army. His words were echoed by another, Rafael Eitan, adviser to the Prime Minister on the 'War against Terror', who urged that

> every Israeli who enters the territories, and even the Old City of Jerusalem, should carry arms and know how to use them. In my judgement more Israeli civilians must be allowed to carry weapons all the time. Some argue that such a state of affairs will be exploited for the worst purposes. My reply: already hundreds of thousands of guns are in the hands of the IDF (army) personnel, the police and the Israeli civilian sector. An addition of several thousand weapons more will not change matters for good or bad in this respect.[27]

Thus armed and encouraged the settlers were not merely content with enforcing the law, increasingly they violated it. All took place within that cycle of violence and counter-violence, repression and resistance which, though continuous since 1967, had intensified with the rise of the *Likud* and the Palestinians' realization that Begin's objective was to deprive them not merely of the right to self-determination and national independence but of the territorial base from which that independence might arise. The struggle for land therefore became the central theme of the almost daily clashes between the occupier and the occupied. The Israeli-Egyptian peace treaty provoked widespread disturbances on the West Bank. In the course of them two young demonstrators were killed in Halhul. Although settlers, not soldiers, had shot them, the affair was shelved.

Yet when, about the same time, a soldier-settler from Kiryat Arba was murdered in response to acts of gross provocation and land-grabbing, the whole town of Hebron was placed under harsh curfew for thirteen days—and still the settlers said it was not enough. What was needed, they maintained, was the same 'iron fist' that General Sharon had used to smash resistance in Gaza in 1970. They demanded what they called an appropriate 'Zionist response', that they should move into the heart of the city itself. What that was likely to mean was already clear enough. 'You sit there', wrote Israeli journalist Amon Kapeliouk from Hebron during the curfew, 'and listen to endless stories about the provocations by the settlers, their arrogance and cruelty. They hit at the holy places, such as the Ibrahimi Mosque. They desecrate the Koran, cut the mosque microphones and at times openly provoke the people praying there.'[28] Yet even as it was expelling the last Arab inhabitants from the reconstructed 'Jewish Quarter' of Jerusalem, the government authorized the 'Zionist response'—the establishment of two schools in the centre of Hebron—in a move which even some cabinet ministers called 'pointless' and a 'mistake', which the opposition denounced as yet another submission to the 'manoeuvres of a group of fanatics', and which Arab mayors likened to 'putting a match to gunpowder'.

And so, in fact, it proved. On 2 May 1980, in the worst episode of its kind since 1967, three or four Palestinian gunmen hurled grenades and fired into a crowd of about a hundred Jewish worshippers as they walked home from the Tomb of Abraham. Among the six dead was Eli Hazeev, a member of Rabbi Meir Kahan's fanatical Jewish Defence League, an immigrant from the United States and a Vietnam veteran. Hazeev, the 'Wolf', held the opinion that 'the only good Arab is a dead one'—but he never had the chance to point the M-16 rifle slung over his shoulder the night he died. Several thousand civilians attended his funeral in the centre of Hebron. Many of them, armed with automatic rifles, fired into the air as they passed through the deserted streets. At the graveside, after soldiers had unleashed a farewell volley and the Chief of Staff and the nation's leading rabbis had paid their last respects, a Soviet immigrant with an Uzi sub-machine-gun shouted, 'Revenge, revenge.'

A month later on 2 June three Arab mayors fell victim to a highly sophisticated, simultaneous terrorist plot that spanned four cities. Mayor Bassam Shak'a of Nablus, injured by a bomb that exploded as he got into his car, lost both his legs above the knees. Mayor Karim Khallaf of Ramallah lost part of his foot in a similar explosion. Mayor Ibrahim Tawil of El Bireh, warned by the military government to stay away from his car, escaped unscathed. At the same time seven Arabs were injured when a hand grenade of Israeli manufacture exploded in the heart of Hebron. The three mayors were held to be the most 'radical' members of the pro-PLO Committee of National Guidance, which had come into being in order to combat the 'autonomy' to be conferred on the Palestinians under the Camp David agreements. There was open rejoicing among the West Bank settlers. Mourners who had gathered for a service in memory of the six killed a month before were united in declaring that it was not revenge enough. Rabbi Moshe Levinger, spiritual head of Kiryat Arba, said he felt 'safer' and expressed his 'understanding of the men who did it'. Yossi Weiner, the Secretary of Kiryat Arba, said he was not sad. 'What a miss,' exclaimed another settler about the grenade in the heart of Hebron. 'To lay explosives in the Hebron casbah and end up with only seven injured Arabs is a shame. If it had gone off as planned, it would have hit dozens and perhaps even hundreds of them.'[29] For his part Rabbi Meir Kahan said that all he knew about the assassination attempts was that 'good and capable Jews avenged the blood of good Jews spilled in Hebron'. Those behind it were 'very professional'. They had done 'very good work. . . . As soon as the Arabs leave the country, they'll have fewer troubles. There's room in this land for only one nation. Anyone who thinks Jews and Arabs can co-exist is a fool.'[30]

Begin denounced the terrorist attacks as crimes of the gravest kind and promised a thorough investigation. It did not materialize. Instead of imposing an immediate curfew on such a hotbed of *Gush Emunim* activism as Kiryat Arba, the government sent the army to protect its memorial service. There were official admonitions against jumping to conclusions about the national identity of the terrorists; indeed, it was repeatedly suggested that the deed might have been done by the PLO itself. No arrests were made, no action taken against extremist organizations, and no questions were asked in the quarters where any serious investigation should have begun: among the mayors themselves, their families, friends and colleagues. Within a few weeks a leading Israeli journalist, a senior reserve officer with good intelligence connections, reported that the head of the general security services, the *Shin Beth*, had resigned because the Prime Minister had been systematically obstructing his request for special surveillance of the *Gush Emunim*.[31]

So far as the *Gush Emunim* was concerned violent clashes between Arabs and Jews were a good thing. Since they proved that 'the two cannot co-exist,' said Hanan Porat, head of the movement, 'they will bring about the expulsion of all the Arabs.'[32] The settlers, individually and collectively, were deliberately seeking to create those conditions that would force the Arabs out, either gradually or in one great convulsion. Some people, warned Aharon Yariv, the former director of Military Intelligence, 'hope to exploit a situation of war to expel 7–800,000 . . . things are being said to this effect and the means prepared.'[33]

Each new settler, therefore, was an additional piece of dynamite, both in himself and as an accretion to the power which the dissidents wielded inside Israel proper. For, given the key place which the 'conquest of the land' has always occupied in Zionist theory and practice, those engaged in it have always held a disproportionate influence over everyone else. And if the settlers have always tended to be militant by temperament, the *Gush Emunim* went even further than their predecessors by explicitly repudiating, where necessary, the authority of the state institutions, the courts and parliament in the name of a divine authority of which they were the messengers. A newcomer from the Soviet Union declared on television that 'Greater Israel is preferable to democracy and its laws. When they prevent the settlement of Eretz Israel a dictatorship must be installed.' When the Supreme Court decreed a temporary cessation of settlement activity at Elon Moreh near Nablus the *Gush Emunim* denounced it as 'an instrument in the hands of the terrorists'.[34]

A collision between state and dissidents grew less and less likely, however, as the ruling establishment fell more and more under the influence of its own extremists. Within the establishment the army was asserting itself increasingly over the civilian sector. The Chief of Staff, General Eitan, enjoyed more political power than any of his predecessors. He was openly scornful of the politicians. A group of officers formally opined that soldiers 'have greater moral authority and carry more qualitative weight than civilians'. Reserve General Beni Peled, a former air force commander, proposed the disbandment of the Knesset and its replacement by a political structure based on biblical law. Many civilians shared the officers' disenchantment with democracy. According to an opinion poll, 40 per cent of the public considered that the Knesset was not working properly, 66 per cent believed that politics and parties were unnecessary and 40 per cent agreed that, 'to come to grips with the difficult problems of Israel, it is necessary to totally change the political régime in the country and to establish a strong régime of leaders who will not be dependent upon parties'.[35]

Fears began to be expressed that, with such ideas gaining ground and with the existence of a not-so-secret armed underground that was ready to promote them, there could be a war between the Jews themselves. As Yehuda Litani of *Haaretz* wrote:

> Ariel Sharon knows what he is talking about when he warns of a civil war. The West Bank settlers constitute military units. . . . They will disrupt any political move towards concessions to the Arabs, even the implementation of the *Likud*'s autonomy plan in the West Bank and the Gaza Strip. There can be no doubt that the settlers and their supporters plan to fight these developments by all means. Their well-stocked ammunition stores in the West Bank will be of great help in the struggle.[35]

But would the new dissidents really pit Jew against Jew? It was not inconceivable, some Israelis suggested, pointing out that the extreme right still sought vengeance for the sinking of the *Irgun* arms ship *Altalena*. In their view Jews who condoned the break-up of Greater Israel were worse than the Arabs themselves. *Likud* thugs had taken to attacking 'traitors' with crowbars, whips and razor blades. Assassination threats were made on the telephone against journalists, lawyers, members of parliament and human rights activists. Children were warned that their parents might be killed if they did not stop supporting the Palestinians. The way the security forces dealt with Jewish demonstrators showed that they did not rate them much more highly than the Arabs.[37] The Deputy Prime Minister Yigal Yadin forecast that if Labour returned to power a civil war was indeed possible. In effect, he thereby assured the extreme right that their threat to the state and the rule of law had its rewards in that its deterrent effect was so great that the institutions would not be put to the test.[38] Sure enough, the country was temporarily saved from further domestic strife by Begin's return to power in the June 1981 general election. With every poll more and more Sephardi Jews of Oriental origin had been turning to *Likud* and this time about two in every three *Likud* voters were drawn from their ranks, while Ashkenazi Jews of European origin constituted 70 per cent of Labour's constituency.[39] The new coalition government which Begin now formed, though still overwhelmingly Ashkenazi in composition, pandered even more flagrantly to the rising forces of chauvinism and religious fanaticism. Within the cabinet itself the principal illustration of that was the promotion, to the Defence Ministry which he had so long coveted, of General Ariel Sharon.

Menachim Milson, Civil Administration and the Village Leagues

Begin called his second electoral triumph 'a mandate from the people to preserve Eretz Israel in its entirety'. Some parties in his ruling coalition, such as the National Religious Party, patron of the *Gush Emunim*, had lost seats, but only because others, even more extreme than themselves, had gained at their expense. Among them, for example, was the newly created *Tehiya* (Renewal) party, which won three seats. Steeped in a mystical nationalism which had much in common with classical European fascism, *Tehiya* advocated the abrogation of the peace treaty with Egypt and the annexation of all the occupied territories. Its solution to the problem of the Palestinian refugees was simple: 'evacuation of all the camps and the deportation of all the refugees to Saudi Arabia and the oil-producing countries which have urgent manpower needs'. Its leader, Professor Yuval Ne'eman, considered that the Israeli army had shown 'great laxity' during the 1973 War, because it had failed to take this opportunity 'to empty the Gaza Strip of all its [450,000] Palestinian inhabitants once and for all'.[40]

Much unseemly haggling went into the formation of Begin's new cabinet. But it was not the concessions he had to make to the minority religious parties, those bastions of medieval obscurantism, which cost him such qualms and misgivings, it was the elevation of General Ariel Sharon, hawk of hawks, to the Ministry of Defence, that fateful step which he had finally brought himself to take. Since the resignation of Ezer Weizmann, anything but a dove himself, Sharon had been the obvious, openly aspiring successor. Rather than gratify him, however, Begin, no military man himself despite his terrorist past, had taken on the job. Weizmann had written of Sharon that 'in war I'd follow him through fire and flood'. He was also, however, to all but a few faithful stalwarts within the military establishment, ambitious to the point of megalomania, ruthless with all who stood in his way, impervious to any view but his own, an opportunist, a liar and a blackguard. 'Never before', wrote the *Jerusalem Post*'s military correspondent, 'has any person been accused by so many, so harshly of being totally devoid of loyalty, and so dedicated to his own future.'[41] A popular Israeli maxim said of the swashbuckling, fifty-three-year-old general that he was 'a war looking for a place to happen'. So to put such a man at the head of the most powerful military machine in the Middle East, and one of the most powerful in the world, was obviously pregnant with the gravest possible consequences. There had been other reasons for Begin's hesitations. When once asked why he had delayed so long before moving Sharon from the Agriculture to the Defence Ministry, Begin had replied that it would only be a matter of time before he sent tanks to surround the Prime Minister's office. The reported slight was denied, wrote Weizmann in his memoirs, but the denial had a hollow ring. 'Begin really believes Sharon capable of such a thing.'[42] Sharon was a clear and obvious danger to what the Americans still so fondly called 'the only democracy in the Middle East'.

For the *Gush Emunim* and the 'dissidents', some of whom had now discovered that Begin himself was too soft, Sharon was the godsend they awaited, the 'strong man' who would deal with the 'enemy within' and restore the nation's honour. He did not hide it: he was of the opinion that 'the state is above everything else', security above (the still non-existent) constitution.[43] 'Our country,' Sharon told the Knesset, 'is in a condition of weakness and self-destruction, a climate of suicide whose reasons are hard to explain. The real danger is not our economic or military situation, but the lack of national objectives and values.'[44] 'The most dangerous enemies,' he went on, 'are not the *Gush Emunim*—real pioneers, would that there were more of them—our enemy is servility before the foreigner, the self-hatred that you ceaselessly cultivate, the sick motives that sustain it. You want us all to be reduced to nothings, but you won't succeed.' To which deputy Shulamit Aloni, civil libertarian, replied: 'That is how all fascists come to power'.[45]

An aggravation of their plight was all that the Arabs of the occupied territories could expect from the man who had been removed from the command of Gaza in 1970 because his 'pacification' of it had been so brutal that even the country's most hardened soldiers could not tolerate it.[46] In the opinion of a retired general, Sharon would try to reduce the population of the West Bank and Gaza 'by a variety of measures which will fall short of forcible deportation or open atrocities'.[47]

Yet barely had the new cabinet been sworn in than its new Defence Minister announced a series of measures designed to lighten the heavy hand of military rule in the occupied territories. Soldiers no longer had the right to enter schools and universities in the course of demonstrations, roadblocks were to be reduced, there were to be no more 'collective punishments', no more arrests at the slightest incident. The military authorities, it was put about unofficially, would refrain from all actions calculated to 'degrade' or 'humiliate' the local population.[48]

The Egypt of President Sadat, anxious for anything to show that its efforts on the Palestinians' behalf were at last yielding fruit, welcomed this unlooked-for display of concern for their welfare by the last man anyone expected it of. The Palestinians were, however, sceptical, not to say downright cynical, from the outset. It quickly turned out that they were right. Unable to agree on a form of autonomy which the infinitely accommodating Sadat, let alone King

Hussein, the other Arab states or the Palestinians themselves could accept, the Israelis decided to impose their own new order pure and simple. Even General Sharon, though, thought he had better have a Palestinian 'cover' of sorts. The course he chose was characteristically unsubtle—the carrot and the stick. From now on there were good Palestinians and bad: those who opposed his plans, in whatever degree, would be punished and penalized, those who acquiesced would win their due reward.

The theoretical foundations of this new policy were laid out, at scholarly length, in an article entitled 'How to Make Peace with the Palestinians', which appeared in *Commentary*, the high-brow American Jewish monthly, three months before Sharon began to put it into effect.[49] The author was Menachim Milson, a professor of Arabic literature and Chairman of the Institute of Asian and African Studies at the Hebrew University of Jerusalem. He was also a colonel in the Israeli army and since 1976 had been Adviser on Arab Affairs to the military government.

The thesis that Milson expounded was that Arab and Palestinian opposition to Camp David and the failure of the 'autonomy' talks had nothing to do with Israel's policy of establishing new settlements in the occupied territories, 'a favoured explanation' of the Western press. The three Camp David signatories, he maintained, had seriously expected to find Palestinians who would join the talks; they had refused to believe that 'the PLO rejection of the Camp David accords' was 'not a response to this or that interpretation of the autonomy plan or to the policy of the Begin government'. But, in truth, this rejection was 'absolute, an expression in concrete political behavior of the refusal to recognize Israel's right to exist as a sovereign state'. And the fact was that the PLO had 'come to control the West Bank and Gaza politically at a time when these areas are controlled militarily and administratively by Israel'. So it was that the municipal elections of 1976 had been a landslide victory for the PLO. At the time the Labour government had hailed the outcome, however distasteful, as a triumph of Israeli democracy. Not so, argued Milson. It had been the PLO's propaganda which had swept its men into office. For the elections had been preceded by 'an intensive campaign conducted by PLO radio stations in Syria and Lebanon calling on the people to vote *en masse* for the candidates who supported the PLO'. 'Serious disorders in the major West Bank towns' had been stirred up in order to 'prove to the people that the PLO had control of the streets'. Thereafter, it was a 'twofold' pressure; 'the offer of patronage money' on the one hand, 'physical terror and intimidation' on the other, which had enabled the PLO to achieve 'what has been described in the media as "the unanimous support of the people" '.

However—and this was the nub—'the situation was not inevitable and is not irreversible'.

> In order to effect progress towards a peaceful settlement, one must create conditions within which moderates in the territories will be able to express their views openly . . . one *can* reach an agreement with those who are willing to work within the necessities and constraints of reality and accept the political consequences. Such people . . . who are ready for a compromise solution, require moral and political support against the extremists.

The only way of helping the moderates was by 'freeing the population of the territories from the grip of the PLO. This must be done by Israel, with the support and cooperation of the US. During the next year . . . Israel will have to engage in a persistent political campaign against PLO domination in the territories.'

On 1 November 1981, General Sharon established a newfangled 'civil administration' for the West Bank and Gaza, and put Professor Milson at the head of it. The new administration, though formally in charge of the military government, did not do away with it. The army retained full control over security affairs, but civilians replaced soldiers in various posts, such as health, education and agriculture. The purpose, officials let it be known, was to show 'good will', to create a new 'climate of confidence', of 'cooperation with the local population'.

The people of the occupied territories immediately rejected the new measures which the mayors, their elected representatives, condemned as another landmark on the road to that complete annexation which, the Begin government had made abundantly clear, would sooner or later come to pass. They also saw it as the beginning of Sharon's policy of creating an alternative puppet leadership that would furnish the necessary Palestinian 'cover' for all his designs. The mayors refused to recognize the authority of Milson and his new administration. Strikes and demonstrations broke out immediately throughout the occupied territories. They were met with the traditional response: the demolition of houses, curfews, searches, the closure of Bir Zeit University, arrests, restrictions on the movement of community leaders, the banning of *al-Fajr* newspaper, and so on. Sharon's new liberal policies had proved short-lived. On 9 November he promised 'exemplary punishment' for all trouble-makers and by 20 November the newspaper *Davar* described the Defence Minister's policies as 'the most brutal and violent' since the beginning of the occupation.[50]

In spite of this opposition, Milson pressed ahead with the strategy he had foreshadowed in his *Commentary* article. He sought to promote those 'moderates' who, shielded from PLO terror, would take their place as the natural leaders of the Palestinian community, ready to play any political and administrative role that he cared to assign them. To this end he developed and expanded an experiment in colonial manipulation which he had first introduced in 1978 in his capacity as adviser to the military government. It was his contention that since 70 per cent of the population lived in villages, they should have a greater say in running affairs than the 30 per cent who lived in the towns. The villagers, conservative, simple, parochial in outlook, were more easily manipulated than the townspeople. It was in the Hebron area, the most conservative in the West Bank, that the first of his Village Leagues had come into being. It was headed by Mustafa Dudeen, a man who commanded little respect in his own neighbourhood and almost none at all in the West Bank as a whole. He had been a devoted servant of King Hussein, doing brief service as a Jordanian cabinet minister—in 'Black September' 1970 when the King's troops broke the back of guerilla power in Jordan. A Jordanian court had sentenced his brother *in absentia* to five years' imprisonment for the theft of municipal funds. It was notorious that, ever since 1967, the Israeli authorities had starved the inhabitants of funds and services—lavishing them instead on their own illegal Jewish settlements—but if the Village Leagues were to get anywhere, Israel had to offer something by way of material incentive. So, whereas before 1978 it was calculated that the military authorities had spent only $3,000 on some seventy-five villages in the Hebron area, they increased it to $2 million on Dudeen's behalf. In raising up Dudeen, the authorities debased the Hebron municipality. West Bankers needed a permit for everything—from the installation of a telephone to the right to cross the Jordan bridge—and it was made clear to the people that if they went to Dudeen they would not only have a much better chance of securing such routine services, they would get special favours too. Israeli television's Arabic programme would show the governor of Hebron or some other important personage donating a cheque to their protégé, who in turn handed it over to this or that village notable of his choosing.

Village Leagues were now destined to spring up all over the West Bank. Uri Avneri, editor of the campaigning weekly *Ha'olam Hazeh*, described it thus:

> You take an ambitious local personality, who commands no respect in his village till now and will sell himself to the devil for power—and these, for the most part, are very primitive people, who cannot read or write. . . . You then give this local potentate your favour—the prospect of easy money and lording it over his family foes, in the hope that this will excite his neighbours' jealousy and that they will emulate him in their turn. But the word 'moderates' is a pretty one. What is really meant is 'toadies', people who will abase themselves before their Israeli masters. . . . It is impossible to bribe a whole people.[51]

Suddenly there was a Village League for the Bethlehem area. Its head, Bishara Qumsiyah, was virtually unknown there; he went on television and applauded the demolition of Arab homes.[52] There was another one for the Ramallah area too; but Yusif Khatib and his son were killed in an ambush. So at the beginning of December Sharon decided that the Leagues should be armed; they could then defend themselves against 'terrorist revenge'. In fact they already had been armed in a small way, but now they were to hire bodyguards, trained by the Israelis, communications equipment and jeeps. They careered around the West Bank, these hirelings of the oppressor, with their Uzi submachine-guns. Sometimes they even manned flying roadblocks alongside the *Gush Emunim*. 'And so,' commented Uri Avneri, 'the

West Bank is being transformed into a small-scale Lebanon.'[53] But it was to no avail. The Leagues were dealt another heavy blow when, on 9 March 1982, the Jordanian government solemnly proclaimed that unless their members renounced all dealings with them, they would face trial and possible execution for 'treason'. Many of the Leaguers had been the King's men in times past, and this frightened them. Although Mustafa Dudeen went on Israel Radio to urge his former master, King Hussein, to end these 'childish' antics and warned all Jordanian agents that 'we can take revenge on them whenever we see fit', the Leaguers began to resign in droves.[54] Sharon warned the Jordanians that if they carried out their threats, Israel would 'treat them just like it treats the terrorists', but the more the Israelis supported them, the more the Leaguers looked like 'agents' and 'traitors' in the eyes of the population.[55]

The campaign against the authentic Palestinian leadership came to a head in March and April 1982 on the eve of the final withdrawal from Sinai. On 19 March Milson dismissed the mayor of El Bireh, Ibrahim Tawil, who had escaped unscathed from the car-bomb plot two years before, along with his entire council. His pretext was that Tawil, boycotting the civil administration, had refused to meet him to discuss the affairs of his town. The dismissal provoked a general strike.

A week later Milson sent armoured cars into Nablus and Ramallah, whose mayors, the legless Bassam Shak'a and Karim Khallaf, were taken at dawn to military headquarters and informed that they, too, had been dismissed. According to an army spokesman, they had also refused to cooperate with the civil administration and 'incited' the population to 'revolt'.

The campaign became a crusade. This 'struggle' against PLO supporters in the occupied territories, Milson declared, was 'the most important political battle since the creation of Israel'. And it was the struggle not only of Israel but of 'the entire Jewish people'. Ten of the twenty-five municipalities were controlled by the PLO, whose behaviour and that of its 'agents' in Judea and Samaria was 'immoral', 'vicious' and 'diabolical'. Once the Arabs had been 'liberated' from the influence of the PLO 'fanatics', 'plenty' of them would come forward to seek the 'political solution', on the basis of Camp David, against which the PLO had set its face. Peace with the

'Palestinian Arabs' *was* possible.[56] The PLO, added the Minister of Justice, had decided 'a long time ago' to foment trouble in retaliation against 'the growing influence of the Village Leagues'. In the view of the Foreign Minister Yitzhak Shamir, the PLO had 'planned the uprising down to the smallest detail'. It was, he said, scheduled to take place after the withdrawal from Sinai, coinciding with an expected new American initiative to revive the 'autonomy' talks.[57]

Most inhabitants of the occupied territories did indeed look upon the PLO as their 'sole, legitimate representative'. It was the symbol to which they clung. Arafat and his men would have been happy to command the direct, operational influence which the Israeli government attributed to them. But they did not, nor did they wish it to appear so now. They had made large claims in the past, but, for tactical reasons, they now found themselves deprecating their own importance. Arafat said that he was 'not directing' the unrest, and his 'Foreign Minister', Farouk Kaddoumi, called it 'a semi-surprise to our leadership'.[58]

The disturbances were by far the most serious in fifteen years of occupation. Similar outbreaks in each of the three previous years had resulted in a total of some five deaths and fifteen injuries. This time, over a period of some six weeks, about twenty were killed, some in sinister circumstances, and about three hundred wounded. It was a very one-sided affair. 'There is no uprising,' said General Uri Orr, commander of the West Bank, 'only stone throwing.'[59] That is essentially what it was: stones against guns. Day after day youngsters, armed with nothing more lethal than these stones and slings, would venture out in protest demonstrations, only to be met with a fusillade of bullets which, supposedly fired above their heads, hit them in the arms and chest. Brutalities were not just the involuntary excesses of soldiers under strain. General Eitan himself encouraged them in written orders which the leading newspaper *Haaretz* called 'astonishing' and 'manifestly illegal'. *Haaretz* also described as highly alarming a directive which authorized Jewish settlers to open fire—without any warning to do so sparingly.[60]

Most sinister of all was the wave of mysterious killings that accompanied the disturbances. On 19 March the body of a young Arab was found near a settlement at Ramallah. Suspicion fell on the settlers and in the Knesset left-wing deputy Yossi Sarid called for an inquiry, pointing out that, as in the terrorist attacks on the three mayors, the perpetrators of crimes against the Arabs never seemed to be caught. In a document submitted to the diplomatic community the Mayor of Ramallah claimed that the settlers had tortured their victim for three days before putting a bullet through his head. A few days later, in retaliation for a stone-throwing episode, Kiryat Arba settlers went out and shot a seventeen-year-old villager. In April, two more young Palestinians were found dead in the fields, one beheaded, the other cut in two. In May yet another mangled corpse was discovered, and a girl was shot by civilians from a passing car.[61]

A year later it all came out: the settlers had indeed been committing crimes of vandalism, sabotage, assault and murder with the blessing of the highest authorities in the land. That, in essence, was the finding of the official inquiry carried out by the Deputy Attorney General Yehudit Karp into Jewish 'vigilantism' in the occupied territories. In April 1983 Karp resigned as chairman of the investigating committee in protest against her superiors' effective shelving of her report and ignoring of its recommendations. The report was never made public but according to the Israeli press it documented 'the two systems of justice, one for the Jews and one for the Arabs', which had grown up in the occupied territories. 'Jewish terrorism', as the police openly called it, had become a scourge to which every responsible quarter, by default or design, was an accomplice. That, of course, included the settlers to a man. Their leadership instructed them not to cooperate with the police. 'Out there,' said a senior police officer gesturing towards the West Bank, 'there is a see no evil, hear no evil, speak no evil attitude among Jews about Jewish vigilantism.' It included the military government, effective rulers of the occupied territories, who were 'ready to impose all sorts of collective punishment on Arabs . . . but encouraged the Jews—in *all* their activities'. It included the government itself, 'senior members' of Begin's ruling coalition and members of parliament. 'Since it takes place in the territories,' said a senior police officer, 'they intervene with the army', which essentially 'calls off' the inquiry. 'Somebody calls up and says, "This boy has a good Jewish heart, you shouldn't bother him" and the military government steps back, taking us with it.' In the Knesset, Shulamit Aloni, civil libertarian, said that for four years General Sharon had lent his personal protection to 'Israeli murderers and vandals', and the newspaper *Davar* said that the Arabs of the occupied territories were not even second-rate citizens. They were 'more or less fifth-rate citizens. . . . The only first-rate citizens are the Jewish residents of the territories, who can commit almost any crime wherever they are and get away with it, so long as the victims are Arabs.'[62]

The campaign was backfiring. No 'moderate' stepped forward to run Palestinian affairs or to negotiate the future of the occupied territories. It would have been pointless, Israel Radio reported after the dismissal of Ibrahim Tawil, to appoint a Village Leaguer in his place, because 'no one would cooperate with him'. The civil administration found itself running the municipalities itself, bringing a few workers to their desks every day in military vehicles. As for 'autonomy', Mustafa Dudeen told Israel Radio that the Village Leagues could have no part in establishing that: 'If world leaders cannot reach a solution, who am I to pride myself on doing that?'[63] If anything Milson was achieving the opposite of what he had set out to do: uniting all the Palestinians in desperate protest against the occupation. Leading Israelis scoffed at the idea of PLO instigation. Twenty-five members of the military government accused the new administration of undermining everything they had achieved. According to the leader of the Labour opposition, Shimon Peres, it was throwing the whole population 'into the arms of the PLO'. 'We are creating a situation', said a former administrator of the occupied territories, 'in which there will be no moderates to talk to at all.'[64]

The disturbances were eventually crushed by General Sharon's 'iron fist'. But with the 'political solution' as far away as ever, it was time to strike at the heart of the cancer, the PLO itself, in its last, Lebanese sanctuary. On 26 April Israel completed its evacuation of Sinai. In the weeks before 3,000 partisans of the Stop the Withdrawal movement had entrenched themselves in the coastal township of Yamit and other settlements on Egyptian soil in order to 'resist' their abandonment. Followers of Rabbi Meir Kahan, barricading themselves in a basement, threatened collective suicide. But, spitting and screaming abuse at the 20,000 soldiers who came to evict them, they finally left without bloodshed and bulldozers ground the settlements back into the desert sand. Begin and Sharon, of all people, had presided over the desecration of a basic article of Zionist faith: territory on which the Jews settle is territory they will forever hold. But hardly had they made full and final peace on their southern front than they went to war on the northern one.

Notes

1. *Maariv*, 23 March 1979.
2. Shaham, David, *Yediot Aharonot* supplement, 13 April 1979, cited in Donald S. Will, 'Zionist Settlement Policy', *Journal of Palestine Studies*, Beirut, Vol. XI, No. 3, 1979, p. 40.
3. *Jerusalem Post*, 25 March 1983.
4. Bulletin 9–10, United Nations Special Unit on Palestinian Rights, September–October 1979, p. 8.
5. United Nations Document A/36/341, 23 June 1981.
6. Abu-Lughod, Janet, 'Israeli Settlements in Occupied Arab Lands: Conquest to Colony', *Journal of Palestine Studies*, Beirut, Vol. XI, No. 2, 1982, pp. 25–7; see also *Gun and Olive Branch*, pp. 229–41.
7. *Ibid.*
8. Bulletin, *op. cit.*
9. Abu-Lughod, *op. cit.*, pp. 45–8.
10. Will, *op. cit.*, citing *Haaretz*, 23 March 1981.
11. Harris, William Wilson, 'Taking Root: Israeli Settlement in the West Bank, the Golan Gaza-Sinai, 1967–80', New York and Chichester: Research Studies Press, a division of John Wiley and Sons, 1980, cited in Abu-Lughod, *op. cit.*, p. 37.
12. See MERIP Report, No. 59, 1977, cited in Abu-Lughod, *ibid.*, p. 43.
13. *The Times*, 11 April 1983.
14. *Ibid.*
15. *Jerusalem Post*, 10 September 1982.
16. *The Times*, 11 April 1983.
17. See *Jerusalem Post*, 10 September 1982, *International Herald Tribune*, 2 October 1982, *Middle East International*, 10 December 1982.
18. *Israel and Palestine Monthly Review*, No. 79, cited in Abu-Lughod, *op. cit.*, p. 49.
19. *Hamakar* (official *Gush Emunim* bulletin, cited in *Journal of Palestine Studies*, Beirut, Vol. X, No. 1, 1980, p. 151.
20. *Jerusalem Post*, International edition, 8–14 June 1980.

21. *Jerusalem Post*, 10 September 1982.
22. *Maariv*, cited in *International Herald Tribune*, 26 January 1981.
23. *Jerusalem Post*, 25 March 1983.
24. See Kapeliouk, Amnon, *Le Monde Diplomatique*, June 1980; also *Le Monde*, 19 June 1980.
25. See *Journal of Palestine Studies*, Beirut, Vol. X, No. 4, p. 139.
26. *Haaretz*, 16 May 1981, see *Journal of Palestine Studies*, Beirut, Vol. XI, No. 3, p. 48.
27. *Maariv*, 18 September 1979, see *ibid.*
28. *Al-Hamishmar*, 8 February 1980.
29. *Davar*, 6 June 1980, see *Journal of Palestine Studies*, Beirut, Vol. X, No. 1, p. 147.
30. *International Herald Tribune*, 3, 4 June 1980.
31. See *Middle East International*, 15 August 1980.
32. Kapeliouk, Amnon, *Le Monde Diplomatique*, June 1980.
33. *Al-Hamishmar*, 16 May 1980, *Journal of Palestine Studies*, Beirut, Vol. XI, No. 3, p. 52.
34. Kapeliouk, Amnon, *Le Monde Diplomatique*, December 1979.
35. *Monitin*, February 1981, see *Journal of Palestine Studies*, Beirut, Vol. XI, No. 3, p. 49.
36. See Pallis, Elfi, *Middle East International*, 24 April 1981.
37. *Ibid.*
38. *Yediot Aharonot*, 6 June 1980, see *Journal of Palestine Studies*, Beirut, Vol. X, No. 1, p. 147.
39. *The Economist*, 30 July 1983.
40. Kapeliouk, Amnon, *Le Monde Diplomatique*, August 1981.
41. Goodman, Hirsh, *Jerusalem Post*, 26 June 1981.
42. *International Herald Tribune*, 6 June 1981.
43. *Yediot Aharonot*, 30 October 1979, see Kapeliouk, Amnon, *Le Monde Diplomatique*, December 1979; *Haaretz*, 13 June 1980, see *Journal of Palestine Studies*, Beirut, Vol. XI, No. 3, p. 52.
44. *Ibid.*
45. *Ibid.*
46. *Jerusalem Post*, 26 June 1981.
47. Peled, Mattityahu, *Middle East International*, 14 August 1981.
48. *Le Monde*, 15 August 1981.
49. *Commentary*, New York, May 1981.
50. Kapeliouk, Amnon, *Le Monde Diplomatique*, December 1981.
51. *Ha'olam Hazeh*, 17 March 1982.
52. *Al-Hamishmar*, 22 March 1982.
53. *Ha'olam Hazeh*, 17 March 1982, see *The Economist*, 27 March 1982.
54. Israel Radio, 10, 11 March 1982.
55. *Le Monde*, 24 March 1982.
56. Israel Radio, 27 March 1982.
57. See *Le Monde*, 26, 27 March 1982; Israel Radio, 28, 29 March 1982.
58. *Middle East Reporter*, 30 March, 5 April 1982.
59. *Le Monde*, 24 March 1982.

60. *Haaretz*, 20 January 1983.
61. *Le Monde*, 22, 26 March, 18 May, *The Economist*, 15 May 1982.
62. *Jerusalem Post*, 12, 16, 17 May 1982; *The Guardian*, 26 May 1983; *Los Angeles Times*, 26 May 1983.
63. Israel Radio, 22, 23 March 1982.
64. *Le Monde*, 3 April 1982.

12 · THE INVASION OF LEBANON

Begin Offers Peace and Plots War

There would be no more 'sacrifices' like Yamit, no more territorial withdrawals for the sake of peace. Begin and his ministers were adamant about that. It would be impossible to annex the West Bank, Begin said, 'because it is already part of our land'. And, upon his urging, the Knesset passed a law prohibiting evacuation of any settlement in the West Bank or Gaza which amounted to annexation in all but name.

Consolidation of existing gains was not enough, however. Zionism is an energetic creed and Begin was a particularly energetic practitioner of it. The Jewish State could not rest until it had won the acceptance of the region in which it had implanted itself and if this acceptance was not voluntarily conferred it would have to be forcibly extracted. Israel's invasion of Lebanon—the fifth full-scale war in its thirty-five-year history—marked a new peak of military strength and of the irresistible, almost biological urge of its leaders to use it, in the guise of self-defence, to achieve yet another breakthrough in Zionism's unfolding purpose.

The invasion had been a long time in the making but, as a deliberate act of policy, it grew out of the Israeli-Egyptian peace treaty. It was in May 1979, shortly after the conclusion of the treaty, that Begin made the first of a series of theatrical 'peace offers' to Lebanon. It came, characteristically, after a bloody reprisal raid. Striking at what they may have thought were Palestinian and Syrian military targets, Israeli warplanes had killed Lebanese civilians instead, among them the bride and four of her guests at a wedding. Israel, Begin pledged, would go on hitting these 'Palestinian murderers' by land, sea and air in order 'to destroy them completely'.

Then, after the threat, the offer—'I hereby invite President Sarkis to come to meet me here in Jerusalem.' He himself was 'ready to go in an aircraft to Beirut or any neutral place to meet President Sarkis . . . and the only subject we would discuss would be the signing of a peace treaty between Israel and Lebanon'. Turning to the Syrians, he said that their 'army of occupation must leave at once'. It was 'destroying Lebanese villages and firing on innocent Christians'. As for the Palestinian refugees, they should all be resettled in Saudi Arabia, Syria, Iraq and Libya, 'very big countries rich in resources and petroleum, with millions of square kilometres of land'. Neither Lebanon nor Israel had any territorial claims on each other and a peace treaty could be worked out 'in two days or so of talks'. Jordan, he forecast, 'would also then make peace with us'.[1] Lebanon's right-wing Christian leaders, or rather the Israeli-backed 'ultras' led by Bashir Gemayel, commander of the Phalangist militia, welcomed the peace offer. President Sarkis spurned it, while the Prime Minister, Selim al-Hoss, said that Israel, through 'blackmail, terrorism and brute force', was planning to tear Lebanon away from its Arab moorings. In the words of the Beirut newspaper *al-Safir* it was intended 'to blow up Lebanon from within'.

That Lebanon, with its military weakness, confessional tensions and *laissez-faire* traditions, was particularly vulnerable to external subversion was an idea that had long commended itself to Israel's imperial dreamers. As early as 1954 David Bengurion had urged that one of the 'central duties' of Israel's foreign policy should be to push the Maronite Christians to 'proclaim a Christian state'. He had won the enthusiastic support of his disciple Moshe Dayan, then Chief of Staff, who said that 'the only thing that is necessary is to find an officer, even just a major. We should either win his heart or buy him with money, to make him agree to declare himself the saviour of the Maronite population. Then the Israeli army will enter Lebanon, will occupy the necessary territory, and will create a Christian régime which will ally itself with Israel.' In the event, what Moshe Sharett, Israel's first Foreign Minister, described as this 'crazy adventure' against an entirely peaceable neighbour was superseded by another mad-cap scheme—the 1956 invasion of Egypt—but when, a quarter of a century later, Begin revived Dayan's blueprint of the 1950s,

Lebanon, ravaged by civil war and foreign occupation, was about as ripe for it as it ever could be.[2]

By 1979 the behaviour of both Palestinians and Israelis was already deeply influenced by that shift in the Middle East balance of power wrought chiefly by Egypt's defection from Arab ranks.

Through most of the decade the Palestinians had been on the offensive, while the Israelis had only retaliated. It was true that, apart from occasional, spectacular 'suicide' missions, the guerillas' trans-frontier raids had been small-scale and sporadic, that the Israeli retribution had been massive, that thousands—more civilian than military, more Lebanese than Palestinian—had died, and scores of thousands had fled their devastated towns and villages. But now Yasser Arafat and the principal guerilla organization, *Fatah*, had all but renounced trans-frontier raids; there had only been two, he said, in the past two years.[3] There were other types of operations—mounted from other Arab countries, from inside Israel or the occupied territories—and these would continue, but those which clearly emanated from *Fatahland*, the PLO's last independent politico-military base, Arafat intended to avoid. He knew how vulnerable he was. For his part, Begin, conscious of Israel's strength, proclaimed himself on permanent offensive. Israel would no longer wait, he warned, for the Palestinians 'to come and kill our women and children'. It would hit them 'any time, any place'. For his Chief of Staff, General Rafael Eitan, the 'war on the terrorists' was one that knew 'no limits, rules or laws'.[4]

The imbalance was accompanied and reinforced by an alliance which Israel had forged within Lebanon itself. The *Likud* government had stepped up that support for the Phalangists, quintessential expression of Maronite Christian militancy, which its Labour predecessors had first provided in the early years of the civil war. At its most blatant, however, the intervention took the very form that Dayan had recommended. In March 1978, following the most murderous of the guerillas' 'suicide' missions, Israel had invaded Lebanon up to the Litani River. It had made only a partial withdrawal and confined the newly created UNIFIL buffer force to a small portion of the invaded territory, placing the vast bulk of it, a border enclave some five to ten kilometres broad by some sixty long, under the control of a Greek Catholic major, Saad Haddad, and his rag-tag militia. Furthermore the Israelis enjoyed secret complicities among the Moslem population. For this Arafat and his men were partly to blame. In Lebanon, as in Jordan a decade before, the guerillas had alienated their Arab environment by something more than their mere presence and the Israeli fire it inevitably attracted: by misdemeanours which the leadership usually attributed to 'undisciplined' elements but which, in the eyes of the population, it rarely attempted to discipline—theft and confiscations, petty warlordism, protection rackets and the levying of 'taxes' on local produce; the hamfisted exploitation of parish pump politics and above all an egoistic indifference to the suffering which the southerners underwent in the name of Palestine.

By 1979 South Lebanon had become one of the world's most explosive flashpoints. On to this complex microcosm was grafted the macrocosm of Middle Eastern, indeed global, conflict. South Lebanon ramified through Arabia, all Arabia converged on South Lebanon. There could be no settlement in the south without a general Lebanese settlement and no Lebanese settlement without a general Middle East settlement. The Israelis could exploit the south to prevent a Lebanese or Middle East settlement which they did not like or, more ambitiously, exploit it to change the whole political and strategic map of the Middle East. Everyone knew it. For the Maronite 'ultras' it was an exhilarating prospect. Their leader, Bashir Gemayel, was waiting for what he called the 'historic opportunity'.[5] A full-scale Israeli invasion was the likeliest form it would take. With Major Haddad following in the wake of the Israeli army, the Phalangist militia would effect a junction with him from the north, thereby restoring the old Maronite Christian ascendancy over the whole country. Others were afraid. The Palestinians. In an ironic reversal of roles, it was they who, under Israel's relentless offensive, now confined themselves to 'reprisals'—rocket and artillery salvoes, inaccurate and generally ineffectual—on Israel's northern towns and settlements. The Syrian Baathists. Military defeat might bring about the long-expected collapse, perhaps in Lebanese-style civil war, of President Asad's highly unpopular régime. The pro-Western, oil-producing countries of the Gulf. A cataclysm on the eastern front would gravely imperil them. Any threat to the Gulf would be a threat to the vital interests of the United States.

The Americans knew it and they too were afraid. The Israelis knew it and brandished their sword of Damocles over the heads of friends and enemies alike, including their one and only indispensable ally. Israel had become by far the most important actor on the Lebanese stage. It alone had the initiative; all the others, the US included, merely reacted. Throughout the 1970s the PLO had been scoring success after success in the international diplomatic arena. Paradoxically, however, it was these triumphs that most endangered it now, because they, more than anything else, were pushing a man like Begin into taking full, adventurous advantage of the PLO's physical and military weakness on the ground. The more moderate, the more 'civilized' the PLO became, the more this alarmed Begin and his superhawks. For the Israeli government, wrote Professor Porath, Arafat's ability to persuade his guerillas, even the most radical among them, to respect a year-long ceasefire presaged a 'real catastrophe'. For it meant also that they could approve a longer-term solution, 'and if, in the future, we approach a period of negotiations between ourselves and certain Arab parties other than Egypt, will our government be able to claim that the PLO is a gang of uncompromising assassins who are not legitimate interlocutors?' The government wanted the PLO to 'return to its earlier terrorist exploits, to plant bombs all over the world, to hijack plenty of aeroplanes and to kill many Israelis'.[6]

The Sharon Plan

After Begin's 'peace offer' it was essentially a question of how and when he would make war. Such was the debate—within the ranks of the ruling *Likud*, between the *Likud* and the opposition and among the political intelligentsia in general—that the invasion, when it finally did come, was no surprise at all. Nor were its dimensions. The range of possible objectives had been endlessly rehearsed. The minimum aim was to create a 'security belt', about twenty-five miles wide, that would protect Israel's northern towns and settlements against Palestinian rocket and artillery bombardment. To achieve that the Israelis would have to conquer another slice of *Fatahland*, already reduced by the Litani Operation of 1978, driving the guerillas north of the Zahrani or Awali rivers, which flow into the sea to the south and north of Sidon respectively. A more ambitious, much-canvassed objective was, as its proponents usually put it, to 'destroy the PLO infrastructure'. More ambitious still was the so-called Sharon Plan. This was a characteristically grandiose scheme to engineer a whole new geopolitical order in and around Israel's frontiers. Israel should reconstitute Lebanon as a Christian or Christian-dominated state ready to make peace with it; more important, the Palestinians should be driven out from there to Jordan. That the final solution to the Palestinian problem lay in Jordan had long been one of Sharon's obsessions. Palestinians already made up at least half its population and all they had to do, with Israel's assistance, in order to satisfy their national aspirations, was to bring down the Hashemite monarchy, whose power base was essentially Transjordanian, and replace it with a régime of their own. If driving the Palestinians out of Lebanon involved a full-scale war against Syria, then so be it; Sharon frequently advocated pre-emptive attack on the neighbour which Israel regarded as its most implacable foe. In his view the destruction of the PLO, the embodiment of Palestinian nationalism and the struggle for self-determination, would break the resistance of the elected West Bank leadership to the Village Leagues and 'autonomy' Israeli-style. The West Bankers should be induced to cross the Jordan and become citizens of their very own Palestinian state on the East Bank.[7]

The Sharon Plan was not even the most far-reaching of the projects which, with the rise of the extreme right, were now entering mainstream Zionist thinking. It has been abundantly demonstrated that, with Zionism, even the most fantastic conceits are apt to become official policy in the end. The learned article entitled 'A Strategy for Israel in the Nineteen Eighties' which appeared in the World Zionist Organization's periodical *Kivunim* cannot, therefore, be dismissed as the ravings of a lunatic fringe. For the author, Oded Yinon, formerly a senior Foreign Ministry official, the 'dissolution' of Jordan, the consequent 'termination of the problem of the territories densely populated with Arabs west of the Jordan, whether in war or under conditions of peace, emigration from the territories and economic, demographic freeze in them', and the recognition by 'the indigenous Arabs' of Israel's 'existence in security borders to the Jordan *and* beyond them', was but 'an immediate strategic target in the short run'. The long-run objectives encompassed the entire Middle East. On 'the Western front', re-invading Sinai and 'breaking Egypt territorially into separate geographical districts is the political goal of Israel in the 1980s.' As for the Eastern front:

> There all the events which are only our wish on the Western front are happening before our eyes today. The total disintegration of Lebanon into five regional, localized governments is the precedent for the entire Arab world. . . . The dissolution of Syria, and later Iraq, into districts of ethnic and religious minorities following the example of Lebanon is Israel's main long-range objective on the Eastern front. The present military weakening of these states is the short-range objective. Syria will disintegrate into several states along the lines of its ethnic and sectarian structure. . . . As a result there will be a Shi'ite Alawi state, the district of Aleppo will be a Sunni state, and the district of Damascus another state which is hostile to the northern one. The Druzes—even those of the Golan—should form a state in Hauran and in northern Jordan. . . . The oil-rich but very divided and internally strife-ridden Iraq is certainly a candidate to fit Israel's goals. . . . Every kind of inter-Arab confrontation will help us to persevere in the short run and will hasten the achievement of the supreme goal, namely breaking up Iraq into elements like Syria and Lebanon. There will be three states or more, around the three major cities, Basra, Baghdad and Mosul, while Shi'ite areas in the south will separate from the Sunni north, which is mostly Kurdish. . . . The entire Arabian Peninsula is a natural candidate for dissolution. . . .[8]

War was all but inevitable but none the less Begin hesitated again and again to launch it. These hesitations were expedient not moral, inspired by higher diplomatic considerations—such as American fears that, with Israel yet to complete its withdrawal from Sinai, the Camp David agreements might collapse—or domestic ones, above all the fear that this was a military adventure which might divide rather than unite Israeli society.

The coming of President Reagan, with his militant, anti-Soviet view of the universe and Israel's pride of place in it, gave the slide towards war a hefty push. With the encouragement of the new Secretary of State, Alexander Haig, Israel's most powerful champion within the new Administration, Begin stepped up support for Bashir Gemayel and the Phalangist 'ultras' in their struggle against the Syrian 'peace-keeping' force which were said to be perpetrating atrocities the like of which had not been seen since the Holocaust. But even an official military spokesman, not to mention the Labour opposition, called Christian 'genocide' claims propaganda, and the *Jerusalem Post* complained that Begin, governing the country like an 'exorcist', made no distinction between 'the demons that haunt him personally (the Holocaust) and the objectives of Israeli policy'.[9]

In April 1981 Israeli aircraft shot down two Syrian helicopters over Lebanon's Beka'a Valley. They were supposedly on their way to 'kill Christians'; subsequently it was conceded that this was not the case. In retaliation the Syrians introduced SAM (surface-to-air missiles) into the Beka's, and Begin—declaring this to be a threat to Israel's security which his Chief of Staff subsequently said it was not—warned that 'under no circumstances' could they stay. Thanks largely to American pressure, stay, however, they did. Then, in a diversion from the 'missile crisis', Begin made another incautious pledge. No more Palestinian rockets would fall on Kiryat Shmona. But they soon did. Begin himself provoked the heaviest bombardment that Kiryat Shmona and other northern towns and settlements had ever experienced, although so disproportionate was the rival fire-power that even this amounted to a mere hundredth part of the death and destruction suffered on the other side. In the ten-day air and artillery duels, the Palestinians killed some six Israelis, while the Israelis killed about 300 Lebanese and Palestinians in a single air raid on Beirut, and 500 or 600 altogether.

The hostilities were brought to an end by the exertions of Philip Habib, President Reagan's special Middle East envoy. He negotiated a ceasefire so vague and laconic—'all hostile activities between Lebanese and Israeli territory will cease'—that in due course the

Israelis, again straining at the leash, evolved their own, highly elastic interpretation of it. That was necessary because, whereas the PLO was determined to respect the truce, the Israelis were looking for any opportunity to break it. For this inconvenient ceasefire, Chief of Staff General Rafael Eitan later disclosed, had merely postponed an invasion originally scheduled for July 1981.[10] According to Ariel Sharon, he had been preparing for the invasion ever since he became Defence Minister in August.[11]

For more than eight months following the ceasefire, the UNIFIL forces reported no hostile acts directed against Israel from Lebanon. Nor could Israel prove any. So, as Begin and company orchestrated a steady crescendo of threats to 'destroy', 'crush', 'annihilate' or 'finish off' what one of them called 'those bastards on the other side of the northern frontier',[12] they simultaneously manufactured the pretexts for doing so. When, at the end of January 1982, five guerillas crossing from Jordan managed to plant mines in the West Bank, Israel denounced this as 'a grave violation of the ceasefire'. The United States disagreed: this was not 'reason enough' for Israeli retaliation. The Labour opposition accused the government of deliberately exaggerating the affair in order to portray it as a ceasefire violation. 'Never', wrote the *Haaretz* military correspondent Zeev Schiff, 'has there been such a crisis of confidence between Defence officials and the public.'[13] According to two Israeli newspapers, an attack on Lebanon was called off at the last minute;[14] Begin, though now very close to the brink, was still hesitating. On 3 April, the Second Secretary of the Israeli embassy in Paris was assassinated. Israel promptly blamed the PLO; the perpetrators had come from 'the centre of terrorism' in Lebanon; it was therefore another ceasefire violation. Not so, said a State Department spokesman, while the opposition accused the government of 'demagogy' that threatened to drag Israel into a conflict for which there was no 'national consensus'. Again the Israelis mobilized for an invasion which, American television networks forecast, might carry them to Beirut. Pleading American pressure, Begin again called it off.

It was the Israelis themselves who, on 21 April, first violated the ceasefire, demolished it rather, with an air raid on a string of Palestinian positions between Sidon and the suburbs of Beirut. Twenty-five people were killed and eighty wounded. What, according to Chief of Staff Eitan, had finally 'broken the camel's back' was the death of an Israeli officer on a land mine in Major Saad Haddad's border enclave. For Eitan, the question of what the officer was doing in Lebanese territory was apparently beside the point. *Haaretz* suggested that the main purpose of the raid was to show the Israeli public that 'if Israel had been forced to withdraw from Sinai, it could still strike elsewhere'.[15] The Palestinians did not reply. In spite of objections from hardliners, Arafat promised that, having given his word to respect the ceasefire, he would do his best to keep it. After the raid the Israelis blithely asserted that, so far as they were concerned, the ceasefire was still in effect. Three weeks later a boy and a girl were injured by a bomb blast in Jerusalem. For the Israelis terrorist operations anywhere in Israel or the occupied territories also constituted violations of the South Lebanese ceasefire. So the planes struck again, killing eleven and wounding twenty-eight. This time the Palestinians did reply with rockets and artillery but, according to observers in Israel, they deliberately avoided population centres and there were no casualties. The Israeli cabinet now decided, however, that Palestinian violations had rendered the ceasefire 'null and void'. Eitan could not hide his eagerness for the fray: 'Now that I have built a military machine which costs billions of dollars I have to use it,' he said. 'It is possible that I will be in Beirut tomorrow.'[16]

Clearly the Israelis had just about dispensed with pretexts altogether. For form's sake, however, they did await one for the launching of the fifth Arab-Israeli war. The attempted assassination of the Israeli ambassador in Britain, Shlomo Argov, was not the doing of the PLO, which promptly denounced it. It was another exploit of Arafat's arch-enemy, the notorious, Baghdad-based *Fatah* dissident Abu Nidal, who directed his particular brand of pure, unbridled terrorism more against the mainstream PLO leadership, particularly moderates within its ranks, than against the 'Zionist enemy'. One of the assassins was actually a colonel in Iraqi intelligence; for reasons of their own the Iraqi Baathists were desperately anxious to provoke an Israeli onslaught on their Syrian rivals. The Israelis scorned such distinctions. Arabs had attacked a Jew. It did not matter where. That, too, had become a violation of the South

Lebanese ceasefire.[17] This time Begin did not hesitate. The assassination attempt, said his spokesman, had 'put an end to a long period of Israeli restraint. Those who believed that the ceasefire concluded a year ago on the Lebanese front meant that everywhere else Jewish blood could flow with impunity are mistaken.' He unleashed his air force on Sabra and Chatila, the two Palestinian camps in Beirut, where the PLO had its headquarters. Sixty to a hundred people were killed and some 275 wounded. Palestinian artillery opened up on northern Israel. One person was killed and four wounded. The planes come back the next day: 130 die. Palestinian artillery kills three in northern Israel. An Israeli minister goes to Galilee and tells the inhabitants: 'Begin pledged that not a single rocket will fall on Kiryat Shmona. *Tsahal* (the Israeli army) will ensure that this pledge is respected.'

The Battle of Beirut

On Sunday, 6 June Israeli ground forces crossed the frontier at three points and pushed, unresisted, through the UNIFIL lines, while others made amphibious landings near Tyre and Sidon. Operation Peace for Galilee was under way with the purpose, according to the first official communiqué, of 'placing the whole of the civilian population of Galilee out of range of the terrorists who have concentrated their base and their headquarters in Lebanon'. This, therefore, was the minimum objective of any invasion, the 'security belt', as both government and opposition had anticipated it. It meant the seizure of about a third of Lebanon. Within twenty-four hours the invaders had taken possession of most of that. 'Tyre [the guerilla pocket south of the Litani River], Beaufort [the celebrated medieval fortress that commands the central approaches to Galilee] Fall As Israel Defence Forces Operation Nears Completion' was the *Jerusalem Post* headline of Tuesday, 8 June. Evidently the newspaper really believed what Begin had said: that the campaign would be over within seventy-two hours.[18]

In confining itself to this minimum objective, the government was only seeking to mollify the opposition and those among the public who, though very uneasy, were ready to support a military action that went no further than that. It was also seeking to reassure the United States. It was doubtless true, as Begin himself had said, that there had never been an Administration as favourable to Israel as Reagan's, and there are legitimate suspicions that Secretary of State Alexander Haig approved or even encouraged an attack which, directed against the Soviet-supported Syrian-Palestinian presence in Lebanon, would in his view serve America's higher strategic interests. Former President Jimmy Carter was later to claim that Haig—though he himself denied it—had given the green light for the invasion. On 20 May Sharon had gone to Washington, where he closeted himself alone with the Secretary of State, and subsequently claimed that he had told him that the invasion was going ahead in any case.[19] Haig lent a sympathetic ear to Israel's repeated complaints that the Palestinians were receiving large quantities of Soviet weaponry and contended that this posed 'a potential threat' to the South Lebanese ceasefire.[20] During the Defence Minister's visit Haig made a key Middle East policy speech that must have rung sweetly in his ears. Singling out Lebanon as a particularly deserving candidate for a more activist American diplomacy, he said: 'The world cannot stand aside, watching in morbid fascination, as this small nation . . . slides further into the abyss of violence and chaos. The time has come to take concerted action in support of both Lebanon's territorial integrity within its internationally recognized borders and a strong central government capable of promoting a free, open, democratic and traditionally pluralist society.' Shortly before the invasion additional aircraft carriers were ordered to reinforce the Sixth Fleet in the east Mediterranean. All the same, the Americans, as always, were afraid that their unruly protégé would go too far. They did not want a full-scale war on the Eastern Front.

But the real, larger ambition was already implicit in that first cabinet communiqué. Israel, it said, would not attack the Syrians unless the Syrians attacked it and it 'aspires to the signing of a peace treaty with an independent Lebanon whose territorial integrity has been preserved'. And sure enough, no sooner had Sharon's troops reached the twenty-five-mile line, investing Lebanon's third city, Sidon, on the way, than they were racing along the highway to the outskirts of

Beirut and slicing through the thinly defended Chouf mountains, from where they were poised to cut the Beirut-Damascus highway and Syrian communications with the capital. The Syrians did their best to keep out of the way, ignominiously retreating from some of their forwardmost positions, but it was not enough. The Israelis bore down on their central strongholds and even as Begin and Sharon were calling on the Syrians to refrain from battle, insisting that Israel's only target was 'the terrorists', they were simultaneously instructing their army to draw them into war and 'settle accounts with them'.[21] On 11 August the Israeli air force, in a long-promised *tour de force*, took out the SAM missiles in the Beka's Valley and shot down some eighty aircraft, about a quarter of the Syrian air force, for the loss of only one of their own. On 13 June General Sharon led a column of tanks into Baabda, where a hapless President Elias Sarkis, overlooking a blitzed and burning Beirut from his palace, enjoyed sovereignty over about six square miles of his country. Ostensibly, with the Beirut-Damascus highway now cut and the capital encircled, Sharon was linking up with his Christian allies. The symbolism was plain, however: henceforward Israel would shape its neighbour's destiny through the Presidency itself.

This and related objectives were now emerging as public policy. Ever since his 'peace offer' of three years before Begin had been uncharacteristically discreet about his heart's desire—a peace treaty with a second Arab country—but now, once again, he was ready to go to Beirut and sign one 'tomorrow'. The pro-government press began to talk about 'a new political order in Lebanon', and *Likud* deputies bluntly asserted that 'a Lebanese government must be formed under the protection of Israeli bayonets'.[22] All the 'terrorist organizations', Begin went on, must leave the country with their Soviet, Syrian and Libyan weapons. And, although this was never clearly enunciated policy, it appeared that Palestinian civilians should go with them. The reason why the invading army set about demolishing refugee camps in South Lebanon with bulldozers and dynamite after it had bombarded them with artillery was not merely to finish off the 'terrorists' who continued to resist from bases there, it was to break up and scatter the whole community from which they sprang. 'Push them east to Syria,' said Yaacov Meridor, the minister responsible for refugee affairs, with an appropriate gesture. 'Let them go, and don't let them come back.'[23] The Syrian army, Begin now announced for the first time, would also have to leave. As for the Israelis, he and his officials never tired of repeating that they would leave as soon as the Syrians and the 'terrorists' did. For they did not covet an inch of Lebanese territory. Yet some Israelis clearly did. They included Yuval Ne'eman, leader of the neo-fascist *Tehiya* party, who became a cabinet minister during the invasion. Israel should prepare for 'a long stay in Lebanon', he urged, and 'could possibly even reach an agreement on border rectification' in a region 'which geographically and historically is an integral part of Eretz Israel'.[24] Naturally the *Gush Emunim* rushed in with their biblico-strategic claims. Had not the conquered territory once belonged to the tribes of Asher and Naftali? 'In the wake of our soldiers will come our settlers,' pledged Rabbi Ariel, the 'hero of Yamit', 'Lebanon is no less sacred to us than Sinai. We do not accept borders. Amman, too, is Eretz Israel.'[25] Israel's 'next duty' was not only to ensure peace for Galilee, but 'also to do her best in order to uproot the source of evil from the entire world'.[26]

Older conquests were not forgotten in the excitement of the new one. On the contrary General Sharon vigorously enacted his conviction that the harder he hit the PLO the readier the West Bankers and Gazans would be to acquiesce in the new order he had in store for them. He announced that he would begin 'immediate' contacts with 'moderate elements' to establish 'an autonomy as Israel understands it'. To that end, the Village Leaguers were urged to 'seize the opportunity' created by the war. Two more mayors, including Rashad Shawa of Gaza, perhaps the most conciliatory of all, were dismissed and the municipal councils of Nablus and Tulkaram dissolved. 'Uncooperative' schoolteachers were also sacked as part of a general assault on individuals and institutions. 'We can do anything we want now in the territories,' exulted a senior official, 'and no one will be able to stop us. If they didn't stop us from going to Beirut, then we will certainly be able to install an order favourable to us in Judea, Samaria and Gaza.'[27]

The attitude of the United States seemed to keep pace with the expanding objectives of its protégé. In contrast with former President

Jimmy Carter's disapproval of the much less ambitious, much less indefensible invasion of 1978, the Reagan Administration refused, again and again, to go along with Security Council draft resolutions calling for Israel's immediate withdrawal. Secretary of State Haig said that there should be an evacuation of 'all foreign forces', thereby putting the Israelis on the same footing as the Syrians and the Palestinians who, however unwelcome, were at least Arabs in an Arab country with Arab and Lebanese sanction for their presence.

It was not surprising that Begin exulted, and his supporters with him. The 'King of Israel' had made good his election promise. No more rockets on Kiryat Shmona, of course—but that, by now, was subsumed within the infinitely grander, demonstrated fact of Israel's power and impregnability. 'There is no other country around us that is capable of attacking us,' the Prime Minister told the National Defence Council with a pride which, on this occasion, did not impair his objectivity. 'We have destroyed the best tanks and planes the Syrians had . . . Jordan cannot attack us . . . and the peace treaty [with Egypt] stood the test.' More than that, the King of Israel had acquired an empire that now reached beyond the bounds of Eretz Israel proper, or, at least, an ability to prosecute quasi-imperialist grand designs. Gone were the days when the Israeli Defence Forces at least appeared to justify their name, when this people's army only mobilized and fought for the nation's very survival in wars of its enemies' choosing. True, there had always been a goodly portion of myth in this. Now, however, the myth itself was all but abandoned. Coolly and deliberately, when opportunity beckoned, Israel, a regional superpower, now went to war to shape the destiny of the neighbours which used to threaten it. There were 'chosen' and 'unchosen' wars. Peace for Galilee belonged to the first category. The 'terrorists' had not threatened Israel's existence, only the lives of its citizens. But there was no moral obligation to launch a war only when there was no choice. 'On the contrary, a free people . . . which hates war, loves peace, but insists on its security must create conditions in which its war—though necessary—is not unchosen.' He forecast forty years of peace—more or less.[28]

It was as humbling for 150 million Arabs as it was intoxicating for 3 million Israelis. It was known of course that, quite apart from

Egypt's virtual defection from the common cause, the Arab nation, 'which stretches from the Atlantic to the Gulf', had sunk to deplorable depths of division and disarray; that Iraq, the most powerful country of the eastern Arab world, was locked in a life-and-death struggle with non-Arab Iran; that the monarchies and sheikhdoms of the Gulf, terrified of the possible repercussions of that struggle, were debilitatingly dependent on American protection; that, in its isolation and domestic decay, Syria, the 'front-line' state *par excellence*, was pursuing ostensibly militant policies far beyond its resources to sustain.

These, after all, added up to the golden opportunity that persuaded Israel to attack. It could hardly have been foreseen, however, to what nadir of hypocrisy and impotence the Arab régimes would sink when it did. Only the Palestinians salvaged something from the wreckage of Arab dignity. When General Sharon's troops reached the outskirts of Beirut in three extraordinary days, it looked as though they would storm the city itself, rout the guerillas in their last redoubt, kill or capture their leaders, and, as a Lebanese politician put it, 'carry off Arafat like Adolph Eichmann in a cage'. But whatever Sharon had originally planned or desired, those initial lightning advances had obscured a painful, unforeseen reality. Some of the guerillas may have been the cowards so many Israelis always said they were. Others were not. Surrounded in the camps of Tyre, Sidon and other southern strongholds, outnumbered and hugely outgunned, they fought till the end. The casualties they inflicted were a warning of what awaited the Israelis if they tried to take the capital itself, a sprawling high-rise jungle, a street-fighter's dream, on which the guerillas were falling back, organizing and fortifying it for their last stand.

So the Israelis halted at the gates of the guerilla-held Western half of the city. The Chief of Staff, General Eitan, said that, though his men had not been given orders to enter it, they would 'encircle and completely destroy the terrorists' nerve centre'. Their leaders had already fled, he said. That, it seems, was wish-fulfilment, for Arafat was very much in evidence. He popped up all over the place, touring his front-line positions, even playing chess with foreign correspondents. His men would never leave, or, if they did, only for Palestine. He would sooner die at his post. That, however, was as rhetorical as the Israelis' threat to come and get him. For at the same time, through negotiations via Lebanese intermediaries with Philip Habib, President Reagan's special envoy, he sought a diplomatic solution, one in which he preserved at least something, if only the shadow of his state-within-a-state.

Sharon would not have it. The PLO must 'disappear', he told the Knesset. There must be no military presence—even just to protect the refugee camps of Sabra, Chatila and Bourj al-Brajneh—nor a political, or symbolic one. As the wrangling dragged on the Israelis, in their frustration, repeatedly threatened to storm the city. That was rhetoric too. Indeed the siege degenerated into the very antithesis of the *Blitzkrieg* brilliance in which the Israelis, and no one more than the daredevil Defence Minister himself, had once taken such pride. Instead of those swift, clean victories in the uninhabited wastes of Sinai or the sparsely populated Golan, here they were, reduced to the same tactics that the Syrians and every other party to the Lebanese conflict had used before them: stationary wars of attrition, endless artillery duels which slaughtered civilians by the hundred but achieved no military objectives. Occasionally, under cover of massive bombardment, ground troops did push forward into guerilla-held territory, but whether they held what little gains they made or were forced to relinquish them, they got more, very unpleasant foretastes of what awaited them if they attempted to take the whole of it. Indeed, if anything it was the guerillas who, in their particular form of combat, were displaying the panache, daring and ingenuity that the Israelis used to display in the past. 'We don't want to sound arrogant,' said Abu Khalid, a front-line commander at the international airport, 'but it is we who are teaching the Israelis now. It is we who have mobility. They wait in their tanks with their electronically controlled machine-guns. They have become cowards, really. And they lie about their casualties.'[29]

In time, however, Yasser Arafat and the guerilla leadership decided that they would have to withdraw, leaving no military and very little political and symbolic presence behind. The enemy's firepower and overall strategic advantage were too great and it was ready to use them, it appeared, to destroy the whole city over the heads of its inhabitants. 'If this had been Jerusalem', it was said, 'we would have stayed to the end. But it is not ours to destroy.' So withdraw—under the protection of a multi-national force of Americans, French and Italians—11,500 Palestinians and 2,700 Syrians trapped with them finally did. The PLO leaders bravely called it a victory. For had they not survived a campaign that was meant to annihilate them? Had they not held out for seventy-seven days against all that the most powerful army in the Middle East—and one of the most powerful in the world—could throw against them? They went by sea to a variety of farflung destinations or overland to Damascus. As their convoys made their way to the port, where Marines and French Legionaries saw them aboard almost under the noses of the Israelis and their Phalangist allies, they were greeted with ceremonial salvoes the like of which even Beirut, accustomed to such pyrotechnics, had never seen before and—since this really was the end of an era—would very likely never see again.

It is not altogether clear why the PLO leadership finally did decide to leave. The rank and file were against it and there were murmurings of 'treason' from some of Arafat's harsher critics. For if they had held on the Israelis would surely have been forced, under mounting international pressure, to retreat themselves or to take the decision they clearly dreaded, to invest the city, street by blitzed, blood-drenched street. Compassion for the Lebanese and fear that even their Moslem-leftist friends and allies would eventually turn against them were no doubt part of it. Assuredly the Arabs were also another, more important, part. Here, for the first time in the history of the Arab-Israeli struggle, was the hated 'Zionist enemy' besieging an Arab capital. Its arrogance and brutality had surpassed all limits. It would have been better for the Arab régimes if Arafat *had* fled or his fighting forces crumbled beneath the initial onslaught. But for almost two and a half months the siege went on, and for two and a half months they could do nothing, through use of either arms or diplomacy, to halt the crescendo of high explosives delivered from land, sea and air, the concussion, cluster and phosphorous bombs, the slaughter of innocents blown to bits on the streets or buried beneath the rubble of multi-storey buildings flattened at a stroke.

The Arab régimes could not even rise to that old stand-by, an emergency summit conference, let alone decide on a collective course of action. President Mubarak of Egypt denounced the invasion as 'illegal, inhumane, and contrary to the spirit of the Camp David agreements', but he resisted all guerilla appeals to repudiate the agreements in retaliation. King Fahd said that Saudi Arabia was putting 'all its resources and potentials' at the disposal of the Palestinians, but, as Israel rained down death and destruction with American-supplied weapons, this champion of *Pax Americana* in the Middle East just as steadfastly resisted guerilla appeals to use its oil and financial power against Israel's incorrigible superpower supporter. Syria, self-styled protector of Lebanon and the Palestinian resistance movement, did fight for a while. After their first devastating blows—which knocked out Syria's SAM missiles and all but achieved the encirclement of Beirut—the Israelis declared a unilateral ceasefire. The Baathist régime promptly accepted it—and held victory celebrations in Damascus. For this, it said, was the first time in the history of the Arab-Israeli struggle that Israel rather than an Arab country had asked for a ceasefire. When the Israelis proceeded to break their own ceasefire, not once but a dozen times—for every ceasefire was a ruse—the Syrians, withdrawing from the fray themselves, told the Palestinians to stand, fight and turn Beirut into 'a cemetery for the invaders'. Any agreement achieved through Philip Habib, they said, would be 'like Sadat and Camp David'. Syria, for its part, would never take the evacuated guerillas in. Seeing everyone else do so, however, it then had to itself, with concomitant proclamations that, with Syria as its principal base, the Palestinian struggle had now been reinforced 'by the support of the Arab masses everywhere'. As for Colonel Gadafi of Libya, patriot of patriots, he only had advice to offer: the Palestinians should commit suicide rather than withdraw.

No wonder that, as they left Beirut, the guerillas reserved their bitterest curses not for Israel—whose villainies they took for granted—but for the Arab rulers, whose 'betrayal', the latest instalment of what Arafat once called 'an Arab plot', surpassed their worst fears. Their emotions were mixed and many: pride and sadness, frustration, resignation and despair, but the one that unified them all was anger at the Arabs. 'Save your tears for the Arab rulers,' shouted one departing fighter to his weeping kinsfolk. 'Ask them, ask Gadafi,' shouted another, 'where were their MiGs and Mirages.' At the port, within earshot of clean-faced young Marines come to protect the 'stability' of the Middle East, a third fighter, younger even than they but hardened beyond his years, swore that, 'we are going to put Israel aside for five years and clean up the Arab world. All our rulers are traitors. There must be vengeance, assassinations.' He clearly planned to be among the assassins. Gentler comrades smiled but did not dissent.

Beirut was to pass quickly into heroic legend. It was none the less a military and political defeat, the latest and perhaps the greatest in the history of the Palestine 'revolution'. It was not only Israeli might, American complicity and Arab pusillanimity that conspired to produce it. The resistance movement's own abiding 'inner sickness' had made its contribution too.[30] Had the movement been a healthier organism in the first place, it would never have been obliged to fight from such a corner. Arafat had come a long way, politically and diplomatically, since *Fatah* first emerged as a potent force on the Middle East stage. Paradoxically, though, his territorial power base had been continually shrinking and with it the reliance on 'armed struggle' which had been his organization's original *raison d'être*. In 1970 his guerillas were driven out of Jordan. In 1976 the Syrians dealt them a cruel blow in Lebanon. Thereafter the armed struggle became essentially defensive in nature. Arafat had at all costs to preserve his last, Lebanese sanctuary as an independent base, not for raids into Israel but for the diplomatic struggle on which he now almost exclusively relied. Now that last base was gone too and his fighters exiled to no fewer than eight Arab countries, some of them—the two Yemens, Sudan, Tunis and Algeria—a good thousand miles and more from the Palestine it was their mission to liberate.

Arafat chose Tunis rather than Damascus as his headquarters. For Syria, the country from which he most desired to assert his independence by means of this far-flung dispersal of his men, was the very one which, on account of its geographical location and militant traditions, was best qualified to help him. It was there that his revolution had begun; it was there, he feared, that it might end. There was one guiding principle from which President Asad never veered: exploiting his country's special position to secure a preponderant influence over the PLO, inciting it against any peace plan of which he disapproved, sacrificing it for any of which he did not. After the débâcle in Lebanon he was more than ever jealous of his frayed but only trump and were Arafat to have rebased in Syria, Asad would certainly have reduced him, behind a façade of continued independence, to an abject extension of his will.

Preserving the PLO's internal cohesion and independence of Arab régimes was going to tax Arafat's diplomatic and manipulative skills to the limit, all the more so because after such an upheaval there was bound to be a revival of the Middle East 'peace process' and the PLO, thus emasculated, was bound to come under intense pressure to join it. The West, Egypt and—*sotto voce*—various other Arab countries had been saying that it was time for the PLO to 'renounce terrorism', to turn itself into a purely political organization. As the Beirut evacuation negotiations proceeded Arafat desperately sought an appropriate 'political compensation' in exchange for a sacrifice that was coming anyway. Already, of course, the Palestinian cause had won an international publicity and sympathy it had never enjoyed before. But sympathy without tangible gains was not enough. What Arafat needed was hard-and-fast guarantees that Palestinian self-determination and ultimate statehood would be incorporated into America's conception of a just and lasting peace in the Middle East.

What Arafat got fell far short of what he needed but at least it was something. It came in the shape of the new American 'peace plan' which President Reagan solemnly unveiled a mere twenty-four hours after the last guerilla had left Beirut. He pinned American colours to the so-called 'Jordanian option' which was already implicit in Camp David. The departure from Beirut, he said, had 'dramatized more than ever the homelessness of the Palestinian people'. Tragic though it was, the war in Lebanon had ushered in a new opportunity for a broader Middle East settlement. The United States, he said, would not support the establishment of an independent Palestinian State in the West Bank and Gaza, but neither would it support annexation and permanent control by Israel, which should place an immediate 'freeze' on its settlement of Arab land. What he proposed was 'self-government by the Palestinians of the West Bank and Gaza in association with Jordan'.

Begin promptly and indignantly rejected the plan; the West Bank would 'never again become part of the Hashemite Kingdom of Jordan'. For his part Arafat managed never to reject it outright. If anything, he fought harder—for moderation—on the verbal battlefields of the conference chambers than he did on the military ones of Lebanon. But he could not accept the plan either. He could not hand over to King Hussein the role which Reagan wanted to confer on him. That would have been to renounce his whole *raison d'être* and to repudiate the resolutions of the 1974 Rabat summit conference, which had anointed the PLO in place of King Hussein as 'the sole legitimate representative of the Palestinian people'. All the same he was to make of the King, the man who had driven him out of Jordan in Black September 1970, his closest Arab partner. For months a Palestinian-Jordanian 'committee for coordination of political action' strove to devise the magic formula which the Reagan plan required: a form of Palestinian-Jordanian representation in peace negotiations that satisfied the PLO without incurring the inevitable Israeli-American veto, reconciling the PLO's demand for independent statehood in the newly liberated West Bank and Gaza with American insistence on their subordination to Jordan.

King Hussein always sought more than Arafat could give. The more Arafat gave, the more he excited opposition within his own ranks and the more Syria, furious at a go-it-alone diplomacy which aligned Arafat ever more closely with the conservative, pro-Western Arab camp, sought to exploit that opposition. The King argued that, however inadequate the Reagan plan, at least it furnished an opportunity, a working mechanism on which the Arabs should seize; it was the 'last chance' of saving what was left of the West Bank from Zionist depredations. Arafat appreciated the argument but, in the end, he could not make enough concessions. After the collapse in April 1983 of a make-or-break summit with the King, Jordan announced that it was 'now leaving it up to the PLO and the Palestinian people to determine their own course of action, to save themselves and their land. . . .' An embittered and frustrated King said that—in addition to the arch-rejectionist, Begin himself—the United States was 'partly to blame', because it had refused a 'direct dialogue' with the PLO, rejected any Soviet Union role in Middle East peacemaking,[31] and lost 'credibility' by its failure to secure the withdrawal of Israeli forces from Lebanon and bring about a 'freeze' of Israeli land settlement.

Begin's men rejoiced. They pronounced the Reagan plan dead and, despite brave American protestations to the contrary, dead it seemed to be. They could now expect American pressures to cease, enabling them to push ahead, unimpeded, with the Judaization of Greater Israel. Sure enough the Americans put all the blame on the PLO. Secretary of State George Shultz told a press conference that, in granting exclusive negotiating authority to the PLO at the Rabat summit nine years before, the Arab governments had made a mistake, and now they should tell the PLO 'to use it or lose it'. A Beirut newspaper called it 'open war' on the PLO.

The Syrian Baathists were pleased too. Events had proved, said Damascus Radio, that America 'does not hold the key to a solution in the region'. With Arafat's diplomatic path blocked and his inter-Arab room for manoeuvre reduced almost to nothing, he was now in grave danger of falling completely under the thumb of the Syrians whom he detested but could not do without. For the first time since the evacuation from Beirut Arafat and Asad met to reaffirm their 'strategic relationship'.

It did not last long. Within a few days Arafat was reeling under the most grievous blow of his career, a blow from within. In early May, 1983, he committed a historic blunder—a blunder which none the less grew naturally out of his whole style of leadership. He put two new commanders, Abu Hajim and Haj Ismail, in charge of the *Fatah* forces in those parts of Lebanon, the Syrian-occupied Beka'a Valley and the northern Tripoli district, where they had retained a presence. These men were not merely Arafat loyalists to the core, they were the very two who, more than anyone else, had disgraced themselves in the Israeli invasion of the previous summer. Their appointment provoked a full-scale rebellion within *Fatah*. Rebel leader Abu Musa and his followers called it 'a military and organizational *coup d'état*' which 'makes no distinction between courage and cowardice, the thief and the honest man, the struggler and the suspect, the hero and the spy'. Arafat had replaced the best officers with 'deviationists and defeatists'. The two men were quintessential embodiments of that 'inner sickness' which had now come virulently and calamitously into the open. Of them, and their kind, Abu Musa said that:

> These people did not want to fight in the Lebanese war. We knew that this would be their role—that they would desert their men. Because they never cared about them. They were busy with their own affairs, their commerce, money, banks. Many of them have millions of Lebanese pounds, and gold, which they speculate with on the stock exchange. He who has millions is not prepared to die. Arafat was told, but he did nothing about them. They are near to him. Everyone who errs gets near to him. Why? Because he knows that they cannot quarrel with him.[32]

The appointments were not merely a dire provocation and an insult to those guerillas who had truly fought and wanted to do so again, they were a portent, in the rebels' eyes, that, after the collapse of the 'Jordanian option', Arafat was seeking to pre-empt the fierce opposition within his own ranks that fresh diplomatic retreats would bring. For they were persuaded that, in sheer desperation, Arafat was about to carry moderation to even greater lengths, that he was planning to renounce the 'armed struggle' altogether, to withdraw from Lebanon, just as he had done from Beirut, in return for assurances, American and Arab, that would never be honoured. Only through the likes of Abu Hajim and Haj Ismail could he impose such retreats.

For Abu Musa and his men were 'rejectionists', indeed fundamentalists, who opposed all Arafat's diplomacy of the past decade and the basic objective which he had set himself: the establishment of a Palestinian state, co-existent with Israel, in the West Bank and Gaza. 'We began with complete liberation,' Abu Musa said, 'then we sought the liberation of any portion of Palestine, and now we are dealing with the Reagan plan as if it were a patriotic plan.' He wanted a return to first principles, to the Palestine National Charter which, never formally abjured, enunciated those principles; he wanted the establishment of a Palestine State in the whole land of Palestine and the return to their countries of all those Jews who were not Palestinian by birth or parentage; and he wanted a rededication to 'armed struggle' as the only means of achieving these full-blooded, original aims of the Palestine 'revolution'.

Arafat had faced 'rejectionism' before. But publicly, at least, it had been confined largely to those lesser, left-wing groups, such as George Habash's Popular Front, whose bark was to prove much worse than their bite. What he faced now was entirely different, an uprising within

Fatah—the original guerilla organization, the largest and his very own—which struck at the very foundations of his power and prestige. The rebellion quickly spread and it led to a small-scale civil war. Most of the Beka'a Valley fell into the rebels' hands as more and more guerillas went over to their cause. The Arafat loyalists were left in exclusive control of a last pathetic redoubt around the northern Lebanese city of Tripoli.

The Syrians favoured the rebels. Just how much they assisted them physically is controversial. What is clear is that, as the rebellion increased, Arafat grew more and more strident in blaming it all on Libya, then on Syria itself, which had 'shot us in the back'. And so it came about in 24 June, Syria, original sponsor and principal base of the Palestinian resistance movement, expelled Arafat from its soil. His spokesman called it a disaster and it was.

In December, he sailed under international protection from Tripoli. It was his second such flight, after a military defeat, in a year, and an even more distressing one in that, this time, it had been inflicted on him not by the historic Zionist foe but by his very own Arab and Palestinian brethren. He remained the Chairman of the PLO—the rebels had never sought his removal, only root-and-branch reforms in *Fatah*, the PLO's principal component. The 'revolution' he had pioneered was in ruins and, in an Arab world without even the pretence of a collective Palestinian strategy, the cause he represented had never looked so forlorn since the original exodus of 1948. If there were any consolation, it was that Israel was suffering grave and deepening troubles of its own.

Sabra and Chatila

It had been inherently likely that the Israeli invasion of Lebanon would bring some such ghastly climax as Sabra and Chatila; all the same, it came as something of a surprise even to some of those who had anticipated it.[33] The Palestinian and Syrian combatants had all left without a hitch. On 30 August 1982, Yasser Arafat had bid his emotional farewell. The Israelis seemed to be satisfied; General Eitan told the Committee of Foreign Affairs and Defence that 'all that remains in West Beirut is a few terrorists and a small office of the PLO.'[34] A few days later the American, French and Italian contingents of the multinational force set up to supervise the evacuation had also departed—even earlier than, under their mandate, they need have. The Americans, last in, were first out, with a smiling Marine holding up for the photographers a sign reading 'mission accomplished'. A start had been made on the 'pacification' of West Beirut; the Moslem-leftist militias, former allies of the Palestinians, had given some ground to the Lebanese army and to the state authority which, however embryonically, the army represented. Earlier, on 23 August, even before the evacuation of the guerillas got under way, the Lebanese parliament had succeeded in electing a new president. True, Bashir Gemayel, commander of the Israeli-supported Phalangist militia, was the very embodiment of Maronite Christian militancy, widely feared and loathed for the violence and brutality which had stained his rise to supreme office. His election, marred by bribery, intimidation and intrigue, observed the forms rather than the true spirit of democracy. There were at least hopes, however, that, under a strong man who might now feel able to woo and conciliate, Lebanon would achieve that order and stability for which almost all its citizens craved.

Via Lebanese intermediaries the PLO leadership had secured written guarantees from Philip Habib for the safety of Palestinian civilians whom the fighting men were leaving behind. Farouk Kaddoumi, the PLO 'Foreign Minister', said that the United States had given its 'word of honour' that Israel would not enter West Beirut and State Department officials were later to confirm that this was so, on the strength of numerous oral assurances from the Israelis.[35] Habib had written to the Lebanese Prime Minister, Shafiq Wazzan:

> The governments of Lebanon and the United States will provide appropriate guarantees for the safety . . . of law-abiding Palestinian non-combatants left in Beirut, including the families of those who have departed. . . . The United States will provide its guarantees on the basis of assurances received from the government of Israel and the leaders of certain Lebanese groups with which it has been in contact.[36]

These commitments were critical to the PLO's agreement to evacuate.

There were, of course, forebodings. The Lebanese Prime Minister considered that the mandate of the multi-nationals was not far-reaching enough. They should have been authorized to stay longer in order to cope with the chaos that was likely to ensue when local militiamen, stronger and more determined than the as yet feeble and uncertain Lebanese army, sought to fill the vacuum created by the withdrawal of the guerillas. His and others' misgivings were reinforced when the Israeli army, encamped on the outskirts of the city, made a 600-yard advance, on the pretext of demining roads, from the international airport to the very edge of Sabra and Chatila, where the PLO headquarters had been located. This violation of the Habib agreement took place directly after President Reagan had unveiled his 'peace plan' and it was a way of expressing displeasure. It was clear that for the Israelis Lebanon, as ever, furnished the means by which they asserted themselves *vis-à-vis* any diplomatic initiative they did not like.

And then on 14 September a remote-controlled bomb went off at the headquarters of the Phalange party in Christian East Beirut. Of all the innumerable terrorist exploits that Beirut had endured, this one was to have the most fateful consequences. For in the building, holding his weekly meeting, was President-elect Bashir Gemayel and when, a few hours later, it was announced that 'sheikh Bashir', the idol of the Maronite Christians (or most of them), had indeed been dragged, dead and disfigured, from the rubble, panic and stupefaction swept the country. Though no one knew who had planted the bomb there were fears of terrible vengeance against any available target by Bashir's supporters.

In further contemptuous disregard for Habib and all his works Begin and Sharon decided, without consulting their colleagues, to invade West Beirut. It had been a heavy blow for them. Had not Begin told a huge rally on 17 July that 'before the end of this year we shall have signed a peace treaty with Lebanon'? Bashir was to have been the man with whom they would sign it.

At three-thirty in the morning of Wednesday, 15 September, General Eitan and General Amir Drori, commander of Israel's northern region, met with Phalangist leaders at the East Beirut headquarters of the militia which Bashir had built with Israeli assistance. Together with Fadi Frem, the commander-in-chief of the 'Lebanese Forces', the Phalangist-dominated militia, and Elias Hobeika, the head of their intelligence, they drew up a plan for Phalangist participation in the seizure of West Beirut. It was decided that, to spare Israeli lives, the Phalangists would be exclusively entrusted with 'searching and mopping up' the refugee camps.[37]

At five o'clock that morning the Israelis began their entry. It was easy: the multi-nationals had conveniently removed mines and barricades and resistance from the Moslem-leftists was little more than symbolic. In the entire operation the Israelis lost only seven killed and a hundred wounded.[38]

At nine o'clock Begin, receiving Habib's deputy Morris Draper, greeted him with these words: 'Mister Ambassador, I have the honour to inform you that, since five o'clock this morning, our forces have been advancing and taking up positions inside West Beirut. Our objective is to maintain order in the town. With the situation created by the assassination of Bashir Gemayel, there could be pogroms.'[39]

What the Phalangists would do when they entered the camps was obvious to any reasonably observant Israeli who knew anything about them. And there were Israelis who knew them very well indeed. They had been training them in Israel itself since 1976. The military correspondent of *Yediot Aharonot* called them 'an organized mob, with uniforms, vehicles, training camps, who have been guilty of abominable cruelties'.[40] It was common knowledge, too, that the Palestinians were the particular object of their hatred. For Bashir Gemayel, there was 'one people too many: the Palestinian people'.[41] In his dealings with the Israelis he left no doubt that, when he came to power, he would 'eliminate the Palestinian problem'—even if that meant resorting to 'aberrant methods against the Palestinians in Lebanon'.[42] His militiamen never concealed their murderous ambitions. When a group of Israeli parliamentarians visited Israeli-occupied South Lebanon, one such militiaman told them: 'One dead Palestinian is a pollution, the death of all Palestinians, that is the solution.' *Bamahane*, the army newspaper, wrote on 1 September, two weeks *before* the massacre:

> A senior Israeli officer heard the following from the lips of a Phalangist: the question we are putting to ourselves is—how to begin, by

> raping or killing? If the Palestinians had a bit of nous, they would try to leave Beirut. You have no idea of the slaughter that will befall the Palestinians, civilians or terrorists, who remain in the city. Their efforts to mingle with the population will be useless. The sword and the gun of the Christian fighters will pursue them everywhere and exterminate them once and for all.'[43]

Political objectives as well as mere blood lust drove the Phalangists. In their meetings with Israeli representatives their leaders confided that it would be necessary to resort to violence in order to bring about a Palestinian exodus from Lebanon.[44] 'We knew that they wanted to destroy the camps,' said General Amos Yaron, commander of the Beirut area.[45] They pinned their hopes on General Sharon's scheme to overthrow King Hussein and dump all Lebanon's Palestinians on Jordan.[46]

The Israeli army also knew, at the highest level, just what vengeful feelings had taken possession of the militiamen after the assassination of their idol. Even after seeing to the Phalangists' entry into the camps, the Chief of Staff told a cabinet meeting that Phalangist officers had 'just one thing left to do, and that is revenge; and it will be terrible . . . it will be an eruption the like of which has never been seen; I can already see in their eyes what they are waiting for.'[47] They knew also what a free rein it was that the commander of the operation was likely to give his men. Elias Hobeika had once been sent to South Lebanon by Bashir Gemayel at the request of the Israelis in order to support the activities of Major Saad Haddad. Hobeika proved his mettle—killing several Lebanese and Palestinian civilians—so much so in fact that the Israelis decided to send him back where he came from, lest his 'excesses' prove an embarrassment. After Sharon had decided to 'cleanse the camps', someone proposed that an Israeli liaison officer be seconded to the Phalangists. But a superior, aware of Hobeika's past, vetoed the idea, arguing that the Israeli army should not get itself mixed up in atrocities.[48]

After passing through the Israeli roadblocks set up at its entrance the first unit of 150 Phalangists entered Chatila camp at sunset. Some carried knives and axes as well as firearms. The carnage began immediately. It was to continue without interruption for forty-eight hours. Night brought no respite: the Israelis lit up the camp with flares. Anything that moved in the narrow alleyways the Phalangists shot. They broke into houses and killed their occupants who were gathered for their evening meal, watching television or already in bed. Sometimes they tortured before they killed, gouging out eyes, skinning alive, disembowelling. Women and small girls were raped, sometimes half a dozen times, before, breasts severed, they were finished off with axes. Babies were torn limb from limb and their heads smashed against walls. Entering Akka hospital the assailants assassinated the patients in their beds. They tied other victims to vehicles and dragged them through the streets alive. They cut off hands to get at rings and bracelets. They killed Christians and Moslems, Lebanese as well as Palestinians. They even killed nine Jewesses who, married to Palestinians, had been living in the camps since 1948. Bulldozers were brought in to bury their victims and demolish houses which Israeli aircraft had not already destroyed; for, roofless as well as terrorized, all the Palestinians would surely have to flee.[49]

What was going on in the camps could hardly escape the attention of the Israeli soldiers surrounding them. Their forward command post was a mere 200 yards from the main killing ground and from the roof of this seven-storey building they had a direct line of sight into the heart of the camps. It was, said one officer, 'like the front row at the theatre'.[50] Elias Hobeika spent Thursday night on the roof of the command post. At 8 P.M. Lieutenant Elul, General Yaron's *chef de bureau*, overheard a radio conversation in which a Phalangist officer inside the camp asked Hobeika what he should do with a group of fifty women and children. 'This is the last time you're going to ask me a question like that,' Hobeika replied, 'you know exactly what to do.' Raucous laughter broke out among the Phalangist personnel on the roof and Lieutenant Elul understood that the women and children were to be murdered. He informed General Yaron.[51] Later the commander of the Phalangist forces in Chatila sent a message to Yaron to the effect that 'up till now 300 civilians and terrorists have been killed'.[52] This information was immediately despatched to military headquarters in Tel Aviv.

As dawn broke on Friday, 17 September, Israeli officers and men atop the command post could see the bodies piling up. Later they were to see bulldozers, at least one or two of them Israeli-supplied, shovelling them into the ground. Soldiers from an armoured unit, stationed a mere hundred yards from the camp, recalled how clearly they had been able to see the killing. Their report went to the higher authorities, who were receiving similar ones from other points around the camp.[53] Lieutenant Avi Grabowski, second-in-command of a tank company, said that he had seen Phalangists killing civilians, and that one of them told him that 'pregnant women will give birth to terrorists'. Israeli solders were instructed to do nothing. 'We don't like it,' an officer told his men, 'but I forbid any of you to intervene in what is happening in the camps.'[54] The soldiers blocked the entrances to the camps, several times turning back refugees trying to get out, and on one occasion a tank pointed its cannon at a group of 500 who, white flags held aloft, tried to explain that the marauders were 'assassinating everybody'.[55]

At about four o'clock on Friday afternoon General Eitan and the Chief of Northern Command, General Drori, met with Phalangist commanders, some of them fresh from the camps. Eitan congratulated them on their operation and the Phalangists, explaining that the Americans had called on them to stop, asked the Israelis for 'just a bit more time to clean the place up'.[56] It was agreed that all Phalangists would have left the camps by Saturday morning and that, meanwhile, no extra forces would be sent in. However, even as Eitan left Beirut airport for Tel Aviv, a new Phalangist unit of some 200 men set off for Chatila, mowed down a group of women and children as soon as they got there, massacred all the occupants of the first house they came across and demolished it with a bulldozer. All accounts agreed: this new operation was well planned and coolly executed.[57]

About the same time, General Sharon and Foreign Minister Yitzhak Shamir were again meeting American envoy Morris Draper, who asked that the Israeli army hand over its positions to the Lebanese army immediately. Sharon told him that nothing could be done because of the Jewish New Year. Besides the presence of the army was 'preventing a massacre of the Palestinian population in the Western part of the city'.[58] Later that evening the military correspondent of Israeli television, after hearing stories of summary executions and other 'horrors' from Israeli officers, telephoned the Defence Minister and told him that something had to be done immediately. 'In a few hours,' he added, 'the press of the entire world will know about it, and then we'll be in a real mess.' Sharon listened attentively and asked if Ben Yishai had any more details. He supplied some. 'The Minister did not react', he was later to recall. 'He thanked me and wished me a happy New Year. My impression was that he knew what was going on in the camps.'[59]

The next day the world did indeed learn. Journalists descended on Sabra and Chatila to find the hundreds of bodies which the Phalangists had not had time to bury, the limbs which protruded from the hastily dug graves of those they had, the naked women with hands and feet tied behind their backs, the victims of car-dragging, one of them with his genitals cut off, piled in a garage, the baby whose limbs had been carefully laid out in a circle, head crowning the whole. They stumbled across evidence of resistance, the sporting shotgun that lay by the body of a young boy.[60]

The Lebanese army, local and international relief and medical teams attempted to count the putrefying remains as they buried them. But these did not include the many bodies that lay undiscovered in the mass graves and the rubble of demolished homes. Nor did it include those of the missing—those who, during the massacre, had been taken away to an unknown destination. How many had died? a Phalangist commander was asked. 'You'll find out', he replied, 'if they ever build a subway in Beirut.'[61] It was a good 3,000 or more.[62]

Israel's Shame—And Redemption

After Beirut's foreign press corps had sent their first, grisly reports, an embarrassed Israeli government denied any knowledge of the carnage. Then, in a first official, but crassly mendacious statement, it conceded that the Phalangists had indeed penetrated the 'far edge' of Chatila camp on Friday (the day after they had actually gone in). On their return they had reported to the Israeli Defence Forces that there had been a hard battle in which both sides had incurred casualties. 'The Israeli army intervened to put an end to the hostilities. Rather than reproaching our army, it would have been better to congratulate it for intervening, even belatedly, where it was not obliged to intervene, thereby preventing an even greater tragedy. . . .'

Indignation was instantaneous and worldwide. In a rebuke of unprecedented severity President Reagan himself pointed out that Israel had justified its entry into West Beirut on the ground that it would thereby forestall just the kind of tragedy which had now taken place. It was no secret that Reagan was extremely angry and that he felt a very personal sense of betrayal. America's honour, its pledges for the safety of the Palestinian refugees, had been trampled underfoot. He believed that Begin should go.

There followed a succession of official justifications that merely succeeded in piling falsehood on falsehood. A military source said that the assailants had infiltrated through a breach in the eastern part of the camp, where the Lebanese army was supposed to be in control. The press recalled Sharon and Eitan's boasts that 'the refugee camps of West Beirut are completely encircled and sealed off by the Israeli army'—not to mention Israel Radio broadcasts, in the early hours of Friday morning, that the Israelis themselves had authorized the Phalangists to go in and cleanse the camps. Then, at an improvised press conference in Beirut, Eitan contended that 'we don't give Phalangists orders and we're not responsible for them. The Phalangists are Lebanese, and Lebanon is theirs, and they act as they see fit. The Phalangists went fighting within this camp here, Chatila, according to their guidelines, if you can call them that, of warfare.' And how was a force of about 150 Phalangists to cope with the '2,000 terrorists' whom, the Israelis suddenly discovered, the PLO had left behind? To that question there was no answer at all.

Israel's Peace Now movement, originally established to protest against official policies in the West Bank, went into action immediately with a first, thousand-strong demonstration outside Begin's residence. 'Begin terrorist', 'Begin assassin', 'Beirut-Deir Yassin 1982' were their slogans. Among them was the eighty-year-old Professor Epstein, who sobbed: 'After what happened in Beirut I am ashamed to be an Israeli. It reminds me too much of the Nazis who brought Ukrainians into the ghetto to massacre the Jews. I don't understand how that could happen to us.'[63]

On the evening of Sunday, 19 September, Begin chaired an

emergency cabinet meeting whose agenda was not the massacre but 'the frontal assault against the State of Israel and its people'. 'Goyim are killing goyim,' he told his assembled ministers, 'and the world is trying to hang the Jews for the crime.' At a cost of $54,000 the government took a full-page advertisement in the *New York Times* and the *Washington Post* to denounce the 'blood libel' against Israel, its government and army: 'Any direct or implicit accusation that the Israeli Defence Force bears any blame whatsoever for this human tragedy is entirely baseless and without foundation. The government rejects such accusations with the contempt they deserve. The people of Israel are proud of the IDF's ethics and respect for human life.'[64]

Protest, in Israel and abroad, rose to a crescendo. 'War Crime in Beirut', headlined *Haaretz*, Israel's leading news-paper, above an article by its military correspondent Zeev Schiff, who wrote that, with the knowledge of the Israeli authorities, the Phalangists had done to death men, women and children 'in exactly the same way as the pogroms against the Jews'. *Davar* said that 'We shall never be able to cleanse ourselves of this stain. What has been done by the perpetrator of Deir Yassin [Begin], the commander of Qibya [Sharon] . . . today besmirches the whole people.' *Al-Hamishmar* said: 'This massacre has made of the war in Lebanon the greatest misfortune to befall the Jewish people since the Holocaust.' 'Until today', wrote one columnist, 'the word *pogrom* had a connotation which concerned us Jews directly, as victims. Prime Minister Begin has "widened" the term; there was Babi-Yar, Lidice, Oradour, and now there is Sabra and Chatila.'[65]

The Labour opposition joined the hue and cry calling upon the government to resign. For expedient reasons—it had been popular with the majority of the electorate—Labour, with certain exceptions, had at first supported the invasion. Later, as its misgivings grew, it was very restrained in its public expression of them. Now, however, in the Knesset Shimon Peres, the party leader, threw away all such constraints. 'The Jewish people,' he declared, 'is face to face with its conscience. We feel that underneath those blocks of concrete that covered the corpses of infants, women and old men lies a moral collapse. The ground is trembling beneath our feet. . . . The fate of Israel, David Bengurion said, is dependent on its strength and righteousness. Righteousness, not just strength, has to guide our deeds.'

In the rest of the world, like President Reagan, Israeli supporters everywhere felt a kind of betrayal. This was not the Israel they thought they knew. Nowhere was this more dangerous than in the United States—in the Administration, the powerful Jewish community or the public at large. There was a feeling, among politicians and experts, that this was a turning-point. In the *Jerusalem Post* Wolf Blitzer called the massacre 'a disaster for Israel in Washington—indeed throughout the United States. It will take many years—if ever—to regain its once very high moral image in America.' Israel had squandered much of the moral credit on which it had so often to draw in order to wrest political, military and economic support from a sometimes reluctant Administration. Senator Alan Cranston, whose devotion to Israel was second to none, appeared on television 'visibly disturbed, even shaken. It was as if his best friend had stabbed him in the back.'[66] In the words of another Congressman, Jesse Helms: 'Begin has done the impossible in the eyes of the American people—he's almost made Yasser Arafat look palatable.' The Israeli embassy, in its review of US newspapers, concluded that Israel's standing in the media had reached an all-time low. Making matters worse was Begin's ill-tempered defence. The $54,000 advertisements were an indication of just how low his popularity had fallen. That American bogeyman, Colonel Gadafi of Libya, had done the same thing the previous year to deny that he was behind a terrorist plot to kill the President. 'The comparison', remarked Blitzer, 'was devastating.'

However, all was by no means lost, Israel was still able to rehabilitate itself. The official inquiry into the massacre—which Begin adamantly rejected on the ground that it would constitute an admission of guilt—would certainly help. Thirty-one of Israel's staunchest congressional supporters urged that course upon him. Failure to heed their advice would be interpreted in the United States as 'indicative of involvement', and this could have 'very grave consequences for the future relationship'.

America's Jews were plunged into moral and emotional turmoil. To be sure there were those, especially community leaders, who argued that Israel was not responsible for the massacre, simply because it was not in the Jews, with their high moral tradition, to do such things. Thus, according to Julius Berman, the Chairman of the Conference of the Presidents of Major Jewish Organizations, 'the injunctions of Jewish law are too powerful a force in Jewish consciousness to have permitted or even countenanced a Jewish role in this awful incident. Any suggestion that Israel took part in it or permitted it to occur must be categorically rejected'.[67] And they elaborated on what, since the beginning of the invasion, had become a familiar complaint: the partisanship of the American media. Charlotte Jacobson, Chairman of the American section of the World Zionist Organization, denounced the 'trigger-quick eagerness of the world to lay the blame for this terrible event at Israel's door'. It was 'a revolting display of bias and double-standard hypocrisy by those who were silent at the magnanimity and spirit of forbearance of the Israeli soldiers who paid in lives and wounds for doing their utmost to spare the civilian hostages of the PLO'. Rabbi Norman Lamm of the Yeshiva University called it 'a rhetorical pogrom, a journalistic mugging of the state'.

Reactions such as these one Rabbi Jacob Neusner, a professor of Judaic Studies at Brown University, called 'craven, cowardly, hypocritical . . . a parade of people lacking all moral commitment'.[68] Ordinary Jews were sorely troubled. Traditionally, where Israel was concerned, they kept their moral scruples to themselves, motivated by emotional solidarity, the belief that the Israelis should decide what was best for themselves and the fear of encouraging anti-Semitism. Uncritical community-wide support for leaders like Begin and Sharon was, however, no longer possible. 'For the American Jewish community', argued Richard Cohen,

> to defend the indefensible would only isolate it from the American community at large and transform a moral force in this country into nothing more than a lobby—for Israel when it is right and when it is wrong. The age-old dream of an Israel that incorporates the very best of Judaism—the dream that propelled kids like me out of the house with a canister for the Jewish National Fund is turning very slowly into a nightmare.[69]

The Jewish establishment, however Zionized, could not fly in the face of prevailing sentiment, whether Jewish or Gentile, and within a few days three major secular organizations (the American Jewish Congress, the American Jewish Committee and B'nai B'rith International), as well as representatives of the three major branches of American Judaism (orthodox, conservative and reform), were joining Israeli demonstrators and US Congressmen in calling on the Begin régime to hold an independent inquiry into the massacre. Rabbi Arthur Herzberg, Vice-President of the American Jewish Congress, declared that it was time for Begin and Sharon to go. It was the first time that so prominent a member of the Jewish community had made so vehement a public attack on an Israeli government.

Begin continued to oppose the holding of an official inquiry, but finally, on 28 September, after a demonstration by anything up to 400,000 people in Tel Aviv, he bowed to Israeli and international pressures. The mere formation of the Commission of Inquiry eased American Jewish consciences. The Israelis, said the *New York Times*, have 'affirm[ed] their humanity . . . shame[d] the killers of their own children . . . expose[d] the hypocrisy of many of their critics'.[70]

A few days later the Kahan Commission—so called after its Chairman, Itzhak Kahan, President of the Supreme Court—began its hearings with the prescribed task of bringing to light 'all the facts and factors connected with the atrocity carried out by a unit of the Lebanese Forces against the civilian population in the Sabra and Chatila camps'.

With the publication of the Kahan Commission's report in February 1983 it seemed as if Israel, in its own and much of the world's eyes, had all but redeemed itself of the sins it had committed. The *Jerusalem Post* hailed it as a 'splendid example of Israeli—not to say Jewish—justice at work'. The *New York Times* proclaimed the advent of a 'Jerusalem ethic'; 'how rare the nation that seeks salvation by revealing such shames.'[71] Western leaders and politicians, including President Reagan, added their praises. Yet the Kahan Report, though not without merits, was by and large a whitewash. It fell into that tradition of moral and intellectual sophistry by which, since the earliest days, the official keepers of the Zionist conscience have persuaded themselves that, in practice as well as theory, theirs has always been a humane and righteous creed.

The Kahan Report

The Kahan Commission established a distinction between direct and indirect responsibility for the massacre. The responsibility of the Phalangists was the direct one, that of the Israeli authorities, military and political, indirect. Any suggestion that Israeli soldiers actually participated in the killing, it contended, was 'groundless' and constituted 'a baseless libel'. There had also been accusations that 'even if the IDF personnel had not shed the blood of the massacred . . . all those who had enabled the entry of the Phalangists into the camps should be regarded as accomplices to the acts of slaughter and sharing in direct responsibility.' These accusations were 'unfounded' too.[72] The reason for sending in the Phalangists had been the one the authorities said it had been: to prevent further losses in the war and to take advantage of the Phalangists' professional skills. There was no intention to harm the non-combatant population in the camps. In the Commission's view, therefore, the responsibility of the Israeli authorities, onerous though it was, was only an indirect one, and in this context it singled out nine persons for particular blame, including Prime Minister Begin, Defence Minister Sharon and Chief of Staff Eitan. Their guilt lay in the fact that 'the decision on the entry of the Phalangists into the camps was taken without consideration of the danger—which the makers and executors of the decision were obligated to foresee as probable—that the Phalangists would commit massacres and pogroms against the inhabitants of the camps', and without 'proper heed' being taken of the reports of killings as they came in and without 'energetic and immediate action' being taken to restrain the Phalangists. 'This both reflects and exhausts Israel's indirect responsibility for what occurred in the refugee camps.'[73]

In its investigation of 'all the facts and factors' involved, the Commission in reality confined itself to the narrowest of spheres, treating the massacre as an isolated, exceptional event, unrelated to the whole conduct of the Lebanese War, about which it barely had a critical word to say, let alone to the larger moral, ideological and historical context in which the war took place. Furthermore, as the distinguished Israeli journalist, Amon Kapeliouk, author of his own book on the massacre, has pointed out, the Commission's report contained some inexplicable omissions, contradictions and errors. The three members of the Commission, he commented, belonged to the Israeli establishment and did not wish to plunge the country into a 'moral and political crisis'. One of the Commission's most grievous errors was its assertion that 'it was impossible to see what was happening within the alleys in the camp from the roof of the [forward] command post'. This assertion was based on the evidence of the soldiers concerned, who would have incriminated themselves if they had admitted it was possible. According to other, independent witnesses, the seven-storey building [not five-storey as the Commission had it] provided a direct, grandstand view of Phalangist activities.[74] None the less, in the light of the 'facts and factors' which the Commission did expose, it was very hard to understand how it reached the exceedingly indulgent conclusion that Israeli responsibility was 'indirect' only. When the massacres were placed in that larger context which the Commission ignored or distorted, it became even harder to understand.

'In all the testimony we have heard', the Report said, 'there has been unanimity regarding [the fact] that the battle ethics of the Phalangists differ greatly from those of the IDF.' Higher standards were naturally to be expected from a regular army than from a private militia, but after that was taken into account, was the difference all that great? Since when had 'purity of arms' become anything more than a nostalgic legend? Not for a very long time, according to General Mordecai Gur, the Chief of Staff during the 1978 invasion of South Lebanon—in a dress rehearsal for that of his successor, General Eitan. In a newspaper interview he was asked whether the Israeli army had bombarded Lebanese civilians 'without discrimination'.

> 'I've been in the army thirty years. Do you think I don't know what we've been doing all those years? What did we do the entire length of the Suez Canal? A million and a half refugees! Really, where do you live? Since when has the population of South Lebanon been so sacred? They know very well what the terrorists were doing. After the massacre of Avivim, I had four villages in South Lebanon bombarded without authorization.'
>
> 'Without discrimination?'

'What discrimination? What had the inhabitants of Irbid [a non-Palestinian town in North Jordan] done to deserve being bombarded by us?'

'But the military communiqués always spoke of returning fire and counterstrikes against terrorist targets?'

'Be serious. . . . You don't know that the whole Jordan Valley was evacuated during the War of Attrition?'

'You maintain that the civilian population should be punished?'

'And how! I am using Sabra language: and how! I never doubted it, not for one moment. When I said . . . bring in tanks as quickly as possible and hit them from far off before the boys reach a face-to-face battle, didn't I know what I was doing? I gave that order. Of course, that was not the first time that I had given that order. For thirty years, from the War of Independence to this day, we have been fighting against a population that lives in villages and in towns and the question that accompanies us endlessly each time from the beginning is whether or not to hit the civilians. . . .'[75]

General Gur was a pillar of the 'moderate', Labour establishment. What was to be expected of the *Likud* 'extremist' who succeeded him? There was a difference, certainly, but it was one of degree, not kind, of posture rather than conduct. Ethically speaking, what the army did under Eitan represented an aggravation, no more, of what it had done under Gur. It was Begin himself who, in the Knesset, deftly and deliberately stressed the essential continuities of Zionist military practice. When, sixty-eight days into the invasion, the Labour opposition was growing restive at the brutalities of the campaign and the bad impression they were making on the outside world, all that Begin had to do, in his own defence, was to cite the text of that famous interview.

There were two ways to get at the 'terrorists'. One was to track them down and kill them individually, street by street, orange grove by orange grove. The other was to bomb, bomb and bomb them again. Those were hypothetical extremes, but the Israeli commanders were overwhelmingly predisposed to the latter—'to hit them from far off before [their] boys reach a face-to-face battle'. That was to be expected of an army that was desperately anxious to minimize its own casualties and disposed of such a formidable array of long-range weaponry. It also fitted into the familiar pattern of contemporary conflicts that pit an established régime, technologically advanced in its own right or by courtesy of a great-power patron, against a revolutionary movement of relatively primitive means. It is a form of warfare of which the people, as distinct from the combatants who move among them, are the principal victims, terrorism of a scale and indiscriminateness which the real 'terrorists' cannot begin to rival.

An Israeli writer, Amnon Dankner, castigated the attempt to draw a distinction between 'two sorts of brutality'.

> The first kind . . . are the personal atrocities, committed face to face. This is condemned by all. Thus, for example, it is forbidden to kill prisoners of war, forbidden to shoot civilians once you can see them with your eyes. On the other hand, the brutality that is far from sight is accepted and regarded as proper, though 'unpleasant'. The pilots throw bombs, the rest of the soldiers use long-range cannon against the civilian population and they are not brutal, they are not performing atrocities, because they are not emotionally involved, they cannot see the 'clients' of their actions with their naked eyes. So you should say: a soldier who shoots an old Palestinian woman from a distance of two metres is a brute who has lost his human image and should be tried. On the other hand, the Phantom pilot who releases a 250 kg bomb over a civilian quarter or a soldier who fires a phosphorous shell that burns women and children is not cruel but a good soldier. This attempt to distinguish between two kinds of war acts, which are both immoral, is an artificial attempt that can be accepted only by the meek minds that have been brainwashed by the sticky mixture of Israeli piety.[76]

It is not known how many people died in the invasion but it was at least 20,000.[77] Of these the great majority were civilians. If the Lebanese among them were, so to speak, 'incidental' victims, the same cannot be said of the Palestinians who, whether civilian or combatant, were deliberate targets. For Israeli spokesmen used the word 'terrorist' in such a way that the distinction between the two virtually disappeared. It encompassed any person or institution that fell under the aegis of the PLO. 'It seems to me,' said Deputy Chief of Staff Moshe Levi, 'that we are dealing with an organizational-military establishment which conducts a wide range of activities—beginning with acts of sabotage or incitement and demonstrations which, although not involving weapons, disturb life in our territories through acts of terror—and has relations with terrorist organizations throughout the world.'[78]

In defining their war aims the Israelis favoured a contemptuous, racist terminology replete with genocidal overtones. Begin himself called the Palestinian fighters 'two-legged beasts'. He never tired of Nazi analogies. The alternative to the invasion of Lebanon was Treblinka.[79] 'I feel', he told President Reagan, 'as a Prime Minister empowered to instruct a valiant army facing Berlin where, among innocent civilians, Hitler and his henchmen hide in a bunker deep beneath the surface.'[80] 'If, in World War II, Adolf Hitler had taken shelter in some apartment along with a score of innocent civilians, nobody would have had any compunction about shelling the apartment, even if it endangered the lives of innocent civilians as well.'[81] In a statement entitled 'Life and Death in the Hands of the Language', published early in the invasion, a group of Israeli 'doves' discussed the pernicious influence of such expressions as 'nests of terrorists', their 'purification', and the 'extermination' of the 'two-legged beasts' who inhabited them. Uri Avneri wrote that 'Every child now killed in the bombardment of Beirut, every child buried under the ruins of a shelled house, is being murdered by an Israeli journalist.' Those journalists' 'original sin' was the very use of the word 'terrorist', first to denote 'all PLO fighters', then 'all PLO members—diplomats, officials, teachers, physicians, nurses in the Palestinian Red Crescent'—and finally 'the whole Palestinian people'.[82] An Israeli soldier who had fought his way to Beirut did not conceal the effect which this insidious propaganda had made on him. 'Listen,' he said,

> I know you are tape-recording this, but personally I would like to see them all dead . . . because they are a sickness wherever they go. . . . Seeing dead children and women here is not really nice, but everyone is involved in this kind of war, the women too, so we can't always

> punish exactly the right people because otherwise it would cost us a lot of deaths. And for us, I guess, I hope you understand this, the death of one Israeli soldier is more important than the death of even several hundred Palestinians.'[83]

So it was that the Israelis, deliberately and systematically, concentrated their heaviest artillery bombardments on the Palestinian refugee camps. The consequences, for five such camps in South Lebanon, were drily summarized in an UNRWA report three weeks after the invasion began: 'Mieh Mieh camp slightly damaged. Bourj al-Shemali: 35% of refugee houses destroyed. . . . Rashidieh camp: 70% of refugee houses destroyed. . . . Ain Hilweh camp: totally destroyed.'[84] The camps had to be destroyed, in the final analysis, simply because they were there, scattered, vestigial strongholds of Palestinian nationalism. In addition to the general devastation of the camps as such, in their fury the Israelis appeared to single out the targets, notably hospitals, which, by all the rules of war, they should have done all in their power to spare.[85] These were the characteristic, long-range brutalities of a high-technology military power. But there was no dearth of personal atrocities, the ones that 'are condemned by all', and of the various forms which these might take, the most characteristic, perhaps, being the maltreatment of captives. The Israelis, deeming all PLO members to be 'terrorists' and 'criminals', denied them prisoner-of-war status. Norwegian and Canadian doctors have testified that they witnessed Israeli soldiers beating Palestinian prisoners to death and that Colonel Arnon Mozer, commander of the Sidon region, saw the beatings but did nothing to stop them.[86] As for the murder of prisoners and civilians, there were some claims that this was less widespread than in the invasion of 1978, when the army had been instructed 'not to take prisoners', but human rights activists such as Israel Shahak contended that in reality it was much more widespread, the difference being that this time the job was given to allies: Saad Haddad's men, Phalangist units, other militias or Israel's own Border Guards. Early in the war, the press reported that Haddad's soldiers 'pass from house to house in the villages which were conquered by the Israeli army exterminating the last nests of terrorists'. Haddad's soldiers were reported to be 'very busy', having been 'awakened to life with the beginning of the Peace for Galilee war. . . . And do not ask in what they are busy.'[87]

The Israelis and the Phalangists, in fact, differed very little in their hatred of the Palestinians. They also had very similar ideas about how the Palestinian problem should be solved. The difference was one of technique. Israel, the high-technology power, tried to drive the Palestinians out of the camps with long-range artillery; the Phalangists, their low-technology auxiliaries, went into the camps, as General Eitan put it, 'to fight according to their guidelines of warfare'. This was not an aberration; it was a culmination. The finding of 'indirect responsibility' was founded on one 'fact' alone: that the Israeli soldiers did not actually pull the triggers. The Kahan Report, said Amon Kapeliouk, 'does not close this horrible affair. All those directly responsible must be punished. Contrary to what this document affirms, they are not exclusively Lebanese.'[88]

The Murder of Emil Grunzweig

The moral impulse that produced the Kahan Commission did not reform and re-invigorate Israel. It divided and weakened it further. There had been significant opposition to a war of any kind in the north even before it began. By and large, however, public opinion was ready for a campaign confined to pushing the guerillas out of the twenty-five-mile 'security belt'. That was as much as the precious 'national consensus' could take. As soon as it proved that General Sharon's ambitions were much larger, that he planned to go all the way to Beirut, it broke down. The protest swelled quickly, and, most disturbing for the government, it came from soldiers who were fighting the war. These were often men of impeccable credentials, such as, for example, thirty-five members of the unit which had carried out the famous raid on Entebbe airport in 1976, rescuing passengers from Palestinian terrorists. In a letter to Begin they said that the war was 'a catastrophe for our reputation and our morality'. The climax came when Colonel Eli Geva, who had led the attack on Sidon and was considered to be the hero of the campaign, asked to be relieved of his command. 'I don't have the courage,' he said, 'to look bereaved parents in the face and tell them their men fell in an operation which, in my opinion, we could have done without.' The soldiers joined in anti-war demonstrations. These were unprecedented. Hitherto, in times of war and emergency, the Israelis had closed ranks. Less than a month into the invasion the Peace Now movement was able to mobilize as many as 100,000 people to demonstrate in favour of an immediate end to the war.

Impressive though these manifestations were, the Begin régime was still able to command spectacular displays of support. A quarter of a million turned out to hear him speak at a rally on 17 July under banners reading 'One People, One Army, One Government'. They revelled in the demagogic oratory of the 'King of Israel'. For, under his auspices, the language of political debate had become coarse, colourful, strident and vituperative, replete with what President Itzhak Navon reprovingly called 'verbal violence'. There were now, in effect, two Israels, two political cultures. One was Begin and the *Likud*'s. Its leadership was furnished by Ashkenazis, Jews of European origin, but its power base consisted of Sephardis, the Oriental Jews who now constituted the bulk of the Israeli population. It was a marriage of the doctrinaire religious-nationalist fanaticism of the Ashkenazis with the adulation of the Sephardis—poor, oppressed, resentful and volatile—for the charismatic 'strong man', for force and 'bashing' the Arabs. The other Israel, Labour's Israel, was one that clung to the ideals of the Zionist 'founding fathers', an Israel that deemed itself enlightened, rational and humane, the Israel of the *kibbutz*, social democracy, purity of arms. This Israel, though never itself true to its ideals, was nonetheless alarmed to discover just how far, under Begin, the country had moved away from them. The origins of this extraordinary upsurge of cross-cultural allegiances were complicated, but it made for an explosive mixture.

For Begin's Israel the other side were 'traitors', 'defeatists', 'self-haters', 'Arafat-lovers' who 'stabbed the nation in the back'. The war camp organized a virulent offensive against them. Groups such as The Voice of the Silent Majority and Families of Terrorist Victims sprang mysteriously into being. They put 'patriotic' advertisements in the newspapers. One of the earliest of these exhorted all those 'beautiful souls' to 'stop striking the army from the rear. Our sons are giving their lives to destroy the heart of the PLO viper, and, now, just as a chance of peace beckons on our northern frontier, we ask you to stop supporting the enemies of our people.'[89] A group calling itself Citizens for the Reinforcement of Israel warned against the 'internal danger' and announced its intention of collecting half a million signatures on a petition calling for a ban on the expression of 'defeatist' opinions, and a penalty of five years in prison for all offenders.

For the other side, Begin and Sharon were 'men of blood', 'fascists', 'terrorists'. For Professor Yeshayahu Leibowitz, a literary critic, the war was an outgrowth of Israel's Judeo-Nazification. In the first six years of his rule, 'Hitler did not perpetrate mass murder, he only prepared it, and, in Israel, the present government is doing exactly what Hitler did in those first six years. The Israeli policy today is Judeo-Nazification.'[90]

With the publication of the Kahan Report, the verbal violence turned into physical violence. As Begin and his cabinet debated whether and in what way to accept the Commission's findings, the two Israels confronted each other in the streets outside. Passions rose. In one camp the loyalists called for outright rejection of the report. They hurled abuse at their opponents, the Peace Now demonstrators with their placards reading 'Begin and Sharon Out', 'No to the Butchers of Beirut'. 'I would rather sit with the Nazi Arafat,' shouted one. 'You are whores, you are destroying the country. You must be liquidated.' The insults were heavy with ethnic overtones. 'Ashkenazis, your place is in the Yad Vashem; they should have left you in Auschwitz.'[91]

As night fell on a cabinet still locked in agonizing deliberations, the last of the Peace Now demonstrators were folding their banners and preparing to disperse. Among them was Emil Grunzweig, a thirty-three-year-old *kibbutznik* recently returned from the war in Lebanon. Suddenly the dreadful deed was done and Grunzweig lay dead in a pool of his own blood. The grenade flung out of the darkness had killed him and wounded ten others, including the son of the Interior Minister Joseph Burg. 'Incredible, incredible,' murmured a policeman on the spot, 'Jews have killed other Jews.' It was the first time since the founding of the state, and it shook it to its foundations.

But it had been all but pre-ordained. 'You cannot spew out so much hatred,' said Tsali Resheff, Peace Now's spokesman, 'without there being dead one day.'[92]

For *Davar*, mouthpiece of the Labour opposition,

> The hands were those of the person who threw the grenade, but the voice belongs to Ariel Sharon who, by hateful pronouncements of demagogy, allowed his followers to stir themselves up to the brink of civil war. The tenth of February is liable to be marked in the calendar as the day on which the last of the dam was broken, the day on which Israel integrated itself, in a final and bitter way, into its surrounding region. Today, Israel is divided into two camps, a bloc of grenades on the one hand and, on the other, a tremendous fear for the future of democracy—and in the middle a chasm.[93]

According to President Navon, 'the danger of civil war is a more serious threat than war against the PLO. Either the situation will continue to deteriorate, dragging us into civil war, or the fatal hand grenade that was thrown will be the last.'[94] For Avraham Shatira, a member of the ultra-orthodox Agudat Israel, and President of the *Likud* parliamentary coalition, this was 'how the Second Temple crumbled'.[95]

A few hours after Grunzweig's death, the Begin cabinet accepted the findings of the Kahan Commission by sixteen votes to one. Among those nine persons whom, in its attribution of 'indirect responsibility', the Commission said that Begin had shown 'indifference', and 'absolutely no interest' in what was going on in the camps for two days. The Commission did not call on him to resign—which, by any truly democratic reckoning, he should promptly have done. But it did call on General Sharon, the chief culprit, to do so; failing which the Prime Minister should dismiss him.

It was a highly specious acceptance. All that Begin did was to move Sharon from one cabinet seat to another. Instead of Minister of Defence he became Minister without Portfolio. To have ditched Sharon might have endangered the ruling coalition's majority. The new Defence Minister, Moshe Arens, was a superhawk who differed from his predecessor in manner and style only.

This hypocrisy cried out to heaven, commented the leading

newspaper *Haaretz*. It none the less accorded with the dominant mood of the country. Things had indeed changed since the publication of the last such report, which had looked into the shortcomings in the conduct of the 1973 war. Although the report had praised the then Prime Minister, Golda Meir, Begin had eloquently and emphatically declared that she should resign. The fact was, wrote a *Haaretz* commentator, that the three Commissioners were applying the standards of a different era. Today, he said, it was the mob that ruled, and the niceties of law, justice and personal responsibility no longer applied where non-Jews were involved.[96] A report in the *Jerusalem Post* did indeed conclude that the street was largely indifferent to Grunzweig's death. 'You should put them all up against the wall and shoot them,' said a taxi-driver about the Peace Now movement. 'I wouldn't be surprised if the Peace Now people threw the grenade themselves as a provocation,' said a typesetter near the Mahane Yehuda market.[97] The polls showed that 51.7 per cent of the population thought the Commission had been too harsh. Only 31.4 per cent deemed it just, while a tiny minority, 2.17 per cent, deemed it too lenient.[98] Within two months of the publication of the Report, another poll showed that Begin's popularity was on the increase, with 45.6 per cent of the people considering him the best man for the job, compared with 44.7 per cent two months before. This was in line with the growing extremism of Israeli public opinion, 50.2 per cent of which rejected any territorial concessions over the West Bank in exchange for peace with Jordan, compared with 43.4 per cent the previous December.[99] It all bore out the forecast of Yoel Marcus, who, under a column entitled 'The Commission Will Finish—The Government Will Remain', wrote that:

> In the matter of Sabra and Chatila, a large part of the community, perhaps the majority, is not at all troubled by the massacre itself. Killing of Arabs in general, and Palestinians in particular, is quite popular, or at least 'doesn't bother anyone', in the words of the youth these days. Ever since the massacre I have been surprised more than once to hear from educated, enlightened people, 'the conscience of Tel Aviv', the view that the massacre itself, as a step towards removing the remaining Palestinians from Lebanon, is not terrible. It is just too bad that we were in the neighbourhood.[100]

Notes

1. Speeches, 7, 14 May 1979.
2. Rokach, Livia, *Israel's Sacred Terrorism, A Study Based on Moshe Sharett's Personal Diary and Other Documents*, Association of Arab-American University Graduates, Inc., Belmont, Massachusetts, 1980, pp. 24–30.
3. *Al-Hawadith*, 1 June 1979.
4. *Maariv*, 25 May 1979.
5. *Le Reveil*, 25 July 1977.
6. *Haaretz*, 25 June 1982.
7. See, for example, *Ha'olam Hazeh*, 15 April 1981; Shipler, David, *International Herald Tribune*, 29 April 1982; Schiff, Zeev, *Haaretz*, cited in *Middle East International*, 16 June 1982; Frankel, Jonathan, *Jerusalem Post*, 27 June 1982.
8. *Kivunim* (A Journal for Judaism and Zionism), Jerusalem, February 1982.
9. *Jerusalem Post*, 7 May 1981.
10. *Financial Times*, 3 July 1982.
11. Kapeliouk, Amnon, *Le Monde Diplomatique*, July 1982.
12. Israel Radio, 12 May 1982.
13. *Haaretz*, 7 February 1982.
14. *Yediot Aharonot, Maariv*, 6 February 1982.
15. *Haaretz*, 22 April 1982.
16. *Yediot Aharonot*, 14 May 1982.
17. See, for example, statements by Israeli cabinet ministers Gideon Patt, Mordecai Zippori, Israel Radio, 12 May, 4 June 1982.
18. See Jansen, Michael, *The Battle of Beirut*, Zed Press, London, 1982, p. 7.
19. Randal, Jonathan, *Going All the Way: Christian Warlords, Israeli Adventurers, and the War in Lebanon*, Viking Press, New York, 1983, p. 247.
20. *Washington Post*, 26 February 1982.
21. *Haaretz*, 5 July 1982.
22. Kapeliouk, Amnon, *Le Monde Diplomatique*, July 1982.
23. *Al-Hamishmar*, 5 August 1982.
24. *Jerusalem Post*, 24 June 1982.
25. *Haaretz*, 13 August 1982.
26. *Maariv*, 3 October 1982.
27. *Middle East International*, 16 July 1982.
28. *Maariv*, 20 August 1982.
29. *The Guardian*, 13 July 1982.
30. See p. 300.
31. *Al-Nahar*, 30 April 1983; *al-Sayyad* (Beirut weekly), 11 May 1983.
32. *The Guardian*, 4 July 1983.
33. Randal, *op. cit.*, p. 16.

34. Kapeliouk, *Enquete Sur Un Massacre, op. cit.*, p. 30.
35. See Kapeliouk, *ibid.*, p. 33; MacBride, *op. cit.*, p. 166.
36. Cockburn, Alexander, *Village Voice*, 9 November 1982.
37. The Kahan Report, *Jerusalem Post* supplement, 9 February 1983.
38. Kapeliouk, *op. cit.*, p. 26.
39. *Ibid.*, p. 29.
40. *Ibid.*, p. 41.
41. *Nouvel Observateur*, 19–25 June 1982.
42. Kahan, *op. cit.*, p. 4.
43. Kapeliouk, *op. cit.*, p. 41.
44. Kahan, *op. cit.*, p. 4.
45. Kapeliouk, *op. cit.*, p. 70.
46. Randal, *op. cit.*, p. 281.
47. Kahan, *op. cit.*, p. 7.
48. Kapeliouk, *op. cit.*, p. 38.
49. *Ibid.*, pp. 47–51, 64–7; MacBride *op. cit.*, pp., 162–83, 268–80.
50. Kapeliouk, *op. cit.*, p. 47.
51. Kahan, *op. cit.*, p. 6.
52. Kapeliouk, *op. cit.*, p. 54.
53. *Ibid.*, p. 59.
54. *Ibid.*, p. 60.
55. *Ibid.*
56. *Ibid.*, p. 64.
57. *Ibid.*, p. 70.
58. *Ibid.*, p. 74.
59. *Ibid.*, p. 75.
60. MacBride, *op. cit.*, p. 170.
61. Randal, *op. cit.*, p. 16.
62. See Kapeliouk, *op. cit.*, p. 92; MacBride, *op. cit.*, p. 176.
63. Kapeliouk, *op. cit.*, p. 101.
64. *Washington Post*, 21 September 1982.
65. *Ibid.*, p. 111.
66. Blitzer, Wolf, *Jerusalem Post*, 24 September 1982.
67. *Jewish Week*, 24 September 1982.
68. *Newsweek*, 4 October 1982.
69. *Washington Post*, 26 September 1982.
70. *New York Times*, 29 September 1982.
71. *New York Times*, 9 February 1982.
72. Kahan, *op. cit.*, p. 12.
73. *Ibid.*, p. 13.
74. Kapeliouk, *Le Monde Diplomatique*, July 1983; see *New York Times*, 26 September 1982, *Newsweek*, 4 October 1982.
75. *Al-Hamishmar*, 10 May 1978.
76. *Haaretz*, 5 August 1982.
77. MacBride, *op. cit.*, p. 19.
78. *Ibid.*, p. 56.
79. Kapeliouk, *Le Monde Diplomatique*, July 1982.

80. Jansen, *op. cit.*, p. 71.
81. *Jerusalem Post* (weekly), 20–6 June 1982.
82. *Ha'olam Hazeh*, 4 August 1982.
83. *The Times*, 17 June 1982.
84. Jansen, *op. cit.*, p. 19.
85. See MacBride, *op. cit.*, introduction, p. xvii, pp. 259–62; *The Guardian*, 22 June 1982.
86. MacBride, *op. cit.*, p. 240; *Sunday Star*, Toronto, 27 June 1982; *Village Voice*, 27 July 1982.
87. *Haaretz*, 11 June 1982; *Yediot Aharonot*, 18 June 1982.
88. Kapeliouk, *Le Monde Diplomatique*, June 1983.
89. *Maariv*, 25 June 1982.
90. *Yediot Aharonot*, 21 June 1982.
91. *Jewish Week*, 18 February 1983.
92. *Le Matin*, Paris, 12 February 1983.
93. *Davar*, 11 February 1983.
94. *Nouvel Observateur*, 24 February 1983.
95. *Le Matin*, 12 February 1983.
96. See *Middle East International*, 18 February 1983.
97. *Jerusalem Post*, 13 February 1983.
98. *Jerusalem Post*, 1 April 1983.
99. *Jerusalem Post*, 15 April 1983.
100. *Haaretz*, 19 November 1982.

EPILOGUE

On 28 August 1983, Begin told his cabinet that he was resigning, and, resisting all the appeals of stunned colleagues and distraught supporters, resign he did. After six years as Prime Minister, six years full of sound and fury, the 'King of Israel' confided that 'I simply cannot go on.' He withdrew from the world; press reports had it that, shrunken, weeping, unshaven, he seemed to lose interest in his very existence.[1]

It was above all the war in Lebanon that precipitated Begin's miserable exit from history. According to his personal secretary, he had really imagined that, after invading, the Israelis would 'be out in the blink of an eye'.[2] They were still there a year later. Begin perceived the disaster, and, emotionally unstable man that he was, he simply could not live with it. The portents of ultimate breakdown had long been there. He had never gone to the funerals of the fallen—'for fear', said the opposition newspaper *Davar*, 'of being confronted by the gaze of those who remain'.[3] For it was the casualties that hurt most. And he was cruelly, daily, reminded of them by the demonstrators who, in a round-the-clock vigil outside his home, posted up the latest death toll. In the year before the invasion not a single person had been killed (other than in the full-scale border war of July 1981) in northern Israel. A year after it, by June 1983, 492 soldiers had perished in Lebanon. Three months after that, Begin himself became, as it were, the 518th victim of his own aggression. 'Perhaps,' commented the *Jerusalem Post*, 'it is Mr Begin's resignation that best signifies the darkness brought upon the nation by a leadership consumed by the arrogance of power. With nothing left to say to the people, with no guidance left to bequeath his government or his party, he chose to slip silently into the shadows, hoping history would remember him, forgivingly, for other days.'[4]

Israel's fifth unnecessary war may have brought peace to Galilee—for the time being at least—but it did not bring peace to Israel. On the contrary, it has laid bare and exacerbated conflicts and tensions *inside* a country which hitherto, in the thirty-five years of its existence, had lived, or so it seemed to itself and the world, under dire and relentless threat from outside. A French writer found these conflicts so profound and pervasive that he entitled his book on the subject, quite simply, *La Déchirure*. 'From the development towns to the universities,' wrote Jean-Francis Held, 'from the bank counters to the *moshavs*, from the docks at Ashdod to the luxurious villas of Caesarea, I pursued the Schism. I found it in the restaurants of Dizengoff, in the synagogues of the West Bank, on the snow-covered heights of Lebanon where the Merkava tanks stand guard. . . .'[5]

The central schism was between the Ashkenazis and the Sephardis. But it was impossible to isolate that ethnic-cultural antagonism from the others which, individually or collectively, imperiled the Jewish State from within. The invasion of Lebanon, gratuitous assault on the external threat that was hardly a threat any more, grew out of the domestic divide. Without the infatuated, unreasoning support of the Sephardis, Begin, the calculating Ashkenazi fanatic, would never have embarked on the geopolitical adventure which his megalomaniac general, Ariel Sharon, had laid before him. It was the Sephardi masses who had thrived on, and fuelled, his boastful rhetoric, his grandiose promises, his Gentile-baiting defiance as he concluded his victor's peace with Egypt, mocked President Carter over the West Bank settlements, made Jerusalem Israel's indivisible capital, effectively annexed the Golan Heights, bombed Iraq's nuclear reactor and the PLO headquarters in the populous heart of Beirut, goaded the Syrians in the Beka'a Valley and then flung himself into the last great military enterprise which would have completed his Zionist destiny. Success in the Lebanese war, and the con-sequent apotheosis of the 'King of Israel', would have at least temporarily eased the Schism. Failure could not but deepen it.

Failure it was. Begin's Israel had overreached itself at last. It did not possess the intrinsic strength, the manpower and economic resources, to sustain this quasi-imperialist grand design. True, it broke the back of Yasser Arafat's guerilla state-within-in-a-state, with ultimately disastrous consequences for the internal cohesion of his resistance movement, his independence of decision and freedom of diplomatic manoeuvre. But Begin did not get the fully-fledged Lebanese peace treaty on which he had set his heart. Bashir Gemayel, the 'dear friend' who was to sign it, was assassinated before he took office. Though a Phalangist too, Amin, the brother who promptly succeeded him, owed the Israelis nothing. He set his face firmly against any agreement which, like the one between Israel and Egypt, would have invited the reprisals and anathemas of the Arab world. With the backing of the United States, he resisted the crude pressures which the Israeli leadership, desperate to salvage something from the wreckage, now brought to bear against their Phalangist allies. Outraged Lebanese Christians discovered that the Israelis were 'no better than the Syrians'.

On 17 May 1983 Israel and Lebanon concluded an agreement providing for an end to the state of war between them and the withdrawal of Israeli troops. It was little more than a security arrangement, a mere shadow of what Begin and Sharon had originally sought. Yet they were not even to get the shadow, for Syria, angered at the political and strategic gains which the agreement did bring Israel, pronounced it 'more dangerous than Camp David'. The agreement must fall, Syria said, 'whatever the consequences'. So the Lebanese government was never to ratify it. In September the exasperated Israelis staged a partial withdrawal; they abandoned the central Chouf Mountains, making the Awali river their new front line. When those doughty warriors, the Druzes, inflicted crushing defeats on the Phalangists in the war for the Chouf that inevitably ensued, gravely imperilling the Gemayel régime itself, the Israelis did not lift a finger to help the 'Christian minority' for whose survival, in a hostile environment, they had professed such anguished concern in the past. The Palestinian guerillas were still solidly entrenched in the Beka'a Valley. Yasser Arafat returned to the northern city of Tripoli until Syrians and rebels drove him out. Some Palestinians participated in the Chouf war, amid growing Israel fears that before long they would be returning in triumph to Beirut itself. The Israeli army continued to come under terrorist attack in the regions it still occupied—'war of attrition' of a kind which, in the past, successive Israeli governments had said they would never tolerate. Worse still, Syria, after its humiliation of the year before, was savouring a quiet revenge. Far from knocking out the war-making capacity of Israel's most redoubtable foe for years to come, as General Sharon had dreamed, the invasion had actually enhanced it. For Syria's Russian backers, humiliated too, had stepped in decisively to redress the balance. Massively rearmed—and supplied with a formidable new air-defence system and long-range ground-to-ground missiles—Syria worked tirelessly, through Lebanese proxies, to undermine all the gains which Israel had secured from its military adventure. Not just Begin but the whole nation was demoralized.

While the war in Lebanon supplanted the occupied territories as the most divisive issue in Israeli public life, it was in the territories that, in the long run, the greatest danger lay. They remained the heart of the struggle—between Arab and Jew, and between the Jews themselves. The blow dealt to the PLO in Lebanon—and especially the internal Schism to which it led—was deeply demoralizing to the West Bankers. But, for all that, they did not acquiesce in the new order, autonomy Israel-style, which General Sharon intended for them. Sharon's protégé, civil administrator Menachim Milson, resigned at the time of the Sabra and Chatila massacre; a year later, Mustafa Dudeen, the head of the Village Leagues, resigned too.

So it was the Jewish settlers, led by the fanatics of the *Gush Emunim*, who continued to set the pace, and it was in the holy city of Hebron, scene of most of their triumphs over the government, that they were setting it. In early July 1983, a Jewish seminarist was stabbed to death in the centre of the city. It was inevitable retaliation, and seen as such by reasonable Israeli opinion, against the unpunished crimes and brutalities of the settlers. After a mob had set fire to the old Arab market under the noses of Israeli soldiers, Rabbi Moshe Levinger and his followers sent up their old familiar, hysterical cry for an appropriate 'Zionist response'. They got it. The new Defence Minister, Moshe Arens, caved in to their demand—which a week before he had called 'ridiculous'—for the dismissal of Mustafa Natshe, the very moderate mayor of Hebron, whose only real crime was that, through appeals to the Israeli courts, he was holding up the illegal seizure of Arab property which the settlers coveted. Then, in another great victory for the zealots' cause, the cabinet announced plans for a 600-family Jewish quarter in the heart of the city.

At the end of July, four men ran from an Israeli-registered car on to Hebron university campus. Six minutes, two hand-grenades and hundreds of automatic rifle rounds later, three Arabs—two teachers and a visitor—were dead and thirty-eight were wounded. 'One must be blind,' commented the leading daily *Haaretz*, 'not to see that the crime was planned and carried out as an act of retaliation for the murder of Aharon Gross.'[6] While they condemned this 'despicable crime', the authorities, true to form, suggested that it grew out of an inter-Arab feud, and the security services, while fully aware of the probable culprits, did no more to investigate and bring them to justice than they had done in the case of terrorist attacks on the three West Bank mayors three years before.

In *Davar*, Dani Rubinstein warned that all was now clear: the struggle was developing 'into a struggle to deport the Arabs'. This was inevitable.

> Today the settlers and their representatives in the government demand the expulsion of Arabs from the Jewish Quarter of Hebron and the deportation of the families of those who throw stones. In the light of past experience we may well assume that other demands will be fulfilled. In the past, important decisions concerning the West Bank were taken by Dayan and Golda Meir. Today they are made at the meetings of the Judea and Samaria Settlers Council and the Kiryat Arba Committee, while government ministries have become just operational bodies.[7]

In *Haaretz*, Eliayahu Salpeter wrote:

> One thing should be clear: the organization of terror groups and gangs of political murderers on one side of the Green Line is a matter for concern for everyone of us on the other side of the Green Line.

> Because if we don't eliminate terror, terror will destroy us as a free democratic society.[8]

Nearly a year after Emil Grunzweig died in a Peace Now demonstration, the police had had no more success in securing justice for this first Jewish victim of Jewish terror than for its many Arab ones.

Yitzhak Shamir succeeded Begin. In his personal style, dour, secretive—he was no orator at all—he could hardly have been more different from his predecessor; in his politics, a nationalist fanatic of the same school, he was, if anything, more extreme than Begin. In pre-independence days, he had been a leader of the *Stern Gang*, the most vicious of the terrorist undergrounds. During Begin's premiership, he had opposed Camp David and the peace treaty with Egypt.

Nominated for the premiership, he managed, after the usual unseemly haggling, to preserve the Begin coalition cabinet essentially intact. In his swearing-in speech before the Knesset, he pledged to continue the 'holy work' of settlement on the West Bank; and there would be no softness over Lebanon.

Israel's seventh prime minister took office in the midst of the worst economic crisis in its thirty-five-year history. A panic run on the shares of the country's main banks had brought them to the brink of bankruptcy; a stock market crash loomed. Two hours after its swearing-in, the new cabinet held an emergency, all-night session. Among other things, in an austerity package of unprecedented severity, it raised the price of basic foodstuffs by 50 per cent. That was part—for there had to be yet more draconian measures to come—of the crippling price the duped Israeli public now had to pay for the profligate economics, the fake prosperity, of the Begin era. The underlying facts were frightening. Since 1977, Israel's foreign debt had risen from $11 billion to $21.5 billion, its rate of inflation from 48 per cent to more than 150 per cent. Its economic growth rate was stagnant and, for the first time in its history, its exports were falling.

The crisis had its roots in doctrinaire Zionism, Begin-style—in the one-third of a $24 billion budget that went on defence, in $1 million dollars a day on the continued occupation of Lebanon, in $300 million a year on West Bank settlement. But, paradoxcially, even the deliberately induced, recklessly irresponsible consumer boom—the riot of imported videos, colour televisions, new cars and holidays abroad—served the higher cause; it was the very antithesis of pioneering Zionism, but it bought the indispensable votes of those, mainly the underprivileged Sephardis, who enabled Begin and the zealots to pursue their extravagant, Ashkenazi obsession with the 'upbuilding' of Greater Israel.

Israel survived its economic follies by courtesy of the United States. It was by far the greatest beneficiary of American aid. Regular subsidies, some $250 million a year after the 1967 war, rose to $1,500 million after the 1973 war and exceeded $2,500 million by 1983. A report by the US General Accounting Office warned that the United States 'confronts a rising spiral in financing Israel that may be impossible to stop'. Israel would be seeking more and more aid, and other favours, simply in order to service its existing debt to the American taxpayer. By 1993, the report forecast, it will need an additional $995 million for debt-servicing alone.[9]

The economic shambles was but another manifestation of the deepening crisis, the multi-faceted Schism, which threatened the Jewish state from within. It was a luxury which it could only afford, as it went from Begin to Shamir—and as the maniacal Sharon aspires to be next—because of the even deeper divisions and degeneracy of the Arab world.

But the Arabs' abasement cannot last for ever. A new order will eventually emerge which is better able to mobilize the vast potential at their disposal and—if *Fatah* rebel leader Abu Musa and his neo-rejectionism represent the shape of things to come—more determined to use it for the final, military solution out of sheer despair of ever achieving a peaceful one.

It is the outside world, the US above all, which sustains and pays for Israel's inflated living standards, its wars, conquests and its purblind intransigence, which poses a permanent threat to Western interests throughout the Middle East. In the final analysis, only the United States, by bringing Israel to its senses, can save it from itself. Without that salvation, the olive branch will never replace the gun. Without it, the last act of violence in the Middle East will be nuclear; the fatal Zionist propensity for the extreme solution, which we have seen in action, at every stage of this history, all but guarantees it. Israel has not signed the Non-Proliferation Treaty; it possesses the Bomb; and the further development of its nuclear capacity is the only way that it can match its enemies' conventional strength. The logic of force on which it has always relied is ultimately a self-destroying one. But without a peaceful settlement nothing can stand in the way of its apocalyptic appeal:

> From time to time the US Administration wonders [in] all innocence why we're so greedy. From time to time it plays dumb and pretends not to know of this tragic situation where 3 million weary Jews who've just begun building their home in the desert are being forced to maintain a huge military force to defend themselves against 100 million millionaires building up an army of Nato size. The US Administration acts as if it had no idea that nearly half our Gross National Product lies under wraps in our military emergency stores, and that if it weren't for this back-breaking burden we wouldn't be standing like beggars at their door.
>
> All this generous American assistance, even when it's called economic, goes directly or indirectly to sustain a losing arms race. All the parties involved have an interest in this race, each for his own reasons—except Israel who can never win it. To be sure, Israel won't be defeated in battle: it'll collapse—economically and socially—under the fearful load of endless arms purchases. . . .
>
> It's a fully planned vicious circle: when the Arabs have 10,000 tanks, we'll need at least 6,000; when they have 20,000, we'll need 12,000, and so on *ad infinitum*. Interim agreements or not, the race will go on, and our total dependence on the US.
>
> And this total dependence will mean total retreat to the 1967 frontiers and the sticking of a Palestinian State in our throats, *without peace*. . . .
>
> Our one and only alternative to our gradual destruction by arms race is to develop a nuclear deterrent of our own. It's our single chance for telling our many enemies and our one friend: that's it, we're not playing any more, we refuse to go on running for ever in the circles you've drawn for us. We want no more of your arms, we want a sophisticated educational system.
>
> Sooner or later we'll have to say it out loud. Sooner or later we'll have to announce: if any Arab army crosses this green line, we reserve

the right to use atomic weapons, and if he crosses the red line, we'll drop the bomb automatically, even if this whole country is blown up by nuclear retaliation. You don't believe it? Try us!

Shocking? It's exactly what an inferior West has been saying to a mighty Soviet bloc for the past thirty years. It's what has saved its skin, and it's what will keep the free world free when China and the USSR join forces—the bloody bomb.

Israel has no better ally.

We know the arguments of the sanctimonious peace camp, who abominate any bomb that isn't in their own arsenal. We also know the Arabs will have one of their own eventually, whether we do develop ours or not. Still, for our neighbours it will mean the *novel* threat of a mass holocaust; for us it'll just be a difference in method, since we have been living under the threat of annihilation from the moment this State was born.

True, the nuclear arms balance may wipe out the *entire area* or it may not—but the present arms race is going to finish *us* for certain.[10]

Notes

1. *Haaretz*, 15 September 1983.
2. Associated Press, 23 September 1983.
3. *Davar*, 12 June 1982.
4. *Jerusalem Post*, 7 September 1983.
5. Held, Jean-Francis, *La Déchirure*, Ransay, Paris, 1983, p. 25.
6. *Haaretz*, 27 July 1983.
7. *Davar*, 29 July 1983.
8. *Haaretz*, 10 August 1983.
9. *Jerusalem Post*, 10 July 1983.
10. Kison, Ephraim, *Jerusalem Post*, 25 April 1976.

Index